CRITICAL CONVERGENCES

SECOND EDITION

Edited by the Writing Program Committee
Syracuse University

Pearson
Custom
Publishing

Cover Art: "Train Track," by Kay Canavino.

Printed in the United States of America

10 9 8 7 6 5 4 3 2 1

Please visit our web site at www.pearsoncustom.com

ISBN 0–536–68665–3

BA 995390

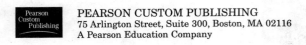

PEARSON CUSTOM PUBLISHING
75 Arlington Street, Suite 300, Boston, MA 02116
A Pearson Education Company

Excerpt from *The Way to Rainy Mountain* by N. Scott Momaday, reprinted by permission of University of New Mexico Press.

"Mommy, What Does 'Nigger' Mean?" by Gloria Naylor, reprinted from the *New York Times*, (1986), by permission of Sterling Lord Literistic, Inc.

"Language and Literature from a Pueblo Indian Perspective," by Leslie Marmon Silko, reprinted from *English Literature: Opening Up the Canon*, edited by Leslie Fiedler & Houston Baker, (1979), by permission of Johns Hopkins University Press.

"Lullaby," by Leslie Marmon Silko, reprinted from *Storyteller*, (1981), by permission of the Wylie Agency.

Excerpt from *On Photography* by Susan Sontag, (1995), Farrar, Straus & Giroux.

"Black Men and Public Space," by Brent Staples, reprinted from *Ms. Magazine*, (1986), by permission of the author.

"Heroin/e," by Cheryl Strayed, reprinted from *DoubleTake*, Spring 1999, by permission of the publisher.

"What's So Bad About Hate?" by Andrew Sullivan, reprinted from the *New York Times Magazine*, September 26, 1999, by permission of the Wylie Agency.

"Men and Women Talking on the Job," by Deborah Tannen, reprinted from *Talking 9 to 5: How Women's and Men's Conversational Styles Affect Who Gets Heard,* (1994), HarperCollins Publishers.

"Doonesbury" cartoon, by Garry B. Trudeau, by permission of Universal Press Syndicate.

"Tense Present: Democracy, English, and the Wars Over Usage," by David Foster Wallace, reprinted from *Harper's Magazine*, April 2001, by permission of the publisher.

"Ode to an Orange," by Larry Woiwode, 1985, reprinted by permission of Donadio & Ashworth, Inc.

The Key of Dreams, by Rene Magritte, 1927, courtesy of Artists Rights Society/Art Resource.

Regents of the Old Men's Alms House, 1664, by Frans Hals, courtesy of the Frans Hals Museum.

Regentesses of the Old Man's Alms House, 1664, by Frans Hals, courtesy of the Frans Hals Museum.

Still Life with Wicker Chair, by Pablo Picasso, 1912, courtesy of Artists Rights Society/Art Resource.

Virgin of the Rocks, by Leonardo da Vinci, 1503, courtesy of Corbis Images and Art Resource. *The Virgin and Child with St. Anne and St. John the Baptist*, by Leonardo da Vinci, 1501, by permission of Art Resource.

Venus and Mars, by Sondro Botticelli, 1487, courtesy of Art Resource.

Procession to Calvary, by Pieter Brueghel, 1564, courtesy of Art Resource.

Wheatfield with Crows, by Vincent Van Gogh, 1890, courtesy of Art Resource.

The Milkmaid, by Jan Vermeer, 1658, courtesy of Rijksmuseum-Stichting.

CONTENTS

Really Great Essays!

Contents

Contents

Webliography

Congressional Research Service Reports
gwis2.circ.gwu.edu/~gprice/crs.htm

Images
images.google.com

Library of Congress' American Memory Collection
memory.loc.gov/ammem

National Public Radio
npr.org

Official Modern Language Association Website
mla.org

Research Central
awlonline.com/researchcentral

Syracuse University Libraries
libwww.syr.edu

FOREWORD

Critical Convergences (2nd edition)

Margaret Himley

The decision to design a second edition for *Critical Convergences: Readings for Analysis, Argument, and Academic Writing* was prompted by our desire to make this book useful in both WRT 105 and WRT 205.

We have organized this edition in three sections;

- On Writing and Research

  Here you will find essays on composing on style, on organization, on responding to others' essays, and on critical research.

- Really Great Essays!

  Here you will find essays (and actually poems and cartoons) that take up provocative, current, and compelling topics and that require and reward careful, critical reading.

  The essays are listed alphabetically by author's last, cover a range of topics, and offer many possibilities for teachers to combine or juxtapose them based on topic, organization, style.

  We have added essays on seeing and visual literacy (and eliminated the essays on education).

- Webliography

  This listing of websites provides students and teachers with lots of images for analysis and use in classroom discussion and in written assignments.

We think this edition continues to offer teachers essays that are richly complex and varied, and so provide productive opportunities for doing rhetorical analysis. There are lots of different formats, intriguing claims, types of evidence, and varied ethical appeals. We think too that this edition aligns well with the goals of WRT 105 and WRT 205.

I want to thank Scott Love for all his hard and imaginative work in re-thinking the contents of *Critical Convergences,* and LouAnn Payne for her extraordinary and helpful organizational skills. Thanks too to Eileen Moeller and MK Babock and all the other teachers in the program who provided suggestions and advice. We got a lot done in a short amount of time.

I look forward to teaching with *Critical Convergences* next year and to learning from my talented colleagues the creative ways they put this reader to work in their courses.

Margaret Himley
Director of Undergraduate Studies
The Writing Program
Syracuse University
April 25, 2002

INTRODUCTIONS ALL AROUND

E. S. Love

in.tro.duce 1a: to lead, bring, conduct, or usher in, especially for the first time b: to cause to take part or be involved 2a: to bring into play: bring forward in the course of an action or sequence: add or contribute as a new element or feature b: to bring into practice or use 3: to cause to exist: bring into being 4: to lead to or make known by a formal act or announcement

Dear Reader,

I have been asked (as a writer of this "text") to introduce you (as the reader of this "text") to this new book *Analysis, Argument, and Academic Writing* (which you are now holding in your hands).

At this point in time, you could say we are all complete strangers to each other.

> I have never met you.
> You have never met me.
> And the book is new.

You could also say, I am simply a voice speaking to you across space and time.

But as your host, so to speak, I feel some proper introductions are needed all around before we can become better acquainted.

A proper introduction, I feel, is a necessary custom or convention we are all familiar with.

You know what I mean:

> "Hello, Mrs. Jones. I would like you to meet a friend of mine, Carl Smith."
>
> "Carl, this is Betty Jones. I believe you share a common interest in . . ."

However, writing the introduction to a book (this book) is not as simple as I first imagined. In fact, I am a little bit nervous about introducing you, two, complete strangers, to each other for the first time.

If truth be known, I imagine myself in the uncustomary and quite awkward (perhaps even

As I write this introduction, I am sitting at home at my desk in my study. I'm using my new, blue, iMac OS computer with 32MB of built in memory. I don't usually compose while at the computer, but to meet my deadline, I am willing to break several old habits of mine to write this introduction using a process with which you, as members of the "computer generation," are, perhaps, more familiar. Few of you, I'm sure, write essays in longhand anymore. I'm not that comfortable with composing on a computer. The end product, though, I imagine, will be both more informal and direct than an introduction I would have composed over a longer period of time using different, perhaps archaic from your point of view, technologies. Times are changing. Writing is changing.

Actually, to be more accurate, I am sitting at one of two desks in my study. One desk (the desk where I am now seated) is a modern, wooden, computer work station. I use my computer, mostly, for email, to keep in touch with my students and to maintain a website for my writing classes. The other desk is an old, massive, metal, Shaw Walker, leather topped, executive's desk, which once belonged to my father, now a retired Methodist minister. My mother bought this desk as a present for my father's ordination. As a small child, I would play underneath this desk on Saturday nights (bath night) as my father prepared his Sunday sermon. I write stories at this desk, using a process of writing and revising drafts in longhand on alternate pages in notebooks, skipping lines to provide space for revisions. Using this system, one notebook usually holds the first four drafts of a story.

nightmarish) position of acting as the host at a very important and fancy black tie dinner party and having to extend the introductions all around between the very special and very distinguished guests, all the time while wearing a blindfold.

You see, at this stage of the process, I have not yet seen the book you are now holding in your hands. For me, the book has no physical substance nor visual certainty yet. The word "book," however, when I see, read, or hear the word, serves as a complex linguistic sign providing a link between a culturally familiar, written inscription and a sound pattern with a culturally conditioned concept of this object we call "book" in my mind. This process provides me with a wide range of shapes and forms of "books" for me to consider based on my prior experiences with this physical reality I know and name a "book." In fact, as I try to find the words to introduce you both to each other, I am literally surrounded by boxes of books. Books I know quite well, which I could describe more accurately to you. But I don't yet have a picture of *this concrete* book you are now holding in your hands in my mind. I have not yet seen a copy from the printers. For this reason, I do not feel I know this book well enough to provide a proper and full introduction to you.

And this bothers me.

Yet, at the same time, I also realize, as the reader of this introduction, although you have a distinct advantage over me, the writer, by being able to hold and read the physical text of this book, which I, at this moment in time as I sit here writing this introduction, can only imagine, that you are also in a similar, unknown situation with me. Neither one of us has a very clear picture of the other. I suppose you could say, we are both wearing the blindfold.

So, who do I imagine you, the reader, to be?

If my research and experiences as a teacher in the Syracuse Writing Program are correct, you, the reader of this text are a young, undergraduate

As I sit here thinking about writing this introduction, I look around my study for ideas—for inspiration. Besides the two desks, the room contains several bookcases overflowing with books about writing, rhetoric, composition, or literary criticism. In fact, I even have bookcases in the closet. The floor is also completely covered with stacks of books I have been reading, papers I have been writing, and newspaper clippings which I will, when I find time, eventually stuff into file folders and label by subject in black marker. There are also at least three boxes full of books and papers on the floor (although you can't be sure of the exact number of boxes because one box might really be a box within a box). There are also several paper bags full of notes and clippings waiting to be sorted into files.

I have also tacked post it notes and index cards to the wall above my desk, a habit I inherited from one of my writing teachers a long time ago. Some serve as reminders to get to work.

A card tacked at eye level proclaims in black ink a favorite quotation of my former teacher from another famous writer, Isak Dinesen:

> Write a little every day, without hope and without despair.

But enough about me. I'm simply stalling. Let's get back to the task at hand.

With all these books about writing, why do we need a new one? What can I say about this textbook?

(I really dislike the word textbook. Sounds so prescriptive. Take two of these! and you'll be a writer in the morning! I think everybody on the committee would prefer to call this book of selected "texts" a reader).

So, let's say something about this committee . . .

The Textbook Committee, as we were called, was asked to design a new book for our undergraduate writing classes. This book would be used by a diverse group of teachers (including all first year Writing Program graduate teaching assistants). As a group, the committee met weekly for fifteen weeks. The committee was comprised of eight current teachers in the Writing Program: Joan Marcus, Sue

student (between the ages of 17 and 20) attending Syracuse University.

According to the most current statistics available to me (2001), this means you are a member of a diverse student population of over 12,000 undergraduate students who have defined themselves as follows:

54.8% female
45.2% male
7.3% African American
0.4% American Indian/Alaskan Native
4.5% Asian/Pacific Islander
3.8% Latino American
3.4% Nonresident Alien
68.8% White, Non-Hispanic
11.9% Unknown

I also know that nearly 60% of all high school graduates in America attend college; 77% of the students at Syracuse University were ranked in the top quarter of their high school classes; and the middle 50% of SAT scores for entering freshmen attending Syracuse University ranged from 1130 to 1300. Based on these statistics of high school academic performance, Syracuse University is considered one of the top 50 private universities in the United States. This makes you, as an SU student, and reader of this text, a very privileged individual.

This privilege is quite evident when you look at literacy statistics for the United States. Close to 40% or nearly 70 million Americans cannot read this introduction as you are doing so now.

And your ability to access and use the internet, makes you a member of a very privileged two percent of the world's population.

In addition, in comparison to the composite picture of the average citizen of the over six billion people in the world, who earn less than $2.00 a day, live in an 8' x 10' home, with no indoor plumbing nor electricity . . . the idea of privilege takes on a larger scope.

Cronin, Amy Robillard, Melissa Kaplan, Margaret Himley, Shane Seely, Steve Feikes, and myself, with office help from Sonya Pollard.

As a group, we first discussed what we did or did not like about books we currently used, or had used in the past, for our classes. Some of us no longer required textbooks for our classes stating that textbooks were often unsatisfactory for several reasons: high cost to students, poor quality of essays available, the outdatedness of essays, and a lack of interesting essays. Others of us still used textbooks, but frequently found students disinterested in most of the essays. A few of us depended entirely on students gathering materials on their own or were already providing readers for students of materials we selected ourselves.

Eventually, this initial discussion of texts turned into a very complex and interesting conversation about how and why we used readings in writing classes. We agreed that we used most readings for two major purposes. The first was to generate lively discussions in the class room about ideas which could be used as possible topics for student writings. The second was to use readings which would help illustrate for students the various methods, strategies, and techniques used by writers when creating texts.

We also realized, in being asked to create a reader for undergraduates at Syracuse University, we were, in effect, being asked to create a book which would reflect the unique position of the Writing Program here at SU, and thereby reflect our program's interests in the disciplines of composition studies and comparative rhetoric.

So we began looking for pieces of writing which would be both interesting and challenging to teachers and students. We divided the work of reading hundreds of suggested essays between us, collected and grouped essays according to several themes which we felt were interesting, and prepared a tentative list of potential readings for inclusion. We slowly whittled a very lengthy list down to about sixty-five pieces, give or take, to send to the publisher's representatives. Then, the publishers would check with the holders of the copyrights of each individual piece to estimate the costs involved for using our chosen texts. Then we would need

But this is only part of the picture I have of you as my reader. By way of further introduction, I think I can provide you with some more background as to how we have all come to meet together here on this page engaged in this conversation.

First off, by choosing to attend Syracuse University, you have chosen to attend a college which requires you, as an undergraduate, to take at least two writing courses. This is why you are, at this moment in time, (fortunately or unfortunately depending upon your perspective) reading this text.

This decision also means you have chosen, as a member of the university community, to enter a dynamic conversation about what it means to be a writer and what it means to write for and from within a multitude of rhetorical situations, both as a student and as a citizen, and both now and in the future.

For example, as a university, and especially as a Writing Program, we are constantly reexamining the changing meaning of literacy in our society. How are ideas expressed? Who is allowed to express these ideas? What texts will you read in your classes? How will these texts be selected for you? How will these texts be presented to you? What texts will you be asked to create? What shapes and forms will they take? What language can you use?

As you can see, this conversation impacts you already as a student, most immediately in the design and use of this textbook in your writing class.

Will I like this book?

I don't know.

This is a question both of us will eventually come to answer for ourselves in our own ways. I hope we can all, at least, agree, at the end of the semester that the book was both interesting and engaging; that somehow, in some way, this book enables you to look at your writing and the ideas you now have about writing, in a much deeper way.

to decide on the arrangement of the text and the presentation.

Somehow, we managed to accomplish all of this before the deadline (barely).
I'm not quite sure how.

However, what we ended up with is a reader which we feel both teachers and students will find engaging and useful; a reader which we feel will be a true complement to classroom and individual writing activities; and a reader which we feel will challenge students to become better critical readers and writers.

The readings included in this reader represent a variety of genres, political perspectives, and styles of writing. Some of the content in the readings may make you angry or trouble you or you may find yourself agreeing wholeheartedly with an author's viewpoint. All, in some fashion, represent what we believe is "good" writing.

The readings also reflect several large themes or topics we feel are rich areas for inquiry which we hope will engage your interest. There are readings about writing and composing, education, language, and the body. Your individual instructors will combine these readings in unique interesting ways for you to consider.

So. . . .

Introductions, I hope, have been satisfactorily made.

Now, it's time to more fully become acquainted with each other and more fully enter the conversation.

"BUILDING A MYSTERY": ALTERNATIVE RESEARCH WRITING AND THE ACADEMIC ACT OF SEEKING

Robert Davis and Mark Shadle

Alternative forms of research writing that displace those of modernism are unfolded, ending with "multi-writing," which incorporates multiple genres, disciplines, cultures, and media to syncretically gather post/modern forms. Such alternatives represent a shift in academic values toward a more exploratory inquiry that honors mystery.

Research writing is disrespected and omnipresent, trite and vital, central to modern academic discourse, yet a part of our own duties as teachers of writing that we seldom discuss.[1] For nearly thirty years, the conventional construct of research writing, the "research paper," has seemed ready to collapse, undercut by the charge that it is an absurd, "non-form of writing" (Larson). Still, the research paper goes on. In a 1982 survey, James Ford and Dennis R. Perry found that the research paper is taught in 84 percent of first-year composition courses and 40 percent of advanced composition courses (827). The survey has not been repeated, but our own informal research suggests that the research paper is still taught in most composition curriculums, typically at the end of a first-year composition course or course sequence, and thus it is positioned as the final, even climactic, step for students entering the communities of academic discourse.[2]

This notable status has not kept the research paper from being notoriously vacant, clichéd, and templated. Research writing textbooks, despite their earnest good intentions, tend to reinforce unoriginal writing by providing students not only with maps through the conventional routes of academic research, but also a standardized concept of how academic research writing should look and sound: textbooks typically provide sample papers, and stock advice on the "rules" of logical argumentation, linear organization, acceptable evidence, and the proper way to cite sources.

In this essay, we will present a series of alternatives to the modernist research paper: the argumentative research paper, the personal research paper, the research essay, and the multi-genre/media/disciplinary/cultural research paper. Part of our purpose is practical—we want to suggest new choices to teachers and students of research writing. However, we are also interested in the theoretical implications of alternative research writing strategies. We see in these strategies movement away from the modernist ideals of

---

[1] James E. Ford notes that the 1995 volume he edited, *Teaching the Research Paper: From Theory to Pedagogy, from Research to Writing* is the first book on research paper instruction. His introduction provides additional counts: only 2 sessions on research writing have been presented at the MLA Convention, only 1 published bibliography has appeared on the subject (1). Further "[Research paper instruction] has beeb ignored in the periodic overview of the profession conducted by the MLA, NCTE, and CEA. . . . The annual and semiannual bibliographies published in the major writing journals omit it completely" (2). This inattention is striking, especially given Ford's estimate that 56 percent of first-year composition teachers devote an average of 29 percent of their time to research paper instruction (1–2).

expertise, detachment, and certainty, and toward a new valuation of uncertainty, passionate exploration, and mystery. We also see an increased rhetorical sophistication. Alternative research writing often asks students to compose within a large range of strategies, genres, and media. Our students, whose work we will highlight at the end of this essay, create research projects that use and mix not only multiple genres and media, but also multiple disciplines and cultures. This work overcomes not only students' fear of, and boredom with, traditional research writing, but also some of the false oppositions prevalent in composition studies and academic culture. These include the divisions between: academic and expressive writing; competing canons; fiction and nonfiction; high, pop, and folk culture; and the methods and jargons of different fields.

Escaping Posusta

Research writing instruction in its current state has begun to spawn parasitic parodies. What "Cliff Notes" has done for literature, Steven Posusta's *Don't Panic: The Procrastinator's Guide to Writing an Effective Term Paper (You know who you are)* does for research writing manuals. Posusta is a snowboarder and mountain biker with an M.A. who tutored at UCLA. His book is at once a spoof of other research writing texts; an exposé of the emptiness of "academic discourse," at least as practiced by cynics; and perhaps the best guide to research writing in that it makes full, explicit use of the value that hovers at the edges of other, more polite, texts: sheer efficiency. The writing "process" Posusta outlines can be completed in just one night, although he admits that two are best.

This efficiency took time to develop. Posusta recounts his own painful lessons as an academic outsider learning to, in David Bartholomae's phrase, "invent the university":

> Writing papers for college or university professors can be terrifying. The first paper I ever wrote came back to me flowing with red ink. A note on the first page read: "Why did you ignore my instructions? Rewrite!" I had unfortunately interpreted the professor's instructions as mere suggestions. Papers are personal, aren't they? If I answer the question and speak my mind, I'll do fine, right? Wrong. (7)

To better invent, Posusta had to learn the academy's customs, rules, and practices. He eventually did this well enough to become a writing tutor, where he encountered students like the one he had been, struggling to write in the ways of the academy. Further, he found that most students put off their writing until the last minute. Rather than attempt to help them enact longer writing processes, he instead suggested methods for quickly creating acceptable discourse.

His book is a continuation of his tutoring. At a sleek 62 pages (with large print), it claims a special ability to help students quickly get up to speed. Devices such as the Instant Thesis Maker help:

THE INSTANT THESIS
#1. Although _____,
     (general statement, opposite opinion)
#2. Nevertheless _____,
     (thesis, your idea)
#3. Because _____,
     (examples, evidence, #1, #2, #3, etc.) (12)

---

[2]In Oregon, for instance, the research paper is most often taught in the third of a three-course sequence in first-year writing.

The only thing more efficient would be to let an expert like Posusta or a computer program do the work for you, filling in the blanks in the Instant Thesis, Body, and Conclusion. Posusta, however, stands guard against forms of cheating even he considers too efficient. He cannot keep students from downloading research papers from the Internet, but he can foil their plans to pass off as their own the sample paper provided in *Don't Panic.* While other authors blather about the evils of plagiarism, Posusta takes protective measures. Instructors reading the photocopies of his sample paper, handed in by students who have failed to read it, will find the following sentence in the midst of the competent prose: "I am plagiarizing, please fail me" (9).

As the many cases of plagiarism and Posusta's Instant Book suggest, the research paper has become a stationary target. We would like to believe that research writing teaches valuable skills and encourages students to commit to the academic ideals of inquiry and evidentiary reasoning. However, it may be as often the case that the research paper assignment teaches students little more than the act of producing, as effortlessly as possible, a drab discourse, vacant of originality or commitment.

Defenses of the research paper often rely on its preparatory function. We must teach the research paper, the argument goes, because students are likely to encounter it again in other courses across the disciplines. While this argument has validity, it can be countered by noting that teaching the research paper as the sole example of research writing will fail to prepare students for a myriad of other research-based writings: lab reports, case studies, news stories, position papers, take-home exams, and research proposals. Further, one can argue, the research paper is solely academic. In a culture overrun with data, the public often remains uninterested in the detached perspective of the modernist research paper. As Sharon Crowley and Debra Hawhee point out, facts take on meaning within networks of interpretation, which enable and shape cultural debates (6).

Richard Larson's well-known criticism goes further, charging that, theoretically speaking, the research paper does not exist:

> Research can inform virtually any writing or speaking if the author wishes it to do so; there is nothing of substance or content that differentiates one paper that draws on data from outside the author's own self from another such paper—nothing that can enable one to say that this paper is a "research paper" and that paper is not. (Indeed even an ordered, interpretative reporting of altogether personal experiences and responses can, if presented purposively, be a reporting of research.) I would assert therefore that the so-called "research paper," as a generic, cross-disciplinary term, has no conceptual or substantive identity. If almost any paper is potentially a paper incorporating the fruits of research, the term "research paper" has virtually no value as an identification of a kind of substance in a paper. Conceptually, the generic term "research paper" is for practical purposes meaningless. (813)

Larson's erasure of the research paper's grounding, however, reveals the omnipresence and importance of research writing. He opens his essay with a defense of research-based learning as part of any literate education:

> Let me begin by assuring you that I do not oppose the assumption that student writers in academic and professional settings, whether they be freshmen or sophomores or students in secondary school or intend to be journalists or lawyers or scholars or whatever, should engage in research . . . and that appropriately informed people should help them learn to engage in research in whatever field these writers happen to be studying. (811)

Larson is joined by advocates of research writing, and the authors of sincere, non-Posusta research writing textbooks, in stressing the importance of research in our infoculture and the necessity of teaching research skills. Research writing, we are told, should teach students about how data is generated and expertise gained. It should also allow them to cultivate their intellectual curiosity and expand their knowledge. The issue becomes method and form—how to do research and how to write it in ways that will allow students to embrace academic ideals and escape the cynicism of Posusta.

In alternative research writing, Larson's claim that research can inform nearly all discourse becomes the ground on which research writing is re-made. The models of composing we will present often involve choosing among, mixing, and juxtaposing a grand variety of discourses. The field of composition is here constituted as the study of all utterances—communicative, persuasive, expressive—in any genre, media, discipline, or culture. Seen in this light, research writing begins to enact the vision of composition theorist Derek Owens:

> Feasibly, taken in this broadest sense, composition studies is a crossroads discipline, a catalytic zone where a motley assemblage of discourse communities and arenas for intellectual exploration converge, metamorphose, and regenerate. At the same time, we cannot study multiple disciplines without being brought back somehow to the art of composing: musically, syntactically, lexically, orally, dialogically, socially, politically, poetically. (160)

As well as a broadened field for composing, the practices of alternative research writing enact a revised understanding of the purposes of academic work. According to its original ideal, modern research writing was to inscribe an act of seeking by presenting the knowledge the act secured. Seeking was made to consist of creating the conditions under which knowledge could present itself to the mind ready to receive it. But, as critiques of modernism have shown, knowledge cannot "present itself" to the mind because the mind and the world around it cannot be separated. Research has never been the hollow act of recording dead facts in a static world, and research writing has never been a mirror of nature. As James Elkins says in *The Object Stares Back: On the Nature of Seeing,* the gaze into the mirror is always an act of desire:

> When I say, "Just looking," I mean I am searching, I have my "eye out" for something. Looking is hoping, desiring, never just taking in light, never merely collecting patterns and data. Looking is possessing or the desire to possess—we eat food, we own objects, and we "possess" bodies—and there is no looking without thoughts of using, possessing, repossessing, owning, fixing, appropriating, keeping, remembering and commemorating, cherishing, borrowing, and stealing. I cannot look at *anything*—any object, any person—without the shadow of the thought of possessing that thing. Those appetites don't just accompany looking: they are looking itself. (22)

In the modern academy, the possessive gaze is expressed as the desire for expertise, which hides the passionate need to control the world. Werner Muensterberger has seen a similar drive in exacting and prestigious collectors. In *Collecting: An Unruly Passion,* he writes:

> I have followed the trail of these emotional conditions in the life histories of many collectors. . . . They like to pose or make a spectacle of their possessions. But one soon realizes that these possessions, regardless of their value or significance, are but stand-ins for themselves. And while they use their objects for inner security and outer applause, their deep inner function is to screen off self-doubt and unassimilated memories. (13)

Alternative research writing may offer hope for resisting the will to possess without returning to illusory claims to detachment, objectivity, and pure reflection. Such research writing does not seek claims to constant truth or an unassailable perspective, but instead asks us to take comfort in contingency, and thrill at mystery. Desire here is enacted as a restlessness reversing the libidinal economy of ownership; instead of wanting to possess, or even "know" the other, we want to sustain the experiential excitement of not knowing, the seductive wonder we feel at discovering that the other is beyond us, unknown, inexhaustible. The ideal of alternative research writing is exploration freed from its historical weight of conquest and enslavement.

Alternative research writing then, is not only a set of pedagogic strategies, but also a series of expressions of an altered conception of inquiry. Knowledge here plays leapfrog with mystery; meanings are made to move beyond, and writing traces this movement. Research becomes seeking as a mode of being. As academic seekers, we journey toward a state of understanding that subsumes both ignorance and knowledge, a state in which we "know" more deeply our own incapacity for certainty and find that it is uncertainty that keeps us alive and thinking. Alternative research writing is what William Covino calls a form of wondering: a way not to end thinking, but to generate and sustain it.[3] This discursive inquiry has a literal parallel in many world cultures. Whether we think of Australian aborigines on walkabout or East Indian men on sunyata, intellectual wondering is enacted as physical wandering.

Alternative research writing is intensely academic, but it also strives to reconstitute the academy by reaching beyond the disciplinary thinking, logos-dominated arguing, and nonexpressive writing we have come to call "academic." Alternative research writing inscribes an inclusive cross-disciplinary academy, which mixes the personal and the public and values the imagination as much as the intellect. Such writing thus helps us to regather creative work as inquiry, recalling, for instance, the moral charge Milan Kundera has given the novel: it must operate within the unknown to rediscover our world and ourselves. The plight of the alternative research writer is like the one Donald Barthelme sees in the novelist beginning a work:

> Writing is a process of dealing with not-knowing, a forcing of what and how. We have all heard novelists testify to the fact that, beginning a new book, they are utterly baffled as to how to proceed, what should be written and how it might be written, even though they've done a dozen. At best there's a slender intuition, not much greater than an itch. (486)

Student research writers may be working on a writing project that is, in some ways, different from a novel—still, we want them to have, and heed, an itch.[4] We want them to use research writing to follow questions wherever they lead and write this winding trail in discourse that is dialogic, Protean, and playful, while also passionately engaged—in the act of seeking itself, the work of the restless, wandering mind.

Ours, then, is an Instant Thesis after vitamins:

1. The research paper may be a vacant (non) form;
2. nevertheless, research writing remains a valuable activity, central to the academy in an infoculture—
3. as evidenced by alternative research writing strategies, which we will discuss here.
4. Further, we want to suggest, these alternative strategies may be read as inscriptions of the field of composition and academic culture revising themselves, reclaiming mystery as the heart of academic experience and discourse.

The Research Paper as Modernism Diminished

But first, #0, some history. We will trace the research paper as a historical construct, in part to attach it to a modern era, now passing. We also want to suggest, however, a more complicated set of relations,

---

[3]See Covino's *Forms of Writing: A Dialogue of Writing,* for Writers, a textbook on writing enacted through a series of dialogic forms. For Covino's re-reading of the Western rhetorical and philosophic tradition as a series of wonderings, see *The Art of Wondering.*

[4]See Kundera's *The Art of the Novel.*

in which the ghost of the original modern spirit lives on, rekindled in alternative research writing. At the advent of modern research writing, we find an egalitarian respect for the act of seeking, a desire to inscribe the passage into the unknown. Research writing was conceived in the modern era as a way of writing the making of knowledge, and this writing was, at least in theory, open to all.[5] Anyone, according to this modern mythology, was capable of making a breakthrough, given the right disposition, intelligence, and training. The research paper as we now teach it, like many things modern, scarcely lives up to this promise. It is, typically, an apprentice work, not making knowledge as much as reporting the known.

Curricular histories cast the research paper as the product of the modern American university and modern society. In *Writing in the Academic Disciplines, 1870–1990,* David R. Russell notes, "The research paper, like the American university itself, is a grafting of certain German traditions onto what was originally a British system of college education" (79). The idea of requiring students to do text-based scholarship, a thesis or dissertation, began to take hold in the United States as early as the 1860s. In many cases, theses supplanted the earlier forensic speechmaking toward which much of undergraduate education was geared. The change in forms signaled a change in values as well: "Oral performance for a local academic community demanded only a *display* of learning, but the new text-based standards demanded an *original contribution* to a disciplinary community in written form: a research paper" (Russell 80).

Research writing prospered in a climate favoring originality and calling for the creation of knowledge. Such writing was to demonstrate the writer's place in the society of knowers by increasing the society's store of knowledge. As a written embodiment of modernist values, research writing proliferated. By the early 20th century, it was central to college writing courses. Its widespread adoption in these courses, however, may have stemmed from motivations very different from the stress on knowledge-making with which modern research writing began. In *Composition-Rhetoric,* Robert Connors writes:

> The rise of the "research paper" as a genre in freshman composition is another way teachers tried to transcend the personal writing that occupied the early stages of any course. Library research—often unconnected to any writing purpose other than amassing brute facts for regurgitation into a "research" paper—became very popular around 1920 and has remained a staple in writing courses since. (321)

The research paper came to be chiefly a vehicle for training—not in the creation of knowledge, but in the recording of existing knowledge. Connors describes the state-of-being of the student research paper writer:

> He is, finally, a medium, not an originator. His task is to explore the library or the words of the world, not timeless wisdom or his own experience. He is to be trained to pick and choose carefully among myriad facts, coming ideally to that selfless position of knowing secondary materials so well that he merges with them. As Canby et al., wrote in 1933, "Now if your paper is to be worth reading this must be the expression of information that has finally become so thoroughly digested that it truly comes from your own storehouse" (Canby et al., 300–01). The research writer is meant, in other words, to give himself up absolutely to a discourse community. (322–23)

A student writer given over to a discourse community may be ready for originality, ready to make the knowledge that will take the community to a new place. However, this potential was often lost in a tangle

---

[5]Of course, the practices of the modern academy were exclusionary—sexist, racist, and classist. Still, the direction of the academy at this stage was, roughly, toward greater inclusion.

of legalistic concerns. Freshman research writing was not only to introduce students to the already known, it also sought to enforce a set of rules about the ownership of the known. As Connors notes, the research paper assignment "meant to teach the entire process of 'ethical' research—giving proper space to varied sources and proper crediting of sources. These concerns were just a formalization of the growing concern with intellectual property that had become a notable part of nineteenth-century law and jurisprudence" (321). The emerging conventions of the research paper "presented teachers with a grateful mass of practical formal material for which they could hold students responsible—the minutiae of formats, footnotes, bibliographies, citation forms, and so on" (322).

Russell notes that teacher/regulators saw poor writing as caused by poor thinking, and saw poor thinking as a threat to the academy:

> The "undisciplined" gropings of student prose were of course far from the research ideal held up by the disciplines. As faculty never tired of pointing out, student papers were replete with ignorance and errors of all sorts, which could seemingly never be entirely eradicated. Because faculty tended to regard poor writing as evidence of poor thinking, not as evidence of a student's incomplete assimilation into a disciplinary community, faculty sensed that the discipline's "store knowledge," acquired at great sacrifice, was "tarnished" by poor writing. (74)

The writing teacher thus becomes part guard, part dishwasher. "'Scouring' student writing for 'mistakes of fact and expression' became the goal, and writing instruction 'professional scullery'" (Wolverton 407, quoted in Russell 74).

The history of research writing in the American university is one of failed promise for students, teachers, and discourse. Begun with the egalitarian ideal of the making of knowledge, modern research writing has become the fallen "research paper," an apprentice work piecing together what is known, and presenting this piecing in a form that is also known, at least by the teacher. The teaching of research writing has remained tied to a contrived and templated way of writing, and to the self-imposed charge of safeguarding the university's store of knowledge—from those who do not know, and may never know, the words and thoughts that will grant them admittance to the society of knowers.

Some students seem to experience the culture of expertise as Kafka's land surveyor does the castle—as impenetrable, governed either by inexplicable whims or rules that defy surveying. Those students who learn the rules, however, often suffer another dilemma—an apparent unwillingness or inability to think imaginatively or originally. Many of the teachers we know complain that even advanced students are content to do what they know how to do: present the knowledge made by others, write within set conventions, and produce what they have been conditioned to believe teachers want. The teaching of research writing is often part of this conditioning: by asking students to stick to researching the known, we teach them to fear the unknown. We also make possible Steven Posusta, who would make the research process and product generic, repeatable, and instant.

The alternative ways of researching writing we survey below challenge the conditioned fear of the unknown and the banalities of "efficient" research writing. These methods embrace the modernist value of collegial work within the unknown. At least two of the methods, the research essay and the multi-genre/media/disciplinary/cultural research project, recall the intellectual wandering of early modernists, such as Montaigne. As ways of working within contingency, methods that use multiple genres and media may seem in sync with postmodern literature and art.

Beyond this entwinement of the modern and postmodern, we prefer, however, to see these methods as neither modern nor postmodern, but instead as historical time-travelers, regathering habits of mind and ways of writing, while attempting to stage intellectual experience as seeking and saying in the heart of mystery.[6] Inside "heart" is the "ear" and "hear"; it is thus what we heed in listening to poet Charles Olson's call to pay attention to the life passing through us mysteriously. Throughout *The Special View of History,* Olson also reminds us of the consequences of practicing Herodotus's original translation of "istorin" as "to find out for yourself." Such a perspective need not lead to a post-modern nihilism and relativism; instead, in an ever-changing world where every person is imperfect, and each event is an incomplete palimpsest we select or build from the shards at our disposal, the importance of the rhetorical process and critical thinking are amplified. When no researcher can have the "best facts or interpretations," it becomes crucial to carefully assess the audience, occasion, message, purpose, and logic of our writing.

In teaching alternative research writing, we ask our students to practice not only this rhetorical sophistication, but also the gathering and syncretism found in so many cultures pre-dating and leaking into Western Civilization. In his novel *The Mapmaker's Dream,* James Cowan has his Italian Renaissance mapmaker monk, while researching the geography of earth, describe this syncretism of an either/and (rather than either/or) world/consciousness in these words:

> Every man who had ever lived became a contributor to the evolution of the earth, since his observations were a part of its growth. The world was thus a place entirely constructed from thought, ever changing, constantly renewing itself through the process of mankind's pondering its reality for themselves. (60)

Similarly we recall the "nomadic" thought of Deleuze and Guattari, which inscribes "plateaus" of intense conductivity without center or fixed form. This is the kind of practice we envision for, and begin to see enacted by, alternative research writing. Like the surprising transformation of traditional nomadic life into the itinerancy of our own, we see such research writing as committed, its practitioners engaged in a sustained, "lifelong" learning in which the spirit is always at stake precisely because the individual's journey does matter in a world that is always changing and uncertain.[7]

Survey of Alternative Research Writing Methods

When taken in turn, the alternative research writing methods we will present—the research argument, research essay, personal research paper, and multi-genre/media/disciplinary/cultural research project—enact a gradual reopening of the purpose of research writing reminiscent of a closed fist opening finger-by-finger. Viewed consecutively, these methods trace a movement away from the templated discourse of the research paper and into an increasingly complex world of rhetorical choices. This movement also performs what Zygmunt Bauman calls a "re-enchantment of the world," supplanting the will to power with a sense of playfulness and wonder.[8] Alternative research writing, as we read and enact it, inscribes an enchanted world that is a continual source of wonder. The stunted will to know is here eclipsed by its shadow: the academic act of seeking inspired by the endless seductions of mystery and the shimmering promise of syncretic mapping.

---

[6]Historian Daniel J. Boorstin identifies seeking as the great communal human act: ". . . While the finding, the belief that we have found the Answer, can separate us and make us forget our humanity, it is the seeking that continues to bring us together" (1). Philosopher Steven R. L. Clark brings together seeking and saying ". . . the pursuit of knowledge through the exchange of ideas is something that we must assume we have been about since we were talking beasts" (4).

[7]For examples of nomadic thought, see especially Deleuze and Guattari's *A Thousand Plateaus: Capitalism and Schizophrenia.*

[8]Bauman identifies this reenactment with postmodernity, seeing it as a way of relating to the world that comes after the tragic history of modernism, in which power-supported structures of cultural meaning are repeatedly erected only to be demolished.

The Research Argument

Research writing has always *argued;* persuasion is needed, even in discourses aimed at exposition, to hold the writing together and provide an understanding of what the data means. Robert E. Schwegler and Linda K Shamoon, however, argue that research papers may contain arguments, but are nonetheless distinct from persuasive writing. Instead, they claim, the overall structure and aim of research papers fit the category James Kinneavy called scientific discourse: "writing that makes interpretive statements about some aspect of reality . . . and demonstrates the validity of these statements" (Kinneavy 88–89, quoted in Schwegler and Shamoon 818).

Still, most research writing textbooks now include some elements of argumentation, often in complex relation to the informational and interpretive intents of the modern research paper. In *The Craft of Research,* Wayne C. Booth, Greg G. Colomb, and Joseph M. Williams suggest that copious notes and collections of facts take on meaning only when writers discover the claims they want to make. These authors then provide an explication of the Toulminian scheme of claims, warrants, qualifications, and evidence. They further note that arguing in research writing can shift the emphasis of the paper from the information presented to the significance of the information, and even the authorial self projected on the page. The authors recommend that research writers imagine themselves in conversation with their readers: ". . . you making claims, your readers asking good questions, you answering them as best you can" (89).

In *Doing Research: The Complete Research Paper Guide,* Dorothy Seyler delineates three modes of research writing: the expository research paper, the analytic research paper; and the argumentative research essay. Each is animated by different kinds of questions and yields different sorts of discourse. She suggests the differences in a list of topics:

EXPOSITORY:
Report on debate over relationship of modern birds to dinosaurs.
Report on recent literature on infant speech development.

ANALYTIC:
Account of the processes used to identify and classify animals based on the fossil record.
Explanation of process of infant speech development.

ARGUMENTATIVE:
Support of claim that modern birds descended from dinosaurs.
Argument for specific actions by parents to aid infant speech development. (6)

Seyler's first argumentative topic would allow its writer to enter a current debate about evolution: far from reporting the known, this paper would stake a claim in a hotly contested area. The second topic functions on a personal level: it appeals to the parent, and/or future parent in its writer and reader. In each case, we can easily imagine that the student writer's claims would not be seen as pure knowledge, or even accepted as correct. Others in the class might suggest that birds evolved from another source, or that evolution does not make new families, phyla, or species. Advice about speech development could be supplemented or challenged by other research or the experience of the reader. Research and writing, here, become fodder for continuing debate.

The "research argument" constructs the academy as a site for informed conversation. Writers of the research argument seek to become experts, taking in the research they need to formulate and support an intelligent position. They are not, however, charged with ending dialogue and establishing set truth.

Instead, their responsibility is to use research to inform debate, and to position themselves as reasonable persuaders.

Further, the research argument can call on students to consider, and use, a range of rhetorical strategies. While some books may stress a fairly rigid approach to argumentation—stressing, for instance, the appeal to reason, using factual evidence or probabilities—teachers and students can also adopt a more varied approach, stressing diverse appeals and showing how they can be integrated.[9]

The research argument pushes toward, then, an academic environment that values debate, and calls for the appropriate and strategic use of a wide rhetorical repertoire. However, the research argument can also be criticized for requiring the defense of a claim or position, rather than a detached examination of data, as in the modernist research paper, or a more open exploration of a series of claims, as in the alternative methods of research writing explicated below. These methods allow writers to examine a range of viewpoints, but without forcing them to adopt a single position to defend. They make conversations not only communal, but also internal.

The Personal Research Paper

While the research argument asks students to at least simulate informed entry into public debate, the personal research paper allows students to research and inscribe a personal issue. In his textbook *Research: The Student's Guide to Writing Research Papers*, Richard Veit suggests that the advantage of the personal research paper is that it allows students to formally think about subjects to which they feel intimately connected. Veit acknowledges that his personal research paper is Macrorie's "I-Search" paper renamed and offers the same opportunity to answer existential, or practical needs; Veit and Macrorie's samples include papers on choosing the right camera and becoming a creative writer. Research sources include both written materials and interviews with those who can shed light on the question being pursued. In form, personal research papers often use a narrative structure and chronological order to recreate the writer's unfolding search. The papers typically end with either a tentative, perhaps temporary, conclusion, or the redirection of the question: "Should I be a writer?" becomes "Are the rewards of writing worth the sacrifices?"

The personal nature of these papers, it seems, might lead to writing that means much to the writer but little to readers. Veit and Macrorie, however, each stress that lively writing makes these papers captivating. Perhaps so, but the well-known criticism of Macrorie's approach—that it largely misses the social dimension of writing—still has force, even if the I-Search does seem a powerful method for helping students direct their own lives.[10]

Approaches are needed that preserve the spirit of the I-Search in discourse that explores questions that are more explicitly intellectual and public. For instance, recasting "Should I be a disc jockey?" as "Why

---

[9]A work such as Sharon Crowley and Debra Hawhee's *Ancient Rhetorics for Contemporary Students,* while not nominally a research writing text, could be helpful in showing students the range of argumentative strategies.

[10]James Berlin's "Contemporary Composition: The Major Pedagogical Theories" and Lester Faigley's "Competing Theories of Process: A Critique and a Proposal" brand Macrorie's work "expressionist." Berlin argues that expressionist pedagogies typically encourage students to use writing to reach toward a deep, personal truth. While students in expressionist classrooms often work together, the purpose of this collaboration is for students to help each other come to realizations that are finally individual. Expressionist practices are thus reminiscent of Platonic dialectics.

In Textual Carnivals, Susan Miller carries the critique of expressionism further, suggesting that such pedagogic strategies perpetuate the dominant order by enacting writing as an individual act, separate from social concerns and constraints.

Expressionist discourse fares better, however, in Geoffrey Sirc's "Never Mind the Tagmemics: Where's the Sex Pistols?" Here, Macrorie is cast as something of a punk compositionist, whose work is finally devalued because it does not ask students to bow to the dominant discursive order of academic convention.

does radio fascinate?" may lead to interdisciplinary research that is both library and interview-based and writing that is more likely to apply to readers as well as its writer. Such public/private work preserves the notion that learning is autobiographical, while also sustaining one of the chief lessons of rhetoric—that even the personal scripts in which we think are socially constructed and keep us connected to a shared, if conflicted, world. It also seems wise to preserve, while transforming, the idea that open questions are to be pursued and explored, rather than avoided, or terminally answered. As Theodore Zeldin argues in *An Intimate History of Humanity,* the ability and willingness to hold an open and continuing conversation is a defining act of consciousness, necessary for becoming human. We might add that it is what we may most need to escape from the current barbarisms in which our world abounds.

The alternative methods of research writing described below typically make use of open-ended questions that are both personal and public. These methods are notably inclusive, allowing writers to use material from different kinds of research as well as personal experience. Further, they are syncretic discourses—using a variety of modes, genres, and, in some cases, media, and bringing together material from a number of disciplines and perspectives. We cannot claim that any of these methods will save the world, but done well, they can help enliven the worlds of the students who use them.

The Research Essay

We refer to essaying in the Montaignian sense of attempting, wondering, or as Scott Russell Sanders puts it, creating "experiments in making sense of things" (*Paradise* xiii):

> The "essay is the closest thing we have, on paper, to a record of the individual mind at work and play . . . [it is] the spectacle of a single consciousness making sense of a part of the chaos" of experience. The essay works by "following the zigzag motions of the inquisitive mind. . . . The writing of an essay is like finding one's way through a forest without being quite sure what game you are chasing, what landmark you are seeking." ("Singular" 660, quoted in Heilker 89)

Paul Heilker argues that the essay counters the "thesis/support form," which he finds restrictive to students' development as thinkers and writers, and in conflict with current theories of social epistemology and rhetoric. These theories, he notes, tend to see truth and reality as multiple, provisional, dialogic, and dialectical. The essay better fits such theories in that it allows for multiple viewpoints, puts these viewpoints into dialogue with one another, and arrives, like the I-Search, at a provisional conclusion to be questioned in the dialectic's next round, or a recasting of the question.

Potentially, the essay can include all of experience. As Susan Griffin suggests in "The Red Shoes," and enacts in many of her works, essays can make the private public, erasing the lines we draw between parts of our experience. In this way, Griffin says, the essay is like the novel, which she finds to have discovered the legitimacy of private worlds for public writing. In form, the essay also resembles the novel by being varied in structure and often radically mixed in form. As Lydia Fakundiny notes, "Every essay is the only one of its kind. There are no rules for making beginnings, or middles, or endings; it is a harder, a more original discipline than that" (2). Further, essays typically collect many different kinds of discourse: personal narratives, philosophic speculations, textual interpretations, parables, legends, folk wisdom, jokes, dialogues, complaints, rants, and arguments. Essay writing requires fluid thinking, rhetorical flexibility, and the ability to orchestrate.

The essay is brought to research writing in the work of Bruce Ballenger. In *The Curious Researcher,* Ballenger says that students who write research essays shape, and are shaped by, the information they encounter. A broad range of topics is possible, since the writer is not limited to arguing a single position. Topic development often leads to the expansion of thinking as the writer takes in and reflects on various viewpoints. It also offers an element of risk, as writers must mediate between views and work toward their own developing understanding. However, with risk can come intellectual growth—as well as academic enculturation. By inscribing themselves in the midst of a dialogue, debate, or search, students cast themselves within a culture of seeking.

An objection to assigning the research essay stems from compositionists' concerns with preparing students for college writing. Students are unlikely to write this hybrid post-Montaignian, research-enhanced form (or collection of forms) in other courses. It may be, however, that the research essay prepares students for the diverse literacies of the academy precisely through its variety of information and discourse. It can be used to teach students various modes and genres, while also showing how this variety can function together. The research essay can prepare students for further academic and intellectual work by helping them to cultivate the ability and desire to engage multiple perspectives on issues that remain open for further inquiry.[11]

The Multi-Genre/Media/Disciplinary/Cultural Research Project

The final alternative strategy we survey here, the multi-genre/media/disciplinary/cultural research project, further expands the field of seeking. Here, students explore topics of interest or fascination and use a variety of sources to inform projects that combine multiple genres and, in some cases, different media, disciplines, and cultures. These projects often resist, suspend, and/or decanter the master consciousness or central perspective inscribed in the essay as a unifying voice. They instead suggest a wandering consciousness, the traces of which we read in the various, linked, echoing pieces it has left behind for us to find.

These traces may come in the form of words, or in other media. In *The Electronic Word,* Richard Lanham calls print "an act of perceptual self-denial," and says that electronic textuality makes us aware of that "self-denial at every point and in all the ways in which print is at pains to conceal" (74). Multi-media research writing also points out these denials, but offering a full world of expression and communication in which the visual arts, video, music, noise, textures, even smells and tastes work in complex relations with writing. Like Web sites and other electronic discourses, multi-media research writing enacts a process of intertextual linking that erases the boundaries between texts, and between author and audience. Multi-media research projects gather material from many sources and often inspire readers to contribute more, or to do related work.

The act of gathering can also go beyond genres and media. The wandering, and wondering, consciousness is connected to the traits Julie Thompson Klein ascribes to interdisciplinary thinkers: "reliability, flexibility, patience, resilience, sensitivity to others, risk taking, a thick skin, and a preference for diversity and new social roles" (182–83). Klein also claims that "the tendency to follow problems across disciplinary boundaries" is ". . . a normal characteristic of highly active researchers" (183). The wandering/wondering consciousness knows no boundaries because its focus is on the questions it pursues. Such pursuit is not careless, for it requires great concentration as well as openness. Enacting such a mind is a sign of great "discipline," but not that which requires us to stick to bounded fields.

A combination of flexibility and focus is also often seen in the multicultural codeswitchers who have finally begun to gain recognition as the margins of culture become central sites for intellectual study. In *Borderlands/La Frontera,* Gloria Anzaldúa writes of the new *mestiza,* who "operates in a pluralistic mode—

---

[11]If our suggestions of the value of wondering and the uses of mystery seem to suggest a purely humanistic or philosophic viewpoint on research writing, consider an episode of *Nova* in which scientists confront the thrilling mysteries of the planet Venus. Venus, these scientists say, was traditionally thought to be very similar to Earth, close in size and, probably, composition. It was even thought that Venus might have oceans and rich oil deposits. Data from various, probes, however, suggest not only that Venus is not like Earth, but that things happen there that could not happen on Earth, at least given our current understanding of natural processes and laws. The Earth's surface, for instance, is thought (and verifiably proven) to have been made over time, through the mechanics of volcanic eruption and plate tectonics. The surface of Venus appears to be all one age. By Earthly standards, this can't be.

nothing is thrust out, the good, the bad and the ugly, nothing rejected, nothing abandoned. Not only does she sustain contradictions, she turns the ambivalence into something else" (79).

This "something else" is a state of consciousness and discourse that the multi-genre/media/disciplinary/cultural/research project begins to work toward. Such projects can create intellectual spaces that allow for various information, mindsets, and ideas—as well as diverse methods of thinking and ways of expressing, arguing, and communicating—to question and deepen one another and together make a greater, but still dissonant, whole. These projects work by making, but not forcing, connections; as such, they model the holistic learning that most formal schooling, with its disciplinary structure and many exclusions, too often works against.

David Jolliffe's work on multi-genre inquiry offers a starting point for considering how to enact multi-genre/disciplinary/cultural research writing. Jolliffe asks students to make an "inquiry contract" in which they agree to research and write several different pieces about a subject. Example topics, listed in Jolliffe's *Inquiry and Genre: Writing to Learn in College,* include the history of the seeding system in tennis, the relationship between the stock market and the defense industry, and the roles of women in American wars. Students pursue their topics using a range of rhetorical strategies, including: the contract proposal; the clarification project, in which students write reflectively about what they already know; the information project, in which they report on things they learn; the exploration project, with an essay raising additional questions; and the working documents project, which results in public writing designed to change people's minds.

Pieces within Jolliffe's method are reminiscent of the expository modernist research paper, the research argument, and the research essay, and—since each project begins with students' own interests—the overall agenda is similar to that of the personal research paper. By using these varied strategies, students strive to build a rhetorical repertoire. They also learn how to better recognize that their thinking is conditioned by the genres they write in, and that inquiry can extend across a range of singular, but related, texts.

Tom Romano describes multi-genre research projects that are potentially even more student-driven and open-ended. Romano's idea for what he came to call the Multi-Genre Research Paper surfaced after reading Michael Ondaatje's multi-genre "novel," *The Collected Works of Billy the Kid,* the reading of which Romano compared to listening to jazz: ". . . the reader feels something satisfying and meaningful, but may not be able to articulate what it is right away" (124). Romano asked his high school students to make biographical research projects using a style similar to Ondaatje's. The students wrote on subjects including Elvis Presley, Jimi Hendrix, Jim Thorpe, Marilyn Monroe, and Maya Angelou. Romano reports on the results:

> I have never read anything like these papers. Although four or five [of 26] were disappointing, showing little depth, breadth, or commitment, the rest were good, genuinely interesting in style and content, with seven or eight papers astonishingly superior. The visions were complex, the writing versatile. (130–131)

These students' projects are portfolios of diverse writing on a common subject. Each piece echoes the others, as an inner dynamic or theme emerges. A sample paper on John Lennon focuses especially on Lennon's love for Yoko Ono. The project is linked, in part, by a continuing series of poems about Lennon's murder called "Unfinished Music." It also contains other genres, including a news story, several narratives, and a meditation on the number "9" and its repeating presence in John and Yoko's lives. The author, Brian McNight calls the project a "play," perhaps because it manages multiple voices (132–37).

Our students at Eastern Oregon University have gone beyond the multi-genre research paper to compose research projects that incorporate multiple genres, media, disciplines, and cultures. This approach originated in a 200-level Applied Discourse Theory course. It came out of long meditation on the way our students often found research sterile and theory either incomprehensible or dry. While initial resistance to the multi-genre/media/disciplinary/cultural approach was great—as the only thing more terrifying than slavery is sometimes freedom—students quickly found the excitement in research and theory directed toward projects that linked their academic and personal lives.

"Multi-writing," as we have come to call it, has now spread at our university to a 400-level capstone seminar in English/Writing; 300-level courses in Writing Theory, Electronic Literary, and American Folklore; 200-level courses in Argumentation and Methods of Tutoring Writing; and a 100-level Exploratory Writing course. It has also expanded to courses in other disciplines, including a 100-level American Government course, and a 300-level Spanish Literature course. Next year, the university is planning a holistic revision of general education that will cast multi-writing as a central method for helping students to learn across disciplines and connect academic issues to their personal concerns. We see this sort of work early in college as an important retention effort, as well as a way of breaking intellectual ground for further work at the higher levels.

Through conference presentations and workshops, multi-writing has now been taken up on other campuses in our state and nationally and has moved into K-12 classes, especially those taught by fellows of the Oregon Writing Project, many of whom have participated in multi-writing workshops. At the primary and secondary levels, multi-writing helps students generate rich work samples, demonstrating multiple proficiencies for assessment.[12]

In teaching multi-writing in our discourse theory course, we first open students up to a sense of either a multi-dimensional self or multiple selves, in order to create in a postmodern world. We have used texts like Daniel Halpern's *Who's Wining This?*, where dozens of famous writers rewrite the little self-portrait of Jorge Luis Borges in their own surprisingly different ways. Often students move from writing traditional and summative autobiographical pieces, where the older and wiser narrator looks back, to multi-cultural and generative ones, where the writer creates a new incarnation to grow into. Also successful has been a variation of autoethnography where students interview three people about themselves, then affirm or rebut the comments. We even invented two new kinds of multi-autobiography: "ought-to" and "want-to" biography—where students with a difficult childhood they would rather not delve into can imagine a different past: struggling artist in Paris, Tibetan monk, Earth Goddess, architect, blues musician.

In our most recent term of teaching, multi-autobiography projects included: Frank Kaminski's recycling box of personal obsessions from banal pop culture (*Star Wars,* the *Dukes of Hazzard,* the *Alien* movies); Katie McCann's cast-a-way project in which she imagines she is stranded on an island (her writings and drawings are contained in bottles); and Cara Kobernik's project on shoes. Shoes have been an important part of the author's life since she was baby, due originally to medical problems with her feet. The project includes a mock shoe catalogue and an illuminated manuscript called "Shoe Stories," as well as a beloved pair of sandals. In another memorable project, Lisa Rodgers split her self into three emanations with very different personalities and had the three escape from the dictatorial "Lisa" and journey on an improbable adventure, reminiscent of *Thelma and Louise.*

To keep the self from becoming too abstract and imaginary, we then require a mini-body project. Texts like Diane Ackerman's *A Natural History of the Senses* help students see how to combine facts with stylish prose. Student projects on the body often counter the typical images of the body prevalent in our culture, searching for other, richer views. Recent examples include Aubree Tipton's study of the relation of mind to disease and Sherry McGeorge's elaborate project on a feminist philosophy of belly dancing.

Finally, students create their own "multi-research project" on a theme they select. Some of these projects are biographical, like those of Romano's students. Subjects of recent "multi-biographies" include Adrienne Rich, Howard Hughes, Georgia O'Keefe, and Kurt Cobain. Other students find different themes,

---

[12]For more on using multi-writing to meet proficiency standards, see "Multi-Genre Writing and State Standards," an article in the *Oregon English Journal,* which we wrote with high school teachers Tom Lovell, Jennifer Pambrun, and John Scanlan.

including: angels, Schoedinger's cat experiment, theories of the end of the world, massage, autism, the mysteries of tea, the Grand Canyon, the color blue, the Shroud of Turin, the Taiwanese language/dialect, the religion of television, masks, islands, Proppian interpretation of dreams, the concept of the "soulmate," the birth of punk rock, and debates over the literary canon.

The works show remarkable syncretism. Aubree Tipton's project on the Grand Canyon brings together courses she has taken in history, geology, and literature. Linnea Simon's project on tea is a cross-cultural dialogue, while Jakob Curtis studies Taiwan as a multiculture. Shirley Crabtree's interdisciplinary/multicultural project on fleas inscribes the history of this tiny but durable animal as part of a wider narrative of attempts by various imperial and fascistic entities to kill those seen as lesser.

The projects are widely varied in form. Like Romano's students, ours typically employ a range of genres: narratives, interpretive essays, letters, poems, wills, employment applications, lab reports, ethnographic and archeological field notes, prophecies, aphorisms, monologues, and dialogues, to name just a few. Cara Kobernik's project on the meanings of spring includes poems, personal and historical narratives, myths, folktales, monologues (including one by the Easter bunny), scripture and scriptural exegesis, aphorisms, science writing, philosophic reflection, and recipes.

Various media also abound. Judith Darrow's project on the fresco includes several original paintings in a style that might be called postmodern gothic. Kobernik's project on spring is very nearly a coffeetable book, with many photographs and drawings and an elegant design, as well as a lovely, floral smell. Nearly all of Jan Harris' project on blue is displayed in blue, on blue. The Grand Canyon project includes music, as does the project on blue, and many others. Videos are also common. Project containers are often interesting. We have received projects in folders, books, albums, boxes, crates, ovens, and even the back of a pickup truck. The project on blue comes in a binder covered with a blue suit. Eric Hutchinson's project on train travel is contained in its own kerchief-and-pole hobo bag. McGeorge's project on belly dancing comes wrapped in a beautiful scarf.

Some of the projects include strong elements of parody, often with serious intent: Sherri Edvalson's "A Feminist Education for Barbie" explores the effectiveness of gender theory and pedagogy in a continually sexist culture; it is enacted through a series of mock assignments for various courses and contained in a Barbie bookbag. Sue Ruth's EmpTV Guide, which is written in the form of a mock *TV Guide,* includes substantial research on television programming and cultural criticism, as well as scripts for mock commercials and Barnie's appearance on the Home Shopping Network. The project shows us locked into a media culture from which even parody cannot quite grant us escape.

In the midst of a grand variety of possible subjects, purposes, and forms, choices must be made. In his project on Houdini, Randy Kromwall saw and wanted to show intensity, obsession, awe, and passion in the magician's relationship to one of his most famous and dangerous tricks, the Water Torture Cell. Kromwall crafted a discourse that is part dialogue, part interior monologue, part lyric poem. The machine speaks, claiming that it is loved, and Houdini answers: "Yes, I love you / But you also terrify me. . . ." Kromwall gives his project a sensational tone and circus-like aura through the use of gothic type and several colorful posters advertising Houdini.

In her project on theories of good and evil, Judy Cornish used genres and media creatively to represent the ways in which her sources, and Cornish herself, have seen the two forces interlocking, and even becoming one. Her project design employed only black, white, and gray for its many images from high art and pop culture. Cornish made some images from scratch, and processed others into collages and striking juxtapositions. Among her writings is a dialogue in which the Kenpo concept of "push/pull," a way of absorbing violence, is explicated by a master and absorbed by a student, physically and spiritually. At the end, a provisional peace is realized when master and student redirect violence in a dance of acceptance.

In a reflective essay we typically assign at the end of a project, Cornish writes that her work on good and evil grew from her own hard life choices, which have made her question whether she was "good" or "evil," or if these words refer to anything real. Her project makes use of views on good and evil from writers of various time periods and cultures, including Toni Morrison, John Barth, Niccolo Machiavelli, and Kitaro Nishida. Cornish has told us that her personal connection to the material not only prompted the project, but pushed her toward doing more research and writing, even after she had clearly gone far beyond the requirements of the assignment. She was intellectually exploring a question that she was also urgently living

A similar personal impetus motivates many of our students' projects, and sometimes leads them to work beyond the project. For Michelle Skow, a project on the Japanese American Internment grew into a larger capstone project, to which she has continued to add, even now that she has graduated. Skow realized that her own identity was deeply entwined with her grandparents' experience during the Internment. In her reflective essay, she wrote:

> The Japanese American Internment experience is something my grandparents rarely discuss. When they do, they refer to their internment as "camp"—a euphemism for unlawful incarceration. Both claim to remember little of what happened during this time, even though my grandma was eleven and my grandpa was fourteen. . . . I have urged them to share, in-depth, this part of their lives with me, but they cling tightly to their vow of silence. I cannot say I disagree with their desire to forgive and forget, but I feel a part of me is missing.

Skow's project became an act of historical memory and re-creation. It begins dramatically, with a stark copy of the internment order (see Figure 1).[13] The project also includes a conventional historical narra-

---

[13]The text of Executive Order No. 9066 is as follows:

Instructions to All Persons of Japanese Ancestry Living in the Following Area:

All that portion of the City and County of San Francisco, State of California, lying generally west of the north-south line established by Junipero Serra Boulevard, Worchester Avenue, and Nineteenth Avenue, and lying generally north of the east-west line established by California Street, to the intersection of Market Street, and thence on Market Street to San Francisco Bay.

All Japanese persons, both alien and non-alien, will be evacuated from the above designated area by 12:00 o'clock noon Tuesday, April 7, 1942.

No Japanese person will be permitted to enter or leave the above described area after 8:00 a.m., Thursday, April 2, 1942, without obtaining special permission from the Provost Marshall at the Civil Control Station located at:

1701 Van Ness Avenue
San Francisco, California

The Civil Control Station is equipped to assist the Japanese population affected by this evacuation in the following ways:

1. Give advice and instructions on the evacuation.
2. Provide services with respect to the management, leasing, sale, storage or other disposition of most kinds of property including: real estate, business and professional equipment, buildings, household goods, boats, automobiles, livestock, etc.
3. Provide temporary residence elsewhere for all Japanese in family groups.
4. Transport persons and a limited amount of clothing and equipment to their new residence, as specified below.

The Following Instructions Must Be Observed:

1. A responsible member of each family, preferably the head of the family, or the person in whose name most of the property is held, and each individual living alone, will report to the Civil Control Station to receive further instructions. This must be done between 8:00 a.m. and 5:00 p.m. Thursday, April 2, 1942, or between 8:00 a.m. and 5:00 p.m., Friday, April 3, 1942.

EXECUTIVE ORDER NO. 9066

**WESTERN DEFENSE COMMAND AND FOURTH ARMY
WARTIME CIVIL CONTROL ADMINISTRATION**
Presidio of San Francisco, California
April 1, 1942

INSTRUCTIONS
TO ALL PERSONS OF
JAPANESE
ANCESTRY

Living in the Following Area:

All that portion of the City and County of San Francisco, State of California, lying generally west of the north-south line established by Junipero Serra Boulevard, Worchester Avenue, and Nineteenth Avenue, and lying generally north of the east-west line established by California Street, to the intersection of Market Street, and thence on Market Street to San Francisco Bay.

All Japanese persons, both alien and non-alien, will be evacuated from the above designated area by 12:00 o'clock noon Tuesday, April 7, 1942.

No Japanese person will be permitted to enter or leave the above described area after 8:00 a. m., Thursday, April 2, 1942, without obtaining special permission from the Provost Marshal at the Civil Control Station located at:

1701 Van Ness Avenue
San Francisco, California

The Civil Control Station is equipped to assist the Japanese population affected by this evacuation in the following ways:

1. Give advice and instructions on the evacuation.
2. Provide services with respect to the management, leasing, sale, storage or other disposition of most kinds of property including: real estate, business and professional equipment, buildings, household goods, boats, automobiles, livestock, etc.
3. Provide temporary residence elsewhere for all Japanese in family groups.
4. Transport persons and a limited amount of clothing and equipment to their new residence, as specified below.

The Following Instructions Must Be Observed:

1. A responsible member of each family, preferably the head of the family, or the person in whose name most of the property is held, and each individual living alone, will report to the Civil Control Station to receive further instructions. This must be done between 8:00 a. m. and 5:00 p. m., Thursday, April 2, 1942, or between 8:00 a. m. and 5:00 p. m., Friday, April 3, 1942.

2. Evacuees must carry with them on departure for the Reception Center, the following property:
(a) Bedding and linens (no mattress) for each member of the family;
(b) Toilet articles for each member of the family;
(c) Extra clothing for each member of the family;
(d) Sufficient knives, forks, spoons, plates, bowls and cups for each member of the family;
(e) Essential personal effects for each member of the family.

All items carried will be securely packaged, tied and plainly marked with the name of the owner and numbered in accordance with instructions received at the Civil Control Station.

The size and number of packages is limited to that which can be carried by the individual or family group.

No contraband items as described in paragraph 6, Public Proclamation No. 3, Headquarters Western Defense Command and Fourth Army, dated March 24, 1942, will be carried.

3. The United States Government through its agencies will provide for the storage at the sole risk of the owner of the more substantial household items, such as iceboxes, washing machines, pianos and other heavy furniture. Cooking utensils and other small items will be accepted if crated, packed and plainly marked with the name and address of the owner. Only one name and address will be used by a given family.

4. Each family, and individual living alone, will be furnished transportation to the Reception Center. Private means of transportation will not be utilized. All instructions pertaining to the movement will be obtained at the Civil Control Station.

Go to the Civil Control Station at 1701 Van Ness Avenue, San Francisco, California, between 8:00 a. m. and 5:00 p. m., Thursday, April 2, 1942, or between 8:00 a. m. and 5:00 p. m., Friday, April 3, 1942, to receive further instructions.

J. L. DeWITT
Lieutenant General, U. S. Army
Commanding

Figure 1. Executive Order No. 9066 as it appeared in 1942. The full text is repeated in Note 13.

2. Evacuees must carry with them on departure for the Reception Center, the following property:
   (a) Bedding and linens (no mattress) for each member of the family;
   (b) Toilet articles for each member of the family;
   (c) Extra clothing for each member of the family;
   (d) Sufficient knives, forks, spoons, plates, bowls and cups for each member of the family;
   (e) Essential personal effects for each member of the family.

tive about the Internment; found texts, such as James Masao Mitsui's poems written from photographs; Skow's own poems; diary entries written by Skow from the point of view of her grandparents during the Internment; photographs; and a poster announcing Executive Order 9066, the Internment order.

At times, we are taken to the camps; at other times, we are looking back at them. Gradually, Skow comes to better understand not only the Internment, but also her older relatives' attitude about it. She writes:

> I want to forget Okasan as she sits.
> Silently crocheting doily after doily.
> Tablecloth after tablecloth.
> Her nymph-like hands, cracked and withered
> From the burning sum and stinging dust.
> Working consciously, stitching a contract of silence:
> Never forsake, never look back, never forget.

She has circled back to her grandmother's silence, with a new understanding. But not a full one. Skow followed up her fast "multi-project" with another on first generation Japanese Americans that grew into a capstone for her English/History double major. Now that she has graduated, she continues to tell us about new reading and writing that she has done, including essays on her "third generation" cultural heritage, and more writings from her grandparents' point of view. She says that she sees herself trying to mesh the first-generation world view and her own.

As well as asking students to write reflectively about (and often, within) their projects, we also ask students to refract, to think about projects deflected from the original, threads left hanging, questions remaining, or questions not yet asked.[14] Several of our students have followed Skow in creating linked projects. Michael McClure began with an autobiographic project, modeled after Gregory Ulmer's concept of

---

All items carried will be securely packaged, tied and plainly marked with the name of the owner and numbered in accordance with instructions received at the Civil Control Station.

The size and number of packages are limited to that which can be carried by the individual or family group.

No contraband items as described in paragraph 6, Public Proclamation No. 3. Headquarters Western Defense Command and Fourth Army, dated March 24, 1942, will be carried.

3. The United States Government through its agencies will provide for the storage at the sole risk of the owner of the more substantial household items, such as iceboxes, washing machines, pianos and other heavy furniture. Cooking utensils and other small items will be accepted if crated, packed and plainly marked with the name and address of the owner. Only one name and address will be used by a given family.

4. Each family and individual living alone, will be furnished transportation to the Reception Center. Private means of transportation will not be utilized. All instructions pertaining to the movement will be obtained at the Civil Control Station.

Go to the Civil Control Station at 1701 Van Ness Avenue, San Francisco, California, between 8:00 a.m. and 5:00 p.m., Thursday, April 2,1942, or between 8:00 a.m., and 5:00 p.m. Friday, April 3, 1942, to receive further instructions.

J. L. DeWITT
Lieutenant General, U. S. Army Commanding

[14]A similar view of revision as refraction is held by Nancy Welch in *Getting Restless*. Welsh argues that composition teachers have failed to ask questions such as "something missing, something else?" in responding to student drafts, instead conceiving of revision mainly as a way to narrow foci, correct inappropriate tones, and achieve clarity. For Welch, revision should strive not to eliminative dissonance, but instead use it as "the start of a reproductive struggle that can lead to a change of direction, a change of thesis, and re-envisioning of the text, its meaning and intentions" (30).

"mystory," held in a trunk full of texts and objects supposedly recovered in an archeological dig.[15] Mc-Clure followed this project with another on the artist Joseph Cornell, who made art in and from boxes, cases, and trunks. McClure's project includes a Cornellesque box of found and made objects, including an old gold watch, and several expository, interpretive, and creative writings, including a meditation on archeological time in Cornell's work.

These projects continue to evolve in the minds of their viewers/readers as well as their makers. We return to them again and again, trying to understand them in full, but also finding pleasure in knowing that we will not, that they will remain fertile mysteries. This is an experience far different from reading modernist research papers, where all meanings are to be made immediately clear and the product is considered acceptable in large measure because it follows the rules. In multi-writing "rules" are few. Students are shown some of the earlier projects, then asked to do something better. We assess them according to what they demonstrate as researchers, writers, and thinkers. We ask them to find a variety of sources, show us some of their range and depth as a rhetor, and reach for a philosophic understanding of their subject and their own project that will allow the work to hang together and make each piece part of the same web.

Less Efficiency, More Mystery

It would be possible, perhaps even desirable, to deconstruct the progression we have presented. One could easily cast the alternatives listed above as simply a series of possibilities to be mixed and matched as supplements of, or replacements for, the modernist research papers. It might be quite sound pedagogically, for instance, to ask students to write a research paper, then a research argument, essay or multi-writing research project; or to continue teaching the research paper at the 100-level, and then move on to alternative methods later; or to use alternative methods in introductory courses to get students started researching with fervor, and then require the research paper as they progress toward graduation. Such methods would satisfy consciences that believe the modernist paper ought still to be taught, but also allow students valuable new experiences.

For our purposes, however, establishing a progression is vital, for it shows the purpose and nature of research writing changing to meet the demands of a fluid world of complex relationships. If we want to describe a fixed world as others have described it, the modernist research paper will do. The research argument allows us to move beyond exposition of the unchanging to inscribe a human world continually remade by argument, in which research supports the will to stake and defend a claim. The personal research paper allows an inward turn from this culture of conflict, asking its writer to explore and mediate personal conflicts, contradictions, and questions.

The research essay provides an important reconnection with the social scene of writing, taking as its purpose the personal exploration of an issue or theme of collective concern. The essay can be seen as a discourse of the question, in which a variety of genres of writing are used to wander the terrain of a subject matter through which the writer may have tread before, but which she or he cannot claim to finally "know." The research essay thus foregrounds a shift in priorities—begun in the research argument and personal research paper—away from claims to, or descriptions of, verifiable knowledge, and toward a more open stance on the part of writers aware of uncertainty and contingency.

---

[15]Ulmer presents "mystory" as a writing-after-video that combines personal, professional, and historic elements and utilizes the jump-cut logic of television. Ulmer's own mystory. "Derrida at Little Bighorn," can be seen as a work of personal and public research writing for the electronic age.

The multi-writing research project makes visible use of possibilities implicit in the research essay. Here, the trail of a question or questions leads through a range of connected material, including different genres of writing and, in some cases, different media, disciplines, and cultures. The maker of the multi-writing project is a collector, but not in the way of Muensterberger's collector/possessor. Instead, the intent here is to lay out a portion of what is potentially an inexhaustible, and radically open, network, to which the project's maker, and its readers/viewers, can add. One can imagine an infinite multi-writing which would call into its fold, bit by bit, all of discourse. Even the other methods of research writing—the research paper, the research argument, the personal research paper, the research essay—would be subsumed by this syncretic, ravenous multi-text.

Are we arguing that facts are useless, or that the discourses of expository intent, such as the modernist research paper, be abandoned? No. We are suggesting, however, that facts and expository writing have limits; they allow only certain types of inquiry to take place. What we envision, finally, is a discourse that will not have limits, that will allow for various kinds and levels of inquiry to echo, question, and deepen one another. Cornish's Kenpo scene may end with a brief bit of peace, but her project on good and evil settles nothing. Theories are both upheld and negated, as they challenge, question, and dance with one another. And yet, something important has happened. A student, an intellectual, a person has (re-)engaged an important, open question—one of the fascinations/terrors/joys through which she shapes, repeatedly and anew, her examined life.

Above all, we want our students to view mystery as a source of inquiry, research, and writing. Mystery is an academic value; what good would an institute of inquiry be if everything was already known? A collective appreciation of mystery can also be a basis for revising the academy, making it truly a place of free inquiry, where the unknown is approached from many directions, using a variety of ways of thinking, writing, and making. In this academy, we envision the research writer learning many traditions of inquiry and discourse, while also learning to use these traditions syncretically in the composition classroom. Here, students can begin to write the eclectic and multiple texts of their learning; they can, in singer Sarah McLachlan's oxymoronic words, mix craft and inspiration, and "build a mystery."

Works Cited

Ackerman, Diane. *A Natural History of the Senses.* New York: Random House, 1990.

Anzaldúa, Gloria. *Borderlands/La Frontera: The New Mestiza.* San Francisco: Aunt Lute Books, 1991.

Ballenger, Bruce. *The Curious Researcher: A Guide to Writing Research Papers.* Boston: Allyn and Bacon, 1994.

Barthelme, Donald. "Not-Knowing." *The Art of the Essay.* Ed. Lydia Fakundiny. Boston: Houghton Mifflin, 1991, 485–97.

Bartholomae, David. "Inventing the University." *When a Writer Can't Write: Studies in Writer's Block and Other Composing-Process Problems.* Ed. Mike Rose, New York: Guilford P, 1985, 134–65.

Bauman, Zygmunt, *Intimations of Postmodernity.* London: Routledge, 1992.

Berlin, James. "Contemporary Composition: The Major Pedagogical Theories." *College English* 44 (1982): 343–48.

Boorstin, Daniel J. *The Seekers: The Story of Alan's Continuing Quest to Understand His World.* New York: Random House, 1998.

Booth, Wayne C., Gregory G. Colomb, and Joseph M. Williams. *The Craft of Research.* Chicago: U of Chicago P, 1995.

Canby, Henry S., et al. *English Composition in Theory and Practice.* 3rd ed. New York: Macmillan, 1933.

Clark, Steven R. L. "Ancient Philosophy." *The Oxford History of Western Philosophy.* Ed. Anthony Kenny. Oxford: Oxford UP, 1994, 1–54.

Connors, Robert J. *Composition-Rhetoric: Backgrounds, Theory, and Pedagogy.* Pittsburgh: U of Pittsburgh P, 1997.

Covino, William A. *The Art of Wondering: A Revisionist Return to the History of Rhetoric.* Portsmouth, NH: Heinemann, 1988.

_____. *Forms of Wondering: A Dialogue of Writing for Writers.* Portsmouth. NH: Heinemann, 1990.

Cowan, James. *A Mapmaker's Dream: The Meditations of Fra Mauro, Cartographer to the Court of Venice.* New York: Warner, 1996.

Crowley, Sharon, and Debra Hawhee. *Ancient Rhetorics for Contemporary Students.* 2nd ed. Boston: Allyn and Bacon, 1999.

Davis, Robert L., Tom Lovell, Jennifer Pambrun, John Scanlan, and Mark Shadle. "Multi-Genre Writing and State Standards." *Oregon English Journal* 20.2 (1988): 5–10.

Deleuze, Gilles, and Félix Guattari. *A Thousand Plateaus: Capitalism and Schizophrenia.* Trans. Brian Massumi. Minneapolis: U of Minnesota P, 1987.

Elkins, James. *The Object Stares Back: On the Nature of Seeing.* New York: Simon and Schuster, 1996.

Faigley, Lester. "Competing Theories of Process: A Critique and a Proposal." *College English* 48 (1986): 527–42.

Fakundiny, Lydia. "On Approaching the Essay." *The Art of the Essay.* Ed. Lydia Fakundiny. Boston: Houghton Mifflin, 1991, 1–19.

Ford, James E. "Introduction: The Need for *The Research Paper.*" *Teaching the Research Paper: From Theory to Practice, from Research to Writing.* Ed. James E. Ford, Metuchen, NJ: Scarecrow 1995, 1–5.

Ford, James E., and Dennis R. Perry "Research Paper Instruction in Undergraduate Writing Programs: National Survey." *College English* 44 (1982): 825–31.

Griffin, Susan. "The Bed Shoes." *The Eros of Everyday Life: Essays on Ecology, Gender, and Society.* New York: Doubleday, 1995, 161–76.

Halpern, Daniel, ed. *Who's Writing This? Notations on the Authorial I, with Self-Portraits.* Hopewell, NJ: Ecco P, 1995.

Heilker, Paul. *The Essay Theory and Pedagogy for an Active Form.* Urbana, IL: NCTE, 1996.

Jolliffe, David A. *Inquiry and Genre: Writing to Learn in College.* Boston: Allyn and Bacon, 1999.

Kafka, Franz. *The Castle.* Trans. Edwin and Willa Muir. New York: Knopf, 1941.

Kinneavy, James. *A Theory of Discourse.* Englewood Cliffs, NJ: Prentice-Hall, 1971.

Klein, Julie Thompson. *Interdisciplinarity: History, Theory and Practice.* Detroit: Wayne State UP, 1990.

Kundera, Milan. *The Art of the Novel.* Trans. Linda Asher. Now York: Grove P, 1988.

Lanham, Richard. *The Electronic Word: Democracy, Technology, and the Arts.* Chicago: U of Chicago P, 1993.

Larson, Richard L. "The 'Research Paper' in the Writing Course: A Non-Form of Writing." *College English* 44 (1982): 811–16.

Macrorie, Ken. *The I-Search Paper.* Portsmouth, NH: Heinemann, 1998.

Miller, Susan. *Textual Carnivals: The Politics of Composition.* Carbondale: Southern Illinois UP, 1991.

Muensterberger, Werner. *Collecting: An Unruly Passion: Psychological Perspectives.* NJ: Princeton UP, 1994.

Olson, Charles. *The Special View of History.* Berkeley: Oyez. 1970.

Ondaatje, Michael. *The Collected Works of Billy the Kid.* New York: Norton. 1974.

Owens, Derek. "Composition as the Voicing of Multiple Fictions." *Into the Field: Sites of Composition Studies.* Ed. Anne Ruggles Gere. New York: MLA, 1993, 159-75.

Posusta, Steven. *Don't Panic: The Procrastinator's Guide to Writing an Effective Term Paper (You know who you are).* Santa Barbara: Bandanna, 1996.

Romano, Tom. *Writing with Passion: Life Stories, Multiple Genres.* Portsmouth, NH: Heinemann, 1995.

Russell, David R. *Writing in the Academic Disciplines 1870–1990: A Curricular History.* Carbondale: Southern Illinois UP, 1991.

Sanders, Scott Russell. *The Paradise of Bombs.* Athens: U of Georgia P, 1987.

_____. "The Singular First Person." *Sewanee Review* 96 (1988) 658–72.

Schwegler, Robert E., and Linda K. Shamoon. "The Aims and Process of the Research Paper." *College English* 44 (1982): 817–24.

Seyler, Dorothy U. *Doing Research: The Complete Research Paper Guide.* 2nd ed. Boston: McGraw-Hill, 1999.

Sirc, Geoffrey. "Never Mind the Tagmemics: Where's the Sex Pistols?" *College Composition and Communication* 48 (1997): 9–29.

Ulmer, Gregory. *Teletheory: Grammatology in the Age of Video.* New York: Routledge, 1989.

Veit, Richard. *Research: The Student's Guide to Writing Research Papers.* 2nd ed. Boston: Allyn and Boom 1998.

"Venus Unveiled." *Nova.* PBS. Oct.17, 1995.

Welch, Nancy. *Getting Restless: Rethinking Revision in Writing Instruction.* Portsmouth, NH: Heinemann-Boynton/Cook, 1997.

Wolverton, S. F. "Professional Scullery." *Educational Review* 60 (1920): 407.

Zeldin, Theodore. *An Intimate History of Humanity.* New York: Harper, 1966.

Robert Davis and Mark Shadle

Robert Davis and Mark Shadle are associate professors of English-Writing at Eastern Oregon University in La Grande, where Davis directs the writing program and Shadle directs the Writing Lab. Davis's teaching and research interests include postmodern theory, ancient rhetoric, carnivalisque discourse, exploratory writing, and teacher education. He has published articles and book chapters on cultural simulations, multigenre approaches to writing pedagogy, and electronic writing. Shadle's teaching and research interests include writing center theory and practice, postmodern and post-colonial theory, exploratory writing, American and Caribbean Studies, environmental literature, multicultural and contemporary world literature. He has published articles and book chapters on writing center staffing, online writing labs, blues/jazz, and the work of Wendell Berry, Ishmael Reed, David Rubadiri, and Simon Schama. Together, Davis and Shadle have spread the use of multi-writing in multiple genres, disciplines, cultures, and media from their own courses and campus throughout the Pacific Northwest and the country through conference presentations and National Writing Project workshops. Currently, they are at work on a textbook on research writing that presents multi-writing alongside traditional forms.

❧ ON KEEPING A NOTEBOOK ❧

Joan Didion

"'That woman Estelle,'" the note reads, "'is partly the reason why George Sharp and I are separated today.' *Dirty crépe-de-Chine wrapper, hotel bar, Wilmington RR, 9:45 A.M. August Monday morning.*"

Since the note is in my notebook, it presumably has some meaning to me. I study it for a long while. At first I have only the most general notion of what I was doing on an August Monday morning in the bar of the hotel across from the Pennsylvania Railroad station in Wilmington, Delaware (waiting for a train? missing one? 1960? 1961? why Wilmington?), but I do remember being there. The woman in the dirty crépe-de-Chine wrapper had come down from her room for a beer, and the bartender had heard before the reason why George Sharp and she were separated today. "Sure," he said, and went on mopping the floor. "You told me." At the other end of the bar is a girl. She is talking, pointedly, not to the man beside her but to a cat lying in the triangle of sunlight cast through the open door. She is wearing a plaid silk dress from Peck & Peck, and the hem is coming down.

Here is what it is: the girl has been on the Eastern Shore, and now she is going back to the city, leaving the man beside her, and all she can see ahead are the viscous summer sidewalks and the 3 A.M. long-distance calls that will make her lie awake and then sleep drugged through all the steaming mornings left in August (1960? 1961?). Because she must go directly from the train to lunch in New York, she wishes that she had a safety pin for the hem of the plaid silk dress, and she also wishes that she could forget about the hem and the lunch and stay in the cool bar that smells of disinfectant and malt and make friends with the woman in the crépe-de-Chine wrapper. She is afflicted by a little self-pity, and she wants to compare Estelles. That is what that was all about.

Why did I write it down? In order to remember, of course, but exactly what was it I wanted to remember? How much of it actually happened? Did any of it? Why do I keep a notebook at all? It is easy to deceive oneself on all those scores. The impulse to write things down is a peculiarly compulsive one, inexplicable to those who do not share it, useful only accidentally, only secondarily, in the way that any compulsion tries to justify itself. I suppose that it begins or does not begin in the cradle. Although I have felt compelled to write things down since I was five years old, I doubt that my daughter ever will, for she is a singularly blessed and accepting child, delighted with life exactly as life presents itself to her, unafraid to go to sleep and unafraid to wake up. Keepers of private notebooks are a different breed altogether, lonely and resistant rearrangers of things, anxious malcontents, children afflicted apparently at birth with some presentiment of loss.

My first notebook was a Big Five tablet, given to me by my mother with the sensible suggestion that I stop whining and learn to amuse myself by writing down my thoughts. She returned the tablet to me a few years ago; the first entry is an account of a woman who believed herself to be freezing to death in the Arctic night, only to find, when day broke, that she had stumbled onto the Sahara Desert, where she would die of the heat before lunch. I have no idea what turn of a five-year-old's mind could have prompted so insistently "ironic" and exotic a story, but it does reveal a certain predilection for the extreme which has dogged me into adult life; perhaps if I were analytically inclined I would find it a truer story than any

I might have told about Donald Johnson's birthday party or the day my cousin Brenda put Kitty Litter in the aquarium.

So the point of my keeping a notebook has never been, nor is it now, to have an accurate factual record of what I have been doing or thinking. That would be a different impulse entirely, an instinct for reality which I sometimes envy but do not possess. At no point have I ever been able successfully to keep a diary; my approach to daily life ranges from the grossly negligent to the merely absent, and on those few occasions when I have tried dutifully to record a day's events, boredom has so overcome me that the results are mysterious at best. What is this business about "shopping, typing piece, dinner with E, depressed"? Shopping for what? Type what piece? Who is E? Was this "E" depressed, or was I depressed? Who cares?

In fact I have abandoned altogether that kind of pointless entry; instead I tell what some would call lies. "That's simply not true," the members of my family frequently tell me when they come up against my memory of a shared event. "The party was not for you, the spider was *not* a black widow, *it wasn't that way at all.*" Very likely they are right, for not only have I always had trouble distinguishing between what happened and what merely might have happened, but I remain unconvinced that the distinction, for my purposes, matters. The cracked crab that I recall having for lunch the day my father came home from Detroit in 1945 must certainly be embroidery, worked into the day's pattern to lend verisimilitude; I was ten years old and would not now remember the cracked crab. The day's events did not turn on cracked crab. And yet it is precisely that fictitious crab that makes me see the afternoon all over again, a home movie run all too often, the father bearing gifts, the child weeping, an exercise in family love and guilt. Or that is what it was to me. Similarly, perhaps it never did snow that August in Vermont; perhaps there never were flurries in the night wind, and maybe no one else felt the ground hardening and summer already dead even as we pretended to bask in it, but that was how it felt to me; and it might as well have snowed, could have snowed, did snow.

How it felt to me: that is getting closer to the truth about a notebook. I sometimes delude myself about why I keep a notebook, imagine that some thrifty virtue derives from preserving everything observed. See enough and write it down, I tell myself and then some morning when the world seems drained of wonder, some day when I am only going through the motions of doing what I am supposed to do, which is write—on that bankrupt morning I will simply open my notebook and there it will be, a forgotten account with accumulated interest, paid passage back to the world out there: dialogue overheard in hotels and elevators and at the hatcheck counter in Pavillon (one middle-aged man shows his hat check to another and says, "That's my old football number"); impressions of Bettina Aptheker and Benjamin Sonnenberg and Teddy ("Mr. Acapulco") Stauffer; careful *aperçus* about tennis bums and failed fashion models and Greek shipping heiresses, one of whom taught me a significant lesson (a lesson I could have learned from F. Scott Fitzgerald, but perhaps we all must meet the very rich for ourselves) by asking, when I arrived to interview her in her orchid-filled sitting room on the second day of a paralyzing New York blizzard, whether it was snowing outside.

I imagine, in other words, that the notebook is about other people. But of course it is not. I have no real business with what one stranger said to another at the hatcheck counter in Pavillon; in fact I suspect that the line "That's my old football number" touched not my own imagination at all, but merely some memory of something once read, probably "The Eighty-Yard Run." Nor is my concern with a woman in a dirty crêpe-de-Chine wrapper in a Wilmington bar. My stake is always, of course, in the unmentioned girl in the plaid silk dress. *Remember what it was to be me:* that is always the point.

It is a difficult point to admit. We are brought up in the ethic that others, any others, all others, are by definition more interesting than ourselves; taught to be diffident, just this side of self-effacing. ("You're the least important person in the room and don't forget it," Jessica Mitford's governess would hiss in her ear on the advent of any social occasion; I copied that into my notebook because it is only recently that I have been able to enter a room without hearing some such phrase in my inner ear.) Only the very young and the very old may recount their dreams at breakfast, dwell upon self, interrupt with memories of beach picnics and favorite Liberty lawn dresses and the rainbow trout in a creek near Colorado Springs. The rest of us are expected, rightly, to affect absorption in other people's favorite dresses, other people's trout.

And so we do. But our notebooks give us away, for however dutifully we record what we see around us, the common denominator of all we see is always, transparently, shamelessly, the implacable "I." We are not talking here about the kind of notebook that is patently for public consumption, a structural conceit for binding together a series of graceful *pensées;* we are talking about something private, about bits of the mind's string too short to use, an indiscriminate and erratic assemblage with meaning only for its maker.

And sometimes even the maker has difficulty with the meaning. There does not seem to be, for example, any point in my knowing for the rest of my life that, during 1964, 720 tons of soot fell on every square mile of New York City, yet there it is in my notebook, labeled "FACT." Nor do I really need to remember that Ambrose Bierce liked to spell Leland Stanford's name "£eland $tanford" or that "smart women almost always wear black in Cuba," a fashion hint without much potential for practical application. And does not the relevance of these notes seem marginal at best?:

In the basement of the Inyo County Courthouse in Independence, California, sign pinned to a mandarin coat: "This MANDARIN COAT was often worn by Mrs. Minnie S. Brooks when giving lectures on her TEAPOT COLLECTION."

Redhead getting out of car in front of Beverly Wilshire Hotel, chinchilla stole, Vuitton bags with tags reading:

> Mrs Lou Fox
> Hotel Sahara
> Vegas

Well, perhaps not entirely marginal. As a matter of fact, Mrs. Minnie S. Brooks and her MANDARIN COAT pull me back into my own childhood, for although I never knew Mrs. Brooks and did not visit Inyo County until I was thirty, I grew up in just such a world, in houses cluttered with Indian relics and bits of gold ore and ambergris and the souvenirs my Aunt Mercy Farnsworth brought back from the Orient. It is a long way from that world to Mrs. Lou Fox's world where we all live now, and is it not just as well to remember that? Might not Mrs. Minnie S. Brooks help me to remember what I am? Might not Mrs. Lou Fox help me to remember what I am not?

But sometimes the point is harder to discern. What exactly did I have in mind when I noted down that it cost the father of someone I know $650 a month to light the place on the Hudson in which he lived before the Crash? What use was I planning to make of this line by Jimmy Hoffa: "I may have my faults, but being wrong ain't one of them"? And although I think it interesting to know where the girls who travel with the Syndicate have their hair done when they find themselves on the West Coast, will I ever make suitable use of it? Might I not be better off just passing it on to John O'Hara? What is a recipe for sauerkraut doing in my notebook? What kind of magpie keeps this notebook? *"He was born the night the* Titanic *went down."* That seems a nice enough line, and I even recall who said it, but is it not really a better line in life than it could ever be in fiction?

But of course that is exactly it: not that I should ever use the line, but that I should remember the woman who said it and the afternoon I heard it. We were on her terrace by the sea, and we were finishing the wine left from lunch, trying to get what sun there was, a California winter sun. The woman whose husband was born the night the *Titanic* went down wanted to rent her house, wanted to go back to her children in Paris. I remember wishing that I could afford the house, which cost $1,000 a month. "Someday you will," she said lazily. "Someday it all comes." There in the sun on her terrace it seemed easy to believe in someday but later I had a low-grade afternoon hangover and ran over a black snake on the way to the supermarket and was flooded with inexplicable fear when I heard the checkout clerk explaining to the man ahead of me why she was finally divorcing her husband. "He left me no choice," she said over and over as she punched the register. "He has a little seven-month-old baby by her, he left me no choice." I would like to believe that my dread then was for the human condition, but of course it was for me, because I wanted a baby and did not then have one and because I wanted to own the house that cost $1,000 a month to rent and because I had a hangover.

It all comes back. Perhaps it is difficult to see the value in having one's self back in that kind of mood, but I do see it; I think we are well advised to keep on nodding terms with the people we used to be, whether we find them attractive company or not. Otherwise they turn up unannounced and surprise us, come hammering on the mind's door at 4 A.M. of a bad night and demand to know who deserted them, who betrayed them, who is going to make amends. We forget all too soon the things we thought we could never forget. We forget the loves and the betrayals alike, forget what we whispered and what we screamed, forget who we were. I have already lost touch with a couple of people I used to be; one of them, a seventeen-year-old, presents little threat, although it would be of some interest to me to know again what it feels like to sit on a river levee drinking vodka-and-orange-juice and listening to Les Paul and Mary Ford and their echoes sing "How High the Moon" on the car radio. (You see I still have the scenes, but I no longer perceive myself among those present, no longer could even improvise the dialogue.) The other one, a twenty-three-year-old, bothers me more. She was always a good deal of trouble, and I suspect she will reappear when I least want to see her, skirts too long, shy to the point of aggravation, always the injured party, full of recriminations and little hurts and stories I do not want to hear again, at once saddening me and angering me with her vulnerability and ignorance, an apparition all the more insistent for being so long banished.

It is a good idea, then, to keep in touch and I suppose that keeping in touch is what notebooks are all about. And we are all on our own when it comes to keeping those lines open to ourselves: your notebooks will never help me, nor mine you. *"So what's new in the whiskey business?" What could that possibly mean to you? To me it means a blonde in a* Pucci bathing suit sitting with a couple of fat men by the pool at the Beverly Hills Hotel. Another man approaches, and they all regard one another in silence for a while. "So what's new in the whiskey business?" one of the fat men finally says by way of welcome, and the blonde stands up, arches one foot and dips it in the pool, looking all the while at the cabana where Baby Pignatari is talking on the telephone. That is all there is to that, except that several years later I saw the blonde coming out of Saks Fifth Avenue in New York with her California complexion and a voluminous mink coat. In the harsh wind that day she looked old and irrevocably tired to me, and even the skins in the mink coat were not worked the way they were doing them that year, not the way she would have wanted them done, and there is the point of the story. For a while after that I did not like to look in the mirror, and my eyes would skim the newspapers and pick out only the deaths, the cancer victims, the premature coronaries, the suicides, and I stopped riding the Lexington Avenue IRT because I noticed for the first time that all the strangers I had seen for years—the man with the seeing-eye dog, the spinster who read the classified pages every day, the fat girl who always got off with me at Grand Central—looked older than they once had.

It all comes back. Even that recipe for sauerkraut: even that brings it back. I was on Fire Island when I first made sauerkraut, and it was raining, and we drank a lot of bourbon and ate the sauerkraut and went to bed at ten, and I listened to the rain and the Atlantic and felt safe. I made the sauerkraut again last night and it did not make me feel any safer, but that is, as they say, another story.

SHE TRIES TO REASON IT OUT

Susan Griffin

No thinking occurs this way of course. Along a perfectly clear, straight line leading from one point to another, to the next and then the next, until there is a neat conclusion. The idea of an irrefutable finding discovered by unbroken increments of logic is an illusion. Even the most analytical thought is more serpentine than this. Time interposes. Sleep. Dreams. You muse. You stare. In the course of two hours you follow several leads, meet several dead ends and then, defeated and hungry, you stop to take a meal. Which will be something you threw together cleverly using the last bit of lettuce, since you have not driven down the hill to the market in several days, and there isn't any lettuce in the garden; there is hardly any garden at all, because you need to improve the soil and you can't do that now, it's been raining, which is just as well since you haven't the money to spend; and though you miss that connection between the ground you are standing on and the food you eat you're glad for these last three leaves, and the bit of leftover chicken you can add.

But the meal, the filled feeling, the good taste of it, makes you a bit sleepy. You lie down maybe on the bed or maybe on the couch. You look at catalogs. You like to do this because the content of them is sufficiently far away from what you're trying to think through, and you are distracted. Which seems appropriate. To go any further now you have somehow got to untie the knot of yourself. There is the gardener's catalog with its beautiful clay-sculpted borders you know you will never buy yet you like looking at the picture of them. Thinking. Imagining how they would be in your garden. Too stiff you think. A bit too formal. Then you shut your eyes. The pillow seems to swim but you know it's really you, your consciousness, moving off into that other space, the sleepy space and then suddenly you are awake again.

And what is it? You can hardly remember what the problem was. What you were thinking about. So you shake the last remnants of sleep off and climb the stairs and there it is, a bit bracing, the last sentence. And you can see that this was the problem. This last sentence turns you in the wrong direction. It sailed out of the sentence before without skipping even a beat but that was the problem. It was rote. As sleek and shiny as you were able to make it, the words too facile, it had lost contact with the ground of your thought. And you knew it not because you could see the illogic of it, which you couldn't then, not yet, but because it had a certain dullness under the shine. That spark of recognition which only comes when the words somehow hold a trace of all that you know that cannot quite be put into words was missing.

And from this false start, this mistaken direction there would have been no way to make that parabolic curve, the roundness, like a hill, a path around a lake, the eyes circumscribing, embracing, surrounded and held by, and at the same time encircling, the return, after a journey, back to where you started, except that you have traveled, and all the texture of your trip, the uneven ground you have tread, the knowledge in the soles of your feet, has changed you, so that coming back, you are both different and more yourself. Though the false start would have come back on you too, had already shown itself as defeat and exhaustion, the flat lands of despair from which no escape seems possible, and in which you believe you just have to continue, spiritless and doomed to the same direction. But now you are released from that fate. You have seen the error. Like a punch-drunk boxer who plugs away at every shadow, you were stuck in argument. Defensive, aggressive, overzealous in your effort, lurching forward too fast, you failed to notice what was there. Just in the sentence before. Something beautiful still to be teased open. A motion more subtle than speed. And from that discovery you are able to detect a delicate trace of the erotic. The slight scent that can change an atmosphere by the smallest degree. But this, of course, is everything.

FORGET ABOUT POLICING PLAGIARISM: JUST *TEACH*

Rebecca Moore Howard

If you are a professor in the United States and you have a pulse, you have heard about the problems of Internet plagiarism. Exactly what you have heard may vary, depending on what you have read, whom you have been listening to, and how you have been filtering the information or opinions that you have encountered. But everyone is worried about it—and for good reason.

Students can gain easy online access to an astonishing array of ready-made term papers, and for a fee, they can get custom-written papers within 48 hours from online sites. Send in the assignment and a credit-card number, download the attachment when the finished paper comes back two days later, print it out, and presto! Assignment completed. Fifteen-page paper on Plato's attitudes toward Homer? No problem.

Professors cannot always spot plagiarism, especially if a student gets a paper from a closed, subscribers-only Web site or hires an online ghostwriter. But often, they manage a digitized gotcha. No longer do they need to spend arduous days in the library, searching for the sources of a suspect paper. In faculty lounges, professors brag to each other about the speed and ease with which they located downloaded papers.

Actually, a whole gotcha industry has sprung up. Turnitin.com, Plagiarism.org—each week brings news of another Web site that will help catch the miscreants. Never mind that some of the sites fail to distinguish between quoting and unattributed copying; never mind that they blur the distinctions between omitting quotation marks and downloading an entire paper; never mind that some require the professor to violate students' intellectual-property rights by contributing students' papers to the program's database.

What drives all the new sites and the professors' anxiety is the concern that ethics, integrity, and honesty are flying out the window on digitized wings. That is a legitimate concern to which we must collectively attend.

But professors should also be worried about even more compelling issues. In our stampede to fight what *The New York Times* calls a "plague" of plagiarism, we risk becoming the enemies rather than the mentors of our students; we are replacing the student-teacher relationship with the criminal-police relationship. Further, by thinking of plagiarism as a unitary act rather than a collection of disparate activities, we risk categorizing all of our students as criminals. Worst of all, we risk not recognizing that our own pedagogy needs reform. Big reform.

I use the word "stampede" deliberately. We are in danger of mass hysteria on the plagiarism issue, hysteria that simplifies categories and reduces multiple choices to binaries. It appears that the Internet is making cheating easier; hence, it appears that the Internet is encouraging bad morals; hence, it appears that morality is in precipitous decline. And there we are at the ramparts, trying to hold back the attack. We see ourselves in a state of siege, holding the line against the enemy.

All those who worked to get advanced academic degrees in order to police young adults, please raise your hands. No hands? Then let's calm down and get back to the business of teaching.

We like the word "plagiarism" because it seems simple and straightforward: Plagiarism is representing the words of another as one's own, our college policies say, and we tell ourselves, "There! It's clear. Students are responsible for reading those policies and observing their guidelines."

Then, when a "plague" of plagiarism comes along and we believe academic integrity itself is under attack,

Rebecca Moore Howard is an associate professor of writing and rhetoric, and director of the writing program, at Syracuse University.

things get even simpler. Encouraged by digital dualisms, we forget that plagiarism means many different things: downloading a term paper, failing to give proper credit to the source of an idea, copying extensive passages without attribution, inserting someone else's phrases or sentences—perhaps with small changes—into your own prose, and forgetting to supply a set of quotation marks.

If we ignore those distinctions, we fail to see that most of us have violated the plagiarism injunctions in one way or another, large or small, intentionally or inadvertently, at one time or another. The distinctions are just not that crisp. We have to pull back from the mass hysteria and remember that the P-word covers a wide variety of behaviors, circumstances, and motivations. Accidentally omitting a set of quotation marks is not the same as submitting a downloaded paper.

Now, a downloaded paper is something that no professor should tolerate. It has to be punished. We assign papers so that our students will learn from the experience of writing them; if they do not write them, they do not learn. We have to protect education; we have to demand that our students learn. But even as we're catching and punishing plagiarists in our classes, we have to ask ourselves why they are plagiarizing. Some of the possible answers to that question are not very appealing. But just as we cannot ignore students' plagiarism, we cannot ignore these possibilities, either.

- It is possible that students are cheating because they don't value the opportunity of learning in our classes. Some of that is cultural, of course. Today's students are likely to change jobs many times before they retire, so they must earn credentials for an array of job possibilities, rather than immersing themselves in a focused, unchanging area of expertise. The fact that many of them are working long hours at outside jobs only exacerbates the problem.
- It is possible that our pedagogy has not adjusted to contemporary circumstances as readily as have our students. Rather than assigning tasks that have meaning, we may be assuming that students will find meaning in performing assigned tasks. How else can one explain giving the same paper assignment semester after semester in a lecture class of 100 students? Such assignments expect that students will gain something from the act of writing, but they do not respond to the needs and interests of the students in a particular section of the class. They are, in that sense, inauthentic assignments.

We expect authentic writing from our students, yet we do not write authentic assignments for them. We beg our students to cheat if we assign a major paper and then have no further involvement with the project until the students turn in their work. Assigning and grading a paper leaves out a crucial middle: working and talking with students while they draft those papers. You're too busy? Then what about dividing your students into small groups that you, a teaching assistant, or a tutor can meet with, or that can respond to their members' work before the papers reach you?

We deprive our students of an authentic audience if we assign papers that are due at the end of the term and that the students never see again. We deprive them of an interested audience if we scrawl a grade and "good work" on a paper—and nothing else. We deprive them of a respectful audience if we tear apart the style, grammar, and mechanics of their papers, marking every error and accusing them of illiteracy for their split infinitives, without ever talking with them about what they were trying to accomplish, how they might achieve their goals, and why all the style, grammar, and mechanics matter anyhow.

I raise those possibilities for myself as well as for my colleagues. I have not only witnessed those practices; I have engaged in them. They are, in fact, temptations to which we regularly succumb, just as our students may succumb to the temptation to plagiarize.

Do professors' shortcomings excuse students' textual transgressions? No. But they do demand that we recognize and reform pedagogy that encourages plagiarism because it discourages learning. We have to be ethical, too.

So do our institutions. If professors' working conditions are such that they cannot give, work with students on, and respond to authentic writing assignments, then the working conditions need to change—whether that means cutting class size, reducing teaching load, or placing more emphasis on teaching in decisions about hiring and promotion. Writing is an invaluable means of learning. Professors must demand that their students do the writing that they are submitting as their own; professors must assign essays that foster learning; and institutions must ensure that their professors' working conditions make good teaching possible.

HELPING STUDENTS USE TEXTUAL SOURCES PERSUASIVELY

Margaret Kantz

Although the researched essay as a topic has been much written about, it has been little studied. In the introduction to their bibliography, Ford, Rees, and Ward point out that most of the over 200 articles about researched essays published in professional journals in the last half century describe classroom methods. "Few," they say, "are of a theoretical nature or based on research, and almost none cites even one other work on the subject" (2). Given Ford and Perry's finding that 84% of freshman composition programs and 40% of advanced composition programs included instruction in writing research papers, more theoretical work seems needed. We need a theory-based explanation, one grounded in the findings of the published research on the nature and reasons for our students' problems with writing persuasive researched papers. To understand how to teach students to write such papers, we also need a better understanding of the demands of synthesis tasks.

As an example for discussing this complex topic, I have used a typical college sophomore. This student is a composite derived from published research, from my own memories of being a student, and from students whom I have taught at an open admissions community college and at both public and private universities. I have also used a few examples taken from my own students, all of whom share many of Shirley's traits. Shirley, first of all, is intelligent and well-motivated. She is a native speaker of English. She has no extraordinary knowledge deficits or emotional problems. She comes from a home where education is valued, and her parents do reading and writing tasks at home and at their jobs. Shirley has certain skills. When she entered first grade, she knew how to listen to and tell stories, and she soon became proficient at reading stories and at writing narratives. During her academic life, Shirley has learned such studying skills as finding the main idea and remembering facts. In terms of the relevant research, Shirley can read and summarize source texts accurately (cf. Spivey; Winograd). She can select material that is relevant for her purpose in writing (Hayes, Waterman, and Robinson; Langer). She can make connections between the available information and her purpose for writing, including the needs of her readers when the audience is specified (Atlas). She can make original connections among ideas (Brown and Day; Langer). She can create an appropriate, audience-based structure for her paper (Spivey), take notes and use them effectively while composing her paper (Kennedy), and she can present information clearly and smoothly (Spivey), without relying on the phrasing of the original sources (Atlas; Winograd). Shirley is, in my experience, a typical college student with an average academic preparation.

Although Shirley seems to have everything going for her, she experiences difficulty with assignments that require her to write original papers based on textual sources. In particular, Shirley is having difficulty in her sophomore-level writing class. Shirley, who likes English history, decided to write about the Battle

College English, Volume 52, Number 1, January 1990

Margaret Kantz is assistant professor of English at Central Missouri State University. She has presented papers at CCCC and published on composing processes in resarched student papers.

of Agincourt (this part of Shirley's story is biographical). She found half a dozen histories that described the circumstances of the battle in a few pages each. Although the topic was unfamiliar, the sources agreed on many of the facts. Shirley collated these facts into her own version, noting but not discussing discrepant details, borrowing what she assumed to be her sources' purpose of retelling the story, and modelling the narrative structure of her paper on that of her sources. Since the only comments Shirley could think of would be to agree or disagree with her sources, who had told her everything she knew about the Battle of Agincourt, she did not comment on the material; instead, she concentrated on telling the story clearly and more completely than her sources had done. She was surprised when her paper received a grade of C-. (Page 1 of Shirley's paper is given as Appendix A.)

Although Shirley is a hypothetical student whose case is based on a real event, her difficulties are typical of undergraduates at both private and public colleges and universities. In a recent class of Intermediate Composition in which the students were instructed to create an argument using at least four textual sources that took differing points of view, one student, who analyzed the coverage of a recent championship football game, ranked her source articles in order from those whose approach she most approved to those she least approved. Another student analyzed various approaches taken by the media to the Kent State shootings in 1970, and was surprised and disappointed to find that all of the sources seemed slanted, either by the perspective of the reporter or by that of the people interviewed. Both students did not understand why their instructor said that their papers lacked a genuine argument.

The task of writing researched papers that express original arguments presents many difficulties. Besides the obvious problems of citation format and coordination of source materials with the emerging written product, writing a synthesis can vary in difficulty according to the number and length of the sources, the abstractness or familiarity of the topic, the uses that the writer must make of the material, the degree and quality of original thought required, and the extent to which the sources will supply the structure and purpose of the new paper. It is usually easier to write a paper that uses all of only one short source on a familiar topic than to write a paper that selects material from many long sources on a topic that one must learn as one reads and writes. It is easier to quote than to paraphrase, and it is easier to build the paraphrases, without comment or with random comments, into a description of what one found than it is to use them as evidence in an original argument. It is easier to use whatever one likes, or everything one finds, than to formally select, evaluate, and interpret material. It is easier to use the structure and purpose of a source as the basis for one's paper than it is to create a structure or an original purpose. A writing-from-sources task can be as simple as collating a body of facts from a few short texts on a familiar topic into a new text that reproduces the structure, tone, and purpose of the originals, but it can also involve applying abstract concepts from one area to an original problem in a different area, a task that involves learning the relationships among materials as a paper is created that may refer to its sources without resembling them.

Moreover, a given task can be interpreted as requiring an easy method, a difficult method, or any of a hundred intermediate methods. In this context, Flower has observed, "The different ways in which students [represent] a 'standard' reading-to-write task to themselves lead to markedly different goals and strategies as well as different organizing plans" ("Role" iii). To write a synthesis, Shirley may or may not need to quote, summarize, or select material from her sources; to evaluate the sources for bias, accuracy, or completeness; to develop original ideas; or to persuade a reader. How well she performs any of these tasks—and whether she thinks to perform these tasks—depends on how she reads the texts and on how she interprets the assignment. Shirley's representation of the task, which in this case was easier than her teacher had in mind, depends on the goals that she sets for herself. The goals that she sets depend on her awareness of the possibilities and her confidence in her writing skills.

Feeling unhappy about her grade, Shirley consulted her friend Alice. Alice, who is an expert, looked at the task in a completely different way and used strategies for thinking about it that were quite different from Shirley's.

"Who were your sources?" asked Alice. "Winston Churchill, right? A French couple and a few others. And they didn't agree about the details, such as the sizes of the armies. Didn't you wonder why?"

"No," said Shirley. "I thought the history books would know the truth. When they disagreed, I figured that they were wrong on those points. I didn't want to have anything in my paper that was wrong."

"But Shirley," said Alice, "you could have thought about why a book entitled *A History of France* might present a different view of the battle than a book subtitled *A History of British Progress*. You could have asked if the English and French writers wanted to make a point about the history of their countries and looked to see if the factual differences suggested anything. You could even have talked about Shakespeare's *Henry V*, which I know you've read—about how he presents the battle, or about how the King Henry in the play differs from the Henrys in your other books. You would have had an angle, a problem. Dr. Boyer would have loved it."

Alice's representation of the task would have required Shirley to formally select and evaluate her material and to use it as proof in an original argument. Alice was suggesting that Shirley invent an original problem and purpose for her paper and create an original structure for her argument. Alice's task is much more sophisticated than Shirley's. Shirley replied, "That would take me a year to do! Besides, Henry was a real person. I don't want to make up things about him."

"Well," said Alice, "You're dealing with facts, so there aren't too many choices. If you want to say something original you either have to talk about the sources or talk about the material. What could you say about the material? Your paper told about all the reasons King Henry wasn't expected to win the battle. Could you have argued that he should have lost because he took too many chances?"

"Gee," said Shirley, "That's awesome. I wish I'd thought of it."

This version of the task would allow Shirley to keep the narrative structure of her paper but would give her an original argument and purpose. To write the argument, Shirley would have only to rephrase the events of the story to take an opposite approach from that of her English sources, emphasizing what she perceived as Henry's mistakes and inserting comments to explain why his decisions were mistakes—an easy argument to write. She could also, if she wished, write a conclusion that criticized the cheerleading tone of her British sources.

As this anecdote makes clear, a given topic can be treated in more or less sophisticated ways—and sophisticated goals, such as inventing an original purpose and evaluating sources, can be achieved in relatively simple versions of a task. Students have many options as to how they can fulfill even a specific task (cf. Jeffery). Even children can decide whether to process a text deeply or not, and purpose in reading affects processing and monitoring of comprehension (Brown). Pichert has shown that reading purpose affects judgments about what is important or unimportant in a narrative text, and other research tells us that attitudes toward the author and content of a text affect comprehension (Asch; Hinze; Shedd; Goldman).

One implication of this story is that the instructor gave a weak assignment and an ineffective critique of the draft (her only comment referred to Shirley's footnoting technique; cf. Appendix A). The available research suggests that if Dr. Boyer had set Shirley a specific rhetorical problem such as having her report on her material to the class and then testing them on it, and if she had commented on the content of Shirley's paper during the drafts, Shirley might well have come up with a paper that did more than repeat its source material (Nelson and Hayes). My teaching experience supports this research finding. If Dr.

Boyer had told Shirley from the outset that she was expected to say something original and that she should examine her sources as she read them for discrepant facts, conflicts, or other interesting material, Shirley might have tried to write an original argument (Kantz, "Originality"). And if Dr. Boyer had suggested that Shirley use her notes to comment on her sources and make plans for using the notes, Shirley might have written a better paper than she did (Kantz, "Relationship").

Even if given specific directions to create an original argument, Shirley might have had difficulty with the task. Her difficulty could come from any of three causes: 1) Many students like Shirley misunderstand sources because they read them as stories. 2) Many students expect their sources to tell the truth; hence, they equate persuasive writing in this context with making things up. 3) Many students do not understand that facts are a kind of claim and are often used persuasively in so-called objective writing to create an impression. Students need to read source texts as arguments and to think about the rhetorical contexts in which they were written rather than to read them merely as a set of facts to be learned. Writing an original persuasive argument based on sources requires students to apply material to a problem or to use it to answer a question, rather than simply to repeat it or evaluate it. These three problems deserve a separate discussion.

Because historical texts often have a chronological structure, students believe that historians tell stories and that renarrating the battle cast them as a historian. Because her sources emphasized the completeness of the victory/defeat and its decisive importance in the history of warfare, Shirley thought that making these same points in her paper completed her job. Her job as a reader was thus to learn the story, i.e., so that she could pass a test on it (cf. Vipond and Hunt's argument that generic expectations affect reading behavior. Vipond and Hunt would describe Shirley's reading as story-driven rather than point-driven). Students commonly misread texts as narratives. When students refer to a textbook as "the story," they are telling us that they read for plot and character, regardless of whether their texts are organized as narratives. One reason Shirley loves history is that when she reads it she can combine her story-reading strategies with her studying strategies. Students like Shirley may need to learn to apply basic organizing patterns, such as cause-effect and general-to-specific, to their texts. If, however, Dr. Boyer asks Shirley to respond to her sources in a way that is not compatible with Shirley's understanding of what such sources do, Shirley will have trouble doing the assignment. Professors may have to do some preparatory teaching about why certain kinds of texts have certain characteristics and what kinds of problems writers must solve as they design text for a particular audience. They may even have to teach a model for the kind of writing they expect.

The writing version of Shirley's problem, which Flower calls "writer-based prose," occurs when Shirley organizes what should be an expository analysis as a narrative, especially when she writes a narrative about how she did her research. Students frequently use time-based organizing patterns, regardless of the task, even when such patterns conflict with what they are trying to say and even when they know how to use more sophisticated strategies. Apparently such common narrative transitional devices such as "the first point" and "the next point" offer a reassuringly familiar pattern for organizing unfamiliar material. The common strategy of beginning paragraphs with such phrases as "my first source," meaning that it was the first source that the writer found in the library or the first one read, appears to combine a story-of-my-research structure with a knowledge-telling strategy (Bereiter and Scardamalia, *Psychology*). Even when students understand that the assignment asks for more than the fill-in-the-blanks, show-me-you've-read-the-material approach described by Schwegler and Shamoon, they cling to narrative structuring devices. A rank ordering of sources, as with Mary's analysis of the football game coverage with the sources listed in an order of ascending disapproval, represents a step away from storytelling and toward synthesizing because it embodies a persuasive evaluation.

In addition to reading texts as stories, students expect factual texts to tell them "the truth" because they have learned to see texts statically, as descriptions of truths, instead of as arguments. Shirley did not understand that nonfiction texts exist as arguments in rhetorical contexts. "After all," she reasoned, "how can one argue about the date of a battle or the sizes of armies?" Churchill, however, described the battle in much more detail than Shirley's other sources, apparently because he wished to persuade his readers to take pride in England's tradition of military achievement. Guizot and Guizot de Witt, on the other hand, said very little about the battle (beyond describing it as "a monotonous and lamentable repetition of the disasters of Crecy and Poitiers" [397]) because they saw the British invasion as a sneaky way to take advantage of a feud among the various branches of the French royal family. Shirley's story/study skills might not have allowed her to recognize such arguments, especially because Dr. Boyer did not teach her to look for them.

When I have asked students to choose a topic and find three or more sources on it that disagree, I am repeatedly asked, "How can sources disagree in different ways? After all, there's only pro and con." Students expect textbooks and other authoritative sources either to tell them the truth (i.e., facts) or to express an opinion with which they may agree or disagree. Mary's treatment of the football coverage reflects this belief, as does Charlie's surprise when he found that even his most comprehensive sources on the Kent State killings omitted certain facts, such as interviews with National Guardsmen. Students' desire for truth leads them to use a collating approach whenever possible, as Shirley did (cf. Appendix A), because students believe that the truth will include all of the facts and will reconcile all conflicts. (This belief may be another manifestation of the knowledge-telling strategy [Bereiter and Scardamalia, *Psychology*] in which students write down everything they can think of about a topic.) When conflicts cannot be reconciled and the topic does not admit a pro or con stance, students may not know what to say. They may omit the material altogether, include it without comment, as Shirley did, or jumble it together without any plan for building an argument.

The skills that Shirley has practiced for most of her academic career—finding the main idea and learning content—allow her to agree or disagree. She needs a technique for reading texts in ways that give her something more to say, a technique for constructing more complex representations of texts that allow room for more sophisticated writing goals. She also needs strategies for analyzing her reading that allow her to build original arguments.

One way to help students like Shirley is to teach the concept of rhetorical situation. A convenient tool for thinking about this concept is Kinneavy's triangular diagram of the rhetorical situation. Kinneavy, analyzing Aristotle's description of rhetoric, posits that every communicative situation has three parts: a speaker/writer (the Encoder), an audience (the Decoder), and a topic (Reality) (19). Although all discourse involves all three aspects of communication, a given type of discourse may pertain more to a particular point of the triangle than to the others, e.g., a diary entry may exist primarily to express the thoughts of the writer (the Encoder); an advertisement may exist primarily to persuade a reader (the Decoder). Following Kinneavy, I posit particular goals for each corner of the triangle. Thus, the primary goal of a writer doing writer-based discourse such as a diary might be originality and self-expression; primary goals for reader-based discourse such as advertising might be persuasion; primary goals for topic-based discourse such as a researched essay might be accuracy, completeness, and mastery of subject matter. Since all three aspects of the rhetorical situation are present and active in any communicative situation, a primarily referential text such as Churchill's *The Birth of Britain* may have a persuasive purpose and may depend for some of its credibility on readers' familiarity with the author. The term "rhetorical reading," then (cf. Haas and Flower), means teaching students to read a text as a message sent by someone to somebody for a reason. Shirley, Mary, and Charlie are probably practiced users of rhetorical persuasion in non-academic contexts. They may never have learned to apply this thinking in a conscious and deliberate way to academic tasks (cf. Kroll).

The concept of rhetorical situation offers insight into the nature of students' representations of a writing task. The operative goals in Shirley's and Alice's approaches to the term paper look quite different when mapped onto the points on the triangle. If we think of Shirley and Alice as Encoders, the topic as Reality, and Dr. Boyer as the Decoder, we can see that for Shirley, being an Encoder means trying to be credible; her relationship to the topic (Reality) involves a goal of using all of the subject matter; and her relationship to the Decoder involves an implied goal of telling a complete story to a reader whom Shirley thinks of as an examiner—to use the classic phrase from the famous book by Britton et al.—i.e., a reader who wants to know if Shirley can pass an exam on the subject of the Battle of Agincourt. For Alice, however, being an Encoder means having a goal of saying something new; the topic (Reality) is a resource to be used; and the Decoder is someone who must be persuaded that Alice's ideas have merit. Varying task representations do not change the dimensions of the rhetorical situation: the Encoder, Decoder, and Reality are always present. But the way a writer represents the task to herself does affect the ways that she thinks about those dimensions—and whether she thinks about them at all.

In the context of a research assignment, rhetorical skills can be used to read the sources as well as to design the paper. Although teachers have probably always known that expert readers use such strategies, the concept of rhetorical reading is new to the literature. Haas and Flower have shown that expert readers use rhetorical strategies "to account for author's purpose, context, and effect on the audience . . . to recreate or infer the rhetorical situation of the text" (176; cf also Bazerman). These strategies, used in addition to formulating main points and paraphrasing content, helped the readers to understand a text more completely and more quickly than did readers who concentrated exclusively on content. As Haas and Flower point out, teaching students to read rhetorically is difficult. They suggest that appropriate pedagogy might include "direct instruction . . . modeling, and . . . encouraging students to become contributing and committed members of rhetorical communities" (182). One early step might be to teach students a set of heuristics based on the three aspects of the communicative triangle. Using such questions could help students set goals for their reading.

In this version of Kinneavy's triangle, the Encoder is the writer of the source text, the Decoder is the student reader, and Reality is the subject matter. Readers may consider only one point of the triangle at a time, asking such questions as "Who are you (i.e., the author/Encoder)?" or "What are the important features of this text?" They may consider two aspects of the rhetorical situation in a single question, e.g., "Am I in your intended (primary) audience?"; "What do I think about this topic?"; "What context affected your ideas and presentation?" Other questions would involve all three points of the triangle, e.g., "What are you saying to help me with the problem you assume I have?" or "What textual devices have you used to manipulate my response?" Asking such questions gives students a way of formulating goals relating to purpose as well as content.

If Shirley, for example, had asked a Decoder-to-Encoder question—such as "Am I in your intended audience?"—she might have realized that Churchill and the Guizots were writing for specific audiences. If she had asked a Decoder-to-Reality question—such as "What context affected your ideas and presentation?"—she might not have ignored Churchill's remark, "All these names [Amiens, Boves, Bethencourt] are well known to our generation" (403). As it was, she missed Churchill's signal that he was writing to survivors of the First World War, who had vainly hoped that it would be war to end all wars. If Shirley had used an Encoder-Decoder-Reality question—such as "What are you saying to help me with the problem you assume I have?"—she might have understood that the authors of her sources were writing to different readers for different reasons. This understanding might have given her something to say. When I gave Shirley's source texts to freshmen students, asked them to use the material in an original argument, and taught them this heuristic for rhetorical reading, I received, for example, papers that warned undergraduates about national pride as a source of authorial bias in history texts.

A factual topic such as the Battle of Agincourt presents special problems because of the seemingly intransigent nature of facts. Like many people, Shirley believes that you can either agree or disagree with issues and opinions, but you can only accept the so-called facts. She believes that facts are what you learn from textbooks, opinions are what you have about clothes, and arguments are what you have with your mother when you want to stay out late at night. Shirley is not in a position to disagree with the facts about the battle (e.g., "No, I think the French won"), and a rhetorical analysis may seem at first to offer minimal rewards (e.g., "According to the Arab, Jewish, and Chinese calendars the date was really . . ."').

Alice, who thinks rhetorically, understands that both facts and opinions are essentially the same kind of statement: they are claims. Alice understands that the only essential difference between a fact and an opinion is how they are received by an audience. (This discussion is derived from Toulmin's model of an argument as consisting of claims proved with data and backed by ethical claims called warrants. According to Toulmin, any aspect of an argument may be questioned by the audience and must then be supported with further argument.) In a rhetorical argument, a fact is a claim that an audience will accept as being true without requiring proof, although they may ask for an explanation. An opinion is a claim that an audience will not accept as true without proof, and which, after the proof is given, the audience may well decide has only a limited truth, i.e., it's true in this case but not in other cases. An audience may also decide that even though a fact is unassailable, the interpretation or use of the fact is open to debate.

For example, Shirley's sources gave different numbers for the size of the British army at Agincourt; these numbers, which must have been estimates, were claims masquerading as facts. Shirley did not understand this. She thought that disagreement signified error, whereas it probably signified rhetorical purpose. The probable reason that the Guizots give a relatively large estimate for the English army and do not mention the size of the French army is so that their French readers would find the British victory easier to accept. Likewise, Churchill's relatively small estimate for the size of the English army and his high estimate for the French army magnify the brilliance of the English victory. Before Shirley could create an argument about the Battle of Agincourt, she needed to understand that, even in her history textbooks, the so-called facts are claims that may or may not be supported, claims made by writers who work in a certain political climate for a particular audience. She may, of course, never learn this truth unless Dr. Boyer teaches her rhetorical theory and uses the research paper as a chance for Shirley to practice rhetorical problem-solving.

For most of her academic life, Shirley has done school tasks that require her to find main ideas and important facts; success in these tasks usually hinges on agreeing with the teacher about what the text says. Such study skills form an essential basis for doing reading-to-write tasks. Obviously a student can only use sources to build an argument if she can first read the sources accurately (cf. Brown and Palincsar; Luftig; Short and Ryan). However, synthesizing tasks often require that readers not accept the authors' ideas. Baker and Brown have pointed out that people misread texts when they blindly accept an author's ideas instead of considering a divergent interpretation. Yet if we want students to learn to build original arguments from texts, we must teach them the skills needed to create divergent interpretations. We must teach them to think about facts and opinions as claims that are made by writers to particular readers for particular reasons in particular historical contexts.

Reading sources rhetorically gives students a powerful tool for creating a persuasive analysis. Although no research exists as yet to suggest that teaching students to read rhetorically will improve their writing, I have seen its effect in successive drafts of students' papers. As mentioned earlier, rhetorical reading allowed a student to move from simply summarizing and evaluating her sources on local coverage of the championship football game to constructing a rationale for articles that covered the fans rather than the game. Rhetorical analysis enabled another student to move from summarizing his sources to understanding why each report about the Kent State shootings necessarily expressed a bias of some kind.

As these examples suggest, however, rhetorical reading is not a magical technique for producing sophisticated arguments. Even when students read their sources rhetorically, they tend merely to report the results of this analysis in their essays. Such writing appears to be a college-level version of the knowledge-telling strategy described by Bereiter and Scardamalia *(Psychology)* and may be, as they suggest, the product of years of exposure to pedagogical practices that enshrine the acquisition and expression of information without a context or purpose.

To move students beyond merely reporting the content and rhetorical orientation of their source texts, I have taught them the concept of the rhetorical gap and some simple heuristic questions for thinking about gaps. Gaps were first described by Iser as unsaid material that a reader must supply to/infer from a text. McCormick expanded the concept to include gaps between the text and the reader; such gaps could involve discrepancies of values, social conventions, language, or any other matter that readers must consider. If we apply the concept of gaps to Kinneavy's triangle, we see that in reading, for example, a gap may occur between the Encoder-Decoder corners when the reader is not a member of the author's intended audience. Shirley fell into such a gap. Another gap can occur between the Decoder-Reality corners when a reader disagrees with or does not understand the text. A third gap can occur between the Encoder-Reality points of the triangle if the writer has misrepresented or misunderstood the material. The benefit of teaching this concept is that when a student thinks about a writer's rhetorical stance, she may ask "Why does he think that way?" When a student encounters a gap, she may ask, "What effect does it have on the success of this communication?" The answers to both questions give students original material for their papers.

Shirley, for example, did not know that Churchill began writing *The Birth of Britain* during the 1930s, when Hitler was rearming Germany and when the British government and most of Churchill's readers ardently favored disarmament. Had she understood the rhetorical orientation of the book, which was published eleven years after the end of World War II, she might have argued that Churchill's evocation of past military glories would have been inflammatory in the 1930s but was highly acceptable twenty years later. A gap between the reader and the text (Decoder-Reality) might stimulate a reader to investigate whether or not she is the only person having this problem; a gap between other readers and the sources may motivate an adaptation or explanation of the material to a particular audience. Shirley might have adapted the Guizots' perspective on the French civil war for American readers. A gap between the author and the material (Encoder-Reality) might motivate a refutation.

To discover gaps, students may need to learn heuristics for setting rhetorical writing goals. That is, they may need to learn to think of the paper, not as a rehash of the available material, but as an opportunity to teach someone, to solve someone's problem, or to answer someone's question. The most salient questions for reading source texts may be "Who are you (the original audience of Decoders)?"; "What is your question or problem with this topic?"; and "How have I (the Encoder) used these materials to answer your question or solve your problem?" More simply, these questions may be learned as "Why," "How," and "So what?" When Shirley learns to read sources as telling not the eternal truth but a truth to a particular audience and when she learns to think of texts as existing to solve problems, she will find it easier to think of things to say.

For example, a sophomore at a private university was struggling with an assignment that required her to analyze an issue and express an opinion on it, using two conflicting source texts, an interview, and personal material as sources. Using rhetorical reading strategies, this girl discovered a gap between Alfred Marbaise, a high school principal who advocates mandatory drug testing of all high school students, and students like those he would be testing:

> Marbaise, who was a lieutenant in the U.S. Marines over thirty years ago . . . makes it very obvious that he cannot and will not tolerate any form of drug abuse in his school. For example, in paragraph seven he claims, "When students become involved in illegal activity, whether they realize it or not, they are violating other students . . . then I become very, very concerned . . . and I will not tolerate that."
>   Because Marbaise has not been in school for nearly forty years himself, he does not take into consideration the reasons why kids actually use drugs. Today the social environment is so drastically different that Marbaise cannot understand a kid's morality, and that is why he writes from such a fatherly but distant point of view.

The second paragraph answers the So what? question, i.e., "Why does it matter that Marbaise seems by his age and background to be fatherly and distant?" Unless the writer/reader thinks to ask this question, she will have difficulty writing a coherent evaluation of Marbaise's argument.

The relative success of some students in finding original things to say about their topics can help us to understand the perennial problem of plagiarism. Some plagiarism derives, I think, from a weak, non-rhetorical task representation. If students believe they are supposed to reproduce source material in their papers, or if they know they are supposed to say something original but have no rhetorical problem to solve and no knowledge of how to find problems that they can discuss in their sources, it becomes difficult for them to avoid plagiarizing. The common student decision to buy a paper when writing the assignment seems a meaningless fill-in-the-blanks activity (cf. Schwegler and Shamoon) becomes easily understandable. Because rhetorical reading leads to discoveries about the text, students who use it may take more interest in their research papers.

Let us now assume that Shirley understands the importance of creating an original argument, knows how to read analytically, and has found things to say about the Battle of Agincourt. Are her troubles over? Will she now create that A paper that she yearns to write? Probably not. Despite her best intentions, Shirley will probably write another narrative/paraphrase of her sources. Why? Because by now, the assignment asks her to do far more than she can handle in a single draft. Shirley's task representation is now so rich, her set of goals so many, that she may be unable to juggle them all simultaneously. Moreover, the rhetorical reading technique requires students to discover content worth writing about and a rhetorical purpose for writing; the uncertainty of managing such a discovery task when a grade is at stake may be too much for Shirley.

Difficult tasks may be difficult in either (or both of) two ways. First, they may require students to do a familiar subtask, such as reading sources, at a higher level of difficulty, e.g., longer sources, more sources, a more difficult topic. Second, they may require students to do new subtasks, such as building notes into an original argument. Such tasks may require task management skills, especially planning, that students have never developed and do not know how to attempt. The insecurity that results from trying a complex new task in a high-stakes situation is increased when students are asked to discover a problem worth writing about because such tasks send students out on a treasure hunt with no guarantee that the treasure exists, that they will recognize it when they find it, or that when they find it they will be able to build it into a coherent argument. The paper on Marbaise quoted above earned a grade of D because the writer could not use her rhetorical insights to build an argument presented in a logical order. Although she asked the logical question about the implications of Marbaise's persona, she did not follow through by evaluating the gaps in his perspective that might affect the probable success of his program.

A skillful student using the summarize-the-main-ideas approach can set her writing goals and even plan (i.e., outline) a paper before she reads the sources. The rhetorical reading strategy, by contrast, requires writers to discover what is worth writing about and to decide how to say it as or after they read their sources. The strategy requires writers to change their content goals and to adjust their writing plans as their understanding of the topic develops. It requires writers, in Flower's term, to "construct" their purposes for writing as well as the content for their paper (for a description of constructive planning, see Flower, Schriver, Carey, Haas, and Hayes). In Flower's words, writers who construct a purpose, as opposed to writers who bring a predetermined purpose to a task, "create a web of purposes . . . set goals, toss up possibilities . . . create a multidimensional network of information . . . a web of purpose . . . a bubbling stew of various mental representations" (531–32). The complex indeterminacy of such a task may pose an intimidating challenge to students who have spent their lives summarizing main ideas and reporting facts.

Shirley may respond to the challenge by concentrating her energies on a familiar subtask, e.g., repeating material about the Battle of Agincourt, at the expense of struggling with an unfamiliar subtask such as creating an original argument. She may even deliberately simplify the task by representing it to herself as calling only for something that she knows how to do, expecting that Dr. Boyer will accept the paper as close enough to the original instructions. My students do this frequently. When students decide to write a report of their reading, they can at least be certain that they will find material to write about.

Because of the limits of attentional memory, not to mention those caused by inexperience, writers can handle only so many task demands at a time. Thus, papers produced by seemingly inadequate task representations may well be essentially rough drafts. What looks like a bad paper may well be a preliminary step, a way of meeting certain task demands in order to create a basis for thinking about new ones. My students consistently report that they need to marshal all of their ideas and text knowledge and get that material down on the page (i.e., tell their knowledge) before they can think about developing an argument (i.e., transform their knowledge). If Shirley's problem is that she has shelved certain task demands in favor of others, Dr. Boyer needs only to point out what Shirley should do to bring the paper into conformity with the assignment and offer Shirley a chance to revise.

The problems of cognitive overload and inexperience in handling complex writing tasks can create a tremendous hurdle for students because so many of them believe that they should be able to write their paper in a single draft. Some students think that if they can't do the paper in one draft that means that something is wrong with them as writers, or with the assignment, or with us for giving the assignment. Often, such students will react to their drafts with anger and despair, throwing away perfectly usable rough drafts and then coming to us and saying that they can't do the assignment.

The student's first draft about drug testing told her knowledge about her sources' opinions on mandatory drug testing. Her second draft contained the rhetorical analysis quoted above, but presented the material in a scrambled order and did not build the analysis into an argument. Only in a third draft was this student able to make her point:

> Not once does Marbaise consider any of the psychological reasons why kids turn away from reality. He fails to realize that drug testing will not answer their questions, ease their frustrations, or respond to their cries for attention, but will merely further alienate himself and other authorities from helping kids deal with their real problems.

This comment represents Terri's answer to the heuristic "So what? Why does the source's position matter?" If we pace our assignments to allow for our students' thoughts to develop, we can do a great deal to build their confidence in their writing (Terri raised her D + to an A). If we treat the researched essay as a sequence of assignments instead of as a one-shot paper with a single due date, we can teach our students to build on their drafts, to use what they can do easily as a bridge to what we want them to learn to do. In this way, we can improve our students' writing habits. More importantly, however, we can help our students to see themselves as capable writers and as active, able, problemsolvers. Most importantly, we can use the sequence of drafts to demand that our students demonstrate increasingly sophisticated kinds of analytic and rhetorical proficiency.

Rhetorical reading and writing heuristics can help students to represent tasks in rich and interesting ways. They can help students to set up complex goal structures (Bereiter and Scardamalia, "Conversation"). They offer students many ways to think about their reading and writing texts. These tools, in other words, encourage students to work creatively.

And after all, creativity is what research should be about. If Shirley writes a creative paper, she has found a constructive solution that is new to her and which other people can use, a solution to a problem that she and other people share. Creativity is an inherently rhetorical quality. If we think of it as thought leading to solutions to problems and of problems as embodied in questions that people ask about situations, the researched essay offers infinite possibilities. Viewed in this way, a creative idea answers a question that the audience or any single reader wants answered. The question could be, "Why did Henry V win the Battle of Agincourt?" or, "How can student readers protect themselves against nationalistic bias when they study history?" or any of a thousand other questions. If we teach our Shirleys to see themselves as scholars who work to find answers to problem questions, and if we teach them to set reading and writing goals for themselves that will allow them to think constructively, we will be doing the most exciting work that teachers can do, nurturing creativity.

Appendix A: Page 1 of Shirley's paper

The battle of Agincourt ranks as one of England's greatest military triumphs. It was the most brilliant victory of the Middle Ages, bar none. It was fought on October 25, 1414, against the French near the French village of Agincourt.

Henry V had claimed the crown of France and had invaded France with an army estimated at anywhere ~~between~~ *from* 10,000[1] ~~and~~ *to* 45,000 men.[2] During the siege of Marfleur dysentery had taken 1/3 of them[3], his food supplies had been depleted[4], and the fall rains had begun. In addition the French had assembled a huge army and were marching toward him. Henry decided to march to Calais, where his ships were to await him[5]. He intended to cross the River Somme at the ford of Blanchetaque[6], but, falsely informed that the ford was guarded, he was forced to follow the flooded Somme up toward its source. The French army was shadowing him on his right. Remembering the slaughters of Crecy and <u>Poictiers</u>, the French constable, Charles d'Albret, hesitated to fight[8], but when Henry forded the Somme just above Amiens[9] and was just

---

1. Carl Stephinson, <u>Medieval History</u>, p. 529.

2. Guizot, (Monsieur and Guizot, Madame.) <u>World's Best Histories-France, Volume II,</u> p. 211.

3. Cyrid E. Robinson. <u>England-A History of British Progress,</u> p. 145.

4. Ibid.

5. Winston Churchill. <u>A History of the English-Speaking Peoples. Volume 1: The Birth of Britain</u>, p. 403.

6. <u>Ibid.</u>

7. <u>Ibid.</u>

you footnote material that does not need to be footnoted

8. Robinson, p. 145.

9. Churchill. p. 403.

Works Cited

Asch, Solomon. *Social Psychology.* New York: Prentice, 1952.

Atlas, Marshall. *Expert-Novice Differences in the Writing Process.* Paper presented at the American Educational Research Association, 1979. ERIC ED 107 769.

Baker, Louise, and Ann L. Brown. "Metacognitive Skills and Reading." *Handbook of Reading Research.* Eds. P. David Person, Rebecca Barr, Michael L. Kamil, and Peter Mosenthal. New York: Longman, 1984.

Bazerman, Charles. "Physicists Reading Physics: Schema-Laden Purposes and Purpose-Laden Schema." *Written Communication* 2.1 (1985): 3–24.

Bereiter, Carl, and Marlene Scardamalia. "From Conversation to Composition: The Role of Instruction in a Developmental Process." *Advances in Instructional Psychology.* Ed. R. Glaser. Vol. 2. Hillsdale, NJ: Lawrence Erlbaum Associates, 1982. 1–64.

_____. *The Psychology of Written Composition.* Hillsdale, .NJ: Lawrence Erlbaum Associates, 1987.

Briscoe, Terri. "To test or not to test." Unpublished essay. Texas Christian University, 1989.

Britton, James, Tony Burgess, Nancy Martin, Alex McLeod, and Harold Rosen. *The Development of Writing Abilities (11–18).* Houndmills Basingstoke Hampshire: Macmillan Education Ltd., 1975.

Brown, Ann L. "Theories of Memory and the Problem of Development: Activity, Growth, and Knowledge." *Levels of Processing in Memory.* Eds. Laird S. Cermak and Fergus I. M. Craik. Hillsdale, NJ: Laurence Erlbaum Associates, 1979, 225–258.

_____, Joseph C. Campione, and L. R. Barclay. *Training Self-Checking Routines for Estimating Test Readiness: Generalizations from List Learning to Prose Recall.* Unpublished manuscript. University of Illinois, 1978.

_____ and Jeanne Day. "Macrorules for Summarizing Texts: The Development of Expertise." *Journal of Verbal Learning and Verbal Behavior* 22.1 (1983): 1–14.

_____ and Annmarie S. Palincsar. *Reciprocal Teaching of Comprehension Strategies: A Natural History of One Program for Enhancing Learning.* Technical Report #334. Urbana, IL: Center for the Study of Reading, 1985.

Churchill, Winston S. *The Birth of Britain.* New York: Dodd, 1956. Vol. 1 of *A History of the English-Speaking Peoples.* 4 vols. 1956–58.

Flower, Linda. "The Construction of Purpose in Writing and Reading." *College English* 50.5 (1988): 528–550.

_____. *The Role of Task Representation in Reading to Write.* Berkeley, CA: Center for the Study of Writing, U of California at Berkeley and Carnegie Mellon. Technical Report, 1987.

_____. "Writer-Based Prose: A Cognitive Basis for Problems in Writing." *College English* 41 (1979): 19–37.

Flower, Linda, Karen Schriver, Linda Carey, Christina Haas, and John R. Hayes. *Planning in Writing: A Theory of the Cognitive Process.* Berkeley, CA: Center for the Study of Writing, U of California at Berkeley and Carnegie Mellon. Technical Report, 1988.

Ford, James E., and Dennis R. Perry. "Research Paper Instruction in the Undergraduate Writing Program." *College English* 44 (1982): 825–31.

Ford, James E., Sharla Rees, and David L. Ward. *Teaching the Research Paper: Comprehensive Bibliography of Periodical Sources,* 1980. ERIC ED 197 363.

Goldman, Susan R. "Knowledge Systems for Realistic Goals." *Discourse Processes* 5 (1982): 279–303.

Guizot and Guizot de Witt. *The History of France from Earliest Times to 1848.* Trans. R. Black. Vol. 2. Philadelphia: John Wanamaker (n.d.).

Haas, Christina, and Linda Flower. "Rhetorical Reading Strategies and the Construction of Meaning." *College Composition and Communication* 39 (1988): 167–84.

Hayes, John R., D. A. Waterman, and C. S. Robinson. "Identifying the Relevant Aspects of a Problem Text." *Cognitive Science* 1 (1977): 297–313.

Hinze, Helen K. "The Individual's Word Associations and His Interpretation of Prose Paragraphs." *Journal of General Psychology* 64 (1961): 193–203.

Iser, Wolfgang. *The act of reading: A theory of aesthetic response.* Baltimore: The Johns Hopkins UP, 1978.

Jeffery, Christopher. "Teachers' and Students' Perceptions of the Writing Process." *Research in the Teaching of English* 15 (1981): 215–28.

Kantz, Margaret. *Originality and Completeness: What Do We Value in Papers Written from Sources?* Conference on College Composition and Communication. St. Louis, MO, 1988.

_____. *The Relationship Between Reading and Planning Strategies and Success in Synthesizing: It's What You Do with Them that Counts.* Technical report in preparation. Pittsburgh: Center for the Study of Writing, 1988.

Kennedy, Mary Louise. "The Composing Process of College Students Writing from Sources." *Written Communication* 2.4 (1985): 434–56.

Kinneavy, James L. *A Theory of Discourse.* New York: Norton, 1971.

Kroll, Barry M. "Audience Adaptation in Children's Persuasive Letters." *Written Communication* 1.4 (1984): 407–28.

Langer, Judith. "Where Problems Start: The Effects of Available Information on Responses to School Writing Tasks." *Contexts for Learning to Write: Studies of Secondary School Instruction.* Ed. Arthur Applebee. Norwood, NJ: ABLEX Publishing Corporation, 1984. 135–48.

Luftig, Richard L. "Abstractive Memory, the Central-Incidental Hypothesis, and the Use of Structural Importance in Text: Control Processes or Structural Features?" *Reading Research Quarterly* 14.1 (1983): 28–37.

Marbaise, Alfred. "Treating a Disease." *Current Issues and Enduring Questions.* Eds. Sylvan Barnet and Hugo Bedau. New York: St. Martin's, 1987. 126–27.

McCormick, Kathleen. "Theory in the Reader: Bleich, Holland, and Beyond." *College English* 47.8 (1985): 836–50.

McGarry, Daniel D. *Medieval History and Civilization.* New York: Macmillan, 1976.

Nelson, Jennie, and John R. Hayes. *The Effects of Classroom Contexts on Students' Responses to Writing from Sources: Regurgitating Information or Triggering Insights.* Berkeley, CA: Center for the Study of Writing, U of California at Berkeley and Carnegie Mellon. Technical Report, 1988.

Pichert, James W. "Sensitivity to Importance as a Predictor of Reading Comprehension." *Perspectives on Reading Research and Instruction.* Eds. Michael A. Kamil and Alden J. Moe. Washington, D.C.: National Reading Conference, 1980. 42–46.

Robinson, Cyril E. *England: A History of British Progress from the Early Ages to the Present Day.* New York: Thomas Y. Crowell Company, 1928.

Schwegler, Robert A., and Linda K. Shamoon. "The Aims and Process of the Research Paper." *College English* 44 (1982): 817–24.

Shedd, Patricia T. "The Relationship between Attitude of the Reader Towards Women's Changing Role and Response to Literature Which Illuminates Women's Role." *Diss.* Syracuse U, 1975. ERIC ED 142 956.

Short, Elizabeth Jane, and Ellen Bouchard Ryan. "Metacognitive Differences between Skilled and Less Skilled Readers: Remediating Deficits through Story Grammar and Attribution Training." *Journal of Education Psychology* 76 (1984): 225–35.

Spivey, Nancy Nelson. *Discourse Synthesis: Constructing Texts in Reading and Writing.* Diss. U Texas, 1983. Newark, DE: International Reading Association, 1984.

Toulmin, Steven E. *The Uses of Argument.* Cambridge: Cambridge UP, 1969.

Vipond, Douglas, and Russell Hunt. "Point-Driven Understanding: Pragmatic and Cognitive Dimensions of Literary Reading." *Poetics* 13, (1984): 261–77.

Winograd, Peter. "Strategic Difficulties in Summarizing Texts." *Reading Research Quarterly* 19 (1984): 404–25.

THE HISTORICAL STRUCTURE OF
SCIENTIFIC DISCOVERY

Thomas Kuhn

[handwritten: he is stating historic picture / his topic]

My object in this article is to isolate and illuminate one small part of what I take to be a continuing historiographic revolution in the study of science. The structure of scientific discovery is my particular topic, and I can best approach it by pointing out that the subject itself may well seem extraordinarily odd. Both scientists and, until quite recently, historians have ordinarily viewed discovery as the sort of event which, though it may have preconditions and surely has consequences, is itself without internal structure. Rather than being seen as a complex development extended both in space and time, discovering something has usually seemed to be a unitary event, one which, like seeing something, happens to an individual at a specific time and place.

This view of the nature of discovery has, I suspect, deep roots in the nature of the scientific community. One of the few historical elements recurrent in the textbooks from which the prospective scientist learns his field is the attribution of particular natural phenomena to the historical personages who first discovered them. As a result of this and other aspects of their training, discovery becomes for many scientists an important goal. To make a discovery is to achieve one of the closest approximations to a property right that the scientific career affords. Professional prestige is often closely associated with these acquisitions.[1] Small wonder, then, that acrimonious disputes about priority and independence in discovery have often marred the normally placid tenor of scientific communication. Even less wonder that many historians of science have seen the individual discovery as an appropriate unit with which to measure scientific progress and have devoted much time and skill to determining what man made which discovery at what point in time. If the study of discovery has a surprise to offer, it is only that, despite the immense energy and ingenuity expended upon it, neither polemic nor painstaking scholarship has often succeeded in pinpointing the time and place at which a given discovery could properly be said to have "been made."

That failure, both of argument and of research, suggests the thesis that I now wish to develop. Many scientific discoveries, particularly the most interesting and important, are not the sort of event *[handwritten: claim]* about which the questions "Where?" and, more particularly, "When?" can appropriately be asked. Even if all conceivable data were at hand, those questions would not regularly possess answers. That we are persistently driven to ask them nonetheless is symptomatic of a fundamental inappropriateness in our image of discovery. That inappropriateness is here my main concern, but I approach it by considering first the historical problem presented by the attempt to date and to place a major class of fundamental discoveries.

---

[1] For a brilliant discussion of these points, see R. K. Merton, "Priorities in Scientific Discovery: A Chapter in the Sociology of Science," *American Sociological Review* 22 (1957): 635. Also very relevant, though it did not appear until this article had been prepared, is F. Reif, "The Competitive World of the Pure Scientist," *Science* 134 (1961): 1957.

The troublesome class consists of those discoveries—including oxygen, the electric current, X rays, and the electron-which could not be predicted from accepted theory in advance and which therefore caught the assembled profession by surprise. That kind of discovery will shortly be my exclusive concern, but it will help first to note that there is another sort and one which presents very few of the same problems. Into this second class of discoveries fall the neutrino, radio waves, and the elements which filled empty places in the periodic table. The existence of all these objects had been predicted from theory before they were discovered, and the men who made the discoveries therefore knew from the start what to look for. That foreknowledge did not make their task less demanding or less interesting, but it did provide criteria which told them when their goal had been reached.[2] As a result, there have been few priority debates over discoveries of this second sort, and only a paucity of data can prevent the historian from ascribing them to a particular time and place. Those facts help to isolate the difficulties we encounter as we return to the troublesome discoveries of the first class. In the cases that most concern us here there are no benchmarks to inform either the scientist or the historian when the job of discovery has been done.

As an illustration of this fundamental problem and its consequences, consider first the discovery of oxygen. Because it has repeatedly been studied, often with exemplary care and skill, that discovery is unlikely to offer any purely factual surprises. Therefore it is particularly well suited to clarify points of principle.[3] At least three scientists—Carl Scheele, Joseph Priestley, and Antoine Lavoisier—have a legitimate claim to this discovery, and polemicists have occasionally entered the same claim for Pierre Bayen.[4] Scheele's work, though it was almost certainly completed before the relevant researches of Priestley and

---

[2]Not all discoveries fall so neatly as the preceding into one or the other of my two classes. For example, Anderson's work on the positron was done in complete ignorance of Dirac's theory from which the new particle's existence had already been very nearly predicted. On the other hand, the immediately succeeding work by Blackett and Occhialini made full use of Dirac's theory and therefore exploited experiment more fully and constructed a more forceful case for the positron's existence than Anderson had been able to do. On this subject see N. R. Hanson, "Discovering the Positron," *British Journal for the Philosophy of Science* 12 (1961): 194; 12 (1962): 299. Hanson suggests several of the points developed here. I am much indebted to Professor Hanson for a preprint of this material.

[3]I have adapted a less familiar example from the same viewpoint in "The Caloric Theory of Adiabatic Compression," *Isis* 49 (1958): 132. A closely similar analysis of the emergence of a new theory is included in the early pages of my essay "Energy Conservation as an Example of Simultaneous Discovery," in *Critical Problems in the History of Science,* ed. M. Clagett (Madison: University of Wisconsin Press, 1959), pp. 321–56. . . . Reference to these papers may add depth and detail to the following discussion.

[4]The still classic discussion of the discovery of oxygen is A. N. Meldrum, *The Eighteenth Century Revolution in Science: The First Phase* (Calcutta, 1930), chap. 5. A more convenient and generally quite reliable discussion is included in J. B. Conant, *The Overthrow of the Phlogiston Theory: The Chemical Revolution of 1775–1789,* Harvard Case Histories in Experimental Science, case 2 (Cambridge: Harvard University Press, 1950). A recent and indispensable review which includes an account of the development of the priority controversy, is M. Daumas, *Lavoisier, théoricien et expérimentateur* (Paris, 1955), chaps. 2 and 3. H. Guerlac has added much significant detail to our knowledge of the early relations between Priestley and Lavoisier in his "Joseph Priestley's First Papers on Gases and Their Reception in France," *Journal of the History of Medicine* 12 (1957): I and in his very recent monograph, *Lavoisier: The Crucial Year* (Ithaca: Cornell University Press, 1961). For Scheele see J. R. Partington, *A Short History of Chemistry,* 2d ed. (London, 1951), pp. 104–09.

[5]For the dating of Scheele's work, see A. E. Nordenskjöld, *Carl Wilhelm Scheele, Nachgelessene Briefe und Aufzeichmungen* (Stockholm, 1892).

Lavoisier, was not made public until their work was well known.[5] Therefore it had no apparent causal role, and I shall simplify my story by omitting it.[6] Instead, I pick up the main route to the discovery of oxygen with the work of Bayen, who, sometime before March 1774, discovered that red precipitate of mercury (HgO) could, by heating, be made to yield a gas. That aeriform product Bayen identified as fixed air (CO_2), a substance made familiar to most pneumatic chemists by the earlier work of Joseph Black.[7] A variety of other substances were known to yield the same gas.

At the beginning of August 1774, a few months after Bayen's work had appeared, Joseph Priestley, repeated the experiment, though probably independently. Priestley, however, observed that the gaseous product would support combustion and therefore changed the identification. For him the gas obtained on heating red precipitate was nitrous air (N_2O), a substance that he had himself discovered more than two years before.[8] Later in the same month Priestley made a trip to Paris and there informed Lavoisier of the new reaction. The latter repeated the experiment once more, both in November 1775 and in February 1774. But, because he used tests somewhat more elaborate than Priestley's, Lavoisier again changed the identification. For him, as of May 1775, the gas released by red precipitate was neither fixed air nor nitrous air. Instead, it was "[atmospheric] air itself entire without alteration . . . even to the point that . . . it comes out more pure."[9] Meanwhile, however, Priestley had also been at work, and, before the beginning of March 1775, he, too, had concluded that the gas must be "common air." Until this point all of the men who had produced a gas from red precipitate of mercury had identified it with some previously known species.[10]

The remainder of this story of discovery is briefly told. During March 1775 Priestley discovered that his gas was in several respects very much "better" than common air, and he therefore reidentified the gas once more, this time calling it "dephlogisticated air," that is, atmospheric air deprived of its normal complement of phlogiston*. This conclusion Priestley published in the *Philosophical Transactions,* and it was apparently that publication which led Lavoisier to reexamine his own results.[11] The reexamination began during February 1776 and within a year had led Lavoisier to the conclusion that the gas was actually a

---

*Phlogiston. Was once believed to be the element that caused combustion and that was given off by anything burning.

[6]U. Bocklund ("A Lost Letter from Scheele to Lavoisier," *Lychnos,* 1957–58, pp. 39–62) argues that Scheele communicated his discovery of oxygen to Lavoisier in a letter of 30 Sept. 1774. Certainly the letter is important, and it clearly demonstrates that Scheele was ahead of both Priestley and Lavoisier at the time it was written. But I think the letter is not quite so candid as Bocklund supposes, and I fail to see how Lavoisier could have drawn the discovery of oxygen from it. Scheele describes a procedure for reconstituting common air, not for producing a new gas, and that, as we shall see, is almost the same information that Lavoisier received from Priestley at about the same time. In any case, there is no evidence that Lavoisier performed the sort of experiment that Scheele suggested.

[7]Bayen, "Essai d'experiences chymiques, faites sur quelques précipités de mercure, dans la vue de découvrir leur nature, Seconde partie," *Observations sur la physique* 3 (1774): 280–95, particularly pp. 289–91.

[8]J. B. Conant, *The Overthrow of the Phlogiston Theory,* pp. 34–40.

[9]Ibid., p. 23. A useful translation of the full text is available in Conant.

[10]For simplicity I use the term *red precipitate* throughout. Actually, Bayen used the precipitate; Priestley used both the precipitate and the oxide produced by direct calcination of mercury; and Lavoisier used only the latter. The difference is not without importance, for it was not unequivocally clear to chemists that the two substances were identical.

[11]There has been some doubt about Priestley's having influenced Lavoisier's thinking at this point, but, when the latter returned to experimenting with the gas in February 1776, he recorded in his notebooks that he had obtained "l'air dephlogistique de M. Priestley" (M. Daumas, *Lavoisier,* p. 36).

separable component of the atmospheric air which both he and Priestley had previously thought of as homogeneous. With this point reached, with the gas recognized as an irreducibly distinct species, we may conclude that the discovery of oxygen had been completed.

But to return to my initial question, when shall we say that oxygen was discovered and what criteria shall we use in answering that question? If discovering oxygen is simply holding an impure sample in one's hands, then the gas had been "discovered" in antiquity by the first man who ever bottled atmospheric air. Undoubtedly, for an experimental criterion, we must at least require a relatively pure sample like that obtained by Priestley in August 1774. But during 1774 Priestley was unaware that he had discovered anything except a new way to produce a relatively familiar species. Throughout that year his "discovery" is scarcely distinguishable from the one made earlier by Bayen, and neither case is quite distinct from that of the Reverend Stephen Hales, who had obtained the same gas more than forty years before.[12] Apparently to discover something one must also be aware of the discovery and know as well what it is that one has discovered.

But, that being the case, how much must one know? Had Priestley come close enough when he identified the gas as nitrous air? If not, was either he or Lavoisier significantly closer when he changed the identification to common air? And what are we to say about Priestley's next identification, the one made in March 1775? Dephlogisticated air is still not oxygen or even, for the phlogistic chemist, a quite unexpected sort of gas. Rather it is a particularly pure atmospheric air. Presumably, then, we wait for Lavoisier's work in 1776 and 1777, work which led him not merely to isolate the gas but to see what it was. Yet even that decision can be questioned, for in 1777 and to the end of his life Lavoisier insisted that oxygen was an atomic "principle of acidity" and that oxygen *gas* was formed only when that "principle" united with caloric, the matter of heat.[13] Shall we therefore say that oxygen had not yet been discovered in 1777? Some may be tempted to do so. But the principle of acidity was not banished from chemistry until after 1810 and caloric lingered on until the 1860s. Oxygen had, however, become a standard chemical substance long before either of those dates. Furthermore, what is perhaps the key point, it would probably have gained that status on the basis of Priestley's work alone without benefit of Lavoisier's still partial reinterpretation.

I conclude that we need a new vocabulary and new concepts for analyzing events like the discovery of oxygen. Though undoubtedly correct, the sentence "Oxygen was discovered" misleads by suggesting that discovering something is a single simple act unequivocally attributable, if only we knew enough, to an individual and an instant in time. When the discovery is unexpected, however, the latter attribution is always impossible and the former often is as well. Ignoring Scheele, we can, for example, safely say that oxygen had not been discovered before 1774; probably we would also insist that it had been discovered by 1777 or shortly thereafter. But within those limits any attempt to date the discovery or to attribute it to an individual must inevitably be arbitrary. Furthermore, it must be arbitrary just because discovering a new sort of phenomenon is necessarily a complex process which involves recognizing both *that* something is and *what* it is. Observation and conceptualization, fact and the assimilation of fact to theory, are inseparably linked in the discovery of scientific novelty. Inevitably, that process extends over time and may often involve a number of

---

[12]J. R. Partington, *A Short History of Chemistry,* p. 91.

[13]For the traditional elements in Lavoisier's interpretations of chemical reactions, see H. Metzger, *La philosophie de la matière chez Lavoisier* (Paris, 1935), and Daumas, Lavoisier, chap. 7.

people. Only for discoveries in my second category—those whose nature is known in advance—can discovering *that* and discovering *what* occur together and in an instant.

Two last, simpler, and far briefer examples will simultaneously show how typical the case of oxygen is and also prepare the way for a somewhat more precise conclusion. On the night of 13 March 1781, the astronomer William Herschel made the following entry in his journal: "In the quartile near Zeta Tauri . . . is a curious either nebulous star or perhaps a comet.[14] That entry is generally said to record the discovery of the planet Uranus, but it cannot quite have done that. Between 1690 and Herschel's observation in 1781 the same object had been seen and recorded at least seventeen times by men who took it to be a star. Herschel differed from them only in supposing that, because in his telescope it appeared especially large, it might actually be a *comet*! Two additional observations on 17 and 19 March confirmed that suspicion by showing that the object he had observed moved among the stars. As a result, astronomers throughout Europe were informed of the discovery, and the mathematicians among them began to compute the new comet's orbit. Only several months later, after all those attempts had repeatedly failed to square with observation, did the astronomer Lexell suggest that the object observed by Herschel might be a planet. And only when additional computations, using a planet's rather than a comet's orbit, proved reconcilable with observation was that suggestion generally accepted. At what point during 1781 do we want to say that the planet Uranus was discovered? And are we entirely and unequivocally clear that it was Herschel rather than Lexell who discovered it?

Or consider still more briefly the story of the discovery of X rays, a story which opens on the day in 1895 when the physicist Roentgen interrupted a well-precedented investigation of cathode rays because he noticed that a barium platinocyanide screen far from his shielded apparatus glowed when the discharge was in process.[15] Additional investigations—they required seven hectic weeks during which Roentgen rarely left the laboratory—indicated that the cause of the glow traveled in straight lines from the cathode ray tube, that the radiation cast shadows, that it could not be deflected by a magnet, and much else besides. Before announcing his discovery Roentgen had convinced himself that his effect was not due to cathode rays themselves but to a new form of radiation with at least some similarity to light. Once again the question suggests itself: When shall we say that X rays were actually discovered? Not, in any case, at the first instant, when all that had been noted was a glowing screen. At least one other investigator had seen that glow and, to his subsequent chagrin, discovered nothing at all. Nor, it is almost as clear, can the moment of discovery be pushed back to a point during the last week of investigation. By that time Roentgen was exploring the properties of the new radiation he had *already* discovered. We may have to settle for the remark that X rays emerged in Würzburg between 8 November and 28 December 1895.

The characteristics shared by these examples are, I think, common to all the episodes by which unanticipated novelties become subjects for scientific attention. I therefore conclude these brief remarks by discussing three such common characteristics, one which may help to provide a framework for the further study of the extended episodes we customarily call "discoveries."

In the first place, notice that all three of our discoveries—oxygen, Uranus, and X rays—began with the experimental or observational isolation of an anomaly, that is, with nature's failure to conform entirely to expectation. Notice, further, that the process by which that anomaly was educed displays simultaneously the apparently incompatible characteristics of the inevitable and the accidental. In the case of X rays, the anomalous

---

[14]P. Doig, *A Concise History of Astronomy* (London: Chapman, 1950), pp. 115–16.

[15]L. W. Taylor, *Physics, the Pioneer Science* (Boston: Houghton Mifflin Co., 1941), p. 790.

☙ glow which provided Roentgen's first clue was clearly the result of an accidental disposition of his apparatus. But by 1895 cathode rays were a normal subject for research all over Europe; that research quite regularly juxtaposed cathode-rays tubes with sensitive screens and films; as a result, Roentgen's accident was almost certain to occur elsewhere, as in fact it had. Those remarks, however, should make Roentgen's case look very much like those of Herschel and Priestley. Herschel first observed his oversized and thus anomalous star in the course of a prolonged survey of the northern heavens. That survey was, except for the magnification provided by Herschel's instruments, precisely of the sort that had repeatedly been carried through before and that had occasionally resulted in prior observations of Uranus. And Priestley, too—when he isolated the gas that behaved almost but not quite like nitrous air and then almost but not quite like common air—was seeing something unintended and wrong in the outcome of a sort of experiment for which there was much European precedent and which had more than once before led to the production of the new gas.

These features suggest the existence of two normal requisites for the beginning of an episode of discovery. The first, which throughout this paper I have largely taken for granted, is the individual skill, wit, or genius to recognize that something has gone wrong in ways that may prove consequential. Not any and every scientist would have noted that no unrecorded star should be so large, that the screen ought not to have glowed, that nitrous air should not have supported life. But that requisite presupposes another which is less frequently taken for granted. Whatever the level of genius available to observe them, anomalies do not emerge from the normal course of scientific research until both instruments and concepts have developed sufficiently to make their emergence likely and to make the anomaly which results recognizable as a violation of expectation.[16] To say that an unexpected discovery begins only when something goes wrong is to say that it begins only when scientists know well both how their instruments and how nature should behave. What distinguished Priestley, who saw an anomaly, from Hales, who did not, is largely the considerable articulation of pneumatic techniques and expectations that had come into being during the four decades which separate their two isolations of oxygen.[17] The very number of claimants indicates that after 1770 the discovery could not have been postponed for long.

The role of anomaly is the first of the characteristics shared by our three examples. A second can be considered more briefly, for it has provided the main theme for the body of my text. Though awareness of anomaly marks the beginning of a discovery, it marks only the beginning. What necessarily follows, if anything at all is to be discovered, is a more or less extended period during which the individual and often many members of his group struggle to make the anomaly lawlike. Invariably that period demands additional observation or experimentation as well as repeated cogitation. While it continues, scientists repeatedly revise their expectations, usually their instrumental standards, and sometimes their most fundamental theories as well. In this sense discoveries have a proper internal history as well as prehistory and a posthistory. Furthermore, within the rather vaguely delimited interval of internal history, there is no single moment or day which the historian, however complete his data, can identify as the point at which the discovery was made. Often, when several individuals are involved, it is even impossible unequivocally to identify any one of them as the discoverer.

Finally, turning to the third of these selected common characteristics, note briefly what happens as the period of discovery draws to a close. A full discussion of that question would require additional evi-

---

[16]Though the point cannot be argued here, the conditions which make the emergence of anomaly likely and those which make anomaly recognizable are to a very great extent the same. That fact may help us understand the extraordinarily large amount of simultaneous discovery in the sciences.

[17]A useful sketch of the development of pneumatic chemistry is included in Partington, *A Short History of Chemistry,* chap. 6.

dence and a separate paper, for I have had little to say about the aftermath of discovery in the body of my text. Nevertheless, the topic must not be entirely neglected, for it is in part a corollary of what has already been said.

Discoveries are often described as mere additions or increments to the growing stockpile of scientific knowledge, and that description has helped make the unit discovery seem a significant measure of progress. I suggest, however, that it is fully appropriate only to those discoveries which, like the elements that filled missing places in the periodic table, were anticipated and sought in advance and which therefore demanded no adjustment, adaptation, and assimilation from the profession. Though the sorts of discoveries we have here been examining are undoubtedly additions to scientific knowledge, they are also something more. In a sense that I can now develop only in part, they also react back upon what has previously been known, providing a new view of some previously familiar objects and simultaneously changing the way in which even some traditional parts of science are practiced. Those in whose area of special competence the new phenomenon falls often see both the world and their work differently as they emerge from the extended struggle with anomaly which constitutes the discovery of that phenomenon.

William Herschel, for example, when he increased by one the time-honored number of planetary bodies, taught astronomers to see new things when they looked at the familiar heavens even with instruments more traditional than his own. That change in the vision of astronomers must be a principal reason why, in the half century after the discovery of Uranus, twenty additional circumsolar bodies were added to the traditional seven.[18] A similar transformation is even clearer in the aftermath of Roentgen's work. In the first place, established techniques for cathode-ray research had to be changed, for scientists found they had failed to control a relevant variable. Those changes included both the redesign of old apparatus and revised ways of asking old questions. In addition, those scientists most concerned experienced the same transformation of vision that we have just noted in the aftermath of the discovery of Uranus. X rays were the first new sort of radiation discovered since infrared and ultraviolet at the beginning of the century. But within less than a decade after Roentgen's work, four more were disclosed by the new scientific sensitivity (for example, to fogged photographic plates) and by some of the new instrumental techniques that had resulted from Roentgen's work and its assimilation.[19]

Very often these transformations in the established techniques of scientific practice prove even more important than the incremental knowledge provided by the discovery itself. That could at least be argued in the cases of Uranus and of X rays; in the case of my third example, oxygen, it is categorically clear. Like the work of Herschel and Roentgen, that of Priestley and Lavoisier taught scientists to view old situations in new ways. Therefore, as we might anticipate, oxygen was not the only new chemical species to be identified in the aftermath of their work. But, in the case of oxygen, the readjustments demanded by assimilation were so profound that they played an integral and essential role—though they were not by themselves the cause—in the gigantic upheaval of chemical theory and practice which has since been

---

[18]R. Wolf, *Geschichte der Astronomie* (Munich, 1877), pp. 513–15, 683–93. The prephotographic discoveries of the asteroids is often seen as an effect of the invention of Bode's law. But that law cannot be the full explanation and may not even have played a large part. Piazzi's discovery of Ceres, in 1801, was made in ignorance of the current speculation about a missing planet in the "hole" between Mars and Jupiter. Instead, like Herschel, Piazzi was engaged on a star survey. More important, Bode's law was old by 1800 (ibid., p. 683), but only one man before that date seems to have thought it worthwhile to look for another planet. Finally, Bode's law, by itself, could only suggest the utility of looking for additional planets; it did not tell astronomers where to look. Clearly, however, the drive to look for additional planets dates from Herschel's work on Uranus.

[19]For α-, β-, and γ-radiation, discovery of which dates from 1896, see Taylor, *Physics*, pp. 800–804. For the fourth new form of radiation, N rays, see D. J. S. Price, *Science Since Babylon* (New Haven: Yale University Press, 1961), pp. 84–89. That N rays were ultimately the source of a scientific scandal does not make them less revealing of the scientific community's state of mind.

known as the chemical revolution. I do not suggest that every unanticipated discovery has consequences for science so deep and so far-reaching as those which followed the discovery of oxygen. But I do suggest that every such discovery demands, from those most concerned, the sorts of readjustment that, when they are more obvious, we equate with scientific revolution. It is, I believe, just because they demand readjustments like these that the process of discovery is necessarily and inevitably one that shows structure and that therefore extends in time.

STYLE: THE HIDDEN AGENDA IN COMPOSITION CLASSES OR ONE READER'S CONFESSION

Kate Ronald

In some ways I see this essay as a confession. I have been teaching writing and theorizing about how it should be taught for almost fifteen years now. During those fifteen years, you, the students reading this essay, have been in school, taking English classes and writing compositions. I have been teaching those classes and reading those compositions; plus I've been teaching some of your teachers for the past ten years, and so I feel responsible to you even though I've never had you in one of my classes. Now I'm going to tell you something you might already know. Since you started school in the first grade, there's been a revolution in the way you've been "taught" to write. It used to be that teachers focused on and evaluated your writing according to two main things: its structure and its correctness. Those were the days of diagramming sentences and imitating types of organization. In the 1960s and '70s, however, many people who studied writing began to talk about teaching the "process" of writing rather than the "products" of writing. In other words, the focus has shifted in the 1980s from organization and correctness to generating ideas, appealing to audiences, and developing a "voice" in writing.

Composition or "rhetoric" as it used to be called, is an ancient discipline going all the way back at least to Plato and Aristotle in the third century BCE. You are the most recent in a long, long line of students sitting in classes where teachers assign writing tasks and evaluate your ability. In ancient times, the art of writing was divided into five steps: invention (coming up with ideas), arrangement (organizing them), style (making them sound right), memory (remembering speeches), and delivery (oratorical ability). One way to think about the history of writing instruction is to look at the different emphases that different eras have put on these five steps. Today, with computers and photocopy machines, we don't worry much anymore about memory, for example, but it was terribly important in the time before the printing press. And we don't "deliver" what we write orally very much anymore, although the kind of font you choose from your word-processing program might be considered a matter of delivery. Of course all writers have to think about invention, arrangement, and style, no matter what age they work in. However, different eras have emphasized different parts of composition. Plato and Aristotle were upset by what they saw as an enchantment with style; they worried that writers could dazzle audiences without caring much about telling them the truth. And so they focused on invention, on figuring out issues by thinking and writing. By the sixteenth and seventeenth centuries, the focus had shifted back to style, going so far as giving students manuals that provided hundreds of ways to say "I enjoyed your letter very much." How a person sounded was more important than what a person had to say.

I see the shift from "product" to "process" while you've been in school as a reaction to that overemphasis on style. Once again, the focus has changed back to make *invention* the most important step in composition. Writing teachers who are up-to-date these days (including me) tell you (our students) not to worry, for example, about grammar or spelling or organization as you write your early drafts. We invite you to choose your own topics for writing and to get feedback from responsive small groups in your classes. We don't grade individual papers, but instead ask you to write multiple drafts and submit for final evaluation the ones you think best represent you as a writer. We don't lecture on punctuation or topic sentences. It's what you say, not how you say it, that counts. No doubt you all are familiar with this kind of teaching—I doubt you'd be reading this essay right now if you weren't in a class with a thoroughly "new rhetoric" teacher. Obviously this whole collection is focused on the *processes* of writing, the main theme of writing instruction in the 1980s.

But here comes my confession. Your teacher, and I, and all the others who were part of this latest revolution in rhetoric, haven't been exactly honest with you about the matter of style. We say we aren't overly interested in style, that your ideas and your growth as writers is uppermost in our minds, but we are still influenced by your writing style more than we admit, or perhaps know. In other words, despite all the research and writing I've done in the past ten years about composing, revising, responding, contexts for writing, personal voice, and all I know about the new rhetoric, I'm still rewarding and punishing my students for their writing styles. And here's the worst part of my confession: I'm not sure that I'm teaching them style. Of course any teacher quickly realizes that she can't teach everything in one semester, but I worry that I'm responding to something in my students' writing that I'm not telling them about—their style, the sound of their voices on paper. This essay is my attempt to atone for that omission in my own teaching. Despite that selfish motive, I also want to suggest to you ways in which you might become aware of your own writing styles and your teachers' agendas about style, as well as show you some strategies for studying and improving your own style in writing.

Let me stop to define what I mean and what I don't mean by "style." I don't mean spelling, grammar, punctuation, or usage, although if I'm going to be completely honest, I'd have to tell you that mistakes along those lines do get in my way when I'm reading. But those can be fixed, easily, by editing and copyreading. By style, I mean what my student, Margaret, said last semester after another student, Paul, had read a paper out loud for the whole class. She got this longing look on her face and cried, "I want to write the way Paul does!" You know students like Paul. He's clever, he surprises with his different perspectives on his topics, and he has a distinctive voice. I call this "writing where somebody's home," as opposed to writing that's technically correct but where there's "nobody home," no life, no voice. Let me give you some examples of these two kinds of voices.

Much Too Young to Be So Old

The neighborhood itself was old. Larger than most side streets, 31st Street had huge cracks that ran continuously from one end to the other of this gray track that led nowhere special. Of the large, lonely looking houses, there were only six left whose original structures hadn't been tampered with in order to make way for inexpensive apartments. Why would a real family continue to live in this place was a question we often asked and none of us could answer. Each stretch of the run-down rickety houses had an alley behind them. These alleys became homes, playgrounds, and learning areas for us children. We treasured these places. They were overgrown with weeds and filled with years of garbage, but we didn't seem to care. Then again, we didn't seem to care about much. (Amy)

The Dog

In 1980 I lived in a green split level house. It was a really ugly green but that is beside the point. The neighborhood was really rather pretty, with trees all over the place and not just little trees. They were huge. My friends and I played football in my backyard right after school every day. The neighbors had a white toy poodle that barked forever. You would walk by the fence and it would bark at you. I had no idea whatsoever that the dog was mean. (Corey)

Even though both these writers begin these essays by describing the settings of their stories, and both end with a suggestion of what's coming next, Amy's opening paragraph appeals to me much more than Corey's. I could point out "flaws" in both openings: I think Corey's suffers from lack of concrete detail, and he takes a pretty long time telling us only that the trees were "huge." Amy uses too much passive voice ("hadn't been tampered with"). However, I'm much more drawn into the world of 31st Street than I am to the neighborhood with huge trees. And I think that's because I know more about Amy from this opening—her words and her rhythm evoke a bittersweet expectation in me—whereas I'm not sure what Corey's up to. In other words, I get the distinct feeling that Amy really wants to tell her readers about her childhood. I don't see that kind of commitment in Corey. I know Corey's going to write a dog story, and usually those are my favorites, but somehow I don't very much want to read on.

But teachers have to read on, and on and on, through hundreds and hundreds of drafts a semester. So I can't just say to Corey, "This is boring." And, being a believer in the "new rhetoric," I'm interested in the process that leads to these two different styles. How does Amy come up with this voice? Was she born clever? And why does Corey make the decision to take himself out of his writing? I can think of many reasons why he would choose to be safe; in fact, he admitted to me later in that course that he had "copped out," choosing to write in what he called his "safe, public style" rather than take chances with what he thought was a more risky, personal style. That makes sense, if you consider the history of writing instruction up until the last fifteen to twenty years. Certainly it's been better to get it right, to avoid mistakes, than to get it good, to try for a voice. And it makes sense that Corey wouldn't want to expose his personal style—writing classrooms traditionally have not been places where students have felt safe. Writing and then showing that writing to someone else for evaluation and response is risky, a lot like asking "Am I OK? Am I a person you want to listen to?"

And so, to play it safe in a risky environment, it's tempting to take on a voice that isn't yours, to try to sound like you know what you're talking about, to sound "collegiate," to be acceptable and accepted. There's also a sort of mystique about "college writing," both in composition courses and in other disciplines. To write in college, this thinking goes, means to be "objective," to make your own opinions, your own stake in the subject, completely out of your writing. That's why people write, "It is to be hoped that" rather than, "I hope" or, "There are many aspects involved" rather than, "This is complicated:" And then there's also a real fear of writing badly, of being thought stupid, and so it's tempting simply to be bland and safe and not call too much attention to yourself.

And teachers have encouraged you, I think, to remain hidden behind your own prose. Remember when you got a "split grade" like this: "C+/B"? One grade for content and another for style. That sends a clear message, I think, that what you say and how you say it can be separated and analyzed differently. That's crazy—we can't split form and content. But teachers tend to encourage you to do that when they ask you to read an essay by Virginia Woolf or E. B. White from an anthology and then tell you to "write like that." Or, we teachers have been so concerned with form that we've discouraged you from real communication with another person. One of my students just yesterday described her English classes this way:

"I wanted to learn how to write and they were trying to teach me what my writing should look like." Preoccupation with correctness, with organization, and with format (margins, typing, neatness, etc.), all get in the way of style and voice. So, too, do prearranged assignments, where each student in the class writes the same essay on the same subject ("Compare high school to college," "Discuss the narrator's attitude in this short story," "My most embarrassing moment"). Such assignments become exercises in competition, in one sense, because you've got somehow to set yourself apart from the rest of the essays your teacher will be reading. But they are also exercises in becoming invisible, for while you want to be noticed, you don't want to be too terribly different, to stick out like a sore thumb. And so you write safely, not revealing too much or taking many chances.

I used to teach that way, giving assignments, comparing one student with another and everyone with the "ideal" paper I imagined in my head (although I never tried writing with my students in those days) correcting mistakes and arriving at a grade for each paper. The new rhetoric classes I teach now have eliminated many of these traps for students, but I've also opened up new ones, I'm afraid. Now my students choose their own topics, writing whatever they want to write. And sometimes I'm simply not interested in their choices. In the old days, when I gave the assignment, naturally I was interested in the topic—it was, after all, *my* idea. Now I read about all sorts of things every week—my students' families, their cars, the joys and sorrows in their love lives, their athletic victories and defeats, their opinions on the latest upcoming election, their thoughts about the future, etc. Frankly, I don't approach each of these topics in the same way. For example, a dog story almost always interests me, while a car story might not. Or, a liberal reading of the latest campus debate on women's issues will grab my attention much more quickly than a fundamentalist interpretation. That's simply the truth. But, as a teacher of "process," I try my best to get interested in whatever my students are writing. And, I'm usually delighted by how much my students can move me with their ideas. So what makes me interested? I'm convinced it has to do with their style. And here I'm defining style not simply as word choice or sentence structure, but as a kind of "presence" on the page, the feeling I get as a reader that, indeed, somebody's home in this paper, somebody wants to say something—to me, to herself, to the class, to the community.

Mine is not the only response students receive in this kind of classroom. Each day, students bring copies of their work-in-progress to their small groups. They read their papers out loud to each other, and we practice ways of responding to each writer that will keep him or her writing, for starts, and that will help the writer see what needs to be added, changed, or cut from the draft. This can get pretty tricky. It's been my experience that showing your writing to another student, to a peer, can be much more risky than showing it to a teacher. We've all had the experience of handing in something we knew was terrible to a teacher, and it's not so painful. People will give writing to teachers that they'd never show to someone whose opinion they valued. But sitting down in a small group with three of four classmates and saying, "I wrote this. What do you think?" is, again, like asking "Do you like me? Am I an interesting person?" And so my classes practice ways of responding to one another's writing without being overly critical, without taking control of the writing out of the writer's hands, and without damaging egos. And they become quite sophisticated as the semester goes along. Still, one of the worst moments in a small group comes when someone reads a draft and the rest of the group responds like this: "It's OK. I don't see anything wrong with it. It seems pretty good." And then silence. In other words, the writer hasn't grabbed their attention, hasn't engaged the readers, hasn't communicated in any meaningful way. What's the difference between this scenario and one where the group comes back with responses like "Where did you get that idea? I really like the way you describe the old man. This reminds me of my grandfather. I think you're right to notice his hands"? I think the difference is in *style,* in the presence of a writer in a group who is honestly trying to communicate to his or her readers.

But I know I still haven't been exactly clear about what I mean by style. That's part of my dilemma, my reason for wanting to write this essay. All of us, teachers and students, recognize good style when we hear it, but I don't know what we do to foster it. And so for the rest of this essay I want to talk to you about how to work on your own writing styles, to recognize and develop your own individual voice in writing, and how to listen for your teachers' agendas in style. Because, despite our very natural desires to remain invisible in academic settings, you *want* to be noticed; you want to be the voice that your teacher becomes interested in. I think I'm telling you that your style ultimately makes the difference. And here I'm talking about not only your writing styles, but the reading styles of your audiences, the agendas operating in the contexts in which you write.

I'll start backward with agendas first. There are several main issues that I think influence English teachers when they are reading students' writing. First, we have a real bent for the literary element, the metaphor, the clever turn of phrase, the rhythm of prose that comes close to the rhythm of poetry. That's why I like sentences like these: "As the big night approached I could feel my stomach gradually easing its way up to my throat. I was as nervous as a young foal experiencing its first thunderstorm" (from an essay about barrel racing) and "Suddenly the University of Nebraska Cornhusker Marching Band takes the field for another exciting half-time performance, and the Sea of Red stands up *en masse* and goes to the concession stand" (from an essay about being in the band). I like the surprise in this last sentence, the unexpectedness of everyone leaving the performance, and I like the comparison to a young foal in the first one, especially since the essay is about horses. I tell my students to "take chances" in their writing. I think these two writers were trying to do just that. And I liked them for taking that chance.

But you don't want to take chances everywhere. Of course this kind of writing won't work in a biology lab report or a history exam, which brings me to another troublesome issue when we talk about style in college writing. You move among what composition researchers call "discourse communities" every day—from English to Biology to Sociology to Music to the dorm to family dinners to friends at bars— you don't talk or write the same way, or in the same voice to each of these groups. You adjust. And yet many professors still believe that you should be learning to write one certain kind of style in college, one that's objective, impersonal, formal, explicit, and organized around assertions, claims, and reasons that illustrate or defend those claims. You know this kind of writing. You produce it in response to questions like "Discuss the causes of the Civil War," or "Do you think that 'nature' or 'nurture' plays the most important role in a child's development?" Here's a student trying out this kind of "academic discourse" in an essay where he discusses what worries him:

> Another outlet for violence in our society is video games. They have renewed the popularity that they had earlier in the 1980's and have taken our country by storm. There is not one child in the country who doesn't know what a Nintendo is. So, instead of running around outside getting fresh air and exercise, most children are sitting in front of the television playing video games. This is affecting their minds and their bodies.

Why wouldn't Jeff just say "Video games are popular again" instead of saying that "they have renewed their popularity" or "Kids are getting fat and lazy" rather than "This is affecting their minds and bodies?" Besides using big words here, Jeff is also trying to sound absolutely knowledgeable: he states that every child in this country knows Nintendo, they are all playing it, when if he thought about that for a minute, he'd know it wasn't true. I don't like this kind of writing very much myself. Jeff is trying so hard to sound academic that "there's nobody home," no authentic voice left, no sense of a real human being trying to say something to somebody. I prefer discourse that "renders experience," as Peter Elbow (1991) puts it, rather than discourse that tries to explain it. He describes this kind of language (or style) as writing where a writer "conveys to others a sense of experience—or indeed, that mirrors back to themselves a sense of their own experience, from a little distance, once it's out there on paper" (137). Here's an example of that kind of "rendering" from Paul's essay about a first date:

> Her mother answers the door. My brain says all kinds of witty and charming things which my larynx translates in a sort of amphibious croak. (Ribbitt, Ribbitt. I can't remember what it was I actually attempted to say.) She materializes at the top of the stairs, cast in a celestial glow. A choir of chubby cherubim, voices lifted into a heavenly chorus, drape her devine body with a thin film of gossamer. (No, not really. She did look pretty lovely, though. I tried to tell her as much. Ribbitt. Ribbitt.)

Now, perhaps Paul goes too far here, trying a little too hard to be clever, but I like this better than the discussion of video games. (And not just because I like the topic of dating better—since I've gotten married, I don't date anymore and I confess I'm addicted to Mario Brothers 3). Paul here is conveying the *feeling* of the moment, the sense of the experience, and he's complicating the memory by moving back and forth between the moment and his interpretation of it. In other words, he's letting me into the story, not explaining something to me. Paul is involved in what he's writing while Jeff is detached. And Paul's funny. Besides dog stories, I like humor in my students' writing.

Now, this brings me to another issue in the matter of style. I prefer the rendering style over the explanatory style, perhaps because I'm an English major and an English teacher, and therefore I like the allusion over the direct reference, description over analysis, narrative over exposition. But perhaps there's another reason I like the more personal style: I'm a woman. There's a whole body of recent research which suggests that men and women have different writing styles, among all sorts of other differences. Theorists such as Pamela Annas and Elizabeth Flynn suggest that women writers in academic situations often are forced to translate their experiences into the foreign language of objectivity, detachment, and authority that the male-dominated school system values. Women strive for connection, this thinking argues, while men value individual power. Feminist theory values writing that "brings together the personal and the political, the private and the public, into writing which is committed and powerful because it takes risks, because it speaks up clearly in their own voices and from their own experiences" (Annas 1985, 370; see also Flynn 1988). Here's an example of that kind of writing, an excerpt from an essay titled, "Grandma, You're Not So Young Anymore":

> My grandma was always so particular about everything. Everything had to be just so. The walls and curtains had to be spotless, the garden couldn't have a weed, the kolaches had to be baked, and the car had to be washed. . . . Each spring she was always the first to have her flowers and garden planted. She could remember the littlest details about our family history and ancestors. . . . There were always kolaches in the oven and cookies in the refrigerator. . . .
>
> I really didn't notice the aging so much at first. . . . When I would come home from college Mom would always say, "Grandma's really lonely now. Grandpa was her company, and now he's gone. You should really go and visit her more often. She won't be around forever."
>
> I had to admit I didn't visit her all that often. . . . I didn't notice how much slower she'd gotten until Thanksgiving Day. Grandma took us to Bonanza because she didn't want to cook that much. I noticed the slower, more crippled steps she took, the larger amount of wrinkles on her face, and most of all, her slowed mental abilities. She sometimes had trouble getting words out as if she couldn't remember what she wanted to say. She couldn't decide what foods she wanted to eat, and when she did eat, she hardly touched a thing. I didn't think my grandma would ever get old. Now I don't think she will last forever anymore.

Here, Deanna uses her own experience and observations to go on and talk about how the elderly are treated in our culture. She could have written a statistical report on nursing homes or a more formal argument about how Americans don't value their old people. But she chose instead to draw from her own life and therefore she draws me into her argument about the "frustration" of getting old. I like old people, and I can identify this woman's deterioration with my own mother's several years ago. But I still think it's more than my personal history that draws me to this essay. I suspect it's Deanna's willingness to explore her own experience on paper. Deanna definitely needs to work on editing this draft to improve her style (something more specific, for example, than "larger amounts of wrinkles" and "slowed mental abilities"). But she doesn't need to work to improve her style in the sense of her commitment to this topic, her presence on the page, or her desire to figure out and to explain her reaction to her grandmother's aging.

Each of these three issues might lead me to advise you that you should write metaphors for English teachers, formal explanations for male teachers in other disciplines, and personal narratives for your women professors. But you know that would be silly, simplistic advice about style. You have to maneuver every day through a complex set of expectations, some of which aren't made explicit, and the whole idea of teacher-as-audience is much more complex than simply psyching out a teacher's background or political agenda. "Style" in writing means different things to different people. I have to be honest and admit that my definition of style as presence on paper is simply my own definition. I hope this essay will lead you to your own thinking about what style means, in all contexts. But I am going to end by giving you some advice about your own style in writing anyway—the teacher in me can't resist. That advice is: Work on your style without thinking about school too much. Here are five suggestions to help you do this.

In School or Out, Write as if You're Actually Saying Something to Somebody. Even if you're not exactly sure who your audience is, try to imagine a real person who's interested in what you have to say. Probably the most important thing I can tell you about working on your style is: Think of your writing as actually saying something to somebody real. Too often in academics we can imagine no audience at all, or at the most an audience with evaluation on its mind, not real interest or response. When I'm able to get interested in my students' writing, no matter what the topic, it's because I hear someone talking to me. My colleague Rick Evans calls this kind of writing "talking on paper," and if you keep that metaphor in mind, I think you'll more often avoid the kind of "academese" or formal language that signals you're hiding or you've disappeared.

I can illustrate the difference in style I'm talking about through two journals that Angie gave me at the beginning and the end of a composition and literature course last year. All through the course, I asked students to write about how the novels we were reading connected to their own lives:

> January 24: Well, I'm confused. I haven't written a paper for an English class that wasn't a formal literary analysis since 8th grade. Now, all of a sudden, the kind of writing my teachers always said would be of no use in college *is,* and what they said *would* be, *isn't.* Go figure. Now, if Kate had asked me to churn out a paper on some passage or symbol in *Beloved*—even one of my own choosing—I could get out 5–8 (handwritten) pages easy. But this life stuff? Who wants to know about that anyway?

> May 1: This portfolio represents the work closest to my guts. It's *my* story, not *Beloved's* or Carlos Rueda's. I hasten to point out that this may not be my best work or even my favorite work, but it's the work that sings my song. My goal was to communicate a set of ideas, to spark a dialogue with *you,* as my reader, to inspire you to think about *what* I have written, not *how* I have written it. So here it is, bound in plastic, unified, in a manner, ready for reading. I hope you like what I have woven.

Notice how Angie's attitude toward me as her reader changed from January to May. At first she referred to "Kate" as if I wouldn't be reading what she had written, even though this was a journal handed in to me; later I become someone she wants to engage in a dialogue. (She had expected the kind of writing class I described at the beginning of this essay, but she found herself writing for a new rhetoric teacher.) Notice, too, how at first she talks about how she could write five to eight pages *even if she had to choose her own topic.* The implication is clear—that it's easier to write when someone else tells her what to do, what to write about. In other words, it's easier to perform rather than to communicate. Notice, finally, Angie's relationship to the literature we were reading in these two journals. At first she wants only to write about the symbols in Toni Morrison's (1987) novel, *Beloved,* focusing all her attention on the literary work and not on herself. At the end of the course, she subordinates the novels almost completely to her own stories. This is an engaged writer, one with a clear sense of her own style, her own presence.

Write Outside of School. Play with writing outside of school. You'll need to write much more than just what's assigned in your classes to develop a beautiful writing style. (Sorry, but it's true.) One of the truisms about good writers is that they are good readers; in other words, they read a lot. (And they were probably read to as kids, but we can't go into that right now.) So, here's an exercise in style that I recommend to my students. Find an author whose writing you admire. Copy out a particular, favorite passage. Then imitate that style, word for word, part-of-speech for part-of-speech. Here's an example from one of my students last semester. We were reading *Beloved,* and Sarah used its opening passage to talk about the first day of class. I'll show you Morrison's passage and then Sarah's:

> 124 was spiteful. Full of a baby's venom. The women in the house knew it and so did the children. For years each put up with the spite in his own way, but by 1873, Sethe and her daughter Denver were its only victims. The grandmother, Baby Suggs, was dead, and the sons, Howard and Buglar, had run away by the time they were thirteen years old—as soon as merely looking in a mirror shattered it (that was the signal for Buglar); as soon as two tiny hand prints appeared in the cake (that was it for Howard). Neither boy waited to see more. (3)

> Andrews 33 was quiet. Full of a new semester's uneasiness. The students in the room knew it and so did the teacher. For a few minutes, everyone took in the tension in their own way, but by 12:45 the roll call and Kate's lame jokes broke the ice a little bit. The course, a new program, was explained, and the syllabus, papers and papers, looked simple enough by the time Kate explained her marvelous approach—as soon as really deciding on a topic excited us (that was the reason for the authority list); as soon as four friendly voices read to each other (that was the reason for small groups). No students lingered too write more. (Sarah)

Sarah told me later that doing this imitation surprised her—she had never written with parentheses before, nor had she stopped sentences in the middle this way ("the syllabus, papers and papers"). She wasn't sure she liked this imitation, but it showed her she could write in different ways. And playing with different voices on paper will help you make choices about your own style in different situations.

Read Your Work-in-progress out Loud, Preferably to a Real Person. Looking back over this essay, I realize that so much of what I've said about style revolves around the sense of sound. Teachers have good ears, and so do you. Listen to your own voice as you read out loud. Do you sound like a person talking to someone? Or a student performing for a grade?

Practice Cutting All the Words You Can out of Your Drafts and Starting from There. This is one of the hardest things for any writer to do, and yet I think it's one of the most effective ways to make your writing more interesting. Most of the time there are simply too many words getting in the way of your meaning, making too much noise for you to be heard. Look closely at your drafts and be hard on yourself. Let me give you a few quick examples:

> The first thing that really upsets me is the destruction of our environment due to ignorance, capitalism, and blindness in the world. The attitude that most people take is that by ignoring the problem it will go away. An example of this attitude is the turnout for elections in America.

> Revision: Ignorance, capitalism, and blindness destroy our environment. Most people look the other way. Many don't even vote.

Once Jim revised this opening sentence from an essay on what worries him, he realized that he hadn't said much yet and that he was moving way too quickly. He learned that he had several ideas he felt strongly about, ideas worth slowing down to develop. Here are two more examples:

> I also think that we need to provide more opportunities for the homeless to receive an education so they can compete in today's job market. Another reason for educating these people is because the increasing numbers of unemployed persons is a factor that is contributing to homelessness in our country. There are declining employment opportunities for unskilled labor in todays job market, and since many homeless are unskilled laborers, they are not able to acquire a decent job. Therefore they cannot afford to buy a home. I think it is critical that these people be educated if the homeless problem in our country is going to be resolved.

> Revision: We need to educate the homeless so they can compete in a market where jobs are becoming more scarce.

> There are so many things that a person can fill their mind with. I find that when talking with friends the majority of their thoughts are filled with worries. I don't really believe that it is all negative to worry unless it becomes an obsession. So many people are worried about so many different things. Some of which are personal while others are more societal. When I try to figure out what worries me most I find it to be on a more personal level.

> Revision: I'm sort of worried that I worry so much about myself.

Each of these last two writers realized that they hadn't said much of anything yet in their initial drafts. Going back to cut words, asking themselves questions about what they meant to say to a reader, allowed them to start over with a different, clearer perspective. I know this isn't easy, especially in school, where you've been trained to "write 1000 words" and, by God, you'll write 1000 words whether you have one or 1000 words to say on the subject. Try to stop padding and counting words in the margins. Cut words. This is probably the most practical piece of advice I have.

Finally, Write About Your Own Writing Style. Keep a record of your reactions to what you write, a list of your favorite sentences, and a reaction to the reactions you get from readers. Most of all, forgive yourself for writing badly from time to time. One of my professors in graduate school told me that I was capable of writing "awkward word piles," and here I am with the nerve to be writing an essay to you about style. I've tried to practice what I preach, and now I'm suggesting that you throw out more than you keep and to notice and remember what works for you. Writing about your own writing is another piece of practical advice.

This is really my last word: don't let *me* fool you here. Even though I understand what Angie meant in her last journal to me about my being more interested in what she has to say than *how* she said it, I'm still very in tune with the how, with her style, I'm happy that her focus has moved away from me as evaluator toward herself as a creator. But I'm still influenced by her style. Don't forget that. And I'm happy that the emphasis in composition has shifted from style back to invention. But I still reward and punish style in my reactions to students' writings. Yes, I try to be an interested reader, but my agendas also include listening for the sound of prose I like.

I suppose what I'm really confessing to you all in this essay is that I am not only a teacher, but I'm also a reader, with her own tastes, preferences, and phobias about what I like to read. And, as a reader, I look for style. There's a play that I love that I think can show you what I mean by style, by presence in writing. *The Real Thing,* by Tom Stoppard (1983) is about real love and real life, but it's also about real writing. At about the end of Act One, Henry, the playwright/hero, talks about good writing. He's picked up a cricket bat (could be a Louisville slugger, but this play is set in London) to make his point. (Read this out loud and listen to the sound):

> This thing here, which looks like a wooden club, is actually several pieces of particular wood cunningly put together in a certain way so that the whole thing is sprung, like a dance floor. It's for hitting cricket balls with. If you get it right, the cricket ball will travel two hundred yards in four seconds, and all you've done is give it a knock like knocking the top off a bottle of stout, and it make a noise like a trout taking a fly. What we're trying to do is write cricket bats, so then when we throw up an idea and give it a little knock, it might . . . *travel.* (22)

This image has stayed with me for seven years, ever since I first saw and read Stoppard's play, and it's an idea that I think all writers and readers understand. "Ideas traveling"—surely that's what I want for myself as a writer and for my students. I love the image of the dance floor too—the idea of a piece of writing as an invitation to movement, a place to join with others, a site of communal passion and joy. But I don't think people in school always think of writing as something that travels, or as a dance floor, and I would like somehow to help you a little toward Henry's vision. Later in the same speech he picks up a badly written play that he's been asked to "fix" and describes it:

> Now, what we've got here is a lump of wood of roughly the same shape trying to be a cricket bat, and if you hit a ball with it, the ball will travel about ten feet and you will drop the bat and dance about shouting "Ouch!" with your hands stuck in your armpits (23).

I've read writing, my own and my students' and professionals', that makes me want to do this different kind of dancing. Many of your textbooks read like "lumps of wood," yes? Henry tells us that no amount of simple editing will fix something that has no life or passion to begin with. But how to transform lumps of wood into cricket bats? It seems to me the key lies in this play's other theme—the "real thing," meaning real love and real passion. When I encourage you to develop your style in writing, I'm inviting you into the game, onto the dance floor, encouraging you to commit yourself to your ideas and to your readers. That's the essence of *style,* which, without knowledge and passion, amounts only to a performance that dazzles without touching its readers, and which, without practice, amounts to very little. In that sense, Plato and Aristotle were right to say that we shouldn't emphasize style over invention, ideas, and voice. And in another sense, my last piece of advice would apply to students in ancient Greece as well as modern America: write about something you care about to someone you care about. Even if you are writing in school, try to have a presence—show them that somebody's home, working. Writers must know and love not only their subjects but their audiences as well, so that ideas will dance, so that ideas will travel.

Works Cited

Annas, Pamela. (1985). "Style as Politics." *College English,* 4, 370.

Elbow, Peter (1991). "Reflections on Academic Discourse." *College English,* 2, 137.

Flynn, Elizabeth (1988). "Composing as Woman." *College Composition and Communication,* 39, 423–435.

Morrison, Toni (1987). *Beloved.* New York: Knopf.

Stoppard, Tom (1983). *The Real Thing.* London: Faber & Faber.

THE SINGULAR FIRST PERSON

Scott Russell Sanders

The first soapbox orator I ever saw was haranguing a crowd beside the Greyhound Station in Providence, Rhode Island, about the evils of fluoridated water. What the man stood on was actually an upturned milk crate, all the genuine soapboxes presumably having been snapped up by antique dealers. He wore an orange plaid sports coat and matching bow tie and held aloft a bottle filled with mossy green liquid. I don't remember the details of his spiel, except his warning that fluoride was an invention of the Communists designed to weaken our bones and thereby make us pushovers for a Red invasion. What amazed me, as a tongue-tied kid of seventeen newly arrived in the city from the boondocks, was not his message but his courage in delivering it to a mob of strangers. I figured it would have been easier for me to jump straight over the Greyhound Station than to stand there on that milk crate and utter my thoughts.

To this day, when I read or when I compose one of those curious monologues we call the personal essay, I often think of that soapbox orator. Nobody had asked him for his two cents' worth, but there he was declaring it with all the eloquence he could muster. The essay, although enacted in private, is no less arrogant a performance. Unlike novelists and playwrights, who lurk behind the scenes while distracting our attention with the puppet show of imaginary characters, unlike scholars and journalists, who quote the opinions of others and shelter behind the hedges of neutrality, the essayist has nowhere to hide. While the poet can lean back on a several-thousand-year-old legacy of ecstatic speech, the essayist inherits a much briefer and skimpier tradition. The poet is allowed to quit after a few lines, but the essayist must hold our attention over pages and pages. It is a brash and foolhardy form, this one-man or one-woman circus, which relies on the tricks of anecdote, conjecture, memory, and wit to enthrall us.

Addressing a monologue to the world seems all the more brazen or preposterous an act when you consider what a tiny fraction of the human chorus any single voice is. At the Boston Museum of Science an electronic meter records with flashing lights the population of the United States. Figuring in the rate of births, deaths, emigrants leaving the country and immigrants arriving, the meter calculates that we add one fellow citizen every twenty-one seconds. When I looked at it recently, the count stood at 249,958,483. As I wrote that figure in my notebook, the final number jumped from three to four. Another mouth, another set of ears and eyes, another brain. A counter for the earth's population would stand somewhere past five billion at the moment, and would be rising in a blur of digits. Amid this avalanche of selves, it is a wonder that anyone finds the gumption to sit down and write one of those naked, lonely, quixotic letters-to-the-world.

A surprising number do find the gumption. In fact, I have the impression there are more essayists at work in America today, and more gifted ones, than at any time in recent decades. Whom do I have in mind? Here is a sampler: Wendell Berry, Carol Bly, Joan Didion, Annie Dillard, Stephen Jay Gould, Elizabeth Hardwick, Edward Hoagland, Phillip Lopate, Barry Lopez, Peter Matthiessen, John McPhee, Cynthia Ozick, Paul Theroux, Lewis Thomas, Tom Wolfe. No doubt you could make up a list of your own—with a greater ethnic range, perhaps, or fewer nature enthusiasts—a list that would provide equally convincing support for the view that we are blessed right now with an abundance of essayists. We do not have anyone to rival Emerson or Thoreau, but in sheer quantity of first-rate work our time stands comparison with any period since the heyday of the form in the mid-nineteenth century.

Why are so many writers taking up this risky form, and why are so many readers—to judge by the statistics of book and magazine publication—seeking it out? In this era of prepackaged thought, the essay is the closest thing we have, on paper, to a record of the individual mind at work and play. It is an amateur's raid in a world of specialists. Feeling overwhelmed by data, random information, the flotsam and jetsam of mass culture, we relish the spectacle of a single consciousness making sense of a portion of the chaos. We are grateful to Lewis Thomas for shining his light into the dark corners of biology, to John McPhee for laying bare the geology beneath our landscape, to Annie Dillard for showing us the universal fire blazing in the branches of a cedar, to Peter Matthiessen for chasing after snow leopards and mystical insights in the Himalayas. No matter if they are sketchy, these maps of meaning are still welcome. As Joan Didion observes in her own collection of essays, *The White Album,* "We live entirely, especially if we are writers, by the imposition of a narrative line upon disparate images, by the 'ideas' with which we have learned to freeze the shifting phantasmagoria which is our actual experience." Dizzy from a dance that seems to accelerate hour by hour, we cling to the narrative line, even though it may be as pure an invention as the shapes drawn by Greeks to identify the constellations.

The essay is a haven for the private, idiosyncratic voice in an era of anonymous babble. Like the blandburgers served in their millions along our highways, most language served up in public these days is textureless, tasteless mush. On television, over the phone, in the newspaper, wherever humans bandy words about, we encounter more and more abstractions, more empty formulas. Think of the pablum ladled out by politicians. Think of the fluffy white bread of advertising. Think, lord help us, of committee reports. By contrast, the essay remains stubbornly concrete and particular: it confronts you with an oil-smeared toilet at the Sunoco station, a red vinyl purse shaped like a valentine heart, a bowlegged dentist hunting deer with an elephant gun. As Orwell forcefully argued, and as dictators seem to agree, such a bypassing of abstractions, such an insistence on the concrete, is a politically subversive act. Clinging to this door, that child, this grief, following the zigzag motions of an inquisitive mind, the essay renews language and clears trash from the springs of thought. A century and a half ago, in the rousing manifesto entitled *Nature,* Emerson called on a new generation of writers to cast off the hand-me-down rhetoric of the day, to "pierce this rotten diction and fasten words again to visible things." The essayist aspires to do just that.

As if all these virtues were not enough to account for a renaissance of this protean genre, the essay has also taken over some of the territory abdicated by contemporary fiction. Whittled down to the bare bones of plot, camouflaged with irony, muttering in brief sentences and grade-school vocabulary, peopled with characters who stumble like sleepwalkers through numb lives, today's fashionable fiction avoids disclosing where the author stands on anything. In the essay, you had better speak from a region pretty close to the heart or the reader will detect the wind of phoniness whistling through your hollow phrases. In the essay you may be caught with your pants down, your ignorance and sentimentality showing, while you trot recklessly about on one of your hobbyhorses. You cannot stand back from the action, as Joyce instructed us to do, and pare your fingernails. You cannot palm off your cockamamie notions on some hapless character.

To our list of the essay's contemporary attractions we should add the perennial ones of verbal play, mental adventure, and sheer anarchic high spirits. To see how the capricious mind can be led astray, consider the foregoing paragraph, which drags in metaphors from the realms of toys, clothing, weather, and biology, among others. That is bad enough; but it could have been worse. For example, I began to draft a sentence in that paragraph with the following words: "More than once, in sitting down to beaver away at a narrative, felling trees of memory and hauling brush to build a dam that might slow down the waters of time. . . ." I had set out to make some innocent remark, and here I was gnawing down trees and building dams, all because I had let that *beaver* slip in. On this occasion I had the good sense to throw out the unruly word. I don't always, as no doubt you will have noticed. Whatever its more visible subject, an essay is also about the way a mind moves, the links and leaps and jigs of thought. I might as well drag in another metaphor—and another unoffending animal—by saying that each doggy sentence, as it noses forward into the underbrush of thought, scatters a bunch of rabbits that go bounding off in all directions. The essayist can afford to chase more of those rabbits than the fiction writer can, but fewer than the poet. If you refuse to chase any of them, and keep plodding along in a straight line, you and your reader will have a dull outing. If you chase too many, you will soon wind up lost in a thicket of confusion with your tongue hanging out.

The pursuit of mental rabbits was strictly forbidden by the teachers who instructed me in English composition. For that matter, nearly all the qualities of the personal essay, as I have been sketching them, violate the rules that many of us were taught in school. You recall we were supposed to begin with an outline and stick by it faithfully, like a train riding its rails, avoiding sidetracks. Each paragraph was to have a topic sentence pasted near the front, and these orderly paragraphs were to be coupled end-to-end like so many boxcars. Every item in those boxcars was to bear the stamp of some external authority, preferably a footnote referring to a thick book, although appeals to magazines and newspapers would do in a pinch. Our diction was to be formal, dignified, shunning the vernacular. Polysyllabic words derived from Latin were preferable to the blunt lingo of the streets. Metaphors were to be used only in emergencies, and no two of them were to be mixed. And even in emergencies we could not speak in the first person singular.

Already as a schoolboy, I chafed against those rules. Now I break them shamelessly, in particular the taboo against using the lonely capital *I*. Just look at what I'm doing right now. My speculations about the state of the essay arise, needless to say, from my own practice as reader and writer, and they reflect my own tastes, no matter how I may pretend to gaze dispassionately down on the question from a hot-air balloon. As Thoreau declares in his cocky manner on the opening page of *Walden:* "In most books the *I,* or first person, is omitted; in this it will be retained; that, in respect to egotism, is the main difference. We commonly do not remember that it is, after all, always the first person that is speaking. I should not talk so much about myself if there were anybody else whom I knew as well." True for the personal essay, it is doubly true for an essay about the essay: one speaks always and inescapably in the first person singular.

We could sort out essays along a spectrum according to the degree to which the writer's ego is on display—with John McPhee, perhaps, at the extreme of self-effacement, and Norman Mailer at the opposite extreme of self-dramatization. Brassy or shy, center stage or hanging back in the wings, the author's persona commands our attention. For the length of an essay, or a book of essays, we respond to that persona as we would to a friend caught up in a rapturous monologue. When the monologue is finished, we may not be able to say precisely what it was about, any more than we can draw conclusions from a piece of music. "Essays don't usually boil down to a summary, as articles do," notes Edward Hoagland, one of the least summarizable of companions, "and the style of the writer has a 'nap' to it, a combination of personality and originality and energetic loose ends that stand up like the nap of a piece of wool and can't be brushed flat" ("What I Think, What I Am"). We make assumptions about that speaking voice, assumptions we cannot validly make about the narrators in fiction. Only a sophomore is permitted to ask if Huckleberry Finn ever had any children; but even literary sophisticates wonder in print about Thoreau's love life, Montaigne's domestic arrangements, De Quincey's opium habit, Virginia Woolf's depression.

Montaigne, who not only invented the form but nearly perfected it as well, announced from the start that his true subject was himself. In his note "To the Reader" at the beginning of the *Essays,* he slyly proclaimed:

> I want to be seen here in my simple, natural, ordinary fashion, without straining or artifice; for it is myself that I portray. My defects will here be read to the life, and also my natural form, as far as respect for the public has allowed. Had I been placed among those nations which are said to live still in the sweet freedom of nature's first laws, I assure you I should very gladly have portrayed myself here entire and wholly naked.

A few pages after this disarming introduction, we are told of the Emperor Maximilian, who was so prudish about exposing his private parts that he would not let a servant dress him or see him in the bath. The Emperor went so far as to give orders that he be buried in his underdrawers. Having let us in on this intimacy about Maximilian, Montaigne then confessed that he himself, although "bold-mouthed," was equally prudish, and that "except under great stress of necessity or voluptuousness," he never allowed anyone to see him naked. Such modesty, he feared, was unbecoming in a soldier. But such honesty is quite becoming in an essayist. The very confession of his prudery is a far more revealing gesture than any doffing of clothes.

A curious reader will soon find out that the word *essay,* as adapted by Montaigne, means a trial or attempt. The Latin root carries the more vivid sense of a weighing out. In the days when that root was alive and green, merchants discovered the value of goods and alchemists discovered the composition of unknown metals by the use of scales. Just so the essay, as Montaigne was the first to show, is a weighing out, an inquiry into the value, meaning, and true nature of experience; it is a private experiment carried out in public. In each of three successive editions, Montaigne inserted new material into his essays without revising the old material. Often the new statements contradicted the original ones, but Montaigne let them stand, since he believed that the only consistent fact about human beings is their inconsistency. In a celebration called "Why Montaigne Is Not a Bore," Lewis Thomas has remarked of him that "He [was] fond of his mind, and affectionately entertained by everything in his head." Whatever Montaigne wrote about—and he wrote about everything under the sun: fears, smells, growing old, the pleasures of scratching—he weighed on the scales of his own character.

It is the *singularity* of the first person—its warts and crotchets and turn of voice—that lures many of us into reading essays, and that lingers with us after we finish. Consider the lonely, melancholy persona of Loren Eiseley, forever wandering, forever brooding on our dim and bestial past, his lips frosty with the chill of the Ice Age. Consider the volatile, Dionysian persona of D. H. Lawrence, with his incandescent gaze, his habit of turning peasants into gods and trees into flames, his quick hatred and quicker love. Consider that philosophical farmer, Wendell Berry, who speaks with a countryman's knowledge and a deacon's severity. Consider E. B. White, with his cheery affection for brown eggs and dachshunds, his unflappable way of herding geese while the radio warns of an approaching hurricane.

E. B. White, that engaging master of the genre, a champion of idiosyncrasy, introduced his own volume of Essays by admitting the danger of narcissism:

> I think some people find the essay the last resort of the egoist, a much too self-conscious and self-serving form for their taste; they feel that it is presumptuous of a writer to assume that his little excursions or his small observations will interest the reader. There is some justice in their complaint. I have always been aware that I am by nature self-absorbed and egotistical; to write of myself to the extent I have done indicates a too great attention to my own life, not enough to the lives of others.

Yet the self-absorbed Mr. White was in fact a delighted observer of the world, and shared that delight with us. Thus, after describing memorably how a circus girl practiced her bareback riding in the leisure moments between shows ("The Ring of Time"), he confessed: "As a writing man, or secretary, I have always felt charged with the safekeeping of all unexpected items of worldly or unworldly enchantment, as though I might be held personally responsible if even a small one were to be lost." That may still be presumptuous, but it is a presumption turned outward on the creation.

This looking outward helps distinguish the essay from pure autobiography, which dwells more complacently on the self. Mass murderers, movie stars, sports heroes, Wall Street crooks, and defrocked politicians may blather on about whatever high jinks or low jinks made them temporarily famous, may chronicle their exploits, their diets, their hobbies, in perfect confidence that the public is eager to gobble up every least gossipy scrap. And the public, according to sales figures, generally is. On the other hand, I assume the public does not give a hoot about my private life. If I write of hiking up a mountain with my one-year-old boy riding like a papoose on my back, and of what he babbled to me while we gazed down from the summit onto the scudding clouds, it is not because I am deluded into believing that my baby, like the offspring of Prince Charles, matters to the great world. It is because I know the great world produces babies of its own and watches them change cloudfast before its doting eyes. To make that climb up the mountain vividly present for readers is harder work than the climb itself. I choose to write about my experience not because it is mine, but because it seems to me a door through which others might pass.

On that cocky first page of *Walden,* Thoreau justified his own seeming self-absorption by saying that he wrote the book for the sake of his fellow citizens, who kept asking him to account for his peculiar experiment by the pond. There is at least a sliver of truth to this, since Thoreau, a town character, had been invited more than once to speak his mind at the public lectern. Most of us, however, cannot honestly say the townspeople have been clamoring for our words. I suspect that all writers of the essay, even Norman Mailer and Gore Vidal, must occasionally wonder if they are egomaniacs. For the essayist, in other words, the problem of authority is inescapable. By what right does one speak? Why should anyone listen? The traditional sources of authority no longer serve. You cannot justify your words by appealing to the Bible or some other holy text, you cannot merely stitch together a patchwork of quotations from classical authors, you cannot lean on a podium at the Atheneum and deliver your wisdom to a rapt audience.

In searching for your own soapbox, a sturdy platform from which to deliver your opinionated monologues, it helps if you have already distinguished yourself at some other, less fishy form. When Yeats describes his longing for Maud Gonne or muses on Ireland's misty lore, everything he says is charged with the prior strength of his poetry. When Virginia Woolf, in *A Room of One's Own,* reflects on the status of women and the conditions necessary for making art, she speaks as the author of *Mrs. Dalloway* and *To the Lighthouse.* The essayist may also lay claim to our attention by having lived through events or traveled through terrains that already bear a richness of meaning. When James Baldwin writes his *Notes of a Native Son,* he does not have to convince us that racism is a troubling reality. When Barry Lopez takes us on a meditative tour of the far north in *Arctic Dreams,* he can rely on our curiosity about that fabled and forbidding place. When Paul Theroux climbs aboard a train and invites us on a journey to some exotic destination, he can count on the romance of railroads and the allure of remote cities to bear us along.

Most essayists, however, cannot draw on any source of authority from beyond the page to lend force to the page itself. They can only use language to put themselves on display and to gesture at the world. When Annie Dillard tells us in the opening lines of *Pilgrim at Tinker Creek* about the tomcat with bloody paws who jumps through the window onto her chest, why should we listen? Well, because of the voice that goes on to say: "And some mornings I'd wake in daylight to find my body covered with paw prints in blood; I looked as though I'd been painted with roses." Listen to her explaining a few pages later what she is up to in this book, this broody, zestful record of her stay in the Roanoke Valley: "I propose to keep here what Thoreau called 'a meteorological journal of the mind,' telling some tales and describing some of the sights of this rather tamed valley, and exploring, in fear and trembling, some of the unmapped dim reaches and unholy fastnesses to which those tales and sights so dizzyingly lead." The sentence not only describes the method of her literary search, but also exhibits the breathless, often giddy, always eloquent and spiritually hungry soul who will do the searching. If you enjoy her company, you will relish Annie Dillard's essays; if you don't, you won't.

Listen to another voice which readers tend to find either captivating or insufferable:

> That summer I began to see, however dimly, that one of my ambitions, perhaps my governing ambition, was to belong fully to this place, to belong as the thrushes and the herons and the muskrats belonged, to be altogether at home here. That is still my ambition. But now I have come to see that it proposes an enormous labor. It is a spiritual ambition, like goodness. The wild creatures belong to the place by nature, but as a man I can belong to it only by understanding and by virtue. It is an ambition I cannot hope to succeed in wholly, but I have come to believe that it is the most worthy of all.

That is Wendell Berry in "The Long-Legged House" writing about his patch of Kentucky. Once you have heard that stately, moralizing, cherishing voice, laced through with references to the land, you will not mistake it for anyone else's. Berry's themes are profound and arresting ones. But it is his voice, more than anything he speaks about, that either seizes us or drives us away

Even so distinct a persona as Wendell Berry's or Annie Dillard's is still only a literary fabrication, of course. The first person singular is too narrow a gate for the whole writer to squeeze through. What we meet on the page is not the flesh-and-blood author, but a simulacrum, a character who wears the label *I*. Introducing the lectures that became *A Room of One's Own,* Virginia Woolf reminded her listeners that "'I' is only a convenient term for somebody who has no real being. Lies will flow from my lips, but there may perhaps be some truth mixed up with them; it is for you to seek out this truth and to decide whether any part of it is worth keeping." Here is a part I consider worth keeping: "Women have served all these centuries as looking-glasses possessing the magic and delicious power of reflecting the figure of man at twice its natural size." It is from such elegant, revelatory sentences that we build up our notion of the "I" who speaks to us under the name of Virginia Woolf.

What the essay tells us may not be true in any sense that would satisfy a court of law. As an example, think of Orwell's brief narrative, "A Hanging," which describes an execution in Burma. Anyone who has read it remembers how the condemned man as he walked to the gallows stepped aside to avoid a puddle. That is the sort of haunting detail only an eyewitness should be able to report. Alas, biographers, those zealous debunkers, have recently claimed that Orwell never saw such a hanging, that he reconstructed it from hearsay. What then do we make of his essay? Or has it become the sort of barefaced lie we prefer to call a story?

Frankly, I don't much care what label we put on "A Hanging,"—fiction or nonfiction, it is a powerful statement either way—but Orwell might have cared a great deal. I say this because not long ago I was bemused and then vexed to find one of my own essays treated in a scholarly article as a work of fiction. Here was my earnest report about growing up on a military base, my heartfelt rendering of indelible memories, being confused with the airy figments of novelists! To be sure, in writing the piece I had used dialogue, scenes, settings, character descriptions, the whole fictional bag of tricks; sure, I picked and chose among a thousand beckoning details; sure, I downplayed some facts and highlighted others; but I was writing about the actual, not the invented. I shaped the matter, but I did not make it up.

To explain my vexation, I must break another taboo, which is to speak of the author's intent. My teachers warned me strenuously to avoid the intentional fallacy. They told me to regard poems and plays and stories as objects washed up on the page from some unknown and unknowable shores. Now that I am on the other side of the page, so to speak, I think quite recklessly of intention all the time. I believe that if we allow the question of intent in the case of murder, we should allow it in literature. The essay is distinguished from the short story, not by the presence or absence of literary devices, not by tone or theme or subject, but by the writer's stance toward the material. In composing an essay about what it was like to grow up on that military base, I *meant* something quite different from what I mean when concocting a story. I meant to preserve and record and help give voice to a reality that existed independently of me. I meant to pay my respects to a minor passage of history in an out-of-the-way place. I felt responsible to the truth as known by other people. I wanted to speak directly out of my own life into the lives of others.

You can see I am teetering on the brink of metaphysics. One step farther and I will plunge into the void, wondering as I fall how to prove there is any external truth for the essayist to pay homage to. I draw back from the brink and simply declare that I believe one writes, in essays, with a regard for the actual world, with a respect for the shared substance of history, the autonomy of other lives, the being of nature, the mystery and majesty of a creation we have not made.

When it comes to speculating about the creation, I feel more at ease with physics than with metaphysics. According to certain bold and lyrical cosmologists, there is at the center of black holes a geometrical point, the tiniest conceivable speck, where all the matter of a collapsed star has been concentrated, and where everyday notions of time, space, and force break down. That point is called a singularity. The boldest and most poetic theories suggest that anything sucked into a singularity might be flung back out again, utterly changed, somewhere else in the universe. The lonely first person, the essayist's microcosmic "I," may be thought of as a verbal singularity at the center of the mind's black hole. The raw matter of experience, torn away from the axes of time and space, falls in constantly from all sides, undergoes the mind's inscrutable alchemy, and reemerges in the quirky, unprecedented shape of an essay.

Now it is time for me to step down, before another metaphor seizes hold of me, before you notice that I am standing, not on a soapbox, but on the purest air.

RESPONDING—REALLY RESPONDING— TO OTHER STUDENTS' WRITING

Richard Straub

Okay. You've got a student paper you have to read and make comments on for Thursday. It's not something you're looking forward to. But that's alright, you think. There isn't really all that much to it. Just keep it simple. Read it quickly and mark whatever you see. Say something about the introduction. Something about details and examples. Ideas you can say you like. Mark any typos and spelling errors. Make your comments brief. Abbreviate where possible: *awk, good intro, give ex, frag*. Try to imitate the teacher. Mark what he'd mark and sound like he'd sound. But be cool about it. Don't praise anything really, but no need to get harsh or cut throat either. Get in and get out. You're okay, I'm okay. Everybody's happy. What's the problem?

This is, no doubt, a way of getting through the assignment. Satisfy the teacher and no surprises for the writer. It might just do the trick. But say you want to do a *good* job. Say you're willing to put in the time and effort—though time is tight and you know it's not going to be easy—and help the writer look back on the paper and revise it. And maybe in the process learn something more yourself about writing. What do you look for? How do you sound? How much do you take up? What exactly are you trying to accomplish? Here are some ideas.

How Should You Look at Yourself as a Responder?

Consider yourself a friendly reader. A test pilot. A roommate who's been asked to look over the paper and tell the writer what you think. Except you don't just take on the role of The Nice Roommate or The Ever-faithful Friend and tell her what she wants to hear. *This all looks good. 1 wouldn't change a thing. There are a couple places that I think he might not like, but I can see what you're doing there. I'd go with it. Good stuff.* You're supportive. You give her the benefit of the doubt and look to see the good in her writing. But friends don't let friends think their writing is the best thing since *The Great Gatsby* and they don't lead them to think that all is fine and well when it's not. Look to help this friend, this roommate writer—okay, this person in your class—to get a better piece of writing. Point to problems and areas for improvement but do it in a constructive way. See what you can do to push her to do even more than she's done and stretch herself as a writer.

What Are Your Goals?

First, don't set out to seek and destroy all errors and problems in the writing. You're not an editor. You're not a teacher. You're not a cruise missile. And don't rewrite any parts of the paper. You're not the writer; you're a reader. One of many. The paper is not yours; it's the writer's. She writes. You read. She is in charge of what she does to her writing. That doesn't mean you can't make suggestions. It doesn't mean you can't offer a few sample rewrites here and there, as models. But make it clear they're samples, models. Not rewrites. Not edits. Not corrections. Be reluctant at first even to say what you would do if the paper were yours. It's not yours. Again: Writers write, readers read and show what they're understanding and maybe make suggestions. What to do instead: Look at your task as a simple one. You're there to play back to the writer how you read the paper: what you got from it; what you found interesting; where you were confused; where you wanted more. With this done, you can go on to point out problems, ask questions, offer advice, and wonder out loud with the writer about her ideas. Look to help her improve the writing or encourage her to work on some things as a writer.

How Do You Get Started?

Before you up and start reading the paper, take a minute (alright, thirty seconds) to make a mental checklist about the circumstances of the writing, the context. You're not going to just read a text. You're going to read a text within a certain context, a set of circumstances that accompany the writing and that you bring to your reading. It's one kind of writing or another, designed for one audience and purpose or another. It's a rough draft or a final draft. The writer is trying to be serious or casual, straight or ironic. Ideally, you'll read the paper with an eye to the circumstances that it was written in and the situation it is looking to create. That means looking at the writing in terms of the assignment, the writer's particular interests and aims, the work you've been doing in class, and the stage of drafting.

- *The assignment:* What kind of writing does the assignment call (or allow) for? Is the paper supposed to be a personal essay? A report? An analysis? An argument? Consider how well the paper before you meets the demands of the kind of writing the writer is taking up.
- *The writer's interests and aims:* What does the writer want to accomplish? If she's writing a personal narrative, say, is she trying to simply recount a past experience? Is she trying to recount a past experience and at the same time amuse her readers? Is she trying to show a pleasant experience on the surface, yet suggest underneath that everything was not as pleasant as it seems? Hone in on the writer's particular aims in the writing.
- *The work of the class:* Try to tie your comments to the concepts and strategies you've been studying in class. If you've been doing a lot of work on using detail, be sure to point to places in the writing where the writer uses detail effectively or where she might provide richer detail. If you've been working on developing arguments through examples and sample cases, indicate where the writer might use such methods to strengthen her arguments. If you've been considering various ways to sharpen the style of your sentences, offer places where the writer can clarify her sentence structure or arrange a sentence for maximum impact. The best comments will ring familiar even as they lead the writer to try to do something she hasn't quite done before, or done in quite the same way. They'll be comforting and understandable even as they create some need to do more, a need to figure out some better way.
- *The stage of drafting:* Is it an early draft? A full but incomplete draft? A nearly final draft? Pay attention to the stage of drafting. Don't try to deal with everything all at once if it's a first, rough draft. Concentrate on the large picture: the paper's focus; the content; the writer's voice. Don't worry about errors and punctuation problems yet. There'll be time for them later. If it's closer to a full draft, go ahead and talk, in addition to the overall content, about arrangement, pacing, and sentence style. Wait till the final draft to give much attention to fine-tuning sentences and dealing in detail with proofreading. Remember: You're not an editor. Leave these sentence revisions and corrections for the writer. It's her paper. And she's going to learn best by detecting problems and making her own changes.

What to Address in Your Comments?

Try to focus your comments on a couple of areas of writing. Glance through the paper quickly first. Get an idea whether you'll deal mostly with the overall content and purpose of the writing, its shape and flow, or (if these are more or less in order) with local matters of paragraph structure, sentence style, and correctness. Don't try to cover everything that comes up or even all instances of a given problem. Address issues that are most important to address in this paper, at this time.

Where to Put Your Comments?

Some teachers like to have students write comments in the margins right next to the passage. Some like to have students write out their comments in an end note or in a separate letter to the writer. I like to recommend using both marginal comments and a note or letter at the end. The best of both worlds. Marginal comments allow you to give a quick moment-by-moment reading of the paper. They make it easy to give immediate and specific feedback. You still have to make sure you specify what you're talking about and what you have to say, but they save you some work telling the writer what you're addressing and allow you to focus your end note on things that are most important. Comments at the end allow you to provide some perspective on your response. This doesn't mean that you have to size up the paper and give it a thumbs up or a thumbs down. You can use the end comment to emphasize the key points of your response, explain and elaborate on issues you want to deal with more fully, and mention additional points that you don't want to address in detail. One thing to avoid: plastering comments all over the writing; in between and over the lines of the other person's writing—up, down, and across the page. Write in your space, and let the writer keep hers.

How to Sound?

Not like a teacher. Not like a judge. Not like an editor or critic or shotgun. (Wouldn't you want someone who was giving you comments not to sound like a teacher's red pen, a judge's ruling, an editor's impatience, a critic's wrath, a shotgun's blast?) Sound like you normally sound when you're speaking with a friend or acquaintance. Talk to the writer. You're not just marking up a text; you're responding to the writer. You're a reader, a helper, a colleague. Try to sound like someone who's a reader, who's helpful, and who's collegial. Supportive. And remember: Even when you're tough and demanding you can still be supportive.

How Much to Comment?

Don't be stingy. Write most of your comments out in full statements. Instead of writing two or three words, write seven or eight. Instead of making only one brief comment and moving on, say what you have to say and then go back over the statement and explain what you mean or why you said it or note other alternatives. Let the writer know again and again how you are understanding her paper, what you take her to be saying. And elaborate on your key comments. Explain your interpretations, problems, questions, and advice.

Is It Okay to Be Short and Sweet?

No. At least not most of the time. Get specific. Don't rely on general statements alone. How much have generic comments helped you as a writer? "Add detail." "Needs better structure." "Unclear." Try to let the writer know what exactly the problem is. Refer specifically to the writer's words and make them a part of your comments. "Add some detail on what it was like working at the beach." "I think we'll need to know more about your high school crowd before we can understand the way you've changed." "This sentence is not clear. Were you disappointed or were *they* disappointed?" This way the writer will see what you're talking about, and she'll have a better idea what to work on.

Do You Praise or Criticize or What?

Be always of two (or three) minds about your response to the paper. You like the paper, but it could use some more interesting detail. You found this statement interesting, but these ideas in the second paragraph are not so hot. It's an alright paper, but it could be outstanding if the writer said what was really bothering her. Always be ready to praise. But always look to point to places that are not working well or that are not yet working as well as they might. Always be ready to expect more from the writer.

How to Present Your Comments?

Don't steer away from being critical. Feel free—in fact, feel obliged—to tell the writer what you like and don't like, what is and is not working, and where you think it can be made to work better. But use some other strategies, too. Try to engage the writer in considering her choices and thinking about possible ways to improve the paper. Make it a goal to write two or three comments that look to summarize or paraphrase what the writer is saying. Instead of *telling* the reader what to do, *suggest* what she might do. Identify the questions that are raised for you as you reader:

- Play back your way of understanding the writing:

    This seems to be the real focus of the paper, the issue you seem most interested in.

    So you're saying that you really weren't interested in her romantically?

- Temper your criticisms:

    This sentence is a bit hard to follow.

    I'm not sure this paragraph is necessary.

- Offer advice:

    It might help to add an example here.

    Maybe save this sentence for the end of the paper.

- Ask questions, especially real questions:

    What else were you feeling at the time?

    What kind of friend? Would it help to say?

    Do you need this opening sentence?

    In what ways were you "a daddy's little girl"?

- Explain and follow up on your initial comments:

    You might present this episode first. This way we can see what you mean when you say that he was always too busy.

    How did you react? Did you cry or yell? Did you walk away?

    This makes her sound cold and calculating. Is that what you want?

- Offer some praise, and then explain to the writer why the writing works:

    Good opening paragraph. You've got my attention.

    Good detail. It tells me a lot about the place.

    I like the descriptions you provide—for instance, about your grandmother cooking, at the bottom of page 1; about her house, in the middle of page 2; and about how she said her rosary at night: "quick but almost pleading, like crying without tears."

How Much Criticism? How Much Praise?

Challenge yourself to write as many praise comments as criticisms. When you praise, praise well. Think about it. Sincerity and specificity are everything when it comes to a compliment.

How Much Should You Be Influenced by What You Know About the Writer?

Consider the person behind the writer when you make your comments. If she's not done so well in class lately, maybe you can give her a pick-me-up in your comments. If she's shy and seems reluctant to go into the kind of personal detail the paper seems to need, encourage her. Make some suggestions or tell her what you would do. If she's confident and going on arrogant, see what you can do to challenge her with the ideas she presents in the paper. Look for other views she may not have thought about, and find ways to lead her to consider them. Always be ready to look at the text in terms of the writer behind the text.

Good comments, this listing shows, require a lot from a reader. But you don't have to make a checklist out of these suggestions and go through each one methodically as you read. It's amazing how they all start coming together when you look at your response as a way of talking with the writer seriously about the writing, recording how you experience the words on the page and giving the writer something to think about for revision. The more you see examples of thoughtful commentary and the more you try to do it yourself, the more you'll get a feel for how it's done.

Here's a set of student comments on a student paper. They were done in the last third of a course that focused on the personal essay and concentrated on helping students develop the content and thought of their writing. The class had been working on finding ways to develop and extend the key statements of their essays (by using short, representative details, full-blown examples, dialogue, and multiple perspectives) and getting more careful about selecting and shaping parts of their writing. The assignment called on students to write an essay or an autobiographical story where they looked to capture how they see (or have seen) something about one or both of their parents—some habits, attitudes, or traits their parents have taken on. They were encouraged to give shape to their ideas and experiences in ways that went beyond their previous understandings and try things they hadn't tried in their writing. More a personal narrative than an essay, Todd's paper looks to capture one distinct difference in the way his mother and father disciplined their children. It is a rough draft that will be taken through one or possibly two more revisions. Readers were asked to offer whatever feedback they could that might help the writer with the next stage of writing.

This is a full and thoughtful set of comments. The responder, Jeremy, creates himself not as a teacher or critic but first of all as a reader, one who is intent on saying how he takes the writing and what he'd like to hear more about:

Good point. Makes it more unlikely that you should be the one to get caught.
Great passage. Really lets the reader know what you were thinking.

Was there a reason you were first or did it just happen that way?
Would he punish you anyway or could you just get away with things?

He makes twenty-two comments on the paper—seventeen statements in the margins and five more in the end note. The comments are written out in full statements, and they are detailed and specific. They make his response into a lively exchange with the writer, one person talking with another about what he's said. Well over half of the comments are follow-up comments that explain, illustrate, or qualify other responses.

The comments focus on the content and development of the writing, in line with the assignment, the stage of drafting, and the work of the course. They also view the writing rhetorically, in terms of how the text has certain effects on readers. Although there are over two dozen wording or sentence-level errors in the paper, he decides, wisely, to stick with the larger matters of writing. Yet even as he offers a pretty full set of comments he doesn't ever take control over the text. His comments are placed unobtrusively on the page, and he doesn't try to close things down or decide things for the writer. He offers praise, encouragement, and direction. What's more, he pushes the writer to do more than he has already done, to extend the boundaries of his examination. In keeping with the assignment and the larger goals of the course, he calls on Todd in several comments to explore the motivations and personalities behind his parents' different ways of disciplining:

> Maybe you could say more as to why you think your mom is like this. Did your dad get into trouble as a kid so he know what it's like? Explain why he reacts as he does.

He is careful, though, not to get presumptuous and make decisions for the writer. Instead, he offers options and points to possibilities:

> Perhaps more on your understanding of why your parents react as they do. What other things did you do to get into trouble? Or is it irrelevant?

From start to finish he takes on the task of reading and responding and leaves the work of writing and revising to Todd.

Jeremy's response is not in a class by itself. A set of comments to end all commentary on Todd's paper. He might have done well, for instance, to recognize how much this paper works because of the way Todd arranges the story. He could have done more to point to what's not working in the writing or what could be made to work better. He might have asked Todd for more details about his state of mind when he got caught by the policeman and while he was being held at the police station. He might have urged him more to make certain changes. He might even have said, if only in a brief warning, something about the number of errors across the writing. But this is moot and just. Different readers are always going to pick up on different things and respond in different ways, and no one reading or response is going to address everything that might well be addressed, in the way it might best be addressed. All responses are incomplete and provisional—one reader's way of reading and reacting to the text in front of him. And any number of other responses, presented in any number of different ways, might be as useful or maybe even more useful to Todd as he takes up his work with the writing.

All this notwithstanding, Jeremy's comments are solid. They are full. They are thoughtful. And they are respectful. They take the writing and the writer seriously and address the issues that are raised responsibly. His comments do what commentary on student writing should optimally do. They turn the writer back into his writing and lead him to reflect on his choices and aims, to consider and reconsider his intentions as a writer and the effects the words on the page will have on readers. They help him see what he can work on in revision and what he might deal with in his ongoing work as a writer.

☙ ME AND MY SHADOW ☙

Jane Tompkins

Iwrote this essay in answer to Ellen Messer-Davidow's "The Philosophical Bases of Feminist Literary Criticisms" which appeared in the Fall 1987 issue of *New Literary History* along with several replies, including a shorter version of this one. As if it weren't distraction enough that my essay depends on someone else's, I want, before you've even read it, to defend it from an accusation. Believing that my reply, which turns its back on theory, constituted a return to the "rhetoric of presence," to an "earlier, naive, untheoretical feminism," someone, whom I'll call the unfriendly reader, complained that I was making the "old patriarchal gesture of representation" whose effect had been to marginalize women, thus "reinforcing the very stereotypes women and minorities have fought so hard to overcome." I want to reply to this objection because I think it is mistaken and because it reproduces exactly the way I used to feel about feminist criticism when it first appeared in the late 1960s.

I wanted nothing to do with it. It was embarrassing to see women, with whom one was necessarily identified, insisting in print on the differences between men's and women's experience, focusing obsessively on women authors, women characters, women's issues. How pathetic, I thought, to have to call attention to yourself in that way. And in such bad taste. It was the worst kind of special pleading, an admission of weakness so blatant it made me ashamed. What I felt then, and what I think my unfriendly reader feels now, is a version of what women who are new to feminism often feel: that if we don't call attention to ourselves as women, but just shut up about it and do our work, no one will notice the difference and everything will be OK.

Women who adopt this line are, understandably, afraid. Afraid of being confused with the weaker sex, the sex that goes around whining and talking about itself in an unseemly way, that can't or won't do what the big boys do ("tough it out") and so won't ever be allowed to play in the big boys' games. I am sympathetic with this position. Not long ago, as organizer of an MLA session entitled "Professional Politics: Women and the Institution," I urged a large roomful of women to "get theory" because I thought that doing theory would admit us to the big leagues and enable us at the same time to argue a feminist case in the most unimpeachable terms—those that men had supplied. I busily took my own advice, which was good as far as it went. But I now see that there has been a price for this, at least there has been for me; it is the subject of my reply to Ellen. I now tend to think that theory itself, at least as it is usually practiced, may be one of the patriarchal gestures women *and* men ought to avoid.

There are two voices inside me answering, answering to, Ellen's essay. One is the voice of a critic who wants to correct a mistake in the essay's view of epistemology. The other is the voice of a person who wants to write about her feelings (I have wanted to do this for a long time but have felt too embarrassed). This person feels it is wrong to criticize the essay philosophically and even beside the point: because a critique of the kind the critic has in mind only insulates academic discourse further from the issues that make feminism matter. That make *her* matter. The critic, meanwhile, believes such feelings, and the attitudes that inform them, are soft-minded, self-indulgent, and unprofessional.

These beings exist separately but not apart. One writes for professional journals, the other in diaries, late at night. One uses words like "context" and "intelligibility," likes to win arguments, see her name in print, and give graduate students hardheaded advice. The other has hardly ever been heard from. She had a short story published once in a university library magazine, but her works exist chiefly in notebooks and manila folders labeled "Journal" and "Private." This person talks on the telephone a lot to her friends, has seen psychiatrists, likes cappuccino, worries about the state of her soul. Her father is ill right now, and one of her friends recently committed suicide.

The dichotomy drawn here is false—and not false. I mean in reality there's no split. It's the same person who feels and who discourses about epistemology. The problem is that you can't talk about your private life in the course of doing your professional work. You have to pretend that epistemology, or whatever you're writing about, has nothing to do with your life, that it's more exalted, more important, because it (supposedly) *transcends* the merely personal. Well, I'm tired of the conventions that keep discussions of epistemology, or James Joyce, segregated from meditations on what is happening outside my window or inside my heart. The public-private dichotomy, which is to say, the public-private *hierarchy*, is a founding condition of female oppression. I say to hell with it. The reason I feel embarrassed at my own attempts to speak personally in a professional context is that I have been conditioned to feel that way. That's all there is to it.

I think people are scared to talk about themselves, that they haven't got the guts to do it. I think readers want to know about each other. Sometimes, when a writer introduces some personal bit of story into an essay, I can hardly contain my pleasure. I love writers who write about their own experience. I feel I'm being nourished by them, that I'm being allowed to enter into a personal relationship with them. That I can match my own experience up with theirs, feel cousin to them, and say, yes, that's how it is.

> When he casts his leaves forth upon the wind [said Hawthorne], the author addresses, not the many who will fling aside his volume, or never take it up, but the few who will understand him. . . . As if the printed book, thrown at large on the wide world, were certain to find out the divided segment of the writer's own nature, and complete his circle of existence by bringing him into communion with it. . . . And so as thoughts are frozen and utterance, benumbed unless the speaker stand in some true relation with this audience—it may be pardonable to imagine that a friend, a kind and apprehensive, though not the closest friend, is listening to our talk. (Nathaniel Hawthorne, "The Custom-House," *The Scarlet Letter*, 5–6).

Hawthorne's sensitivity to the relationship that writing implies is rare in academic prose, even when the subject would seem to make awareness of the reader inevitable. Alison Jaggar gave a lecture recently that crystallized the problem. Western epistemology, she argued, is shaped by the belief that emotion should be excluded from the process of attaining knowledge. Because women in our culture are not simply encouraged but *required* to be the bearers of emotion, which men are culturally conditioned to repress, an epistemology which excludes emotions from the process of attaining knowledge radically undercuts women's epistemic authority. The idea that the conventions defining legitimate sources of knowledge overlapped with the conventions defining appropriate gender behavior (male) came to me as a blinding insight. I saw that I had been socialized from birth to feel and act in ways that automatically excluded me from participating in the culture's most valued activities. No wonder I felt so uncomfortable in the postures academic prose forced me to assume; it was like wearing men's jeans.

Ellen Messer-Davidow's essay participates—as Jaggar's lecture and my précis of it did—in the conventions of Western rationalism. It adopts the impersonal, technical vocabulary of the epistemic ideology it seeks to dislocate. The political problem posed by my need to reply to the essay is this: to adhere to the conventions is to uphold a male standard of rationality that militates against women's being recognized as culturally legitimate sources of knowledge. To break with the convention is to risk not being heard at all.

This is how I would reply to Ellen's essay if I were to do it in the professionally sanctioned way.

The essay provides feminist critics with an overarching framework for thinking about what they do, both in relation to mainstream criticism and in relation to feminist work in other fields. It allows the reader to see women's studies as a whole, furnishing useful categories for organizing a confusing and miscellaneous array of materials. It also provides excellent summaries of a wide variety of books and essays that readers might not otherwise encounter. The enterprise is carried out without pointed attacks on other theorists, without creating a cumbersome new vocabulary, without exhibitionistic displays of intellect or esoteric learning. Its practical aim—to define a field within which debate can take place—is fulfilled by *New Literary History*'s decision to publish it, and to do so in a format which includes replies.

(Very nice, Jane. You sound so reasonable and generous. But, as anybody can tell you, this is just the obligatory pat on the back before the stab in the entrails.)

The difficulty with the essay from a philosophical, as opposed to a practical, point of view is that the theory it offers as a basis for future work stems from a confused notion of what an epistemology is. The author says: "An epistemology . . . consists of assumptions that knowers make about the entities and processes in a domain of study, the relations that obtain among them, and the proper methods for investigating them" (p. 87). I want to quarrel with this definition. Epistemology, strictly speaking, is a *theory* about the origins and nature of knowledge. As such, it is a set of ideas explicitly held and consciously elaborated, and thus belongs to the practice of a subcategory of philosophy called epistemology. The fact that there is a branch of philosophy given over to the study of what knowledge is and how it is acquired is important, because it means that such theories are generated not in relation to this or that "domain of study" but in relation to one another: that is, within the context of already existing epistemological theories. They are rarely based upon a study of the practices of investigators within a particular field.

An epistemology does not consist of "assumptions that knowers make" in a particular field; it is a theory about how knowledge is acquired which makes sense, chiefly, in relation to other such theories. What Messer-Davidow offers as the "epistemology" of traditional literary critics is not *their* epistemology, if in fact they have one, but her description of what she assumes their assumptions are, a description which may or may not be correct. Moreover, if literary critics should indeed elaborate a theory of how they got their beliefs, that theory would have no privileged position in relation to their actual assumptions. It would simply be another theory. This distinction—between actual assumptions and an observer's description of them (even when one is observing one's own practice)—is crucial because it points to an all-important fact about the relation of epistemology to what really gets done in a given domain of study, namely this: that epistemology, a theory about how one gets one's knowledge, in no way determines the particular knowledge that one has.

This fact is important because Messer-Davidow assumes that if we change our epistemology, our practice as critics will change, too. Specifically, she wants us to give up the subject-object theory, in which "knowledge is an abstract representation of objective existence," for a theory which says that what counts as knowledge is a function of situation and perspective. She believes that it follows from this latter theory that knowledge will become more equitable, more self-aware, and more humane.

I disagree. Knowing that my knowledge is perspectival, language-based, culturally constructed, or what have you, does not change in the slightest the things I believe to be true. All that it changes is what I think about how we get knowledge. The insight that my ideas are all products of the situation I occupy in the world applies to all of my ideas equally (including the idea that knowledge is culturally based) and to all of everybody else's ideas as well. So where does this get us? Right back to where we were before, mainly. I still believe what I believe and, if you differ with me, think that you are wrong. If I want to change your mind I still have to persuade you that I am right by using evidence, reasons, chains of inference, citations of authority, analogies, illustrations, and so on. Believing that what I believe comes from my being in a particular cultural framework does not change my relation to my beliefs. I still believe them just as much as if I thought they came from God, or the laws of nature, or my autonomous self.

Here endeth the epistle.

But while I think Ellen is wrong in thinking that a change of epistemology can mean a change in the kinds of things we think, I am in sympathy with the ends she has in view. This sympathy prompts me to say that my professionally correct reply is not on target. Because the target, the goal, rather, is not to be fighting over these questions, trying to beat the other person down. (What the goal is, it is harder to say.) Intellectual debate, if it were in the right spirit, would be wonderful. But I don't know how to be in the right spirit, exactly, can't make points without sounding rather superior and smug. Most of all, I don't know how to enter the debate without leaving everything else behind—the birds outside my window, my grief over Janice, just myself as a person sitting here in stockinged feet, a little bit chilly because the windows are open, and thinking about going to the bathroom. But not going yet.

I find that when I try to write in my "other" voice, I am immediately critical of it. It wobbles, vacillates back and forth, is neither this nor that. The voice in which I write about epistemology is familiar, I know how it ought to sound. This voice, though, I hardly know. I don't even know if it has anything to say. But if I never write in it, it never will. So I have to try. (That is why you see, this doesn't sound too good. It isn't a practiced performance, it hasn't got a surface. I'm asking you to bear with me while I try, hoping that this, what I write, will express something you yourself have felt or will help you find a part of yourself that you would like to express.)

The thing I want to say is that I've been hiding a part of myself for a long time. I've known it was there, but I couldn't listen because there was no place for this person in literary criticism. The criticism I would like to write would always take off from personal experience. Would always be in some way a chronicle of my hours and days. Would speak in a voice which can talk about everything, would reach out to a reader like me and touch me where I want to be touched. Susan Griffin's voice in "The Way of All Ideology." I want to speak in what Ursula LeGuin, at the Bryn Mawr College commencement in 1986, called the "mother tongue." This is LeGuin speaking:

> The dialect of the father tongue that you and I learned best in college . . . only lectures. . . . Many believe this dialect—the expository and particularly scientific discourse—is the highest form of language, the true language, of which all other uses of words are primitive vestiges. . . . And it is indeed a High Language. . . . Newton's Principia was written in it in Latin . . . and Kant wrote German in it, and Marx, Darwin, Freud, Boas, Foucault, all the great scientists and social thinkers wrote it. It is the language of thought that seeks objectivity.
>
> . . . The essential gesture of the father tongue is not reasoning, but distancing—making a gap, a space, between the subject or self and the object or other. . . . Everywhere now everybody speaks [this] language in laboratories and government buildings and headquarters and offices of business. . . . The father tongue is spoken from above. It goes one way. No answer is expected, or heard.
>
> . . . The mother tongue, spoken or written, expects an answer. It is conversation, a word the root of which means "turning together." The mother tongue is language not as mere communication, but as relation, relationship. It connects. . . . Its power is not in dividing but in binding. . . . We all know it by heart. John have you got your umbrella I think it's going to rain. Can you come play with me? If I told you once

I told you a hundred times. . . . O what am I going to do? . . . Pass the soy sauce please. Oh, shit. . . . You look like what the cat dragged in. (3–4)

Much of what I'm saving elaborates or circles around these quotes from LeGuin. I find that having released myself from the duty to say things I'm not interested in, in a language I resist, I feel free to entertain other people's voices. Quoting them becomes a pleasure of appreciation rather than the obligatory giving of credit, because when I write in a voice that is not struggling to be heard through the screen of a forced language, I no longer feel that it is not I who am speaking, and so there is more room for what others have said.

One sentence in Ellen's essay stuck out for me the first time I read it and the second and the third: "In time we can build a synchronous account of our subject matters as we glissade among them and turn upon ourselves" (p.79).

What attracted me to the sentence was the "glissade." Fluidity, flexibility, versatility, mobility. Moving from one thing to another without embarrassment. It is a tenet of feminist rhetoric that the personal is political, but who in the academy acts on this where language is concerned? We all speak the father tongue, which is impersonal, while decrying the fathers' ideas. All of what I have written so far is in a kind of watered-down expository prose. Not much imagery. No description of concrete things. Only that one word, "glissade."

Like black swallows swooping and gliding
  in a flurry of entangled loops and curves

Two lines of a poem I memorized in high school are what the word "glissade" called to mind. Turning upon ourselves. Turning, weaving, bending, unbending, moving in loops and curves.

I don't believe we can ever turn upon ourselves in the sense Ellen intends. You can't get behind the thing that casts the shadow. *You* cast the shadow. As soon as you turn, the shadow falls in another place. It is still your shadow. You have not got "behind" yourself. That is why self-consciousness is not the way to make ourselves better than we are.

Just me and my shadow, walkin' down the avenue.

It is a beautiful day here in North Carolina. The first day that is both cool and sunny all summer. After a terrible summer, first drought, then heat-wave, then torrential rain, trees down, flooding. Now, finally, beautiful weather. A tree outside my window just brushed by red, with one fully red leaf (This is what I want you to see. A person sitting in stockinged feet looking out of her window—a floor to ceiling rectangle filled with green, with one red leaf. The season poised, sunny and chill, ready to rush down the incline into autumn. But perfect, and still. Not going yet.)

My response to this essay is not a response to something Ellen Messer-Davidow has written; it is a response to something within myself. As I reread the opening pages I feel myself being squeezed into a straitjacket; I wriggle, I will not go in. As I read the list "subject matters, methods of reasoning, and epistemology," the words will not go down. They belong to a debate whose susurrus hardly reaches my ears.

The liberation Ellen promises from the straitjacket of a subject-object epistemology is one I experienced some time ago. Mine didn't take the form she outlines, but it was close enough. I discovered, or thought I discovered, that the poststructuralist way of understanding language and knowledge enabled me to say what I wanted about the world. It enabled me to do this because it pointed out that the world I knew was a construct of ways of thinking about it and, as such, had no privileged claim on the truth. Truth in fact would always be just such a construction, and so one could offer another, competing, description and thus help to change the world that was.

The catch was that anything I might say or imagine was itself the product of an already existing discourse. Not something "I" had made up but a way of constructing things I had absorbed from the intellectual surround. Poststructuralism's proposition about the constructed nature of things held good, but that did not mean that the world could be changed by an act of will. For, as we are looking at this or that phenomenon and re-seeing it, re-thinking it, the rest of the world, that part of it from which we do the seeing, is still there, in place, real, irrefragable as a whole, and making visible what we see, though changed by it, too.

This little lecture pretends to something I no longer want to claim. The pretense is in the tone and level of the language, not in what it says about poststructuralism. The claim being made by the language is analogous to what Barthes calls the "reality effect" of historical writing, whose real message is not that this or that happened but that reality exists. So the claim of this language I've been using (and am using right now) lies in its implicit deification of the speaker. Let's call it the "authority effect." I cannot describe the pretense except to talk about what it ignores: the human frailty of the speaker, his body, his emotions, his history; the moment of intercourse with the reader—acknowledgment of the other person's presence, feelings, needs. This "authoritative" language speaks as though the other person weren't there. Or perhaps more accurately, it doesn't bother to imagine who, as Hawthorne said, is listening to our talk.

How can we speak personally to one another and yet not be self centered? How can we be part of the great world and yet remain loyal to ourselves?

It seems to me that I am trying to write out of my experience without acknowledging any discontinuity between this and the subject matter of the profession I work in—and at the same time find that I no longer want to write about that subject matter, as it appears in Ellen's essay. I am, on the one hand, demanding a connection between literary theory and my own life and asserting, on the other, that there is no connection.

But here is a connection. I learned what epistemology I know from my husband. I think of it as more his game than mine. It's a game I enjoy playing but which I no longer need or want to play. I want to declare my independence of it, of him. (Part of what is going on here has to do with a need I have to make sure I'm not being absorbed in someone else's personality.) What I am breaking away from is both my conformity to the conventions of a male professional practice and my intellectual dependence on my husband. How can I talk about such things in public? How can I *not.*

Looking for something to read this morning, I took three books down from my literary theory shelf, in order to prove a point. The first book was Félix Guattari's *Molecular Revolution.* I find it difficult to read, and therefore have read very little of it, but according to a student who is a disciple of Deleuze and Guattari, "molecular revolution" has to do with getting away from ideology and enacting revolution within daily life. It is specific, not programmed—that is, it does not have a "method," nor "steps," and is neither psychoanalytic nor Marxist, although its discourse seems shaped by those discourses, antithetically. From this kind of revolution, said I to myself, disingenuously, one would expect some recognition of the personal. A revolution that started with daily life would have to begin, or at least would have sometimes to reside, at home. So I open at a section entitled "Towards a New Vocabulary," looking for something in the mother tongue, and this is what I find:

> The distinction I am proposing between machine and structure is based solely on the way we use the words; we may consider that we are merely dealing with a 'written device' of the kind one has to invent for dealing with a mathematical problem, or with an axiom that may have to be reconsidered at a particular stage of development, or again with the kind of machine we shall be talking about here.
>
> I want therefore to make it clear that I am putting into parentheses the fact that, in reality, a machine is inseparable from its structural articulations and conversely, that each contingent structure is dominated (and this is what I want to demonstrate) by a system of machines, or at the very least by one logic machine. (111)

At this point, I start to skip, reading only the first sentence of each paragraph.

"We may say of structure that it positions its elements . . ."
  "The agent of action, whose definition here does not extend beyond this principle of reciprocal determination . . ."
  "The machine, on the other hand remains essentially remote . . ."
  "The history of technology is dated . . ."
  "Yesterday's machine, today's and tomorrow's, are not related in their structural determinations . . ."

I find this language incredibly alienating. In fact, the paragraph after the one I stopped at begins: "The individual's relation to the machine has been described by sociologists following Friedmann as one of fundamental alienation." I will return to this essay some day and read it. I sense that it will have something interesting to say. But the effort is too great now. What strikes me now is the incredibly distancing effect of this language. It is totally abstract and impersonal. Though the author uses the first person ("The distinction I am proposing," "I want therefore to make it clear"), it quickly became clear to me that he had no interest whatsoever in the personal, or in concrete situations as I understand them—a specific person, at a specific machine, somewhere in time and space, with something on his/her mind, real noises, smells, aches and pains. He has no interest in his own experience of machines or in explaining why he is writing about them, what they mean to him personally. I take down the next book: *Poetry and Repression* by Harold Bloom.

This book should contain some reference to the self, to the author's self, to ourselves, to how people feel, to how the author feels, since its subject is psychological: repression. I open the book at page 1 and read:

> Jacques Derrida asks a central question in his essay on "Freud and the Scene of Writing": "What is a text, and what must the psyche be if it can be represented by a text?" My narrow concern with poetry prompts the contrary question: "What is a psyche, and what must a text be if it can be represented by a psyche?" Both Derrida's question and my own require exploration of three terms: "psyche," "text," "represented." "Psyche" is ultimately from the Indo-European root. . . . (1)

—and I stop reading.

The subject of poetry and repression will involve the asking and answering of questions about "a text"—a generalized, nonparticular object that has been the subject of endless discussion for the past twenty years—and about an equally disembodied "psyche" in relation to the thing called "a text"—not, to my mind or rather in view of my desires, a very promising relation in which to consider it. Answering these questions, moreover, will "require" (on whose part, I wonder?) the "exploration" of "three terms." Before we get to the things themselves—psyches, texts—we shall have to spend a lot of time looking at them *as words*. With the beginning of the next paragraph, we get down to the etymology of "psyche." With my agenda, I get off the bus here.

But first I look through the book. Bloom is arguing against canonical readings (of some very canonical poems) and for readings that are not exactly personal, but in which the drama of a self is constantly being played out on a cosmic stage—lots of references to God, kingdom, Paradise, the fall, the eternal—a biblical stage on which, apparently, only men are players (God, Freud, Christ, Nietzsche, and the poets). It is a drama that, although I can see how gripping Bloom can make it, will pall for me because it isn't *my* drama.

Book number three, Michel Foucault's *History of Sexuality*, is more promising. Section One is entitled "We 'other Victorians.'" So Foucault is acknowledging his and our implication in the object of the study. This book will in some way be about "ourselves," which is what I want. It begins:

For a long time, the story goes, we supported a Victorian regime, and we continue to be dominated by it even today. Thus the image of the imperial prude is emblazoned on our restrained, mute, and hypocritical sexuality. (3)

Who, exactly, are "we"? Foucault is using the convention in which the author establishes common ground with his reader by using the first person plural—a presumptuous, though usually successful, move. Presumptuous because it presumes that we are really like him, and successful because, especially when an author is famous, and even when he isn't, "our" instinct (I criticize the practice and engage in it too) is to want to cooperate, to be included in the circle the author is drawing so cosily around "us." It is chummy, this "we." It feels good, for a little while, until it starts to feel coercive, until "we" are subscribing to things that "I" don't believe.

There is no specific reference to the author's self, no attempt to specify himself. It continues:

At the beginning of the seventeenth century . . .

I know now where we are going. We are going to history: "At the beginning of the seventeenth century a certain frankness was still common, it would seem." Generalizations about the past, though pleasantly qualified ("a certain frankness," "it would seem "), are nevertheless disappointingly magisterial. Things continue in a generalizing vein—"it was a time of direct gestures, shameless discourse, and open transgressions." It's not so much that I don't believe him as that I am uncomfortable with the level or the mode of discourse. It is everything that, I thought, Foucault was trying to get away from in *The Archaeology of Knowledge*. The primacy of the subject as the point of view from which history could be written, the bland assumption of authority, the taking over of time, of substance, of event, the imperialism of description from a unified perspective. Even though the subject matter interests me—sex, hypocrisy, whether or not our view of Victorianism and of ourselves in relation to it is correct—I am not eager to read on. The point of view is discouraging. It will march along giving orders, barking out commands. I'm not willing to go along for the march, not even on Foucault's say-so (I am, or have been, an extravagant admirer of his).

So I turn to "my" books. To the women's section of my shelves. I take down, unerringly, an anthology called *The Powers of Desire* edited by Christine Stansell, Ann Snitow, and Sharon Thompson. I turn, almost as unerringly, to an essay by Jessica Benjamin entitled "Master and Slave: The Fantasy of Erotic Domination," and begin to read:

This essay is concerned with the violence of erotic domination. It is about the strange union of rationality and violence that is made in the secret heart of our culture and sometimes enacted in the body. This union has inspired some of the holiest imagery of religious transcendence and now comes to light at the porno newsstands, where women are regularly depicted in the bonds of love. But the slave of love is not always a woman, not always a heterosexual; the fantasy of erotic domination permeates all sexual imagery in our culture. (281)

I am completely hooked, I am going to read this essay from beginning to end and proceed to do so. It gets better, much better, as it goes along. In fact, it gets so good, I find myself putting it down and straying from it because the subject is *so* close to home, and therefore so threatening, that I need relief from it, little breathers, before I can go on. I underline vigorously and often. Think of people I should give it to to read (my husband, this colleague, that colleague).

But wait a minute. There is no personal reference here. The author deals, like Foucault, in generalities. In even bigger ones than his: hers aren't limited to the seventeenth century or the Victorian era. She generalizes about religion, rationality, violence. Why am I not turned off by this as I was in Foucault's case? Why don't I reject this as a grand drama in the style of Bloom? Why don't I bridle at the abstractions as I did when reading Guattari? Well?

The answer is, I see the abstractions as concrete and the issues as personal. They are already personal for me without being personalized because they concern things I've been thinking about for some time, struggling with, trying to figure out for myself. I don't need the author to identify her own involvement, I don't need her to concretize, because these things are already personal and concrete for me. The erotic is already eroticized.

Probably, when Guattari picks up an article whose first sentence has the words "machine," "structure," and "determination," he cathects it immediately. Great stuff. Juicy, terrific. The same would go for Bloom on encountering multiple references to Nietzsche, representation, God the Father, and the Sublime. But isn't erotic domination, as a subject, surer to arouse strong feeling than systems of machines or the psyche that can be represented as a text? Clearly, the answer depends on the readership. The people at the convenience store where I stop to get gas and buy milk would find all these passages equally baffling. Though they *might* have uneasy stirrings when they read Jessica Benjamin. "Erotic domination," especially when coupled with "porno newsstands," does call some feelings into play almost no matter who you are in this culture.

But I will concede the point. What is personal is completely a function of what is perceived as personal. And what is perceived as personal by men, or rather, what is gripping, significant, "juicy," is different from what is felt to be that way by women. For what we are really talking about is not the personal as such, what we are talking about is what is important, answers one's needs, strikes one as immediately *interesting*. For women, the personal is such a category.

In literary criticism, we have moved from the New Criticism, which was antipersonal and declared the personal off-limits at every turn—the intentional fallacy, the affective fallacy—to structuralism, which does away with the self altogether—at least as something unique and important to consider—to deconstruction, which subsumes everything in language and makes the self non-self-consistent, ungraspable, a floating signifier, and finally to new historicism which re-institutes the discourse of the object—"In the seventeenth century"—with occasional side glances at how the author's "situatedness" affects his writing.

The female subject par excellence, which is her self and her experiences, has once more been elided by literary criticism.

The question is, why did this happen? One might have imagined a different outcome. The 1960s paves the way for a new personalism in literary discourse by opening literary discussion up to politics, to psychology, to the "reader," to the effects of style. What happened to deflect criticism into the impersonal labyrinths of "language," "discourse," "system," "network," and now, with Guattari, "machine"?

I met Ellen Messer-Davidow last summer at the School of Criticism and Theory where she was the undoubted leader of the women who were there. She organized them, led them (I might as well say us, since, although I was on the faculty as a visiting lecturer, she led me, too). At the end of the summer we put on a symposium, a kind of teach-in on feminist criticism and theory, of which none was being offered that summer. I thought it really worked. Some, people, eager to advertise their intellectual superiority, murmured disappointment at the "level" of discussion (code for, "my mind is finer and more rigorous than yours"). One person who spoke out at the closing session said he felt bulldozed: a more honest and useful response. The point is that Ellen's leadership affected the experience of everyone at the School that summer. What she offered was not an intellectual performance calculated to draw attention to the quality of her mind, but a sustained effort of practical courage that changed the situation we were in. I think that the kind of thing Ellen did should be included in our concept of criticism: analysis that is not an end in itself but pressure brought to bear on a situation.

Now it's time to talk about something that's central to everything I've been saying so far, although it doesn't *show,* as we used to say about the slips we used to wear. If f had to bet on it, I would say that Ellen Messer-Davidow was motivated last summer, and probably in her essay, by anger (forgive me, Ellen, if I am wrong), anger at her, our, exclusion from what was being studied at the School, our exclusion from the discourse of "Western man." I interpret her behavior this way because anger is what fuels my engagement with feminist issues; an absolute fury that has never even been tapped, relatively speaking. It's time to talk about this now, because it's so central, at least for me. I hate men for the way they treat women, and pretending that women aren't there is one of the ways I hate most.

Last night I saw a movie called *Gunfight at the OK Corral,* starring Burt Lancaster and Kirk Douglas. The movie is patently about the love-relationship between the characters these men play—Wyatt Earp and Doc Holliday. The women in the movie are merely pawns that serve in various ways to reflect the characters of the men and to advance the story of their relationship to one another. There is a particularly humiliating part, played by Jo Van Fleet, the part of Doc Holliday's mistress—Kate Fisher—whom he treats abominably (everybody in the movie acknowledges this, it's not just me saying so). This woman is degraded over and over again. She is a whore, she is a drunkard, she is a clinging woman, she betrays the life of Wyatt Earp in order to get Doc Holliday back, she is *no longer young* (perhaps this is her chief sin). And her words are always in vain, they are chaff, less than nothing, another sign of her degradation.

Now Doc Holliday is a similarly degraded character. He used to be a dentist and is now a gambler who lives to get other people's money away from them; he is a drunk, and he abuses the woman who loves him. But his weaknesses, in the perspective of the movie, are glamorous. He is irresistible, charming, seductive, handsome, witty, commanding; it's no wonder Wyatt Earp falls for him, who wouldn't? The degradation doesn't stick to Kirk Douglas; it is all absorbed by his female counterpart, the "slut," Jo Van Fleet. We are embarrassed every time she appears on the screen, because every time, she is humiliated further.

What enrages me is the way women are used as extensions of men, mirrors of men, devices for showing men off, devices for helping men get what they want. They are never there in their own right, or rarely. The world of the Western contains no women.

Sometimes I think *the world* contains no women.

Why am I so angry?

My anger is partly the result of having been an only child who caved in to authority very early on. As a result I've built up a huge storehouse of hatred and resentment against people in authority over me (mostly male). Hatred and resentment and attraction.

Why should poor men be made the object of this old pent-up anger? (Old anger is the best anger, the meanest, the truest, the most intense. Old anger is pure because it's been dislocated from its source for so long, has had the chance to ferment, to feed on itself for so many years, so that it is nothing but anger. All cause, all relation to the outside world, long since sloughed off, withered away. The rage I feel inside me now is the distillation of forty-six years. It has had a long time to simmer, to harden, to become adamantine, a black slab that glows in the dark.)

Are all feminists fueled by such rage? Is the molten lava of millennia of hatred boiling below the surface of every essay, every book, every syllabus, every newsletter, every little magazine? I imagine that I can open the front of my stomach like a door, reach in, and pluck from memory the rooted sorrow, pull it out, root and branch. But where, or rather, who, would I be then? I am attached to this rage. It is a source of identity for me. It is a motivator, an explainer, a justifier, a no-need-to-say-more greeter at the door. If I were to eradicate this anger somehow, what would I do? Volunteer work all day long?

A therapist once suggested to me that I blamed on sexism a lot of stuff that really had to do with my own childhood. Her view was basically the one articulated in Alice Miller's *The Drama of the Gifted Child,* in which the good child has been made to develop a false self by parents who cathect the child narcissistically. My therapist meant that if I worked out some of my problems—as she understood them, on a psychological level—my feminist rage would subside.

Maybe it would, but that wouldn't touch the issue of female oppression. Here is what Miller says about this:

> Political action can be fed by the unconscious anger of children who have been . . . misused, imprisoned, exploited, cramped, and drilled. . . . If, however, disillusionment and the resultant mourning can be lived through. . . , then social and political disengagement do not usually follow, but the patient's actions are freed from the compulsion to repeat. (101)

According to Miller's theory, the critical voice inside me, the voice I noticed butting in, belittling, doubting, being wise, is "the contemptuous introject."—the introjection of authorities who manipulated me, without necessarily meaning to. I think that if you can come to terms with your "contemptuous introjects," learn to forgive and understand them, your anger will go away.

But if you're not angry, can you still act? Will you still care enough to write the letters, make the phone calls, attend the meetings? You need to find another center within yourself from which to act. A center of outgoing, outflowing, giving feelings. Love instead of anger. I'm embarrassed to say words like these because I've been taught they are mushy and sentimental and smack of cheap popular psychology. I've been taught to look down on people who read M. Scott Peck and Leo Buscaglia and Harold Kushner, because they're people who haven't very much education and because they're mostly women. Or if not women, then people who take responsibility, for learning how to deal with their feelings, who take responsibility for marriages that are going bad, for children who are in trouble, for friends who need help, for themselves. The disdain for popular psychology and for words like "love" and "giving" is part of the police action that academic intellectuals wage ceaselessly against feeling, against women, against what is personal. The ridiculing of the "touchy-feely," of the "Mickey Mouse," of the sentimental (often associated with teaching that takes students' concerns into account), belongs to the tradition Alison Jaggar rightly characterized as founding knowledge in the denial of emotion. It is looking down on women, with whom feelings are associated, and on the activities with which women are identified: mother, nurse, teacher, social worker, volunteer.

So for a while I can't talk about epistemology. I can't deal with the philosophical bases of feminist literary criticisms. I can't strap myself psychically into an apparatus that will produce the right gestures when I begin to move. I have to deal with the trashing of emotion and with my anger against it.

This one time I've taken off the straitjacket, and it feels so good.

References

Benjamin, Jessica. "Master and Slave: The Fantasy of Erotic Domination." *The Powers of Desire: The Politics of Sexuality.* Ed. Ann Snitow, Christine Stansell, and Sharon Thompson. New York: Monthly Review Press, 1983. 280–89.

Bloom, Harold. *Poetry and Repression: Revision from Blake to Stevens.* New Haven, Conn.: Yale University Press, 1976.

Foucault, Michel. *The History of Sexuality,* Volume 1: *An Introduction.* Trans. Robert Hurley. New York: Vintage Books, 1980. Copyright 1978 by Random House. [Originally published in French as *La Volonté de Savoir.* Paris: Editions Gallimard, 1976.]

Griffin, Susan. "The Way of All Ideology." *Made from the Earth: An Anthology of Writings.* New York: Harper and Row, 1982. 161–82.

Guattari, Felix. *Molecular Revolution: Psychiatry and Politics.* Trans. Rosemary Sheed, intro. David Cooper. New York: Penguin Books, 1984. [First published as *Psychanalyse et transversalité (1972), and La Revolution moléculaire* (1977).]

Hawthorne, Nathaniel. *The Scarlet Letter and Other Tales of the Puritans.* Ed. with an intro. and notes by Harry Levin. Boston, Mass.: Houghton Mifflin, 1960–61.

LeGuin, Ursula. "The Mother Tongue." *Bryn Mawr Alumnae Bulletin* (Summer 1986): 3–4.

Miller, Alice. *The Drama of the Gifted Child.* New York: Basic Books, 1983.

EXPERIMENTAL CRITICAL WRITING

Marianna Torgovnick

At the 1988 MLA Convention I gave a paper called "Malinowski's Body." Since I was afraid to give this paper, I had announced it in the program by the deliberately neutral title "Looking at Anthropologists" so that I could change my mind up to the last minute and substitute something else instead. I was afraid because "Malinowski's Body" does not resemble the usual MLA paper in style or content. I knew that the audience would listen to it and respond to it, and I knew that some members of the audience would not like it and might even walk out—and not because there was another talk they wanted to hear at the same hour.

"Malinowski's Body" did not begin its life in any of the ways I have been taught to consider legitimate. In fact, I wrote it, almost as a dare, after my writing group found the first material I wrote on Malinowski dull. To prove I could do better I went home and wrote several pages that begin this way:

> Malinowski's body looks like Lord Jim's. It's cased rigidly in white or beige trousers and shirt that sometimes becomes stained a muddy brown. When this happens, Malinowski summons his servants and has the clothes washed, immediately. For his clothes somehow seem to him an important part of his body, not just a covering for it.
>
> It's a small body, well fed but not kindly disposed enough toward itself to put on flesh. It has a narrow chest—pale, with just a few hairs and no nipples to speak of. It has thin legs yearning for massive thighs; in fact, if this man does put on weight in later life (and he may) it will show in his thighs first. The buttocks lie flat, unwelcoming, with maybe a stray pimple. The penis is a center of anxiety for him but is in fact no smaller—and no bigger—than anyone else's. It's one of the few points of identification he can settle on between his body and theirs.
>
> Their bodies—almost naked—unnerve him. His body needs its clothes; his head, its hat. He rarely looks at his body—except when washing it. But he has to look at theirs. The dislike he sometimes feels for the natives comes over him especially when in the presence of their bodies. "Come in and bathe," the natives say from their ponds and rivers. "No, thanks," says Malinowski, retrieving the pith helmet and camera he momentarily laid aside on the grass. He looks at their bodies and takes notes about size, ornamentation, haircuts, and other ethnographic data. He takes photographs. He talks to them about customs, trade, housing, sex. He feels okay about the customs, trade, and housing, but the sex makes him uneasy.

The pages are based on an intuition and a hunch about what Malinowski looked like that were formed before I had found any pictures of him. They begin with an image rather than with the kind of concise generalization that had been my customary opening. And they were designed to loosen my prose by giving my imagination free play. Inevitably, I used what I had read by and about Malinowski—but in an almost unrecognizable way. My premise was that I would undress the ethnographer for study as Malinowski himself undresses subjects in his ethnographies and undresses, in his diary, the women he meets in daily life. When I wrote "Malinowski's Body" I did not intend to use it in the book I was writing. My goals were simply to limber up my style and to get in touch with what I wanted to say. But "Malinowski's Body" makes so many points about the ethnographer's scripting of himself according to conventional ideas of what is moral and manly that I decided to include it in my book. It is a creative piece, risky for the MLA. And yet my audience, or at least most of its members, seemed delighted. They asked questions about my "intentions" and "effects" that made me feel like a writer, not just a critic—a heady moment for me and a reception that gave David Laurence reason to invite me to present my thoughts on experimental critical writing. And it was a moment that had not come easily.

When I began to write my newest book—called *Gone Primitive* and published in the spring of 1990—I knew that I wanted to write something significantly different in tone and style from my first two books. I had recently been tenured and then promoted to full professor, and I felt that I was no longer writing for any committees—I was writing for myself. It was not that I would rewrite the books I had written; I am in fact proud of them. What I wanted was to reach a larger audience and to go somewhere new. What I discovered was that at first I did not know how.

The turning point came when I showed an early chapter to the members of my newly formed writing group. I was writing on an untraditional, uncanonical topic—Edgar Rice Burroughs' Tarzan novels—but my approach was conventional and scholarly. I began by surveying the critical literature on Tarzan and protesting (a little uneasily) that earlier critics either had overidentified with Burroughs or had not taken Tarzan seriously with regard to race and gender relations. I tried to pack lots of statistics and facts in the opening paragraphs to prove that Tarzan was important. In my eagerness to meet accepted standards of academic seriousness, I had succeeded (to borrow a phrase Wayne Booth once used to describe the freshman essay) in being "boring from within."

The members of my group, from whom I had asked no mercy that day, showed none. The chapter was sluggish, they said; the prose was lifeless and cold. It had no momentum, no narrative. Instinctively, I defended myself; I talked about all the interesting things that happened as I was researching and writing the chapter, telling them how I often found articles on the rebirth of the Tarzan phenomenon in issues of magazines that report the assassination of President Kennedy and reproduce those astonishing pictures we all remember of Jackie and little John-John and of Oswald. I had tried in the chapter to place the Tarzan series in the contexts of the twenties (the decade of its first great popularity) and the sixties (the decade of its rebirth). But I had used a style that censored my own experiences and visceral responses and that hid my writing's source of energy. One member of the group said, cannily, "You know, none of what you've just said comes out in this chapter. And there's a huge difference between the things you say and the things you write. You never write anything funny. You often say funny things." She was right. The other members of the group asked me to say more about La, barbarian priestess in the Tarzan novels whom I had mentioned in passing. As I warmed to my description of La's importance and La's wrongs, my friend said, "When you start to get dull, pretend you are La—because you *are* La." And she was also right.

For me, "writing like La" became a metaphor for getting to a place where I was not afraid to write in a voice that had passion as well as information—a voice that wanted to be heard. "Writing like La" meant letting myself out of the protective cage of the style I had mastered—a style I now call the thus-and-therefore style because it naturally tends to include distancing words like those. Before I could change my thus-and-therefore style, I had to defamiliarize it; I had to know my cage so that I could open it at will. A fifteen-minute exercise I did with my writing group was a significant breakthrough. In this exercise, I parodied my own dullest style in a description of grocery stores in Durham, North Carolina. I began the description with just the kind of generalization that was one of my primary tics as a writer: "In Durham, one can shop at Food Lion for bargains, or Kroger's for selection. The most interesting shopping of all, however, is done at Harris Teeter." This exercise made me laugh at my own habits and made it impossible for me afterward to write unknowingly in my usual way. But there were still many low points, when

I found myself unable to do anything but write in my dullest style. In fact, I wrote my excruciatingly bad beginning on Malinowski—the material I replaced with "Malinowski's Body"—roughly eighteen months after I vowed to leave my old style behind.

In preparing this presentation, I discovered in my files my first draft on Malinowski. I would like to share part of its beginning with you as an example of one sort of standard academic prose:

> Implicitly, I have been suggesting that "objectivity" is a delusory principle undergirding both important strands of social scientific and ethnographic thought and aesthetic and artistic-literary theories and methods. Rereading Malinowski, I think I've found a direct and interesting analogy.
>
> Malinowski founded what is called functionalism in anthropology, the theory (and derived method) that explains all elements of a culture in terms of interlocking functions: the ethnographer explicitly "constructs" a model in which all the parts are presumed to contribute to a whole that is organic and unified (though quirkier than a machine). To make his construction, the ethnographer lives inside the culture, inhabits it as a text. He tries to replicate the native's point of view, which is the ground and touchstone of meaning and "accuracy." Functionalism leads, in anthropology, to what is called structural functionalism and then, later, to structuralism.
>
> A point-by-point analogy with New Criticism and other formal approaches exists. Here too the "student" (critic) inhabits the text, assuming the unity of the parts as a whole and constructing an account of that whole in terms of the interlocking functions of its parts. The original ground of meaning is the author's intentions.

What I was doing in these paragraphs was the writerly equivalent of scratching at a scab. I had to say what was closest to the surface of my mind in order to get rid of that content, in order to discover whether it was useful or not, interesting or not. Sometimes, what I write first as a throwaway turns out to contain the intellectual core of my argument; sometimes, as in this real throwaway, it does not. The difference is usually whether I begin with material that I really care about or with material that I think I should care about. In this instance, I began with critical categories and genealogies of influence that I knew, by training, were considered important—and I trotted them out dutifully. Other critics had scratched these scabs; now it was my turn. The paragraphs include a lot of qualifications and distinctions, often inserted in parenthetical remarks, that would be unlikely to interest anyone but me. Sticky academic language coats the whole—"implicitly," "explicitly," "strand of thought." And I explain things in more detail than most people would want to read.

I would be too embarrassed to reproduce this rejected passage if I did not realize that it's representative of the prose that I—and I suspect many of you—habitually write. For this style typifies a great deal of academic writing. How did it come to be a norm? Largely, I think by establishing itself in an era when less criticism was published and the circle of critics was small enough to allow its members to believe they were contributing to the building of a common edifice. In this construction project all the names could and should be named, like those of contributors on a memorial plaque; Professor Z would build on what Professors X and Y had said in their essays; years later, Professors A and B would come along and add some decorative touches or do major renovations.

All of us who write criticism today wrote dissertations yesterday. And our teachers often tried, and succeeded in handing on what they perceived as the correct—that is, the careful, the judicious, the fair—way to write. But the styles we were taught can't work now in the same way as they worked fifty or even fifteen years ago. No one who gets around to writing a book, or even an essay, ever reads everything that has been written about its subject. Yet we cling to the fiction of completeness and coverage that the academic style preserves. This style protects us, we fondly believe, from being careless or subjective or unfair. It prescribes certain moves to ensure that the writer will stay within the boundaries that the academy has drawn.

Like many people who choose an academic life, I have a fundamental need for approval. I needed approval from my graduate advisers, tenure and promotion committees, and reviewers; I need it from my students and colleagues. It has been crucial for me in the last few years to have a writing group that approved of my new writing style: the group provided a different audience from the one I once imagined as my academic superiors, who judged the material I wrote according to more traditional standards. But I have also become aware that I am now not just someone in need of approval but also someone (like many of you) who gives or withholds approval. When we pass on the academic style to our graduate students or newest colleague, we train them to stay within the boundaries, both stylistically and conceptually. When we encourage experimental critical writing, we do not always know what we will get, but we stimulate the profession to grow and to change. We don't control the future of the profession only when we give grades or make hiring or tenure decisions; we control it at the level of the sentence.

At this point I need to back up a bit. It seems pretty clear to me that if all we want to do is to write for professional advancement, to write for a fairly narrow circle of critics who exist within the same disciplinary boundaries as we do, there is nothing really wrong with the traditional academic style. In fact, it's the right style, the inevitable style, because it says, in every superfluous detail and in every familiar move, You don't need to read me except to write your own project; I am the kind of writing that does not want to be heard.

But when critics want to be read, and especially when they want to be read by a large audience, they have to court their readers. And the courtship begins when the critic begins to think of himself or herself as a writer as well, a process that for me, as for some other critics of my generation, means writing as a person with feelings, histories, and desires—as well as information and knowledge. When writers want to be read they have to be more flexible and take more chances than the standard scholarly style allows: often, they have to be more direct and more personal. In a very real way (although my writing includes precious few autobiographical revelations), I could not think of myself as a writer until I risked exposing myself in my writing.

I am not talking here, necessarily, about full-scale autobiographical writing—though I am not ruling it out either. But I am saying that writerly writing is personal writing, whether or not it is autobiographical. Even if it offers no facts from the writer's life, or offers just a hint of them here and there, it makes the reader know some things about the writer—a fundamental condition, it seems to me, of any real act of communication. And real communication is exciting. For me, at any rate, the experience of this new kind of writing—which not only recognizes the pitfalls of the standard academic style but goes out of its way to avoid them—has been exhilarating.

SOCIAL CLASS AND THE HIDDEN CURRICULUM OF WORK

Jean Anyon

Scholars in political economy and the sociology of knowledge have recently argued that public schools in complex industrial societies like our own make available different types of educational experience and curriculum knowledge to students in different social classes. Bowles and Gintis[1] for example, have argued that students in different social-class backgrounds are rewarded for classroom behaviors that correspond to personality traits allegedly rewarded in the different occupational strata—the working classes for docility and obedience, the managerial classes for initiative and personal assertiveness. Basil Bernstein, Pierre Bourdieu, and Michael W. Apple[2] focusing on school knowledge, have argued that knowledge and skills leading to social power and regard (medical, legal, managerial) are made available to the advantaged social groups but are withheld from the working classes to whom a more "practical" curriculum is offered (manual skills, clerical knowledge). While there has been considerable argumentation of these points regarding education in England, France, and North America, there has been little or no attempt to investigate these ideas empirically in elementary or secondary schools and classrooms in this country.[3]

This article offers tentative empirical support (and qualification) of the above arguments by providing illustrative examples of differences in student *work* in classrooms in contrasting social class communities. The examples were gathered *as* part of an ethnographical[4] study of curricular, pedagogical, and pupil evaluation practices in five elementary schools. The article attempts a theoretical contribution as well and assesses student work in the light of a theoretical approach to social-class analysis. . . . It will be suggested that there is a "hidden curriculum" in schoolwork that has profound implications for the theory—and consequence—of everyday activity in education. . . .

The Sample of Schools

. . . The social-class designation of each of the five schools will be identified, and the income, occupation, and other relevant available social characteristics of the students and their parents will be described. The

---

[1]S. Bowles and H. Gintes, *Schooling in Capitalist America: Educational Reform and the Contradictions of Economic Life* (New York: Basic Books, 1976). [Author's note]

[2]B. Bernstein, *Class, Codes and Control, Vol. 3. Towards a Theory of Educational Transmission,* 2d ed. (London: Routledge & Kegan Paul, 1977); P. Bourdieu and J. Passeron, *Reproduction in Education, Society and Culture* (Beverly Hills, Calif : Sage, 1977); M.W. Apple, *Ideology and Curriculum* (Boston: Routledge Kegan Paul, 1979). [Author's note]

[3]But see, in a related vein, M.W. Apple and N. King, "What Do Schools Teach?" *Curriculum Inquiry* 6 (1977); 341–58; R.C. Rist, *The Urban School: A Factory for Failure* (Cambridge, Mass.: MIT Press, 1973). [Author's note]

[4]*ethnographical:* Based on an anthropological study of cultures or subcultures—the "cultures" in this case being the five schools being observed.

first three schools are in a medium-sized city district in northern New Jersey, and the other two are in a nearby New Jersey suburb.

The first two schools I will call *working class schools.* Most of the parents have blue-collar jobs. Less than a third of the fathers are skilled, while the majority are in unskilled or semiskilled jobs. During the period of the study (1978–1979), approximately 15 percent of the fathers were unemployed. The large majority (85 percent) of the families are white. The following occupations are typical: platform, storeroom, and stockroom workers; foundry-men, pipe welders, and boilermakers; semiskilled and unskilled assembly-line operatives; gas station attendants, auto mechanics, maintenance workers, and security guards. Less than 30 percent of the women work, some part-time and some full-time, on assembly lines, in storerooms and stockrooms, as waitresses, barmaids, or sales clerks. Of the fifth-grade parents, none of the wives of the skilled workers had jobs. Approximately 15 percent of the families in each school are at or below the federal "poverty" level; most of the rest of the family incomes are at or below $12,000, except some of the skilled workers whose incomes are higher.[5] The incomes of the majority of the families in these two schools (at or below $12,000) are typical of 38.6 percent of the families in the United States.[6]

The third school is called the *middle-class school,* although because of 5 neighborhood residence patterns, the population is a mixture of several social classes. The parents' occupations can be divided into three groups: a small group of blue-collar "rich," who are skilled, well-paid workers such as printers, carpenters, plumbers, and construction workers. The second group is composed of parents in working-class and middle-class white-collar jobs: women in office jobs, technicians, supervisors in industry, and parents employed by the city (such as firemen, policemen, and several of the school's teachers). The third group is composed of occupations such as personnel directors in local firms, accountants, "middle management," and a few small capitalists (owners of shops in the area). The children of several local doctors attend this school. Most family incomes are between $13,000 and $25,000, with a few higher. This income range is typical of 38.9 percent of the families in the United States.[7]

The fourth school has a parent population that is at the upper income level of the upper middle class and is predominantly professional. This school will be called the *affluent professional school.* Typical jobs are: cardiologist, interior designer, corporate lawyer or engineer, executive in advertising or television. There are some families who are not as affluent as the majority (the family of the superintendent of the district's schools, and the one or two families in which the fathers are skilled workers). In addition, a few of the families are more affluent than the majority and can be classified in the capitalist class (a partner in a prestigious Wall Street stock brokerage firm). Approximately 90 percent of the children in this school are white. Most family incomes are between $40,000 and $80,000. This income span represents approximately 7 percent of the families in the United States.[8]

---

[5]The U.S. Bureau of the Census defines *poverty* for a nonfarm family of four as a yearly income of $6,191 a year or less. U.S. Bureau of the Census, *Statistical Abstract of the United States: 1978* (Washington, D.C.: U.S. Government Printing Office, 1978), p. 465, table 754. [Author's note]

[6]U.S. Bureau of the Census, "Money Income in 1977 of Families and Persons in the United States," *Current Population Reports* Series P-60, no. 118 (Washington, D.C.: U.S. Government Printing Office, 1978), p. 2, table A. [Author's note]

[7]Ibid. [Author's note]

[8]This figure is an estimate. According to the Bureau of the Census, only 2.6 percent of families in the United States have money income of $50,000 or over. U.S. Bureau of the Census, *Current Population Reports* Series P-60. For figures on income at these higher levels, see J.D. Smith and S. Franklin, "The Concentration of Personal Wealth, 1922–1969," *American Economic Review* 64 (1974): 162–67. [Author's note]

In the fifth school the majority of the families belong to the capitalist class. This school will be called the *executive elite school* because most of the fathers are top executives (for example, presidents and vice-presidents) in major United States-based multinational corporations—for example, AT&T, RCA, Citibank, American Express, U.S. Steel. A sizable group of fathers are top executives in financial firms in Wall Street. There are also a number of fathers who list their occupations as "general counsel" to a particular corporation, and these corporations are also among the large multi-nationals. Many of the mothers do volunteer work in the Junior League, Junior Fortnightly, or other service groups; some are intricately involved in town politics; and some are themselves in well-paid occupations. There are no minority children in the school. Almost all the family incomes are over $100,000 with some in the $500,000 range. The incomes in this school represent less than 1 percent of the families in the United States.[9]

Since each of the five schools is only one instance of elementary education in a particular social class context, I will not generalize beyond the sample. However, the examples of schoolwork which follow will suggest characteristics of education in each social setting that appear to have theoretical and social significance and to be worth investigation in a larger number of schools.

The Working Class Schools

In the two working-class schools, work is following the steps of a procedure. The procedure is usually mechanical, involving rote behavior and very little decision making or choice. The teachers rarely explain why the work is being assigned, how it might connect to other assignments, or what the idea is that lies behind the procedure or gives it coherence and perhaps meaning or significance. Available textbooks are not always used, and the teachers often prepare their own dittos or put work examples on the board. Most of the rules regarding work are designations of what the children are to do; the rules are steps to follow. These steps are told to the children by the teachers and are often written on the board. The children are usually told to copy the steps as notes. These notes are to be studied. Work is often evaluated not according to whether it is right or wrong but according to whether the children followed the right steps.

The following examples illustrate these points. In math, when two-digit division was introduced, the teacher in one school gave a four-minute lecture on what the terms are called (which number is the divisor, dividend, quotient, and remainder). The children were told to copy these names in their notebooks. Then the teacher told them the steps to follow to do the problems, saying, "This is how you do them." The teacher listed the steps on the board, and they appeared several days later as a chart hung in the middle of the front wall: "Divide, Multiply, Subtract, Bring Down." The children often did examples of two-digit division. When the teacher went over the examples with them, he told them what the procedure was for each problem, rarely asking them to conceptualize or explain it themselves: "Three into twenty-two is seven; do your subtraction and one is left over." During the week that two-digit division was introduced (or at any other time), the investigator did not observe any discussion of the idea of grouping involved in division, any use of manipulables, or any attempt to relate two-digit division to any other mathematical process. Nor was there any attempt to relate the steps to an actual or possible thought process of the children. The observer did not hear the terms *dividend, quotient,* and so on, used again. The math teacher in the other working-class school followed similar procedures regarding two-digit division and at one point her class seemed confused. She said, "You're confusing yourselves. You're tensing up. Remember, when you do this, it's the same steps over and over again—and that's the way division always is." Several weeks

---

[9]Smith and Franklin, "The Concentration of Personal Wealth." [Author's note]

later, after a test, a group of her children "still didn't get it," and she made no attempt to explain the concept of dividing things into groups or to give them manipulables for their own investigation. Rather, she went over the steps with them again and told them that they "needed more practice."

In other areas of math, work is also carrying out often unexplained fragmented procedures. For example, one of the teachers led the children through a series of steps to make a 1-inch grid on their paper *without* telling them that they were making a 1-inch grid or that it would be used to study scale. She said, "Take your ruler. Put it across the top. Make a mark at every number. Then move your ruler down to the bottom. No, put it across the bottom. Now make a mark on top of every number. Now draw a line from. . . ." At this point a girl said that she had a faster way to do it and the teacher said, "No, you don't; you don't even know what I'm making yet. Do it this way or it's wrong." After they had made the lines up and down and across, the teacher told them she wanted them to make a figure by connecting some dots and to measure that, using the scale of 1 inch equals 1 mile. Then they were to cut it out. She said, "Don't cut it until I check it."

In both working-class schools, work in language arts is mechanics of punctuation (commas, periods, question marks, exclamation points), capitalization, and the four kinds of sentences. One teacher explained to me, "Simple punctuation is all they'll ever use." Regarding punctuation, either a teacher or a ditto stated the rules for where, for example, to put commas. The investigator heard no classroom discussion of the aural context of punctuation (which, of course, is what gives each mark its meaning). Nor did the investigator hear any statement or inference that placing a punctuation mark could be a decision-making process, depending, for example, on one's intended meaning. Rather, the children were told to follow the rules. Language arts did not involve creative writing. There were several writing assign-ments throughout the year but in each instance the children were given a ditto, and they wrote answers to questions on the sheet. For example, they wrote their "autobiography" by answering such questions as "Where were you born?" "What is your favorite animal?" on a sheet entitled "All About Me."

In one of the working-class schools, the class had a science period several times a week. On the three occasions observed, the children were not called upon to set up experiments or to give explanations for facts or concepts. Rather, on each occasion the teacher told them in his own words what the book said. The children copied the teacher's sentences from the board. Each day that preceded the day they were to do a science experiment, the teacher told them to copy the directions from the book for the procedure they would carry out the next day and to study the list at home that night. The day after each experiment, the teacher went over what they had "found" (they did the experiments as a class, and each was actually a class demonstration led by the teacher). Then the teacher wrote what they "found" on the board, and the children copied that in their notebooks. Once or twice a year there are science projects. The project is chosen and assigned by the teacher from a box of 3-by-5-inch cards. On the card the teacher has written the question to be answered, the books to use, and how much to write. Explaining the cards to the observer, the teacher said, "It tells them exactly what to do, or they couldn't do it."

Social studies in the working-class schools is also largely mechanical, rote work that was given little explanation or connection to larger contexts. In one school, for example, although there was a book available, social studies work was to copy the teacher's notes from the board. Several times a week for a period of several months the children copied these notes. The fifth grades in the district were to study United States history. The teacher used a booklet she had purchased called "The Fabulous Fifty States." Each day she put information from the booklet in outline form on the board and the children copied it. The type of information did not vary: the name of the state, its abbreviation, state capital, nickname of the state, its main products, main business, and a "Fabulous Fact" ("Idaho grew twenty-seven billion potatoes in one year. That's enough potatoes for each man, woman, and . . .") As the children finished copying the sentences, the teacher erased them and wrote more. Children would occasionally go to the front to pull down the wall map in order to locate the states they were copying, and the teacher did not dissuade them. But the observer never saw her refer to the map; nor did the observer ever hear her make other than perfunctory remarks concerning the information the children were copying. Occasionally the children colored in a ditto and cut it out to make a stand-up figure (representing, for example, a man roping a cow in the Southwest). These were referred to by the teacher as their social studies "projects."

Rote behavior was often called for in classroom work. When going over 15 math and language art skills sheets, for example, as the teacher asked for the answer to each problem, he fired the questions rapidly, staccato, and the scene reminded the observer of a sergeant drilling recruits: above all, the questions demanded that you stay at attention: "The next one? What do I put here? . . . Here? Give us the next." Or "How many commas in this sentence? Where do I put them . . . The next one?"

The four fifth grade teachers observed in the working-class schools attempted to control classroom time and space by making decisions without consulting the children and without explaining the basis for their decisions. The teacher's control thus often seemed capricious. Teachers, for instance, very often ignored the bells to switch classes—deciding among themselves to keep the children after the period was officially over to continue with the work or for disciplinary reasons or so they (the teachers) could stand in the hall and talk. There were no clocks in the rooms in either school, and the children often asked, "What period is this?" "When do we go to gym?" The children had no access to materials. These were handed out by teachers and closely guarded. Things in the room "belonged" to the teacher: "Bob, bring me my garbage can." The teachers continually gave the children orders. Only three times did the investigator hear a teacher in either working-class school preface a directive with an unsarcastic "please," or "let's" or "would you." Instead, the teachers said, "Shut up," "Shut your mouth," "Open your books," "Throw your gum away—if you want to rot your teeth, do it on your own time." Teachers made every effort to control the movement of the children, and often shouted, "'Why are you out of your seat??!!" If the children got permission to leave the room, they had to take a written pass with the date and time. . . .

Middle-Class School

In the middle-class school, work is getting the right answer. If one accumulates enough right answers, one gets a good grade. One must follow the directions in order to get the right answers, but the directions often call for some figuring, some choice, some decision making. For example, the children must often figure out by themselves what the directions ask them to do and how to get the answer: what do you do first, second, and perhaps third? Answers are usually found in books or by listening to the teacher. Answers are usually words, sentences, numbers, or facts and dates; one writes them on paper, and one should be neat. Answers must be given in the right order, and one cannot make them up.

The following activities are illustrative. Math involves some choice: one may do two-digit division the long way or the short way, and there are some math problems that can be done "in your head." When the teacher explains how to do two-digit division, there is recognition that a cognitive process is involved; she gives you several ways and says, "I want to make sure you understand what you're doing—so you get it right"; and, when they go over the homework, she asks the *children* to tell how they did the problem and what answer they got.

In social studies the daily work is to read the assigned pages in the textbook and to answer the teacher's questions. The questions are almost always designed to check on whether the students have read the assignment and understood it: who did so-and-so; what happened after that; when did it happen, where, and sometimes, why did it happen? The answers are in the book and in one's understanding of the book; the teacher's hints when one doesn't know the answers are to "read it again" or to look at the picture or at the rest of the paragraph. One is to search for the answer in the "context," in what is given.

Language arts is "simple grammar, what they need for everyday life." The language arts teacher says, "They should learn to speak properly, to write business letters and thank-you letters, and to understand what nouns and verbs and simple subjects are." Here, as well, actual work is to choose the right answers, to understand what is given. The teacher often says, "Please read the next sentence and then I'll question you about it." One teacher said in some exasperation to a boy who was fooling around in class, "If you don't know the answers to the questions I ask, then you can't stay in this *class!* [pause] You *never* know the answers to the questions I ask, and it's not fair to me—and certainly not to you!"

Most lessons are based on the textbook. This does not involve a critical perspective on what is given there. For example, a critical perspective in social studies is perceived as dangerous by these teachers because it may lead to controversial topics; the parents might complain. The children, however, are often curious especially in social studies. Their questions are tolerated and usually answered perfunctorily. But after a few minutes the teacher will say, "All right, we're not going any farther. Please open your social studies workbook." While the teachers spend a lot of time explaining and expanding on what the textbooks say, there is little attempt to analyze how or why things happen, or to give thought to how pieces of a culture, or, say, a system of numbers or elements of a language fit together or can be analyzed. What has happened in the past and what exists now may not be equitable or fair, but (shrug) that is the way things are and one does not confront such matters in school. For example, in social studies after a child is called on to read a passage about the pilgrims, the teacher summarizes the paragraph and then says, "So you can see how strict they were about everything." A child asks, "Why?" "Well, because they felt that if you weren't busy you'd get into trouble." Another child asks, "Is it true that they burned women at the stake?" The teacher says, "Yes, if a woman did anything strange, they hanged them. [*sic*] What would a woman do, do you think, to make them burn them? [*sic*] See if you can come up with better answers than my other [social studies] class." Several children offer suggestions, to which the teacher nods but does not comment. Then she says, "Okay, good," and calls on the next child to read.

Work tasks do not usually request creativity. Serious attention is rarely given in school work on *how* the children develop or express their own feelings and ideas, either linguistically or in graphic form. On the occasions when creativity or self-expression is requested, it is peripheral to the main activity or it is "enriched" or "for fun." During a lesson on what similes are, for example, the teacher explains what they are, puts several on the board, gives some other examples herself, and then asks the children if they can "make some up." She calls on three children who give similes, two of which are actually in the book they have open before them. The teacher does not comment on this and then asks several others to choose similes from the list of phrases in the book. Several do so correctly, and she says, "Oh good! You're picking them out! See how good we are?" Their homework is to pick out the rest of the similes from the list.

Creativity is not often requested in social studies and science projects, either. Social studies projects, for example, are given with directions to "find information on your topic" and write it up. The children are not supposed to copy but to "put it in your own words." Although a number of the projects subsequently went beyond the teacher's direction to find information and had quite expressive covers and inside illustrations, the teacher's evaluative comments had to do with the amount of information, whether they had "copied," and if their work was neat.

The style of control of the three fifth-grade teachers observed in this school varied from somewhat easygoing to strict, but in contrast to the working-class schools, the teachers' decisions were usually based on external rules and regulations—for example, on criteria that were known or available to the children. Thus, the teachers always honor the bells for changing classes, and they usually evaluate children's work by what is in the textbooks and answer booklets.

There is little excitement in schoolwork for the children, and the assignments are perceived as having little to do with their interests and feelings. As one child said, what you do is "store facts up in your head like cold storage—until you need it later for a test or your job." Thus, doing well is important because there are thought to be *other* likely rewards: a good job or college.[10]

Affluent Professional School

In the affluent professional school, work is creative activity carried out independently. The students are continually asked to express and apply ideas and concepts. Work involves individual thought and expressiveness, expansion and illustration of ideas, and choice of appropriate method and material. (The class is not considered an open classroom, and the principal explained that because of the large number of discipline problems in the fifth grade this year they did not departmentalize. The teacher who agreed to take part in the study said she is "more structured this year than she usually is.) The products of work in this class are often written stories, editorials and essays, or representations of ideas in mural, graph, or craft form. The products of work should not be like anybody else's and should show individuality. They should exhibit good design, and (this is important) they must also fit empirical reality. The relatively few rules to be followed regarding work are usually criteria for, or limits on, individual activity. One's product is usually evaluated for the quality of its expression and for the appropriateness of its conception to the task. In many cases, one's own satisfaction with the product is an important criterion for its evaluation. When right answers are called for, as in commercial materials like SRA (Science Research Associates) and math, it is important that the children decide on an answer as a result of thinking about the idea involved in what they're being asked to do. Teacher's hints are to "think about it some more."

The following activities are illustrative. The class takes home a sheet requesting each child's parents to fill in the number of cars they have, the number of television sets, refrigerators, games, or rooms in the house, and so on. Each child is to figure the average number of a type of possession owned by the fifth grade. Each child must compile the "data" from all the sheets. A calculator is available in the classroom to do the mechanics of finding the average. Some children decide to send sheets to the fourth-grade families for comparison. Their work should be "verified" by a classmate before it is handed in.

Each child and his or her family has made a geoboard. The teacher asks the class to get their geoboards from the side cabinet, to take a handful of rubber bands, and then to listen to what she would like them to do. She says, "I would like you to design a figure and then find the perimeter and area. When you have it, check with your neighbor. After you've done that, please transfer it to graph paper and tomorrow I'll ask you to make up a question about it for someone. When you hand it in, please let me know whose it is and who verified it. Then I have something else for you to do that's really fun. [pause] Find the average number of chocolate chips in three cookies. I'll give you three cookies, and you'll have to *eat* your way through, I'm afraid!" Then she goes around the room and gives help, suggestions, praise, and admonitions that they are getting noisy. They work sitting, or standing up at their desks, at benches in the back, or on the floor. A child hands the teacher his paper and she comments, "I'm not accepting this paper. Do a

---

[10]A dominant feeling expressed directly and indirectly by teachers in this school, was boredom with their work. They did, however, in contrast to the working-class schools, almost always carry out lessons during class times. [Author's note]

better design." To another child she says, "That's fantastic! But you'll never find the area. Why don't you draw a figure inside [the big one] and subtract to get the area?"

The school district requires the fifth grade to study ancient civilization (in particular, Egypt, Athens, and Sumer). In this classroom, the emphasis is on illustrating and re-creating the culture of the people of ancient times. The following are typical activities: the children made an 8mm film on Egypt, which one of the parents edited. A girl in the class wrote the script, and the class acted it out. They put the sound on themselves. They read stories of those days. They wrote essays and stories depicting the lives of the people and the societal and occupational divisions. They chose from a list of projects, all of which involved graphical presentations of ideas. For example: "Make a mural depicting the division of labor in Egyptian society."

Each wrote and exchanged a letter in hieroglyphics with a fifth grader in another class, and they also exchanged stories they wrote in cuneiform. They made a scroll and singed the edges so it looked authentic. They each chose an occupation and made an Egyptian plaque representing that occupation, simulating the appropriate Egyptian design. They carved their design on a cylinder of wax, pressed the wax into clay, and then baked the clay. Although one girl did not choose an occupation but carved instead a series of gods and slaves, the teacher said, "That's all right, Amber, it's beautiful." As they were working the teacher said, "Don't cut into your clay until you're satisfied with your design."

Social studies also involves almost daily presentation by the children of some event from the news. The teacher's questions ask the children to expand what they say, to give more details, and to be more specific. Occasionally she adds some remarks to help them see connections between events.

The emphasis on expressing and illustrating ideas in social studies is accompanied in language arts by an emphasis on creative writing. Each child wrote a rebus story for a first grader whom they had interviewed to see what kind of story the child liked best. They wrote editorials on pending decisions by the school board and radio plays, some of which were read over the school intercom from the office and one of which was performed in the auditorium. There is no language arts textbook because, the teacher said, "The principal wants us to be creative." There is not much grammar, but there is punctuation. One morning when the observer arrived, the class was doing a punctuation ditto. The teacher later apologized for using the ditto. "It's just for review," she said. "I don't teach punctuation that way. We use their language." The ditto had three unambiguous rules for where to put commas in a sentence. As the teacher was going around to help the children with the ditto, she repeated several times, "Where you put commas depends on how you say the sentence; it depends on the situation and what you want to say." Several weeks later the observer saw another punctuation activity. The teacher had printed a five-paragraph story on an oak tag and then cut it into phrases. She read the whole story to the class from the book, then passed out the phrases. The group had to decide how the phrases could best be put together again. (They arranged the phrases on the floor.) The point was not to replicate the story, although that was not irrelevant, but to "decide what you think the best way is." Punctuation marks on cardboard pieces were then handed out, and the children discussed and then decided what mark was best at each place they thought one was needed. At the end of each paragraph the teacher asked, "Are you satisfied with the way the paragraphs are now? Read it to yourself and see how it sounds." Then she read the original story again, and they compared the two.

Describing her goals in science to the investigator, the teacher said, "We use ESS (Elementary Science Study). It's very good because it gives a hands-on experience—so they can make *sense* out of it. It doesn't matter whether it [what they find] is right or wrong. I bring them together and there's value in discussing their ideas."

The products of work in this class are often highly valued by the children and the teacher. In fact, this was the only school in which the investigator was not allowed to take original pieces of the children's work for her files. If the work was small enough, however, and was on paper, the investigator could duplicate it on the copying machine in the office.

The teacher's attempt to control the class involves constant negotiation. She does not give direct orders unless she is angry because the children have been too noisy. Normally, she tries to get them to foresee the consequences of their actions and to decide accordingly. For example, lining them up to go see a play written by the sixth graders, she says, "I presume you're lined up by someone with whom you want to sit. I hope you're lined up by someone you won't get in trouble with." . . .

One of the few rules governing the children's movement is that no more than three children may be out of the room at once. There is a school rule that anyone can go to the library at any time to get a book. In the fifth grade I observed, they sign their name on the chalkboard and leave. There are no passes. Finally, the children have a fair amount of officially sanctioned say over what happens in the class. For example, they often negotiate what work is to be done. If the teacher wants to move on to the next subject, but the children say they are not ready, they want to work on their present projects some *more*, she very often lets them do it.

Executive Elite School

In the executive elite school, work is developing one's analytical intellectual powers. Children are continually asked to reason through a problem, to produce intellectual products that are both logically sound and of top academic quality. A primary goal of thought is to conceptualize rules by which elements may fit together in systems and then to apply these rules in solving a problem. Schoolwork helps one to achieve, to excel, to prepare for life.

The following are illustrative. The math teacher teaches area and perimeter by having the children derive formulas for each. First she helps them, through discussion at the board, to arrive at $A = W \times L$ as a formula (not *the* formula) for area. After discussing several, she says, "Can anyone make up a formula for perimeter? Can you figure that out yourselves? [pause] Knowing what we know, can we think of a formula?" She works out three children's suggestions at the board, saying to two, "Yes, that's a good one," and then asks the class if they can think of any more. No one volunteers. To prod them, she says, "If you use rules and good reasoning, you get many ways. Chris, can you think up a formula?"

She discusses two-digit division with the children as a decision-making process. Presenting a new type of problem to them, she asks, "What's the *first* decision you'd make if presented with this kind of example? What is the first thing you'd *think?* Craig?" Craig says, "To find my first partial quotient." She responds, "Yes, that would be your first decision. How would you do that?" Craig explains, and then the teacher says, "OK, we'll see how that works for you." The class tries his way. Subsequently, she comments on the merits and shortcomings of several other children's decisions. Later, she tells the investigator that her goals in math are to develop their reasoning and mathematical thinking and that, unfortunately, "there's no time for manipulables."

While right answers are important in math, they are not "given" by the book or by the teacher but may be challenged by the children. Going over some problems in late September the teacher says, "Raise your hand if you do not agree." A child says, "I don't agree with sixty-four." The teacher responds, "OK, there's a question about sixty-four. [to class] Please check it. Owen, they're disagreeing with you. Kristen, they're checking yours." The teacher emphasized this repeatedly during September and October with statements like "Don't be afraid to say you disagree. In the last [math] class, somebody disagreed, and they were right. Before you disagree, check yours, and if you still think we're wrong, then we'll check it out." By Thanksgiving, the children did not often speak in terms of right and wrong math problems but of whether they agreed with the answer that had been given.

There are complicated math mimeos with many word problems. Whenever they go over the examples, they discuss how each child has set up the problem. The children must explain it precisely. On one occasion the teacher said, "I'm more—just as interested in *how* you set up the problem as in what answer you find. If you set up a problem in a good way, the answer is *easy* to find."

Social studies work is most often reading and discussion of concepts and independent research. There are only occasional artistic, expressive, or illustrative projects. Ancient Athens and Sumer are, rather, societies to analyze. The following questions are typical of those that guide the children's independent research. "What mistakes did Pericles make after the war?" "What mistakes did the citizens of Athens make?" "What are the elements of a civilization?" "How did Greece build an economic empire?" "Compare the way Athens chose its leaders with the way we choose ours." Occasionally the children are asked to make up sample questions for their social studies tests. On an occasion when the investigator was present, the social studies teacher rejected a child's question by saying, "That's just fact. If I asked you that question on a test, you'd complain it was just memory! Good questions ask for concepts."

In social studies—but also in reading, science, and health—the teachers initiate classroom discussions of current social issues and problems. These discussions occurred on every one of the investigator's visits, and a teacher told me, "These children's opinions are important—it's important that they learn to reason things through." The classroom discussions always struck the observer as quite realistic and analytical, dealing with concrete social issues like the following: "Why do workers strike?" "Is that right or wrong?" "Why do we have inflation, and what can be done to stop it?" "Why do companies put chemicals in food when the natural ingredients are available?" and so on. Usually the children did not have to be prodded to give their opinions. In fact, their statements and the interchanges between them struck the observer as quite sophisticated conceptually and verbally, and well-informed. Occasionally the teachers would prod with statements such as, "Even if you don't know [the answers], if you think logically about it, you can figure it out." And "I'm asking you [these] questions to help you think this through."

Language arts emphasizes language as a complex system, one that should be mastered. The children are asked to diagram sentences of complex grammatical construction, to memorize irregular verb conjugations (he lay, he has lain, and so on . . .), and to use the proper participles, conjunctions, and interjections in their speech. The teacher (the same one who teaches social studies) told them, "It is not enough to get these right on tests; you must use what you learn [in grammar classes] in your written and oral work. I will grade you on that."

Most writing assignments are either research reports and essays for social studies or experiment analyses and write-ups for science. There is only an occasional story or other "creative writing" assignment. On the occasion observed by the investigator (the writing of a Halloween story), the points the teacher stressed in preparing the children to write involved the structural aspects of a story rather than the expression of feelings or other ideas. The teacher showed them a filmstrip, "The Seven Parts of a Story;" and lectured them on plot development, mood setting, character development, consistency, and the use of a logical or appropriate ending. The stories they subsequently wrote were, in fact, well-structured, but many were also personal and expressive. The teacher's evaluative comments, however, did not refer to the expressiveness or artistry but were all directed toward whether they had "developed" the story well.

Language arts work also involved a large amount of practice in presentation of the self and in managing situations where the child was expected to be in charge. For example, there was a series of assignments in which each child had to be a "student teacher." The child had to plan a lesson in grammar, outlining, punctuation, or other language arts topic and explain the concept to the class. Each child was to prepare a worksheet or game and a homework assignment as well. After each presentation, the teacher and other children gave a critical appraisal of the "student teacher's" performance. Their criteria were: whether the student spoke clearly, whether the lesson was interesting, whether the student made any mistakes, and whether he or she kept control of the class. On an occasion when a child did not maintain control, the teacher said, "When you're up there, you have authority and you have to use it. I'll back you up."

The executive elite school is the only school where bells do not demarcate the periods of time. The two fifth-grade teachers were very strict about changing classes on schedule, however, as specific plans for each session had been made. The teachers attempted to keep tight control over the children during lessons, and the children were sometimes flippant, boisterous, and occasionally rude. However, the children may be brought into line by reminding them that "It is up to you." "You must control yourself," "you are responsible for your work," you must "set your own priorities." One teacher told a child, "You are the only driver of your car and only you can regulate your speed." A new teacher complained to the observer that she had thought "these children" would have more control.

While strict attention to the lesson at hand is required, the teachers make relatively little attempt to regulate the movement of the children at other times. For example, except for the kindergartners the children in this school do not have to wait for the bell to ring in the morning; they may go to their classroom when they arrive at school. Fifth graders often came early to read, to finish work, or to catch up. After the first two months of school, the fifth-grade teachers did not line the children up to change classes or to go to gym, and so on, but, when the children were ready and quiet, they were told they could go—sometimes without the teachers.

In the classroom, the children could get materials when they needed them and took what they needed from closets and from the teacher's desk. They were in charge of the office at lunchtime. During class they did not have to sign out or ask permission to leave the room; they just got up and left. Because of the pressure to get work done, however, they did not leave the room very often. The teachers were very polite to the children, and the investigator heard no sarcasm, no nasty remarks, and few direct orders. The teachers never called the children "honey" or "dear" but always called them by name. The teachers were expected to be available before school, after school, and for part of their lunchtime to provide extra help if needed.

The foregoing analysis of differences in schoolwork in contrasting social class contexts suggests the following conclusion: the "hidden curriculum" of schoolwork is tacit preparation for relating to the process of production in a particular way. Differing curricular, pedagogical, and pupil evaluation practices emphasize different cognitive and behavioral skills in each social setting and thus contribute to the development in the children of certain potential relationships to physical and symbolic capital,[11] to authority, and to the process of work. School experience, in the sample of schools discussed here, differed qualitatively by social class. These differences may not only contribute to the development in the children in each social class of certain types of economically significant relationships and not others but would

---

[11] *Physical and symbolic capital:* Elsewhere Anyon defines capital as "property that is used to produce profit, interest, or rent": she defines symbolic capital as the knowledge and skills that "may yield social and cultural power."

thereby help to reproduce this system of relations in society. In the contribution to the reproduction of unequal social relations lies a theoretical meaning and social consequence of classroom practice.

The identification of different emphases in classrooms in a sample of contrasting social class contexts implies that further research should be conducted in a large number of schools to investigate the types of work tasks and interactions in each to see if they differ in the ways discussed here and to see if similar potential relationships are uncovered. Such research could have as a product the further elucidation of complex but not readily apparent connections between everyday activity in schools and classrooms and the unequal structure of economic relationships in which we work and live.

HOW TO TAME A WILD TONGUE

Gloria Anzaldúa

"We're going to have to control your tongue," the dentist says, pulling out all the metal from my mouth. Silver bits plop and tinkle into the basin. My mouth is a motherlode.

The dentist is cleaning out my roots. I get a whiff of the stench when I gasp. "I can't cap that tooth yet, you're still draining," he says.

"We're going to have to do something about your tongue," I hear the anger rising in his voice. My tongue keeps pushing out the wads of cotton, pushing back the drills, the long thin needles. "I've never seen anything as strong or as stubborn," he says. And I think, how do you tame a wild tongue, train it to be quiet, how do you bridle and saddle it? How do you make it lie down?

> "Who is to say that robbing a people of
> its language is less violent than war?"
>
> —Ray Gwyn Smith[1]

I remember being caught speaking Spanish at recess—that was good for three licks on the knuckles with a sharp ruler. I remember being sent to the corner of the classroom for "talking back" to the Anglo teacher when all I was trying to do was tell her how to pronounce my name. "If you want to be American, speak 'American.' If you don't like it, go back to Mexico where you belong."

"I want you to speak English. *Pa' hallar buen trabajo tienes que saber hablar el inglés bien. Qué vale toda tu educación si todavía hables inglés con un 'accent,'*" my mother would say, mortified that I spoke English like a Mexican. At Pan American University, I, and all Chicano students, were required to take two speech classes. Their purpose: to get rid of our accents.

Attacks on one's form of expression with the intent to censor are a violation of the First Amendment. *El Anglo con cara de inocente nos arrancó la lengua.* Wild tongues can't be tamed, they can only be cut out.

Overcoming the Tradition of Silence

Ahogadas, escupimos el oscuro.
Peleando con nuestra propia sombra
el silencio nos sepulta.

En boca cerrada no entran moscas. "Flies don't enter a closed mouth" is a saying I kept hearing when I was a child. *Ser habladora* was to be a gossip and a liar, to talk too much. *Muchachitas bien criadas,* well-bred girls, don't answer back. *Es una falta de respeto* to talk back to one's mother or father. I remember one of the sins I'd recite to the priest in the confession box the few times I went to confession: talking

---

[1]Ray Gwyn Smith, *Moorland Is Cold Country,* unpublished book.

back to my mother, *hablar pa' 'tras, replar. Hocicona, repelona, chismosa,* having a big mouth, questioning, carrying tales are all signs of being *mal criada.* In my culture they are all words that are derogatory if applied to women—I've never heard them applied to men.

The first time I heard two women, a Puerto Rican and a Cuban, say the word "*nosotras,*" I was shocked. I had not known the word existed. Chicanos use *nosotros* whether we're male or female. We are robbed of our female being by the masculine plural. Language is a male discourse.

> And our tongues have become
> dry   the wilderness has
> dried out our tongues   and
> we have forgotten speech.
>   —Irena Klepfisz[2]

Even our own people, other Spanish speakers *nos quieren poner candados en la boca.* They would hold us back with their bag of *reglas de academia.*

Oyé como ladra: el lenguaje de la frontera

Quien tiene boca se equivoca.
                    —Mexican saying

"*Pocho,* cultural traitor, you're speaking the oppressor's language by speaking English, you're ruining the Spanish language," I have been accused by various Latinos and Latinas. Chicano Spanish is considered by the purist and by most Latinos deficient, a mutilation of Spanish.

But Chicano Spanish is a border tongue which developed naturally. Change, *evolución, enriquecimiento de palabras nuevas por invención o adopción* have created variants of Chicano Spanish, *un nuevo lenguaje. Un lenguaje que corresponde a un modo de vivir.* Chicano Spanish is not incorrect; it is a living language.

For a people who are neither Spanish nor live in a country in which Spanish is the first language; for a people who live in a country in which English is the reigning tongue but who are not Anglo; for a people who cannot identify with either standard (formal, Castilian) Spanish nor standard English, what recourse is left to them but to create their own language? A language which they can connect their identity to, one capable of communicating the realities and values true to themselves—a language with terms that are neither *español ni inglés,* but both. We speak a *patois,* a forked tongue, a variation of two languages.

Chicano Spanish sprang out of the Chicanos' need to identify ourselves as a distinct people. We needed a language with which we could communicate with ourselves, a secret language. For some of us, language is a homeland closer than the Southwest—for many Chicanos today live in the Midwest and the East. And because we are a complex, heterogeneous people, we speak many languages. Some of the languages we speak are:

1. Standard English
2. Working class and slang English

---

[2]Irena Klepfisz, *"Di rayze aheym/*The Journey Home," in *The Tribe of Dina: A Jewish Women's Anthology,* Melanie Kaye/Kantrowitz and Irena Klepfisz, eds. (Montpelier, VT: Sinister Wisdom Books, 1986), 49.

3. Standard Spanish
4. Standard Mexican Spanish
5. North Mexican Spanish dialect
6. Chicano Spanish (Texas, New Mexico, Arizona and California have regional variations)
7. Tex-Mex
8. *Pachuco* (called *caló*)

My "home" tongues are the languages I speak with my sister and brothers, with my friends. They are the last five listed, with 6 and 7 being closest to my heart. From school, the media and job situations, I've picked up standard and working class English. From Mamagrande Locha and from reading Spanish and Mexican literature, I've picked up Standard Spanish and Standard Mexican Spanish. From *los recién llegados,* Mexican immigrants, and *braceros,* I learned the North Mexican dialect. With Mexicans I'll try to speak either Standard Mexican Spanish or the North Mexican dialect. From my parents and Chicanos living in the Valley, I picked up Chicano Texas Spanish, and I speak it with my mom, younger brother (who married a Mexican and who rarely mixes Spanish with English), and aunts and older relatives.

With Chicanas from *Nuevo México* or *Arizona* I will speak Chicano Spanish a little, but often they don't understand what I'm saying. With most California Chicanas I speak entirely in English (unless I forget). When I first moved to San Francisco, I'd rattle off something in Spanish, unintentionally embarrassing them. Often it is only with another Chicana *tejana* that I can talk freely.

Words distorted by English are known as anglicisms or *pochismos.* The *pocho* is an anglicized Mexican or American of Mexican origin who speaks Spanish with an accent characteristic of North Americans and who distorts and reconstructs the language according to the influence of English.[3] Tex-Mex, or Spanglish, comes most naturally to me. I may switch back and forth from English to Spanish in the same sentence or in the same word. With my sister and my brother Nune and with Chicano *tejano* contemporaries I speak in Tex-Mex.

From kids and people my own age I picked up *Pachuco. Pachuco* (the language of the zoot suiters) is a language of rebellion, both against Standard Spanish and Standard English. It is a secret language. Adults of the culture and outsiders cannot understand it. It is made up of slang words from both English and Spanish. *Ruca* means girl or woman, *vato* means guy or dude, *chale* means no, *simón* means yes, *churro* is sure, talk is *periquiar, pigionear* means petting, *qué gacho* means how nerdy, *ponte áquila* means watch out, death is called *la pelona.* Through lack of practice and not having others who can speak it, I've lost most of the *Pachuco* tongue.

Chicano Spanish

Chicanos, after 250 years of Spanish/Anglo colonization, have developed significant differences in the Spanish we speak. We collapse two adjacent vowels into a single syllable and sometimes shift the stress in certain words such as *maíz/maiz, cohete/cuete.* We leave out certain consonants when they appear between vowels: *lado/lao, mojado/mojao.* Chicanos from South Texas pronounce *f* as *j* as in *jue (fue).* Chicanos use

---

[3] R. C. Ortega, *Dialectología Del Barrio,* trans. Hortencia S. Alwan (Los Angeles, CA: R. C. Ortega Publisher & Bookseller, 1977), 132.

"archaisms," words that are no longer in the Spanish language, words that have been evolved out. We say *semos, truje, haiga, ansina,* and *naiden.* We retain the "archaic" *j,* as in *jalar,* that derives from an earlier *h,* (the French *halar* or the Germanic *halon* which was lost to standard Spanish in the 16th century), but which is still found in several regional dialects such as the one spoken in South Texas. (Due to geography, Chicanos from the Valley of South Texas were cut off linguistically from other Spanish speakers. We tend to use words that the Spaniards brought over from Medieval Spain. The majority of the Spanish colonizers in Mexico and the Southwest came from Extremadura—Hernán Cortés was one of them—and Andalucía. Andalucians pronounce *ll* like a *y,* and their *d*'s tend to be absorbed by adjacent vowels: *tirado* becomes *tirao.* They brought *el lenguaje popular, dialectos y regionalismos.*[4])

Chicanos and other Spanish speakers also shift *ll* to *y* and *z* to *s.*[5] We leave out initial syllables, saying *tar* for *estar, toy* for *estoy, hora* for *ahora (cubanos* and *puertorriqueños* also leave out initial letters of some words.) We also leave out the final syllable such as *pa* for *para.* The intervocalic *y,* the *ll* as in *tortilla, ella, botella,* gets replaced by *tortia* or *tortiya, ea, botea.* We add an additional syllable at the beginning of certain words: *atocar* for *tocar, agastar* for *gastar.* Sometimes we'll say *lavaste las vacijas,* other times *lavates* (substituting the *ates* verb endings for the *aste*).

We use anglicisms, words borrowed from English: *bola* from ball, *carpeta* from carpet, *máchina de lavar* (instead of *lavadora*) from washing machine. Tex-Mex argot, created by adding a Spanish sound at the beginning or end of an English word such as *cookiar* for cook, *watchiar* for watch, *parkiar* for park, and *rapiar* for rape, is the result of the pressures on Spanish speakers to adapt to English.

We don't use the word *vosotros/as* or its accompanying verb form. We don't say *claro* (to mean yes), *imagínate,* or *me emociona,* unless we picked up Spanish from Latinas, out of a book, or in a classroom. Other Spanish-speaking groups are going through the same, or similar, development in their Spanish.

Linguistic Terrorism

> Deslenguadas. Somos los del español deficiente. We are your linguistic nightmare, your linguistic aberration, your linguistic mestisaje, the subject of your burla. Because we speak with tongues of fire we are culturally crucified. Racially, culturally and linguistically somos huérfanos—we speak an orphan tongue.

Chicanas who grew up speaking Chicano Spanish have internalized the belief that we speak poor Spanish. It is illegitimate, a bastard language. And because we internalize how our language has been used against us by the dominant culture, we use our language differences against each other.

Chicana feminists often skirt around each other with suspicion and hesitation. For the longest time I couldn't figure it out. Then it dawned on me. To be close to another Chicana is like looking into the mirror. We are afraid of what we'll see there. *Pena.* Shame. Low estimation of self. In childhood we are told that our language is wrong. Repeated attacks on our native tongue diminish our sense of self. The attacks continue throughout our lives.

Chicanas feel uncomfortable talking in Spanish to Latinas, afraid of their censure. Their language was not outlawed in their countries. They had a whole lifetime of being immersed in their native tongue; gen-

---

[4]Eduardo Hernández-Chávez, Andrew D. Cohen, and Anthony F. Beltramo, *El Lenguaje de los Chicanos: Regional and Social Characteristics Used By Mexican Americans* (Arlington, VA: Center for Applied Linguistics, 1975), 39.

[5]Hernández-Chávez, xvii.

erations, centuries in which Spanish was a first language, taught in school, heard on radio and TV, and read in the newspaper.

If a person, Chicana or Latina, has a low estimation of my native tongue, she also has a low estimation of me. Often with *mexicanas y latinas* we'll speak English as a neutral language. Even among Chicanas we tend to speak English at parties or conferences. Yet, at the same time, we're afraid the other will think we're *agringadas* because we don't speak Chicano Spanish. We oppress each other trying to out-Chicano each other, vying to be the "real" Chicanas, to speak like Chicanos. There is no one Chicano language just as there is no one Chicano experience. A monolingual Chicana whose first language is English or Spanish is just as much a Chicana as one who speaks several variants of Spanish. A Chicana from Michigan or Chicago or Detroit is just as much a Chicana as one from the Southwest. Chicano Spanish is as diverse linguistically as it is regionally.

By the end of this century, Spanish speakers will comprise the biggest minority group in the U.S., a country where students in high schools and colleges are encouraged to take French classes because French is considered more "cultured." But for a language to remain alive it must be used.[6] By the end of this century English, and not Spanish, will be the mother tongue of most Chicanos and Latinos.

So, if you want to really hurt me, talk badly about my language. Ethnic identity is twin skin to linguistic identity—I am my language. Until I can take pride in my language, I cannot take pride in myself. Until I can accept as legitimate Chicano Texas Spanish, Tex-Mex and all the other languages I speak, I cannot accept the legitimacy of myself. Until I am free to write bilingually and to switch codes without having always to translate, while I still have to speak English or Spanish when I would rather speak Spanglish, and as long as I have to accommodate the English speakers rather than having them accommodate me, my tongue will be illegitimate.

I will no longer be made to feel ashamed of existing. I will have my voice: Indian, Spanish, white. I will have my serpent's tongue—my woman's voice, my sexual voice, my poet's voice. I will overcome the tradition of silence.

> My fingers
> move sly against your palm
> Like women everywhere, we speak in code. . . .
> —Melanie Kaye/Kantrowitz[7]

"Vistas," corridos, y comida: My Native Tongue

In the 1960s, I read my first Chicano novel. It was *City of Night* by John Rechy, a gay Texan, son of a Scottish father and a Mexican mother. For days I walked around in stunned amazement that a Chicano could write and could get published. When I read *I Am Joaquín*[8] I was surprised to see a bilingual book by a Chicano in print. When I saw poetry written in Tex-Mex for the first time, a feeling of pure joy flashed through me. I felt like we really existed as a people. In 1971, when I started teaching High School English

---

[6]Irena Klepfisz, "Secular Jewish Identity: Yidishkayt in American," in *The Tribe of Dina,* Kaye/Kantrowitz and Klepfisz, eds., 43.

[7]Melanie Kaye/Kantrowitz, "Sign," in *We Speak in Code: Poems and other Writings* (Pittsburgh, PA: Motheroot Publications, Inc., 1980), 85.

[8]Rodolfo Gonzales, *I Am Joaquín/Yo Soy Joaquín* (New York, NY: Bantam Books, 1972). It was first published in 1967.

to Chicano students, I tried to supplement required texts with works by Chicanos, only to be reprimanded and forbidden to do so by the principal. He claimed that I was supposed to teach "American" and English literature. At the risk of being fired, I swore my students to secrecy and slipped in Chicano short stories, poems, a play. In graduate school, while working toward a Ph.D., I had to "argue" with one advisor after the other, semester after semester, before I was allowed to make Chicano literature an area of focus.

Even before I read books by Chicanos or Mexicans, it was the Mexican movies I saw at the drive-in— the Thursday night specials of $1.00 a carload—that gave me a sense of belonging. "*Vámonos a las vistas,*" my mother would call out and we'd all—grandmother, brothers, sister and cousins—squeeze into the car. We'd wolf down cheese and bologna white bread sandwiches while watching Pedro Infante in melodramatic tearjerkers like *Nosotros los pobres,* the first "real" Mexican movie (that was not an imitation of European movies). I remember seeing *Cuando los hijos se van* and surmising that all Mexican movies played up the love a mother has for her children and what ungrateful sons and daughters suffer when they are not devoted to their mothers. I remember the singing-type "westerns" of Jorge Negrete and Miquel Aceves Mejía. When watching Mexican movies, I felt a sense of homecoming as well as alienation. People who were to amount to something didn't go to Mexican movies, or *bailes* or tune their radios to *bolero,* *rancherita,* and *corrido* music.

The whole time I was growing up, there was *norteño* music, sometimes called North Mexican border music, or Tex-Mex music, or Chicano music, or *cantina* (bar) music. I grew up listening to *conjuntos,* three- or four-piece bands made up of folk musicians playing guitar, *baja sexto,* drums and button accordion, which Chicanos had borrowed from the German immigrants who had come to Central Texas and Mexico to farm and build breweries. In the Rio Grande Valley, Steve Jordan and Little Joe Hernández were popular, and Flaco Jiménez was the accordion king. The rhythms of Tex-Mex music are those of the polka, also adapted from the Germans, who in turn had borrowed the polka from the Czechs and Bohemians.

I remember the hot, sultry evenings when *corridos*—songs of love and death on the Texas-Mexican borderlands—reverberated out of cheap amplifiers from the local *cantinas* and wafted in through my bedroom window.

Corridos first became widely used along the South Texas/Mexican border during the early conflict between Chicanos and Anglos. The *corridos* are usually about Mexican heroes who do valiant deeds against the Anglo oppressors. Pancho Villa's song, *"La cucaracha,"* is the most famous one. *Corridos* of John F. Kennedy and his death are still very popular in the Valley. Older Chicanos remember Lydia Mendoza, one of the great border corrido singers who was called *la Gloria de Tejas.* Her *"El tango negro,"* sung during the Great Depression, made her a singer of the people. The ever present *corridos* narrated one hundred years of border history, bringing news of events as well as entertaining. These folk musicians and folk songs are our chief cultural mythmakers, and they made our hard lives seem bearable.

I grew up feeling ambivalent about our music. Country-western and rock-and-roll had more status. In the 50s and 60s, for the slightly educated and *agringado* Chicanos, there existed a sense of shame at being caught listening to our music. Yet I couldn't stop my feet from thumping to the music, could not stop humming the words, nor hide from myself the exhilaration I felt when I heard it.

There are more subtle ways that we internalize identification, especially in the forms of images and emotions. For me food and certain smells are tied to my identity, to my homeland. Woodsmoke curling up to an immense blue sky; woodsmoke perfuming my grandmother's clothes, her skin. The stench of cow manure and the yellow patches on the ground; the crack of a .22 rifle and the reek of cordite. Homemade white cheese sizzling in a pan, melting inside a folded *tortilla.* My sister Hilda's hot, spicy *menudo, chile colorado* making it deep red, pieces of *panza* and hominy floating on top. My brother Carito barbecuing *fajitas* in the backyard. Even now and 3,000 miles away, I can see my mother spicing the ground beef, pork and venison with *chile*. My mouth salivates at the thought of the hot steaming *tamales* I would be eating if I were home.

Si le preguntas a mi mamá, "¿Qué eres?"

> Identity is the essential core of who
> we are as individuals, the conscious
> experience of the self inside.
>
> —Kaufman[9]

Nosotros los chicanos straddle the borderlands. On one side of us, we are constantly exposed to the Spanish of the Mexicans, on the other side we hear the Anglos' incessant clamoring so that we forget our language. Among ourselves we don't say *nosotros los americanos, o nosotros los españoles, o nosotros los hispanos.* We say *nosotros los mexicanos* (by *mexicanos* we do not mean citizens of Mexico; we do not mean a national identity, but a racial one). We distinguish between *mexicanos del otro lado* and *mexicanos de este lado.* Deep in our hearts we believe that being Mexican has nothing to do with which country one lives in. Being Mexican is a state of soul—not one of mind, not one of citizenship. Neither eagle nor serpent, but both. And like the ocean, neither animal respects borders.

> Dime con quien andas y te diré quien eres.
> (Tell me who your friends are and I'll tell you who
> you are.)
>
> —Mexican saying

Si le preguntas a mi mamá, "¿Qué eres?" te dirá. *"Soy mexicana."* My brothers and sisters say the same. I sometimes will answer *"soy mexicana"* and at others will say *"soy chicana" o "soy tejana."* But I identified as *"Raza"* before I ever identified as *"mexicana"* or *"chicana".*

As a culture, we call ourselves Spanish when referring to ourselves as a linguistic group and when copping out. It is then that we forget our predominant Indian genes. We are 70–80% Indian.[10] We call ourselves Hispanic[11] or Spanish-American or Latin-American or Latin when linking ourselves to other Spanish-speaking peoples of the Western hemisphere and when copping out. We call ourselves Mexican-American[12] to signify we are neither Mexican nor American, but more the noun "American" than the adjective "Mexican" (and when copping out).

Chicanos and other people of color suffer economically for not acculturating. This voluntary (yet forced) alienation makes for psychological conflict, a kind of dual identity—we don't identify with the Anglo-American cultural values and we don't totally identify with the Mexican cultural values. We are a synergy of the two cultures with various degrees of Mexicanness or Angloness. I have so internalized the

---

[9]Kaufman, 68.

[10]Hernández-Chávez, 88–90.

[11]"Hispanic" is derived from *Hispania (España),* a name given to the Iberian Peninsula in ancient times when it was part of the Roman Empire, and is a term designated by the U.S. government to make it easier to handle us on paper.

[12]The Treaty of Guadalupe Hidalgo created the Mexican-American in 1848.

borderland conflict that sometimes I feel like one cancels out the other and we are zero, nothing, no one. *A veces no soy nada ni nadie. Pero hasta cuando no lo soy, lo soy.*

When not copping out, when we know we are more than nothing, we call ourselves Mexican, referring to race and ancestry; *mestizo* when affirming both our Indian and Spanish (but we hardly ever own our Black ancestry); Chicano when referring to a politically aware people born and/or raised in the U.S.; *Raza* when referring to Chicanos; *tejanos* when we are Chicanos from Texas.

Chicanos did not know we were a people until 1965 when César Chávez and the farmworkers united and *I Am Joaquín* was published and *la Raza Unida* party was formed in Texas. With that recognition, we became a distinct people. Something momentous happened to the Chicano soul—we became aware of our reality and acquired a name and a language (Chicano Spanish) that reflected that reality. Now that we had a name, some of the fragmented pieces began to fall together—who we were, what we were, how we had evolved. We began to get glimpses of what we might eventually become.

Yet the struggle of identities continues, the struggle of borders is our reality still. One day the inner struggle will cease and a true integration take place. In the meantime, *tenemos que hacer la lucha. ¿Quién está protegiendo los ranchos de mi gente? ¿Quién está tratando de cerrar la fisura entre la india y el blanco en nuestra sangre? El chicano, si, el chicano que anda como un ladrón en su propia casa.*

Los chicanos, how patient we seem, how very patient. There is the quiet of the Indian about us.[13] We know how to survive. When other races have given up their tongue, we've kept ours. We know what it is to live under the hammer blow of the dominant *norteamericano* culture. But more than we count the blows, we count the days the weeks the years the centuries the eons until the white laws and commerce and customs will rot in the deserts they've created, lie bleached. *Humildes* yet proud, *quietos* yet wild, *nosotros los mexicanos-chicanos* will walk by the crumbling ashes as we go about our business. Stubborn, persevering, impenetrable as stone, yet possessing a malleability that renders us unbreakable, we, the *mestizas* and *mestizos,* will remain.

---

[13]Anglos, in order to alleviate their guilt for dispossessing the Chicano, stressed the Spanish part of us and perpetuated the myth of the Spanish Southwest. We have accepted the fiction that we are Hispanic, that is Spanish, in order to accommodate ourselves to the dominant culture and its abhorrence of Indians. Hernández-Chávez, 88–91.

BAMBI: A BOY'S STORY

Russell Banks

Who can say that one and only one movie changed his life? Who can name with confidence *the* movie that accomplished so much? No, there have been many movies—or "films," as I called them in my late teens and twenties—which altered my thinking about the world and thus about myself and which, therefore, could be said, to a greater or lesser degree, to have changed my life. (Although I must say that there have not been as many movies as books that have had this effect—but that's in the nature of a more or less bookish adult life, isn't it?)

Even so, I am an American child of the twentieth century, so that, before books began to change my life books, and then travel, sex, death, and divorce—which is to say, before I reached adolescence, there were surely movies to do the serious work, and in my childhood, in the absence of books, in the absence of even a merely provincial cinematic context against which I could place and measure the movie, and, going back still further, in the absence of any world larger than the one provided by my immediate family, in he absence, then, of church, school, community, in the absence of a conscious culture of any kind, yes, a single movie did have the capacity to alter and then shape my inner life with a power, clarity, end speed that would never be available to me again. Not in movies, anyhow, and certainly not in books.

I was little more than a baby at the time, but a person nonetheless; no tabula rasa, no amorphous unformed amoeba of a consciousness, but a true *person;* and I recently discovered that there was a single winter afternoon at the movies that did indeed change my life, and in such a thoroughgoing way that I am utterly unable to remember today the person I was before the moment I sat down in the Scenic Theater, the only movie house in the small mill town of Pittsfield, New Hampshire, with my younger brother Steve on one side, my cousin Neil, also younger, and Uncle Bud Eastman on the other, and the lights went out. One person—a child very much like the newborn fawn Bambi, of no particular gender, a creature whose destiny was shaped merely by his species—seems to have died that afternoon; and another—a child defined by his gender—got born.

The power and clarity and speed of ritual is what I'm referring to here. My secularized New England Protestant bar mitzvah. Though I had long remembered the event, the name of the movie, the circumstances surrounding my viewing, and a few vivid details, until I happened in recent months to see it again, I recalled little else of it. And exactly who I was before I first saw the movie is lost to me now, except as I'm able to observe him in another child that age or younger; and who I was afterward remains to a disturbing degree the person I am today. That's how powerful it is, or was—*Bambi,* the Disney movie version of the Felix Salten story, which I saw at the age of four.

How do I know this took place, this transformation? The truth is, I was taught it by a child and, in part, by another Disney movie. I have a three-year-old granddaughter, Sarah, and last summer Sarah spent a week, without her parents, visiting my wife and me in our home in the Adirondack Mountains in upstate New York.

I am a relatively young grandfather, and my wife (not Sarah's grandmother) is even younger, but nevertheless we soon tired of carting this energetic, curious, but easily bored child to Santa's Workshop, Frontiertown, and the Great Escape Amusement Park. We began to look for diversions for her that were located closer to home and that we ourselves would find amusing, too.

There is very little television programming for children her age, especially way up in the north country, where the only channel we receive, and receive badly at that, is the NBC affiliate from Plattsburgh. We tuned in, but most of the children's shows seemed alternately hysterical and simple-minded. Sarah was neither, and we liked her that way, as did she.

But she seemed too young for movies—she was barely three, and too sidereal and digressive in her perceptions of time to care for plot, too curious about background to bother distinguishing it from foreground, and too far outside the economy to have her fantasy life targeted for colonization by sexual imagery. She was, we thought, media innocent. Possibly media immune.

We concluded all this when we rented the more popular children's movies and played them for her one after the other on the VCR. She watched them, *Mary Poppins, Cinderella, Peter Pan,* even *The Wizard of Oz;* but she watched them obediently, passively, sleepily, as if narcotized by a little too much cough medicine; and reluctantly (*we* were interested, after all), we rewound the movies halfway through, with no protest from her, and returned them to the video outlet in nearby Elizabethtown.

Then, one evening, for the first time, we ran a movie that instantly seized her attention, drew her forward in her seat and engaged her emotionally in a way that none of the others had so far. She had locked onto it like a heat-seeking missile. It was Disney's *The Little Mermaid.* Relieved, my wife and I brought in a bowl of popcorn and sat down to watch it with her, but after a few moments, to our dismay and slight embarrassment, we realized that *The Little Mermaid* was essentially a dramatized tract designed to promote the virtues and rewards of female submissiveness and silence. Not the sort of thing we wanted our granddaughter to watch while in our care. She was *not* too young, it now seemed, to have her fantasy life structured and rearranged by sexual imagery, not too young to be colonized by the masters of the medium.

She wept when we rewound the film and removed it from the VCR. We replaced it with *Bambi,* the last of the children's films in Elizabethtown that was not science fiction or horror. My wife, born in 1950, had not seen *Bambi* since her own early childhood and remembered it no more clearly than I, although she at least knew that Bambi was a boy, which I did not. All I'd remembered of it, as I said, was that I had seen it at the Scenic in Pittsfield when I was four, with my brother and cousin and uncle. In my memory, it was a *girl's* story about a fawn—Bambi is a girl's name, right?—and there was a forest fire, and Bambi's mother had died somehow. Which was sad, to be sure, but it was only one episode and not the dramatic point of the movie, and the Disney people had handled the tragedy with gentleness and tact, as I recalled. The ending I remembered vaguely as uplifting. There were several memorable secondary characters, a mischievous rabbit with a foot spasm named Thumper and a winsome skunk named Flower. Nothing very promising; certainly nothing dangerous.

I did remember it as having been a visually thrilling movie, however, filled with gorgeously painted scenery—endless northern forests, fields of wildflowers, falling leaves, snow and ice, lofty mountains, and turbulent skies—lyrical pictures of a world not unlike the one that I had grown up in and that actually surrounded us now in the Adirondacks. A world I hoped to honor and celebrate with my granddaughter.

It opened with a trailer for *The Little Mermaid,* a preview. We winced and waited. This stuff is inescapable. Perhaps Sarah thought the trailer was the opening scene of the new movie; or the final scene of the movie we had just removed, a lingering afterimage.

No matter. From the first frame, *Bambi* was of an entirely different aesthetic and moral order than *The Little Mermaid.* We approved of this. We may have been forced to deprive our granddaughter of the pleasure of watching the story of Ariel, the free-swimming mermaid who surrenders her beautiful voice, becomes a bimbo in a bikini—Barbie with fins—and lands her prince, but we had given her instead the story of *Bambi,* which, from the scene unfolding behind the credits, we realized would be a story about love between mother and child, with possibly an early Green theme tossed in—the enemy, the outsider, would be Man, we could see. The central image appeared to be that of the Edenic garden before the arrival of the wars between the species. Nice. We approved. And where *The Little Mermaid* had opened like Andre Agassi's wardrobe, a frantic disco-dance of primary colors, of garish neon red and orange and fluorescent green and purple, the colors and rhythms of *Bambi* were soft and muted, opening slowly like the wings of a butterfly in shades of pale green and blue-gray, shifting to rose to speckled sunlight. This was a visual lyricism we could understand and value, one we wanted to share with Sarah.

It's the slow dawning of a spring day in the deep forest. Behind the images, the voices of a male tenor and chorus, hymnlike, rise up singing. . . .

My obligations to oversee the moral education of my granddaughter met, I was free now to sit back, relax, and watch the movie for myself, and suddenly I was gone, lost inside the world of the movie, and found again inside my four-year-old self. It was a startling transformation, instantaneous and complete. I was at once and once again a country child on the cusp of boyhood, a creature just emerging from the polymorphous envelope of infancy and facing for the first time the beginnings of a terrifying, bewildering male life with others. An owl returns to his huge oak from his nighttime haunts, and flocks of birds waken the rest of the world with song. The dappled forest floor fills with parents and their newborn babes—quail, mice, squirrels, rabbits—all performing their morning ablutions, breaking their fasts, when a bluebird, fluttering from tree to tree, excitedly brings the news, "It's happened! It's happened!" What's happened? we all wonder. "The prince is born!" the bird exclaims. "The prince is born!"

Everyone hurries to what can only be called an adoration scene, a crèche, practically, in the thicket, where a lovely large-eyed doe nudges her newborn fawn into view. It's straight from the New Testament. Like a benign Dr. Johnson, Friend Owl, urging reverence, explains to the excited onlookers, especially the agitated, somewhat bewildered young: "This is quite an occasion. It isn't every day a new Prince is born."

Indeed. And that is why this dawn is different from all other dawns. The story of stories, your own story, if you happen to have just figured out this week that you yourself are a new prince, has begun.

The irrepressible Thumper asks what we all want to ask but don't dare. "Whacha gonna call Him?"

"I think I'll call Him," says his mother, in a voice that can only come from the mouth of a madonna, ". . . Bambi." (Not Jesus, but, to these ears, almost; or, more likely, what I heard was, "I think I'll call Him . . . Russell.")

After we have paused and admired the mother and child, the adoration is appropriately terminated by Friend Owl, and we cut away and move through the tangled woods to a slowly rising shot of a powerful stag on a mountaintop in the distance. It's the magnificent Hartford Insurance stag in profile, silent on a peak in Darien, nobly examining the horizon. The Father. Our gaze has gone from the son to the father, from adoration of the young prince to contemplation of the old. Time and destiny have entered the story.

Strong stuff. At least, for me it was. In seconds, the movie had shattered my personal time, had broken it into bits and swept away all the intervening years in which I had struggled, and mostly failed, to live out the story of Bambi, returning me to the moment when the story first took me over. I suddenly remembered (oddly, remembered with my right hand, which began to move, as if holding a pencil or crayon between thumb and forefinger) how for years I had obsessively drawn that hugely antlered male deer, the old prince of the forest. Seated now on my living room sofa next to my granddaughter and wife, I reproduced the drawing invisibly in air, just as I had done over and over again when I was a boy—a single swift line that traced the outline of the noble stag, covering brown paper grocery bags with it, filling schoolbook margins and endpapers, drawing it all over my notebooks, even in wet sand at Wells Beach and in new snow in the backyard.

The story of Bambi, subtitled in Felix Salter's book "A Life in the Woods," is both simple and amazingly complete. From birth to death, it describes and proscribes the territory of a male life in a sequence that follows exactly the Victorian and modern middle-class view of that life properly lived. It's a rigorous, wholly believable, moral story. Believable because, although it has no irony, no sly winking inside jokes between knowing adults, it has an abundance of humor. And while, as everyone knows, it has heartbreak aplenty, the movie, as few of us remember, is nonetheless not sentimental. It's downright Darwinian. *Bambi* has danger to be faced, great peril, obstacles to be overcome; and, at crucial moments, the movie shows us death. Both kinds—death that is sudden, violent, and inexplicable and death that comes late and is unavoidable, natural, necessary. It has sex, to be sure, but no Hollywood sleaze, no puritanical prurience—males and females are simply drawn to one another, where they go mad with procreative desire ("twitter-pated," Friend Owl explains) and rush off to couple with one another and quickly produce offspring, all done with pleasure, great good gusto, and not a single salacious nudge or apology. No one, after all, wears clothes in this movie. In fact, the pleasures of the body—eating, sleeping, bathing, sport, and sex—are presented as straightforwardly satisfying and natural as in *Tom Jones.*

Bambi makes all the stops on the life-circuit, and does so in a rigorously structured, comprehensive, and rhythmically patterned way, as precise and inclusive as a Catholic mass or a cycle of myths. Which, of course, makes it feel universal. And from that feeling proceeds its moral imperative. *Bambi* may be agitprop, but it's agitprop of a very high order.

Not for everyone, however. Recently, a friend of mine took his son to see the movie in a Manhattan theater. My friend is a large and gentle feminist of a man; his son is a bright six-year-old boy, older perhaps by several lifetimes than I was when I first saw the movie. In the scene that follows the death of Bambi's mother, when Bambi's father arrives at the thicket and, basso profundo, says to him, "Your mother can't be with you any more. . . ," my friend's son asked, "Didn't the father help the mother?" My friend had to say no. After all, the movie said no. "Then we'd better get out of here," the boy said, and they did, father and son, barely a third of the way through the movie.

On Manhattan's Upper West Side in 1990, *Bambi,* the boy's story, was not *their* story, that's for sure. Not the way it had been mine in the middle 1940s in small-town New Hampshire. My father had a rack of antlers and was absent on a hill, too—a plumber working all week on the construction of the weather station at the top of Mount Washington, coming home only on weekends, taking up my mother's time with his needs and watching over me from a vast, powerfully masculine, fixed distance. "Were you a good boy this week? Did you do all your chores? Did you obey your mother, take care of your younger brother, learn the ways of the forest?"

There are the usual differences between the movie and the book that generated it, *Bambi: A Life in the Woods,* by Felix Salten, translated in 1928 by Whittaker Chambers, of all people, with a wry foreword by John Galsworthy ("I particularly recommend it to sportsmen . . ."). The story has been simplified, streamlined, slightly sanitized. But there is, to me, an amazing and shrewd faithfulness to the overall structure of the book (everything is cyclic and occurs in triplets—three acts, three seasonal sequences, three distinct stages of life) and to Salten's realistic description of "a life in the woods." His is not a kind and gentle woods; it's nature with fang and frost, with hunger and hardship, with violence that is natural and necessary (there are carnivores in the forest, after all) and the perverse, gratuitous violence of Man the Hunter. And although there is much in Salten's novel concerning the relations between the genders that is explicit and didactic, in Disney's movie that same material is implicit, is dramatized, and is no less thematically central or seductive for that. Quite the opposite.

At bottom, they are both, novel and movie, moral tales about the proper relations between the genders, told for boys from the Victorian male point of view. In the book, after having seen a passing pair of grown male deer for the first time, Bambi asks his mother, "'Didn't they see us?'

"His mother understood what he meant and replied, 'Of course, they saw all of us.'

"Bambi was troubled. He felt shy about asking questions, but it was too much for him. 'Then why. . . ,' he began, and stopped.

"His mother helped him along. 'What is it you want to know, son?' she asked.

" 'Why didn't they stay with us?'

"'They don't ever stay with us,' his mother answered, 'only at times.'

"Bambi continued, 'But why didn't they speak to us?'

"His mother said, 'They don't speak to us now; only at times. We have to wait till they come to us. And we have to wait for them to speak to us. They do it whenever they like.'"

And a little further on, his mother says, "'If you live, my son, if you are cunning and don't run into danger, you'll be as strong and handsome as your father is sometime, and you'll have antlers like his, too.'

"Bambi breathed deeply. His heart swelled with joy and expectancy."

As did mine. Hunkered down in my seat in the darkness in the Scenic Theater, and now here, forty-six years later, in front of a TV screen in my living room, I was on both occasions located at precisely the age when a child can be most easily colonized by the gender-specific notions of his or her culture, the age when the first significant moves toward individuation are occurring at a recklessly fast rate and in the explicit terms of one's inescapable biology.

At that moment, at the telling of one's story, one's heart cannot help swelling with joy and expectancy. Just as, earlier, Sarah's heart, perhaps, had swelled at the telling of Ariel's story in *The Little Mermaid.* And was apparently not moved in the slightest by the telling of Bambi's and mine. For this was, as she surely knew, a boy's story, and thus was not for her, was irrelevant, if pleasantly distracting. For, after all, the birds were pretty, the thump-footed rabbit funny, the shy skunk sweet, and there was the excitement of the forest fire, the scary presence of the hunters. All that seemed more than mildly interesting to her, but in no way capable of changing her life.

She needed *The Little Mermaid* for that, I'm afraid. I have no regrets that my wife and I kept it from her, however. And though it probably would have done me in the long run no good at all, I wish that someone—my uncle Bud Eastman, maybe, or a kindly grandfather conscious of the pain, confusion, and cruelty that come as soon as a boy marches into such territory—someone, had taken a quick look at the opening scenes of *Bambi* that Saturday afternoon and had said to himself, This movie is only going to drive the kid deeper into sexual stereotyping. It's going to validate the worst attitudes of the adult world that surrounds him. It's going to speed the end of his innocence.

"Let's get out of here, boys," he might then have said to me and my brother Steve and cousin Neil. He'd have needed to know back then only what my friend's six-year-old son knows now. "Let's go down the street to Varney's for an ice cream soda," he might have said, "and come back next week for a Zorro double feature, or maybe for Gene Autry, the Singing Cowboy. Let's come back when they're showing a movie that *won't* change your life."

WAYS OF SEEING

John Berger

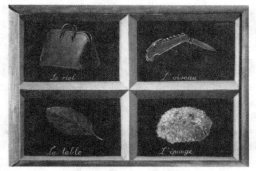

The Key of Dreams by Magritte (1898–1967).

Seeing comes before words. The child looks and recognizes before it can speak.

But there is also another sense in which seeing comes before words. It is seeing which establishes our place in the surrounding world; we explain that world with words, but words can never undo the fact that we are surrounded by it. The relation between what we see and what we know is never settled. Each evening we *see* the sun set. We *know* that the earth is turning away from it. Yet the knowledge, the explanation, never quite fits the sight. The Surrealist painter Magritte commented on this always-present gap between words and seeing in a painting called *The Key of Dreams.*

The way we see things is affected by what we know or what we believe. In the Middle Ages when men believed in the physical existence of Hell the sight of fire must have meant something different from what it means today. Nevertheless their idea of Hell owed a lot to the sight of the consuming and the ashes remaining—as well as to their experience of the pain of burns.

When in love, the sight of the beloved has a completeness which no words and no embrace can match: a completeness which only the act of making love can temporarily accommodate.

Yet this seeing which comes before words, and can never be quite covered by them, is not a question of mechanically reacting to stimuli. (It can only be thought of in this way if one isolates the small part of the process which concerns the eye's retina.) We only see what we look at. To look is an act of choice. As a result of this act, what we see is brought within our reach—though not necessarily within arm's reach. To touch something is to situate oneself in relation to it. (Close your eyes, move round the room and notice how the faculty of touch is like a static, limited form of sight.) We never look at just one thing; we are always looking at the relation between things and ourselves. Our vision is continually active, continually moving, continually holding things in a circle around itself, constituting what is present to us as we are.

Soon after we can see, we are aware that we can also be seen. The eye of the other combines with our own eye to make it fully credible that we are part of the visible world.

If we accept that we can see that hill over there, we propose that from that hill we can be seen. The reciprocal nature of vision is more fundamental than that of spoken dialogue. And often dialogue is an attempt to verbalize this—an attempt to explain how, either metaphorically or literally, "you see things," and an attempt to discover how "he sees things."

In the sense in which we use the word in this book, all images are manmade [see below]. An image is a sight which has been recreated or reproduced. It is an appearance, or a set of appearances, which has been detached from the place and time in which it first made its appearance and preserved—for a few moments or a few centuries. Every image embodies a way of seeing. Even a photograph. For photographs are not, as is often assumed, a mechanical record. Every time we look at a photograph, we are aware, however slightly, of the photographer selecting that sight from an infinity of other possible sights. This is true even in the most casual family snapshot. The photographer's way of seeing is reflected in his choice of subject. The painter's way of seeing is reconstituted by the marks he makes on the canvas or paper. Yet, although every image embodies a way of seeing, our perception or appreciation of an image depends also upon our own way of seeing. (It may be, for example, that Sheila is one figure among twenty; but for our own reasons she is the one we have eyes for.)

Images were first made to conjure up the appearance of something that was absent. Gradually it became evident that an image could outlast what it represented; it then showed how something or somebody had once looked—and thus by implication how the subject had once been seen by other people. Later still the specific vision of the image-maker was also recognized as part of the record. An image became a record of how X had seen Y. This was the result of an increasing consciousness of individuality, accompanying an increasing awareness of history. It would be rash to try to date this last development precisely. But certainly in Europe such consciousness has existed since the beginning of the Renaissance.

No other kind of relic or text from the past can offer such a direct testimony about the world which surrounded other people at other times. In this respect images are more precise and richer than literature. To say this is not to deny the expressive or imaginative quality of art, treating it as mere documentary evidence; the more imaginative the work, the more profoundly it allows us to share the artist's experience of the visible.

Yet when an image is presented as a work of art, the way people look at it is affected by a whole series of learnt assumptions about art. Assumptions concerning:

Beauty	Truth
Genius	Civilization
Form	Status
Taste, etc.	

Regents of the Old Men's Alms House by Hals (1580–1666).

Regentesses of the Old Men's Alms House by Hals (1580–1666).

Many of these assumptions no longer accord with the world as it is. The world-as-it-is is more than pure objective fact, it includes consciousness. Out of true with the present, these assumptions obscure the past. They mystify rather than clarify. The past is never there waiting to be discovered, to be recognized for exactly what it is. History always constitutes the relation between a present and its past. Consequently fear of the present leads to mystification of the past. The past is not for living in; it is a well of conclusions from which we draw in order to act. Cultural mystification of the past entails a double loss. Works of art are made unnecessarily remote. And the past offers us fewer conclusions to complete in action.

When we "see" a landscape, we situate ourselves in it. If we "saw" the art of the past, we would situate ourselves in history. When we are prevented from seeing it, we are being deprived of the history which belongs to us. Who benefits from this deprivation? In the end, the art of the past is being mystified because a privileged minority is striving to invent a history which can retrospectively justify the role of the ruling classes, and such a justification can no longer make sense in modern terms. And so, inevitably, it mystifies.

Let us consider a typical example of such mystification. A two-volume study was recently published on Frans Hals.[1] It is the authoritative work to date on this painter. As a book of specialized art history it is no better and no worse than the average.

The last two great paintings by Frans Hals portray the Governors and the Governesses of an Alms House for old paupers in the Dutch seventeenth-century city of Haarlem. They were officially commissioned portraits. Hals, an old man of over eighty, was destitute. Most of his life he had been in debt. During the winter of 1664, the year he began painting these pictures, he obtained three loads of peat on public charity, otherwise he would have frozen to death. Those who now sat for him were administrators of such public charity.

The author records these facts and then explicitly says that it would be incorrect to read into the paintings any criticism of the sitters. There is no evidence, he says, that Hals painted them in a spirit of bitterness. The author considers them, however, remarkable works of art and explains why. Here he writes of the Regentesses:

> Each woman speaks to us of the human condition with equal importance. Each woman stands out with equal clarity against the *enormous* dark surface, yet they are linked by a firm rhythmical arrangement and the subdued diagonal pattern formed by their heads and hands. Subtle modulations of the *deep,* glowing blacks contribute to the *harmonious fusion* of the whole and form an *unforgettable contrast* with the *powerful* whites and vivid flesh tones where the detached strokes reach a *peak of breadth and strength.* [Berger's italics]

The compositional unity of a painting contributes fundamentally to the power of its image. It is reasonable to consider a painting's composition. But here the composition is written about as though it were in itself the emotional charge of the painting. Terms like *harmonious fusion, unforgettable contrast,* reaching *a peak of breadth and strength* transfer the emotion provoked by the image from the plane of lived experience, to that of disinterested "art appreciation." All conflict disappears. One is left with the unchanging "human condition," and the painting considered as a marvellously made object.

----

[1]Seymour Slive, *Frans Hals*) (Phaidon, London).

Very little is known about Hals or the Regents who commissioned him. It is not possible to produce circumstantial evidence to establish what their relations were. But there is the evidence of the paintings themselves: the evidence of a group of men and a group of women as seen by another man, the painter. Study this evidence and judge for yourself.

The art historian fears such direct judgement:

> As in so many other pictures by Hals, the penetrating characterizations almost seduce us into believing that we know the personality traits and even the habits of the men and women portrayed.

What is this "seduction" he writes of? It is nothing less than the paintings working upon us. They work upon us because we accept the way Hals saw his sitters. We do not accept this innocently. We accept it in so far as it corresponds to our own observation of people, gestures, faces, institutions. This is possible because we still live in a society of comparable social relations and moral values. And it is precisely this which gives the paintings their psychological and social urgency. It is this—not the painter's skill as a "seducer"—which convinces us that we *can* know the people portrayed.

The author continues:

> In the case of some critics the seduction has been a total success. It has, for example, been asserted that the Regent in the tipped slouch hat, which hardly covers any of his long, lank hair, and whose curiously set eyes do not focus, was shown in a drunken state [below].

 This, he suggests, is a libel. He argues that it was a fashion at that time to wear hats on the side of the head. He cites medical opinion to prove that the Regent's expression could well be the result of a facial paralysis. He insists that the painting would have been unacceptable to the Regents if one of them had been portrayed drunk. One might go on discussing each of these points for pages. (Men in seventeenth-century Holland wore their hats on the side of their heads in order to be thought of as adventurous and pleasure-loving. Heavy drinking was an approved practice. Etcetera.) But such a discussion would take us even farther away from the only confrontation which matters and which the author is determined to evade.

In this confrontation the Regents and Regentesses stare at Hals, a destitute old painter who has lost his reputation and lives off public charity; he examines them through the eyes of a pauper who must nevertheless try to be objective; i.e., must try to surmount the way he sees as a pauper. This is the drama of these paintings. A drama of an "unforgettable contrast."

Mystification has little to do with the vocabulary used. Mystification is the process of explaining away what might otherwise be evident. Hals was the first portraitist to paint the new characters and expressions created by capitalism. He did in pictorial terms what Balzac did two centuries later in literature. Yet the author of the authoritative work on these paintings sums up the artist's achievement by referring to

> Hals's unwavering commitment to his personal vision, which enriches our consciousness of our fellow men and heightens our awe for the ever-increasing power of the mighty impulses that enabled him to give us a dose view of life's vital forces.

That is mystification.

In order to avoid mystifying the past (which can equally well suffer pseudo-Marxist mystification) let us now examine the particular relation which now exists, so far as pictorial images are concerned, between the present and the past. If we can see the present clearly enough, we shall ask the right questions of the past.

Today we see the art of the past as nobody saw it before. We actually perceive it in a different way.

This difference can be illustrated in terms of what was thought of as perspective. The convention of perspective, which is unique to European art and which was first established in the early Renaissance, centres everything on the eye of the beholder. It is like a beam from a lighthouse—only instead of light travelling outwards, appearances travel in. The conventions called those appearances *reality*. Perspective makes the single eye the centre of the visible world. Everything converges on to the eye as to the vanishing point of infinity. The visible world is arranged for the spectator as the universe was once thought to be arranged for God.

According to the convention of perspective there is no visual reciprocity. There is no need for God to situate himself in relation to others: he is himself the situation. The inherent contradiction in perspective was that it structured all images of reality to address a single spectator who, unlike God, could only be in one place at a time.

After the invention of the camera this contradiction gradually became apparent.

I'm an eye. A mechanical eye. I, the machine, show you a world the way only I can see it. I free myself for today and forever from human immobility. I'm in constant movement. I approach and pull away from objects. I creep under them. I move alongside a running horse's mouth. I fall and rise with the falling and rising bodies. This is I, the machine, manoeuvring in the chaotic movements, recording one movement after another in the most complex combinations.

Freed from the boundaries of time and space, I coordinate any and all points of the universe, wherever I want them to be. My way leads towards the creation of a fresh perception of the world. Thus I explain in a new way the world unknown to you.[2]

The camera isolated momentary appearances and in so doing destroyed the idea that images were timeless. Or, to put it another way, the camera showed that the notion of time passing was inseparable from the experience of the visual (except in paintings). What you saw depended upon where you were when. What you saw was relative to your position in time and space. It was no longer possible to imagine everything converging on the human eye as on the vanishing point of infinity.

This is not to say that before the invention of the camera men believed that everyone could see everything. But perspective organized the visual field as though that were indeed the ideal. Every drawing or painting that used perspective proposed to the spectator that he was the unique centre of the world. The camera—and more particularly the movie camera—demonstrated that there was no centre.

The invention of the camera changed the way men saw. The visible came to mean something different to them. This was immediately reflected in painting.

For the Impressionists the visible no longer presented itself to man in order to be seen. On the contrary, the visible,

Still from *Man with a Movie Camera* by Vertov (1895–1954).

___

[2]This quotation is from an article written in 1923 by Dziga Vertov, the revolutionary Soviet film director.

Still Life with Wicker Chair by Picasso (1881–1973).

in continual flux, became fugitive. For the Cubists the visible was no longer what confronted the single eye, but the totality of possible views taken from points all round the object (or person) being depicted [left].

The invention of the camera also changed the way in which men saw paintings painted long before the camera was invented. Originally paintings were an integral part of the building for which they were designed. Sometimes in an early Renaissance church or chapel one has the feeling that the images on the wall are records of the building's interior life, that together they make up the building's memory—so much are they part of the particularity of the building [below].

The uniqueness of every painting was once part of the uniqueness of the place where it resided. Sometimes the painting was transportable. But it could never be seen in two places at the same time. When the camera reproduces a painting, it destroys the uniqueness of its image. As a result its meaning changes. Or, more exactly, its meaning multiplies and fragments into many meanings.

This is vividly illustrated by what happens when a painting is shown on a television screen. The painting enters each viewer's house. There it is surrounded by his wallpaper, his furniture, his mementos. It enters the atmosphere of his family. It becomes their talking point. It lends its meaning to their meaning. At the same time it enters a million other houses and, in each of them, is seen in a different context. Because of the camera, the painting now travels to the spectator rather than the spectator to the painting. In its travels, its meaning is diversified.

One might argue that all reproductions more or less distort, and that therefore the original painting is still in a sense unique. Here [right] is a reproduction of the *Virgin of the Rocks* by Leonardo da Vinci.

Having seen this reproduction, one can go to the National Gallery to look at the original and there discover what the reproduction lacks. Alternatively one can forget about the quality of the reproduction and simply be reminded, when one sees the original, that it is a famous painting of which somewhere one has already seen a reproduction. But in either case the uniqueness of the original now lies in it being *the original of a reproduction*. It is no longer what its image shows that strikes one as unique; its first meaning is no longer to be found in what it says, but in what it is.

Church of St. Francis of Assisi.

Virgin of the Rocks by Leonardo da Vinci (1452–1519). Reproduced by courtesy of the Trustees, The National Gallery, London.

This new status of the original work is the perfectly rational consequence of the new means of reproduction. But it is at this point that a process of mystification again enters. The meaning of the original work no longer lies in what it uniquely says but in what it uniquely is. How is its unique existence evaluated and defined in our present culture? It is defined as an object whose value depends upon its rarity. This market is affirmed and gauged by the price it fetches on the market. But because it is nevertheless "a work of art"—and art is thought to be greater than commerce—its market price is said to be a reflection of its spiritual value. Yet the spiritual value of an object, as distinct from a message or an example, can only be explained in terms of magic or religion. And since in modern society neither of these is a living force, the art object, the "work of art," is enveloped in an atmosphere of entirely bogus religiosity. Works of art are discussed and presented as thought they were holy relics: relics which are first and foremost evidence of their own survival. The past in which they originated is studied in order to prove their survival genuine. They are declared art when their line of descent can be certified.

Before the *Virgin of the Rocks* the vistor to the National Gallery would be encouraged by nearly everything he might have heard and read about the painting to feel something like this: I am in front of it. I can see it. This painting by Leonardo is unlike any other in the world. The National Gallery has the real one. If I look at this painting hard enough, I should somehow be able to feel its authenticity. The *Virgin of the Rocks* by Leonard da Vinci is authentic and therefore it is beautiful.

To dismiss such feelings as naïve would be quite wrong. They accord perfectly with the sophisticated culture of art experts for whom the National Gallery catalogue is written. The entry on the *Virgin of the Rocks* is one of the longest entries. It consists of fourteen closely printed pages. They do not deal with the meaning of the image. They deal with who commissioned the painting, legal squabbles, who owned it, its likely date, the families of its owners. Behind this information lie years of research. The aim of the research is to prove beyond any shadow of doubt that the painting is a genuine Leonardo. The secondary aim is to prove that an almost identical painting in the Louvre is a replica of the National Gallery version [right].

French art historians try to prove the opposite.

The National Gallery sells more reproductions of Leonardo's cartoon of *The Virgin and Child with St. Anne and St. John the Baptist* [next page] than any other picture in

Virgin of the Rocks by Leonardo da Vinci (1452–1519). Louvre Museum.

133

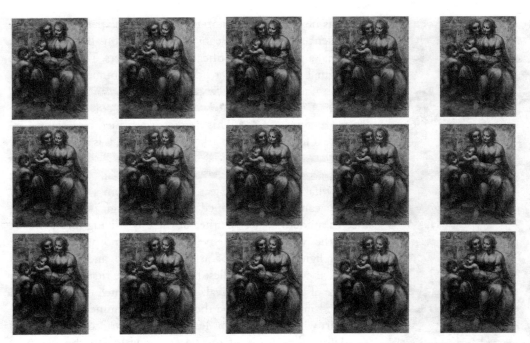

The Virgin and Child with St. Anne and St. John the Baptists by Leonardo da Vinci (1452–1519). Reproduced by courtesy of the Trustees, the National Gallery, London.

their collection. A few years ago it was known only to scholars. It became famous because an American wanted to buy it for two and a half million pounds.

Now it hangs in a room by itself. The room is like a chapel. The drawing is behind bullet-proof perspex. It has acquired a new kind of impressiveness. Not because of what it shows—not because of the meaning of its image. It has become impressive, mysterious, because of its market value.

The bogus religiosity which now surrounds original works of art, and which is ultimately dependent upon their market value, has become the substitute for what paintings lost when the camera made them reproducible. Its function is nostalgic. It is the final empty claim for the continuing values of an oligarchic, undemocratic culture. If the image is no longer unique and exclusive, the art object, the thing, must be made mysteriously so.

The majority of the population do not visit art museums. The following table [next page] shows how closely an interest in art is related to privileged education.

The majority take it as axiomatic that the museums are full of holy relics which refer to a mystery which excludes them: the mystery of unaccountable wealth. Or, to put this another way, they believe that original masterpieces belong to the preserve (both materially and spiritually) of the rich. Another table indicates what the idea of an art gallery suggests to each social class.

In the age of pictorial reproduction the meaning of paintings is no longer attached to them; their meaning becomes transmittable: that is to say it becomes information of a sort, and, like all information, it is either put to use or ignored; information carries no special authority within itself. When a painting is put to use, its meaning is either modified or totally changed. One should be quite clear about what this involves. It is not a question of reproduction failing to reproduce certain aspects of an image faithfully; it is a question of reproduction making it possible, even inevitable, that an image will be used for many different purposes and that the reproduced image, unlike an original work, can lend itself to them all. Let

National proportion of art museum visitors according to level of education: Percentage of each educational category who visit an museums

	Greece	Poland	France	Holland
With no educational qualification	0.02	0.12	0.13	—
Only primary education	0.30	1.50	0.45	0.50
Only secondary education	0.5	10.4	10	20
Further and higher education	11.5	11.7	12.3	17.3

Source. Pierre Bourdieu and Alain Darbel. *L'Amour de l'art,* Editions de Minuit. Paris 1969, Appendix 3, table 4.

Of the places listed below which dots a museum remind you of most?

	Manual workers	Skilled and white collar	Professional and upper managerial
	%	%	%
Church	66	45	30.5
Library	9	34	28
Lecture hall	—	4	4.5
Department store or entrance hall in public building	—	—	2
Church and library	9	2	4.5
Church and lecture hall	4	2	—
Library and lecture hall	—	—	2
None of these	4	2	19.5
No reply	8	4	9
	100(n-53)	100(n=98)	100(n=99)

Source: As left. Appendix 4, table 3.

us examine some of the ways in which the reproduced image lends itself to such usage.

Reproduction isolates a detail of a painting from the whole. The detail is transformed. An allegorical figure becomes a portrait of a girl [see left].

When a painting is reproduced by a film camera it inevitably becomes material for the film-maker's argument.

A film which reproduces images of a painting leads the spectator, through the painting, to the film-maker's own conclusions. The painting lends authority to the film-maker.

Venus and Mars by Botticelli (1445–1510). Reproduced courtesy of the Trustees, The National Gallery, London.

Procession to Calvary by Breughel (1525–1569).

This is because a film unfolds in time and a painting does not. In a film the way one image follows another, their succession, constructs an argument which becomes irreversible. In a painting all its elements are there to be seen simultaneously. The spectator may need time to examine each element of the painting but whenever he reaches a conclusion, the simultaneity of the whole painting is there to reverse or qualify his conclusion. The painting maintains its own authority.

Wheatfield with Crows by Van Gogh (1853–1890).

This is the last picture that Van Gogh painted before he killed himself.

Paintings are often reproduced with words around them.

This is a landscape of a cornfield with birds flying out of it [left]. Look at it for a moment. Then see the painting below.

It is hard to define exactly how the words have changed the image but undoubtedly they have. The image now illustrates the sentence.

In this essay each image reproduced has become part of an argument which has little or nothing to do with the painting's original independent meaning. The words have quoted the paintings to confirm their own verbal authority. . . .

Reproduced paintings, like all information, have to hold their own against all the other information being continually transmitted [see top, next page].

Consequently a reproduction, as well as making its own references to the image of its original, becomes itself the reference point for other images. The meaning of an image is changed according to what one sees immediately beside it or what comes immediately after it. Such authority as it retains, is distributed over the whole context in which it appears [see middle, next page].

Because works of art are reproducible, they can, theoretically, be used by anybody. Yet mostly—in art books, magazines, films, or within gilt frames in living-rooms—reproductions are still used to bolster the illusion that nothing has changed, that art, with its unique undiminished authority, justifies most other forms of authority, that art makes inequality seem noble and hierarchies seem thrilling. For example, the whole concept of the National Cultural Heritage exploits the authority of art to glorify the present social system and its priorities.

Subject and significance in Titian's Death of Actaeon

The means of reproduction are used politically and commercially to disguise or deny what their existence makes possible. But sometimes individuals use them differently [see bottom right].

Adults and children sometimes have boards in their bedrooms or living-rooms on which they pin pieces of paper: letters, snapshots, reproductions of paintings, newspaper cuttings, original drawings, postcards. On each board all the images belong to the same language and all are more or less equal within it, because they have been chosen in a highly personal way to match and express the experience of the room's inhabitant. Logically, these boards should replace museums.

What are we saying by that? Let us first be sure about what we are not saying.

We are not saying that there is nothing left to experience before original works of art except a sense of awe because they have survived. The way original works of art are usually approached—through museum catalogues, guides, hired cassettes, etc.—is not the only way they might be approached. When the art of the past ceases to be viewed nostalgically, the works will cease to be holy relics—although they will never re-become what they were before the age of reproduction. We are not saying original works of art are now useless.

Original paintings are silent and still in a sense that information never is. Even a reproduction hung on a wall is not comparable in this respect for in the original the silence and stillness permeate the actual material, the paint, in which one follows the traces of the painter's immediate gestures. This has the effect of closing the distance in time between the painting of the picture and one's own act of looking at it. In this special sense all paintings are contemporary. Hence the immediacy of their testimony. Their historical moment is literally there before our eyes. Cézanne

made a similar observation from the painter's point of view. "A minute in the world's life passes! To paint it in its reality, and forget everything for that! To become that minute, to be the sensitive plate . . . give the image of what we see, forgetting everything that has appeared before our time. . . ." What we make of that painted moment when it is before our eyes depends upon what we expect of art, and that in turn depends today upon how we have already experienced the meaning of paintings through reproductions.

Nor are we saying that all art can be understood spontaneously. We are not claiming that to cut out a magazine reproduction of an archaic Greek head, because it is reminiscent of some personal experience, and to pin it to a board beside other disparate images is to come to terms with the full meaning of that head.

The idea of innocence faces two ways. By refusing to enter a conspiracy, one remains innocent of that conspiracy. But to remain innocent may also be to remain ignorant. The issue is not between innocence and knowledge, or between the natural and the cultural, but between a total approach to art which attempts to relate it to every aspect of experience and the esoteric

Woman Pouring Milk by Vermeer (1632–1675).

approach of a few specialized experts who are the clerks of the nostalgia of a ruling class in decline. (In decline, not before the proletariat, but before the new power of the corporation and the state.) The real question is: to whom does the meaning of the art of the past properly belong? To those who can apply it to their own lives, or to a cultural hierarchy of relic specialists?

The visual arts have always existed within a certain preserve; originally this preserve was magical or sacred. But it was also physical: it was the place, the cave, the building, in which, or for which, the work was made. The experience of art, which at first was the experience of ritual, was set apart from the rest of life—precisely in order to be able to exercise power over it. Later the preserve of art became a social one. It entered the culture of the ruling class, whilst physically it was set apart and isolated in their palaces and houses. During all this history the authority of art was inseparable from the particular authority of the preserve.

What the modern means of reproduction have done is to destroy the authority of art and to remove it—or, rather, to remove its images which they reproduce—from any preserve. For the first time ever, images of art have become ephemeral, ubiquitous, insubstantial, available, valueless, free. They surround us in the same way as a language surrounds us. They have entered the mainstream of life over which they no longer, in themselves, have power.

Yet very few people are aware of what has happened because the means of reproduction are used nearly all the time to promote the illusion that nothing has changed except that the masses, thanks to reproductions, can now begin to appreciate art as the cultured minority once did. Understandably, the masses remain uninterested and skeptical.

If the new language of images were used differently, it would, through its use, confer a new kind of power. Within it we could begin to define our experiences more precisely in areas where words are inadequate. (Seeing comes before words.) Not only personal experience, but also the essential historical experience of our relation to the past: that is to say the experience of seeking to give meaning to our lives, of trying to understand the history of which we can become the active agents.

The art of the past no longer exists as it once did. Its authority is lost. In its place there is a language of images. What matters now is who uses that language for what purpose. This touches upon questions of copyright for reproduction, the ownership of art presses and publishers, the total policy of public art galleries and museums. As usually presented, these are narrow professional matters. One of the aims of this essay has been to show that what is really at stake is much larger. A people or a class which is cut off from its own past is far less free to choose and to act as a people or class than one that has been able to situate itself in history. This is why—and this is the only reason why—the entire art of the past has now become a political issue.

Many of the ideas in the preceding essay have been taken from another, written over forty years ago* by the German critic and philosopher Walter Benjamin.

His essay was entitled The Work of Art in the Age of Mechanical Reproduction. *This essay is available in English in a collection called* Illuminations *(Cape, London, 1970).*

---

* Now over seventy years ago [eds.].

⮞ THE BODY LIES ⮜

Amy Bloom

What would you go through not to have to live Gregor Samsa's life? Not to realize, early in childhood, that other people perceive a slight, unmistakable bugginess about you which you find horrifying but they claim to find unremarkable? That glimpses of yourself in the mirror are upsetting and puzzling and to be avoided, since they show a self that is not you? That although you can ignore your shell much of the time and your playmates often seem to see you and not your cockroach exterior, teachers and relatives pluck playfully at your antennae with increasing frequency and suggest, not unkindly, that you might be more comfortable with the other insects? And when you say, or cry, that you are not a cockroach, your parents are sad, or concerned, or annoyed, but unwavering in their conviction—how could it be otherwise?—that you are a cockroach, and are becoming more cockroach-like every day? Would you hesitate to pay thirty thousand dollars and experience some sharp but passing physical misery in order to be returned to your own dear, soft, skin-covered self?

Approximately two people in every hundred thousand are diagnosed (first by themselves, then by endocrinologists, family doctors, psychiatrists, or psychologists) as high-intensity transsexuals, meaning that they will be motivated, whether or not they succeed, to have the surgery that will bring their bodies into accord with the gender that they have known themselves, since toddlerhood, to be. Until ten years ago, the clinical literature and the notoriously unreliable statistics suggested that for every four men seeking to become anatomically female, there was one woman seeking the opposite change. Now clinical-evaluation centers report the ratio is almost one to one.

In fifteen years of practice as a clinical social worker, I met men who like to wear women's clothing, women who preferred sex in public conveyances to sex at home, men who were more attracted to shoes than to the people in them; I didn't meet any transsexuals. I encountered transsexuals only the way most people do: in Renée Richards' story, in Jan Morris's "Conundrum," and on afternoon talk shows, in which transsexuals are usually represented by startlingly pretty young women, sometimes holding hands with engagingly shy, love-struck fiancés, sometimes accompanied by defensive, supportive wives turned best friends. I wondered—in the middle of the afternoon—where the female-to-male transsexuals were. Even if there were four times as many male-to-females, there still had to be a few thousand of the other kind somewhere.

I thought there must be a reason that they were invisible. I wondered if their physical transformations were so pitiful that no one could bear to interview them, if women who wished to be men were less interesting, less interview-worthy than men who wished to be women, or if these people were so floridly disturbed that even the talk-show hosts were ashamed to be seen with them.

Much of the early psychiatric literature about transsexuals, from the pre-Christine Jorgensen nineteen-forties until the late nineteen-seventies, leaned heavily toward psychoanalytic explanations and toward clinical descriptions that, however sympathetic to the unhappy patient, emphasized the

From *The New Yorker,* July 18, 1994.

bizarreness not of the biological condition but of the conviction that there was a biological condition. The next psychiatric wave emphasized "personality disorders"—specifically, the popularized borderline-personality syndrome, with its inadequately formed sense of self and frightened yearning for symbiosis—as the root of transsexualism. In "The Transsexual Empire," Janice Raymond's overwrought theories about the training and practice of surgeons who perform transsexual procedures are the feminist equivalent of some of the Mafia-C.I.A.-White Russian-conspiracy theories of Kennedy's assassination, but her essential point—that transsexuals are psychologically unstable victims of a society that overemphasizes the roles of sexual insignia and gender difference—made sense to me. If the people involved were less nuts and society were less rigid, it seemed, neither transsexuals nor the surgery they seek would exist.

Most of us can understand a wish, even a chronic wish, to be the other gender. History and fiction are full of examples—many charming, some heroic—of women who dressed as men throughout their lives. It's the medical procedures that make transsexuals seem crazy: six months to two years of biweekly intramuscular injections of two hundred milligrams of Depo-Testosterone, which cause an outbreak of adolescent acne, the cessation of menstruation, and the development of male secondary sex characteristics; then a double mastectomy, in which most but not all of the breast tissue is removed, the nipple saved, and the chest recontoured for a more masculine, pectorally pronounced look; and then, a year to ten years later (depending on the patient's wishes and financial resources), one of two possible genital surgeries—a phalloplasty or a metoidioplasty—and a hysterectomy. In short, multiple, expensive, and traumatic surgeries to remove healthy tissue. Who would do this?

Lyle and his mother, Jessie, live in a trailer park in suburban Montana, a state in which I'd never imagined suburbs. (The names of these people and some identifying details about them have been altered.) The trailer park is neatly laid out beneath a shocking cobalt sky, and all the culs-de-sac have their own blue-and-white street signs, none of which are bent or rusted or facing the wrong way. The careful hand of people who are used to making do, doing without, and trying again is everywhere. Jessie and Lyle are watching for me from the trailer's little porch, and they come toward the car like a couple of welcoming relatives.

The inside of the trailer is familiar; it is the Montana twin of my mother-in-law's home, in northern Minnesota. Sturdy, slightly bowed Herculon love seat and matching recliner in shades of orange; copper mallards flying across the opposite wall, arching over the TV. The three of us finish two pitchers of iced tea during the afternoon's conversation. Lyle and Jessie allow themselves to be sad and occasionally puzzled by their own story—but not for long. All their painful stories are followed by moments of remembered grief but end in the genuine and ironic laughter of foxhole buddies; they know what they know and they are not afraid anymore.

Lyle is older than I had thought he would be—an adult. He had been a patient of three of the people I had previously interviewed: Dr. Donald Laub, a preëminent plastic surgeon known especially for female-to-male sex-change surgery; Judy Van Maasdam, the counsellor at Laub's surgical center, in Palo Alto; and Dr. Ira Pauly, a prominent psychiatrist, now head of the Department of Psychiatry at the University of Nevada School of Medicine. When they told me about Lyle, they all focussed on how young he was at the time of transition—much younger than most people who apply for surgery. Even though I knew better, I had half expected to meet a teen-ager. He was fourteen when he began hormone treatments, with medical approval, fifteen when he had his mastectomies, but twenty-three before he and his parents had enough money for the phalloplasty, the "bottom" surgery. (That's what the guys say about their surgeries—"my top," "my bottom.") I was horrified when I first heard the stories about this kid, and I imagined meeting his parents and clinically evaluating them as misguided, covertly sadistic, or perversely ignorant, acting out their own unhappiness on their helpless child.

You should have such parents.

When Lyle entered puberty, his mother and his late father took him from doctor to doctor, looking for explanations for Lyle's unhappiness and fierce resistance to being treated like a young woman. An endocrinologist who had worked with Don Laub recognized Lyle as possibly transsexual, and Ira Pauly and Judy Van Maasdam confirmed the diagnosis. Then, after extensive hormone treatments, Laub performed the first surgery and the family moved to another state, to allow Lyle to enter high school as a boy. Later, they nursed him after his hysterectomy and his phalloplasty, and used all their savings, and then some, to pay his medical bills.

Jessie says, "I want everyone to know who reads this that this wasn't easy—it was a really terrible shock. I didn't understand. I said to the first endocrinologist, 'Where did we go wrong?' and he said nowhere, it was biological. I called every single—I'm not kidding you—every single insurance company in the U.S.A., and they said, 'No, it's cosmetic.'"

Lyle interrupts—the only time I'll see him openly angry. "Yeah, right. Like I wanted a nose job. Cosmetic. Well, it was only my life."

Jessie makes soothing hand gestures, reminding him that it's all right now. "And, of course, the money. Our other kids resented it. I understand. But what could I do? What could we do? If your child has a birth defect, you get help. We understood—we understood even when he was little that something wasn't right. And we knew, when the doctors told us what could be done—we just knew what we had to do. When the doctors said he was transsexual, I felt that I *knew* that."

After hearing the stories about the hated girl name, the astonished, frightened tears and protracted battles over party dresses, Mary Janes, and even girl-styled polo shirts, and the deep, early sense of male identity, I ask Lyle about life since the transition. He gives me a glossy, friend-filled account, highlighted by a two-year romance with an older woman (twenty, to his seventeen) and a successful football career cut short by an ankle injury.

And after high school?

Finally, a bit of trouble: "I had a little money problem and a little drug problem. I got some counselling, came back from Las Vegas, started college. Now I'm taking classes, paying off my bills, working for the state. Eventually, I'll get my bachelor's."

He sighs, and Jessie says quickly, "That's all right. Lots of older kids are in college these days. Aren't they?" I say I know quite a few, and we sip our iced tea.

"I did a lot of partying, some wild times," Lyle continues. "I think maybe I was frustrated. I think maybe I did drugs partly because I was so frustrated at not being able to get my bottom surgery right away. Maybe. I just felt not quite right, but the surgery didn't make the difference I thought it would. It just made me feel me—not macho, just *me*. Uh, sexually"—he looks at Jessie—"it helped me out mentally, not really physically. But it cost so much. Not that Don Laub wasn't fair—he was. And when it was over, all I wanted to say was 'Thank you, Dr. Laub, for letting me be reborn.' But if it hadn't been for that I'd have a very nice house by now."

He laughs and Jessie laughs. "Me, too," she says. "We'd have two very nice houses." Not looking at him, she goes on, "There is another surgery he could have, to get all the feeling"—a surgery in which a nerve taken from the forearm is run through the phallus, I learned later—"but we just don't have the money."

I didn't ask any questions, because at that time I didn't know much about the different kinds of phalloplasties and I thought that it was rude to ask people about the working condition of their genitals, constructed or otherwise.

Lyle says, "What does it cost? Another forty grand? To have more sensation? It'd be nice, I guess, but I'd rather pay off my debts and buy a condo. What I have is fine. I need to get back on my feet financially and own my home more than I need to—" He laughs again and looks at his mother, who laughs, too.

Lyle shows me photographs I've asked to see. It seems absurd to describe the child I'm looking at as a little girl; there are no pictures like that. He is a sturdy little boy, looking adoringly at his dad while happily playing with his electric train; a handsome, shaggy graduating senior, being kissed by a pretty girl; a friendly, beefy man with thinning blond hair—exactly the look of most West Coast high-school football stars ten years down the road.

James Green, the transsexual man who has organized a get-together for me at his Oakland condo, sits beside me in the rental car while I look for the dimmer switch. I'm parked in his parking space, since he has chivalrously moved his car a block away to make room for me. I find the headlights, I find the interior light. I find the wipers. I cannot turn off the brights. James reaches across me with his left hand and adjusts the dimmer switch. The brights go down, and he looks at me exactly as my husband has on hundreds of such occasions: affectionate, pleased, a little charmed by this blind spot of mine. We smile at each other and I shrug. He shrugs, too. "It's innate," he says, and he laughs, not taking his eyes off me.

We are dining unfashionably early, in an austerely hip neighborhood café, before the group arrives at James's place. A huge plate of food is put before James, and he hunches over slightly and begins eating. I notice that he does not say, "Gee, this is a lot of food," or anything like that. Like a man, he just starts eating. I ask him how he met the girlfriend he'd mentioned earlier.

James puts his fork down and gives me the full effect of his green eyes. "She's a writer. She was interviewing me." A quick unfolding of a Jack Nicholson smile, and then, with slow mock shyness, he goes back to his dinner. I smile, too.

After dinner, we drive to his condo, which is clearly the home of a writer and a noncustodial father: eclectic reference books spill off the bookshelves, the refrigerator door is bedecked with drawings by and photographs of a cute little girl, dolls and coloring books make a pink-and-purple jumble in a corner of the living room. When James was a lesbian, the woman he lived with had a child, whom he regards as his daughter; after his surgery, they broke up, but he now sees the little girl as much as he can. The doorbell rings, and James introduces me to Loren and Luis, guys from the local transsexual community. (Luis is a pseudonym, and some of the details of his background have been changed.) Loren Cameron, blond bantamweight photographer, is wearing a billowing tank top and black shorts. He has a tight, perfect build, and startling black stripes tattooed across his chest, on both forearms, and on his thighs. A cross between Mercury and Rob Lowe, he looks like a not uncommon type of handsome, cocky, possibly gay man one sees at beaches, on boardwalks, and in other open-air settings.

Luis, thirty-five years old, is a slightly built, gentle South American man, a chemist in Silicon Valley, single and bi-sexual, primarily involved with women. "I was twenty-two when I went to Don Laub for my surgery," Luis says. "It was the right thing for me—I can go to the gym, go swimming, and I don't have to feel vulnerable or be afraid. I was always athletic, and I didn't want to give that up. And it feels right for sex. What I perceive and what my partner perceives match up. Inside and outside, I'm a man. The surgeries made a huge difference for me. I had the genital surgery, not the full phalloplasty. I don't know what Dr. Laub calls the other one now, but that's what I had. The easier one. I have days when I think about it, but I'd rather save my money—for travel, for my future, for investing. The gender issue isn't at the center of my life." He sighs. "I don't get the chance to talk about this—it's not a conversation I'd have with other men. Gender is slippery. I used to see it as black and white—men, women, that's it. I wanted to be perceived as male, in a male role, with male attributes. I don't hold on to that anymore. Male, female—I don't even understand that anymore. And I find, after all this, it doesn't matter much."

The four of us talk for two hours, and Loren and James cheerfully interrupt each other, disagree, raise their voices, point out the holes in each other's logic; Luis and I listen, and from time to time we point out the issues on which James and Loren do agree, which seems to matter to us but not to them. They agree—they both know at first hand—that a number of transsexual men have emerge from the lesbian community, a world in which each of them could maneuver with some success but not with complete ease.

James says, "I was excluded from lesbian events even before I started the transition. I was just too male—not butch but male. I crossed some line somehow, and everyone, the other women, felt that there were things about me, despite my female body, that were just not female."

Loren, somehow irritated by James's calm, even superior acquiescence in the face of rejection by the community that was their world for so many years, adds, "The loss makes me mad, losing the women's community. And the lack of acknowledgment. Transsexuals are never really accepted, by anyone."

Luis says, very quietly, reluctant to antagonize the activists, "I used to hate and fear men, at least all the ones I knew. Now I don't. Probably you don't have to become anatomically male to stop hating men." He smiles. "But it is effective."

I expected to find psychologically disturbed, male-identified women so filled with self-loathing that it had even spilled onto their physical selves, leading them to self-mutilating, self-punishing surgery. Maybe I would meet some very butch lesbians, in ties and jackets and chest binders, who could not, somehow, accept their female bodies. I didn't meet those people. I met men. Some I liked, some I didn't. I met bullshit artists, salesmen, computer programmers, compulsive, misogynistic seducers, pretty boys inviting seduction, cowboys, New Age prophets, good ole boys, shy truck drivers saving their money for a June wedding, and gentle knights. I met men.

Ira Pauly is one of the acknowledged titans of transsexual psychiatry, a pioneering researcher who has shifted his attention to administration. He sits in a bunkerlike office at the University of Nevada and cautions me that he hasn't kept up with everything in the recent literature, which represents a huge body of work and new ideas. He says that he has met a few people who have had regrets after their surgery, but only a few, out of hundreds, and that whatever the etiology of transsexualism may be, there are those for whom surgery is the only true solution.

Pauly is a modest, very smart middle-aged man with big hands and a U.C.L.A. plaque on his desk showing his college football history. He became chairman of the Department of Psychiatry partly on the strength of his research on transsexuals. He is always clear, reasonable, fair, and extremely contained. He showed strong feeling only once during our interview—when he talked about Louis Sullivan. A female-to-male transsexual, Sullivan was also a gay man with AIDS, and he called Pauly in the late eighties in the hope of educating the professionals in the "gender community" about the difference between gender and sexual orientation.

In his search for treatment, Sullivan went to several gender-dysphoria clinics. For transsexuals, Pauly explains, such clinics are the only gateways to reputable surgeons committed to minimal standards of care; under the supervision of a clinic, the patient lives full time as a member of the opposite sex for two years and receives documented treatment by a licensed mental-health-care provider—an arrangement recommended by the Harry Benjamin International Gender Dysphoria Association, the organization of gender-dysphoria professionals: psychologists, social workers, psychiatrists, surgeons, endocrinologists, the occasional lawyer. These clinics rejected Sullivan, because he not only knew that despite his female anatomy he was male, he knew that he was a gay male.

Pauly lent me three hours of videotaped interviews he had conducted with Sullivan. The setup reminded me of public-access TV: a ficus tree keeps brushing Sullivan's ears, the carpeting clashes with the chairs, the camera occasionally seems stuck on the socks sliding down Ira Pauly's bare shins or on Louis Sullivan's pale hands fumbling with the mike. If you missed the sections on surgery and hormones, you would simply be moved by this increasingly gaunt, youngish, mild-mannered man so ferociously determined to make use of his death sentence to educate the rest of us.

"They said, 'It can't be,' and I said, 'It is,'" Sullivan says on one of the tapes. "They told me that I must not really be transsexual. After all, they thought, if I just wanted to sleep with men, why go to all the trouble?"

The notion that gender has a continuum, a fluid range of possibilities, seems to produce such anxious rigidity in many of us that we ignore everything we've learned through our own lives about the complexities of men and women and seek refuge in explanations and expectations of gender which are more magical, romantic, and unrealistic than any attitude I encountered among the transsexuals I met. Ever since Christine Jorgensen, there seems to have been a lot of confusion about what now, thanks to Louis Sullivan, seems so unconfused to Ira Pauly and others in the field. Male is not gay or straight—it's male. We may not know what it is, but we know it's not about whether male or female sexual stimuli inspire your erection. Maybe it's not even about the ability or the equipment to have an erection. Maybe it's closer to the sensation of inner arousal pushed out—a sense of erectness, of intact outerness—than to the source or object of one's erotic desires. There are gay men, heterosexual men, masculine men, feminine men. We know that the object of desire and the fluttering of hands versus the clenching of fists do not make maleness. We don't know what does, and neither do the transsexual men, and neither do the people who treat them, psychologically and surgically.

I ask Dr. Pauly, who has expressed caution about the surgery—and even more caution about those who wish to have it declared a problem rather than a solution—if he would recommend surgery if he had a transsexual child.

"I would hope not to have a transsexual child; that life is no easy thing, with or without the surgery. I *hope* that the follow-up studies support the studies we have now. I *hope* these patients are happier."

I press him.

"I would probably try to intervene early in childhood. But you know, those studies of strongly effeminate boys—a lot of them grow up to be gay, but they don't grow up to be transsexual. You're looking at five in a hundred for male homosexuals, one in fifty thousand for transsexuals."

In the end, after edging up on saying yes half a dozen times, he indicates yes but doesn't say it, and I stop asking.

At Don Laub's surgical center, in Palo Alto, I stand in the doorway of the waiting room, observing two women in the courtyard, wondering if they are "genetically female," and wondering if I can stand to ask such a rude question. But if I believe, as I now find myself believing, that transsexual men and women are men and women, what would make the question rude?

I go into the courtyard, and one of the women, a very pretty blonde, lightly made up and wearing a conservative navy-blue dress and matching pumps, calls my name and introduces herself: Gail Lebovic, Dr. Laub's associate.

We are joined by Dr. Laub, graying and clean-shaven, utterly conventional and conservative in a dark-suited, rep-tie way, except for eyes so brightly intense they seem silver rather than blue-gray. He went to Jesuit schools, has been married forever to the same woman, and has five children, two of whom plan to join his surgical practice, and he is the founder of Interplast, a charitable organization that sends plastic surgeons to underdeveloped countries to provide free corrective surgery for children and adults. Laub has done over six hundred sex-change—or, as he says, "sex confirmation"—surgeries since 1968

Don Laub and Gail Lebovic show me the photograph albums they keep of their patients—dozens of head shots, before, during, and after hormone treatments. Many of the pictures of the same patient at various stages of his transformation look like family portraits—younger, middle, and eldest brother. The faces broaden, the foreheads slope forward and down more roughly to the eyebrows from receding hairlines, the necks and shoulders widen. Strength training is recommended, to deal with the weight gain, but many of the men in the photographs are somewhere between stocky and fat. A few of them are handsome, more than a few are attractive, most are average. One guy looks like Don Ho, another looks like Don Knotts, another like Richard Gere. Some are homely, with bad skin, bad haircuts, cheap eyeglasses and overwashed shirts, ugly mustaches, pouchy eyes, jowly necks. But no one in his right mind would take them for women.

Lebovic clears her throat and shows me the other pictures. I've seen them before—they are the pictures that Laub sent me of phalloplasties and metoidioplasties. I had flipped through them at home and tried to study them, but they were Xeroxes. The originals are in brutal, Polaroid-type color, in which brown skin gets a dappled, froglike quality and white skin has the sheen and color of bad pork.

Lebovic occasionally points out items of interest. "See, with this surgery"—the phalloplasty—"we keep the clitoris. Here, underneath, just above the scrotum, so when the penis is either rubbing against it or pulled out of the way, there's full sexual response. Isn't that great? We make the scrotum with the labia, by inserting skin expanders, just a little bit, week by week. After the skin has expanded, we insert the testicular implants, stitch it up the middle a bit, to create the look. Otherwise you just have one big ball, like this. Picture a small deflated baboon—that's the expander. We put one in each labium, sew the labia together, then expand each compartment so it's just like testicles and put in the implants, just silicone balls."

She describes the painful electrolysis of the abdominal area, and then the surgery. Two vertical incisions are made, three inches apart, stopping short of the navel. The surgeon lifts up the skin and soft tissue—while it's still attached the ends—and rolls it up sidewise into a tube. This inside-out tube is covered with a skin graft from the hip. The soft, skin-covered tube is still attached in two places, at a navel and bikini line, and will be left that way—a pulsing hot dog growing on the abdominal-field—for at least three months, so that it will develop its own blood supply. The second stage requires detaching it at the navel and allowing the tube (the essential phallus) to drop down.

We come to some terrible pictures. These are of men, genetic men, who've had penises created after disease or trauma. "Burn, cancer, tree shredder," Lebovic says gently.

We look at another album of various completed phalloplasties, which is much easier than looking at the squirming reds and yellows and acres of flaccid, anesthetized skin of the surgical procedures used to construct them. The penises from the early days of the procedure are long, blobby tubes, with no real heads, no color. The white ones look like *Weisswurst*. The brown ones seem less blobby but peculiarly speckled.

"These are the early ones," Lebovic says. "You see the shape is not so great. And of course, Dr. Laub was making them huge. I mean, really." She shows me a photograph with a ruler held up to the penis. I'm reluctant to lean closer to read the number of inches. "Nine," she says, laughing. "Well, Dr. Laub is a guy. I guess he figured that if you want one—Anyway, now they're a little closer to average. And there's no erectile tissue, so you wouldn't want it too small."

The penises are starting to look more familiar, more penis-like. I am getting used to the black, hard-looking stitches.

On to the metoidioplasties—a surgery that frees up the testosterone-enlarged clitoris to resemble a small penis. They look, just as Laub's articles say they do, like the penises of small boys, or, as he writes, "what you'd see in a men's locker room on a chilly day."

"I don't really understand why they have this surgery," Lebovic says. "I mean, if you're going to have a penis . . ."

I arrange to meet Don Laub again in New York City, at the Harry Benjamin International Gender Dysphoria Symposium. Harry Benjamin came from Germany in 1911 to do his residency in endocrinology; he stayed in America and began a private practice. In 1966, he published "The Transsexual Phenomenon," still widely used as a reference. He was, by all reports, the most lovable of men. He retired at ninety and died in 1986, at a hundred and one.

At my request, Laub is going to show me the genital surgeries for female-to-male transsexuals, and he's going to do it on lined yellow paper, using his pen point as a scalpel. The four options are the basic phalloplasty, with external devices for erection and urination; two de-luxe models, both of which provide the capacity to urinate in the typical male position (one also affords some physical sensation); and the metoidioplasty. All four are major surgeries, with more than one step.

The conference takes place at the Marriott Marquis Hotel. In a corridor which also functions as a lounge, we sit at a little table, surrounded by large and small yellow penises and one Red Grooms-like paper sculpture, with which Laub has walked me through three stages of the de-luxe phalloplasty that includes the removal of a nerve from the forearm and its placement within the newly created phallus, running from the glans of the new penis to the nerves of the still existing clitoris and allowing a full range of sensation.

"I call this the postmodern one. Like those buildings over there." He waves vaguely toward the newer architecture of Times Square.

Including the mastectomy, the whole procedure for the basic phalloplasty costs twenty thousand dollars; if your insurance company is persuaded that you truly have the psychiatric disorder of transsexualism, for which surgery is a necessary part of the treatment, you might get reimbursement from them—after you've agreed to go through life with an official diagnosis probably comparable in many people's minds to necrophilia.

"This kind of phalloplasty, which allows for natural, unassisted urination, calls for a year of electrolysis in a very sensitive place, the pubic region and lower stomach. But you see"—he quickly makes an incision in the paper and rolls up the tube—"you can't have urination through the tunnel if there's hair. The skin has to be hairless, so you either have to find hairless skin"—he taps my forearm—"or make it."

"Now, metoidioplasty—it's from *meta*, meaning 'toward,' *oidio*, for the male genitals, and *plasty*, 'change.'" He draws and dissects another set of female genitalia, carving out a small penis and folding over the lips of the labia majora to make a very neat, actually rather cute scrotum. "I don't think the patients really prefer this—I mean, if money were no object. Maybe some, some who are not such high-intensity transsexuals. Sometimes their wives don't want the penises—they've been married eight, ten years, and I'm showing them the choices. I sit there like an encyclopedia salesman, showing them the different models, and maybe the wife says, 'We want the metoidioplasty.' And the husband says, 'We do? I don't think so, honey. I want the phalloplasty.' And that relationship is in trouble. Because, for the most part—again, if money's no object and this is a younger man—he wants a penis. Men want penises. But the metoidioplasty mimics nature, and that's appealing. The testosterone enlarges the clitoris. It's the way men and women both are in utero—an enlarged clitoris, which does or doesn't become a penis. And it's one-stage surgery, less expensive than the other, and, obviously, sexual and urinary functioning is intact and they can go on having sex however they had it. Like lesbians do."

"You mean sex without intercourse? That's all that they don't get, right? No penile penetration."

Laub pauses. "Well, yes. It's only about an inch and half, maybe two inches. So they can go on having the kind of sex they had before. Dildos, whatever."

Laub next describes the four different devices that allow the men to have erections. The devices fall into two categories: pumps and inserts. One pump, the most discreet, is small, ball-like, and implanted in the scrotum. When activated, it pumps fluid from inside the ball into the penis, which remains erect for about ten minutes. There is also a syringe-like external pump, which is attached to a condom. When activated, the pump evacuates the air from the hollow tube of the penis, forming a vacuum within it and hardening the outer casing. There are two inserts—one permanent, one that is used only as needed. Laub is wary of the permanent implant, a woven-silver-wire tube within a silicone sheath, which gives the penis some rigidity, whether pointed up or down. "It's dangerous to have implants where you have no feeling," Laub says. He recommends the baculum, slightly thicker than a ballpoint pen, coated with Teflon, and tailor-made, rather inexpensively, for each patient. It is inserted before intercourse, extends from the tip of the penis back to the clitoris and allows for tireless intercourse and full sensation from the pressure on the clitoris, now located above the scrotum.

Laub is more comfortable with the men who choose penises and intercourse and who have clear-cut, easily identifiable heterosexual preferences, but he not only does the metoidioplasties, he does them extremely well and teaches other surgeons to do them. As is so often the case in the medical world, the doctors and the patients involved in these procedures understand their relationships in radically different ways. Many of the men I interviewed preferred metoidioplasties but never for the reasons offered in the literature or by the surgeons. The gender professionals say that patients choose metoidioplasties because they're older and don't want to go through the more complicated surgery, because they have other medical conditions, which contraindicate surgery, or because they were lesbians before transition and their partners don't like the idea of sex with a man. But every transsexual man I spoke to who chose metoidioplasty said, in essence, "I don't need a big, expensive penis; this little one does just fine, and I can use the money to enhance my life." It was like interviewing a bunch of proud and content but slightly bewildered Volkswagen owners and, across town, some slightly miffed and equally bewildered Mercedes dealers.

During the gender-dysphoria symposium, I also talk to psychologists, psychiatrists, even psychoanalysts; collectively, the people I meet have worked with a thousand transsexuals and their families, here and in northern Europe. Dr. Leah Schaefer, a psychologist and a genetic female, is the president of the Harry Benjamin Association and has treated hundreds of people like Loren, James, Luis, and Lyle. She is small and rounded, the right kind of Mitteleuropean figure for full skirts, big belts, and a lace fichu at the neck. We meet at her Manhattan office, which is in her home and is itself homey, *haimish*—dried flowers, ceramic birds, little boxes, family photographs, and a little sculpture of an Orthodox Jewish man studying the Torah. I didn't expect the mezuzah on the doorway, or that she would have spent twelve years singing professionally, or that we would end up talking about her closetful of shoes, talking with the same shared enthusiasm and tenderness you hear in the voices of boat enthusiasts, golfers—and transsexuals comparing surgical work.

"Now there are probably more than five thousand postoperative transsexuals in the United States. You have small-town surgeons setting up shop just like the well-known ones, the ones with years of training.

I've seen over five hundred people, and no one has even interviewed me or asked for my statistics when they're gathering information. I'm afraid I don't know where people get their numbers."

Later, she brightens when she thinks of "a very wonderful scientist" to tell me about.

"Friedemann Pfafflin's everything—an M.D., a psychoanalyst, a practicing clinician. He has a better vantage point than a lot of researchers. He's just wonderful."

And he's attending the Harry Benjamin Symposium in New York City, smoking steadily in the corridor while I interview Don Laub. Dr. Pfafflin absolutely knows where he gets his numbers. Peggy Cohen-Kettenis, a Dutch clinical psychologist I've also arranged to meet, obviously knows Pfafflin well and suggests a joint interview.

Pfafflin doesn't seem to think much of American record-keeping but has found the data banks in Germany, the Netherlands, Australia, and Sweden to be reliable, and has been doing research and follow-up studies for the last twelve years. Pfafflin shows me two studies. The first is based on the Bem Sex Role Inventory, a psychological test, oriented differently for men and women, to determine feelings of masculinity and femininity; one of its underlying assumptions is that a mix of masculine and feminine is normal and healthy in both males and females. It compares female-to-male (F.T.M.) transsexuals before and after hormonal and/or surgical treatment with "normal"—i.e., genetic—females. They test out as high masculine/low feminine before the treatment and afterward as well-adjusted men who accept their feminine side.

The second study, based on a German psychological test similar to the Minnesota Multiphasic Inventory (a psychological personality evaluation widely used in the gender-dysphoria clinics here), has even broader implications. The F.T.M. transsexuals are compared with normal men and with normal women, and I don't need to read German to understand the charts—they are as clear as cartoons. The good-sized gray bar down the middle is normal men on page one, normal women on page two; green lines that run in and out of the gray bars are the untreated transsexuals, and red lines that run square in the center of the male page and close to the middle on the female page are the post-op transsexuals. "They are completely in the normal range, psychologically, for men, after treatment," Pfafflin says, running his finger up and down a gray bar. "Even before treatment, they are not so off the norm for women." The clinical and research studies also show no unusual levels of psychopathology in the families of transsexual teenagers or in the adolescents themselves.

Neither Pfafflin nor Cohen-Kettenis appears to be particularly impressed by the surgeons in their field; Cohen-Kettenis, consistently more tactful, shrugs slightly when I ask about the exchange of ideas between the surgeons and the mental-health people here at the conference. Pfafflin laughs. "Well, they are naïve, like children. They love to build. I will build a little clitoris, I will build a little penis."

Cohen-Kettenis smiles. "Not a little penis. Only big ones."

Although they attend the surgeons' presentations (ten to twenty minutes of endless, blurring slides of penises and vaginas and recontoured chests and abdominal flaps and forearm donor sites and Y-shaped incisions), they don't expect the surgeons to attend the psychological presentations. Laub tells me that the surgeons do. He does.

I talk to Don Laub for the last time in a meeting room filled with energetic, well-dressed men and women whose genetic origins are impossible to know. I ask him about the origin of high-intensity transsexualism—the kind for which surgery seems to be the only solution. "I believe it's biological and behavioral," he says. "A behavioral problem with a surgical solution. There have been a number of experiments, corroborated over and over, at Wisconsin, at Oregon, at Stanford. They injected lab mammals—cats, rats, dogs, and monkeys—with opposite-sex hormones shortly before birth. And that was it. No matter what kind of conditioning you used on those mammals, they behaved consistently like the opposite sex, like the gender of the hormone with which they were injected. And I think that that's what we'll find, eventually. A biological answer.

"When plastic surgeons begin doing this work, a lot of them just see the technical challenge, the professional opportunity. They dislike the whole idea of transsexuals, but they're fascinated by the challenge. But when they meet the patients, they change—they become more empathetic. They see the people and they are forever changed.

"F.T.M. surgery is going to improve, aesthetically and in other ways. I learned something here at the conference. I'm going to start doing it right away. They showed how to construct the glans, how to build up a corona. I'll start doing that. And they tattoo a pinkish color onto the head—that helps, too. I'm going to do that. And in the future there might be transplants, if we can figure out how to reduce rejection. I don't think the government will fund penis transplants, but we'll try to persuade it to."

Until fairly recently, pragmatic, solution-oriented approaches like Don Laub's were anathema to clinical theorists, whose diagnoses and suggestions for treatment focussed primarily on male-to-female transsexuals and on the inevitable opinions about pre-existing family pathology. Absent fathers, over-involved mothers—that was the traditional psychoanalytic explanation for male homosexuality, and for transsexualism, as well. Other clinicians have taken the opposite view: dominant fathers, submissive mothers. The other two major psychological theories are that parents of transsexuals encourage cross-gender identification and play. That about covers it. I can't imagine that with the dominant and absent fathers, the passive and active mothers, the encouraging and discouraging of cross-gender behaviors we've left out too many American families (except the single parents, and they have their own problems). According to these theories, there should be millions of transsexuals in America alone, and McSurgery centers in every good-sized town.

No one cares at all about theory at what I'll call the American Fantasia conference. It's a big get-together of cross-dressing men and their wives and a smaller group of transsexual men and women and their partners, held behind a homemade curtain of pink tablecloths, down the most remote corridor of a smallish motel in a Southern suburb. American Fantasia is organized by a man whose name I can't use: although many at the gathering know that he's transsexual, his neighbors don't, his colleagues don't, the psychiatrists and psychologists and social workers to whom he regularly lectures on transsexualism don't. I don't know, either, until he tells me, halfway through the interview. He looks like a liberal Republican, a social worker, a minister, or a very effective insurance salesman, in his earnest, slightly old-fashioned suit and his very tidy hair and beard. He has a deep, manly chuckle that gets on my nerves, especially as it punctuates his belittling remarks about M.T.F. cross-dressers and the amusement with which F.T.M. transsexuals regard them. I'm annoyed until I realize, with surprise, that he's just another courtly, charming Southern man, whose notion of appropriate physical distance is somewhat narrower than my own—a nice man who doesn't really like women (the ladies, God bless 'em).

I'm at ease with most of these guys, though—even at the end of one of the plastic surgeons' presentations, when the guys compare handiwork and those who are most pleased with their surgery begin lifting their shirts. It's like being in a room full of cardiac-surgery survivors—everyone is telling stories, wagging fingers, showing what his doctor did for him. I see the scars from a distance, but it seems that the men wouldn't mind if I got closer. Aaron, a transsexual man in his late forties—enough like Joe Pesci to be his shorter, Southern brother—is taking photographs and acting as my guide. When I am speechless, he acts as my interpreter. Aaron photographs the men for an F.T.M. newsletter.

One guy whose chest Aaron and I study looks like a blond sailor from the cover of a 1946 *Life* magazine. "It takes about three years for the body to settle down," this guy says, and as he rolls up his T-shirt to show the incision lines, tan and thickly ridged against his muscular torso, another man, middle-aged and narrow-chested, moves his tie and shyly opens his white shirt and shows me the incision marks around his nipples.

I'm cold, but Aaron unbuttons his cuffs. "Look around you," he says. All the guys have loosened ties, rolled-up shirtsleeves. "Testosterone heats up the system. We're all comfortable, but you're gonna freeze your butt off."

After the conference, Aaron provides introductions to some wives and significant others. The first one I talk to is his girlfriend.

Samantha (a pseudonym), forty-two, met Aaron through the personal ads. "I had dated women, and I had a bad dating experience with a genetic man, so I was looking at the personals: gay, straight, and alternative. And this was *alternative.* I didn't have to go through the anguish of his transition—I just met this man. And although I wasn't attracted to him physically right away, I was very attracted to his energy and his vigor. That testosterone—it's really something.

"I thought it would be very different from being with a genetic man, but it turns out to be not so different, after all. There's nothing female about him. Sometimes I wish there were.

"I said to my friend Mitzi that men are all wrapped up with their cocks, whether they have them or not. It's still all testosterone and power and having balls, one way or another."

Bridget (also a pseudonym) is the journalist who became James Green's girlfriend.

"I thought, as a feminist, This is horrible—these are crazy women, self-hating women, who find these unscrupulous, misogynistic surgeons to lop off their breasts. I had met a few of these guys, and I had read a few books by feminists on the subject. Transsexuals seemed pretty wacky.

"After two hours with James, I was very attracted, and I think I fell in love with him the next day. I went for a walk and began fantasizing about him, sexually. I had asked him, for the article, to show me the surgery, and we were both embarrassed, we laughed, but he showed me. And my first, my spontaneous response to what I saw was 'Oh, that's so cute!' And it was. I have friends—straight friends—who think I've given up something important because he doesn't have a regular penis. It wasn't a loss to me. We have a lot more variety. We make love to each other, after all—not to organs."

Her tone of fond reminiscence—the affection she holds not only for the lover but for the joy the lover has given—falters, and her voice tightens to a sharp New York buzz. "I saw him as a combination of female and male, and he was sane and he was a feminist . . . sort of. I thought, I'm tired of men, I'm tired of women, here's someone completely *new.* But now we're dealing with the same old man-woman thing, like with any other man. And we're struggling. Suddenly, I can totally relate to my friend who has been complaining about her husband for years.

"I'm convinced—I know otherwise, but I'm convinced—that he was never *really* a woman."

Michael is the pseudonym he has asked me to use, and I cannot describe his corporate job or comfortable home. He does not go to events like American Fantasia. His former therapist contacted him, and he agreed to talk with me on neutral ground, at a friend's apartment. We're meeting in the late morning, and I buy three sandwiches, a dozen cookies, and two kinds of soda at a fancy deli, but he doesn't eat. He is a serious, dark-skinned black man dressed in corporate casual clothes for a Saturday with his relatives, whom he announces he plans to join before too long. I take him for thirty-eight or so, but he is ten years older than that. I don't know if I have just never noticed that men usually look younger than women their age or if it's something in the skin of these particular men—some vestige of former female smoothness— or if it's having had a second, hormonally powerful adolescence later in life, but all the transsexual men look to me at least five years younger than they are. After two hours, Michael is less nervous than when we began, but he is never relaxed. About half an hour before he leaves, he takes a cookie and a sip of club soda.

"I grew up in a nice, materially comfortable, middle-class life. But I carried a deep, dark secret around with me. I was pretty strange anyway. I was not an easy child to raise—my mother had her times with me. I believed that my feelings mattered, even though I was a child. I was an *offensive* child. I would not be taken advantage of, I would not be ordered about. I know a kid just like that now. Completely obnoxious. I love him.

"I hate to sound like Marlo Thomas, but I just wanted to be free to be me, whatever that was. And I didn't know, although I kept going to the library, trying to find out. Until I was six, I was a happy child. Boy games, boy clothes, even a little girlfriend up the street. And after going off to school, horrified that I had to go in what felt like drag, sure that everyone would laugh at me, I knew that I'd better get used to it, because this body was not becoming male and it clearly made a difference to the world. I tried to do what I was supposed to in adolescence. I didn't even bother trying to be a tomboy—it would have been absurd by then. My breasts were huge—they were ridiculous, size 46 double-Z. But Joan of Arc did it for me, explained me to me, when I encountered her in school, at the age of nine. I thought, Well, here we go, and when I was twelve, finally, I found a book on transsexuals.

"After graduate school," Michael continues, shaking his head over another five wasted years, "I thought, Well, maybe I'm a lesbian. Could be—I know I'm attracted to women. I went to consciousness-raising meetings, and I'd listen and feel like a fraud. One girl said, 'What makes each of us feel like a real woman?' And while they went around the room, answering, I thought, Nothing—absolutely nothing on earth makes me feel like a woman.

"I'm just a plain old heterosexual man, and I didn't want to spend my life having relationships with women who had never, ever been with a woman before and didn't know why they were attracted to me. I wanted a life. I'm not a professional transsexual. I don't think of myself as transsexual anymore. I was one, I made that transition, now I'm just a man."

Michael says, "Let me tell you about my terminally polite family." And although he himself borders on the terminally polite, he tells me funny, sad, outrageous family stories, the kind we all use to entertain company, deflect sympathy, and connect without too much feeling. His father, born early enough in this century to have heard stories of slavery from *his* father, always told Michael that he was entitled to be happy, and that God would not have put such an unusual child on this earth without purpose.

"He said to me, 'You're not the first freak in the family, and you're not likely to be the last.' My poor mother. I'm dead to her. We see each other, we love each other, but the loss of her daughter was terrible. And I feel her pain. But I couldn't do otherwise. I know she would have preferred the husband, the kids, the house, and the Valium, but I couldn't. The first time someone suggested I might want to kiss a man, I thought, Don't be ridiculous."

At funerals and weddings, the old folks who had known him before puberty as a tough little girl nicknamed Butch were comfortable with him. And the young kids would call him over to their table at the party and brag to their friends, "Go on, Uncle Mike. Tell them how you used to be a girl. Tell them." One elderly uncle approached him at a funeral. "So, you're a man now. Well, well. How you doin'? How's your health?" And when Michael said that his health was fine, thank you, the old man sat him down for twenty minutes so they could talk about his rheumatism. "They figured I had my health, I had a job, God bless me," he concluded.

He sits back and opens his tight hands. He makes himself smile and his dimples show. "I was born black. I don't expect people to like me, to accept me. Some transsexuals, especially the white M.T.F.s— they're in shock after the transition. Loss of privilege, loss of status; they think people should be thrilled

153

to work side by side with them. Well, people do not go to work in mainstream America hoping for an educational experience. I didn't expect anyone to be happy to see me—I just expected, I demanded, a little tolerance. Hell, I transitioned on the job. I didn't even tell people what was going on. You remember I said I was an offensive *child*? A friend of mine said, 'Uh, don't you think you ought to say something? People want to know.' And I said, 'Let 'em ask.' The transition was hard, but once I was completely male, people relaxed.

"I'm the same personality—a little more visually responsive erotically, maybe a little more aggressive, but I was always aggressive. You know what's different? I have a toolbox. My whole life, I never thought about one, I'm not a big fixer. But now, every once in a while, I find myself buying another wrench, or one of those very small screwdrivers. That's different.

"I'm prepared to make my own way. And I am. I've been fortunate—I've been loved, I've been married, I'm not an addict, not unemployed, not dysfunctional. I'm a decent person, I'm not ashamed. I don't know why this condition chose me. We, people who have been through this transition—we are among the few people in the world who have overcome obstacles and fulfilled their lifelong dreams. All these obstacles, and I am who I dreamed I'd be, who I wanted to be."

READING THE SLENDER BODY

Susan Bordo

In the late Victorian era, arguably for the first time in the West, those who could afford to eat well began systematically to deny themselves food in pursuit of an aesthetic ideal.[1] Certainly, other cultures had dieted. Aristocratic Greek culture made a science of the regulation of food intake, as a road to self-mastery and the practice of moderation in all things.[2] Fasting, aimed at spiritual purification and domination of the flesh, was an important part of the repertoire of Christian practice in the Middle Ages.[3] These forms of diet can clearly be viewed as instruments for the development of a "self"—whether an "inner" self, for the Christians, or a public self, for the Greeks—constructed as an arena in which the deepest possibilities for human excellence may be realized. Rituals of fasting and asceticism were therefore reserved for the select few, aristocratic or priestly, who were deemed capable of achieving such excellence of spirit. In the late nineteenth century, by contrast, the practices of body management begin to be middle-class preoccupations, and concern with diet becomes attached to the pursuit of an idealized physical weight or shape; it becomes a project in service of body rather than soul. Fat, not appetite or desire, became the declared enemy, and people began to measure their dietary achievements by the numbers on the scale rather than by the level of their mastery of impulse and excess. The bourgeois "tyranny of slenderness" (as Kim Chernin has called it)[4] had begun its ascendancy (particularly over women), and with it the development of numerous technologies—diet, exercise, and, later on, chemicals and surgery—aimed at a purely physical transformation.

Today, we have become acutely aware of the massive and multifaceted nature of such technologies and the industries built around them. To the degree that a popular critical consciousness exists, however, it has been focused largely (and not surprisingly) on what has been viewed as pathological or extreme—on the unfortunate minority who become "obsessed" or go "too far." Television talk shows feature tales of disasters caused by stomach stapling, gastric hobbles, gastrointestinal bypass operations, liquid diets, compulsive exercising. Magazines warn of the dangers of fat-reduction surgery and liposuction. Books and articles about bulimia and anorexia nervosa proliferate. The portrayal of eating disorders by the popular media is often lurid; audiences gasp at pictures of skeletal bodies or at item-by-item descriptions of the

This piece originally appeared in Mary Jacobus, Evelyn Fox Keller, and Sally Shuttleworth, eds., *Body/Politics: Women and the Discourses of Science* (New York: Routledge, 1989). I wish to thank Mary Jacobus, Sally Shuttleworth, and Mario Moussa for comments and editorial suggestions on the original version.

[1]See Keith Walden, "The Road to Fat City: An Interpretation of the Development of Weight Consciousness in Western Society," *Historical Reflections* 12, no. 3 (1985): 331–73.

[2]See Michel Foucault, *The Use of Pleasure* (New York: Random House, 1986).

[3]See Rudolph Bell, *Holy Anorexia* (Chicago: University of Chicago Press, 1985); and Caroline Walker Bynum, *Holy Feast and Holy Fast: The Religious Significance of Food to Medieval Women* (Berkeley: University of California Press, 1987), pp. 31–48.

[4]See Kim Chernin, *The Obsession: Reflections on the Tyranny of Slenderness* (New York: Harper and Row, 1981).

mounds of food eaten luring an average binge. Such presentations create a "side show" relationship between the ("normal") audience and those on view ("the freaks"). To the degree that the audience may nonetheless recognize themselves in the behavior or reported experiences of those on stage, they confront themselves as "pathological" or outside the norm.

Of course, many of these behaviors are outside the norm, if only because of the financial resources they require. But preoccupation with fat, diet, and slenderness are not abnormal.[5] Indeed, such preoccupation may function as one of the most powerful normalizing mechanisms of our century, insuring the production of self-monitoring and self-disciplining "docile bodies" sensitive to any departure from social norms and habituated to self-improvement and self-transformation in the service of those norms. Seen in this light, the focus on "pathology," disorder, accident, unexpected disaster, and bizarre behavior obscures the normalizing function of the technologies of diet and body management. For women, who are subject to such controls more profoundly and, historically, more ubiquitously than men, the focus on "pathology" (unless embedded in a political analysis) diverts recognition from a central means of the reproduction of gender.

In this essay I examine the normalizing role of diet and exercise by analyzing popular representations through which their cultural meaning is crystallized, metaphorically encoded, and transmitted. More specifically, I pursue here Mary Douglas's insight that images of the "microcosm"—the physical body—may symbolically reproduce central vulnerabilities and anxieties of the "macrocosm"—the social body.[6] I will explore this insight by reading, as the text or surface on which culture is symbolically written, some dominant meanings that are connected, in our time, to the imagery of slenderness.[7]

The first step in my argument is a decoding of the contemporary slenderness ideal so as to reveal the psychic anxieties and moral valuations contained within it—valuations concerning correct and incorrect management of impulse and desire. In the process I describe a key contrast between two different symbolic functions of body shape and size: (1) the designation of social position, such as class status or gender role;

---

[5]See Thomas Cash, Barbara Winstead, and Louis Janda, "The Great American Shape-up," *Psychology Today* (April 1986); and "Dieting: The Losing Game," *Time* (Jan. 20, 1986), among numerous other general reports. Concerning women's preoccupation in particular, see note 24 below.

[6]See Mary Douglas, *Natural Symbols* (New York: Pantheon, 1982); and her *Purity and Danger* (London: Routledge and Kegan Paul, 1966).

[7]This approach presupposes, of course, that popular cultural images *have* meaning and are not merely arbitrary formations spawned by the whimsy of fashion, the vicissitudes of Madison Avenue, or the logic of post-industrial capitalism, within which (as has been argued, by Fredric Jameson and others) the attraction of a product or image derives solely from pure differentiation, from its cultural positioning, its suggestion of the novel or new. Within such a postmodern logic, Gail Faurschou argues, "Fashion has become the commodity 'par excellence.' It is fed by all of capitalism's incessant, frantic, reproductive passion and power. Fashion *is* the logic of planned obsolescence—not just the necessity for market survival, but the cycle of desire itself, the endless process through which the body is decoded and recoded, in order to define and inhabit the newest territorialized spaces of capital's expansion." ("Fashion and the Cultural Logic of Postmodernity," *Canadian Journal of Political and Social Theory* 11, no 1–2 [1987]: 72.) While I don't disagree with Faurschou's general characterization of fashion here, the heralding of an absolute historical break, after which images have become completely empty of history, substance, and symbolic determination, seems itself an embodiment, rather than a demystifier, of the compulsively innovative logic of postmodernity. More important to the argument of this piece, a postmodern logic cannot explain the cultural hold of the slenderness ideal, long after its novelty has worn off. Many times, in fact, the principle of the new has made tentative, but ultimately nominal, gestures toward the end of the reign of thinness, announcing a "softer," "curvier" look, and so forth. How many women have picked up magazines whose covers declared such a turn, only to find that the images within remained essentially continuous with prevailing norms? Large breasts may be making a comeback, but they are attached to extremely thin, often athletic bodies. Here, I would suggest, there are constraints on the pure logic of postmodernity—constraints that this essay tries to explore.

and (2) the outer indication of the spiritual, moral, or emotional state of the individual. Next, aided by the significant work of Robert Crawford, I turn to the social body of consumer culture in order to demonstrate how the "correct" management of desire in that culture, requiring as it does a contradictory double-bind construction of personality, inevitably produces an unstable bulimic personality-type as its norm, along with the contrasting extremes of obesity and self-starvation.[8] These symbolize, I will argue, the contradictions of the social body—contradictions that make self-management a continual and virtually impossible task in our culture. Finally, I introduce gender into this symbolic framework, showing how additional resonances (concerning the cultural management of female desire, on the one hand, and female flight from a purely reproductive destiny, on the other) have overdetermined slenderness as the current ideal for women.

Contemporary Anxiety and the Enemy Flab

In the magazine show "20/20," several ten-year-old boys were shown some photos of fashion models. The models were pencil-thin. Yet the pose was such that a small bulge of hip was forced, through the action of the body, into protuberance—as is natural, unavoidable on any but the most skeletal or the most tautly developed bodies. We bend over, we sit down, and the flesh coalesces in spots. These young boys, pointing to the hips, disgustedly pronounced the models to be "fat." Watching the show, I was appalled at the boys' reaction. Yet I could not deny that I had also been surprised at my own current perceptions while re-viewing female bodies in movies from the 1970s; what once appeared slender and fit now seemed loose and flabby. *Weight* was not the key element in these changed perceptions—my standards had not come to favor *thinner* bodies—rather, I had come to expect a tighter, smoother, more contained body profile (see Figure 1, which dramatically captures the essence of this ideal).

The self-criticisms of the anorectic, too, are usually focused on particular soft, protuberant areas of the body (most often the stomach) rather than on the body as a whole. Karen, in Ira Sacker and Marc Zimmer's *Dying to Be Thin,* tries to dispel what she sees as the myth that the anorectic misperceives her whole body as fat:

> I hope I'm expressing myself properly here, because this is important. You have to understand. I don't see my whole body as fat. When I look in the mirror I don't really see a fat person there. I see certain things about me that are really thin. Like my arms and legs. But I can tell the minute I eat certain things that my stomach blows up like a pig's. I know it gets distended. And it's disgusting. That's what I keep to myself—hug to myself.[9]

Figure 1

[8]See Robert Crawford, "A Cultural Account of 'Health'—Self-Control, Release, and the Social Body," in John McKinlay, ed., *Issues in the Political Economy of Health Care* (New York: Methuen, 1985), pp. 60–103.

[9]Ira Sacker and Marc Zimmer, *Dying to Be Thin* (New York: Warner, 1987), p. 57.

Or Barbara, from Dalma Heyn's article on "Body Vision":

> Sometimes my body looks so bloated, I don't want to get dressed. I like the way it looks for exactly two days each month: usually, the eighth and ninth days after my period. Every other day, my breasts, my stomach—they're just awful lumps, bumps, bulges. My body can turn on me at any moment; it is an out-of-control mass of flesh.[10]

Much has been made of such descriptions, from both psychoanalytic and feminist perspectives. But for now I wish to pursue these images of unwanted bulges and erupting stomachs in another direction than that of gender symbolism. I want to consider them as a metaphor for anxiety about internal processes out of control—uncontained desire, unrestrained hunger, uncontrolled impulse. Images of bodily eruption frequently function symbolically in this way in contemporary horror movies and werewolf films (*The Howling, A Teen-Age Werewolf in London*) and in David Cronenberg's remake of *The Fly*. The original *Fly* imagined a mechanical joining of fly parts and person parts, a variation on the standard "half-man, half-beast" image. In Cronenberg's *Fly,* as in the werewolf genre, a new, alien, libidinous, and uncontrollable self literally bursts through the seams of the victims' old flesh. (A related, frequently copied image occurs in *Alien,* where a parasite erupts from the chest of the human host.) In advertisements, the construction of the body as an alien attacker, threatening to erupt in an unsightly display of bulging flesh, is a ubiquitous cultural image.

Figure 2

Until the 1980s, excess weight was the target of most ads for diet products; today, one is much more likely to find the enemy constructed as bulge, fat, or flab. "Now," a typical ad runs, "get rid of those embarrassing bumps, bulges, large stomach, flabby breasts and buttocks. Feel younger, and help prevent cellulite buildup. . . . Have a nice shape with no tummy." To achieve such results (often envisioned as the absolute eradication of body, as in "no tummy") a violent assault on the enemy is usually required; bulges must be "attacked" and "destroyed," fat "burned," and stomachs (or, more disgustedly, "guts") must be "busted" and "eliminated" (Figure 2). The increasing popularity of liposuction, a far from totally safe technique developed specifically to suck out the unwanted bulges of people of normal weight (it is not recommended for the obese), suggests how far our disgust with bodily bulges has gone. The ideal here is of a body that is absolutely tight, contained, "bolted down,"

---

[10]Dalma Heyn, "Body Vision?" *Mademoiselle* (April 1987): 213.

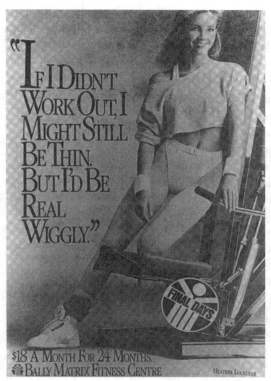

"IF I DIDN'T WORK OUT, I MIGHT STILL BE THIN, BUT I'D BE REAL WIGGLY."

FINAL DAYS

$18 A MONTH FOR 24 MONTHS.
BALLY MATRIX FITNESS CENTRE

HEATHER LOCKLEAR

Figure 3

firm: in other words, a body that is protected against eruption from within, whose internal processes are under control. Areas that are soft, loose, or "wiggly" are unacceptable, even on extremely thin bodies. Cellulite management, like liposuction, has nothing to do with weight loss, and everything to do with the quest for firm bodily margins.

This perspective helps illuminate an important continuity of meaning in our culture between compulsive dieting and body-building, and it reveals why it has been so easy for contemporary images of female attractiveness to oscillate between a spare, "minimalist" look and a solid, muscular, athletic look. The coexistence of these seemingly disparate images does not indicate that a postmodern universe of empty, endlessly differentiating images now reigns. Rather, the two ideals, though superficially very different, are united in battle against a common enemy: the soft, the loose, unsolid, excess flesh. It is perfectly permissible in our culture (even for women) to have substantial weight and bulk—so long as it is tightly managed. Simply to be slim is not enough—the flesh must not "wiggle" (Figure 3). Here we arrive at one source of insight into why it is that the image of ideal slenderness has grown thinner and thinner throughout the 1980s and early 1990s, and why women with extremely slender bodies often still see themselves as fat. Unless one takes to muscle-building, to achieve a flab-free, excess-free body one must trim very near the bone.

Slenderness and the Inner State of the Self

The moral—and, as we shall see, economic—coding of the fat/slender body in terms of its capacity for self-containment and the control of impulse and desire represents the culmination of a developing historical change in the social symbolism of body weight and size. Until the late nineteenth century, the central discriminations marked were those of class, race, and gender; the body indicated social identity and "place." So, for example, the bulging stomachs of successful mid-nineteenth-century businessmen and politicians were a symbol of bourgeois success, an outward manifestation of their accumulated wealth.[11] By contrast, the gracefully slender body announced aristocratic status; disdainful of the bourgeois need to display wealth and power ostentatiously, it commanded social space invisibly rather than aggressively, seemingly above the commerce in appetite or the need to eat. Subsequently, this ideal began to be appropriated by the status-seeking middle class, as slender wives became the showpieces of their husbands' success.[12]

---

[11]See Lois Banner, *American Beauty* (Chicago: University of Chicago Press, 1983), p. 232.

[12]Banner, *American Beauty*, pp. 53–55.

Corpulence went out of middle-class vogue at the end of the century (even William Howard Taft, who had weighed over three hundred pounds while in office, went on a reducing diet). Social power had come to be less dependent on the sheer accumulation of material wealth and more connected to the ability to control and manage the labor and resources of others. At the same time, excess body weight came to be seen as reflecting moral of personal inadequacy, or lack of will.[13] These associations are possible only in a culture of overabundance—that is, in a society in which those who control the production of "culture" have more than enough to eat. The moral requirement to diet depends on the material preconditions that make the *choice* to diet an option and the possibility of personal "excess" a reality. Although slenderness continues to retain some of its traditional class associations ("a woman can never be too rich or too thin"), the importance of this equation has eroded considerably since the 1970s. Increasingly, the size and shape of the body have come to operate as a market of personal, internal order (or disorder)—as a symbol for the emotional, moral, or spiritual state of the individual.

Consider one particularly clear example, that of changes in the meaning of the muscled body. Muscularity has had a variety of cultural meanings that have prevented the well-developed body from playing a major role in middle-class conceptions of attractiveness. Of course, muscles have chiefly symbolized and continue to symbolize masculine power as physical strength, frequently operating as a means of coding the "naturalness" of sexual difference, as a *Time* cover and a Secret ad illustrate (Figures 4 and 5). But at the same time (and as the Secret ad illustrates), they have been associated with manual labor and proletarian status, and they have often been suffused with racial meaning as well (as in numerous film representations of sweating, glistening bodies belonging to black slaves and prizefighters). Under the racial and class biases of our culture, muscles thus have been associated with the insensitive, unintelligent, and animalistic (recall the well-developed Marlon Brando as the emotionally primitive, physically abusive Stanley Kowalski in *A Streetcar Named Desire*). Moreover, as the body itself is dominantly imagined within the West as belonging to the "nature" side of a nature/culture duality, the *more* body one has had, the more uncultured and uncivilized one has been expected to be.

Figure 4

Today, however, the well-muscled body has become a cultural icon; "working out" is a glamorized and sexualized yuppie activity. No longer signifying inferior status (except when developed to extremes, at which point the old association of muscles with brute, unconscious materiality surfaces once more), the firm, developed body has become a symbol of correct *attitude;* it means that one "cares" about oneself and how one appears to others, suggesting willpower, energy, control over infantile impulse, the ability to "shape your life" (Figure 6). "You exercise, you diet," says Heather Locklear, promoting Bally Matrix Fitness Centre on television, "and you can do anything you want." Muscles express sexuality, but controlled,

---

[13]See Walden, "Road to Fat City," pp. 334–35, 353.

Figure 5

Figure 6

managed sexuality that is not about to erupt in unwanted and embarrassing display.[14]

To the degree that the question of class still operates in all this, it relates to the category of social mobility (or lack of it) rather than class *location.* So, for example, when associations of fat and lower class status exist, they are usually mediated by moral qualities of being perceived as indicative of laziness, lack of discipline, unwillingness to conform, and absence of all those "managerial" abilities that, according to the dominant ideology, confer upward mobility (Figure 7). Correspondingly, in popular teen movies such as *Flashdance* and *Vision Quest,* the ability of the (working-class) heroine and hero to pare, prune, tighten, and master the body operates as a clear symbol of successful upward aspiration, of the penetrability of class boundaries to those who have "the right stuff." These movies (as one title makes explicit) are contemporary "quest myths"; like their prototype, *Rocky,* they follow the struggle of an individual to attain a personal grail, against all odds and through numerous trials. But unlike the film quests of a previous era (which sent Mr. Smith to Washington and Mr. Deeds to town to battle the respective social evils of corrupt government and big business), *Flashdance* and *Vision Quest* render the hero's and heroine's commitment, will and spiritual integrity through the metaphors of weight loss, exercise, and tolerance of and ability to conquer physical pain and exhaustion. (In *Vision Quest,* for example, the audience is encouraged to admire the young wrestler's perseverance when he ignores the fainting spells and nosebleeds caused by his rigorous training and dieting.)

---

[14]I thank Mario Moussa for this point, and for the Heather Locklear quotation.

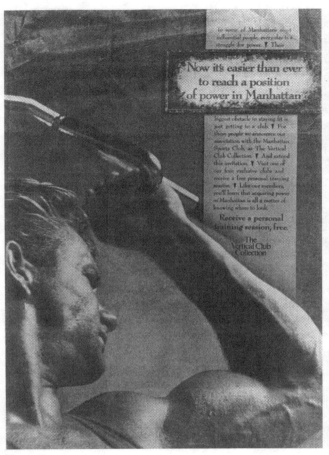

Figure 7

Not surprisingly, young people with eating disorders often thematize their own experience in similar terms, as in the following excerpt from an interview with a young woman runner:

Well, I had the willpower, I could train for competition, and I could turn down food any time. I remember feeling like I was on a constant high. And the pain? Sure, there was pain. It was incredible. Between the hunger and the muscle pain from the constant workouts? I can't tell you how much I hurt.

You may think I was crazy to put myself through constant, intense pain. But you have to remember, I was fighting a battle. And when you get hurt in a battle, you're proud of it. Sure, you may scream inside, but if you're brave and really good, then you take it quietly, because you know it's the price you pay for winning. And I needed to win. I really felt that if I didn't win, I would die . . . all these enemy troops were coming at me, and I had to outsmart them. If I could discipline myself enough—if I could keep myself lean and strong—then I could win. The pain was just a natural thing I had to deal with.[15]

As in *Vision Quest,* the external context is training for an athletic event. But here, too, that goal becomes subordinated to an internal one.

The real battle, ultimately, is with the self. At this point, the limitations of the brief history presented in the opening paragraph of this essay are revealed. In that paragraph, the contemporary preoccupation with diet is contrasted to historical projects of body management that were suffused with moral meaning. In this section, however, I have suggested that examination of even the most shallow representations (teen movies) discloses a moral ideology—one, in fact, seemingly close to the aristocratic Greek ideal described by Foucault in *The Use of Pleasure.* The central element of that ideal, as Foucault describes it, is "an agonistic relation with the self"—aimed, not at the extirpation of desire and hunger in the interests of "purity" (as in the Christian strain of dualism), but at a "virile" mastery of desire through constant "spiritual combat."[16]

For the Greeks, however, the "virile" mastery of desire took place in a culture that valorized moderation. The culture of contemporary body-management, struggling to manage desire in a system dedicated to the proliferation of desirable commodities, is very different. In cultural fantasies such as *Vision Quest* and *Flashdance,* self-mastery is presented as an attainable and stable state; but, as I argue in the next section of this essay, the reality of the contemporary agonism of the self is another matter entirely.

---

[15]Sacker and Zimmer, *Dying to Be Thin,* pp. 149–150.

[16]Foucault, *The Use of Pleasure,* pp. 64–70.

Slenderness and the Social Body

Mary Douglas, looking on the body as a system of "natural symbols" that reproduce social categories and concerns, has argued that anxiety about the maintenance of rigid bodily boundaries (manifested, for example, in rituals and prohibitions concerning excreta, saliva, and the strict delineation of "inside" and "outside") is most evident and intense in societies whose external boundaries are under attack.[17] Let me hypothesize, similarly, that preoccupation with the "internal" management of the body (that is, management of its desires) is produced by instabilities in what could be called the macro-regulation of desire within the system of the social body.

In advanced consumer capitalism, as Robert Crawford has elegantly argued, an unstable, agonistic construction of personality is produced by the contradictory structure of economic life.[18] On the one hand, as producers of goods and services we must sublimate, delay, repress desires for immediate gratification; we must cultivate the work ethic. On the other hand, as consumers we must display a boundless capacity to capitulate to desire and indulge in impulse; we must hunger for constant and immediate satisfaction. The regulation of desire thus becomes an ongoing problem, as we find ourselves continually besieged by temptation, while socially condemned for overindulgence. (Of course, those who cannot afford to indulge their desires as consumers, teased and frustrated by the culture, face a much harsher dilemma.)

Food and diet are central arenas for the expression of these contradictions. On television and in popular magazines, with a flip of the page or barely a pause between commercials, images of luscious foods and the rhetoric of craving and desire are replaced by advertisements for grapefruit diets, low-calorie recipes, and exercise equipment. Even more disquieting than these manifest oppositions, however, are the constant attempts by advertisers to mystify them, suggesting that the contradiction doesn't really exist, that one can "have it all." Diets and exercise programs are accordingly presented with the imagery of instant gratification ("From Fat to Fabulous in 21 Days," "Size 22 to Size 10 in No Time Flat," "Six Minutes to an Olympic-Class Stomach") and effortlessness ("3,000 Sit-Ups Without Moving an Inch . . . 10 Miles of Jogging Lying Flat on Your Back" [Figure 8], "85 Pounds Without Dieting," and even, shamelessly, "Exercise Without Exercise"). In reality, however, the opposition is not so easily reconciled. Rather, it presents a classic double bind, in which the self is torn in two mutually incompatible directions. The contradiction is not an abstract one but stems from the specific historical construction of a "consuming passion" from which all inclinations toward balance, moderation, rationality, and foresight have been excluded.

Conditioned to lose control at the mere sight of desirable products, we can master our desires only by creating rigid defenses against them. The slender body codes the tantalizing ideal of a well-managed self in which all is kept in order despite the contradictions of consumer culture. Thus, whether or not the struggle is played out in terms of food and diet, many of us may find our lives vacillating between a daytime rigidly ruled by the "performance principle" and nights and weekends that capitulate to unconscious "letting go" (food, shopping, liquor, television, and other addictive drugs). In this way, the central contradiction of the system inscribes itself on our bodies, and bulimia emerges as a characteristic modern personality construction. For bulimia precisely and explicitly expresses the extreme development of the hunger for unrestrained consumption (exhibited in the bulimic's uncontrollable food binges) existing in unstable tension alongside the requirement that we sober up, "clean up our act," get back in firm control on Monday morning (the necessity for purge—exhibited in the

---

[17]See Douglas, *Purity and Danger*, pp. 114–28.

[18]See Crawford, "A Cultural Account of 'Health.'"

Figure 8

bulimic's vomiting, compulsive exercising, and laxative purges).

The same structural contradiction is inscribed in what has been termed (incorrectly) the "paradox" that we have an "epidemic" of anorexia nervosa in this country "despite the fact that we have an overweight majority."[19] Far from paradoxical, the coexistence of anorexia and obesity reveals the instability of the contemporary personality construction, the difficulty of finding homeostasis between the producer and the consumer sides of the self. Bulimia embodies the unstable double bind of consumer capitalism, while anorexia and obesity embody an attempted resolution of that double bind. Anorexia could thus be seen as an extreme development of the capacity for self-denial and repression of desire (the work ethic in absolute control); obesity, as an extreme capacity to capitulate to desire (consumerism in control). Both are rooted in the same consumer-culture construction of desire as overwhelming and overtaking the self: Given that construction, we can only respond either with total submission or rigid defense.

Neither anorexia nor obesity is accepted by the culture as an appropriate response. The absolute conquest of hunger and desire (even in symbolic form) can never be tolerated by a consumer system—even if the Christian dualism of our culture also predisposes us to be dazzled by the anorectic's ability seemingly to transcend the flesh. Anorectics are proud of this ability, but, as the disorder progresses, they usually feel the need to hide their skeletal bodies from those around them. If cultural attitudes toward the anorectic are ambivalent, however, reactions to the obese are not. As Marcia Millman documents in *Such a Pretty Face,* the obese elicit blinding rage and disgust in our culture and are often viewed in terms that suggest an infant sucking hungrily, unconsciously at its mother's breast: greedy, self-absorbed, lazy, without self-control or willpower.[20] People avoid sitting next to the obese (even when the space they take up is not intrusive); comics feel no need to restrain their cruelty; socially, they are considered unacceptable at public functions (one man wrote to "Dear Abby," saying that he was planning to replace his brother and sister-in-law as honor attendants at his

---

[19]John Farquhar, Stanford University Medical Center, quoted in "Dieting: The Losing Game," *Time* (Feb. 20, 1986): 57.

[20]See Marcia Millman, *Such a Pretty Face: Being Fat in America* (New York: Norton, 1980), esp. pp. 65–79.

wedding, because "they are both quite overweight"). Significantly, the part of the obese anatomy most often targeted for vicious attack, and most despised by the obese themselves, is the stomach, symbol of consumption (in the case of the obese, unrestrained consumption taking over the organism; one of Marcia Millman's interviewees recalls how the husband of a friend called hers "an awful, cancerous-looking growth").[21]

Slenderness Self-Management, and Normalization

Self-management in consumer culture, I have been arguing, becomes more elusive as it becomes more pressing. The attainment of an acceptable body is extremely difficult for those who do not come by it "naturally" (whether aided by genetics, metabolism, or high activity-level) and as the ideal becomes firmer and tauter it begins to exclude more and more people. Constant watchfulness over appetite and strenuous work on the body itself are required to conform to this ideal, while the most popular means of "correction"—dieting—often insures its own failure, as the experience of deprivation leads to compensatory binging, with its attendant feelings of defeat, worthlessness, and loss of hope. Between the media images of self-containment and self-mastery and the reality of constant, everyday stress and anxiety about one's appearance lies the chasm that produces bodies habituated to self-monitoring and self-normalization.

Ultimately, the body (besides being evaluated for its success or failure at getting itself in order) is seen as demonstrating correct or incorrect attitudes toward the demands of normalization itself. The obese and anorectic are therefore disturbing partly because they embody resistance to cultural norms. Bulimics, by contrast, typically strive for the conventionally attractive body shape dictated by their more "normative" pattern of managing desire. In the case of the obese, in particular, what is perceived as their defiant rebellion against normalization appears to be a source of the hostility they inspire. The anorectic at least pays homage to dominant cultural values, outdoing them in their own terms:

> I wanted people to look at me and see something special. I wanted to look in the face of a stranger and see admiration, so that I would know that I accomplished something that was just about impossible for most people, especially in our society. . . . From what I've seen, more people fail at losing weight than at any other single goal. I found out how to do what everyone else couldn't: I could lose as much or as little weight as I wanted. And that meant I was better than everyone else.[22]

The anorectic thus strives to stand above the crowd by excelling at its own rules; in so doing, however, she exposes the hidden penalties. But the obese—particularly those who claim to be happy although overweight—are perceived as not playing by the rules at all. If the rest of us are struggling to be acceptable and "normal," we cannot allow them to get away with it; they must be put in their place, be humiliated and defeated.

A number of talk shows have made this abundantly clear. On one, much of the audience reaction was given over to disbelief and to the attempt to prove to one obese woman that she was *not* happy: "I can't believe you don't want to be slim and beautiful, I just can't believe it." "I heard you talk a lot about how you feel good about yourself and you like yourself, but I really think you're kidding yourself." "It's hard for me to believe that Mary Jane is really happy . . . you don't fit into chairs, it's hard to get through the doorway. My God, on the subway, forget it." When Mary Jane persisted in her assertion that she was

---

[21]Millman, *Such a Pretty Face,* p. 77.

[22]Sacker and Zimmer, *Dying to Be Thin*, p. 32.

happy, she was warned, in a viciously self-righteous tone, that it would not last: "Mary Jane, to be the way you are today, you had better start going on a diet soon, because if you don't you're going to get bigger and bigger and bigger. It's true."[23] On another show, in an effort to subdue an increasingly hostile and offensive audience one of the doctor-guests kept trying to reassure them that the "fat and happy" target of their attacks did not *really* mean that she didn't *want* to lose weight; rather, she was simply tired of trying and failing. This construction allows people to give their sympathy to the obese, assuming as it does the obese person's acknowledgment that to be "normal" is the most desired goal, elusive only because of personal inadequacy. Those who are willing to present themselves as pitiable, in pain, and conscious of their own unattractiveness—often demonstrated, on these shows, by self-admissions about intimate physical difficulties, orgies of self-hate, or descriptions of gross consumption of food, win the sympathy and concern of the audience.

Slenderness and Gender

It has been amply documented that women in our culture are more tyrannized by the contemporary slenderness ideal than men are, as they typically have been by beauty ideals in general. It is far more important to men than to women that their partner be slim.[24] Women are much more prone than men to perceive themselves as too fat.[25] And, as is by now well known, girls and women are more likely to engage in crash dieting, laxative abuse, and compulsive exercising and are far more vulnerable to eating disorders than males. But eating disorders are not only "about" slenderness, any more than (as I have been arguing) slenderness is only—or even chiefly—about being physically thin. My aim in this section, therefore, is not to "explain" facts about which so much has now been written from historical, psychological, and sociological points of view. Rather, I want to remain with the image of the slender body, confronting it now both as a gendered body (the slender body as female body—the usual form in which the image is displayed) (Figure 9) and as a body whose gender meaning is never neutral. This layer of gender-coded signification, suffusing other meanings, overdetermines slenderness as a contemporary ideal of specifically *female* attractiveness.

The exploration of contemporary slenderness as a metaphor for the correct management of desire must take into account the fact that throughout dominant Western religious and philosophical traditions, the capacity for self-management is decisively coded as male. By contrast, all those bodily spontaneities—

---

[23]These quotations are taken from transcripts of the "Donahue" show, provided by Multimedia Entertainment, Cincinnati, Ohio.

[24]The discrepancy emerges very early. "We don't expect boys to be that handsome," says a nine-year-old girl in the California study cited above. "But boys expect girls to be perfect and beautiful. And skinny." A male classmate agrees: "Fat girls aren't like regular girls," he says. Many of my female students have described in their journals the pressure their boyfriends put on them to stay or get slim. These men have plenty of social support for such demands. Sylvester Stallone told Cornelia Guest that he likes his woman "anorexic"; she immediately lost twenty-four pounds (*Time* [April 18, 1988]: 89). But few men want their women to go that far. Actress Valerie Bertinelli reports (*Syracuse Post-Standard*) how her husband, Eddie Van Halen, "helps keep her in shape": "When I get too heavy, he says, 'Honey, lose weight.' Then when I get too thin, he says, 'I don't like making love with you, you've got to gain some weight.'"

[25]The most famous of such studies, by now replicated many times, appeared in *Glamour* (Feb. 1984): a poll of 33,000 women revealed that 75 percent considered themselves "too fat," while only 25 percent of them were above Metropolitan Life Insurance standards, and 30 percent were *below*. ("Feeling Fat in a Thin Society," p. 198). See also Kevin Thompson, "Larger Than Life," *Psychology Today* (April 1986); Dalma Heyn, "Why We're Never Satisfied with Our Bodies," *McCall's* (May 1982); Daniel Goleman, "Dislike of Own Body Found Common Among Women," *New York Times*, March 19, 1985.

Even a woman in great shape is, on the average, 21% fat.

Which makes our salami look even better —you see, Hebrew National salami is only 17% fat.

That's not only less than our model, Kim Cooper; it's 50% less than the leading Genoa salami.

43% less than Oscar Mayer bologna.

And 8% less than even Best Kosher's "low-salt, low-fat, no-sugar" salami.

Mind you, this is no diet salami. This is good, old-fashioned, 100% beef, kosher salami.

So the next time you feel like a great-tasting, nutritional, low-fat lunch, skip the tuna and cottage cheese, and have some salami. That's what Kim does. How do you think she stays 79% fat free?

There's more fat on her than on our salami.

Kim Cooper 79% Fat Free

HEBREW NATIONAL

"You Should Be So Lean."

Figure 9

hunger, sexuality, the emotions—seen as needful of containment and control have been culturally constructed and coded as female.[26] The management of specifically female desire, therefore, is in phallocentric cultures a doubly freighted problem. Women's desires are by their very nature excessive, irrational, threatening to erupt and challenge the patriarchal order.

Some writers have argued that female hunger (as a code for female desire) is especially problematized during periods of disruption and change in established gender-relations and in the position of women. In such periods (of which our own is arguably one), nightmare images of what Bram Dijkstra has called "the consuming woman" theme proliferate in art and literature (images representing female desire unleashed), while dominant constructions of the female body become more sylph-like—unlike the body of a fully developed woman, more like that of an adolescent or boy (images that might be called female desire unborn). Dijkstra argues such a case concerning the late nineteenth century, pointing to the devouring sphinxes and bloodsucking vampires of *fin-de-siècle* art, and the accompanying vogue for elongated, "sublimely emaciated" female bodies.[27] A commentator of the time vividly describes the emergence of a new body-style, not very unlike our own:

> Women can change the cut of their clothes at will, but how can they change the cut of their anatomies? And yet, they have done just this thing. Their shoulders have become narrow and slightly sloping, their throats more slender, their hips smaller and their arms and legs elongated to an extent that suggest that bed, upon which the robber, Procrustes, used to stretch his victims.[28]

The fact that our own era has witnessed a comparable shift (from the hourglass figure of the fifties to the androgynous, increasingly elongated, slender look that has developed over the past decade) cries out for

---

[26]On cultural associations of male with mind and female with matter, see, for instance, Dorothy Dinnerstein, *The Mermaid and the Minotaur: Sexual Arrangements and Human Malaise* (New York: Harper and Row, 1976); Genevieve Lloyd, *The Man of Reason* (Minneapolis: University of Minnesota Press, 1984); and Luce Irigaray, *Speculum of the Other Woman* (Ithaca: Cornell University Press, 1985).

[27]Bram Dijkstra, *Idols of Perversity* (New York: Oxford University Press, 1986), p. 29.

[28]"Mutable Beauty," *Saturday Night* (Feb. 1, 1892): 9.

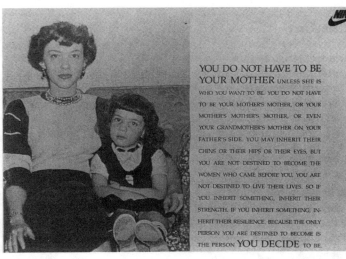

YOU DO NOT HAVE TO BE
YOUR MOTHER UNLESS SHE IS
WHO YOU WANT TO BE. YOU DO NOT HAVE
TO BE YOUR MOTHER'S MOTHER, OR YOUR
MOTHER'S MOTHER'S MOTHER, OR EVEN
YOUR GRANDMOTHER'S MOTHER ON YOUR
FATHER'S SIDE. YOU MAY INHERIT THEIR
CHINS OR THEIR HIPS OR THEIR EYES, BUT
YOU ARE NOT DESTINED TO BECOME THE
WOMEN WHO CAME BEFORE YOU. YOU ARE
NOT DESTINED TO LIVE THEIR LIVES. SO IF
YOU INHERIT SOMETHING, INHERIT THEIR
STRENGTH. IF YOU INHERIT SOMETHING, IN-
HERIT THEIR RESILIENCE. BECAUSE THE ONLY
PERSON YOU ARE DESTINED TO BECOME IS
THE PERSON YOU DECIDE TO BE.

Figure 10

interpretation. This shift, however, needs to be interpreted not only from the standpoint of male anxiety over women's desires (Dijkstra's analysis, while crucial, is only half the story) but also from the standpoint of the women who embrace the "new look." For them it may have a very different meaning; it may symbolize, not so much the containment of female desire, as its liberation from a domestic, reproductive destiny. The fact that the slender female body can carry both these seemingly contradictory meanings is one reason, I would suggest, for its compelling attraction in periods of gender change.[29]

To elaborate this argument in more detail earlier, I presented some quotations from interviews with eating-disordered women in which they describe their revulsion to breasts, stomachs, and all other bodily bulges. At that point I subjected these quotations to a gender-neutral reading. While not rescinding that interpretation, I want to overlay it now with another reading, which I present in "Anorexia Nervosa: Psychopathology as the Crystallization of Culture." There, I suggest that the characteristic anorexic revulsion toward hips, stomach, and breasts (often accompanied by disgust at menstruation and relief at amenorrhoea) might be viewed as expressing rebellion against maternal, domestic femininity—a femininity that represents both the suffocating control the anorectic experiences her own mother as having had over her, and the mother's actual lack of position and authority outside the domestic arena. (A Nike ad [Figure 10] embodies both these elements, as the "strength" of the mother is depicted in the containing arm that encircles her small daughter, while young women reading the ad are reassured that they can exercise their strength in other, nonmaternal ways.) Here we encounter another reason for anxiety over soft, protuberant body-parts. They evoke helpless infancy and symbolize maternal femininity as it has been constructed over the past hundred years in the West. That femininity, as Dorothy Dinnerstein has argued, is perceived as both frighteningly powerful and, as the child comes increasingly to recognize the hierarchical nature of the sexual division of labor, utterly powerless.[30]

The most literal symbolic form of maternal femininity is represented by the nineteenth-century hourglass figure, emphasizing breasts and hips—the markers of reproductive femaleness—against a fragile wasp waist.[31] It is not until the post-World War II period, with its relocation of middle-class women

---

[29]Mary Jacobus and Sally Shuttleworth (personal communication), pointing to the sometimes boyish figure of the "new woman" of late Victorian literature, have suggested to me the appropriateness of this interpretation for the late Victorian era; I have, however, chosen to argue the point only with respect to the current context.

[30]Dinnerstein, *The Mermaid and the Minotaur*, pp. 28–34. See Chernin, *The Obsession*, for an exploration of the connection between early infant experience and attitudes toward the fleshy female body.

[31]Historian LeeAnn Whites has pointed out to me how perverse this body symbolism seems when we remember what a pregnant and nursing body is actually like. The hourglass figure is really more correctly a symbolic advertisement to men of the woman's reproductive, domestic sphere than a representation of her reproductive *body*.

from factory to home and its coercive bourgeois dualism of the happy homemaker-mother and the responsible, provider-father, that such clear bodily demarcation of "male" and "female" spheres surfaces again. The era of the cinch belt, the pushup bra, and Marilyn Monroe could be viewed, for the body, as an era of "resurgent Victorianism."[32] It was also the last coercively normalizing body-ideal to reign before boyish slenderness began its ascendancy in the mid-1960s.

From this perspective, one might speculate that the boys who reacted with disgust or anxiety to fleshy female parts were reacting to evocations of maternal power, newly threatening in an age when women are making their way into arenas traditionally reserved for men: law, business, higher education, politics, and so forth.[33] The buxom Sophia Loren was a sex goddess in an era when women were encouraged to define their deepest desires in terms of service to home, husband, and family. Today, it is required of female desire, loose in the male world, to be normalized according to the professional (and male) standards of that world; female bodies, accordingly, must be stripped of all psychic resonances with maternal power. From the standpoint of male anxiety, the lean body of the career businesswoman today may symbolize such a neutralization. With her body and her dress she declares symbolic allegiance to the professional, white, male world along with her lack of intention to subvert that arena with alternative "female values." At the same time, insofar as she is clearly "dressing up," *playing* male (almost always with a "softening" fashion touch to establish traditional feminine decorativeness, and continually cautioned against the dire consequences of allotting success higher priority than her looks), she represents no serious competition (symbolically, that is) to the real men of the workplace (Figures 11 and 12).

For many women, however, disidentification with the maternal body, far from symbolizing reduced power, may symbolize (as it did in the 1890s and 1920s) freedom from a reproductive destiny and a construction of femininity seen as constraining and suffocating. Correspondingly, taking on the accoutrements of the white, male world may be experienced as empowerment by women themselves, and as their chance to embody qualities—detachment, self-containment,

Is your face paying the price of success?

Figure 11

---

[32]See Banner, *American Beauty*, pp. 283–85.

[33]It is no accident, I believe, that Dolly Parton, now down to one hundred pounds and truly looking as though she might snap in two in a strong wind, opened her new show with a statement of its implicitly anti-feminist premise: "I'll bust my butt to please you!" (Surely she already has?) Her television presence is now recessive, beseeching, desiring only to serve; clearly, her packagers are exploiting the cultural resonances of her diminished physicality. Parton, of course, is no androgynous body-type. Rather, like Vanna White of "Wheel of Fortune" (who also lost a great deal of weight at one point in her career and is obsessive about staying thin), she has tremendous appeal to those longing for a more traditional femininity in an era when women's public presence and power have greatly increased. Parton's and White's large breasts evoke a nurturing, maternal sexuality. But after weight-reduction regimens set to anorexic standards, those breasts now adorn bodies that are vulnerably thin, with fragile, spindly arms and legs like those of young colts. Parton and White suggest the pleasures of nurturant female sexuality without any encounter with its powers and dangers.

Figure 12

Figure 13

self-mastery, control—that are highly valued in our culture. The slender body, as I have argued earlier, symbolizes such qualities. "It was about power," says Kim Morgan, speaking in the documentary *The Waist Land* of the obsession with slenderness that led to her anorexia, "that was the big thing . . . something I could throw in people's faces, and they would look at me and I'd only weigh this much, but I was strong and in control, and hey *you're* sloppy.[34] The taking on of "male" power as self-mastery is another locus where, for all their surface dissimilarities, the shedding of weight and the development of muscles intersect. Appropriately, the new "Joy of Cooking" takes place in the gym, in one advertisement that shamelessly exploits the associations of female body-building with liberation from a traditional, domestic destiny (Figure 13).

In the intersection of these gentler issues and more general cultural dilemmas concerning the management of desire, we see how the tightly managed body—whether demonstrated through sleek, minimalist lines or firmly developed muscles—has been overdetermined as a contemporary ideal of specifically female attractiveness. The axis of consumption/production is gender-overlaid, as I have argued, by the hierarchical dualism that constructs a dangerous, appetitive, bodily "female principle" in opposition to a masterful "male" will. We would thus expect that when the regulation of desire becomes

---

[34] *The Waist Land: Eating Disorders in America*, 1985, Gannett Corporation, MTI Teleprograms. The analysis presented here becomes more complicated with bulimia, in which the hungering "female" self refuses to be annihilated, and feminine ideals are typically not rejected by embraced.

especially problematic (as it is in advanced consumer cultures), women and their bodies will pay the greatest symbolic and material toll. When such a situation is compounded by anxiety about *women's* desires in periods when traditional forms of gender organization are being challenged, this toll is multiplied. It would be wrong to suppose, however, that it is exacted through the simple *repression* of female hunger. Rather, here as elsewhere, power works also "from below," as women associate slenderness with self-management, by way of the experience of newfound freedom (from a domestic destiny) and empowerment in the public arena. In this connection we might note the difference between contemporary ideals of slenderness, coded in terms of self-mastery and expressed through traditionally "male" body symbolism, and mid-Victorian ideals of female slenderness, which symbolically emphasized reproductive femininity corseted under tight "external" constraints. But whether externally bound or internally managed, no body can escape either the imprint of culture or its gendered meanings.

HERMAPHRODITES WITH ATTITUDE: MAPPING THE EMERGENCE OF INTERSEX POLITICAL ACTIVISM

Cheryl Chase

The insistence on two clearly distinguished sexes has calamitous personal consequences for the many individuals who arrive in the world with sexual anatomy that fails to be easily distinguished as male or female. Such individuals are labeled "intersexuals" or "hermaphrodites" by modem medical discourse.[1] About one in a hundred births exhibits some anomaly in sex differentiation,[2] and about one in two thousand is different enough to render problematic the question "Is it a boy or a girl?"[3] Since the early 1960s, nearly every major city in the United States has had a hospital with a standing team of medical experts who intervene in these cases to assign—through drastic surgical means—a male or female status to intersex infants. The fact that this system for preserving the boundaries of the categories male and female has existed for so long without drawing criticism or scrutiny from any quarter indicates the extreme discomfort that sexual ambiguity excites in our culture. Pediatric genital surgeries literalize what might otherwise be considered a theoretical operation: the attempted production of normatively sexed bodies and gendered subjects through constitutive acts of violence. Over the last few years, however, intersex people have begun to politicize intersex identities, thus transforming intensely personal experiences of violation into collective opposition to the medical regulation of bodies that queer the foundations of heteronormative identification and desires.

Hermaphrodites: Medical Authority and Cultural Invisibility

Many people familiar with the ideas that gender is a phenomenon not adequately described by male/ female dimorphism and that the interpretation of physical sex differences is culturally constructed

My appreciation goes to Susan Stryker for her extensive contributions to the structure and substance of this essay.

[1]Claude J. Migeon, Gary D. Berkovitz, and Terry R. Brown, "Sexual Differentiation and Ambiguity," in *Wilkins: The Diagnosis and Treatment of Endocrine Disorders in Childhood and Adolescence,* ed. Michael S. Kappy, Robert M. Blizzard, and Claude J. Migeon (Springfield, Ill.: Charles C. Thomas, 1994), 573–715.

[2]Lalitha Raman-Wilms et al., "Fetal Genital Effects of First-Trimester Sex Hormone Exposure: A Meta-Analysis," *Obstetrics and Gynecology* 85 (1995): 141–48.

[3]Anne Fausto-Sterling, *Body Building: How Biologists Construct Sexuality* (New York: Basic Books, forthcoming).

remain surprised to learn just how variable sexual anatomy is.[4] Though the male/female binary is constructed as natural and presumed to be immutable, the phenomenon of intersexuality offers clear evidence to the contrary and furnishes an opportunity to deploy "nature" strategically to disrupt heteronormative systems of sex, gender, and sexuality. The concept of bodily sex, in popular usage, refers to multiple components including karyotype (organization of sex chromosomes), gonadal differentiation (e.g., ovarian or testicular), genital morphology, configuration of internal reproductive organs, and pubertal sex characteristics such as breasts and facial hair. Because these characteristics are expected to be concordant in each individual—either all male or all female—an observer, once having attributed male or female sex to a particular individual, assumes the values of other unobserved characteristics.[5]

Because medicine intervenes quickly in intersex births to change the infant's body, the phenomenon of intersexuality is today largely unknown outside specialized medical practices. General public awareness of intersex bodies slowly vanished in modern Western European societies as medicine gradually appropriated to itself the authority to interpret—and eventually manage—the category which had previously been widely known as "hermaphroditism." Victorian medical taxonomy began to efface hermaphroditism as a legitimated status by establishing mixed gonadal histology as a necessary criterion for "true" hermaphroditism. By this criterion, both ovarian and testicular tissue types had to be present. Given the limitations of Victorian surgery and anesthesia, such confirmation was impossible in a living patient. All other anomalies were reclassified as "pseudohermaphroditisms" masking a "true sex" determined by the gonads.[6]

With advances in anesthesia, surgery, embryology, and endocrinology, however, twentieth-century medicine moved from merely labeling intersexed bodies to the far more invasive practice of "fixing" them to conform with a diagnosed true sex. The techniques and protocols for physically transforming intersexed bodies were developed primarily at Johns Hopkins University in Baltimore during the 1920s and 1930s under the guidance of urologist Hugh Hampton Young. "Only during the last few years," Young enthused in the preface to his pioneering textbook, *Genital Abnormalities,* "have we begun to get somewhere near the explanation of the marvels of anatomic abnormality that may be portrayed by these amazing individuals. But the surgery of the hermaphrodite has remained a terra incognita." The "sad state of these unfortunates" prompted Young to devise "a great variety of surgical procedures" by which he attempted to normalize their bodily appearances to the greatest extents possible.[7]

Quite a few of Young's patients resisted his efforts. One, a "'snappy' young negro woman with a good figure" and a large clitoris, had married a man but found her passion only with women. She refused "to be made into a man" because removal of her vagina would mean the loss of her "meal ticket," namely, her husband.[8] By the 1950s, the principle of rapid postnatal detection and intervention for intersex infants

---

[4]Judith Butler, *Gender Trouble: Feminism and the Subversion of Identity* (New York: Routledge, 1990); Thomas Laqueur, *Making Sex: Body and Gender from the Greeks to Freud* (Cambridge, Mass.: Harvard University Press, 1990).

[5]Suzanne Kessler and Wendy McKenna, *Gender: An Ethnomethodological Approach* (New York: John Wiley and Sons, 1978).

[6]Alice Domurat Dreger, "Doubtful Sex: Cases and Concepts of Hermaphroditism in France and Britain, 1868–1915," (Ph.D. diss., Indiana University, 1995); Alice Domurat Dreger, "Doubtful Sex: The Fate of the Hermaphrodite in Victorian Medicine," *Victorian Studies* (spring 1995): 336–70; Alice Domurat Dreger, "Hermaphrodites in Love: The Truth of the Gonads," *Science and Homosexualities,* ed. Vernon Rosario (New York: Routledge, 1997), 46–66; Alice Domurat Dreger, "Doctors Containing Hermaphrodites: The Victorian Legacy," *Chrysalis: The Journal of Transgressive Gender Identities* (fall 1997): 15–22.

[7]Hugh Hampton Young, *Genital Abnormalities, Hermaphroditism, and Related Adrenal Diseases* (Baltimore: Williams and Wilkins, 1937), xxxix–xl.

[8]Ibid., 139–42.

had been developed at John Hopkins with the stated goal of completing surgery early enough so that the child would have no memory of it.[9] One wonders whether the insistence on early intervention was not at least partly motivated by the resistance offered by adult intersexuals to normalization through surgery. Frightened parents of ambiguously sexed infants were much more open to suggestions of normalizing surgery, while the infants themselves could of course offer no resistance whatever. Most of the theoretical foundations justifying these interventions are attributable to psychologist John Money, a sex researcher invited to Johns Hopkins by Lawson Wilkins, the founder of pediatric endocrinology.[10] Wilkins's numerous students subsequently carried these protocols to hospitals throughout the United States and abroad.[11] Suzanne Kessler notes that today Wilkins and Money's protocols enjoy a "consensus of approval rarely encountered in science."[12]

In keeping with the Johns Hopkins model, the birth of an intersex infant today is deemed a "psychosocial emergency" that propels a multidisciplinary team of intersex specialists into action. Significantly, they are surgeons and endocrinologists rather than psychologists, bioethicists, representatives from intersex peer support organizations, or parents of intersex children. The team examines the infant and chooses either male or female as a "sex of assignment," then informs the parents that this is the child's "true sex." Medical technology, including surgery and hormones, is then used to make the child's body conform as closely as possible to that sex.

The sort of deviation from sex norms exhibited by intersexuals is so highly stigmatized that the likely prospect of emotional harm due to social rejection of the intersexual provides physicians with their most compelling argument to justify medically unnecessary surgical interventions. Intersex status is considered to be so incompatible with emotional health that misrepresentation, concealment of facts, and outright lying (both to parents and later to the intersex person) are unabashedly advocated in professional medical literature.[13] Rather, the systematic hushing up of the fact of intersex births and the use of violent techniques to normalize intersex bodies have caused profound emotional and physical harm to intersexuals and their families. The harm begins when the birth is treated as a medical crisis, and the consequences of that initial treatment ripple out ever afterward. The impact of this treatment is so devastating that until just a few years ago, people whose lives have been touched by intersexuality maintained silence about their ordeal. As recently as 1993, no one publicly disputed surgeon Milton Edgerton when he wrote that in

---

[9]Howard W. Jones: Jr. and William Wallace Scott, *Hermaphroditism, Genital Anomalies, and Related Endocrine Disorders* (Baltimore: Williams and Wilkins, 1958), 269.

[10]John Money, Joan G. Hampson, and John L. Hampson, "An Examination of Some Basic Sexual Concepts: The Evidence of Human Hermaphroditism," *Bulletin of the Johns Hopkins Hospital* 97 (1955): 301–19; John Money, Joan G. Hampson, and John L. Hampson, "Hermaphroditism: Recommendations Concerning Assignment of Sex, Change of Sex, and Psychologic Management," *Bulletin of Johns Hopkins Hospital* 97 (1955): 284–300; John Money, *Venuses Penuses* (Buffalo: Prometheus, 1986).

[11]Robert M. Blizzard, "Lawson Wilkins," in Kappy et al. *Wilkins*, xi–xiv.

[12]Suzanne Kessler. "The Medical Construction of Gender: Case Management of Intersexual Infants," *Signs: Journal of Women in Culture and Society* 16 (1990): 3–26.

[13]J. Dewhurst and D. B. Grant. "Intersex Problems," *Archives of Disease in Childhood* 59 (1984): 1191–94: Anita Natarajan, "Medical Ethics and Truth-Telling in the Case of Androgen Insensitivity Syndrome," *Canadian Medical Association Journal* 154 (1996): 568–70; Tom Mazur, "Ambiguous Genitalia: Detection and Counseling." *Pediatric Nursing* (1983): 417–22; E. M. E. Slijper et al., "Neonates with Abnormal Genital Development Assigned the Female Sex: Parent Counseling," *Journal of Sex Education and Therapy* 20 (1994): 9–17.

forty years of clitoral surgery on intersexuals, "not one has complained of loss of sensation, *even when the entire clitoris was removed.*"[14]

The tragic irony is that, while intersexual anatomy occasionally indicates an underlying medical problem such as adrenal malfunction, ambiguous genitals are in and of themselves neither painful nor harmful to health. Surgery is essentially a destructive process. It can remove and to a limited extent relocate tissue, but it cannot create new structures. This technical limitation, taken together with the framing of the feminine as a condition of lack, leads physicians to assign 90 percent of anatomically ambiguous infants as female by excising genital tissue. Members of the Johns Hopkins intersex team have justified female assignment by saying, "You can make a hole, but you can't build a pole."[15] Positively heroic efforts shore up a tenuous masculine status for the remaining 10 percent assigned male, who are subjected to multiple operations—twenty-two in one case[16]—with the goal of straightening the penis and constructing a urethra to enable standing urinary posture. For some, the surgeries end only when the child grows old enough to resist.[17]

Children assigned to the female sex are subjected to surgery that removes the troubling hypertrophic clitoris (the same tissue that would have been a troubling micropenis if the child had been assigned male). Through the 1960s, feminizing pediatric genital surgery was openly labeled "clitorectomy" and was compared favorably to the African practices that have been the recent focus of such intense scrutiny. As three Harvard surgeons noted, "Evidence that the clitoris is not essential for normal coitus may be gained from certain sociological data. For instance, it is the custom of a number of African tribes to excise the clitoris and other parts of the external genitals. Yet normal sexual function is observed in these females."[18] A modified operation that removes most of the clitoris and relocates a bit of the tip is variously (and euphemistically) called clitoroplasty, clitoral reduction, or clitoral recession and is described as a "simple cosmetic procedure" to differentiate it from the now infamous clitorectomy. However, the operation is far from benign. Here is a slightly simplified summary (in my own words) of the surgical technique—recommended by Johns Hopkins Surgeons Oesterling, Gearhart, and Jeffs—that is representative of the operation:

> They make an incision around the phallus, at the corona, then dissect the skin away from its underside. Next they dissect the skin away from the dorsal side and remove as much of the corpora, or erectile bodies, as necessary to create an "appropriate size clitoris." Next, stitches are placed from the pubic area along both sides of the entire length of what remains of the phallus; when these stitches are tightened, it folds up like pleats in a skirt, and recesses into a concealed position behind the mons pubis. If the result is still "too large," the glans is further reduced by cutting away a pie-shaped wedge.[19]

---

[14]Milton T. Edgerton. "Discussion: Clitoroplasty for Clitoromegaly due to Adrenogenital Syndrome without Loss of Sensitivity (by Nobuyuki Sagehashi)," *Plastic and Reconstructive Surgery* 91 (1993): 956.

[15]Melissa Hendricks, "Is It a Boy or a Girl?" *Johns Hopkins Magazine*, November, 1993, 10–16.

[16]John E Stecker et al., "Hypospadias Cripples," *Urologic Clinics of North America: Symposium on Hypospadias* 8 (1981): 539–44.

[17]Jeff McClintock, "Growing Up in the Surgical Maelstrom," *Chrysalis: The Journal of Transgressive Gender Identities* (fall 1997): 53–54.

[18]Robert E. Gross. Judson Randolph, and John F. Crigler, "Clitorectomy for Sexual Abnormalities: Indications and Technique," *Surgery* 59 (1966): 300–308.

[19]Joseph E. Oesterling, John P. Gearhart, and Robert D. Jeffs, "A Unified Approach to Early Reconstructive Surgery of the Child with Ambiguous Genitalia," *Journal of Urology* 138 (1987): 1079–84.

For most intersexuals, this sort of arcane, dehumanized medical description, illustrated with close-ups of genital surgery and naked children with blacked-out eyes, is the only available version of *Our Bodies, Ourselves*. We as a culture have relinquished to medicine the authority to police the boundaries of male and female, leaving intersexuals to recover as best they can, alone and silent, from violent normalization.

My Career as a Hermaphrodite: Renegotiating Cultural Meanings

I was born with ambiguous genitals. A doctor specializing in intersexuality deliberated for three days—sedating my mother each time she asked what was wrong with her baby—before concluding that I was male, with a micropenis, complete hypospadias, undescended testes, and a strange extra opening behind the urethra. A male birth certificate was completed for me, and my parents began raising me as a boy. When I was a year and a half old my parents consulted a different set of experts, who admitted me to a hospital for "sex determination." "Determine" is a remarkably apt word in this context, meaning both "to ascertain by investigation" and "to cause to come to a resolution." It perfectly describes the two-stage process whereby science produces through a series of masked operations what it claims merely to observe. Doctors told my parents that a thorough medical investigation would be necessary to determine (in the first sense of that word) what my "true sex" was. They judged my genital appendage to be inadequate as a penis, too short to mark masculine status effectively or to penetrate females. As a female, however, I would be penetrable and potentially fertile. My anatomy having been relabeled as vagina, urethra, labia, and outsized clitoris, my sex was determined (in the second sense) by amputating my genital appendage. Following doctors' orders, my parents then changed my name, combed their house to eliminate all traces of my existence as a boy (photographs, birthday cards, etc.), changed my birth certificate, moved to a different town, instructed extended family members no longer to refer to me as a boy, and never told anyone else—including me—just what had happened. My intersexuality and change of sex were the family's dirty little secrets.

At age eight, I was returned to the hospital for abdominal surgery that trimmed away the testicular portion of my gonads, each of which was partly ovarian and partly testicular in character. No explanation was given to me then for the long hospital stay or the abdominal surgery, nor for the regular hospital visits afterward, in which doctors photographed my genitals and inserted fingers and instruments into my vagina and anus. These visits ceased as soon as I began to menstruate. At the time of the sex change, doctors had assured my parents that their once son/now daughter would grow into a woman who could have a normal sex life and babies. With the confirmation of menstruation, my parents apparently concluded that that prediction had been borne out and their ordeal was behind them. For me, the worst part of the nightmare was just beginning.

As an adolescent, I became aware that I had no clitoris or inner labia and was unable to orgasm. By the end of my teens, I began to do research in medical libraries, trying to discover what might have happened to me. When I finally determined to obtain my medical records, it took me three years to overcome the obstruction of the doctors whom I asked for help. When I did obtain them, a scant three pages, I first learned that I was a "true hermaphrodite" who had been my parents' son for a year and a half and who bore a name unfamiliar to me. The records also documented my clitorectomy. This was the middle 1970s, when I was in my early twenties. I had come to identify myself as lesbian, at a time when lesbianism and a biologically based gender essentialism were virtually synonymous: men were rapists who caused war and environmental destruction; women were good and would heal the earth; lesbians were a superior form of being uncontaminated by "men's energy." In such a world, how could I tell anyone that I had actually possessed the dreaded "phallus"? I was no longer a woman in my own eyes but rather a monstrous and mythical creature. Because my hermaphroditism and long-buried boyhood were the history behind the clitorectomy, I could never speak openly about that or my consequent inability to orgasm. I was so traumatized by discovering the circumstances that produced my embodiment that I could not speak of these matters with anyone.

Nearly fifteen years later, I suffered an emotional meltdown. In the eyes of the world, I was a highly successful businesswoman, a principal in an international high tech company. To myself, I was a freak, incapable of loving or being loved, filled with shame about my status as a hermaphrodite and about my sexual dysfunction. Unable to make peace with myself, I finally sought help from a psychotherapist, who reacted to each revelation about my history and predicament with some version of "no, it's not" or "so what?" I would say, "I'm not really a woman," and she would say, "Of course you are. You look female." I would say, "My complete withdrawal from sexuality has destroyed every relationship I've ever entered." She would say, "Everybody has their ups and downs," I tried another therapist and met with a similar response. Increasingly desperate, I confided my story to several friends, who shrank away in embarrassed silence. I was in emotional agony, feeling utterly alone, seeing no possible way out. I decided to kill myself.

Confronting suicide as a real possibility proved to be my personal epiphany. I fantasized killing myself quite messily and dramatically in the office of the surgeon who had cut off my clitoris, forcibly confronting him with the horror he had imposed on my life. But in acknowledging the desire to put my pain to some use, not to utterly waste my life, I turned a crucial corner, finding a way to direct my rage productively out into the world rather than destructively at myself. I had no conceptual framework for developing a more positive self-consciousness. I knew only that I felt mutilated, not fully human, but that I was determined to heal. I struggled for weeks in emotional chaos, unable to eat or sleep or work. I could not accept my image of a hermaphroditic body any more than I could accept the butchered one the surgeons left me with. Thoughts of myself as a Frankenstein's monster patchwork alternated with longings for escape by death, only to be followed by outrage, anger, and a determination to survive. I could not accept that it was just or right or good to treat any person as I had been treated—my sex changed, my genitals cut up, my experience silenced and rendered invisible. I bore a private hell within me, wretchedly alone in my condition without even my tormentors for company. Finally, I began to envision myself standing in a driving storm but with clear skies and a rainbow visible in the distance. I was still in agony, but I was beginning to see the painful process in which I was caught up in terms of revitalization and rebirth, a means of investing my life with a new sense of authenticity that possessed vast potentials for further transformation. Since then, I have seen this experience of movement through pain to personal empowerment described by other intersex and transsexual activists.[20]

I slowly developed a newly politicized and critically aware form of self-understanding. I had been the kind of lesbian who at times had a girlfriend but who had never really participated in the life of a lesbian community. I felt almost completely isolated from gay politics, feminism, and queer and gender theory. I did possess the rudimentary knowledge that the gay rights movement had gathered momentum only when it could effectively deny that homosexuality was sick or inferior and assert to the contrary that "gay is good." As impossible as it then seemed, I pledged similarly to affirm that "intersex is good," that the body I was born with was not diseased, only different. I vowed to embrace the sense of being "not a woman" that I initially had been so terrified to discover.

---

[20]Kira Triea, "The Awakening," *Hermaphrodites with Attitude* (winter 1994): 1; Susan Stryker, "My Words to Victor Frankenstein above the Village of Chamounix: Performing Transgender Rage," *GLQ* 1 (1994): 237–54.

I began searching for community and consequently moved to San Francisco in the fall of 1992, based entirely on my vague notion that people living in the "queer mecca" would have the most conceptually sophisticated, socially tolerant, and politically astute analysis of sexed and gendered embodiment. I found what I was looking for in part because my arrival in the Bay Area corresponded with the rather sudden emergence of an energetic transgender political movement. Transgender Nation (TN) had developed out of Queer Nation, a post-gay/lesbian group that sought to transcend identity politics. TN's actions garnered media attention—especially when members were arrested during a "zap" of the American Psychiatric Association's annual convention when they protested the psychiatric labeling of transsexuality as mental illness. Transsexual performance artist Kate Bornstein was introducing transgender issues in an entertaining way to the San Francisco gay/lesbian community and beyond. Female-to-male issues had achieved a new level of visibility due in large part to efforts made by Lou Sullivan, a gay FTM activist who had died an untimely death from HIV-related illnesses in 1991. And in the wake of her underground best-selling novel, *Stone Butch Blues,* Leslie Feinberg's manifesto *Transgender Liberation: A Movement Whose Time Has Come* was finding a substantial audience, linking transgender social justice to a broader progressive political agenda for the first time.[21] At the same time, a vigorous new wave of gender scholarship had emerged in the academy.[22] In this context; intersex activist and theoretician Morgan Holmes could analyze her own clitorectomy for her master's thesis and have it taken seriously as academic work.[23] Openly transsexual scholars, including Susan Stryker and Sandy Stone, were visible in responsible academic positions at major universities. Stone's "*Empire* Strikes Back: A Posttranssexual Manifesto" refigured open, visible transsexuals not as gender conformists propping up a system of rigid, binary sex but as "a set of embodied texts whose potential for productive disruption of structured sexualities and spectra of desire has yet to be explored."[24]

Into this heady atmosphere, I brought my own experience. Introduced by Bornstein to other gender activists, I explored with them the cultural politics of intersexuality, which to me represented yet another new configuration of bodies, identities, desires, and sexualities from which to confront the violently normativizing aspects of the dominant sex/gender system. In the fall of 1993, TN pioneer Anne Ogborn invited me to participate in a weekend retreat called the New Woman Conference, where postoperative transsexual women shared their stories, their griefs and joys, and enjoyed the freedom to swim or sunbathe in the nude with others who had surgically changed genitals. I saw that participants returned home in a state of euphoria, and I determined to bring that same sort of healing experience to intersex people.

Birth of an Intersex Movement: Opposition and Allies

Upon moving to San Francisco, I started telling my story indiscriminately to everyone I met. Over the course of a year, simply by speaking openly within my own social circles, I learned of six other intersexuals—including

---

[21]Leslie Feinberg, *Stone Butch Blues* (Ithaca, N.Y.: Firebrand, 1993); Leslie Feinberg, *Transgender Liberation: A Movement Whose Time Has Come* (New York: World View Forum, 1992).

[22]See, for example, Judith Butler, *Bodies That Matter: On the Discursive Limits of "Sex"* (New York: Routledge, 1993); Butler, *Gender Trouble;* Laqueur, *Making Sex;* and Julia Epstein and Kristina Straub, eds., *Body Guards: The Cultural Politics of Gender Ambiguity* (New York: Routledge, 1991).

[23]Morgan Holmes, "Medical Politics and Cultural Imperatives: Intersexuality Beyond Pathology and Erasure" (master's thesis, York University, Toronto, 1994).

[24]Sandy Stone, "The *Empire* Strikes Back: A Posttranssexual Manifesto," in Epstein and Straub, *Body Guards,* 280–304, quotation on 296.

two who had been fortunate enough to escape medical attention. I realized that intersexuality, rather than being extremely rare, must be relatively common. I decided to create a support network. In the summer of 1993, I produced some pamphlets, obtained a post office box, and began to publicize the Intersex Society of North America (ISNA) through small notices in the media. Before long, I was receiving several letters per week from intersexuals throughout the United States and Canada and occasionally some from Europe. While the details varied, the letters gave a remarkably coherent picture of the emotional consequences of medical intervention. Morgan Holmes: "All the things my body might have grown to do, all the possibilities, went down the hall with my amputated clitoris to the pathology department. The rest of me went to the recovery room— I'm still recovering." Angela Moreno: "I am horrified by what has been done to me and by the conspiracy of silence and lies. I am filled with grief and rage, but also relief finally to believe that maybe I am not the only one." Thomas: "I pray that I will have the means to repay, in some measure, the American Urological Association for all that it has done for my benefit. I am having some trouble, though, in connecting the timing mechanism to the fuse."

ISNA's most immediate goal has been to create a community of intersex people who could provide peer support to deal with shame, stigma, grief, and rage as well as with practical issues such as how to obtain old medical records or locate a sympathetic psychotherapist or endocrinologist. To that end, I cooperated with journalists whom I judged capable of reporting widely and responsibly on our efforts, listed ISNA with self-help and referral clearinghouses, and established a presence on the Internet (http://www.isna.org). ISNA now connects hundreds of intersexuals across North America, Europe, Australia, and New Zealand. It has also begun sponsoring an annual intersex retreat, the first of which took place in 1996 and which moved participants every bit as profoundly as the New Woman Conference had moved me in 1993.

ISNA's longer-term and more fundamental goal, however, is to change the way intersex infants are treated. We advocate that surgery not be performed on ambiguous genitals unless there is medical reason (such as blocked or painful urination), and that parents be given the conceptual tools and emotional support to accept their children's physical differences. While it is fascinating to think about the potential development of new genders or subject positions grounded in forms of embodiment that fall outside the familiar male/female dichotomy, we recognize that the two-sex/gender model is currently hegemonic and therefore advocate that children be raised either as boys or girls, according to which designation seems most likely to offer the child the greatest future sense of comfort. Advocating gender assignment without resorting to normalizing surgery is a radical position given that it requires the willful disruption of the assumed concordance between body shape and gender category. However, this is the only position that prevents irreversible physical damage to the intersex person's body, that respects the intersex person's agency regarding his/her own flesh, and that recognizes genital sensation and erotic functioning to be at least as important as reproductive capacity. If an intersex child or adult decides to change gender or to undergo surgical or hormonal alteration of his/her body, that decision should also be fully respected and facilitated. The key point is that intersex subjects should not be violated for the comfort and convenience of others.

One part of reaching ISNA's long-term goal has been to document the emotional and physical carnage resulting from medical interventions. As a rapidly growing literature makes abundantly clear (see the bibliography on our website, http://www.isna.org/bigbib.html), the medical management of intersexuality has changed little in the forty years since my first surgery. Kessler expresses surprise that "in spite of the thousands of genital operations performed every year, there are no meta-analyses from within the medical community on levels of success."[25] They do not know whether postsurgical intersexuals are "silent and happy

---

[25]Suzanne Kessler, *Lessons from the Intersexed* (New Brunswick, N.J.: Rutgers University Press, forthcoming).

or silent and unhappy."[26] There is no research effort to improve erotic functioning for adult intersexuals whose genitals have been altered, nor are there psychotherapists specializing in working with adult intersex clients trying to heal from the trauma of medical intervention. To provide a counterpoint to the mountains of medical literature that neglect intersex experience and to begin compiling an ethnographic account of that experience, *ISNA's Hermaphrodites with Attitude* newsletter has developed into a forum for intersexuals to tell their own stories. We have sent complimentary copies of the newsletter filled with searing personal narratives to academics, writers, journalists, minority rights organizations, and medical practitioners—to anybody we thought might make a difference in our campaign to change the way intersex bodies are managed.

ISNA's presence has begun to generate effects. It has helped politicize the growing number of intersex organizations, as well as intersex identities themselves. When I first began organizing ISNA, I met leaders of the Turner's Syndrome Society, the oldest known support group focusing on atypical sexual differentiation, founded in 1987. Turner's Syndrome is defined by an XO genetic karyotype that results in a female body morphology with nonfunctioning ovaries, extremely short stature, and a variety of other physical differences described in the medical literature with such stigmatizing labels as "web-necked" and "fish-mouthed." Each of these women told me what a profound, life-changing experience it had been simply to meet another person like herself. I was inspired by their accomplishments (they are a national organization serving thousands of members), but I wanted ISNA to have a different focus. I was less willing to think of intersexuality as a pathology or disability, more interested in challenging its medicalization entirely, and more interested still in politicizing a pan-intersexual identity across the divisions of particular etiologies in order to destabilize more effectively the heteronormative assumptions underlying the violence directed at our bodies.

When I established ISNA in 1993, no such politicized groups existed. In the United Kingdom in 1988, the mother of a girl with androgen-insensitivity syndrome (AIS, which produces genetic males with female genital morphologies) formed the AIS Support Group. The group, which initially lobbied for increased medical attention (better surgical techniques for producing greater vaginal depth, more research into the osteoporosis that often attends AIS), now has chapters in five countries. Another group, K. S. and Associates, was formed in 1989 by the mother of a boy with Klinefelter's Syndrome and today serves over one thousand families. Klinefelter's is characterized by the presence of one or more additional X chromosomes, which produce bodies with fairly masculine external genitals. Above-average height, and somewhat gangly limbs. At puberty, people with K. S. often experience pelvic broadening and the development of breasts. K. S. and Associates continues to be dominated by parents, is highly medical in orientation, and has resisted attempts by adult Klinefelter's Syndrome men to discuss gender identity or sexual orientation issues related to their intersex condition.

Since ISNA has been on the scene, other groups with a more resistant stance vis-à-vis the medical establishment have begun to appear. In 1995, a mother who refused medical pressure for female assignment for her intersex child formed the Ambiguous Genitalia Support Network, which introduces parents of intersexuals to each other and encourages the development of pen-pal support relationships. In 1996, another mother who had rejected medical pressure to assign her intersex infant as a female by removing his penis formed the Hermaphrodite Education and Listening Post (HELP) to provide peer support and medical information. Neither of these parent-oriented groups, however, frames its work in overtly political terms. Still, political analysis and action of the sort advocated by ISNA has not been without effect on

---

[26]Robert Jeffs, quoted in Ellen Barry, "United States of Ambiguity," Boston *Phoenix,* 22 November 1996, 6–8, quotation on 6.

the more narrowly defined service-oriented or parent-dominated groups. The AIS Support Group, now more representative of both adults and parents, noted in a recent newsletter,

> Our first impression of ISNA was that they were perhaps a bit too angry and militant to gain the support of the medical profession. However, we have to say that, having read [political analyses of intersexuality by ISNA, Kessler, Fausto-Sterling, and Holmes], we feel that the feminist concepts relating to the patriarchal treatment of intersexuality are extremely interesting and do make a lot of sense. After all, the lives of intersexed people are stigmatized by the cultural disapproval of their genital appearance, [which need not] affect their experience as sexual human beings.[27]

Other more militant groups have now begun to pop up. In 1994, German intersexuals formed both the Workgroup on Violence in Pediatrics and Gynecology and the Genital Mutilation Survivors' Support Network, and Hijra Nippon now represents activist intersexuals in Japan.

Outside the rather small community of intersex organizations, ISNA's work has generated a complex patchwork of alliances and oppositions. Queer activists, especially transgender activists, have provided encouragement, advice, and logistical support to the intersex movement. The direct action group Transsexual Menace helped an ad hoc group of militant intersexuals calling themselves Hermaphrodites with Attitude plan and carry out a picket of the 1996 annual meeting of the American Academy of Pediatrics in Boston—the first recorded instance of intersex public protest in modern history.[28] ISNA was also invited to join GenderPAC, a recently formed national consortium of transgender organizations that lobbies against discrimination based on atypical expressions of gender or embodiment. More mainstream gay and lesbian political organizations such as the National Gay and Lesbian Task Force have also been willing to include intersex concerns as part of their political agendas. Transgender and lesbian/gay groups have been supportive of intersex political activism largely because they see similarities in the medicalization of these various identities as a form of social control and (especially for transsexuals) empathize with our struggle to assert agency within a medical discourse that works to efface the ability to exercise informed consent about what happens to one's own body.

Gay/lesbian caucuses and special interest groups within professional medical associations have been especially receptive to ISNA's agenda. One physician on the Internet discussion group glb-medical wrote:

> The effect of Cheryl Chase's postings—admittedly, after the shock wore off—was to make me realize that THOSE WHO HAVE BEEN TREATED might very well think [they had not been well served by medical intervention]. This matters a lot. As a gay man, and simply as a person, I have struggled for much of my adult life to find my own natural self, to disentangle the confusions caused by others' presumptions about how I am/should be. But, thankfully, their decisions were not surgically imposed on me!

Queer psychiatrists, starting with Bill Byne at New York's Mount Sinai Hospital, have been quick to support ISNA, in part because the psychological principles underlying the current intersex treatment protocols are manifestly unsound. They seem almost willfully designed to exacerbate rather than ameliorate already difficult emotional issues arising from sexual difference. Some of these psychiatrists see the surgical and endocrinological domination of a problem that even surgeons and endocrinologists acknowledge to be psychosocial rather than biomedical as an unjustified invasion of their area of professional competence.

---

[27]AIS Support Group, "Letter to America," *ALIAS* (spring 1996): 3–4.

[28]Barry, "United States of Ambiguity," 7.

ISNA has deliberately cultivated a network of nonintersexed advocates who command a measure of social legitimacy and can speak in contexts where uninterpreted intersex voices will not be heard. Because there is a strong impulse to discount what intersexuals have to say about intersexuality, sympathetic representation has been welcome—especially in helping intersexuals reframe intersexuality in nonmedical terms. Some gender theory scholars, feminist critics of science, medical historians, and anthropologists have been quick to understand and support intersex activism. Years before ISNA came into existence, feminist biologist and science studies scholar Anne Fausto-Sterling had written about intersexuality in relation to intellectually suspect scientific practices that perpetuate masculinist constructs of gender, and she became an early ISNA ally.[29] Likewise, social psychologist Suzanne Kessler had written a brilliant ethnography of surgeons who specialize in treating intersexuals. After speaking with several "products" of their practice, she, too, became a strong supporter of intersex activism.[30] Historian of science Alice Dreger, whose work focuses not only on hermaphroditism but on other forms of potentially benign atypical embodiment that become subject to destructively normalizing medical interventions (conjoined twins. for example), has been especially supportive. Fausto-Sterling, Kessler, and Dreger will each shortly publish works that analyze the medical treatment of intersexuality as being culturally motivated and criticize it as harmful to its ostensible patients.[31]

Allies who help contest the medicalization of intersexuality are especially important because ISNA has found it almost entirely fruitless to attempt direct, nonconfrontational interactions with the medical specialists who themselves determine policy on the treatment of intersex infants and who actually carry out the surgeries. Joycelyn Elders, the Clinton administration's first surgeon general, is a pediatric endocrinologist with many years of experience managing intersex infants but, in spite of a generally feminist approach to health care and frequent overtures from ISNA, she has been dismissive of the concerns of intersexuals themselves.[32] Another pediatrician remarked in an Internet discussion on intersexuality: "I think this whole issue is preposterous. . . . To suggest that [medical decisions about the treatment of intersex conditions] are somehow cruel or arbitrary is insulting, ignorant and misguided. . . . To spread the claims that [ISNA] is making is just plain wrong, and I hope that this [on-line group of doctors and scientists] will not blindly accept them." Yet another participant in that same chat asked what was for him obviously a rhetorical question: "Who is the enemy? I really don't think it's the medical establishment. Since when did we establish the male/female hegemony?" While a surgeon quoted in a *New York Times* article on ISNA summarily dismissed us as "zealots,"[33] there is considerable anecdotal information supplied by ISNA sympathizers that professional meetings in the fields of pediatrics, urology, genital plastic surgery, and endocrinology are

---

[29]Anne Fausto-Sterling, "The Five Sexes: Why Male and Female Are Not Enough," *The Sciences* 33, no. 2 (March/April 1993): 20–25; Anne Fausto-Sterling, *Myths of Gender: Biological Theories about Women and Men,* 2d ed. (New York: Basic Books, 1985), 134–41.

[30]Kessler, "The Medical Construction of Gender"; Suzanne Kessler, "Meanings of Genital Variability," *Chrysalis: The Journal of Transgressive Gender Identities* (fall 1997): 33–38.

[31]Anne Fausto-Sterling, *Building Bodies: Biology and the Social Construction of Sexuality* (New York: Basic Books, forthcoming); Kessler, "Meanings of Genital Variability"; Alice Domurat Dreger, *Hermaphrodites and the Medical Invention of Sex* (Cambridge, Mass.: Harvard University Press, forthcoming).

[32]"Dr. Elders' Medical History," *New Yorker,* 26 September 1994: 45–46; Joycelyn Elders and David Chanoff, *From Sharecropper's Daughter to Surgeon General of the United States of America* (New York: William Morrow, 1996).

[33]Natalie Angier, "Intersexual Healing: An Anomaly Finds a Group," *New York Times,* 4 February 1996, E14.

buzzing with anxious and defensive discussions of intersex activism. In response to the Hermaphrodites with Attitude protests at the American Academy of Pediatrics meeting, that organization felt compelled to issue the following statement to the press: "The Academy is deeply concerned about the emotional, cognitive, and body image development of intersexuals, and believes that successful early genital surgery minimizes these issues." Further protests were planned for 1997.

The roots of resistance to the truth claims of intersexuals run deep in the medical establishment. Not only does ISNA critique the normativist biases couched within most scientific practice, it advocates a treatment protocol for intersex infants that disrupts conventional understandings of the relationship between bodies and genders. But on a level more personally threatening to medical practitioners, ISNA's position implies that they have—unwittingly at best, through willful denial at worst—spent their careers inflicting a profound harm from which their patients will never fully recover. ISNA's position threatens to destroy the assumptions motivating an entire medical subspecialty, thus jeopardizing the ability to perform what many surgeons find to be technically difficult and fascinating work. Melissa Hendricks notes that Dr. Gearhart is known to colleagues as a surgical "artist" who can "carve a large phallus down into a clitoris" with consummate skill.[34] More than one ISNA member has discovered that surgeons actually operated on their genitals at no charge. The medical establishment's fascination with its own power to change sex and its drive to rescue parents from their intersex children are so strong that heroic interventions are delivered without regard to the capitalist model that ordinarily governs medical services.

Given such deep and mutually reinforcing reasons for opposing ISNA's position, it is hardly surprising that medical intersex specialists have, for the most part, turned a deaf ear toward us. The lone exception as of April 1997 is urologist Justine Schober. After watching a videotape of the 1996 ISNA retreat and receiving other input from HELP and the AIS Support Group, she suggests in a new textbook on pediatric surgery that while technology has advanced to the point that "our needs [as surgeons] and the needs of parents to have a presentable child can be satisfied," it is time to acknowledge that problems exist that "we as surgeons . . . cannot address. Success in psychosocial adjustment is the true goal of sexual assignment and genitoplasty. . . . Surgery makes parents and doctors comfortable, but counseling makes people comfortable too, and is not irreversible."[35]

While ISNA will continue to approach the medical establishment for dialogue (and continue supporting protests outside the closed doors when doctors refuse to talk), perhaps the most important aspect of our current activities is the struggle to change public perceptions. By using the mass media, the Internet, and our growing network of allies and sympathizers to make the general public aware of the frequency of intersexuality and of the intense suffering that medical treatment has caused, we seek to create an environment in which many parents of intersex children will have already heard about the intersex movement when their child is born. Such informed parents we hope will be better able to resist medical pressure for unnecessary genital surgery and secrecy and to find their way to a peer-support group and counseling rather than to a surgical theater.

---

[34]Hendricks, "Is It a Boy or a Girl?" 10.

[35]Justine M. Schober, "Long Term Outcomes of Feminizing Genitoplasty for Intersex," in *Pediatric Surgery and Urology: Long Term Outcomes,* ed. Pierre Mouriquant (Philadelphia: W. B. Saunders, forthcoming).

HOMAGE TO MY HAIR

Lucille Clifton

When i feel her jump up and dance
i hear the music! my God
i'm talking about my nappy hair!
she is a challenge to your hand
black man,
she is as tasty on your tongue as good greens
black man,
she can touch your mind
with her electric fingers and
the grayer she do get, good God,
the blacker she do be!

HOMAGE TO MY HIPS

Lucille Clifton

These hips are big hips
they need space to
move around in.
they don't fit into little
petty places, these hips
are free hips.
they don't like to he held back.
these hips have never been enslaved,
they go where they want to go
they do what they want to do.
these hips are mighty hips.
these hips are magic hips.
i have known them
to put a spell on a man and
spin him like a top!

(RE)CONSTRUCTING BODIES: SEMIOTIC SOVEREIGNTY AND THE DEBATE OVER KENNEWICK MAN

Suzanne J. Crawford

On July 28, 1996, two students discovered the half-buried remains of a ninety-three-hundred-year-old skeleton while wading in the Columbia River near Kennewick, Washington. Because of its Caucasian-like features the skeleton was first thought to be that of a nineteenth-century settler, before radiocarbon dating at the University of California at Davis showed the body to be over nine thousand years old. The body was thereafter known as Kennewick Man. Acting under a provision of the Native American Graves Protection and Repatriation Act (NAGPRA), the Army Corps of Engineers, which had jurisdiction over the area, determined to return the body for reburial to five local Native American tribes (the Confederated Tribes of the Umatilla, the Yakima Indian Nation, the Nez Perce tribe, the Wanapum band, and the Colville Confederated Tribes). This decision resulted in a maelstrom of protests from anthropologists and archaeologists throughout the country, eight of whom promptly filed a lawsuit requesting that the bones first be turned over to them for study before reburial. The lawsuit was soon joined by a third parry, the Asatru Folk Assembly (AFA), a religious group located outside of Nevada City, California, that works to revive pre-Christian Celtic, Nordic, and Germanic traditions. Because of Kennewick Man's Caucasian characteristics, the group believes him to be one of their ancestors who migrated to the New World over nine thousand years ago. The five-tribe coalition, however, remains adamant that the body should be reburied as soon as possible. The tribes oppose testing of the body, especially destructive techniques such as DNA analysis and radiocarbon dating, seeing them "as desecration, with devastating spiritual consequences" (*Portland Oregonian* 10/2/97, D1).

The debate has created a series of profound controversies that extend beyond simple legal issues. The furor over Kennewick Man is a moment strikingly illustrative of the manner in which narratives explicating social identity and history are inscribed on the body. At the heart of the AFA'S interest in the body is a firm belief that ancient Caucasians were in fact the first settlers of America, predating the ancestors of contemporary Native American tribes. While insisting that the find is an invaluable source of information about the physical characteristics, health, and lifestyle of America's first people, of the peopling of the Americas, and of human evolution in general, scientists also speculate upon its possible ethnic background. It is these speculations upon his possible European lineage that garner Kennewick Man the most publicity, keeping him in the public eye. All the parties involved approach Kennewick Man with their own economic desires, identity needs, and religio-ethical concerns, all of which are in turn inscribed on the body. The purpose of this paper is to examine the language used to describe Kennewick Man and other early Native American remains, in order to ask several fundamental questions: how does this language reveal the ways non-Natives have constructed the image of the Native American body? And why do we approach these bodies with the questions and agendas that we do? It is my suggestion that the creation of the fictitious "Authentic Indian" of non-Native American lore effectively cuts contemporary Native Americans off from their heritage, enabling the appropriation of Native identity by non-Natives. The ultimate goal of this appropriation is to secure a sense of place, what Yi-Fu Tuan has called "geopiety" (Tuan 1977).

In recent scholarship much attention has been focused on the role of the body within political, economic, and religious institutions. What has not been explored as fully is the relationship between the body and the construction of space and place. Ideologies of identity depend strongly upon understandings of both the body and place and the interaction of the two. A discussion of repatriation and reburial of Native American remains reveals a great deal about the manner in which cultural constructions of the body contribute to the creation of space and a sense of place, especially in dominant white culture. Through the work of feminist critical theorists such as Donna Haraway, Rosemary Hennessy, Judith Butler, and Denise Riley, as well as the work of Michel Foucault, this paper discusses the recent debate over Kennewick Man. As we will see, the Kennewick Man debate demonstrates the manner in which the dominant culture's search for the "Authentic Other," the "Real Indian," facilitates the appropriation of Native identity by non-Natives, legitimating non-Native claims to place and validating non-Native identity. It is not my intent to discuss the validity of any claims made over Kennewick Man, scientific or Native, but rather to explore why the scientific community and the popular press have asked the questions they have. It is in reading the various texts that have been inscribed on this body that latent power relations are made manifest. The debate over Kennewick Man demonstrates the challenges that face the academic community within a postcolonial context and provides an opportunity to create workable solutions to those challenges.

What quickly emerges within the Kennewick Man debate are profoundly different ways of viewing death, the body, history, and cultural identity. Debra Croswell, spokesperson for the Umatillas, argues that the bones should be returned to the ground, regardless of whether the body turns out to be Native or non-Native. "Our feelings on any human remains is that (they) should be reburied. We respect human life, unlike some other cultures, who do not" (*Oregonian* 3/29/97, B2). Horace Axtell, Nez Perce, echoes Croswell's sentiments: "We have an inherent responsibility to care for those who are no longer with us. Our tradition, spiritual beliefs, practices and culture teach us that when a body goes into the ground, it is meant to stay there until the end of time. When remains are disturbed above the ground, their spirits are at unrest. To put those spirits at ease, the remains must be returned to the ground as soon as possible" (*Oregonian* 4/30/97, A14). Armand Minthorn, tribal chairperson of the Umatillas, explained the process further: "Culturally and religiously, our religion tells us that when a body goes into the ground, it is keeping a promise that was made when time began. And the body is to remain in the ground until the end of time. And because these remains have been exposed, this is very sensitive to us, because the remains aren't part of the ground like they should be" (*Oregonian* 10/14/96, A1). The body, for the tribes, serves as a reminder of the intimate tie that exists among themselves, their ancestors, and the land. As Minthorn further explained: "My tribe has ties to this individual because he was uncovered in our traditional homeland, a homeland (in which) we still retain fishing, hunting, gathering and other rights under our 1855 treaty with the U.S. government" (*Oregonian* 10/24/96, C1).[1] The location of the body on Native lands, its residence within the soil for millennia, creates an inherent relationship of reciprocity and respect between the body and the Umatillas, who feel it is their responsibility to care for the land. The body, in its decomposition, is fulfilling a relationship of reciprocity: the earth supports the body during life, and in death, the body supports the earth. Halting this process threatens both ecological and spiritual stability.

---

[1]See also two chapters in this volume: Larry Zimmerman, "A New and Different Archaeology?" (chap. 16), and Kurt E. Dongoske, "NAGPRA: A New Beginning, Not the End, for Osteological Analysis—A Hopi Perspective" (chap. 15).

Native peoples have methods of constructing cultural identity that are quite different from the DNA analysis and radiocarbon dating of university laboratories. Identities here stem from the land base itself, as well as from a complex and honored oral tradition. Adeline Fredin, director and manager of the Colville confederated tribes' history and archaeology department, argues that the oral traditions of the communities do indeed go back ten thousand years. "It's very clear that our ancestral people were there. How can we deny our ancestry? We're living with those kinds of stories and those kinds of Indian legends that tell us about our own ancestry" (*Oregonian* 10/14/96, A1).[2] As Maria Big Boy, an attorney representing the tribes, explains: "It would be wrong to be disturbing this individual. When laid to rest, they are laid to rest. We don't need science to tell us who we are or where our people came from" (*Oregonian* 10/2/97, D7). Larry Zimmerman has argued that the very nature of time and history is perceived radically differently among traditional Native communities: "To Native Americans, the idea that discovery is the only way to know the past is absurd. For the Indian interested in traditional practice and belief, the past lives in the present. Indians know the past because it is spiritually and ritually part of their daily existence and is relevant only as it exists in the present. . . . When archaeologists say that the Native American past is gone, extinct, or lost unless archaeology can find it, they send a strong message that Native Americans themselves are extinct" (Zimmerman 1994; see also Watson et al., 1989, 5–6).

Cultural and religious sentiments aside, the Kennewick Man controversy serves as a reminder to Native peoples of a long history of atrocities perpetrated upon Native communities by archaeologists and anthropologists. For much of U.S. history, professional academics and amateur scavengers have gathered Native remains, some recently deceased, others much older, removing them from burial grounds and shipping them to museums and universities, where they often remained, unstudied, in storage for decades. As of 1996 there were approximately one million such remains still held by public and private institutions (Mihesuah, introduction, this volume). This collection was driven by the notion that the Native peoples of the Americas were doomed to extinction by the onward march of progress in the form of Western capitalism and Christianity and that specimens of Native biology and culture should be preserved for future (white) generations to admire on the shelves of museums. This collecting took little regard for the opinions or sentiments of Native peoples themselves: they were, after all, about to disappear forever.[3] During the Indian wars of the nineteenth century, for example, fallen Native warriors were "decapitated, by order of the Surgeon General of the army for an Indian Crania Study" (Mihesuah, introduction, this volume). In 1900 explorer Alex Hrdlicka dug up the burial ground of a village at Larsen Bay, Alaska, leaving with the remains of eight hundred Konaig Natives, while living villagers watched and protested. There are many such examples, up to the present day, of both academic and amateur "grave robbing" in which bones and grave materials are removed without the permission of local Native tribes (Trafzer, 1997). It is only recently, with NAGPRA, that Native communities have been able to demand the return of their ancestors' and relatives' remains. Kennewick Man, for Native communities, cannot be seen outside of this long history of abuse and disrespect on the part of Euroamerican colonizers.

For those who insist that the body should be subjected to intensive study, however, Kennewick Man is a scientific text, which must be read for the benefit of humanity. As James Chatters, the forensic anthropologist who first studied Kennewick Man, argued in August of 1996: "It's quite exciting to turn up someone who lived then, and whose body tells so many stories" (*Oregonian* 8/28/96, A1). Stephen McNallen of the

---

[2]This statement offers a stark contrast to the sentiment expressed by Grover Krantz of Washington State University: "What the Indians are doing is destroying evidence of their own history" (*Portland Oregonian,* October 14, 1996, A1).

[3]See for example, Theodora Kroeber, *Ishi: A Biography of the Last Wild Indian in North America* (Los Angeles: University of California Press, 1967).

AFA likewise conjured up the image of Kennewick Man as storyteller, when he told reporters: "We share a common ancestry, and we know he has a remarkable story to tell us about how this continent was populated" (*Oregonian* 8/20/97, C1). Kennewick Man's bones "have a message for us. I don't know what that message is . . . our task is to listen" (*Oregonian* 8/28/97, C7). As controversy around the body grew, those opposed to reburial insisted more strongly on the importance of listening to the stories that the body holds, hidden within it. As Chatters told Donald Preston of the *New Yorker*: "We didn't go digging for this man. He fell out—he was actually a volunteer. I think is would be wrong to stick him back in the ground without waiting to hear the story he has to tell. We need to look at things as (human) beings, not as one race or another. The message this man brings to us is one of unification: there may be some commonality in our past that will bring us together" (Preston 1997).

Indeed, the argument most commonly expressed by those in favor of handing Kennewick Man over to a team of anthropologists and archaeologists for intensive study is a universalist and humanistic one reflective of the dominant white culture from which it comes: the body belongs not to Native American tribes but to all humanity. Archaeologists explain that their work is directed not at a certain cultural or national group but at the global human community. This sentiment is found in Landau and Steele's explanation of the necessity of the use of human remains in archaeological study: "In examining our heritage, physical anthropologists seek to understand the biological history and origins of all humans in all geographical areas. Our focus is on all humankind. . . . Each society's biological history is an integral part of the complete and continuing story of all humankind." Landau and Steele are concerned with questions that address "our ancestors," "our ancestral species," and "our understanding of past Native American peoples, and by extension, all humans past and present," because "our total history is who we are" (Landau and Steele, chap. 4, this volume). Pushing cultural distinctions to the side, physical anthropologists claim to address cross-cultural and cross-ethnic questions of biological evolution. Anthropologist Amy Dansie has argued that bones such as those of Kennewick Man are "priceless rare treasures of humanity. The skeleton's features are virtually indistinguishable from white ancestors and Asian ancestors. We share a common ground. These skeletons are important to remind everybody that we're all one people" (*Oregonian* 42/19/96, E10). Chatters also argues for the national appeal of Kennewick Man. "This is knowledge that everyone can have, even the descendants of the tribes. We'd like to know the history of our homeland to the fullest extent. . . . The Kennewick Man is the common heritage of all Americans and should be studied for the benefit of all" (*Chronicle of Higher Education* 5/22/98, A22). And as he pointed out shortly after Kennewick Man's discovery: "This guy's old enough to be everyone's ancestor" (*Oregonian* 8/28/96, A1). Again and again, Kennewick Man and other similar human remains used for osteological study are referred to as "national treasures" and a source from which to gather invaluable information and data to reconstruct the lives and migrations of the "first Americans," for the benefit of all Americans.

This language is found throughout the press coverage of Kennewick Man, from nonacademics as well. Richard Hill, columnist for the Oregonian, wrote soon after the controversy surfaced: "The quest is for our past, for the elusive first Americans" (*Oregonian* 11/27/96, A18). A letter to the editor of the *Oregonian* from Lyle T. Hubbard Jr. of Ridgefield, Washington, reads: "Humans comprise a global community. We need to know about our past so we can have, in common, a vision for our future" (*Oregonian* 11/28/96, B9). Another editorial argues in a similar strain: "This discussion ought to be less about whose ancestor he is than what he can teach all of us. This is a rare discovery that rightfully belongs to all of the people of the Americas and the world." (*Oregonian* 11/1/96, D10). Thomas McClelland, an artist who, in a striking illustration of Foucault's theory of the social construction of the body, (re)constructed Kennewick Man's face from a plaster cast of his skull, told reporters: "The interesting thing about Kennewick Man is that he could be related to anyone. And I think that's part of what this whole controversy is about, too. He does have features that could be tied to any group in the world today. He's kind of like an 'Every-man' if you will" (*Oregonian* 2/28/98, B11). Slade Gorton, the Washington State senator who has attempted to pass legislation that would facilitate the study of the remains, has argued that "My amendment makes the bones available for further scientific study, keeping the interests of all Americans in mind" (*Oregonian* 7/18/97, B7). The Oregonian supported the move in an editorial written soon afterward: "We hope that science prevails in the end. The information from ancient Kennewick Man is simply too important to all peoples to be buried by one people" (*Oregonian* 8/1/97, B10).

Such arguments are clearly reminiscent of an ideology of global monoculture, drawing on the American mythic ideal of the melting pot. All this raises several important questions: How do sovereign Native nations fit into this notion of American monoculture? At what point does a body become common property, and who in reality is this "common humanity" to which they refer? Is it really "all Americans" that are interested in and feel they would benefit from knowing about Kennewick Man? If Kennewick Man is envisioned as a treasure trove of ancient wisdom, one must ask what this information might be, and why do those persons who argue most vehemently in favor of scientific study feel is to be so vastly important? Why the insistence upon overlooking ethnic and cultural distinctions, agendas, and definitions and the repeated argument that Kennewick Man belongs to "all of us," is "our ancestor," and is part of the history of "our homeland"?

These questions become even more important when it is noted that the use of such terms as "Everyman" and "all one people" is immediately and continually contradicted by the argument that the primary use of scientific study of the body will be to determine its racial origin. Alan Schneider, the lawyer acting on behalf of the anthropologists in the lawsuit, argued that study must be done to "determine whether the skeleton is a Native American. . . . We're arguing that we don't know who it belongs to, and that can't be determined without study" (*Oregonian* 1/2/97, A10). The eight anthropologists in the lawsuit have argued that "more science is needed to determine whether Kennewick Man is an American Indian, or related to modern tribes" (*Oregonian* 7/3/97, B11).

Such challenges raise interesting questions about the definition of "Native American." According to Francis R McManamon of the U.S. Department of the Interior, who is also the departmental consulting archaeologist with the National Park Service, the U.S. government understands the term "Native American" to apply to "human remains relating to tribes, peoples, or cultures that lived in what is now the United States before the documented arrival of European explorers. The remains would be considered Native American regardless of when a particular group might have begun to live in this area and regardless of whether these groups were culturally affiliated or biologically related to present-day tribes" (*Oregonian* 4/14/98, B1). By such a standard, Kennewick Man, regardless of the size of his nose, is considered to be Native American and thus subject to NAGPRA. The fact, then, that so many people are demanding that his Native status be reevaluated is extremely revealing. The question of Kennewick Man's ethnicity, of whether he is in fact "Native American," would not be made unless another possibility is being implied. And it is.

For the popular press, Kennewick Man's most glamorous appeal is his "Caucasoid" characteristics. Even those scientists who insist upon a conservative reading of the shape of his skull, arguing that he is most likely part of an earlier but still very Asian migration across the Bering Strait land bridge, cannot help but speculate a little on the possibility that the first Americans were, in fact, white guys. The AFA has requested that the bones be studied to determine whether Kennewick Man is "more closely linked to modern Native Americans, Asians, or Europeans" (*Oregonian* 10/3/97, D3). Senator Slade Gorton and State Representatives Doc Hastings, Jack Metcalf, and George Netherwitt Jr., all of Washington, have argued that preliminary scientific assessments indicate that the remains could be Caucasian. An article in the *New Yorker* does its best to argue that the first Americans may very well have been ancient Europeans: "Kennewick Man's bones are part of a growing quantity of evidence that the earliest inhabitants of the New World may have been a Caucasoid people. . . . these people may have originally come from Europe" (Preston 1997, 72). Preston quotes Chatters's description of what Kennewick Man may have looked like: "On the physical characteristics alone, he could fit on the streets of Stockholm without causing any kind of notice. Or, on the streets of Jerusalem, or New Delhi for that matter. I've been looking around for someone who matches this Kennewick gentleman, looking for weeks and weeks for people on the street, thinking, 'This one's got a little bit here, that one a little bit there.' And then, one evening, I turned on the TV and there was Patrick Stewart—Captain Picard of Star Trek, and I said, 'My God, there he is! Kennewick Man!'" (Preston 1997, 73).

Robson Bonnichsen also argues that the earliest inhabitants of the Americas may not have been those people we currently think of as indigenous. "We're getting some hints from people working with genetic data that these earliest populations might have some shared genetic characteristics with latter-day European populations" (Preston 1997, 78). *U.S. News and World Report* jumped on the sensationalized media appeal of Kennewick Man, clearly demonstrating why the remains have had such a following in popular culture: "Thus continued the dramatics attending One of the Most Startling Science Stories of the Age. K-Man, it happens, is identifiably Caucasoid, and his discovery has rocked all Extant Systems of Belief as anthropologists ponder a large and quite politically incorrect question about The Peopling of North America: Is it possible that the original 'Native Americans' were, um, white guys?" (*U.S. News and World Report* 9/22/97, 10).

Even more interesting, these texts argue that these ancient Europeans in America were wiped out in a genocidal mass by the ancestors of today's contemporary Native Americans, perhaps by warfare, perhaps by the spreading of new and unfamiliar diseases, "just as European diseases wiped out a large percentage of the Native American population after the arrival of Columbus" (Preston 1997, 80). Preston concludes his argument for the prehistoric European conquest of the Americas by posing this question: "It does raise an interesting question: If the original inhabitants of the New World were Europeans who were pushed out by Indians would it change the Indians' position in the great moral landscape?" (Preston 1997, 81). If Native Americans can be accused of prehistoric genocide against early Euroamericans, can the genocide of colonization be re-envisioned as the evening of an old score? As Bruce M. Rowe of Pierce College in Los Angeles said: "If the current Native Americans' ancestors were the second population here, then their legal battles over land based on 'They were here first' might not have as much psychological force" (*Kennewick {WA} Tri-Cities Herald*, 6/1/99).

Similarly, the AFB has argued their belief that Kennewick Man is in fact an ancient European and as such shared religious and cultural traits with ancient Germanic and Nordic peoples. Michael Clinton, lawyer for the AFA, told the *Oregonian*: "It is now thought possible that European-type groups could, in fact, have also made that long walk" (*Oregonian* 10/26/96, D3). An article in the *Runestone,* the quarterly publication of the AFA, in the spring of 1997 argued that: "An entire culture of long-skulled Caucasian proportioned people may have inhabited the American west . . . . the lore of Nevada and California is full of stories about tall, red haired mummies that don't resemble Native Americans in the slightest. . . . Kennewick Man is kin. He represents a branch of our people, a limb of the family tree that grew through America's back door long before our own forebears ever dreamed of sailing the Atlantic. . . . Someday it will be acknowledged that a Caucasoid people did in fact arrive in the Americas thousands of years ago" (McNallan 1997, 7–8).

Such arguments for the presence of ancient Europeans in the New World have been a part of archaeology and anthropology since its inception in the Americas. Enormous earthen mounds in the Midwest were for a long time argued to be the work of "a civilized, white race" that had built the mounds "only to be overrun by red savages" (McGuire 1997, 69). The mound builders were long believed to have been "exterminated by the ancestors of the American Indians." The claim reflected "the widespread belief that the Indians were genocidal savages and made the archaeological record appear to be further justification for the waging of war upon them and the seizure of their land" (Trigger 1980, 665), and to prove beyond doubt that the Native Americans "were not the first inhabitants of the hemisphere" (Zimmerman 1997, 95; see also McGuire 1997, 21).

Such sentiments as these are important to note, I believe, because they take shape within several common stereotypes and symbolic constructions in the popular and academic mind about Native Americans and their place in the history of the United States. Further, they are also descriptive of the ways in which the body becomes constructed as a text upon which dominant cultural norms are inscribed.

The view of the body guiding modern science emerged from the empirical, rational modes of thought of Enlightenment philosophy, in which the body was approached as something to be dissected, analyzed, and eventually mastered. As textbook, the body can be read and comprehended by the rigors of science. It is a material object that follows scientific laws and can be subjected to calculations, experimentations, and evaluation. In many ways, anthropology-as-human-science has approached Native Americans in much the same way. For most of its history, anthropologists approached Native peoples as objects and labeled their Native teachers "informants." Kennewick Man is in keeping with this tradition. He is the ideal informant: He can be read through empirical processes to provide scientifically verifiable data. He cannot speak for himself but must be spoken for. And even better, he cannot mislead researchers through misinformation or poor translations, as living Native "informants" are wont to do. Like the body of the scientific tradition, Kennewick Man is reduced to what Denise Riley has called "an obstinate core of identification" (Riley 1988, 101), that is, a reliable, verifiable source of identifying information, free of cultural or subjective input. The body is thus assumed to be a foundational seal, a place to return to that transcends and precedes discourse.[4]

But such a perception of the body is simplistic. As they have formulated their critique of the modern subject, critical theorists such as Foucault and feminist critical theorists such as Judith Butler, Gayatri Spivak, and Riley have also critiqued the modern empirical view of the body. As these scholars have demonstrated, bodies are constructed, perceivable only through discourse that is influenced by cultural, political, and economic processes. Bodies can only be experienced through discourse, and so the language, narratives, and questions that are used about that body will dictate what sort of body is ultimately perceived. Spivak explains: "If one really thinks about the body, as such, there is no possible outline of the body as such. There are thinkings of the systematiciry of the body, there are value codings of the body. The body, as such, cannot be thought, and I certainly cannot approach it" (qtd. in Butler 1993, 1). The work of Foucault has been foundational in establishing this notion of the body as a culturally constructed force, which conveys knowledge and the power associated with it. This body, for Foucault, acts as a space upon which culture and power relations are clearly inscribed. It acts as the ideal ledger of power. Foucault's body

---

[4]This can be seen among other theorists as well. Jane Gallop quotes Roland Barthes describing the body as "a bedrock given, prior to any subjectivity" (Ebert 1996, 243). And for Julia Kristeva, "the material is matter that exceeds the symbolic function, both the matter of the body and the matter of the objective world" (Hennessy 1993, 50). In much work, the body has thus been imaged as a "presymbolic, corporeal space cut off from the social workings of difference" (Hennessy 1993, 50).

is the "ultimate micro-existence . . . the fundamental materiality on which history has been inscribed . . . a volume in perpetual disintegration" (Hennessy 1993, 44).

Foucault's argument for the body as text led many feminist critical theorists to conclude that the body is only experienced through a culturally constructed discourse, which makes the body as such completely inaccessible. Riley argues that bodies "have slipped away as objects, and become instead almost trace phenomena which are produced by the wheelings about of great technologies and politics. . . . In a strong sense, the body is really constantly altering as a concept" (Riley 1988, 102, 204). Surrounded and encoded by value-laden imagery and political manipulations, the body becomes a potent tool for constructing systems of knowledges and behaviors. Through this dense veil of significations, many theorists argue, the body becomes completely occluded. And as Camilla Griggers has argued in her analysis of the construction of faciality and bodily narratives in the contemporary fashion, media, and medical industries: "The body is not outside textuality; the body is itself a field of signification, a site for the production of cultural meanings and ideological reifications" (Griggers 1997, 54).

These perceptions do not take place in a vacuum: they are the result of political and economic conditions, and is becomes clear that privileged narratives are those that speak on behalf of the privileged class, in this case, that of the colonizer. These narratives that have been constructed about the body reflect significant political and economic concerns, and those narratives that become the privileged, dominant modes of discourse in society reflect privileged political and economic status. In other words, those in power determine which narratives will become the dominant or accepted readings of the body. Scholars in particular, occupying a place of privilege as we do, need to be aware of dominant modes of thought in our own traditions that reduce Native peoples to a farcical stereotype, that would suggest that "real" Indians lived only in prehistory. To begin to reevaluate our position as scholars requires that we first deconstruct the body that we have constructed. What do the discourse and imagery that have arisen around Kennewick Man tell us about the "Indian" body that has been constructed by the dominant culture?

Looking at the brief statements made about Kennewick Man, in light of the work of such scholars as Robert Berkhofer and Fergus M. Bordewich, we see a consistent stereotype of the "noble savage" played out throughout U.S. history, a fetishized image of Native Americans, formed out of projected shadows and needs of white society, which I will call the "Authentic Indian." "Authentic Indians" are seen as being frozen in time, the embodiment of the noble savage, in tune with nature and the mysterious spiritual world that inhabited it prior to the arrival of Western civilization. "Authentic Indians" are one with the land, wear buckskin and feathers, live in tipis, dance with wolves, and hunt buffalo while riding bareback. "Authentic Indians" behave, look like, and live as Hollywood has told us they do. To not look like the stereotype is to not be really "Indian." Indeed, Kennewick Man is said to be of European origin, because, as Douglas Owsley of the Smithsonian Institution has said, he "does not look quite like what you think of when you think about a modern Indian" (*Science* 4/10/98, 190). To any Native American this statement must sound ludicrous. Native people vary vastly in appearance from community to community and generation to generation. But because he does not fit the stereotype, Kennewick Man cannot be considered an ancestor of "our Indians." Concurrent with this stereotype of the "Authentic Indian" is the belief that the "Indian" was doomed to extinction from the moment Columbus set foot in the Americas and that the "Indians," the real ones anyway, have all ceased to exist. And indeed, the "Indian" of Americana mythology no longer exists, nor did she ever. As Rayna Green has commented: "They don't believe in us. They don't believe we're alive because we've changed. They don't believe we can carry briefcases, because the Indians they play are an invention, a figment. And they want us to live up to the Indians they play and the price for that is a mythological and sometimes real death for real Indians. . . . I'm convinced that, in order for them to really successfully play Indian, we need to be dead" (qtd. in Parkhill 1997, 85).

Contemporary Native Americans do not adequately fulfill the stereotypes that American popular culture desires to see embodied: in addition to maintaining deeply held traditional religious and cultural beliefs and practices, living Native Americans also attend college, run casinos, are shrewd legal experts, speak ac academic conferences, and facilitate support groups for recovering Catholics, codependency, or alcoholism. They are not the noble primitive savages that popular American culture, living in its urban, postmodern world, needs to fulfill its fantasies. The "Authentic Indian" is the embodiment of an important part of the non-Native unconscious, and failing to have that stereotype embodied in actuality leaves the non-Native person at a loss. Who will adopt the Boy Scout into his secret ceremonial society, imparting ancient mysterious wisdom that the contemporary city dweller may be feeling hungry for? Where is the Pocahontas who will rescue us from our own spiritual angst? In the absence of "Authentic Indians" Kennewick Man provides a marvelous solution: the "real Indians" are in fact white folks! Wendy Rose has written that "The Whiteshaman reader/performer aspires to 'embody the Indian' in effect 'becoming' the 'real' Indian even when actual Native people are present. Native reality is thereby subsumed and negated by imposition of a greater or 'more universal' contrivance" (Rose 1992, 405).

Kennewick Man, when seen in this light, becomes for non-Natives a crucial and almost mystical link with one's own "inner Indian." Through Kennewick Man, white popular culture can appropriate the role of the "Authentic Indian" that Native Americans have not adequately embodied. White culture can create its own claim to being part of the landscape, to being heirs of the "Indian." And the necessary mediator, who will act to restore American society to the wisdom and strength associated with the preindustrial, preurban, preliterate society of Kennewick Man, is the scientific community. The perception of the "unbridgeable gulf" between the "Indian" in tune with nature and the white, urban, post-World War II individual has grown, and with it has come the notion that there are "rare scholar-mediators who can bridge the gap" (Parkhill 1997, 82). As Randall McGuire has observed: "The notion of the vanishing American Indian allows archaeologists to glorify their object, the Indian past, and yet detach it from the descendants of that past, living Indian people. The heroes of the prehistoric tale become archaeologists that have been able to interpret this past and not the Indian people whose lives flow from it" (McGuire 1992, 827).

It is this context that at times infuses the work of archaeologists and anthropologists with such intense importance. Archaeologists write of their work as a responsibility, duty, and right. "We have a mandate to preserve and protect the past for the future, an obligation to past cultures to tell their story and to future generations to preserve the past for their benefit" (Goldstein and Kintigh, chap. 9, this volume). If the past is to be known, archaeologists must make it known. Clement Meighan writes of the ability and duty of archaeologists to be the sole voice of the vanished "Indian." "Archaeologists have a responsibility to the people they study. They are defining the culture of an extinct group and in presenting their research they are writing a chapter of human history that cannot be written except from archaeological investigation. If the archaeology is not done, the ancient people remain without a history" (Meighan, 1994, 64). Meighan's sentiment effectively cuts contemporary Native peoples away from their predecessors, making archaeologists the true heirs of the prehistoric, "Authentic Indians." Christy Turner's 1986 piece chimes in with Meighan, when Turner argues, "I explicitly assume no living culture, religious interest group, or biological population has any moral or legal right to the exclusive use or regulation of ancient human skeletons since all humans are members of the same species, and ancient skeletons are the remnants of unduplicatable evolutionary events which all living and future peoples have the right to know about and understand" (Turner 1986, 1). The vehicle through which all living and future people will gain this knowledge, it is implied, is through archaeological and osteological investigation. While scientists involved in the debate over Kennewick Man intend for their research to transcend cultural divisions, it in fact proves to reinforce hierarchies of privilege, making the anthropologist the only legitimate voice to speak for indigenous peoples and grant identity to Native peoples, even more so than they themselves. Amy Dansie of the Nevada State Museum argues the point quite well: "We're not trying to offend Native Americans, although they're hostile to us now. . . . It seems they think we're trying to steal their ancestors and their history. We're not; we just think you shouldn't deny these ancient people their identity" (*Science* 4/10/98, 193).

Trigger and others have pointed out the problems inherent in such arguments on behalf of osteological work. Universal agendas and "Everyman" talk inevitably mean that members of the predominantly white, predominantly Western scientific community take possession of the remains and determine the course of investigation.

By treating generalizations about human behavior as being the primary goal of archaeological research, archaeologists have chosen to use data concerning the native peoples of North America for ends that have no special relevance to these people. Instead, the remains are employed in a clinical manner to rest hypotheses that intrigue professional anthropologists and to produce knowledge that is justified as serving the broader interests of Euroamerican society (Trigger 1980, 671).

This tendency is reinforced by the divorce of archaeology from ethnography and the oral traditions of living Native Americans, increasing the sense of an unmendable break between "Indians" of the past and Native Americans of today. As McGuire has pointed out, this belief that "Authentic Indians" had ceased to exist, and the subsequent disarticulation of living Native peoples from their past, "provided the vehicle by which whites took over Native American heritages for nationalistic and scientific purposes. Archaeologists lifted dead Indians from their graves, in part, to help create a national heritage, and the myth of the vanishing Americans. By routing the red savages, the new, civilized white American race inherited the mantle, the heritage, of the old civilization and the legitimate claims to the land" (McGuire 1992, 818, 821).

It is here, I believe, that we begin to understand the implications of the Kennewick Man debate and the reasons behind the intensely emotional determination of non-Native popular and academic culture to glean from this ancient text the wisdom and illumination that they so firmly believe it holds for them. When discussing the work of Charles Godfrey Leland, who collected folklore among Native populations of the Northeast, and Leland's certainty that the Northeast "Indian" myths that he recorded were somehow intimately connected to Norse mythology, Thomas Parkhill turned to Yi Fu Tuan's notion of geopiety, that is, "the sense of country as one's native home, the sense that one had sprung out of its soil and was nurtured by it; the belief that one's ancestors since time immemorial were born in it" (Parkhill 1997, 98). It is this longing for a sense of geopiety that Parkhill believes to be at the root of Leland's desire to see a link between a Maliseet myth and Nordic epics. Parkhill sees Leland's construction as part of "the process by which human beings construct their place by weaving themselves into their landscapes." It is this process that is "part of a larger human endeavor to make Place for themselves" (Parkhill 1997, 99). As Parkhill further explains: "Responding to these Place-driven needs, some of us turn to the timeless, tradition-respecting 'Indian' who has a deep abiding relationship to Mother Earth. Perhaps, their part of our story goes, the 'Indians' can help us to feel a sense of belonging. . . . If the 'Indian' would only teach us some of her or his timeless secrets, we too would have access to this sacred sense of Place" (Parkhill 1997, 111). What we see happening in the battle over Kennewick Man takes Parkhill's experience with Leland's work a step further. With Kennewick Man the mystical "Indian" who will impart the wisdom necessary to restore one's relationship with the land, to achieve a sense of Place, comes one step closer: "The 'Indian' is, in fact, one of us!" And in this instance, the hope that non-Natives are, in fact, the "real Indians" thrives off of a projected need and desire for the "Authentic Indian" that has fed Americana and pop culture since the beginning of U.S. history. Through cinema, advertising, literature, and the numerous image-making techniques of late capitalism, non-Native America has depended upon the power of the "Indian" image, the projection of everything urban industrial civilization is not and secretly (or not so secretly) wishes it was. As Bonnichsen has said: "Kennewick Man has become a public icon. . . . He's pushed peoples' buttons; they are enormously interested in finding out who he is. He could well change our perception of who first settled America" (*Science* 4/10/98, 190).

To the degree that Kennewick Man facilitates the appropriation of the identity of the "Authentic Indian," he gains the attention and fascination of the American public. Parkhill's discussion of the search for Place gives light to the Kennewick Man controversy. When scholars and journalists write about "our ancestor" discovered in "our homeland" who wants to tell us things about "our past," they are weaving themselves and their lives into the history of the Northwest. Thus the body becomes our link with the land. Through the body in question, contemporary Americans will gain a means of creating a sense of Place, and establishing themselves on the land. This is seen clearly in the plans of the AFA to memorialize the site where Kennewick Man was found, to honor "the memory of someone they consider to be a revered ancestor" (*Oregonian* 1/13/98, E3). Thus, cermonially, the AFA will make a claim to space, create Place, and will establish a visible and secure tie that grants them (and other Euroamericans) a legitimacy and authenticity within the land.

Curtis Hinsley Jr. has argued that early archaeologists of the eighteenth and nineteenth centuries struggled to construct a narrative that would lend a definition and sense of identity to the newly forming nation. The bodies of Native Americans became key elements of understanding and incorporating the past into themselves, of becoming part of the landscape in which they lived. "Digging in the prehistoric dirt and constructing heroic tales on what they found, these men . . . faced the challenge of replacing a heritage of heroism built on classical literature with an identity constructed of shards and bones and preliterate silence." They set to work, painstakingly constructing the nation's own identity "by absorbing and domesticating their predecessors into themselves" (Hinsley, chap. 2, this volume). Part and parcel of this process of constructing place has been constructing an "Authentic Indian" body through which Euroamericans can have access to the land. Whether that body was the compliant Indian Maiden or the bloodthirsty savage who must be removed in order for civilization to progress, stereotypes of the "Authentic Indian" have depended upon external constructions of the Native form, which facilitated the appropriation of Native identity and Native land. In an eerie way, Kennewick Man is much the same. As his face was reconstructed from a cast of his skull, Kennewick Man took on the features of a white northern European, looking remarkably like one of the most well-known British actors on television. Mass media, pop culture, and the academic community have already made it very clear. Kennewick Man is one of us. We are the truly "Authentic Indians."[5] Michael Clinton is thus not so very mistaken when he argues that "Kennewick Man is a threat to the Indians because he jeopardizes their moral authority and argument that they were the victims of Europeans which succeeded them" (*New York Times* 4/2/98, A12). That is exactly what the media's reading of Kennewick Man's body, encouraged by academics who have nor considered the political implications of their words, may very well do.

It must of course be pointed out that not all archaeologists or anthropologists participate in the appropriation of Native identities or in the collection and study of human remains without the permission of affiliated tribes. Many scholars have made great strides in becoming responsive to the needs and concerns of Native communities, in working with and for Native communities rather than around them, and

---

[5]David Cournoyer of Denver wrote in response to Chatters's reconstruction: James Chatters, the anthropologist who reconstructed the face of the 9,300 year old skull known as Kennewick Man, likens his facial structure to that of Patrick Stewart, the 'Star Trek' actor. As an American Indian, I see the cheekbones and features of an American Indian" (*New York Times*, 4/8/98, A18) It would be hard to find a clearer illustration of the way in which bodies are constructed and read according to cultural, political, and economic positioning.

in respecting the individuals whom they are studying as individuals and subjects, not as objects. Many also disapprove of the racialized language that has been used surrounding Kennewick Man. Many have insisted that use of the term "Caucasoid" to begin with was an enormous mistake on Chatters's part. In speaking so, "Chatters has given a racial identification to something that may ultimately defy racial categories. As Alan Goodman, professor of anthropology at Hampshire College in Amherst, Mass., put it, 'Kennewick Man has become a textbook example of why race science is bad science'" (*New York Times* 4/2/98. A12). Jonathan Marks of the University of California at Berkeley also challenges Chatters's position.

> Chatters argues that designation of the specimen as "Caucasoid" should be divorced from its racial implications. But how can it, if the term itself is racial and directly implies the peoples of Europe and the Near East? To call the specimen an "atypical Native American" would have been more accurate and less problematic. To call it "Caucasoid" is to connote aspects of ancestry, not simply morphology; it directly suggests that America was settled by Europeans and that those now called "Native Americans" are actually less "native" than they think. This is a strongly political statement requiring an exceptional level of validation. There is an element of responsibility to be considered here; without it, the statement represents anthropology, indeed science in general, very poorly. (Marks 1998, 1)

It must also be pointed out that this desire to construct Place is not criminal or, for that matter, a sign of a culturally impoverished people. The AFA is doing a work that many Native people applaud: encouraging non-Native seekers to seek within their own cultural past before they appropriate Native traditions for their own. The AFC's agenda is neither racist nor hate-driven: they are looking to recover an earth-based faith and tradition that was lost to Christianization. It is a cross-cultural and perhaps universally present need to locate oneself in the place one lives and to feel a sense of connection to the land. It is this assurance of identity and location that many Native peoples of the Pacific Northwest have and that many non-Native peoples crave. Does is mean that non-Native peoples do not have the right to establish a sense of Place? Of course not, nor does it necessarily mean that the readings of Kennewick Man that the academic community or the AFA might make are flawed or wrong. It is nor the veracity of the scientific or religious claims that I question but rather why these claims are made, why these questions are asked to begin with, and why they maintain such a grip on the public's imagination that they continue to occupy headlines nearly three years after the lawsuit over Kennewick Man began. I have argued that it is the need to establish a sense of Place and to find the embodiment of the non-Native projection of the "Authentic Indian" that provides the emotional fascination with Kennewick Man. This projection, carried to its extreme, is most perfectly embodied in a "primitive, noble savage" who is both indigenous to the Americas and of European origin. Here we find the manner in which *cultural constructions of the body contribute to the creation of a sense of place*. With this in mind, is there a resolution to the controversy? If those parties involved recognize their underlying interest in the construction of their identities onto Kennewick Man, can it facilitate a more impartial approach toward a resolution?

Where Do We Go from Here?

The resolution begins, I believe, with recognizing that it is with such histories of archaeological and popular image-making and history-writing that we approach Kennewick Man today. History has ever and always been a narrative, written and rewritten to suit the needs of the day; history is constructed, not discovered. As Thomas Biolsi and Zimmerman have argued: "Anthropology is not a universal 'science of man' [*sic*]. It is a set of questions asked and answered by an 'interested party' in a global and highly unequal encounter, the ultimate results of which are yet to be fully worked out. Anthropology is the academic discipline that makes sense of the Others the West has both created and encountered in its global expansion since 1500" (Biolsi and Zimmerman 1997, 14).

It is this global expansion that must be remembered when we hear arguments that Kennewick Man belongs to the global community. The debate over Kennewick Man itself is a clear indicator of the political and economic forces at work in the cultural construction and reading of the body. Foucault and others have argued that it is as a site and "force of production that the body is invested with relations of power and domination. . . . the body becomes a useful force only if it is both a productive and a subjected body" (Foucault 1977, 26). It is as a tool in the process of colonial capitalism that the body gains power to signify in the contemporary Western world. Kennewick Man is valued and coveted by those fighting for the right to control the reading of his body as text, because he is both a subjected body and a productive body. He is subjected to the gaze and signification of a number of interested parties, and he likewise carries strategic potential within economic hierarchies of production and exploitation of Native lands, research grants, and fellowships, or water, land, and fishing rights. As Teresa Ebert explains: "What makes a body valuable in the world is its economic value" (Ebert 1996, 81, 220).

With this in mind, it becomes clear that approaching corporeality from different modes of thought, with different cultural, political, economic, and spiritual contexts, will radically affect the body that is perceived. Archaeologists and anthropologists who inscribe the body with empiricist Enlightenment agendas ask questions with regard to age, dates, race, migratory patterns, chemical measurements, and radiocarbon dating. The questions are constructed from a history of colonial discourse, which seeks to understand the Other so as to better colonize them: understanding the origins of the Natives, how they fit within the Euroamerican conception of human history, and how to integrate, assimilate, or do away with them most effectively. What must be remembered is that Native peoples are simply asking different questions when approaching their history. For instance, Native peoples may not be asking questions about origins (they know where they came from already) but rather about how best to establish their cultural and semiotic sovereignty. The fact that scientific narratives gain precedence over Native narratives about their own history is indicative of the power differential inherent in colonial relationships. Scientists who would measure craniums, DNA, and radiocarbon emissions and continue to insist that their work emerges from a material body that acts as an essential bedrock of reliable information do not realize that their own processes of inquiry are the result of certain political, economic, and social privileges.[6] We must therefore remember that the global community to which claimants in the lawsuit over Kennewick Man refer is one dominated by Western capitalism and the vestiges of colonialism. We must also remember that the search for Place and the appropriation of the "Authentic Indian" identity cannot be divorced from its economic consequences. The non-Native search for legitimation of land claims has been a source of complex spiritual and emotional paradigms, but is has also been an elementally economic one.

It is in reading this text of the body that relations of power are made manifest. As Foucault has observed, knowledge and power are intimately connected. To know something is to gain power over it. As such, the attempt by the academic community to "know" the history of Native peoples (better than they themselves do), to categorize and map the migration patterns of the past, is to gain power over history. The battle over Kennewick Man becomes a battle over who is to control historical narratives and hence who is to have power over the categories of identity that dominate and control the present and the future. As Alan Schneider, attorney for the anthropologists suing for the body, has said, "It's really a battle

---

[6]For a summary of the history of similar research within anthropology through the nineteenth century that contributed to racist traditions of eugenics and notions of racial evolution, see Robert E. Bieder, chap. 1 this volume.

over who is going to control knowledge about the past" (*Oregonian* 10/14/96, A1). The claim that many well-intentioned academics have made, that their work exists outside of a politicized framework, is naive at best. As Foucault has argued: "We should abandon a whole tradition that allows us to imagine that knowledge can exist only where the power relations are suspended and that knowledge can develop only outside its injunctions, its demands, and its interests . . . power produces knowledge . . . power and knowledge directly imply one another. . . . There is no power relation without the correlative constitution of a field of knowledge, nor any knowledge that does not presuppose and constitute at the same time power relations" (Foucault 1977, 27).

Thus systems of knowledge that are developed as "objective" or "impartial" science can never really be what they claim to be. As children of colonial-expansionist capitalist systems, the academic community that would gaze upon and "know" the passive object can all too easily act to propitiate and further the power relations, land acquisition, and identity appropriation that enabled their work in the first place.

Occupying a place of privilege as we do, scholars within the academy need to be aware of the dominant modes of thought within which our tradition came into being and with which it continues to contend. The debate over Kennewick Man presents us with this challenge to cultivate an attitude of self-reflexive awareness. As members of the economic elite and participants in a colonizing power of political hegemony, scholars can no longer defend a strategic ignorance of our own position within power structures. We must recognize that when the body as such becomes visible to us, it does so "only under some particular gaze, including that of politics" (Riley 1988, 106). Our gaze as intellectuals is never a disembodied gaze, detached from political and economic agendas. We as scholars must scrutinize our own actions and arguments. What right do we have to subject our objects of study to our gaze? What and whose interests are we serving when doing so? And how are those questions and answers informed by our positioning as scholars of privilege?

This is not to suggest that Kennewick Man should be seen as merely a text, scribbled over with the graffiti of culturally relative narratives, none of which have any truth or grounding in reality. As many postmodern critiques have begun to point out, to abandon oneself to notions of cultural relativity and the social construction of everything brings one quickly to an impasse of cultural nihilism. Donna Haraway has argued that when cultural relativity is taken to the extreme, "We end up with a kind of epistemological electric shock therapy, which, far from ushering us into the high stakes cables of the game of contesting public truths, lays us out on the table with self-induced multiple personality disorder" (Haraway 1988, 578). The goal that Haraway suggests, a goal useful to us here, is to have both a "radical contingency for all knowledge claims . . . and a no-nonsense commitment to faithful accounts of a 'real' world, one that can be partially shared." She goes on to argue that the alternative to relativism "is not totalization and single vision, which is always finally the unmarked category whose power depends on systemic narrowing and obscuring. The alternative to relativism is *partial, locatable,* critical knowledges sustaining the possibility of webs of connections called solidarity in politics, and shared conversations in epistemology. . . . It is exactly in the politics and epistemology of partial perspectives that the possibility of sustained, rational, objective inquiry rests" (Haraway 1988, 579, 584).

What Haraway challenges above all is not any particular view of the body but what she calls "the god-trick," that is, "seeing everything from nowhere," the objectivity that much of Western science has made claim to. No sight, Haraway argues, is ever detached and disembodied. "All eyes . . . are active perceptual systems, building on translations and specific ways of seeing. . . . There is no unmediated photograph or passive camera obscura in scientific accounts of bodies and machines; there are only highly specific visual possibilities, each with a wonderfully detailed, active, partial way of organizing worlds" (Haraway 1988,

583). Haraway argues for objectivity that is embodied, objectivity that recognizes it is seen through the eyes of a body that is situated, that sees only partially, and that is positioned within a certain time and space. As she says: "I am arguing for the view from a body, always a complex, contradictory, structuring and structured body, versus the view from above, from nowhere, from simplicity. Only the god trick is forbidden" (Haraway 1988, 589).

The ideal is therefore not to deconstruct bodies out of existence or to suggest that the biological is merely a matter of philosophy. Rather, it is to suggest that culturally distinct agendas within inquiry be given equal value within discourse. When scholars recognize that our own arguments are as much a result of processes of situated construction as those voiced by the objects of study, we will begin the process of productive discourse. It is not, therefore, scientific discourse itself that poses a challenge to political reform but the objectification, dissection, and dismembering of Native identities and the cultivated blindness to the contributions of political hegemony and economic privilege that likewise act to construct our own discourse about the body. By challenging Native notions of identity, which are expressed within their narratives of creation, oral historic traditions, and place-based mythologies, Native peoples are deconstructed as subjects and neatly removed from the political arena. What Haraway's essay calls for in the Kennewick Man debate is that the parties involved recognize their place within a multicultural system of divergent worldviews. Objectivity within the sciences of archaeology and anthropology only exists to the degree that scholars recognize that only a small fragment of the "real" can be seen, and it is necessarily viewed through very embodied, very particularly situated lenses. In the case of Kennewick Man, it means recognizing one's own fixation with projected images of "Authentic Indians," one's failure to recognize contemporary Native Americans as legitimate heirs of their history and tradition, one's own search for Place, spatial legitimacy, and geopiety, and one's attempt to appropriate Native identities for one's own.

With this recognition of one's position as an embodied subject comes the recognition of others as subjects as well. When the god-trick is abandoned, one cannot claim to see or know the whole story. Out of necessity, others are asked to speak, to provide their piece to the greater puzzle. As Haraway argues: "Rational knowledge is power-sensitive conversation . . . ruled by partial sight and limited voice, not partiality for its own sake but, rather, for the sake of the connections and unexpected openings situated knowledges make possible" (Haraway 1988, 590). Zimmerman, following Arnold Krupat's use of the term *ethnocriticism,* defines an ethnocritical archaeology: "Ethnocriticism is concerned with differences rather than oppositions; it seeks to replace oppositional with dialogical models where cultural differences are explored and where interpretations are negotiated rather than declared" (Zimmerman, chap. 16, this volume).

The very presence of a bitter and long-winded court battle indicates that these notions of ethnocriticism, of embodied, situated objectivity, are not currently in effect. It also indicates that until now academics have preferred to declare rather than negotiate interpretations. Situated knowledge grants the object of study her or his own subjectivity, the voice to speak, to provide situated vision nor available to the scholar. "Situated knowledges require that the object of knowledge be pictured as an actor and agent, nor as a screen or ground or a resource, never finally as slave to the master that closes off' the dialectic in his unique agency and his authorship of 'objective' knowledge" (Haraway 1988, 592). This means granting both living and deceased indigenous peoples both agency and subjectivity. It means treating Kennewick Man not merely as a bundle of bone to be radiocarbon dated and DNA to be deconstructed. It means facing the remains with the respect granted to a living human being, and it means granting Native peoples the semiotic sovereignty to speak for themselves, as subjects and not objects; to provide their own equally valued notion of history, rime, space, and ancestry.

The ability to name oneself, to assume a position of subjectivity, is an indicator of power and agency, a reversal in hierarchical systems of exploitation, and Kennewick Man is a revealing illustration of this process. The power to name, describe, and construct narratives around the body has come to be seen as an indicator of authority. To allow Native narratives to have equal voice and authenticity is to place Native use of language on an equal plane with that of Western Enlightenment empiricism and rationalism. To accept Native origin stories and historical narratives as being of equal value to those of Western science is thus to grant Native peoples semiotic sovereignty and as such to grant them subjectivity. It is not a question of who is correct or incorrect, but a matter of respecting the different embodied world views with which people approach their history. Like Kennewick Man, Native Americans have been subjected to study, as objects, throughout the history of their encounter with Euroamericans, and it is time they be granted the semiotic sovereignty to speak for themselves.

For too long academia has not created Native people as subjects with languages and situated rational knowledge of their own. They have instead spoken with other languages, been told to see through eyes embodied by someone else. Cecil King has argued that the language of anthropology "traps us in linguistic cages because we must explain our ways through alien hypothetical constructs and theoretical frameworks. . . . We want to be consulted and respected as not only human beings, at the very least, but as independent nations, with the right to determine what transpires within our boundaries" (King 1997, 116, 118). Vine Deloria, Jr. has argued much the same: "We have been the objects of scientific investigations and publications for too long, and it is our intent to become people once again, not specimens" (Deloria 1992, 595). Kennewick Man calls for a new understanding of ourselves as scholars, of the needs that drive our work, and the inspiration and fascination that guide the questions we ask and the narratives we construct. Finding place and understanding where we are situated within the land in which we live is an important task, one with profound spiritual and psychological consequences, not to mention political, economic, and academic ones. However, what the Kennewick Man debate shows us is that these need-driven searches for place cannot be done at the cost of some very basic principles, the most prominent being respect: respect for others' semiotic sovereignty and for every individual impacted by the work we do and the conclusions we draw. Wendell Johnson of the Colorado River Indian Tribe sums it up well: "The hell with federal laws. When it comes to dealing with people, there has to be that respect. . . . I think that's what this whole reburial thing centers around, is respect" (qtd. in Watson et al 1989, 40).[7]

References

Berkhofer, Robert. 1978. *The White Man's Indian.* New York: Random House.

Biolsi, Thomas, and Larry Zimmerman. 1997. *Indian and Anthropologists: Vine Deloria Jr. and the Critique of Anthropology.* Tucson: University of Arizona Press.

Bordewich, Fergus M. 1996. *Killing the White Man's Indian: Reinventing Native Americans at the End of the Twentieth Century.* New York: Doubleday.

Butler, Judith. 1993. *Bodies That Matter.* New York: Routledge.

Deloria, Vine, Jr. 1992. "Indians, Archaeologists, and the Future." *American Antiquity* 57 (4): 595–98.

Ebert, Teresa. 1996. *Ludic Feminism and After: Postmodernism, Desire, and Labor in Late Capitalism.* Ann Arbor, MI: Michigan University Press.

---

[7] As of 1 July 1999 Kennewick Man's bones have been transferred to the Burke Museum at the University of Washington for preliminary study to determine "cultural affiliation" and if the bones are indeed "Native American." Study has thus far been noninvasive and nondestructive. No conclusions have as of yet been made.

Foucault, Michel. 1977. *Discipline and Punish: The Birth of the Prison.* New York: Random House.

Griggers, Camilla. 1997. *Becoming-Woman.* Minneapolis: University of Minnesota Press.

Haraway, Donna. 1988. "Situated Knowledges: The Science Question in Feminism and the Privilege of Partial Perspective." *Feminist Studies* 14 (3): 575–99.

Hennessy, Rosemary. 1993. *Materialism, Feminism, and the Politics of Discourse.* New York: Routledge.

King, Cecil. 1997. "Here Come the Anthros." In Biolsi and Zimmerman 1997.

Kroeber, Theodora. 1967. *Ishi in Two Worlds: A Biography of the Last Wild Indian in North America.* Berkeley: University of California Press.

Marks, Jonathan. 1998. "Replaying the Race Card." *Anthropology Newsletter* 39 (5): 1–4.

McGuire, Randall. 1997. "Why Have Archaeologists Thought the Real Indians Were Dead, and What Can We Do About It?" In Biolsi and Zimmerman 1997.

_____. 1992. "Archaeology and the First Americans." *American Anthropologist* 94 (4): 8 16–36.

McNallan, Stephen A. 1997. "Ancestral Bones: More on Kennewick Man." *Runestone* (18): 7–8.

Meighan, Clement. 1994. "Burying American Archaeology." *Archaeology* 47 (6): 64–68.

Parkhill, Thomas. 1997. *Weaving Ourselves into the Land: Charles Godfrey Leland, "Indians" and the Study of Native American Religions.* Albany: SUNY Press.

Preston, Donald. 1997. "The Lost Man." *New Yorker* 73 (16: 70–81.

Riley, Denise. 1988. *"Am I That Name?" Feminism and the Category of "Women" in History,* Minneapolis: University of Minnesota Press.

Rose, Wendy. 1992. "The Great Pretenders: Further Reflections on White Shamanism." In *The State of Native America: Genocide, Colonization and Resistance,* ed. M. Annette Jaimes. Boston: South End Press. 403–21.

Trafzer, Clifford E. 1997. *Death Stalks the Yakama.* East Lansing: Michigan State University Press.

Trigger, Bruce. 1980. "Archaeology and the Image of the American Indian." *American Antiquity* 45: 662–76.

Tuan, Yi-Fu. 1977. *Space and Places: The Perspective of Experience.* Minneapolis: University of Minnesota Press.

Turner, Christy. 1986. "What Is Lost with Skeletal Reburial." *Archaeology* 7: 1.

Turner, Frederick W., III. 1971. *I Have Spoken: American History through the Voices of Indians.* Athens, OH: Swallow Press.

Watson, Norman, et al. 1989. "The Present Past: An Examination of Archaeological and Native American Thinking." In *Thinking across Cultures: The Third International Conference of Thinking,* ed. Donald Topping, Doris Crowell, and Victor Kobayashi. Hove, NJ: Lawrence Erlbaum Associates. 33–42.

Zimmerman, Larry. 1997. "Anthropology and Responses to the Reburial Issue." In Biolsi and Zimmerman 1997.

_____. 1994. "Sharing Control of the Past." *Archaeology* 47 (6): 65–68.

_____. 1992. "Archaeology, Reburial, and the Tactics of a Discipline's Self Delusion." *American Indian Culture and Research Journal* 16 (2): 37–56.

❧ BLUE JEANS ❧

Fred Davis

The new clothes [jeans] express profoundly democratic values. There are no distinctions of wealth or status, no elitism; people confront one another shorn of these distinctions.

—Charles A. Reich,
The Greening of America

Throughout the world, the young and their allies are drawn hypnotically to denim's code of hope and solidarity—to an undefined vision of the energetic and fraternal Americanness inherent in them all.

—Kennedy Frasier
"That Missing Button"

Karl Lagerfeld for Chanel shapes a classic suit from blue and white denim, $960, with denim bustier, $360, . . . and denim hat, $400. All at Chanel Boutique, Beverly Hills.

—Photograph caption in *Los Angeles Times Magazine* for article "Dressed-Up Denims," April 19, 1987

Since the dawn of fashion in the West some seven hundred years ago, probably no other article of clothing has in the course of its evolution more fully served as a vehicle for the expression of status ambivalences and ambiguities than blue jeans. Some of the social history supporting this statement is by now generally well known.[1] First fashioned in the mid-nineteenth-century American West by Morris Levi Strauss, a Bavarian Jewish peddler newly arrived in San Francisco, the trousers then as now were made from a sturdy, indigo-dyed cotton cloth said to have originated in Nimes, France. (Hence the anglicized contraction to *denim* from the French *de Nimes.*) A garment similar to that manufactured by Levi Strauss for goldminers and outdoor laborers is said to have been worn earlier in France by sailors and dockworkers from Genoa, Italy, who were referred to as "genes"; hence the term *jeans.* The distinctive copper riveting at the pants pockets and other stress points were the invention of Jacob Davis, a tailor from Carson City, Nevada, who joined the Levi Strauss firm in 1873, some twenty years after the garment's introduction.

More than a century went by, however, before this working man's garment attained the prominence and near-universal recognition it possesses today. For it was not until the late 1960s that blue jeans, after several failed moves in previous decades into a broader mass market, strikingly crossed over nearly all class, gender, age, regional, national, and ideological lines to become the universally worn and widely accepted item of apparel they are today. And since the crossover, enthusiasm for them has by no means been confined to North America and Western Europe. In former Soviet bloc countries and much of the Third World, too, where they have generally been in short supply, they remain highly sought after and hotly bargained over.

---

[1] Excellent, sociologically informed accounts of the origins and social history of blue jeans are to be found in Belasco (n.d.) and Friedmann (1987).

A critical feature of this cultural breakthrough is, of course, blue jeans' identity change from a garment associated exclusively with work (and hard work, at that) to one invested with many of the symbolic attributes of leisure: ease, comfort, casualness, sociability, and the outdoors. Or, as the costume historians Jasper and Roach-Higgins (1987) might put it, the garment underwent a process of cultural authentication that led to its acquiring meanings quite different from that with which it began. In bridging the work/leisure divide when it did, it tapped into the new, consumer-goods-oriented, postindustrial affluence of the West on a massive scale. Soon thereafter it penetrated those many other parts of the world that emulate the West.

But this still fails to answer the questions of why so rough-hewn, drably hued, and crudely tailored a piece of clothing should come to exercise the fascination it has for so many diverse societies and peoples, or why within a relatively short time of breaking out of its narrow occupational locus it spread so quickly throughout the world. Even if wholly satisfactory answers elude us, these questions touch intimately on the twists and turns of status symbolism. . . .

To begin with, considering its origins and longtime association with workingmen, hard physical labor, the outdoors, and the American West, much of the blue jeans' fundamental mystique seems to emanate from populist sentiments of democracy, independence, equality, freedom, and fraternity. This makes for a sartorial symbolic complex at war, even if rather indifferently for nearly a century following its introduction, with class distinctions, elitism, and snobbism, dispositions extant nearly as much in jeans-originating America as in the Old World. It is not surprising, therefore, that the first non-"working stiffs" to become attached to blue jeans and associated denim wear were painters and other artists, mainly in the southwest United States, in the late 1930s and 1940s (Friedmann 1987). These were soon followed by "hoodlum" motorcycle gangs ("bikers") in the 1950s and by New Left activists and hippies in the 1960s (Belasco n.d.). All these groups (each in its own way, of course) stood strongly in opposition to the dominant conservative, middle-class, consumer-oriented culture of American society. Blue jeans, given their origins and historic associations, offered a visible means for announcing such antiestablishment sentiments. Besides, jeans were cheap, and, at least at first, good fit hardly mattered.

Whereas by the late 1950s one could in some places see jeans worn in outdoor play by middle-class boys, until well into the 1960s a truly ecumenical acceptance of them was inhibited precisely because of their association with (more, perhaps, through media attention than from firsthand experience) such disreputable and deviant groups as bikers and hippies. Major sales and public relations campaigns would be undertaken by jeans manufacturers to break the symbolic linkage with disreputability and to convince consumers that jeans and denim were suitable for one and all and for a wide range of occasions (Belasco n.d.). Apparently such efforts helped; by the late 1960s blue jeans had achieved worldwide popularity and, of greater relevance here, had fully crossed over the occupation, class, gender, and age boundaries that had circumscribed them for over a century.

What was it—and, perhaps, what is it still—about blue jeans? Notwithstanding the symbolic elaborations and revisions (some would say perversions) to which fashion and the mass market have in the intervening years subjected the garment, there can be little doubt that at its crossover phase its underlying symbolic appeal derived from its antifashion significations: its visually persuasive historic allusions to rural democracy, the common man, simplicity, unpretentiousness, and, for many, especially Europeans long captivated by it, the romance of the American West with its figure of the free-spirited, self-reliant cowboy.[2]

---

[2]This is not to put forward some absurd claim to the effect that everyone who donned a pair of jeans was swept up by this imagery. Rather, it is to suggest that it was such imagery that came culturally to be encoded in the wearing of blue jeans (Berger 1984, 80–82), so that whether one wore them indifferently or with calculated symbolic intent, imitatively or in a highly individual manner, they would "on average" be viewed in this light.

But as the history of fashion has demonstrated time and again, no vestmental symbol is inviolable. All can, and usually will be, subjected to the whims of those who wish to convey more or different things about their person than the "pure" symbol in its initial state of signification communicates. Democratic, egalitarian sentiments notwithstanding, social status still counts for too much in Western society to permanently suffer the proletarianization that all unmodified blue-jean declaration of equality and fraternity projected. No sooner, then, had jeans made their way into the mass marketplace than myriad devices were employed for muting and mixing messages, readmitting evicted symbolic allusions, and, in general, promoting invidious distinctions among classes and coteries of jean wearers. Indeed, to the extent that their very acceptance was propelled by fashion as such, it can be said an element of invidiousness was already at play. For, other things being equal and regardless of the "message" a new fashion sends, merely to be "in fashion" is to be one up on those who are not as yet.[3]

Elite vs. Populist Status Markers

Beyond this metacommunicative function, however, the twists, inversions, contradictions, and paradoxes of status symbolism to which blue jeans subsequently lent themselves underscore the subtle identity ambivalences plaguing many of their wearers. In a 1973 piece titled "Denim and the New Conservatives," Kennedy Fraser (1981, 92) noted several such, perhaps the most ironic being this:

> Some of the most expensive versions of the All-American denim theme have come bouncing into our stores from European manufacturers. The irresistible pull of both European fashion and denim means that American customers will pay large sums for, say, French blue jeans despite the galling knowledge that fashionable young people in Saint-Tropez are only imitating young people in America, a country that can and does produce better and cheaper blue jeans than France.

By 1990 a nearly parallel inversion seemed about to occur in regard to the garment's post-1950s image as leisure wear, although for destination other than fields and factories. With the introduction of men's fall fashions for the year featuring "urban denim," a spokesman for the Men's Fashion Association said (Hofmann 1990): "It's not just about cowboys and country and western anymore. It used to be that denim meant play clothes; now men want to wear it to the office the next day."

Framing the garment's status dialectic was the contest of polarities, one pole continuing to emphasize and extend blue jeans' "base-line" symbolism of democracy, utility, and classlessness, the other seeking to reintroduce traditional claims to taste, distinction, and hierarchical division. (Any individual wearer, and often the garment itself, might try to meld motifs from both sides in the hope of registering a balanced, yet appropriately ambivalent, statement.)

---

[3]From this perspective, assumed by such important French critics as Barthes (1983) and Baudrillard (1984), all fashion, irrespective of the symbolic content that animates one or another manifestation of it, gravitates toward "designification" or the destruction of meaning. That is to say, because it feeds on itself (on its ability to induce others to follow the fashion "regardless"), it soon neutralizes or sterilizes whatever significance its signifiers had before becoming objects of fashion. Sheer display displaces signification; to take the example of blue jeans, even people hostile to their underlying egalitarian message can via fashion's mandate wear them with ease and impunity and, contrary to the garment's symbolic anti-invidious origins, score "status points" by doing so. This argument is powerful but in my view posits, in a manner similar to the claim that fashion is nothing more than change for the sake of change, too complete a break between the symbolic content of culture and the communication processes that embody and reshape it.

Conspicuous Poverty: Fading and Fringing

From the "left" symbolic (and not altogether apolitical) pole came the practice of jean fading and fringing. Evocative of a kind of conspicuous poverty, faded blue jeans and those worn to the point of exposing some of the garment's warp and woof were soon more highly prized, particularly by the young, than new, well-blued jeans. Indeed, in some circles worn jeans commanded a higher price than new ones. As with Chanel's little black dress, it cost more to look "truly poor" than just ordinarily so, which new jeans by themselves could easily accomplish. But given the vogue that fading and fringing attained, what ensued in the marketplace was predictable: Jeans manufacturers started producing prefaded, worn-looking, stone- or acid-washed jeans.[4] These obviated, for the average consumer if not for the jeans connoisseur disdainful of such subterfuge, the need for a long break-in period.

Labeling, Ornamentation, and Eroticization

From the "right" symbolic pole emerged a host of strategems and devices, all of which sought in effect to de-democratize jeans while capitalizing on the ecumenical appeal they had attained: designer jeans, which prominently displayed the label of the designer; jeans bearing factory sewn-in embroidering, nailheads, rhinestones, and other decorative additions; specially cut and sized jeans for women, children, and older persons; in general, jeans combined (with fashion's sanction) with items of clothing standing in sharp symbolic contradiction of them, e.g., sports jackets, furs, dress shoes, spiked heels, ruffled shirts, or silk blouses.

Paralleling the de-democratization of the jean, by the 1970s strong currents toward its eroticization were also evident. These, of course, contravened the unisex, de-gendered associations the garment initially held for many: the relative unconcern for fit and emphasis on comfort; the fly front for both male and female; the coarse denim material, which, though it chafed some, particularly women, was still suffered willingly. Numerous means were found to invest the jean and its associated wear with gender-specific, eroticized meaning. In the instance of women—and this is more salient sociologically, since it was they who had been defeminized by donning the blatantly masculine blue jeans in the first place—these included the fashioning of denim material into skirts, the "jeans for gals" sales pitches of manufacturers, the use of softer materials, cutting jeans so short as to expose the buttocks, and, in general, the transmogrification of jeans from loose-fitting, baggy trousers into pants so snugly pulled over the posterior as to require some women to lie down to get into them. So much for comfort, so much for unisexuality! Interestingly, in the never-ending vestmental dialectic on these matters baggy jeans for women again became fashionable in the mid-1980s.

Designer Jeans

Of all of the modifications wrought upon it, the phenomenon of designer jeans speaks most directly to the garment's encoding of status ambivalences. The very act of affixing a well-known designer's label—and some of the world's leading hautes couturiers in time did so—to the back side of a pair of jeans has to be interpreted, however else it may be seen, along Veblenian lines, as an instance of conspicuous consumption; in effect, a muting of the underlying rough-hewn proletariat connotation of the garment through the intro-

---

[4]A yet later variation on the same theme was "shotgun washed" jeans manufactured by a Tennessee company that blasted its garments with a twelve-gauge shotgun (Hochswender 1991).

duction of a prominent status marker.[5] True, sewing an exterior designer label onto jeans—a practice designers never resort to with other garments—was facilitated psychologically by the prominent Levi Strauss & Co. label, which had from the beginning been sewn above the right hip pocket of that firm's denim jeans and had over the years become an inseparable part of the garment's image. It could then be argued, as it sometimes was, that the outside sewing of a designer label was consistent with the traditional image of blue jeans. Still, Yves Saint Laurent, Oscar de la Renta, or Gloria Vanderbilt, for that matter, are not names to assimilate easily with Levi Strauss, Lee, or Wrangler, a distinction hardly lost on most consumers.

But as is so characteristic of fashion, every action elicits its reaction. No sooner had the snoblike, status-conscious symbolisms of designer jeans made its impact on the market than dress coteries emerged whose sartorial stock-in-trade was a display of disdain for the invidious distinctions registered by so obvious a status ploy. This was accomplished mainly through a demonstration of hyperloyalty to the original, underlying egalitarian message of denim blue jeans. As Kennedy Fraser (1981, 93) was to observe of these countercyclicists in 1973:

> The denim style of the more sensitive enclaves of the Village, the West Side, and SoHo is the style of the purist and neo-ascetic. Unlike the "chic" devotee of blue jeans, this loyalist often wears positively baggy denims, and scorns such travesties as embroideries and railheads. To underline their association with honesty and toil, the denims of choice are often overalls.

Not long after, the "positively baggy denims" of which Fraser speaks—this antifashion riposte to fashion's prior corruption of denim's 1960s-inspired rejection of status distinctions—were themselves, with that double reflexive irony at which fashion is so adept, assimilated into the fashion cycle. Then those "into" denim styles could by "dressing down" stay ahead of—as had their older, first-time-around denim-clad siblings of the sixties—their more conformist, "properly dressed" alters.

Conclusion

And so . . . do the dialectics of status and antistatus, democracy and distinction, inclusiveness and exclusiveness pervade fashion's twists and turns: as much, or even more, with the workingman's humble blue jeans as with formal dinner wear and the evening gown.

But such is fashion's way. If it is to thrive it can only feed off the ambiguities and ambivalences we endure in our daily lives and concourse, not only over those marks of social status considered here but equally over such other key identity pegs as age, gender, and sexuality, to mention but the most obvious. Were it the case, as some scholars have maintained, that fashion's sole symbolic end was registering and re-registering invidious distinctions of higher and lower, or better and lesser—that is, distinctions of class and social status—it would hardly have enough "to talk about": certainly not enough to account for its having thrived in Western society for as long as it has. But, as we have already seen. . . , it does have more to say: about our

---

[5]Everyone, without exception, whom I interviewed and spoke with in the course of my research on fashion (designers, apparel manufacturers, buyers, persons of the fashion press, fashion-conscious laypersons) interpreted designer jeans in this light. Most felt that status distinctions were the *only* reasons for designer jeans because, except for the display of the designer label, they could detect no significant difference between designer and nondesigner jeans. Not all commentators, however, are of the opinion that the prominent display of an outside label can be attributed solely to invidious status distinctions. Some (Black 1985) find in the phenomenon overtones of a modernist aesthetic akin, for example, to Bauhaus design, exoskeletal building, construction, action painting, and certain directions in pop art wherein the identity of the creator and the processual markings of his/her creation are visibly fused with the art work itself.

masculinity and femininity, our youth and age, our sexual scruples or lack thereof, our work and play, our politics, national identity, and religion. This said, one need not take leave of what has engaged us here, that rich symbolic domain that treats of the deference and respect we accord and receive from others (what Max Weber meant by *status*), in order to appreciate that fashion is capable of much greater subtlety, more surprises, more anxious backward glances and searching forward gazes than we credit it with.

Works Cited

Back, Kurt W. 1985. "Modernism and Fashion: A Social Psychological Interpretation," in Michael R. Solomon, ed., *The Psychology of Fashion.* Lexington, Mass.: Heath.

Barthes, Roland. 1983. *The Fashion System.* Translated by Matthew Ward and Richard Howard. New York: Hill and Wang.

Baudrillard, Jean. 1984. "La Mode or la féerie du code." *Traveres* 3 (October): 7–19.

Belasco, Warren A. n.d. "Mainstreaming Blue Jeans: The Ideological Process, 1945–1980." Unpublished.

Berger, Arthur Asa. 1984. *Signs in Contemporary Culture.* New York: Longman.

Fraser, Kennedy. 1981. *The Fashionable Mind.* New York: Knopf.

Friedmann, Daniel. 1987. *Une Histoire du blue jean.* Paris: Ramsay.

Hochswender, Woody. 1991. "Patterns." *New York Times,* Jan. 8.

Hofmann, Deborah. 1990. "New Urbanity for Denim and Chambray." *New York Times,* Sept. 24.

Jasper, Cynthia R., and Mary Ellen Roach-Higgins. 1987. "History of Costume: Theory and Instruction." *Clothing and Textile Research Journal* 5, no. 4 (Summer): 1–6.

Reich, Charles A. 1970. *The Greening of America.* New York: Crown.

SEEING

Annie Dillard

When I was six or seven years old, growing up in Pittsburgh, I used to take a precious penny of my own and hide it for someone else to find. It was a curious compulsion; sadly, I've never been seized by it since. For some reason I always "hid" the penny along the same stretch of sidewalk up the street. I would cradle it at the roots of a sycamore, say, or in a hole left by a chipped-off piece of sidewalk. Then I would take a piece of chalk, and, starting at either end of the block, draw huge arrows leading up to the penny from both directions. After I learned to write I labeled the arrows: SURPRISE AHEAD or MONEY THIS WAY. I was greatly excited, during all this arrow-drawing, at the thought of the first lucky passer-by who would receive in this way, regardless of merit, a free gift from the universe. But I never lurked about. I would go straight home and not give the matter another thought, until, some months later, I would be gripped again by the impulse to hide another penny.

It is still the first week in January, and I've got great plans. I've been thinking about seeing. There are lots of things to see, unwrapped gifts and free surprises. The world is fairly studded and strewn with pennies cast broadside from a generous hand. But—and this is the point—who gets excited by a mere penny? If you follow one arrow, if you crouch motionless on a bank to watch a tremulous ripple thrill on the water and are rewarded by the sight of a muskrat kit paddling from its den, will you count that sight a chip of copper only, and go your rueful way? It is dire poverty indeed when a man is so malnourished and fatigued that he won't stoop to pick up a penny. But if you cultivate a healthy poverty and simplicity, so that finding a penny will literally make your day, then, since the world is in fact planted in pennies, you have with your poverty bought a lifetime of days. It is that simple. What you see is what you get.

I used to be able to see flying insects in the air. I'd look ahead and see, not the row of hemlocks across the road, but the air in front of it. My eyes would focus along that column of air, picking out flying insects. But I lost interest, I guess, for I dropped the habit. Now I can see birds. Probably some people can look at the grass at their feet and discover all the crawling creatures. I would like to know grasses and sedges—and care. Then my least journey into the world would be a field trip, a series of happy recognitions. Thoreau, in an expansive mood, exulted, "What a rich book might be made about buds, including, perhaps, sprouts!" It would be nice to think so. I cherish mental images I have of three perfectly happy people. One collects stones. Another—an Englishman, say—watches clouds. The third lives on a coast and collects drops of seawater which he examines microscopically and mounts. But I don't see what the specialist sees, and so I cut myself off, not only from the total picture, but from the various forms of happiness.

Unfortunately, nature is very much a now-you-see-it, now-you-don't affair. A fish flashes, then dissolves in the water before my eyes like so much salt. Deer apparently ascend bodily into heaven; the brightest oriole fades into leaves. These disappearances stun me into stillness and concentration; they say of nature that it conceals with a grand nonchalance, and they say of vision that it is a deliberate gift, the revelation of a dancer who for my eyes only flings away her seven veils. For nature does reveal as well as conceal: now-you-don't-see-it, now-you-do. For a week last September migrating red-winged blackbirds were feeding heavily down by the creek at the back of the house. One day I went out to investigate the racket; I walked up to a tree, an Osage orange, and a hundred birds flew away. They simply materialized out of the tree. I saw a tree, then a whisk of color, then a tree again. I walked closer and another hundred blackbirds took flight. Not a branch, not a twig budged: The birds were apparently weightless as well as invisible. Or, it was as if the leaves of the Osage orange had been freed from a spell in the form of red-winged blackbirds; they flew from the tree, caught my eye in the sky, and vanished. When I looked again at the tree the leaves had reassembled as if nothing had happened. Finally I walked directly to the trunk of the tree and a final hundred, the real diehards, appeared, spread, and vanished. How could so many hide in the tree without my seeing them? The Osage orange, unruffled, looked just as it had looked from the house, when three hundred red-winged blackbirds cried from its crown. I looked downstream where they flew, and they were gone. Searching, I couldn't spot one. I wandered downstream to force them to play their hand, but they'd crossed the creek and scattered. One show to a customer. These appearances catch at my throat; they are the free gifts, the bright coppers at the roots of trees.

It's all a matter of keeping my eyes open. Nature is like one of those line drawings of a tree that are puzzles for children: Can you find hidden in the leaves a duck, a house, a boy, a bucket, a zebra, and a boot? Specialists can find the most incredibly well-hidden things. A book I read when I was young recommended an easy way to find caterpillars to rear: You simply find some fresh caterpillar droppings, look up, and there's your caterpillar. More recently an author advised me to set my mind at ease about those piles of cut stems on the ground in grassy fields. Field mice make them; they cut the grass down by degrees to reach the seeds at the head. It seems that when the grass is tightly packed, as in a field of ripe grain, the blade won't topple at a single cut through the stem; instead, the cut stem simply drops vertically, held in the crush of grain. The mouse severs the bottom again and again, the stem keeps dropping an inch at a time, and finally the head is low enough for the mouse to reach the seeds. Meanwhile, the mouse is positively littering the field with its little piles of cut stems into which, presumably, the author of the book is constantly stumbling.

If I can't see these minutiae, I still try to keep my eyes open. I'm always on the lookout for antlion traps in sandy soil, monarch pupae near milkweed, skipper larvae in locust leaves. These things are utterly common, and I've not seen one. I bang on hollow trees near water, but so far no flying squirrels have appeared. In flat country I watch every sunset in hopes of seeing the green ray. The green ray is a seldom-seen streak of light that rises from the sun like a spurting fountain at the moment of sunset; it throbs into the sky for two seconds and disappears. One more reason to keep my eyes open. A photography professor at the University of Florida just happened to see a bird die in midflight; it jerked, died, dropped, and smashed on the ground. I squint at the wind because I read Stewart Edward White: "I have always maintained that if you looked closely enough you could *see* the wind—the dim, hardly-made-out, fine debris fleeing high in the air." White was an excellent observer, and devoted an entire chapter of *The Mountains* to the subject of seeing deer: "As soon as you can forget the naturally obvious and construct an artificial obvious, then you too will see deer."

But the artificial obvious is hard to see. My eyes account for less than one percent of the weight of my head; I'm bony and dense; I see what I expect. I once spent a full three minutes looking at a bullfrog that was so unexpectedly large I couldn't see it even though a dozen enthusiastic campers were shouting directions. Finally I asked, "What color am I looking for?" and a fellow said, "Green." When at last I picked out the frog, I saw what painters are up against: The thing wasn't green at all, but the color of wet hickory bark.

The lover can see, and the knowledgeable. I visited an aunt and uncle at a quarter-horse ranch in Cody, Wyoming. I couldn't do much of anything useful, but I could, I thought, draw. So, as we all sat around the kitchen table after supper, I produced a sheet of paper and drew a horse. "That's one lame horse," my aunt volunteered. The rest of the family joined in: "Only place to saddle that one is his neck"; "Looks like we better shoot the poor thing, on account of those terrible growths." Meekly, I slid the pencil and paper down the table. Everyone in that family, including my three young cousins, could draw a horse. Beautifully. When the paper came back it looked as though five shining, real quarter horses had been corraled by mistake with a papier-mâché moose; the real horses seemed to gaze at the monster with a steady, puzzled air. I stay away from horses now, but I can do a creditable goldfish. The point is that I just don't know what the lover knows; I just can't see the artificial obvious that those in the know construct. The herpetologist asks the native, "Are there snakes in that ravine?" "Nosir." And the herpetologist comes home with, yessir, three bags full. Are there butterflies on that mountain? Are the bluets in bloom, are there arrowheads here, or fossil shells in the shale?

Peeping through my keyhole I see within the range of only about thirty percent of the light that comes from the sun; the rest is infrared and some little ultraviolet, perfectly apparent to many animals, but invisible to me. A nightmare network of ganglia, charged and firing without my knowledge, cuts and splices what I do see, editing it for my brain. Donald E. Carr points out that the sense impressions of one-celled animals are *not* edited for the brain: "This is philosophically interesting in a rather mournful way, since it means that only the simplest animals perceive the universe as it is."

A fog that won't burn away drifts and flows across my field of vision. When you see fog move against a backdrop of deep pines, you don't see the fog itself, but streaks of clearness floating across the air in dark shreds. So I see only tatters of clearness through a pervading obscurity. I can't distinguish the fog from the overcast sky; I can't be sure if the light is direct or reflected. Everywhere darkness and the presence of the unseen appalls. We estimate now that only one atom dances alone in every cubic meter of intergalactic space. I blink and squint. What planet or power yanks Halley's Comet out of orbit? We haven't seen that force yet; it's a question of distance, density, and the pallor of reflected light. We rock, cradled in the swaddling band of darkness. Even the simple darkness of night whispers suggestions to the mind. Last summer, in August, I stayed at the creek too late.

Where Tinker Creek flows under the sycamore log bridge to the tear-shaped island, it is slow and shallow, fringed thinly in cattail marsh. At this spot an astonishing bloom of life supports vast breeding populations of insects, fish, reptiles, birds, and mammals. On windless summer evenings I stalk along the creek bank or straddle the sycamore log in absolute stillness, watching for muskrats. The night I stayed too late I was hunched on the log staring spellbound at spreading, reflected stains of lilac on the water. A cloud in the sky suddenly lighted as if turned on by a switch; its reflection just as suddenly materialized on the water upstream, flat and floating, so that I couldn't see the creek bottom, or life in the water under the cloud. Downstream, away from the cloud on the water, water turtles smooth as beans were gliding down with the current in a series of easy, weightless push-offs, as men bound on the moon. I didn't know whether to trace the progress of one turtle I was sure of, risking sticking my face in one of the bridge's spider webs made invisible by the gathering dark, or take a chance on seeing the carp, or scan the mudbank in hope of seeing a muskrat, or follow the last of the swallows who caught at my heart and trailed it after them like streamers as they appeared from directly below, under the log, flying upstream with the tails forked, so fast.

But shadows spread, and deepened, and stayed. After thousands of years we're still strangers to darkness, fearful aliens in an enemy camp with our arms crossed over our chests. I stirred. A land turtle on the bank, startled, hissed the air from its lungs and withdrew into its shell. An uneasy pink here, an unfathomable blue there, gave great suggestion of lurking beings. Things were going on. I couldn't see whether that sere rustle I heard was a distant rattlesnake, slit-eyed, or a nearby sparrow kicking in the dry flood debris slung at the foot of a willow. Tremendous action roiled the water everywhere I looked, big action, inexplicable. A tremor welled up beside a gaping muskrat burrow in the bank and I caught my breath, but no muskrat appeared. The ripples continued to fan upstream with a steady, powerful thrust. Night was knitting over my face an eyeless mask, and I still sat transfixed. A distant airplane, a delta wing out of nightmare, made a gliding shadow on the creek's bottom that looked like a stingray cruising upstream. At once a black fin slit the pink cloud on the water, shearing it in two. The two halves merged together and seemed to dissolve before my eyes. Darkness pooled in the cleft of the creek and rose, as water collects in a well. Untamed, dreaming lights flickered over the sky. I saw hints of hulking underwater shadows, two pale splashes out of the water, and round ripples rolling close together from a blackened center.

At last I stared upstream where only the deepest violet remained of the cloud, a cloud so high its underbelly still glowed feeble color reflected from a hidden sky lighted in turn by a sun halfway to China. And out of that violet, a sudden enormous black body arced over the water. I saw only a cylindrical sleekness. Head and tail, if there was a head and tail, were both submerged in cloud. I saw only one ebony fling, a headlong dive to darkness; then the waters closed, and the lights went out.

I walked home in a shivering daze, up hill and down. Later I lay open-mouthed in bed, my arms flung wide at my sides to steady the whirling darkness. At this latitude I'm spinning 836 miles an hour round the earth's axis; I often fancy I feel my sweeping fall as a break-neck arc like the dive of dolphins, and the hollow rushing of wind raises hair on my neck and the side of my face. In orbit around the sun I'm moving 64,800 miles an hour. The solar system as a whole, like a merry-go-round unhinged, spins, bobs, and blinks at the speed of 43,200 miles an hour along a course set east of Hercules. Someone has piped, and we are dancing a tarantella until the sweat pours. I open my eyes and I see dark, muscled forms curl out of water, with flapping gills and flattened eyes. I close my eyes and I see stars, deep stars giving way to deeper stars, deeper stars bowing to deepest stars at the crown of an infinite cone.

"Still," wrote van Gogh in a letter, "a great deal of light falls on everything." If we are blinded by darkness, we are also blinded by light. When too much light falls on everything, a special terror results. Peter Freuchen describes the notorious kayak sickness to which Greenland Eskimos are prone. "The Greenland fjords are peculiar for the spells of completely quiet weather, when there is not enough wind to blow out a match and the water is like a sheet of glass. The kayak hunter must sit in his boat without stirring a finger so as not to scare the shy seals away. . . . The sun, low in the sky, sends a glare into his eyes, and the landscape around moves into the realm of the unreal. The reflex from the mirrorlike water hypnotizes him, he seems to be unable to move, and all of a sudden it is as if he were floating in a bottomless void, sinking, sinking, and sinking. . . . Horror-stricken, he tries to stir, to cry out, but he cannot, he is completely paralyzed, he just falls and falls." Some hunters are especially cursed with this panic, and bring ruin and sometimes starvation to their families.

Sometimes here in Virginia at sunset low clouds on the southern or northern horizon are completely invisible in the lighted sky. I only know one is there because I can see its reflection in still water. The first time I discovered this mystery I looked from cloud to no-cloud in bewilderment, checking my bearings over and over, thinking maybe the ark of the covenant was just passing by south of Dead Man Mountain. Only much later did I read the explanation: Polarized light from the sky is very much weakened by reflection, but the light in clouds isn't polarized. So invisible clouds pass among visible clouds, till all slide over the mountains; so a greater light extinguishes a lesser as though it didn't exist.

In the great meteor shower of August, the Perseid, I wail all day for the shooting stars I miss. They're out there showering down, committing hara-kiri in a flame of fatal attraction, and hissing perhaps at last into the ocean. But at dawn what looks like a blue dome clamps down over me like a lid on a pot. The stars and planets could smash and I'd never know. Only a piece of ashen moon occasionally climbs up or down the inside of the dome, and our local star without surcease explodes on our heads. We have really only that one light, one source for all power, and yet we must turn away from it by universal decree. Nobody here on the planet seems aware of this strange, powerful taboo, that we all walk about carefully averting our faces, this way and that, lest our eyes be blasted forever.

Darkness appalls and light dazzles; the scrap of visible light that doesn't hurt my eyes hurts my brain. What I see sets me swaying. Size and distance and the sudden swelling of meanings confuse me, bowl me over. I straddle the sycamore log bridge over Tinker Creek in the summer. I look at the lighted creek bottom: Snail tracks tunnel the mud in quavering curves. A crayfish jerks, but by the time I absorb what has happened, he's gone in a billowing smokescreen of silt. I look at the water: minnows and shiners. If I'm thinking minnows, a carp will fill my brain till I scream. I look at the water's surface: skaters, bubbles, and leaves sliding down. Suddenly, my own face, reflected, startles me witless. Those snails have been tracking my face! Finally, with a shuddering wrench of the will, I see clouds, cirrus clouds. I'm dizzy, I fall in. This looking business is risky.

Once I stood on a humped rock on nearby Purgatory Mountain, watching through binoculars the great autumn hawk migration below, until I discovered that I was in danger of joining the hawks on a vertical migration of my own. I was used to binoculars, but not, apparently, to balancing on humped rocks while looking through them. I staggered. Everything advanced and receded by turns; the world was full of unexplained foreshortenings and depths. A distant huge tan object, a hawk the size of an elephant, turned out to be the browned bough of a nearby loblolly pine. I followed a sharp-shinned hawk against a featureless sky, rotating my head unawares as it flew, and when I lowered the glass a glimpse of my own looming shoulder sent me staggering. What prevents the men on Palomar from falling, voiceless and blinded, from their tiny, vaulted chairs?

I reel in confusion; I don't understand what I see. With the naked eye I can see two million light-years to the Andromeda galaxy. Often I slop some creek water in a jar and when I get home I dump it in a white china bowl. After the silt settles I return and see tracings of minute snails on the bottom, a planarian or two winding round the rim of water, roundworms shimmying frantically, and finally, when my eyes have adjusted to these dimensions, amoebae. At first the amoebae look like muscae volitantes, those curled moving spots you seem to see in your eyes when you stare at a distant wall. Then I see the amoebae as drops of water congealed, bluish, translucent, like chips of sky in the bowl. At length I choose one individual and give myself over to its idea of an evening. I see it dribble a grainy foot before it on its wet, unfathomable way. Do its unedited sense impressions include the fierce focus of my eyes? Shall I take it outside and show it Andromeda, and blow its little endoplasm? I stir the water with a finger, in case it's running out of oxygen. Maybe I should get a tropical aquarium with motorized bubblers and lights, and keep this one for a pet. Yes, it would tell its fissioned descendants, the universe is two feet by five, and if you listen closely you can hear the buzzing music of the spheres.

Oh, it's mysterious lamplit evenings, here in the galaxy, one after the other. It's one of those nights when I wander from window to window, looking for a sign. But I can't see. Terror and a beauty insoluble are a ribband of blue woven into the fringes of garments of things both great and small. No culture explains, no bivouac offers real haven or rest. But it could be that we are not seeing something. Galileo thought comets were an optical illusion. This is fertile ground: Since we are certain that they're not, we can look at what our scientists have been saying with fresh hope. What if there are *really* gleaming, castellated cities hung upside-down over the desert sand? What limpid lakes and cool date palms have our caravans always passed untried? Until, one by one, by the blindest of leaps, we light on the road to these places, we must stumble in darkness and hunger. I turn from the window. I'm blind as a bat, sensing only from every direction the echo of my own thin cries.

I chanced on a wonderful book by Marius von Senden, called *Space and Light.* When Western surgeons discovered how to perform safe cataract operations, they ranged across Europe and America operating on dozens of men and women of all ages who had been blinded by cataracts since birth. Von Senden collected accounts of such cases; the histories are fascinating. Many doctors had tested their patients' sense perceptions and ideas of space both before and after the operations. The vast majority of patients, of both sexes and all ages, had, in von Senden's opinion, no idea of space whatsoever. Form, distance, and size were so many meaningless syllables. A patient "had no idea of depth, confusing it with roundness." Before the operation a doctor would give a blind patient a cube and a sphere; the patient would tongue it or feel it with his hands, and name it correctly. After the operation the doctor would show the same objects to the patient without letting him touch them; now he had no clue whatsoever what he was seeing. One patient called lemonade "square" because it pricked on his tongue as a square shape pricked on the touch of his hands. Of another postoperative patient, the doctor writes, "I have found in her no notion of size, for example, not even within the narrow limits which she might have encompassed with the aid of touch. Thus when I asked her to show me how big her mother was, she did not stretch out her hands, but set her two index-fingers a few inches apart." Other doctors reported their patients' own statements to similar effect. "The room he was in . . . he knew to be but part of the house, yet he could not conceive that the whole house could look bigger"; "Those who are blind from birth . . . have no real conception of height or distance. A house that is a mile away is thought of as nearby, but requiring the taking of a lot of steps. . . . The elevator that whizzes him up and down gives no more sense of vertical distance than does the train of horizontal."

For the newly sighted, vision is pure sensation unencumbered by meaning: "The girl went through the experience that we all go through and forget, the moment we are born. She saw, but it did not mean anything but a lot of different kinds of brightness." Again, "I asked the patient what he could see; he answered that he saw an extensive field of light, in which everything appeared dull, confused, and in motion. He could not distinguish objects." Another patient saw "nothing but a confusion of forms and colours." When a newly sighted girl saw photographs and paintings, she asked, "'Why do they put those dark marks all over them?' 'Those aren't dark marks,' her mother explained, 'those are shadows. That is one of the ways the eye knows that things have shape. If it were not for shadows many things would look flat.' 'Well, that's how things do look,' Joan answered. 'Everything looks flat with dark patches.'"

But it is the patients' concepts of space that are most revealing. One patient, according to his doctor, "practiced his vision in a strange fashion; thus he takes off one of his boots, throws it some way off in front of him, and then attempts to gauge the distance at which it lies; he takes a few steps toward the boot and tries to grasp it; on failing to reach it, he moves on a step or two and gropes for the boot until he finally gets hold of it." "But even at this stage, after three weeks' experience of seeing," von Senden goes on, "'space,' as he conceives it, ends with visual space, i.e., with color-patches that happen to bound his view. He does not yet have the notion that a larger object (a chair) can mask a smaller one (a dog), or that the latter can still be present even though it is not directly seen."

In general the newly sighted see the world as a dazzle of color-patches. They are pleased by the sensation of color, and learn quickly to name the colors, but the rest of seeing is tormentingly difficult. Soon after his operation a patient "generally bumps into one of these color-patches and observes them to be substantial, since they resist him as tactual objects do. In walking about it also strikes him—or can if he pays attention—that he is continually passing in between the colors he sees, that he can go past a visual object, that a part of it then steadily disappears from view; and that in spite of this, however he twists and turns—whether entering the room from the door, for example, or returning back to it—he always has a visual space in front of him. Thus he gradually comes to realize that there is also a space behind him, which he does not see."

The mental effort involved in these reasonings proves overwhelming for many patients. It oppresses them to realize, if they ever do at all, the tremendous size of the world, which they had previously conceived of as something touchingly manageable. It oppresses them to realize that they have been visible to people all along, perhaps unattractively so, without their knowledge or consent. A disheartening number of them refuse to use their new vision, continuing to go over objects with their tongues, and lapsing into apathy and despair. "The child can see, but will not make use of his sight. Only when pressed can he with difficulty be brought to look at objects in his neighborhood; but more than a foot away it is impossible to bestir him to the necessary effort." Of a twenty-one-year-old girl, the doctor relates, "Her unfortunate father, who had hoped for so much from this operation, wrote that his daughter carefully shuts her eyes whenever she wishes to go about the house, especially when she comes to a staircase, and that she is never happier or more at ease than when, by closing her eyelids, she relapses into her former state of total blindness." A fifteen-year-old boy, who was also in love with a girl at the asylum for the blind, finally blurted out, "No, really, I can't stand it any more; I want to be sent back to the asylum again. If things aren't altered, I'll tear my eyes out."

Some do learn to see, especially the young ones. But it changes their lives. One doctor comments on "the rapid and complete loss of that striking and wonderful serenity which is characteristic only of those who have never yet seen." A blind man who learns to see is ashamed of his old habits. He dresses up, grooms himself, and tries to make a good impression. While he was blind he was indifferent to objects unless they were edible; now, "a sifting of values sets in . . . his thoughts and wishes are mightily stirred and some few of the patients are thereby led into dissimulation, envy, theft and fraud."

On the other hand, many newly sighted people speak well of the world, and teach us how dull is our own vision. To one patient, a human hand, unrecognized, is "something bright and then holes." Shown a bunch of grapes, a boy calls out, "It is dark, blue and shiny. . . . It isn't smooth, it has bumps and hollows." A little girl visits a garden. "She is greatly astonished, and can scarcely be persuaded to answer, stands speechless in front of the tree, which she only names on taking hold of it, and then as 'the tree with the lights in it.'" Some delight in their sight and give themselves over to the visual world. Of a patient just after her bandages were removed, her doctor writes, "The first things to attract her attention were her own hands; she looked at them very closely, moved them repeatedly to and fro, bent and stretched the fingers, and seemed greatly astonished at the sight." One girl was eager to tell her blind friend that "men do not really look like trees at all," and astounded to discover that her every visitor had an utterly different face. Finally, a twenty-two-year-old girl was dazzled by the world's brightness and kept her eyes shut for two weeks. When at the end of that time she opened her eyes again, she did not recognize any objects, but, "the more she now directed her gaze upon everything about her, the more it could be seen how an expression of gratification and astonishment overspread her features; she repeatedly exclaimed: 'Oh God! How beautiful!'"

I saw color-patches for weeks after I read this wonderful book. It was summer; the peaches were ripe in the valley orchards. When I woke in the morning, color-patches wrapped round my eyes, intricately, leaving not one unfilled spot. All day long I walked among shifting color-patches that parted before me like the Red Sea and closed again in silence, transfigured, wherever I looked back. Some patches swelled and loomed, while others vanished utterly, and dark marks flitted at random over the whole dazzling sweep. But I couldn't sustain the illusion of flatness. I've been around for too long. Form is condemned to an eternal danse macabre with meaning: I couldn't unpeach the peaches. Nor can I remember ever having seen without understanding; the color-patches of infancy are lost. My brain then must have been smooth as any balloon. I'm told I reached for the moon; many babies do. But the color-patches of infancy swelled as meaning filled them; they arrayed themselves in solemn ranks down distance which unrolled and stretched before me like a plain. The moon rocketed away. I live now in a world of shadows that shape and distance color, a world where space makes a kind of terrible sense. What gnosticism is this, and what physics? The fluttering patch I saw in my nursery window—silver and green and shape-shifting blue—is gone; a row of Lombardy poplars takes its place, mute, across the distant lawn. That humming oblong creature pale as light that stole along the walls of my room at night, stretching exhilaratingly around the corners, is gone, too, gone the night I ate of the bittersweet fruit, put two and two together and puckered forever my brain. Martin Buber tells this tale: "Rabbi Mendel once boasted to his teacher Rabbi Elimelekh that evenings he saw the angel who rolls away the light before the darkness, and mornings the angel who rolls away the darkness before the light. 'Yes,' said Rabbi Elimelekh, 'in my youth I saw that too. Later on you don't see these things any more.'"

Why didn't someone hand those newly sighted people paints and brushes from the start, when they still didn't know what anything was? Then maybe we all could see color-patches too, the world unraveled from reason, Eden before Adam gave names. The scales would drop from my eyes; I'd see trees like men walking; I'd run down the road against all orders, hallooing and leaping.

Seeing is of course very much a matter of verbalization. Unless I call my attention to what passes before my eyes, I simply won't see it. It is, as Ruskin says, "not merely unnoticed, but in the full, clear sense of the word, unseen." My eyes alone can't solve analogy tests using figures, the ones which show, with increasing elaborations, a big square, then a small square in a big square, then a big triangle, and expect me to find a small triangle in a big triangle. I have to say the words, describe what I'm seeing. If Tinker Mountain erupted, I'd be likely to notice. But if want to notice the lesser cataclysms of valley life, I have to maintain in my head a running description of the present. It's not that I'm observant; it's just that I talk too much. Otherwise, especially in a strange place, I'll never know what's happening. Like a blind man at the ball game, I need a radio.

When I see this way I analyze and pry. I hurl over logs and roll away stones; I study the bank a square foot at a time, probing and tilting my head. Some days when a mist covers the mountains, when the muskrats won't show and the microscope's mirror shatters, I want to climb up the blank blue dome as a man would storm the inside of a circus tent, wildly, dangling, and with a steel knife claw a rent in the top, peep, and, if I must, fall.

But there is another kind of seeing that involves a letting go. When I see this way I sway transfixed and emptied. The difference between the two ways of seeing is the difference between walking with and without a camera. When I walk with a camera I walk from shot to shot, reading the light on a calibrated meter. When I walk without a camera, my own shutter opens, and the moment's light prints on my own silver gut. When I see this second way I am above all an unscrupulous observer.

It was sunny one evening last summer at Tinker Creek; the sun was low in the sky, upstream. I was sitting on the sycamore log bridge with the sunset at my back, watching the shiners the size of minnows who were feeding over the muddy sand in skittery schools. Again and again, one fish, then another, turned for a split second across the current and flash! the sun shot out from its silver side. I couldn't watch for it. It was always just happening somewhere else, and it drew my vision just as it disappeared: flash, like a sudden dazzle of the thinnest blade, a sparking over a dun and olive ground at chance intervals from every direction. Then I noticed white specks, some sort of pale petals, small, floating from under my feet on the creek's surface, very slow and steady. So I blurred my eyes and gazed toward the brim of my hat and saw a new world. I saw the pale white circles roll up, roll up, like the world's turning, mute and perfect, and I saw the linear flashes, gleaming silver, like stars being born at random down a rolling scroll of time. Something broke and something opened. I filled up like a new wineskin. I breathed an air like light; I saw a light like water. I was the lip of a fountain the creek filled forever; I was ether, the leaf in the zephyr; I was flesh-flake, feather, bone.

When I see this way I see truly. As Thoreau says, I return to my senses. I am the man who watches the baseball game in silence in an empty stadium. I see the game purely; I'm abstracted and dazed. When it's all over and the white-suited players lope off the green field to their shadowed dugouts, I leap to my feet; I cheer and cheer.

But I can't go out and try to see this way. I'll fail, I'll go mad. All I can do is try to gag the commentator, to hush the noise of useless interior babble that keeps me from seeing just as surely as a newspaper dangled before my eyes. The effort is really a discipline requiring a lifetime of dedicated struggle; it marks the literature of saints and monks of every order East and West, under every rule and no rule, discalced and shod. The world's spiritual geniuses seem to discover universally that the mind's muddy river, this ceaseless flow of trivia and trash, cannot be dammed, and that trying to dam it is a waste of effort that might lead to madness. Instead you must allow the muddy river to flow unheeded in the dim channels of consciousness; you raise your sights; you look along it, mildly, acknowledging its presence without interest and gazing beyond it into the realm of the real where subjects and objects act and rest purely, without utterance. "Launch into the deep," says Jacques Ellul, "and you shall see."

The secret of seeing is, then, the pearl of great price. If I thought he could teach me to find it and keep it forever I would stagger barefoot across a hundred deserts after any lunatic at all. But although the pearl may be found, it may not be sought. The literature of illumination reveals this above all: Although it comes to those who wait for it, it is always, even to the most practiced and adept, a gift and a total surprise. I return from one walk knowing where the killdeer nests in the field by the creek and the hour the laurel blooms. I return from the same walk a day later scarcely knowing my own name. Litanies hum in my ears; my tongue flaps in my mouth Ailinon, alleluia! I cannot cause light; the most I can do is try to put myself in the path of its beam. It is possible, in deep space, to sail on solar wind. Light, be it particle or wave, has force: you rig a giant sail and go. The secret of seeing is to sail on solar wind. Hone and spread your spirit till you yourself are a sail, whetted, translucent, broadside to the merest puff.

When her doctor took her bandages off and led her into the garden, the girl who was no longer blind saw "the tree with the lights in it." It was for this tree I searched through the peach orchards of summer, in the forests of fall and down winter and spring for years. Then one day I was walking along Tinker Creek thinking of nothing at all and I saw the tree with the lights in it. I saw the backyard cedar where the mourning doves roost charged and transfigured, each cell buzzing with flame. I stood on the grass with the lights in it, grass that was wholly fire, utterly focused and utterly dreamed. It was less like seeing than like being for the first time seen, knocked breathless by a powerful glance. The flood of fire abated, but I'm still spending the power. Gradually the lights went out in the cedar, the colors died, the cells unflamed and disappeared. I was still ringing. I had been my whole life a bell, and never knew it until at that moment I was lifted and struck. I have since only very rarely seen the tree with the lights in it. The vision comes and goes, mostly goes, but I live for it, for the moment when the mountains open and a new light roars in spate through the crack, and the mountains slam.

THE THIN RED LINE

Jennifer Egan

One Saturday night in January, Jill McArdle went to a party some distance from her home in West Beverly, a fiercely Irish enclave on Chicago's South Side. She was anxious before setting out; she'd been having a hard time in social situations—parties, especially. At 5 feet 10 inches with long blond hair, green eyes and an underbite that often makes her look as if she's half-smiling, Jill cuts an imposing figure for 16; she is the sort of girl boys notice instantly and are sometimes afraid of. And the fear is mutual, despite her air of confidence.

Jill's troubles begin with her own desire to make everyone happy, a guiding principle that yields mixed results in the flirtatious, beer-swilling atmosphere of teen-age parties. "I feel I have to be all cute and sexy for these boys," she says. "And the next morning when I realize what a fool I looked like, it's the worst feeling ever. . . . 'Oh God, what did I do? Was I flirting with that boy? Is his girlfriend in school tomorrow going to give me a hard time? Are they all going to hate me?'"

Watching Jill in action, you would never guess she was prone to this sort of self-scrutiny. Winner of her cheerleading squad's coveted Spirit Award last year, she is part of a Catholic-school crowd consisting mostly of fellow cheerleaders and the male athletes they cheer for, clean-cut kids who congregate in basement rec rooms of spare, working-class houses where hockey sticks hang on the walls and a fish tank sometimes bubbles in one corner. Jill is a popular, even dominating presence at these parties; once she introduced a series of guys to me with the phrase, "This is my boy," her arm slung across the shoulders of some shy youth in a baseball cap, usually shorter than she, whose name invariably seemed to be Kevin or Patrick.

But in truth, the pressures of adolescence have wreaked extraordinary havoc in Jill's life. "Around my house there's this park, and there used to be like a hundred kids hanging out up there," she says, recalling her first year in high school, two years ago. "And the boys would say stuff to me that was so disgusting . . . perverted stuff, and I'd just be so embarrassed. But the older girls assumed that I was a slut. . . . They'd give me dirty looks in school." Blaming herself for having somehow provoked these reactions, Jill began to feel ashamed and isolated. Her unease spiraled into panic in the spring of that year, when a boy she'd trusted began spreading lies about her. "He goes and tells all of his friends that I did all this sexual stuff with him, and I was just blown away. It made me feel dirty, like I was absolutely nothing."

Jill, then 14, found herself moved to do something she had never done before. "I was in the bathroom going completely crazy, just bawling my eyes out, and I think my mom was wallpapering—there was a wallpaper cutter there. I had so much anxiety, I couldn't concentrate on anything until I somehow let that out, and not being able to let it out in words, I took the razor and started cutting my leg and I got excited about seeing my blood. It felt good to see the blood coming out, like that was my other pain leaving, too. It felt right and it felt good for me to let it out that way."

Jill had made a galvanizing discovery: cutting herself could temporarily ease her emotional distress. It became a habit. Once, she left school early, sat in an alley and carved "Life Sucks" into her leg with the point of a compass. Eventually, her friends got wind of her behavior and told her parents, who were frightened and mystified. They took Jill to Children's Memorial Hospital, where she was treated for depression

223

and put on Prozac, which she took for a few months until she felt better. By last summer she was cutting again in secret and also burning—mostly her upper thighs, where her mother, who by now was anxiously monitoring Jill's behavior, wouldn't see the cuts if she emerged from the family bathroom in a towel. Last summer, Jill wore boxers over her bathing suit even to swim. By January, her state was so precarious that one bad night would have the power to devastate her.

No one recognized Jill's behavior as self-mutilation, as it is clinically known (other names include self-injury, self-harm, self-abuse and the misnomer delicate self-cutting), a disorder that is not new but, because it is finally being properly identified and better understood, is suddenly getting attention. Princess Diana shocked people by admitting that she cut herself during her unhappy marriage. Johnny Depp has publicly revealed that his arms bear scars from self-inflicted wounds. The plot of "Female Perversions," a recent movie that fictionalized the book of the same name by Louise Kaplan, a psychiatrist, hinges on the discovery of a young girl cutting herself. And Steven Levenkron, a psychotherapist who wrote a best-selling novel in the 1970's about an anorexic, recently published "The Luckiest Girl in the World," about a teen-age self-injurer.

"I'm afraid, here we go again," Levenkron says, likening the prevalence of self-injury to that of anorexia. "Self-injury is probably a bit epidemic." Dr. Armando Favazza, a professor of psychiatry at the University of Missouri-Columbia medical school, estimates the number of sufferers at 750 per 100,000 Americans, or close to two million, but suggests that the actual figure may be higher.

Long dismissed by the psychiatric community as merely a symptom of other disorders—notably borderline personality disorder—self-mutilation is generating new interest as a subject of study. Dr. Barbara Stanley of the New York State Psychiatric Institute explains: "Some of us said, maybe we shouldn't be focusing so much on diagnostic studies. . . . Maybe this behavior means something unto itself."

Indeed it does. Favazza, whose book "Bodies Under Siege" was the first to comprehensively explore self-mutilation, defines it as "the direct, deliberate destruction or alteration of one's own body tissue without conscious suicidal intent." His numbers apply to what he calls "moderate/ superficial self-mutilation" like Jill's, rather than involuntary acts like the head banging of autistic or retarded people, or "coarse" self-mutilations like the eye enucleations and self-castrations that are occasionally performed by psychotics. Moderate self-mutilation can include cutting, burning, plucking hairs from the head and body (known as trichotillomania), bone breaking, head banging, needle poking, skin scratching or rubbing glass into the skin.

The fact that awareness of self-mutilation is growing at a time when tattooing, piercing, scarification and branding are on the rise has not been lost on researchers. While experts disagree on the relationship between the behaviors, the increasing popularity of body modification among teenagers, coupled with the two million people injuring in secret, begins to make us look like a nation obsessed with cutting. Marilee Strong, who interviewed nearly 100 injurers for her book, "A Bright Red Scream," to be published in 1998, calls it "the addiction of the 90's."

On that Saturday night in January, despite Jill's anxious resolutions, things at the party ultimately went awry. "It was really late," she says, "and I was supposed to stay at my best friend's house, but she left and I didn't go with her. I was drunk, and it was me down there in the basement with all these boys. . . . I'd walk by and they'd grab my butt or something, so I sat on a chair in the corner. And they tipped the chair over and made me fall off of it."

Realizing she was in a situation she would punish herself for later, Jill went upstairs and tried in vain to get a friend to leave the party with her. She had nowhere to stay—no way to get home without calling her parents—so she ended up at the home of her friend's brother, who was in his 20's and lived near the party. This proved to be another mistake. "I wake up there the next morning, and these guys were basically dirty 20-year-olds," she says, "and they tell me: 'You want a job living here with us? We'll pay you a hundred bucks if you strip for us once a week.' . . . I was just like: 'I have to go home! I have to go home!'"

But by now, a cycle of shame and self-blame was already in motion. On finally arriving at the two-story brick house where she lives with her parents and brothers (one older, one younger), Jill learned that she was being grounded for not having called home the night before. Her bedroom, right off the kitchen, is a small, makeshift room with accordion doors that do not seal off the noise from the rest of the house. "All Sunday I just slept and slept, and I was just so depressed, so disgusted with myself. . . . I felt like the dirtiest thing ever because of everything that had happened the night before."

For all her popularity, Jill felt too fragile that morning to ask her friends for reassurance. "I feel really inferior to them, like they're so much better at everything than me," she says of the other cheerleaders. "I feel like I have to be the pleaser, and I can never do anything wrong. When I fail to make other people happy, I get so angry with myself."

That Sunday, no one was happy with Jill: her parents, the friend whose house she hadn't slept at and, in her fearful imagination, countless older girls who by now had heard of her sloppy conduct at the party and were waiting to pounce. "Monday morning came and I was scared to death to have to go to school and see people," she says. "I started cutting myself. First I used a knife—I was in the bathroom doing it and then I told my mom because I was scared. She was like, 'Why the hell are you doing this? You're going to give me and your father a heart attack: . . . She took the knife away. So then I took a candle holder and went outside and cracked it against the ground and took a piece of glass and started cutting myself with that, and then I took fingernail clippers and was trying to dig at my skin and like pull it off, but it didn't help anymore, it wasn't working. . . . That night, I was like, 'My mom is so mad at me, she doesn't even care that I was doing this,' so that's when I took all the aspirin."

Jill isn't sure how many aspirin she took, but estimates it was around 30. "That night was like the scariest night in my life," she says. "I was puking and sweating and had ringing in my ears and I couldn't focus on anything." Still, she slept through a second day before telling her parents what was really ailing her. They rushed her to a hospital, where she wound up in intensive care for three days with arrhythmia while IV's flushed out her system, and she was lucky not to have permanently damaged her liver.

"That was very shocking, to think that she was going through so much pain without us being aware of it," says her father, Jim McArdle, a ruddy-faced police lieutenant with a soft voice, who chooses his words carefully. "There's a ton of denial," he admits. "It's like: 'It happened once, it's never going to happen again. It happened twice, it's not going to happen three times.' The third time you're like. . . ." He trails off helplessly.

Self-injury rarely stops after two or three incidents. According to the only large-scale survey ever taken of self-injurers (240 American females), in 1989, the average practitioner begins at 14—as Jill did—and continues injuring, often with increasing severity into her late 20's. Generally white, she is also likely to suffer from other compulsive disorders like bulimia or alcoholism. Dr. Jan Hart, who surveyed 87 high-functioning self-injurers for her 1996 doctoral dissertation at UC.L.A., found their most common professions to be teacher and nurse, followed by manager.

The notion of teachers, nurses and high-school students like Jill seeking out ways to hurt themselves in a culture where the avoidance of pain and discomfort is a virtual obsession may seem paradoxical. But it isn't. People harm themselves because it makes them feel better; they use physical pain to obfuscate a deeper, more intolerable psychic pain associated with feelings of anger, sadness or abandonment. Often, the injury is used to relieve the pressure or hysteria these emotions can cause, as it did for Jill; it can also jolt people out of states of numbness and emptiness—it can make them feel alive.

These mood-regulating effects, along with a certain addictive quality (over time, the injurer usually must hurt herself more frequently and more violently to achieve the same degree of relief) have prompted many clinicians to speculate that cutting, for example, releases the body's own opiates, known as beta-endorphins. According to Lisa Cross, a New Haven psychotherapist who has treated self-injurers, patients have for centuries described the sensation of being bled in the same terms of relief and release as she hears from self-injurers. And people who have been professionally scarred or pierced sometimes describe feeling high from the experience.

Women seeking treatment for self-injury far outnumber men. There are many speculations as to why this might be, the most common of which is that women are more likely to turn their anger inward. Dusty Miller, author of "Women Who Hurt Themselves," believes that self-injury reflects a culturally sanctioned antagonism between women and their bodies: "Our bodies are always too fat, our breasts are too small. . . . The body becomes the object of our own violence."

But the fact that few men are treated for self-injury doesn't mean they aren't hurting themselves, too. Among adolescent injurers, the ratio of boys to girls is near equal, and cutting is rampant among both male and female prisoners. Self-Mutilators Anonymous, a New York support group, was initiated 11 years ago by two men, one of whom, Sheldon Goldberg, 59, gouged his face with cuticle scissors, "deep digging" to remove ingrown hairs. "I would have so many bandages on my face from cutting that I would sit on the subway all dressed up to go to work," says Goldberg, a former advertising art director, "and people would look at me and I would realize a wound had opened up and I was bleeding all over my shirt." Now, five reconstructive operations later, the lower half of Goldberg's face is solid scar tissue. "But men can get away with it," he says. "When people ask me what happened, I say: 'I was in the war. I was in a fire.' Men can use all the macho stuff."

It's February, and a frigid midwestern wind thumps at the windows of Keepataw Lodge at the Rock Creek Center, a general psychiatric institution in Lemont, Ill. It is the home of the SAFE (Self-Abuse Finally Ends) Alternatives Program, the nation's only in-patient treatment center for self-injurers, started in 1985. Jill, in jeans, hiking boots and a Pucci-style shirt, lounges on an upholstered banquette in the lodge's skylighted atrium. She has been here 10 days, spending her mornings in the hospital's adolescent program completing assignments her school has faxed in, dividing her afternoons between individual and group therapy.

She's ebullient—partly from sheer relief at being surrounded by people with her same problem. "It's really weird how many people in the group have my same kind of thinking," she says, repeatedly removing and replacing a pen cap with hands scarred by cigarette-lighter burns. "How they grew up feeling like they didn't deserve to feel their feelings, like they had to keep people happy. . . . I don't even know who I am anymore, because everything I do depends on what other people want."

Her cheerleading friends have visited, bearing get-well cards and magazines, but Jill finds playing hostess on the grounds of a mental hospital a tall order. "I'd make up things like, 'Oh, I have a group in 10 minutes, so you guys better leave,' because I couldn't take it to have them sitting there and me not knowing how to make them happy in such a weird environment," she says.

Her parents arrive to meet with her doctor and then take Jill home after her group therapy; for insurance reasons, she must continue the 30-day SAFE program from home as an outpatient. (Blue Cross refused to cover her hospitalization costs before SAFE because her problem was "self-inflicted"; the family is appealing.) Jim and Nancy McArdle are warm, open people who seem a little shell-shocked by their sudden immersion in the mental-health system. Jim, who in happier times likes to kid and joke, sits tentatively at a table with his hands folded. Jill is the most animated of the three. "I'll just turn it off, like I never even knew what that was," she says of the behavior that landed her in the hospital only three weeks ago. An anxious glance from her mother, an attractive woman with reddish brown hair who works as a respiratory therapist, gives Jill pause. "Last time we thought it was going to be fine too," she reflects. "But then eventually it just all fell back even worse than it was before. It's scary to think about. I don't want to spend my life in hospitals."

This is a reasonable fear. Most of Jill's fellow patients at SAFE are women in their late 20's and early 30's, many of whom have been hospitalized repeatedly since their teen-age years, some of whom have children. (SAFE accepts men, but its clientele is 99 percent female.) In free moments during the program's highly structured day, many of these patients can be found on the outdoor smoking deck, perched on white lawn chairs under an overhead heating lamp beside a thicket of spiky trees. (Unlike many psychiatric wards, SAFE does not lock its doors.) The deck's cynosure is a white plastic bucket clogged with what look to be thousands of cigarette butts; even when the deck is empty of smokers, the air reeks.

"Hi! What's your diagnosis?" Jane C., a Southerner in her early 30's, cheerfully queries a patient who has just arrived. "Bipolar? Me, too! Although that can mean a lot of different things. What're your symptoms?" Jane, who insisted her last name not be used, is one of those people who can't bear to see anyone left out. She has olive skin, an animated, birdlike face and wide, dark eyes like those in Byzantine paintings. She smiles even while she's talking.

The patient bums a cigarette from her, and Jane lights it. "Cheers," she says, and the two women touch cigarettes as if they were wine glasses.

Jane once made a list called Reasons for Cutting, and the reasons numbered more than 30. But the word she uses most often is power. Like many self-injurers (65 percent according to the 1989 survey; some believe it is much higher), Jane reports a history of sexual abuse that began when she was 7. Shortly thereafter, she raked a hairbrush across her face. By age 10, she was in her parents' bathroom making her own discovery of the razor blade. "I cut right in the fold of a finger," she says. "It was so sharp and so smooth and so well hidden, and yet there was some sense of empowerment. If somebody else is hurting me or making me bleed, then I take that instrument away and 1 make me bleed. It says: 'You can't hurt me anymore. I'm in charge of that.'"

Sometimes Jane pounds her head repeatedly against a wall. "When my head's spinning, when I'm near hysteria, it's like a slap in the face," she says. "I've had multitudes of concussions—it's amazing I have any sense at all." It is virtually impossible to imagine this polished, friendly young woman doing any of these things. Much like Jill, Jane, herself a former cheerleader, masks her vulnerabilities with an assertive and jovial persona. "She's created this face to the world that's totally in control when there's really chaos going on underneath," says Dr. Wendy Friedman Lader, SAFE's clinical director. "There's something very adaptive about that, but it's a surreal kind of existence." Even Jane's many scars are well hidden, thanks to what she calls her "scar-erasing technique," which sounds something like dermabrasion.

Like many victims of early trauma, Jane is plagued by episodes of dissociation, when she feels numb or dead or separate from her body. Cross, the New Haven psychotherapist, explains the genesis of dissociation this way: "When you are abused, the natural thing to do is to take yourself out of your body. Your body becomes the bad part of you that's being punished, and you, the intact, positive part, are far away." But what begins as a crucial self-protective device can become an inadvertent response to any kind of stress or fear. "There have been times when I don't even feel like I'm alive," Jane says. "I'll do something to feel—anything. And that's usually cutting. Just seeing blood. . . . I don't know why."

At SAFE, Jane C. is often in the company of Jamie Matthews, 20, a quiet, watchful young woman with pale skin and long brown hair who seems to bask in her friend's overabundant energy. Cutting herself, Jamie says, is a way of coping with her rage. "I would get so angry and upset and so tense, so all I could think about was the physical pain, doing it harder and doing it more. And then afterwards it was a relief . . . sometimes I would sleep."

As a student at a small college in upstate New York, Jamie lived in a dormitory, so privacy was a major preoccupation. "I would lie in bed at school—that was the best place for me to do it because if my roommate walked in, she would think I was sleeping—and I would lay on my back with the knife underneath me, and then pull it out the side, across my back." Jamie already completed the SAFE program once, last summer, but relapsed back at school. The last time she injured herself, she says, was when it felt best. "It was actually pleasureful. It gave me chills; it was that kind of feeling. I sat there smiling, watching myself bleed." Descriptions like these, along with the intimate rituals that accompany some people's injuring—candles, incense, special instruments—have led some clinicians to compare self-injury to masturbation.

Jamie's self-injury has caused her a multitude of problems, yet there is almost a tenderness in her voice when she speaks of her self-harming acts. "It's all mine," she says. "It's nothing that anybody can experience with me or take from me. I guess it's like my little secret. I've got physical scars. . . . It shows that my life isn't easy. I can look at different scars and think, yeah, I know when that happened, so it tells a story. I'm afraid of them fading."

Self-injury can appear, at first, to be a viable coping mechanism; the wounds are superficial, no one else is getting hurt and the injurer feels in control of her life. But what begins as an occasional shallow cut can progress to sliced veins and repeated visits to the emergency room. As with any compulsion, the struggle to resist one's urges can eclipse all other thoughts and interests, and despair over the inability to control the behavior can even lead to suicide attempts. "It's like a cancer," says Cross. "It just seems to start eating into more and more of your life."

Jane C. managed to hide her problems for many years. She was married and had a successful career as a sales executive at a medical-supply company, whose wares she frequently used to suture and bandage her self-inflicted wounds. Eventually, despite her vigilant secrecy, Jane got caught—her mother appeared at her house unexpectedly and found her in the bathroom, drenched in blood. Weakened by her emotional turmoil and a severe eating disorder, Jane ultimately almost passed out on the highway while driving home from a sales call, and finally left her job three and a half years ago. "I went on disability, which was really hard on my pride," she says. "I've never not worked in my whole life."

Jane C.'s discovery by her mother is a fairly routine step in the life cycle of self-injury—for all the secrecy surrounding it, it is finally a graphic nonverbal message. "I think that there's a wish implicit in the injury that someone else will notice and ask about it," says Christine Sterkel, a psychologist with SAFE. This was clearly true in Jill's case; after burning her hands, she covered the wounds with band-aids until Christmas morning, then appeared before her family without them. "In the park, she cracked a bottle and cut both her wrists," a friend of Jill's told me. "Everyone gathered around her, and I think that's what she wanted. She was crying and I'd be hugging her and stuff and then she'd raise her head and be laughing."

Later in the afternoon, Jill, Jane C., Jamie and the other SAFE patients settle on couches and chairs for one of the many focused group therapy sessions they participate in throughout the week. Patients must sign a "no-harm contract" before entering the program; group therapy is a forum for grappling with the flood of feelings they would normally be numbing through self-injury. It is not, as I had envisioned, an occasion for trading gruesome tales of the injuring itself. Karen Conterio, SAFE's founder, has treated thousands of patients and rejects the public confessional that is a staple of 12-step programs. "Self-mutilation is a behavior, it's not an identity," she says, and encourages patients to save their war stories for individual therapy.

Beyond that caveat, Conterio, 39, a lithe, athletic woman with short blond hair, lets her patients set the agenda. Today, Jill and the others discuss their feelings of shame—shame they repressed by injuring, shame over the injuring itself. At emergency rooms, their wounds were often mistaken for suicide attempts, which in most states requires that a patient be locked up in a psychiatric ward, often in physical restraints.

Later, in a small office adorned with mementos given to her by former patients—a knit blanket, a papier-mâché mask—Conterio tells me that she's less concerned with guiding patients toward a specific cause for their self-injury than with helping them learn to tolerate their feelings and express them verbally—in other words, begin functioning as adults. Still, revisiting one's past is a key step in this process. As Maureen Ford, a psychologist at SAFE, puts it: "Self-injury is a kind of violence. So how is it that violence has entered their life in some way previously?"

In Jill McArdle's case, the answer isn't obvious. She is part of an intact, supportive family; as far as she knows, she has never been sexually abused. But there were problems. Jill's brother, a year older than she, was born with health troubles that cost him one kidney and left him only partial use of the other. Today he is well, but, Nancy McArdle says: "It was three, four years of just not knowing from one day to the next how he was going to do, in the hospital all the time. . . . Jill picked up on it right away and tried to make everything easy on us where she was concerned." (Jamie Matthews also grew up with a chronically ill sibling.) Beyond worrying constantly about her ill son, Nancy McArdle, whose own childhood was marked by alcoholism in her family, admits to feeling a general sense of impending catastrophe while her children were young. "I wouldn't drive on expressways—I'd take a different route," she says. "If I saw a storm coming, I'd think it was a tornado." Giggling at the memory, Jill says: "She'd make us all go into the basement with pillows and blankets. I've been petrified of storms ever since then."

Nancy McArdle has since been given a diagnosis of obsessive-compulsive disorder and is on Prozac, and she and Jill can now laugh about those old fears. But it's easy to see how Jill, as a child with a terrified mother, a chronically ill sibling and a father who kept a certain distance from the emotional upheavals in the household, might have felt isolated and imperiled. She quickly developed an unusual tolerance for pain. "I'd fall and I'd never cry. . . . I never felt any pain, really. It was there, but I pushed it back." Triumphing over physical pain was something she could excel at—distinguishing herself from her physically weak older brother, while at the same time reassuring her mother that she, anyway, would always be strong.

This mix of toughness and a hypervigilant desire to please is still the engine of Jill's social persona, which mingles easy affection with an opacity that seals off her real thoughts. "She never tells anybody how she feels—ever," Nancy McArdle says. Jill agrees: "I turn it all inside. I just think I have to help myself, it all has to be up to me."

But paradoxically, the child who feels that she must be completely self-sufficient, that no one can help her or that she doesn't deserve help is uniquely ill equipped for the independence she seeks. Terrified to express emotions like sadness or rage for fear of driving everyone away from her, such a person becomes more easily overwhelmed by those feelings and turns them on herself. "I and my razors and my pieces of glass and the pins and the needles are the only things I can trust to bring relief," paraphrases Dr. Kaplan, author of "Female Perversions." "These are their care givers. These have the power to soothe and bring relief of the tension building up inside. . . . They don't expect the environment to hold them." Tending to their own wounds, which many injurers do solicitously, is the final part of the experience.

In a sense, self-injury becomes a perverse ritual of self-caretaking in which the injurer assumes all roles of an abusive relationship: the abuser, the victim and the comforting presence who soothes her afterward.

In someone like Jane C., whose childhood was severely traumatic, physiology may be partly to blame; trauma can cause lasting neurological changes, especially if it occurs while the central nervous system is still developing. Dr. Bessel van der Kolk, a professor of psychiatry at Boston University who specializes in trauma, explains: "The shock absorbers of the brain are shot. If everything is running smoothly, if it crawls along just fine—as it does in nobody's life—you're fine. But the moment you get hurt, jealous, upset, fall in love, fall out of love, your reaction becomes much stronger."

It is for this reason, many people believe, that self-injury begins during adolescence. "They go through early childhood developing very poor capacities to deal with states of internal disruption," says Dr. Karen Latza, a Chicago psychologist who does diagnostic work for SAFE. "I can't think of a single thing that involves more internal upheaval than the adolescent years. The changes that come with their menstrual cycles or with sexual arousal engender panic in the young self-injurer."

Jill fits such a model: for all her popularity, she steers clear of romance out of an apprehension she attributes to the friend who lied about her. "I just think that every boy would be like that, just make up stuff," she says. But there is a second danger for Jill: her irrepressible impulse to please, which could make her vulnerable to unwanted sexual attention. As if sensing this, Jill tends to develop a distaste for boys who take an interest in her.

The next time I see Jill at SAFE, the weather is warmer, the ice on the ponds at Rock Creek is melting, and she seems antsy to resume her old life. "I'm just sick of having to wake up every morning and go to therapy, therapy, therapy," she says. Cheerleading tryouts are that night; the following week, she will begin easing back into school. The thought of facing her peers en masse fills her with anxiety. "Last Thursday I went to a hockey game and I saw all these boys, and seriously, my skin was crawling. . . . They'd give me looks, and I couldn't even look at them."

After the SAFE group, Jill and I drive to Mt. Carmel High School, in a run-down neighborhood on Chicago's South Side, for her tryouts. Her fellow cheerleaders greet her enthusiastically; Jill brings one of them a birthday present. Another girl fawns over Jill in a fanged display of unctuous sweetness. "That's the bitch I hate," Jill says matter-of-factly. The girl, still within earshot, shoots her a look. "She thinks I'm kidding, but I'm not," Jill says.

With glitter over their eyes and tiny mirrored hearts pasted to their cheeks, these incumbent cheerleaders huddle in a stairwell outside the gymnasium, awaiting the chance to defend their positions on the squad. Their coach, Suzy Davy, assures me privately that Jill will be chosen. "She was just so cute and energetic," Davy says of Jill's performance last year, which earned her the Spirit Award during the same period when she was cutting and burning herself in secret. "She wasn't fake. She was just out there and she said, 'This is me!'"

Finally the girls file into the gym, shoes squeaking on the varnished wood, and spread out on the floor to stretch. Some of them seem to be vying for Jill's attention; others keep a respectful distance. And it strikes me that by cutting herself—by getting caught and hospitalized Jill has freed herself from her own tough persona, at least for a time. Everyone knows that something is wrong, that no matter how happy and confident she may seem, there is unhappiness, too, and a need to be cared for. She has revealed herself in the only way she was able.

There is nothing new about self-injury. As Favazza documents in "Bodies Under Siege," from the Christian flagellant cults of the 13th and 14th centuries to male Australian Aborigines who undergo subcision, or the slicing open of the penis along the urethra, as a rite of passage, the equation of bodily mortification with transcendence and healing is repeated across cultures. Many such rituals occur in the context of adolescent initiation rites—ceremonies involving youths about the same age as most boys and girls who begin cutting themselves. "We've done away with rites of passage, but the pattern can still exist," says Favazza. "And the younger teenagers who are seeking to become adults, the ones who can't make it the ordinary way, somehow tap into that."

One group that consciously seeks to tap into primitive rituals and vanished rites of passage are practitioners of what is called new tribalism or extreme body arts, who embrace such forms of body modification as tattooing, piercing and, more recently, scarification and branding. Some of these practices are performed as public rituals of a sort, particularly in gay S & M culture, where they are known as bloodsports. Ron Athey, an H.I.V-positive performance artist, cuts and pierces himself before audiences while reading aloud from autobiographical texts. An entirely different sort of performance is practiced by Orlan, a French woman who has undergone repeated facial plastic surgeries on video.

More often, body modification takes place in private studios like Modern American Bodyarts in Bay Ridge, Brooklyn, a small, scrupulously clean storefront bedecked with African masks. Here, a multiply pierced and heavily tattooed artist, Keith Alexander, pierces clients, cuts designs into them using scalpels and brands them with sheet metal bent into designs, heated up to 1,800 degrees and "pressed firmly and quickly into the flesh."

Partly, the purpose of these practices is to create a decorative scar. Raelyn Gallina, a body artist in San Francisco, takes impressions of her blood designs with Bounty paper towels and has a portfolio of hundreds. But the experience and the scar itself are also symbolic. Gallina says: "You know that you're going to endure some pain, you're going to shed your blood. . . . That act, once it happens and you come out victorious, makes you go through a transformation. We have so little control over what goes on around us. . . . It comes down to you and your body."

Of course "control," or the illusion of control, is perhaps the primary motivation behind self-injury too. And the parallels don't end there. Gallina, like many body modifiers, says that a high proportion of her female clients report having been sexually abused. Rebecca Blackmon, 35, a slim, fair-haired woman with a gentle voice, was such a person. "I wanted to heal all the sexual parts of my body," she says. She began in 1989 by having her clitoral hood pierced; now, her pubic bone and stomach are branded, her nipples, tongue and belly button are pierced and a crescent moon of thick scar tissue from repeated cuttings encircles the lower half of both her breasts. "It's made me a lot more aware of my body; it's made me a lot more sexual," Blackmon says. Her feelings about her abuse have changed, too. "It's not so present in my mind all the time."

Clearly, body modifiers like Blackmon share the urge of many self-injurers to return to the site of their abuse—the body—and alter it in a manner that feels symbolically curative. And as with self-injury, "aftercare," or tending to one's wounds, is an important part of the process. "The ritual part to me is the daily taking care of it," says Blackmon. "The daily cleansing it, pampering it, putting heat packs on it." Among body modifiers who cut, there is great concern over scar enhancement, or thwarting the body's healing process. Common scarring techniques include dousing the freshly cut skin in rubbing alcohol and setting it afire; rubbing cigar ash or ink into the open wounds and advising clients to pick off their newly formed scabs each day.

But the many resonances of motive and procedure between self-injurers and body modifiers can obscure a crucial difference: control. Getting an occasional brand or cut design in the course of a functional life is not the same as slashing at one's flesh—or fighting the urge to do so—on a daily basis. One is a shared act of pride; the other a secretive act steeped in shame. And many body modifiers—perhaps the majority, now that piercing and tattooing have become so commonplace—are motivated not by the process at all but by the simple desire to belong to a group that is visibly outside the mainstream.

One of the most famous body modifiers is Fakir Musafar, 66, who spent much of his early life secretly indulging his own urges to do such things as bind his waist to 19 inches and sew together parts of himself with needle and thread. As a teenager in South Dakota, he assembled a photography dark room in his mother's fruit cellar so that "if she knocked and I was in there putting needles in myself or ripping flesh, I'd say, 'Sorry, I'm developing film and I can't open the door now.'" Now a certified director of a state-licensed school for branding and body piercing in San Francisco, Fakir, as he is known, has seen his secret practices embraced by a growing population of young people. He performs rituals around the world, including the O-Kee-Pa, in which he hangs suspended from two giant hooks that penetrate permanent holes near his pectorals.

Favazza asked Fakir to contribute an epilogue to the second edition of "Bodies Under Siege," published recently. In it, Fakir suggests that self-mutilation and body modification share a common root in a collective human unconscious. "There's an undercurrent in everybody that's quite universal," Fakir says, "to experience in the body self-initiation or healing. If there is some way socially that these urges can be faced, they don't overpower people and get them into mental hospitals." The argument makes a kind of sense, but there is a lot it doesn't explain: if these longings are so universal, why are those cutting themselves, and being cut, so often the victims of trauma and neglect? And using Fakir's logic, couldn't one argue that anorexics and bulimics are merely performing their own symbolic body manipulations? Surely the coexistence of urges, symbolism and a sense of meaning or empowerment is not enough to make a practice healthy.

But Fakir has led a long, rich life, and Blackmon feels she has reclaimed her body, so perhaps there may be a context in which "self-injury" controlled and guided along safe paths, could serve as part of a healing process. Favazza seems to think so." "If it can be controlled and relabeled and not get out of hand, everybody would be better off," he says. "There's less shame associated with it, there's less possibility for bad accidents to occur. . . . But we're dealing with a lot of ifs, ands and buts here."

It's a sunny, springlike St. Patrick's Day, and the McArdle household is teeming with relatives and small children eating corned beef and green-frosted cupcakes from a generous spread on the dining-room table. Jill's bedroom smells of styling gel and electric curlers, and her cheerleading outfit is heaped in one corner. Her hair, which spirals in curls down her back, is crowned with a ring of metallic green and silver shamrocks. With a friend at her side, she works the family phone, trying to figure out where the best parties will take place during the South Side Irish parade.

Soon we're wandering through a neighborhood awash in Irish pride. Jill and her friend sneak cans of beer from the pockets of their windbreakers and guzzle them as we walk. "I love this day," Jill says. She finished the SAFE program two weeks ago but returns twice each week to see her therapist. "I'm feeling so much better," she says, smoking a cigarette as we pass Monroe Park, where the boys used to tease her. "Usually I'd be afraid to go somewhere because maybe somebody wouldn't want me. Now I don't care. Now it's like I'm O.K. with myself. It's their own problem."

We begin a desultory journey from party to party that leads from a cramped back porch beside a half-frozen portable swimming pool to a basement rec room with a hanging wicker chair and a bubble-hockey set. Jill cheerfully explains my presence to anyone with an interest: "She's writing an article on self-mutilation. That's what I was in the hospital for," seeming mildly amused by the double takes this bombshell induces. An old friend of hers, a boy, informs me that Jill is "a nice, friendly person who likes to talk."

She waits for him to say more. "Remember in eighth grade when you used to say to me, 'You have a thousand faces'?" she prompts. "Remember that?"

The boy looks puzzled. "Eighth grade was a long time ago," he says.

Finally we head to Western Avenue for a glimpse of the parade. As we walk in the bright sunlight, I notice that Jill's friend has fresh scars covering her forearms. She tells me rather proudly that she went on a recent binge of cutting herself, but insists she did not get the idea from Jill. Jill tells me privately that she thinks her friend did it to get attention, because the day after, she wore a short-sleeved shirt in the dead of winter, and everyone saw. Jill has been urging her friend to seek help.

The riotous spectators seem almost to drown out the tail end of the parade. Jill plunges into the drunken crowd, tripping over her untied shoelace, her friend straining to keep up with her. Men gape at her under her crown of shamrocks; she cheerily bellows hello at them and then swirls out of sight. We turn onto an alley, and in the sudden quiet, Jill stops a group of strangers and lights her cigarette off one of theirs. Her friend seizes this moment to kneel down and carefully tie Jill's shoelace.

Outside Jill's house, the girls hide their beers and cigarette butts in the bushes, then go inside to exchange a few pleasantries with Jill's family. The openness Jill showed toward her parents at SAFE has vanished behind a sheen of wary cheerfulness. Watching her, I find myself wondering whether self-injury will wind up as a mere footnote to her adolescence or become a problem that will consume her adulthood, as it has Jane C.'s. Often, particularly in someone with an intact family and friends, the behavior will simply fade away. "This disorder does tend to burn out, for some reason," says Cross. "Life takes over." And Jill knows where to get treatment, should she need it again. Jamie Matthews felt like a failure when she relapsed, until she talked to a friend who has repeatedly sought help with her eating disorder. "She said it's like a spiral staircase," Jamie says. "You keep going around in circles, but each time you're at a different level."

As for Jane C., she returned home shortly after Jill left SAFE and reports that the azaleas are blooming. It's hard, she says, returning to a place where she has always felt she was wearing a mask. "One night I was incredibly close," she says. "I mean, I had the blade to the skin. I sat there and I thought, It doesn't matter to anybody else. And I was just about hysterical, but I stopped myself. I thought, This isn't the only way that works."

Jill, too, seems to be making a kind of staggered progress. "I know I have to take care of myself more instead of other people," she says. "I'm at peace with myself." Since leaving the program, she says, she has had no impulses to hurt herself. "Part of me always used to want to do it, but that part of me dissolved."

Her mother, admittedly a worrier by nature, is less sure, and says she has resorted to sneaking into Jill's room in the wee hours with a penlight, lifting the covers while her daughter sleeps to check for new cuts or burns. So far, she's pleased to say, there has been nothing to report. As Jill and her friend finally burst from the house and clamber arm in arm down the block into the late afternoon, Nancy McArdle watches them from the living-room window and says, "You can't ever relax."

❧ HARD BODIES ❧

Stuart Ewen

Writing in 1934, the sociologists George A. Lundberg, Mirra Komarovsky, and Mary Alice McInerny addressed the question of "leisure" in the context of an emerging consumer society. Understanding the symbiotic relationship between mass-production industries and a consumerized definition of leisure, they wrote of the need for society to achieve a compatibility between the worlds of work and daily life. "The ideal to be sought," they proposed, "is undoubtedly the gradual obliteration of the psychological barrier which today distinguishes work from leisure."[1]

That ideal has been realized in the daily routine of Raymond H——, a thirty-four-year-old middle-management employee of a large New York City investment firm. He is a living cog in what Felix Rohatyn has termed the new "money culture," one in which making things" no longer counts; "making money," as an end in itself, is the driving force.[2] His days are spent at computer terminal, monitoring an endless flow of numerical data.

When his workday is done, he heads toward a local health club for the relaxation of a "workout." Three times a week this means a visit to the Nautilus room, with its high, mirrored walls, and its imposing assembly line of large, specialized "machines." The workout consists of exercises for his lower body and for his upper body, twelve "stations" in all. As he moves from Nautilus machine to Nautilus machine, he works on his hips, buttocks, thighs, calves, back, shoulders, chest, upper arms, forearms, abdomen, and neck, body part by body part.

At the first station, Raymond lies on the "hip and back machine," making sure to align his hip joints with the large, polished, kidney-shaped cams which offer resistance as he extends each leg downward over the padded roller under each knee. Twelve repetitions of this, and he moves on to the "hip abduction machine," where he spreads his legs outward against the padded restraints that hold them closed. Then leg extensions on the "compound leg machine" are followed by leg curls on the "leg curl machine." From here, Raymond H—— proceeds to the "pullover/torso arm machine," where he begins to address each piece of his upper body. After a precise series of repetitions on the "double chest machine," he completes his workout on the "four-way neck machine."

While he alternates between different sequential workouts, and different machines, each session is pursued with deliberate precision, following exact instructions.

Raymond H—— has been working on his body for the past three years, ever since he got his last promotion. He is hoping to achieve the body he always wanted. Perhaps it is fitting that this quintessential, single, young, urban professional—whose life has become a circle of work, money culture, and the cultivation of an image—has turned himself, literally, into a piece of work. If the body ideal he seeks is *lean*, devoid of fatty tissue, it is also *hard*. "Soft flesh," once a standard phrase in the American erotic lexicon, is now—within the competitive, upscale world he inhabits—a sign of failure and sloth.

---

[1]George A. Lundberg et al., *Leisure: A Suburban Study* (1934), p. 3.

[2]*New York Times,* 3 June 1987, p. A27.

The hard shell is now a sign of achievement, visible proof of success in the "rat race." The goal he seeks is more about *looking* than *touching*.

To achieve his goal, he approaches his body piece by piece; with each machine he performs a discrete task. Along the way he also assumes the job of inspector, surveying the results of each task in the mirrors that surround him. The division of labor, the fragmentation of the work process, and the regulating function of continual measurement and observation—all fundamental to the principles of "scientific management" are intrinsic to this form of recreation. Like any assembly line worker, H—— needs no overall knowledge of the process he is engaged in, only the specific tasks that comprise that process. "You don't have to understand *why* Nautilus equipment works," writes bodybuilder Mike Mentzer in the foreword to one of the most widely read Nautilus manuals. "With a tape measure in hand," he promises, "you will see what happens."[3]

The body ideal Raymond H—— covets is, itself, an aestheticized tribute to the broken-down work processes of the assembly line. "I'm trying to get better definition," H—— says. "I'm into Nautilus because it lets me do the necessary touchup work. Free weights [barbells] are good for building up mass, but Nautilus is great for definition."[4] By "definition," H—— is employing the lingo of the gym, a reference to a body surface upon which each muscle, each muscle group, appears segmented and distinct. The perfect body is one that ratifies the fragmentary process of its construction, one that mimics—in flesh—the illustrative qualities of a schematic drawing, or an anatomy chart.

Surveying his work in the mirror, H—— admires the job he has done on his broad, high pectorals, but is quick to note that his quadriceps "could use some work." This ambivalence, this mix of emotions, pursues him each time he comes for a workout, and the times in between. He is never quite satisfied with the results. The excesses of the weekend-past invariably leave their blemish. An incorrectly struck pose reveals an over-measure of loose skin, a sign of weakness in the shell. Despite all efforts, photogenic majesty is elusive.

The power of the photographic idiom, in his mind's eye, is reinforced, again and again, by the advertisements and other media of style visible everywhere. The ideal of the perfectly posed machine—the cold, hard body in response—is paraded, perpetually, before his eyes and ours. We see him, or her, at every glance.

An advertisement for home gym equipment promises a "Body By Soloflex." Above is the silent, chiaroscuro portrait of a muscular youth, his torso bare, his elbows reaching high, pulling a thin-ribbed undershirt up over his head, which is faceless, covered by shadow. His identity is situated below the neck, an instrumentally achieved study in brawn. The powerful expanse of his chest and back is illuminated from the right side. A carefully cast shadow accentuates the paired muscle formations of his abdominal wall. The airbrush has done its work as well, effecting a smooth, standardized, molded quality, what John Berger has termed "the skin without a biography." A silent, brooding hulk of a man, he is the unified product of pure engineering. His image is a product of expensive photographic technology, and expensive technical expertise. His body—so we are informed—is also a technical achievement. He has reached this captured moment of perpetual perfection on a "machine that fits in the corner" of his home. The machine, itself, resembles a stamping machine, one used to shape standardized, industrial products. Upon this machine, he has routinely followed instructions for "twenty-four traditional iron pumping exercises, each correct in form and balance." The privileged guidance of industrial engineering, and the mindless obedi-

---

[3]Ellington Darden, *The Nautilus Bodybuilding Book* (1986), pp. viii–ix.

[4]Style Project, interview 1–13.

ence of work discipline, have become legible upon his body; yet as it is displayed, it is nothing less than a thing of beauty, a transcendent aspiration.

This machine-man is one of a generation of desolate, finely tuned loners who have cropped up as icons of American style. Their bodies, often lightly oiled to accentuate definition, reveal their inner mechanisms like costly, open-faced watches, where one can see the wheels and gears moving inside, revealing—as it were—the magic of time itself. If this is eroticism, it is one tuned more to the mysteries of technology than to those of the flesh.

In another magazine advertisement, for Evian spring water from France, six similarly anatomized figures stand across a black and white two-page spread. From the look of things, each figure (three men and three women) has just completed a grueling workout, and four of them are partaking of Evian water as part of their recovery. The six are displayed in a lineup, each one displaying a particularly well-developed anatomical region. These are the new icons of beauty, precisely defined, powerful machines. Below, on the left, is the simple caption: "Revival of the Fittest." Though part of a group, each figure is conspicuously alone.

Once again, the modern contours of power, and the structures of work discipline, are imprinted upon the body. In a world of rampant careerism, self-absorption is a rule of thumb. If the division of labor sets each worker in competition with every other, here that fragmentation is aestheticized into the narcissism of mind and body.

Within this depiction, sexual equality is presented as the meeting point between the anorectic and the "nautilized." True to gender distinctions between evanescent value and industrial work discipline, the three women are defined primarily by contour, by the thin lines that their willowy bodies etch upon the page. Although their muscles are toned, they strike poses that suggest pure, disembodied form. Each of the men, situated alternately between the women, gives testimony on behalf of a particular fraction of segmented flesh: abdomen, shoulders and upper arms, upper back. In keeping with the assembly line approach to muscle building, each man's body symbolizes a particular station within the labor process.

Another ad, for a health and fitness magazine, contains an alarmingly discordant statement: "Today's women workers are back in the sweat shop." There is a basis to this claim. In today's world, powerful, transnational corporations search the globe looking for the cheapest labor they can find. Within this global economy, more and more women—from Chinatown to Taiwan—are employed at tedious, low-paying jobs, producing everything from designer jeans to computer parts.

Yet this is not the kind of sweatshop the ad has in mind. The photographic illustration makes this clear. Above the text, across the two-page color spread, is the glistening, heavily muscled back of a woman hoisting a chrome barbell. Her sweat is self-induced, part of a "new woman" lifestyle being promoted in *Sport* magazine, "the magazine of the new vitality." Although this woman bears the feminine trademark of blonde, braided hair, her body is decidedly masculine, a new body aesthetic in the making. Her muscles are not the cramped, biographically induced muscles of menial labor. Hers is the brawn of the purely symbolic, the guise of the middle-class "working woman."

While the text of the advertisement seems to allude to the real conditions of female labor, the image transforms that truth into beauty, rendering it meaningless. Real conditions are copywritten into catchy and humorous phrases. The harsh physical demands of women's work are reinterpreted as regimented, leisure-time workouts at a "health club." Real sweat is reborn as photogenic body oil.

The migration of women into the social structures of industrial discipline is similarly aestheticized in an ad for Jack LaLanne Fitness Centers. A black and white close-up of a young woman wrestling with a fitness "machine" is complemented by the eroticized grimace on her face. Once again, the chiaroscuro technique accentuates the straining muscles of her arms. The high-contrast, black and white motif may also suggest the "night and day" metamorphosis that will occur when one commits to this particular brand of physical discipline.

In large white letters, superimposed across the shadowy bottom of the photograph, are the words: "Be taut by experts." With a clever play on words the goal of education moves from the mind to the body. Muscle power is offered as an equivalent substitute for brain power. No problem. In the search for the perfectly regulated self, it is implicit that others will do the thinking. This woman, like the Soloflex man, is the product of pure engineering, of technical expertise:

> We were building bodies back when you were building blocks. . . . We know how to perfectly balance your workout between swimming, jogging, aerobics and weight training on hundreds of the most advanced machines available. . . . Sure it may hurt a little. But remember. *You only hurt the one you love.* [Emphasis added.]

These advertisements, like Raymond H——'s regular visits to the Nautilus room, are part of the middle-class bodily rhetoric of the 1980s. Together they mark a culture in which self-absorbed careerism, conspicuous consumption, and a conception of *self* as an object of competitive display have fused to become the preponderant symbols of achievement. The regulated body is the nexus where a cynical ethos of social Darwinism, and the eroticism of raw power, meet.

EXCERPT FROM
"PEDAGOGY OF THE OPPRESSED"

Paulo Freire

A careful analysis of the teacher—student relationship at any level, inside or outside the school, reveals its fundamentally *narrative* character. This relationship involves a narrating Subject (the teacher) and patient, listening objects (the students). The contents, whether values or empirical dimensions of reality, tend in the process of being narrated to become lifeless and petrified. Education is suffering from narration sickness.

The teacher talks about reality as if it were motionless, static, compartmentalized, and predictable. Or else he expounds on a topic completely alien to the existential experience of the students. His task is to "fill" the students with the contents of his narration—contents which are detached from reality, disconnected from the totality that engendered them and could give them significance. Words are emptied of their concreteness and become a hollow, alienated, and alienating verbosity.

The outstanding characteristic of this narrative education, then, is the sonority of words, not their transforming power. "Four times four is sixteen; the capital of Pará is Belém." The student records, memorizes, and repeats these phrases without perceiving what four times four really means, or realizing the true significance of "capital" in the affirmation "the capital of Pará is Belém," that is, what Belém means for Pará and what Pará means for Brazil.

Narration (with the teacher as narrator) leads the students to memorize mechanically the narrated content. Worse yet, it turns them into "containers," into "receptacles" to be "filled" by the teacher. The more completely she fills the receptacles, the better a teacher she is. The more meekly the receptacles permit themselves to be filled, the better students they are.

Education thus becomes an act of depositing, in which the students are the depositories and the teacher is the depositor. Instead of communicating, the teacher issues communiqués and makes deposits which the students patiently receive, memorize, and repeat. This is the "banking" concept of education, in which the scope of action allowed to the students extends only as far as receiving, filing, and storing the deposits. They do, it is true, have the opportunity to become collectors or cataloguers of the things they store. But in the last analysis, it is the people themselves who are filed away through the lack of creativity, transformation, and knowledge in this (at best) misguided system. For apart from inquiry, apart from the praxis, individuals cannot be truly human. Knowledge emerges only through invention and re-invention, through the restless, impatient, continuing, hopeful inquiry human beings pursue in the world, with the world, and with each other.

In the banking concept of education, knowledge is a gift bestowed by those who consider themselves knowledgeable upon those whom they consider to know nothing. Projecting an absolute ignorance onto others, a characteristic of the ideology of oppression, negates education and knowledge as processes of inquiry. The teacher presents himself to his students as their necessary opposite; by considering their ignorance absolute, he justifies his own existence. The students, alienated like the slave in the Hegelian dialectic, accept their ignorance as justifying the teacher's existence—but, unlike the slave, they never discover that they educate the teacher.

The *raison d'être* of libertarian education, on the other hand, lies in its drive towards reconciliation. Education must begin with the solution of the teacher-student contradiction, by reconciling the poles of the contradiction so that both are simultaneously teachers *and* students.

This solution is not (nor can it be) found in the banking concept. On the contrary, banking education maintains and even stimulates the contradiction through the following attitudes and practices, which mirror oppressive society as a whole:

(a) the teacher teaches and the students are taught;

(b) the teacher knows everything and the students know nothing;

(c) the teacher thinks and the students are thought about;

(d) the teacher talks and the students listen—meekly;

(e) the teacher disciplines and the students are disciplined;

(f) the teacher chooses and enforces his choice, and the students comply;

(g) the teacher acts and the students have the illusion of acting through the action of the teacher;

(h) the teacher chooses the program content, and the students (who were not consulted) adapt to it;

(i) the teacher confuses the authority of knowledge with his or her own professional authority, which she and he sets in opposition to the freedom of the students;

(j) the teacher is the Subject of the learning process, while the pupils are mere objects.

It is not surprising that the banking concept of education regards men as adaptable, manageable beings. The more students work at storing the deposits entrusted to them, the less they develop the critical consciousness which would result from their intervention in the world as transformers of that world. The more completely they accept the passive role imposed on them, the more they tend simply to adapt to the world as it is and to the fragmented view of reality deposited in them.

The capability of banking education to minimize or annul the students' creative power and to stimulate their credulity serves the interests of the oppressors, who care neither to have the world revealed nor to see it transformed. The oppressors use their "humanitarianism" to preserve a profitable situation. Thus they react almost instinctively against any experiment in education which stimulates the critical faculties and is not content with a partial view of reality but always seeks out the ties which link one point to another and one problem to another.

Indeed, the interests of the oppressors lie in "changing the consciousness of the oppressed, not the situation which oppresses them";[1] for the more the oppressed can be led to adapt to that situation, the more easily they can be dominated. To achieve this end, the oppressors use the banking concept of education in conjunction with a paternalistic social action apparatus, within which the oppressed receive the euphemistic title of "welfare recipients." They are treated as individual cases, as marginal persons who deviate from the general configuration of a "good, organized, and just" society. The oppressed are regarded as the pathology of the healthy society, which must therefore adjust these "incompetent and lazy" folk to its own patterns by changing their mentality. These marginals need to be "integrated," "incorporated" into the healthy society that they have "forsaken."

The truth is, however, that the oppressed are not "marginals," are not people living "outside" society. They have always been "inside"—inside the structure which made them "beings for others." The solution is not to "integrate" them into the structure of oppression, but to transform that structure so that they

---

[1]Simone de Beauvoir, *La Pensée de Droite, Aujord'hui* (Paris); ST, *El Pensamiento político de la Derecha* (Buenos Aires, 1963), p. 34.

can become "beings for themselves." Such transformation, of course, would undermine the oppressors' purposes; hence their utilization of the banking concept of education to avoid the threat of student *conscientização*.

The banking approach to adult education, for example, will never propose to students that they critically consider reality. It will deal instead with such vital questions as whether Roger gave green grass to the goat, and insist upon the importance of learning that, on the contrary, *R*oger gave green grass to the *r*abbit. The "humanism" of the banking approach masks the effort to turn women and men into automatons—the very negation of their ontological vocation to be more fully human.

Those who use the banking approach, knowingly or unknowingly (for there are innumerable well-intentioned bank-clerk teachers who do not realize that they are serving only to dehumanize), fail to perceive that the deposits themselves contain contradictions about reality. But, sooner or later, these contradictions may lead formerly passive students to turn against their domestication and the attempt to domesticate reality. They may discover through existential experience that their present way of life is irreconcilable with their vocation to become fully human. They may perceive through their relations with reality that reality is really a *process,* undergoing constant transformation. If men and women are searchers and their ontological vocation is humanization, sooner or later they may perceive the contradiction in which banking education seeks to maintain them, and then engage themselves in the struggle for their liberation.

But the humanist, revolutionary educator cannot wait for this possibility to materialize. From the outset, her efforts must coincide with those of the students to engage in critical thinking and the quest for mutual humanization. His efforts must be imbued with a profound trust in people and their creative power. To achieve this, they must be partners of the students in their relations with them.

The banking concept does not admit to such partnership—and necessarily so. To resolve the teacher-student contradiction, to exchange the role of depositor, prescriber, domesticator, for the role of student among students would be to undermine the power of oppression and serve the cause of liberation.

Implicit in the banking concept is tie assumption of a dichotomy between human beings and the world: a person is merely *in* the world, not *with* the world or with others; the individual is spectator, not re-creator. In this view, the person is not a conscious being *(corpo consciente);* he or she is rather the possessor of *a* consciousness: an empty "mind" passively open to the reception of deposits of reality from the world outside. For example, my desk, my books, my coffee cup, all the objects before me—as bits of the world which surround me—would be "inside" me, exactly as I am inside my study right now. This view makes no distinction between being accessible to consciousness and entering consciousness. The distinction, however, is essential: the objects which surround me are simply accessible to my consciousness, not located within it. I am aware of them, but they are not inside me.

It follows logically from the banking notion of consciousness that the educator's role is to regulate the way the world "enters into" the students. The teacher's task is to organize a process which already occurs spontaneously, to "fill" the students by making deposits of information which he or she considers to constitute true knowledge.[2] And since people "receive" the world as passive entities, education should make them more passive still, and adapt them to the world. The educated individual is the adapted person, because she or he is better "fit" for the world. Translated into practice, this concept is well suited to the purposes of the

---

[2]This concept corresponds to what Sartre calls the "digestive" or "nutritive" concept of education, in which knowledge is "fed" by the teacher to the students to "fill them out." See Jean-Paul Sartre, "Une idée fundamentale de la phénoménologie de Husserl: L'intentionalité," *Situations* I (Paris, 1947).

oppressors, whose tranquility rests on how well people fit the world the oppressors have created, and how little they question it.

The more completely the majority adapt to the purposes which the dominant minority prescribe for them (thereby depriving them of the right to their own purposes), the more easily the minority can continue to prescribe. The theory and practice of banking education serve this end quite efficiently. Verbalistic lessons, reading requirements,[3] the methods for evaluating "knowledge," the distance between the teacher and the taught, the criteria for promotion: everything in this ready-to-wear approach serves to obviate thinking.

The bank-clerk educator does not realize that there is no true security in his hypertrophied role, that one must seek to live *with* others in solidarity. One cannot impose oneself, nor even merely co-exist with one's students. Solidarity requires true communication, and the concept by which such an educator is guided fears and proscribes communication.

Yet only through communication can human life hold meaning. The teacher's thinking is authenticated only by the authenticity of the students' thinking. The teacher cannot think for her students, nor can she impose her thought on them. Authentic thinking, thinking that is concerned about *reality,* does not take place in ivory tower isolation, but only in communication. If it is true that thought has meaning only when generated by action upon the world, the subordination of students to teachers becomes impossible.

Because banking education begins with a false understanding of men and women as objects, it cannot promote the development of what Fromm calls "biophily," but instead produces its opposite: "necrophily."

> While life is characterized by growth in a structured, functional manner, the necrophilous person loves all that does not grow, all that is mechanical. The necrophilous person is driven by the desire to transform the organic into the inorganic, to approach life mechanically, as if all living persons were things. . . . Memory, rather than experience; having, rather than being, is what counts. The necrophilous person can relate to an object—a flower or a person—only if he possesses it; hence a threat to his possession is a threat to himself; if he loses possession he loses contact with the world. . . . He loves control, and in the act of controlling he kills life.[4]

Oppression—overwhelming control—is necrophilic; it is nourished by love of death, not life. The banking concept of education, which serves the interests of oppression, is also necrophilic. Based on a mechanistic, static, naturalistic, spatialized view of consciousness, it transforms students into receiving objects. It attempts to control thinking and action, leads women and men to adjust to the world, and inhibits their creative power.

When their efforts to act responsibly are frustrated, when they find themselves unable to use their faculties, people suffer. "This suffering due to impotence is rooted in the very fact that the human equilibrium has been disturbed."[5] But the inability to act which causes people's anguish also causes them to reject their impotence, by attempting

---

[3]For example, some professors specify in their reading lists that a book should be read from pages 10 to 15—and do this to "help" their students!

[4]Fromm, *op. cit.,* p. 41.

[5]*Ibid.,* p. 31.

. . . to restore [their] capacity to act. But can [they], and how? One way is to submit to and identify with a person or group having power. By this symbolic participation in another person's life, [men have] the illusion of acting, when in reality [they] only submit to and become a part of those who act.[6]

Populist manifestations perhaps best exemplify this type of behavior by the oppressed, who, by identifying with charismatic leaders, come to feel that they themselves are active and effective. The rebellion they express as they emerge in the historical process is motivated by that desire to act effectively. The dominant elites consider the remedy to be more domination and repression, carried out in the name of freedom, order, and social peace (that is, the peace of the elites). Thus they can condemn—logically, from their point of view—"the violence of a strike by workers and [can] call upon the state in the same breath to use violence in putting down the strike."[7]

Education as the exercise of domination stimulates the credulity of students, with the ideological intent (often not perceived by educators) of indoctrinating them to adapt to the world of oppression. This accusation is not made in the naïve hope that the dominant elites will thereby simply abandon the practice. Its objective is to call the attention of true humanists to the fact that they cannot use banking educational methods in the pursuit of liberation, for they would only negate that very pursuit. Nor may a revolutionary society inherit these methods from an oppressor society. The revolutionary society which practices banking education is either misguided or mistrusting of people. In either event, it is threatened by the specter of reaction.

Unfortunately, those who espouse the cause of liberation are themselves surrounded and influenced by the climate which generates the banking concept, and often do not perceive its true significance or its dehumanizing power. Paradoxically, then, they utilize this same instrument of alienation in what they consider an effort to liberate. Indeed, some "revolutionaries" brand as "innocents," "dreamers," or even "reactionaries" those who would challenge this educational practice. But one does not liberate people by alienating them. Authentic liberation—the process of humanization—is not another deposit to be made in men. Liberation is a praxis: the action and reflection of men and women upon their world in order to transform it. Those truly committed to the cause of liberation can accept neither the mechanistic concept of consciousness as an empty vessel to be filled, nor the use of banking methods of domination (propaganda, slogans—deposits) in the name of liberation.

Those truly committed to liberation must reject the banking concept in its entirety, adopting instead a concept of women and men as conscious beings, and consciousness as consciousness intent upon the world. They must abandon the educational goal of deposit-making and replace it with the posing of the problems of human beings in their relations with the world. "Problem-posing" education, responding to the essence of consciousness—*intentionality*—rejects communiqués and embodies communication. It epitomizes the special characteristic of consciousness: being *conscious of,* not only as intent on objects but as turned in upon itself in a Jasperian "split"—consciousness as consciousness *of* consciousness.

Liberating education consists in acts of cognition, not transferrals of information. It is a learning situation in which the cognizable object (far from being the end of the cognitive act) intermediates the cognitive actors—teacher on the one hand and students on the other. Accordingly, the practice of problem-posing

---

[6]*Ibid.*

[7]Reinhold Niebuhr, *Moral Man and Immoral Society* (New York, 1960), p. 130.

education entails at the outset that the teacher-student contradiction to be resolved. Dialogical relations—indispensable to the capacity of cognitive actors to cooperate in perceiving the same cognizable object are otherwise impossible.

Indeed, problem-posing education, which breaks with the vertical patterns characteristic of banking education, can fulfill its function as the practice of freedom only if it can overcome the above contradiction. Through dialogue, the teacher-of-the-students and the students-of-the-teacher cease to exist and a new term emerges: teacher-student with students-teachers. The teacher is no longer merely the-one-who-teaches, but one who is himself taught in dialogue with the students, who in turn while being taught also teach. They become jointly responsible for a process in which all grow. In this process, arguments based on "authority" are no longer valid; in order to function, authority must be *on the side of* freedom, not *against* it. Here, no one teaches another, nor is anyone self-taught. People teach each other, mediated by the world, by the cognizable objects which in banking education are "owned" by the teacher.

The banking concept (with its tendency to dichotomize everything) distinguishes two stages in the action of the educator. During the first, he cognizes a cognizable object while he prepares his lessons in his study or his laboratory; during the second, he expounds to his students about that object. The students are not called upon to know, but to memorize the contents narrated by the teacher. Nor do the students practice any act of cognition, since the object towards which that act should be directed is the property of the teacher rather than a medium evoking the critical reflection of both teacher and students. Hence in the name of the "preservation of culture and knowledge" we have a system which achieves neither true knowledge nor true culture.

The problem-posing method does not dichotomize the activity of the teacher-student: she is not "cognitive" at one point and "narrative" at another. She is always "cognitive," whether preparing a project or engaging in dialogue with the students. He does not regard cognizable objects as his private property, but as the object of reflection by himself and the students. In this way, the problem-posing educator constantly re-forms his reflections in the reflection of the students. The students—no longer docile listeners—are now critical co-investigators in dialogue with the teacher. The teacher presents the material to the students for their consideration, and re-considers her earlier considerations as the students express their own. The role of the problem-posing educator is to create, together with the students, the conditions under which knowledge at the level of the *doxa is* superseded by true knowledge, at the level of the *logos*.

Whereas banking education anesthetizes and inhibits creative power, problem-posing education involves a constant unveiling of reality. The former attempts to maintain the *submersion* of consciousness; the latter strives for the *emergence* of consciousness and *critical intervention* in reality.

Students, as they are increasingly posed with problems relating to themselves in the world and with the world, will feel increasingly challenged and obliged to respond to that challenge. Because they apprehend the challenge as interrelated to other problems within a total context, not as a theoretical question, the resulting comprehension tends to be increasingly critical and thus constantly less alienated. Their response to the challenge evokes new challenges, followed by new understandings; and gradually the students come to regard themselves as committed.

Education as the practice of freedom—as opposed to education as the practice of domination—denies that man is abstract, isolated, independent, and unattached to the world; it also denies that the world exists as a reality apart from people. Authentic reflection considers neither abstract man nor the world without people, but people in their relations with the world. In these relations consciousness and world are simultaneous: consciousness neither precedes the world nor follows it.

"La conscience et le monde sont dormés d'un même coup: extérieur par essence à la conscience, le monde est, par essence relatif à elle.[8]

example

In one of our culture circles in Chile, the group was discussing (based on a codification[9]) the anthropological concept of culture. In the midst of the discussion, a peasant who by banking standards was completely ignorant said: "Now I see that without man there is no world." When the educator responded: "Let's say, for the sake of argument, that all the men on earth were to die, but that the earth itself remained, together with trees, birds, animals, rivers, seas, the stars . . . wouldn't all this be a world?" "Oh no," the peasant replied emphatically. "There would be no one to say: 'This is a world'."

The peasant wished to express the idea that there would be lacking the consciousness of the world which necessarily implies the world of consciousness. *I* cannot exist without a *non-I*. In turn, the *not-I* depends on that existence. The world which brings consciousness into existence becomes the world *of* that consciousness. Hence, the previously cited affirmation of Sartre: *"La conscience et le monde sont dormés d'un même coup."*

As women and men, simultaneously reflecting on themselves and on the world, increase the scope of their perception, they begin to direct their observations towards previously inconspicuous phenomena:

> In perception properly so-called, as an explicit awareness *[Gewahren]*, I am turned towards the object, to the paper, for instance. I apprehend it as being this here and now. The apprehension is a singling out, every object having a background in experience. Around and about the paper lie books, pencils, inkwell, and so forth, and these in a certain sense are also "perceived", perceptually there, in the "field of intuition"; but whilst I was turned towards the paper there was no turning in their direction, nor any apprehending of them, not even in a secondary sense. They appeared and yet were not singled out, were not posited on their own account. Every perception of a thing has such a zone of background intuitions or background awareness, if "intuiting" already includes the state of being turned towards, and this also is a "conscious experience", or more briefly a "consciousness of" all indeed that in point of fact lies in the co-perceived objective background.[10]

That which had existed objectively but had not been perceived in its deeper implications (if indeed it was perceived at all) begins to "stand out," assuming the character of a problem and therefore of challenge. Thus, men and women begin to single out elements from their "background awareness" and to reflect upon them. These elements are now objects of their consideration, and, as such, objects of their action and cognition.

In problem-posing education, people develop their power to perceive critically *the way they exist* in the world *with which* and *in which* they find themselves; they come to see the world not as a static reality, but as a reality in process, in transformation. Although the dialectical relations of women and men with the world exist independently of how these relations are perceived (or whether or not they are perceived at all), it is also true that the form of action they adopt is to a large extent a function of how they perceive themselves in the world. Hence, the teacher-student and the students-teachers reflect simultaneously on themselves and the world without dichotomizing this reflection from action, and thus establish an authentic form of thought and action.

---

[8]Sartre, *op. cit.*, p. 32.

[9]See chapter 3. Translators note.

[10]Edmund Husserl, *Ideas—General Introduction to Pure Phenomenology* (London, 1969), pp. 105–106.

Once again, the two educational concepts and practices under analysis come into conflict. Banking education (for obvious reasons) attempts, by mythicizing reality, to conceal certain facts which explain the way human beings exist in the world; problem-posing education sets itself the task of demythologizing. Banking education resists dialogue; problem-posing education regards dialogue as indispensable to the act of cognition which unveils reality. Banking education treats students as objects of assistance; problem-posing education makes them critical thinkers. Banking education inhibits creativity and domesticates (although it cannot completely destroy) the *intentionality* of consciousness by isolating consciousness from the world, thereby denying people their ontological and historical vocation of becoming more fully human. Problem-posing education bases itself on creativity and stimulates true reflection and action upon reality, thereby responding to the vocation of persons as beings who are authentic only when engaged in inquiry and creative transformation. In sum: banking theory and practice, as immobilizing and fixating forces, fail to acknowledge men and women as historical beings; problem-posing theory and practice take the people's historicity as their starting point.

Problem-posing education affirms men and women as beings in the process of *becoming*—as unfinished, uncompleted beings in and with a likewise unfinished reality. Indeed, in contrast to other animals who are unfinished, but not historical, people know themselves to be unfinished; they are aware of their incompletion. In this incompletion and this awareness lie the very roots of education as an exclusively human manifestation. The unfinished character of human beings and the transformational character of reality necessitate that education be an ongoing activity.

Education is thus constantly remade in the praxis. In order to *be*, it must *become*. Its "duration" (in the Bergsonian meaning of the word) is found in the interplay of the opposites *permanence* and *change*. The banking method emphasizes permanence and becomes reactionary; problem-posing education—which accepts neither a "well-behaved" present nor a predetermined future—roots itself in the dynamic present and becomes revolutionary.

Problem-posing education is revolutionary futurity. Hence it is prophetic (and, as such, hopeful). Hence, it corresponds to the historical nature of humankind. Hence, it affirms women and men as beings who transcend themselves, who move forward and look ahead, for whom immobility represents a fatal threat, for whom looking at the past must only be a means of understanding more clearly what and who they are so that they can more wisely build the future. Hence, it identifies with the movement which engages people as beings aware of their incompletion—an historical movement which has its point of departure, its Subjects and its objective.

The point of departure of the movement lies in the people themselves. But since people do not exist apart from the world, apart from reality, the movement must begin with the human-world relationship. Accordingly, the point of departure must always be with men and women in the "here and now," which constitutes the situation within which they are submerged, from which they emerge, and in which they intervene. Only by starting from this situation—which determines their perception of it—can they begin to move. To do this authentically they must perceive their state not as fated and unalterable, but merely as limiting—and therefore challenging.

Whereas the banking method directly or indirectly reinforces men's fatalistic perception of their situation, the problem-posing method presents this very situation to them as a problem. As the situation becomes the object of their cognition, the naïve or magical perception which produced their fatalism gives way to perception which is able to perceive itself even as it perceives reality, and can thus be critically objective about that reality.

A deepened consciousness of their situation leads people to apprehend that situation as an historical reality susceptible of transformation. Resignation gives way to the drive for transformation and inquiry, over which men feel themselves to be in control. If people, as historical beings necessarily engaged with other people in a movement of inquiry, did not control that movement, it would be (and is) a violation of their humanity. Any situation in which some individuals prevent others from engaging in the process of inquiry is one of violence. The means used are not important; to alienate human beings from their own decision-making is to change them into objects.

This movement of inquiry must be directed towards humanization—the people's historical vocation. The pursuit of full humanity, however, cannot be carried out in isolation or individualism, but only in fellowship and solidarity; therefore it cannot unfold in the antagonistic relations between oppressors and oppressed. No one can be authentically human while he prevents others from being so. Attempting *to be more* human, individualistically, leads to *having more*, egotistically, a form of dehumanization. Not that it is not fundamental *to have* in order *to be* human. Precisely because it is necessary, some men's *having* must not be allowed to constitute an obstacle to others' *having*, must not consolidate the power of the former to crush the latter.

Problem-posing education, as a humanist and liberating praxis, posits as fundamental that the people subjected to domination must fight for their emancipation. To that end, it enables teachers and students to become Subjects of the educational process by overcoming authoritarianism and an alienating intellectualism; it also enables people to overcome their false perception of reality. The world—no longer something to be described with deceptive words—becomes the object of that transforming action by men and women which results in their humanization.

Problem-posing education does not and cannot serve the interests of the oppressor. No oppressive order could permit the oppressed to begin to question: Why? While only a revolutionary society can carry out this education in systematic terms, the revolutionary leaders need not take full power before they can employ the method. In the revolutionary process, the leaders cannot utilize the banking method as an interim measure, justified on grounds of expediency, with the intention of *later* behaving in a genuinely revolutionary fashion. They must be revolutionary—that is to say, dialogical—from the outset.

SCHOOL IS HELL: LESSON 4

Matt Groening

SCHOOL IS HELL: LESSON 19

Matt Groening

☙ MEMORY WORK ☙

Wendy S. Hesford

To remember in a critical mode . . . *means, in Freirean terms, to confront the social amnesia of generations in flight from their own collective histories. (McLaren and Tadeu da Silva, 73–74)*

In the basement of my parents' home is a photograph that was once prominently displayed on the fireplace mantel in the family room with other representations of such rites of passage as weddings and school graduations. The photograph stood beside the sacred family heirloom, a large, black, leatherbound Holy Bible, with pressed birth announcements, engagements, and obituaries crumbling between the pages. It is a "portrait" of my maternal great-grandfather, Edward William Trevenan, who left his wife, Amelia, and their five children in Cornwall, England, in 1910 to work as a supervisor of operations at one of the gold mines in Johannesburg, South Africa [see figure, next page]. Edward, in his midthirties, is seated in a small room on a simple wooden chair. The other furnishings are well-worn and merely functional: two low cots, a small wooden table, two battered steamer trunks. The floorboards are rough and paint is peeling off the walls. Edward wears black leather shoes, dark cuffed pants, a button-down shirt (without a collar), and what he would have called "braces" to hold his pants up. He has rolled his shirtsleeves up to his elbows, which are placed casually on the chair back and tabletop. His legs are comfortably crossed, and his shoes shine in the camera's light. His appearance suggests a sense of control over his modest domain.

On the table are what appear to be the deliberately chosen necessities of an English workingman's life at the turn of the century: two tobacco pipes, two brushes (one for shoes, one for hair), a pot of ink containing a pen, a tin canister and several bottles, some papers (letters home?). The walls, too, are covered with "civilizing" touches: a pocket watch and chain hanging where a clock might be kept at home, a felt pincushion (identifiable as such only because my grandmother, Edward's daughter, still has the memento). Most prominent, however, are what appear to be pages torn from newspapers or magazines of British popular culture, which are tacked up in rather random fashion on the wall behind the beds. For example, one of the images seems to be a cover from *The Graphic,* a popular magazine of the British middle-class in the early twentieth century, the contemporary equivalent of our *Life* and *People* magazines. In addition, there is a page of nine portraits of formally dressed white men and women, each accompanied by a printed caption, illegible at this distance; a full-page photograph of a woman, perhaps a popular actress or singer in costume for some role; and two indistinct images, one of which appears to be men on horseback, some with arms in slings and others with guns. Finally, behind Edward's right arm is an image of two smiling women leaning coyly toward each other.

Before Edward, perched on the edge of a steamer trunk beside the cot on the left, sits a young black man in his mid-teens. My great-grandfather looks neither at the camera nor at anything within the frame of the picture, but gazes out, over, and beyond the visual field; the black youth, on the other hand, looks directly into the camera. He is dressed in baggy plaid pants that end above the knee and a plain longsleeved shirt. His clothes do not fit well: the pants are clearly too large, gathered at the waist by a thick

Edward William Trevenan with young man, Johannesburg, South Africa.

black belt, and his shirt is too small and rises up his back. Upon his head sits a misshapen felt slouch hat turned up in the front, and on his feet are scuffed and poorly soled white boots.

This description of the photograph may appear fairly straightforward and objective. But, in truth, it is far from neutral, because I have highlighted certain details and rejected or ignored others. In fact, one could argue that my description, like the photograph, reinvents the all-powerful gaze of the white European patriarch, because it does not question or reveal the logic of representation or the moral economy of the photograph and its relation to material realities. For instance, the description does not mention that there are no pictures of my great-grandmother or their children, nor does it shed any light on other social systems or relations that are not in the immediate field of vision. What exists on the other side of the interior walls is not known. Neither the photograph nor the description depicts the struggles that my great-grandmother Amelia must have faced in raising five children on her own or what must have been conflicting emotions over her husband's absence, which lasted more than eighteen months. Through omission, the description, like the photograph itself, also ignores the dangerous working conditions in the mines and the black workers' resistance to these conditions, as expressed in riots, strikes, and work stoppages, as well as the brutal suppression of such acts by those in power. The opening description and its focus on what can be seen could be interpreted as a controlling act that reinforces the domestic order of the room—a kind of cartography of the privileged—to see only what we want to see. Yet what is *not* seen is as much a part of the context of the photograph as what *is* seen. And in that respect, the opening description mirrors the patterns of detachment common to the Western ethnographic and autobiographic gaze of which the photograph is emblematic.

Unlike this image of my great-grandfather, which could be seen as a study in detachment, one of my primary goals is to show how autobiographical acts can only be understood by means other than detachment. An engaged, critically reflexive reading of the photograph illustrates how detachment has become part of the social memory. This photograph and the process of reading it provide an opportunity for me to present the governing theme of this chapter: the relationship between self-representation and historical realities and the implication of this relationship for understanding "the complexity of the momentarily situated subject" (Faigley, 239). It also serves to further highlight the critical gestures I bring to my study of autobiographical acts in the contact zones of the academy. Thus, this chapter is both critique and construct—a lesson in point of view. My interest is heuristic rather than documentary. I propose that we take a rhetorical approach to the study of autobiography, investigating its pedagogical and cultural dynamics at particular historical moments and within specific material circumstances (Mailloux, 83). As Steven Mailloux suggests in "Rhetorically Covering Conflict," a study of cultural rhetoric "attempts to read the tropes, arguments, and narratives of its object texts (whether literary or nonliterary) within their socio-political contexts of cultural production and reception" (83). What I propose is a cultural material-ist approach that investigates how one attempts to position oneself, or is positioned, among competing discourses and that relocates autobiography in the rhetorical and historical moments of its production and reception. Moreover, as a mode of analysis, cultural-materialist reading practices that foreground rhetoric open up the space to consider how autobiographical subjects negotiate and claim a sense of agency among contrary discourses and how the autobiographical subject and material body are cultural and linguistic sites of contestation.

The photograph and the process of interpreting it can serve as a heuristic for thinking about my shift-ing roles as author—great-granddaughter and keeper of the tales (a generational space that involves feel-ings of betrayal as much as pride), teacher, and social critic—and the cultural and social narratives that shape my authorial location. I began with a reading of this photograph and its accompanying narratives of interpretation to demonstrate that autobiography is a situated, fragmented, and negotiated perfor-mance, which has an "ambiguous relation to reference" (M. Hirsch, 83). I thus use the mobile and inter-secting visual and verbal narratives to interrupt any naturalized temptation to construe autobiographical acts as static or mimetic. In the second part of the chapter, I focus on theories of autobiography informed by deconstruction and poststructuralism, and I argue that positions adopted by critics such as Roland Barthes and Paul de Man theoretically parallel the social posture that my great-grandfather exhibits in the photograph. I call for a theory of autobiography that accounts for the socially constructed positions of the critic, autobiographer, and reader and an understanding of the historical context in which these con-structions are produced. In the last section of the chapter, I reveal how tropes of detachment and privi-lege, which characterize both the production and reception of the family photograph and the theoretical stances of critics of autobiography, are common pedagogical stances, and I argue for a pedagogy that en-ables teachers and students to become sensitive to the autobiographical scripts and cultural narratives that share their relations to each other. The intent of this chapter, then, is to perform autobiography as a form of cultural criticism (N. Miller's coinage) and to cross disciplinary boundaries and blend personal obser-vations with social critique, cultural theory, and political analysis common to such projects.

Let us turn, then, to the logic of representation and its relationship to material and economic reali-ties, which are no less constructed than the stories we tell about them. Consider, for example, how my description of the photograph simultaneously reinforces and lessens my great-grandfather's position of privilege. First, I call the image a "portrait" of my great-grandfather, which highlights his presence and awards him ownership of the image. Second, I suggest that his self-assured posture conveys a "sense of control over his modest domain" (referring to the actual space, although surely both the space and the black youth were considered part of his "domain"). Third, my use of the term "modest"—a minimizing phrase—places limits on my great-grandfather's power and suggests he was not the "grand colonizer" (a descriptor that is informed by the knowledge that my great-grandfather was in a lower-management po-sition in the mining company).

Hygiene is another cultural concept that seeps into the description by separating order from disorder and distinguishing the powerful from the powerless. My great-grandfather's well-fitted clothing and shoes—shined, I suspect, by the black youth—contrast with the black youth's ill-fitted clothing and worn-out boots. The white male body is presented as neat and controlled, whereas the black male body appears ill-kempt. In other words, the clothing and descriptions of the subjects indicate social boundaries of race and class. Whether the photograph was commissioned by the mining company as a promotional piece or taken at the request of my great-grandfather, the construction of the room—namely, the parallel alignment of beds and trunks—conveys an ideal of domestic order. Interestingly, this image of domesticity lacks women, although the black youth is effeminized in the colonial, homosocial domestic relationship. In this instance *domesticate* is akin to *dominate*. The pocket watch, caught by the camera at 10:35, is an emblem of mechanical time and, along with the light bulb, reflects industrial progress, scientific advance, and the functionalism of male colonialists. By visually reproducing an image of imperial aggression and capitalist civilization, the photograph is a vivid reminder of the privileged group's anxiety and discomfort over changing social boundaries and its need to create a "home" far from home.

This photograph of my great-grandfather recalls nineteenth-century portraiture and foregrounds the paradoxical status of photography in bourgeois culture. In the early 1800s, within the developing context of global economy and a professionalized penal climate in Britain, photography was used as a technology of surveillance that "fixed" an image of the "other" through the photographic regulation of the subproletariat in police procedures and anthropological records. Paradoxically, photography both promised the "mastery of nature" and threatened to level the existing cultural order—that is, it represented the "triumph of a mass culture" (Sekula, 4). Photography, as a technology of representation and power, thus was used both to repress and signify the "other" through the imperatives of medical and anatomical illustration and of criminal documentation (which was informed by constructs of deviance and social pathology) and to celebrate the bourgeois tradition through the honorific portrait tradition (Sekula, 7). As Allan Sekula points out, in the nineteenth century, photography "introduce[d] the panoptic principle into daily life" (10). For example, criminal identification photographs were used to "facilitate the *arrest* of their referent" (7) and, presumably, to "unmask the disguises, the alibis, the excuses, and multiple biographies of those who find or place themselves on the wrong side of the law" (Sekula, 6). However, the moral economy of the photographic image served socially cohesive functions, particularly in the United States, where "family photographs sustained sentimental ties in a nation of migrants" and articulated a "nineteenth-century familialism that would survive and become an essential ideological feature of American mass culture" (8–9).

As the photograph of my great-grandfather and his black servant vividly illustrates, "photography welded the honorific and repressive functions together" (Sekula, 10). The family photograph of my great-grandfather and the black youth placed on the mantelpiece—the family shrine—"took its place within a social and moral hierarchy" (10); it monumentalized, commemorated, and reproduced an idealized image of the family and its value—that is, its accomplishment of social conventionality and status. The seemingly private moment of sentimentality and individualization was shadowed by the two other, more public looks: the averted gaze of my great-grandfather and the black youth's arrested gaze at the camera (Sekula, 10). As the family narratives that accompany this photograph suggest, photography asserts its instrumental power by "naturalizing cultural practices" (M. Hirsch, 7). Presumably, the photograph unveils, captures, and *arrests* the truth. But, we must ask, whose truth does the photograph of my great-grandfather and his black servant capture? Who is looking? Who is being seen? To whom does the terrain of representation belong? Is the black youth's look back at the camera an oppositional gaze?

Historically, in the visual structure of representation, black slaves were punished by white slave owners for looking back; as hooks puts it, "The politics of slavery, of racialized power relations were such that the slaves were denied their right to gaze" (1992, 115). Ironically, the black youth's gaze at the camera is not an unequivocally insurgent act of looking back, but rather his visibility produces a kind of public invisibility. Within the framework of late-nineteenth and early-twentieth-century photographic conventions, he is positioned as an object to be surveyed and regulated. He is caught in the exploiters' (both my great-grandfather and the photographer) production of him as "other." As a colonized subject, he is also positioned as a feminized object, capable only of offering himself up to the gaze of the paternal state (Tagg, 11–12). His gaze at the camera is not, then, an act of resistance. As David Spurr points out in *The Rhetoric of Empire*, "For the observer, sight confers power; for the observed, visibility is a trap" (16). The black youth's gaze at the camera contrasts with my great-grandfather's posture, which intentionally refuses the camera's probe and expresses the omniscience of Western European male culture. His commanding view suggests the colonialist surveying his dominion; it is a statement of control. From this perspective, one could look at the "portrait" of my great-grandfather as a use of visualizing technology for the self-authorization of the proto-typical Western white male, what Mary Louise Pratt calls "the monarch of all I survey" (quoted in Shohat and Stam, 156).

One challenge of reading this photograph is recognizing how it situates me, heir to my great-grandfather, as if I too were looking through the eyes of the colonizer. Here, we see how the context of imperial power shaped the uses of visual technology and how the I/Eye of empire traveled around the globe (156). Reading this photograph is like entering an autobiographical contact zone, a space where the narratives of my great-grandfather's generation and my own connect. More particularly, it is a space where the narratives that shape our lives collide. This is not to suggest that I'm caught in the grip of my great-grandfather's historical consciousness or that my gaze simply replicates his, but rather that I face the challenge of unsettling the historic and familial impulse to position myself at the center and of turning the "othering" gaze back on itself (Ellsworth, 9). In order to expose and transform the family narrative, I must resist the historical impulse to construct myself as a neutral cartographer recharting the circumspective force of the colonial gaze and must, instead, move beyond self-centering ethnocentrism. Moreover, I must avoid inscribing the same privileged mobility that my great-grandfather brought to his supervision of South African gold mines. Mary Louise Pratt claims that the representational phenomena of contact zones produce texts that are heterogeneous in their production as well as their reception. Reading a visual text, which to a certain degree circumvents narrative, nevertheless reinforces a kind of discursive mobility and academic literacy that casts an illusionary meta-narrative of control and coherence. My challenge is to inflect heterogeneity in my re-creation and to simulate it in narrative form by constantly unsettling the narratives themselves by showing how they are transformed as they move from one historical, cultural, and familial space to another. In this chapter, I appropriate Pratt's spatial metaphor in order to examine the production and reception of the family photograph and the clashing and collision of family identities, narratives, and networks of looking.

Despite the temporal, spatial, and cultural distance that separates me from the historical location of this photograph, the passage of the unframed "portrait" from one generation in my family to the next (it has traveled from my great-grandmother to my grandmother in Cornwall, England, to my mother in Essex County, New Jersey, to me in Oberlin, Ohio) indicates a lingering commitment to a sense of public history and the power of self-representation. This photograph can be described in Pratt's terms as an "ethnographic text" that captures my family's privilege and historical role in the objectification of the "other." My goal in this chapter is not to re-create yet another dominant ethnographic reading but to reach beyond a historical dominating sensibility to a reading that does not reproduce a colonial encounter. But in writing my first description of the photograph, I learned I cannot interpret it within the culture I live "without also apprehending the imperial contest itself" (Said, 217). "And," as Edward Said rightfully points out, "This . . . is a cultural fact of extraordinary political as well as interpretive importance" (217). In other words, "representations bear as much on the representer's world as on who or what is represented" (224). Spurr elaborates on the metaphorical relation between the writer and the colonizer":

> The problem of the colonizer is in some sense the problem of the writer: in the face of what may appear as a vast cultural and geographical blankness, colonization is a form of self-inscription onto the lives of people who are conceived of as an extension of the landscape. For the colonizer as for the writer, it becomes a question of establishing authority through the demarcation of identity and difference. (7)

While my opening description of the photograph illustrates the power of self-representation and my own role in the reconstruction of my family's history, it also suggests, as revealed through my analysis, that points of contact and collision lie within the "social moment of making memory" (Kuhn, 13). The challenge of reading this photograph is recognizing that the contact zone is *within* my gaze. Indeed, my goal in this chapter is to articulate the dominant narratives that define the historical moments of the photograph's production and reception and to consider how these narratives are now shaped by and mediated through my gaze.

Having presented some of the basic tenets of Pratt's concept of the contact zone in the Introduction and how it shapes my approach to autobiography—namely, my focus on the production and reception of autobiographical acts—I will now consider the particular narratives that shaped my reading of this family photograph as a young girl. This photograph has always fascinated and, at times, embarrassed me. My fascination sprang originally from wanting to know about the lives of my ancestors: where they lived, what they did, whom they knew. My sense of embarrassment is less readily identifiable, although I suspect it stems in part from guilt. When I asked members of my family about the relationship of the young black man to my great-grandfather, I was told that he was one of my great-grandfather's friends. Although I wanted to believe this interpretation, something about the image told me otherwise. Even at age ten, I knew the world was not that simple: a fairly well-dressed white man in South Africa was not likely to be "friends" with a black youth dressed in rags. My lingering sense of guilt arose from the nagging fear that the young black man seated across from my great-grandfather was actually some kind of indentured servant, or worse.

Perhaps it *is* possible that my great-grandfather Edward and the black youth were friends, although the fact that the latter was never named in this narrative of friendship is telling and perhaps another sign of colonial rule. As Spurr points out, "The very process by which one culture subordinates another begins in the act of naming and leaving unnamed, of marking on an unknown territory the lines of division and uniformity, of boundary and continuity" (4). Indeed, as Edward's only living son told me, the youth was referred to as my great-grandfather's "valet," a title that simultaneously suggests the imposition of British social norms onto the South African life and efforts to legitimize the relationship between the two: a personal valet is, after all, no mere servant. Not only is the young man's name unknown, but there is no definitive way to identify his language or place of origin. The colonial government recruited white miners from overseas, but most of its labor came from the indigenous black populations in southern and northern parts of Africa. Perhaps my great-grandfather's servant was initially recruited to work in the mines, but after a cursory medical examination revealed he was unfit or underage, he was relegated to employment outside the mines.[1]

This narrative of friendship may provide a paradigm for the rhetoric of colonial rule, because it allowed certain members of my family to deny their historical position of privilege and, at the same time, reinforced it. But because this narrative emerged in the contact zone of colonial relations, it rewrites the colonial situation in curious and complex ways. For example, reading their relationship as one of friendship or camaraderie rewrites the national colonial narrative at a time when colonial discourse constructed native black South Africans as savages. In other words, the South African youth gets reclassified from the "primitive savage" class into a Europeanized South African—a valet, part of an "advanced" community within the national and local hierarchy. Even if they did share the same living space, which is unlikely (the black youth probably lived with other black workers in overcrowded and unsanitary barracks), this imag-

---

[1]See Jeeves for a discussion of the history of labor and mining in South Africa.

ined fraternity nonetheless speaks to the economic dependency of British imperialism on black African men's labor.

This narrative of friendship is also complicated by and intertwined with national narratives of immigration. In fact, the very multiplicity of the friendship narrative lies in its capacity to absorb distinct cultural and national narratives together (Jameson, 142). For instance, the constructed parallelism and imagined fraternity between my maternal great-grandfather and the South African youth, a reading that was formed well after my great-grandfather and his family had immigrated to America, rewrites my great grandfather's privileged status as colonizer, replacing it with a narrative about his subordinate status as an immigrant "other" in the United States. By immigrating to this country, Edward became the "other" when his position relative to the culture in which he worked changed: in South Africa, he was situated as the foreigner as colonizer, yet in the United States, he was reconstituted as the foreigner as immigrant (a position of considerably less power). These positions of "otherness" are not historical equivalents. In fact, the allegory of alliance and projected fraternity actually disguises neocolonial relationships between First and Third World powers. I suspect, however, that my great-grandfather regarded immigration as an abandonment of the colonial system. Thus, in this friendship narrative, we see both anxiety and hope—a kind of double-sided consciousness.

Like most European immigrants in the late nineteenth and early twentieth century, my great-grandfather sought a better life for his family. For example, he was adamant about living where his sons would not have to work in the mines. As it was, they lived in New Jersey and worked for Du Pont, a plastics company. Although the friendship narrative may reflect the family's anxiety over its own differences in America, as white Anglo-Saxons they were less subordinate than other immigrants. They did not have to learn another language or a new economic system. Nevertheless, we may read into the family's interpretation of this photograph the double-sidedness of my great-grandfather's movements between England and South Africa and, later, the family's immigration to America. More particularly, the narrative of friendship between my great-grandfather and the South African distances my great-grandfather from the British social system of which he was originally a part, and contributes to the process by which he and his family were to invent and assimilate themselves as Americans. Reading this photograph at the moments of its production and reception involves reading into it the colonial relationship and expansion of Western interests, as well as the family's reconception of itself as Americans. When taken together, the friendship and immigration narratives challenge understandings of power relations that are constructed as fixed binaries (white/other, colonized/colonizer), and call for an understanding of the contradictory nature of subject positions, different national and cultural systems of stratification, and the historically situated nature of power (Friedman, 7).

The anxiety over the unsettling of cultural and geographical boundaries between the "First" and "Third" Worlds created narratives that constructed South Africa as a place where England (and Europe more generally) "projected its forbidden sexual desires and fears" (McClintock, 22). Similar narratives of sexual desire shaped my family's reading of this photograph and its understanding of my great-grandfather's movement abroad. For instance, when I visited Cornwall, England, in the mid-1980s on a foreign-exchange program in my senior year of college, I was told surreptitiously of Edward's lust for the bottle and women. This family secret—perhaps better termed a cultural myth—reflects a national narrative that eroticizes the land as well as the women of South Africa. The image of South Africa as seductive temptress is based on the notion that the land has qualities associated with the female body. As Spurr points out, however, what we see in such narratives is how "the traditions of colonialist and phallocentric discourses coincide" (Spurr, 170). This narrative of sexual desire is also about colonial conquest and imperial aggression. The family's construction of this "secret" mirrors a national sexual anxiety and the eroticization of the colonized, and invokes larger cultural anxieties and fantasies of seduction. That this narrative is framed as a secret or myth and my retelling as a betrayal of family privacy is an example of the cultural coding of disloyalty. Annette Kuhn puts it this way: "Secrets haunt our memory-stories, giving them pattern and shape. Family secrets are the other side of the family's public face, of the stories families tell themselves, and the world, about themselves" (2).

The photograph not only represents a discourse on the imperial "progress" of a nation but it also situates the white male as the father at the head of the "global family." The photograph was taken at a time when social crises were reverberating throughout Britain and its colonies. For instance, Britain experienced crises in gender and race relations on both domestic and international fronts. White masculinity was being contested. Middle-class women were seeking better educations and the right for paid work, and working-class women were fighting for fair employment rights and conditions. In contrast to these social challenges and the weakening of gender, race, and class boundaries, the photograph suggests that history and "progress" belong to white European men. This rendition of *his*-story is also shaped by the way science constructed race, which the medium of photography captured; more particularly, by the discourses of evolution and Social Darwinism, wherein racial ranking was prolific and black people were deemed genetically inferior (see Harding, Stepan and Gilman). Interestingly, these visual and verbal narratives of biological and social superiority and competition parallel those that characterize the rise of autobiography as a genre, which is deeply connected to the historical evolution of Western male self-consciousness and the capitalist ideology of possessive individualism. For instance, early critics of the genre claimed that peoples of the "Third World" were "primitive," that they lacked autobiography and feared their images in the mirror. Gusdorf, for one, argued that "primitives" "lag[ged] behind the Western 'child of civilization' and . . . that they have not emerged from 'the mythic framework of traditional teachings . . . into the perilous domain of history'" (Gusdorf quoted in McClintock, 313). These patterns of objectification continue through Western mappings of the "other" and the consumption of testimonial literature of Third World women in the First World marketplace (see Grewal and Kaplan).

How Far Have We Come?

The movement of the photograph from its prominent location in the family room to the basement of my parents' house is yet another rewriting of the progress narrative. The fact that this photograph of my great-grandfather was displayed in the family room of our newly purchased colonial home in a white, upper-middle-class New England suburb in the late 1970s confirms the family's status and upward mobility. The placement of the photograph carries an implicit message: "Look how far we've come from our humble beginnings."

The landscapes of my childhood and my family's geographical movement prompt questions about how I "encountered the other," how I did or did not acknowledge the presence of certain groups, and how what I experienced as home, my safe space, was secured on the basis of historical exclusions, violence, and omissions. I spent my childhood and early adolescence in a segregated suburb of Newark, New Jersey. Class and racial differences were geographically demarcated: the white working class and people of color, mostly African-American families, lived on the west banks of the Passaic River. Unlike the white residents on the Hill, who enjoyed a commanding view, people of color lived in a part of town known as the Valley. People on the Hill projected themselves onto people in the Valley: geographically, "whiteness" rose above and projected itself onto "blackness," or, as Ruth Frankenberg puts it, "Whiteness . . . comes to self-name, invents itself, by means of its declaration that it is *not* that which it projects as Other" (1996, 7). White middle-class families in my hometown were in a position of visual advantage, a location that presumably spared them from dealing with problems of race or class. We lived in a three-bedroom, stone-faced colonial house about midway up the Hill. Like most residents on the Hill, we defined ourselves by what we were not. Whiteness was "the invisible norm, the standard against which the dominant culture measures its own worth" constructed as both "everything and nothing" (McLaren 1995, 133). This monolithic construction of whiteness not only obscures ethnic and class differences among whites but also reinscribes the self-other binary; that is, we needed the "other" in order to see ourselves as unified subjects at the center. Like the gaze of my great-grandfather in the photograph, the spectatorial view from the hill functioned like a long chain of signifiers; the projection of blackness was construed as the necessary construct and counterpart for the establishment of whiteness. A social pecking order also existed among whites, particularly between first- and second-generation immigrants. Italian-American families lived along the crowded maple-lined streets, and a few Jewish families, mostly households headed by doctors and lawyers, dotted the larger lots on the corners. I grew up in a climate of anti-Semitism, which essentialized Jews as part of the white power structure, masked class differences among Jewish families in town, and erased historical memories of struggle.

Washington Street marked the racial boundary between the Valley and the Hill. Most small businesses were located here: an Italian grocer, a Jewish bakery. The border was not a place we inhabited, but a place we traveled through. Like clockwork, my father pulled into Meyer's Bakery after he picked my brother and me up from the Methodist Sunday school on the other side of the Passaic river; crumb buns and donuts would sweeten our return from what always struck me as an alienating experience. Although members of my extended family ran the church, as Sunday-school teachers and treasurer, and sang in the choir, I always felt as if I was just passing through; my presence was a symbolic way for me and my family to uphold an image of goodness. The only other time we stopped on Washington Street—the border—was for my mother to buy fruit and vegetables from an old Italian man, who ran his business from the back of a dilapidated truck. Our experiences of the border were our purchasing power, consumption of ethnicity, and commodification of the "other."

Meanwhile, across the railroad tracks on the south border of town, racial uprisings devastated whole neighborhoods. If I had known that more than fifteen hundred people were injured during the 1967 racial uprisings in Newark, that there were more than three hundred fires, and that the town was under military occupation, I may have been frightened and certainly confused. But I felt nothing. My daily life went on as usual. The only time we went into Newark was to pick my father up at the trolley station on the edge of town. Unlike my friends' fathers, who were policemen, firemen, or truck drivers, my father was a white-collar suit-and-tie man who commuted into Manhattan daily. My little brother and I were proud of our father, and we waited anxiously in the backseat of the family car, eager to see his face appear in the cable-car window. If my childhood years can be defined through narratives of protection and control, my adolescent years revealed the paradoxes of these narratives. For example, the ethic of control and anxieties about dating and relationships led me to excessive concern over body image and dieting—an embodiment of this trope of control.

My family left our house on the Hill in New Jersey when my father's company transferred him from New York to Connecticut. At first, we all seemed happy to move to another state and buy a bigger house, which was our chance to differentiate ourselves from most of the working- and lower-middle-class residents in our New Jersey hometown. My English immigrant grandparents had to work hard to assimilate, whereas my family, born in America, displayed our class difference, as our crossing the border zones suggests, through our consumerism—our construction of market identities—and our mobility. There are compelling parallels between my family's economic and geographic mobility and my own mobility, represented by the position I held while gathering research for this book. For six years after completing graduate school, I was a visiting assistant professor of writing at a college far removed from the blue-collar destiny of many of my childhood friends. Working at an elite college meant learning to deal with the privileges and paradoxes of my position, this movement, and its pedagogical implications. Although I grew up in a privileged white, middle-class environment, at Oberlin I struggled with the sense of entitlement shared by many upper-class students. At this time, the continuation of my family's progress narrative was defined not so much by my economic stability as by my cultural and intellectual status as a college professor, albeit in a visiting position. My authority was tied to my advanced academic literacy, which continues to distance me from my family. I am the first woman in my immediate family to go to college and the only person in my family to obtain a doctorate. Now, as an assistant professor at Indiana University with the privilege of being a new homeowner and adoptive parent, I'm rewriting this personal and professional narrative yet again.

The theme of upward mobility was entangled with another cultural narrative about a presumed lack of what might be called "ethnicity." As English immigrants, my family was not visibly or, because they quickly lost their accents, audibly "other." One might think, as I did as a child, that Anglo-British customs were not alive in America—except for certain foods, like the Cornish pasties and saffron buns my grandmother made. To me, these customs, class, and patterns of communication were invisible, naturalized. My family members had the privilege of situating themselves beyond forms of ethnic signification. As the photograph of my maternal great-grandfather suggests, we occupied the position of the privileging signifier. For instance, Italian-American life was "other" to us, as were the lives of Latinos, Jewish-Americans, South Asians, and African-Americans. But because as an adolescent most of my friends were Italian-Americans, I was comfortable with the Italian-American culture. I craved what seemed like exotic foods: chicken savoy (marinated in vinegar, olive oil, and oregano), cavatelli with ricotta, tiramisu, and red table wine. I yearned for animated conversations at dinnertime and elaborate Catholic rituals and ceremonies, for incense and ornate altars. I always wanted to escape what I saw as the "sterility" of my own family heritage. My desire for the "other"—Argerio, Basto, de Angelo, de Giordano, Donatello, Esposito, Giovanni, Santantonio, Rizzo, Zanfini—was defined by the privilege of not being "other," of knowing the likeness would never be complete. Perhaps in my desire for the "other," the legacy of my great-grandfather's privilege and the self-other binary of imperial subjectivity played out most vividly. As Fredric Jameson puts it, this desire for and impulse to impersonate the "other" are inextricably bound with the historical treatment of ethnic groups as objects of prejudice (146). In fact, these two impulses reinforce each other; a single and centered subject (image of my great-grandfather) needs the self-other, subject-object binary for its formation (Grewal, 234). Reading this photograph and my family's reception of it involves not only the historical contextualization of the colonial gaze and photographic conventions but also a recognition of the cultural narratives of immigration, ethnicity, and upward mobility and of how the material history and shifting categories of the "other" are subsumed within these narratives. My yearning for the Italian-American "other" was, in some sense, a continuation of the historical impulse to impersonate the "other" and construct friendship narratives that erase privilege.

Throughout the 1980s, the photograph, part of a collection of portraits on the mantel, was an accepted part of the family history. But in the early 1990s, when attention to race relations in the United States increased, the photograph disappeared to the basement, where things go if they're out of style or on their way to the Salvation Army or a rummage sale. The deauthorization of the photograph as a family heirloom is telling. It suggests a growing awareness about the historical context of our privilege, albeit an awareness manifested by rendering invisible our most visible yet unspoken secret—our white privilege. Paradoxically, the removal of the photograph to the basement at once represents an awareness of our privilege yet constitutes that privilege as an absence: the family can't bear to witness itself as a negative presence. This denial is tinged, of course, with white guilt about our role within the colonial situation and the historical process of othering. It is also a narrative, like the friendship narrative, that seeks to avoid the problems of white privilege by foregrounding other things—for example, that we can put such experiences aside. The movement of the photograph to the basement, one might argue, is a way of maintaining order and of not "losing face." My adolescent yearning for the Italian-American "other" was also a narrative with whiteness at the center, as the defining core. My reach toward the "other" could thus be interpreted as a reinscription of the white Anglo-American identity that it set out to displace.

The process of reframing these stories imposes new narrative trajectories and autobiographical scripts onto the photograph. Two implied narrative lines in my reconstruction include a redemptive narrative that emphasizes the recuperation of lost memories and the transformation of personal consciousness. The transformation narrative is embedded in a larger narrative about the academy as a radicalizing agent. Although neither narrative is about a triumph over adversity per se, each refers to an increased level of critical consciousness. My reframing of the family photograph and its narratives might be read as emblematic of the movement through Freirean levels of consciousness—that is, the move from "intransitive thought" (where the individual experiences a lack of agency) to "semi-transitive" (a state wherein one claims a sense of agency yet continues to isolate and individualize social problems) to "critical transitivity" (a stage wherein one thinks about one's condition holistically and critically) (Shor 1993, 32). One could argue, for instance, that my reading of the family photograph reflects a certain level of critical transitivity; the constructed analytical narratives go beneath the impressions of the photographic surface to challenge the consequences of representation. However, as the storyteller, I cannot escape the contours of the framing apparatuses or their historical impulses.

Freirean principles encourage critical educators to create pedagogical narratives and forums for sharing and engaging stories of struggle and hope with an awareness of "how, as subjects, we have become disproportionately constituted within dominative regimes of discourses and social practices through race, class, and gender identities" (McLaren and Tadeu da Silva, 68). However, in our creation of these public narratives and spaces we must be careful not to position ourselves as saviors (enlightened beings) and students as mere victims to be saved; not only does this pedagogical narrative uncritically project a state of false consciousness onto our students, but it also fails to acknowledge the "invisible" or masked literacies and levels of critical consciousness that students readily practice and claim both inside and outside the classroom.

This brings me to the second implied narrative trajectory of the academy as a radicalizing agent. It was within the academy, a site of relative privilege and entitlement that sanctions and legitimates middle-class values, that I was first exposed to Freire.[2] That the process of re-education has taken place, and continues to take place, within the structures of the academy suggests that the academy is a place conducive to such growth and transformation. This narrative, of course, is idealistic. But it is a pedagogical narrative of *hope* that I refuse to resign, a narrative that nonetheless must account for the fact that the academy is not an equally accessible or safe place for everyone to articulate social struggles or social dreaming. Thus, we must constantly work to comprehend our own and our students' social and political locations and how institutional relations are shaped by historical understandings and personal and generational biographies.

---

[2] See L. Bloom for a discussion of the midlle-class values in relation to the field of composition.

STRAIGHTENING OUR HAIR

bell hooks

On Saturday mornings we would gather in the kitchen to get our hair fixed, that is straightened. Smells of burning grease and hair, mingled with the scent of our freshly washed bodies, with collard greens cooking on the stove, with fried fish. We did not go to the hairdresser. Mama fixed our hair. Six daughters—there was no way we could have afforded hairdressers. In those days, this process of straightening black women's hair with a hot comb (invented by Madame C. J. Waler) was not connected in my mind with the effort to look white, to live out standards of beauty set by white supremacy. It was connected solely with rites of initiation into womanhood. To arrive at that point where one's hair could be straightened was to move from being perceived as child (whose hair could be neatly combed and braided) to being almost a woman. It was this moment of transition my sisters and I longed for.

Hair pressing was a ritual of blak women's culture—of intimacy. It was an exclusive moment when black women (even those who did not know one another well) might meet at home or in the beauty parlor to talk with one another, to listen to the talk. It was as important a world as that of the male barber shop—mysterious, secret. It was a world where the images constructed as barriers between one's self and the world were briefly let go, before they were made again. It was a moment of creativity, a moment of change.

I wanted this change even though I had been told all my life that I was one of the "lucky" ones because I had been born with "good hair"—hair that was fine, almost straight—not good enough but still good. Hair that had no nappy edges, no "kitchen," that area close to the neck that the hot comb could not reach. This "good hair" meant nothing to me when it stood as a barrier to my entering this secret black woman world. I was overjoyed when mama finally agreed that I could join the Saturday ritual, no longer looking on but patiently waiting my turn. I have written of this ritual: "For each of us getting our hair pressed is an important ritual. It is not a sign of our longing to be white. There are no white people in our intimate world. It is a sign of our desire to be women. It is a gesture that says we are approaching womanhood . . . Before we reach the appropriate age we wear braids, plaits that are symbols of our innocence, our youth, our childhood. Then, we are comforted by the parting hands that comb and braid, comforted by the intimacy and bliss. There is a deeper intimacy in the kitchen on Saturdays when hair is pressed, when fish is fried, when sodas are passed around, when soul music drifts over the talk. It is a time without men. It is a time when we work as women to meet each other's needs, to make each other feel good inside, a time of laughter and outrageous talk."

Since the world we lived in was racially segregated, it was easy to overlook the relationship between white supremacy and our obsession with hair. Even though black women with straight hair were perceived to be more beautiful than those with thick, frizzy hair, it was not overtly related to a notion that white women were a more appealing female group or that their straight hair set a beauty standard black women were struggling to live out. While this was probably the ideological framework from which the process of straightening black women's hair emerged, it was expanded so that it became a real space of black woman bonding through ritualized, shared experience. The beauty parlor was a space of consciousness raising, a space where black women shared life stories—hardship, trials, gossip; a place where one could be comforted and one's spirit renewed. It was for some women a place of rest where one did not need to meet the demands of children or men. It was the one hour some folk would spend "off their feet," a soothing, restful time of mediation and silence, These positive empowering implications of the ritual of hair pressing mediate but do not change negative implications. They exist alongside all that is negative.

Within white supremacist capitalist patriarchy, the social and political context in which the custom of black folks straightening our hair emerges, it represents an imitation of the dominant white group's appearance and often indicates internalized racism, self-hatred, and/or low self-esteem. During the 1960s black people who actively worked to critique, challenge, and change white racism pointed to the way in which black people's obsession with straight hair reflected a colonized mentality. It was at this time that the natural hairdo, the "afro," became fashionable as a sign of cultural resistance to racist oppression and as a celebration of blackness. Naturals were equated with political militancy. Many young black folks found just how much political value was placed on straightened hair as a sign of respectability and conformity to societal expectations when they ceased to straighten their hair. When black liberation struggles did not lead to revolutionary change in society the focus on the political relationship between appearance and complicity with white racism ceased and folks who had once sported afros began to straighten their hair.

In keeping with the move to suppress black consciousness and efforts to be self-defining, white corporations began to acknowledge black people and most especially black women as potential consumers of products they could provide, including hair-care products. Permanents specially designed for black women eliminated the need for hair pressing and the hot comb. They not only cost more but they also took much of the economy and profit out of black communities, out of the pockets of black women who had previously reaped the material benefits (see Manning Marable's *How Capitalism Underdeveloped Black America,* South End Press). Gone was the context of ritual, of black woman bonding. Seated under noisy hair dryers black women lost a space for dialogue, for creative talk.

Stripped of the positive binding rituals that traditionally surrounded the experience, black women straightening our hair seemed more and more to be exclusively a signifier of white supremacist oppression and exploitation. It was clearly a process that was about black women changing their appearance to imitate white people's looks. This need to look as much like white people as possible, to look safe, is related to a desire to succeed in the white world. Before desegregation black people could worry less about what white folks thought about their hair. In a discussion with black women about beauty at Spelman College, students talked about the importance of wearing straight hair when seeking jobs. They were convinced and probably rightly so that their chances of finding good jobs would be enhanced if they had straight hair. When asked to elaborate they focused on the connection between radical politics and natural hairdos, whether natural or braided. One woman wearing a short natural told of purchasing a straight wig for her job search. No one in the discussion felt black women were free to wear our hair in natural styles without reflecting on the possible negative consequences. Often older black adults, especially parents, respond quite negatively to natural hairdos. I shared with the group that when I arrived home with my hair in braids shortly after accepting my job at Yale my parents told me I looked disgusting.

Despite many changes in racial politics, black women continue to obsess about their hair, and straightening hair continues to be serious business. It continues to tap into the insecurity black women feel about our value in this white supremacist society. Talking with groups of women at various college campuses and with black women in our communities there seems to be general consensus that our obsession with hair in general reflects continued struggles with self-esteem and self-actualization. We talk about the extent to which black women perceive our hair as the enemy, as a problem we must solve, a territory we must conquer. Above all it is a part of our black female body that must be controlled. Most of us were not raised in environments where we learned to regard our hair as sensual or beautiful in an unprocessed state. Many of us talk about situations where white people ask to touch our hair when it is unprocessed then show surprise that the texture is soft or feels good. In the eyes of many white folks and other non-black folks, the natural afro looks like steel wool or a helmet. Responses to natural hairstyles worn by black women usually reveal the extent to which our natural hair is perceived in white supremacist culture as not only ugly but frightening. We also internalize that fear. The extent to which we are comfortable with our hair usually reflects on our overall feelings about our bodies. In our black women's support group, *Sisters of the Yam,* we talk about the ways we don't like our bodies, especially our hair. I suggested to the group that we regard our hair as though it is not part of our body but something quite separate—again a territory to be controlled. To me it was important for us to link this need to control with sexuality, with sexual repression. Curious about what black women who had hot-combed or had permanents felt about the relationship between straightened hair and sexual practice I asked whether people worried about their hairdo, whether they feared partners touching their hair. Straightened hair has always seemed to me to call attention to the desire for hair to stay in place. Not surprisingly many black women responded that they felt uncomfortable if too much attention was focused on their hair, if it seemed to be too messy. Those of us who have liberated our hair and let it go in whatever direction it seems fit often receive negative comments.

Looking at photographs of myself and my sisters when we had straightened hair in high school I noticed how much older we looked than when our hair was not processed. It is ironic that we live in a culture that places so much emphasis on women looking young, yet black women are encouraged to change our hair in ways that make us appear older. This past semester we read Toni Morrison's *The Bluest Eye* in a black women's fiction class. I ask students to write autobiographical statements which reflect their thoughts about the connection between race and physical beauty. A vast majority of black women wrote about their hair. When I asked individual women outside class why they continued to straighten their hair, many asserted that naturals don't look good on them, or that they required too much work. Emily, a favorite student with very short hair, always straightened it and I would tease and challenge her. She explained to me convincingly that a natural hairdo would look horrible with her face, that she did not have the appropriate forehead or bone structure. Later she shared that during spring break she had gone to the beauty parlor to have her perm and as she sat there waiting, thinking about class reading and discussion, it came to her that she was really frightened that no one else would think she was attractive if she did not straighten her hair. She acknowledged that this fear was rooted in feelings of low self-esteem. She decided to make a change. Her new look surprised her because it was so appealing. We talked afterwards about her earlier denial and justification for wearing straightened hair. We talked about the way it hurts to realize connection between racist oppression and the arguments we use to convince ourselves and others that we are not beautiful or acceptable as we are.

In numerous discussions with black women about hair one of the strongest factors that prevent black women from wearing unprocessed hairstyles is the fear of losing other people's approval and regard. Heterosexual black women talked about the extent to which black men respond more favorably to women with straight or straightened hair. Lesbian women point to the fact that many of them do not straighten their hair, raising the question of whether or not this gesture is fundamentally linked to heterosexism and a longing for male approval. I recall visiting a woman friend and her black male companion in New York years ago and having an intense discussion about hair. He took it upon himself to share with me that I could be a fine sister if I would do something about my hair (secretly I thought mama must have hired him). What I remember is his shock when I calmly and happily asserted that I like the touch and feel of unprocessed hair.

When students read about race and physical beauty, several black women describe periods of childhood when they were overcome with longing for straight hair as it was so associated with desirability, with being loved. Few women had received affirmation from family, friends, or lovers when choosing not to straighten their hair and we have many stories to tell about advice we receive from everyone, including total strangers, urging to understand how much more attractive we would be if we would fix (straighten) our hair. When I interviewed for my job at Yale, white female advisers who had never before commented on my hair encouraged me not to wear braids or a large natural to the interview. Although they did not say straighten your hair, they were suggesting that I change my hairstyle so that it would most resemble theirs, so that it would indicate a certain conformity. I wore braids and no one seemed to notice. When I was offered the job I did not ask if it mattered whether or not I wore braids. I tell this story to my students so that they will know by this one experience that we do not always need to surrender our power to be self-defining to succeed in an endeavor. Yet I have found the issue of hairstyle comes up again and again with students when I give lectures. At one conference on black women and leadership I walked into a packed auditorium, my hair unprocessed wild and all over the place. The vast majority of black women seated there had straightened hair. Many of them looked at me with hostile contemptuous stares. I felt as though I was being judged on the spot as someone out on the fringe, an undesirable. Such judgments are made particularly about black women in the United States who choose to wear dreadlocks. They are seen and rightly so as the total antithesis of straightening one's hair, as a political statement. Often black women express contempt for those of us who choose this look.

Ironically, just as the natural unprocessed hair of black women is the subject of disregard and disdain we are witnessing return of the long dyed, blonde look. In their writing my black women students described wearing yellow mops on their heads as children to pretend they had long blonde hair. Recently black women singers who are working to appeal to white audiences, to be seen as crossovers, use hair implanting and hair weaving to have long straight hair. There seems to be a definite connection between a black female entertainer's popularity with white audiences and the degree to which she works to appear white, or to embody aspects of white style. Tina Turner and Aretha Franklin were trend setters; both dyed their hair blonde. In everyday life we see more and more black women using chemicals to be blonde. At one of my talks focusing on the social construction of black female identity within a sexist and racist society, a black woman came to me at the end of the discussion and shared that her seven-year-old daughter was obsessed with blonde hair, so much so that she had made a wig to imitate long blonde curls. This mother wanted to know what she was doing wrong in her parenting. She asserted that their home was a place where blackness was affirmed and celebrated. Yet she had not considered that her processed straightened hair was a message to her daughter that black women are not acceptable unless we alter our appearance or hair texture. Recently I talked with one of my younger sisters about her hair. She uses bright colored dyes, various shades of red. Her skin is very dark. She has a broad nose and short hair. For her these choices of straightened dyed hair were directly related to feelings of low self-esteem. She does not like her features and feels that the hairstyle transforms her. My perception was that her choice of red straightened hair actually called attention to the features she was trying to mask. When she commented that this look receives more attention and compliments, I suggested that the positive feedback might be a direct response to her own projection of a higher level of self-satisfaction. Folk may be responding to that and not her altered looks. We talked about the messages she is sending her dark-skinned daughters—that they will be most attractive if they straighten their hair.

A number of black women have argued that straightened hair is not necessarily a signifier of low self-esteem. They argue that it is a survival strategy; it is easier to function in this society with straightened hair. There are fewer hassles. Or as some folk stated, straightened hair is easier to manage, takes less time. When I responded to this argument in our discussion at Spelman by suggesting that perhaps the unwillingness to spend time on ourselves, caring for our bodies, is also a reflection of a sense that this is not important or that we do not deserve such care. In this group and others, black women talked about being raised in households where spending too much time on appearance was ridiculed or considered vanity. Irrespective of the way individual black women choose to do their hair, it is evident that the extent to which we suffer from racist and sexist oppression and exploitation affects the degree to which we feel capable of both selflove and asserting an autonomous presence that is acceptable and pleasing to ourselves. Individual preferences (whether rooted in self-hate or not) cannot negate the reality that our collective obsession with straightening black hair reflects the psychology of oppression and the impact of racist colonization. Together racism and sexism daily reinforce to all black females via the media, advertising, etc. that we will not be considered beautiful or desirable if we do not change ourselves, especially our hair. We cannot resist this socialization if we deny that white supremacy informs our efforts to construct self and identity.

Without organized struggles like the ones that happened in the 1960s and early 1970s, individual black women must struggle alone to acquire the critical consciousness that would enable us to examine issues of race and beauty, our personal choices, from a political standpoint. There are times when I think of straightening my hair just to change my style, just for fun. Then I remind myself that even though such a gesture could be simply playful on my part, an individual expression of desire, I know that such a gesture would carry other implications beyond my control. The reality is: straightened hair is linked historically and currently to a system of racial domination that impresses upon black people, and especially black women, that we are not acceptable as we are, that we are not beautiful. To make such a gesture as an expression of individual freedom and choice would make me complicit with a politic of domination that hurts us. It is easy to surrender this freedom. It is more important that black women resist racism and sexism in every way; that every aspect of our self-representation be a fierce resistance, a radical celebration of our care and respect for ourselves.

Even though I have not had straightened hair for a long time, this did not mean that I am able to really enjoy or appreciate my hair in its natural state. For years I still considered it a problem. (It wasn't naturally nappy enough to make a decent interesting afro. It was too thin.) These complaints expressed my continued dissatisfaction. True liberation of my hair came when I stopped trying to control it in any state and just accepted it as it is. It has been only in recent years that I have ceased to worry about what other people would say about my hair. It has been only in recent years that I could feel consistent pleasure washing, combing, and caring for my hair. These feelings remind me of the pleasure and comfort I felt as a child sitting between my mother's legs feeling the warmth of her body and being as she combed and braided my hair. In a culture of domination, one that is essentially anti-intimacy, we must struggle daily to remain in touch with ourselves and our bodies, with one another. Especially black women and men, as it is our bodies that have been so often devalued, burdened, wounded in alienated labor. Celebrating our bodies, we participate in a liberatory struggle that frees mind and heart.

INCLOSER

Susan Howe

EN-CLŌSE. See Inclose.

IN-CLŌSE,' *v.t.* [Fr. *enclos;* Sp. It. *incluso;* L. *inclusus, includo; in* and *claudo,* or *cludo.*]

1. To surround; to shut in; to confine on all sides; as, to *inclose* a field with a fence; to *inclose* a fort or an army with troops; to *inclose* a town with walls.
2. To separate from common grounds by a fence; as, to *inclose* lands.
3. To include; to shut or confine; as, to *inclose* trinkets in a box.
4. To environ; to encompass.
5. To cover with a wrapper or envelope; to cover under seal; as, to *inclose* a letter or a bank note.

IN\-CLŌS'ER, n. He or that which incloses; one who separates land from common grounds by a fence.
—Noah Webster, *An American Dictionary of the English Language*

Thomas Shepard
Anagram: O, a map's thresh'd
(W 3:513)

The first and least of those books [by Shepard] is called; "The Sincere Convert:" which the Author would commonly call, *his ragged child;* and once, even after its fourth edition, wrote unto Mr. Giles Firmin thus concerning it: "That which is called, *'The Sincere Convert:'* I have not the book: I once saw it: it was a collection of such notes in a dark town in *England,* which one procuring of me, published them without my will or my privity. I scarce know what it contains, nor do I like to see it; considering the many Σφαλματα *Typographica,* most absurd; and the confession of him that published it, that it comes out much altered from what was first written (M I:389)
—Cotton Mather, *Magnalia Christi Americana*

My writing has been haunted and inspired by a series of texts, woven in shrouds and cordage of classic American nineteenth-century works; they are the buried ones, they body them forth.

The selection of particular examples from a large group is always a social act. By choosing to install certain narratives somewhere between history, mystic speech, and poetry, I have enclosed them in an organization, although I know there are places no classificatory procedure can reach, where connections between words and things we thought existed break off. For me, paradoxes and ironies of fragmentation are particularly compelling.

Every statement is a product of collective desires and divisibilities. Knowledge, no matter how I get it, involves exclusion and repression. National histories hold ruptures and hierarchies. On the scales of global power, what gets crossed over? Foreign accents mark dialogues that delete them. Ambulant vagrant bastardy comes looming through assurance and sanctification.

THOMAS SHEPARD: A long story of conversion, and a hundred to one if some lie or other slip not out
of it. Why, the secret meaning is, I pray admire me. (W 2:284)

When we move through the positivism of literary canons and master narratives, we consign ourselves
to the legitimation of power, chains of inertia, an apparatus of capture.

BROTHER CRACKBONE HIS WIFE: So I gave up and I was afraid to sing because to sing a lie, Lord
teach me and I'll follow thee and heard Lord will break the will of His last work. (C 140)

* * *

A printed book enters social and economic networks of distribution. Does the printing modify an author's intention, or does a text develop itself? Why do certain works go on saying something else? Pierre
Macherey says, in *A Theory of Literary Production,* "The work has its beginnings in a break from the usual
ways of speaking and writing—a break which sets it apart from all other forms of ideological expression"
(TP 52). Roman Jakobson says, in "Dialogue on Time in Language and Literature": "One of the essential differences between spoken and written language can be seen clearly. The former has a purely temporal character, while the latter connects time and space. While the sounds that we hear disappear, when
we read we usually have immobile letters before us and the time of the written flow of words is reversible"
(V 20). Gertrude Stein says, in "Patriarchal Poetry": "They said they said. / They said they said when they
said men. / Men many men many how many many many many men men men said many here" (YS 132).
Emily Dickinson writes to her sister-in-law, Susan Gilbert Dickinson: "Moving on in the Dark like
Loaded Boats at Night, though there is no Course, there is Boundlessness—" (I 871).

Strange translucencies: letters, phonemes, syllables, rhymes, shorthand segments, alliteration, asso-
nance, meter, form a ladder to an outside state outside of States. Rungs between escape and enclosure are
confusing and compelling.

BROTHER CRACKBONE HIS WIFE: And seeing house burned down, I thought it was just and mercy
to save life of the child and that I saw not after again my children there. And as my spirit was fiery
so to burn all I had, and hence prayed Lord would send fire of word, baptize me with fire. And since
the Lord hath set my heart at liberty. (C 140)

* * *

There was the last refuge from search and death; so here. (W 2: 196)

I am a poet writing near the close of the twentieth century.

Little by little sound grew to be meaning. I cross an invisible line spoken in the first word "Then."
Every prescriptive grasp assertion was once a hero reading Samson. There and here I encounter one
vagabond formula another pure Idea. To such a land. Yet has haunts. The heart of its falls must be crossed
and re-crossed. October strips off cover and quiet conscience.

New England is the place I am. Listening to the clock and the sun whirl dry leaves along. Distinguishing first age from set hour. The eternal and spirit in them.

A poem can prevent onrushing light going out. Narrow path in the teeth of proof. Fire of words will
try us. Grace given to few. Coming home though bent and bias for the sake of why so. Awkward as I am.
Here and there invincible things as they are.

I write quietly to her. She is a figure of other as thin as paper.

Sorrow for uproar and wrongs of this world. You covenant to love.

* * *

EMILY DICKINSON:
Master.
    If you saw a bullet
hit a Bird—and he told you
he was'nt shot—you might weep
at his courtesy, but you would
certainly doubt his word—
(ML 32)

If history is a record of survivors, Poetry shelters other voices.

Dickinson, Melville, Thoreau, and Hawthorne guided me back to what I once thought was the distant seventeenth century. Now I know that the arena in which Scripture battles raged among New Englanders with originary fury is part of our current American system and events, history and structure.

GOODWIFE WILLOWS: Then I had a mind for New England and I thought I should know more
    of my own heart. So I came and thought I saw more than ever I could have believed that I wondered earth swallowed me not up. And 25 Matthew 5—foolish virgins saw themselves void of all grace. I thought I was so and was gone no farther. And questioned all that ever the Lord had wrought, I'll never leave thee. I could now apprehend that yet desired the Lord not to leave me nor forsake me and afterward I thought I was now discovered. Yet hearing He would not hide His face forever, was encouraged to seek. But I felt my heart rebellious and loathe to submit unto Him. (C 151)

An English relation of conversion spoken at a territorial edge of America is deterritorialized and deterred by anxiety crucial to iconoclastic Puritan piety. Inexplicable acoustic apprehension looms over assurance and sanctification, over soil subsoil sea sky.

Each singular call. As the sound is the sense is. Severed on this side. Who would know there is a covenant. In a new world morphologies are triggered off. . . .

* * *

Finding is the First Act (MBED 1043)

After the beaver population in New England had been decimated by human greed, when roads were cut through unopened countryside, the roadbuilders often crossed streams on abandoned beaver dams, instead of taking time to construct wooden bridges. When other beaver dams collapsed from neglect, they left in their wake many years' accumulation of dead bark, leaves, twigs, and silt. Ponds they formed disappeared with the dams, leaving rich soil newly opened to the sun. These old pond bottoms, often many acres wide, provided fertile agricultural land. Here grass grew as high as a person's shoulder. Without these natural meadows many settlements could not have been established as soon as they were.

Early narratives of conversion and first captivity narratives in New England are often narrated by women. A woman, afraid of not speaking well, tells her story to a man who writes it down. The participant reporters follow and fly out of Scripture and each other. All testimonies are bereft, brief, hungry, pious, *authorized.*

Shock of God's voice speaking English.

Sound moves over the chaos of place in people. In this hungry world anyone may be eaten. What a nest and litter. A wolf lies coiled in the lamb.

Silence becomes a Self. Open your mouth.

In such silence women were talking. Undifferentiated powerlessness swallowed them. When did the break at this degree of distance happen?

Silence calls me himself. Open your mouth.

Whosoever. Not found written in the book of life.

During a later Age of Reason eighteenth-century Protestant gentlemen signed the Constitution in the city of Philadelphia. These first narratives from wide-open places re-place later genial totalities.

During the 1850s, when the Republic was breaking apart, newly exposed soil from abandoned narratives was as rich and fresh as a natural meadow.

Emily Dickinson and Herman Melville are bridge builders. Their writing vaults the streams. They lead me in nomad spaces. They sieve cipherings, hesitations, watchings, survival of sound-meaning associations: the hound and cry, track and call. So much strangeness from God. What is saved to be said.

Once dams, narratives are bridges.

In 1850, when Melville wrote about American literary expression, he called the essay "Hawthorne and His Mosses" and chose a fragment from Hawthorne's story of Puritan doubt.

"'Faith!' shouted Goodman Brown, in a voice of agony and desperation; and the echoes of the forest mocked him, crying—'Faith! Faith!' as if bewildered wretches were seeking her all through the wilderness" (PT 251).

* * *

THOMAS SHEPARD:

Object. But Christ is in heaven; how can I receive him and his love?

Ans. A mighty prince is absent from a traitor; he sends his herald with a letter of love, he gives it him to read; how can he receive the love of the prince when absent? *Ans.* He sees his love in his letter, he knows it came from him, and so at a distance closeth with him by this means; so here, he that was dead, but now is alive, writes, sends to thee; O, receive his love here in his word; this is receiving "him by faith." (W 2:599–600)

In Europe, Protestant tradition since Luther had maintained that no one could fully express her sins. In New England, for some reason hard to determine, Protestant strictures were reversed. Bare promises were insufficient. Leaders and followers had to voice the essential mutability they suddenly faced. Now the minister's scribal hand copied down an applicant for church membership's narrative of mortification and illumination.

In *The Puritan Conversion Narrative: The Beginnings of American Expression,* Patricia Caldwell points out that during the 1630s, in the Bay Colony, a disclaimer about worthlessness and verbal inadequacy had to be followed by a verbal performance strong enough to convince the audience-congregation of the speaker's sincerity.

New England's first isolated and independent clerics must have wrestled with many conflicting impulses and influences. Rage against authority and rage for order, desire for union with the Father and the guilty knowledge they had abandoned their own mothers and fathers. In the 1630s a new society was being shaped or shaping itself. Oppositional wreckers and builders considered themselves divine instruments committed to the creation of a holy commonwealth. In 1636 the antinomian controversy erupted among this "Singular Prospect of Churches erected in an *American* Corner of the World, on purpose to express and pursue the Protestant *Reformation*" (MC 172).

The antinomian controversy circled around a woman, Anne Hutchinson, and what was seen to be "the Flewentess of her Tonge and her Willingness to open herselfe and to divulge her Opinions and to sowe her seed in us that are but highway side and Strayngers to her" (AC 353). Thomas Shepard made this accusation. Paradoxically, he was one of the few ministers who required women to recite their confessions of faith publicly, before the gathered congregation. Hugh Peter lectured Anne Hutchinson in court: "You have stept out of your place, *you have rather bine a Husband than a Wife and a preacher than a Hearer; and a Magistrate than a Subject.* And soe you have thought to carry all Thinges in Church and Commonwealth, as you would and have not bine humbled for this" (AC: 382–83).

Peter, Cotton, Winthrop, Eliot, Wilson, Dudley, Shepard, and other men had stepped out of their places when they left England. She was humbled by them for their Transgression. Anne Hutchinson was the community scapegoat. "'The Mother Opinion of all the rest. . . . From the womb of this *fruitful opinion,* and from the countenance here by given to immediate and unwarranted revelations, 'tis not easie to relate how many monsters, worse than African, arose in these regions of *America:* But a *synod* assembled at *Cambridge,* whereof Mr. Shepard was no small part, most happily crushed them all" (M I: 386).

*   *   *

NOAH WEBSTER:
SCĀPE'-GŌAT. n. [*escape* and *goat*] In *the Jewish ritual,* a goat which was brought to the door of the tabernacle, where the high priest laid his hands upon him, confessing the sins of the people, and putting them on the head of the goat; after which the goat was sent into the wilderness, bearing the iniquities of the people. Lev. xvi. (WD 986)

Kenneth Burke says, in *A Grammar of Motives,* "Dialectic of the Scapegoat": "When the attacker chooses for himself the object of attack, it is usually his blood brother; the debunker is much closer to the debunked than others are; Ahab was pursued by the white whale he was pursuing" (GM 406–7).

René Guard says, in *The Scapegoat,* "What is a Myth?": "Terrified as they [the persecutors] are by their own victim, they see themselves as completely passive, purely reactive, totally controlled by this scapegoat at the very moment when they rush to his attack. They think that all initiative comes from him. There is only room for a single cause in their field of vision, and its triumph is absolute, it absorbs all other causality: it is the scapegoat" (S 43).

I say that the Scapegoat Dialectic and mechanism is peculiarly open to violence if the attacker is male; his bloodbrother, female. Kenneth Burke and René Girard dissect grammars and mythologies in a realm of discourse structured, articulated, and repeated by men.

THOMAS SHEPARD: We are all in Adam, as a whole country in a parliament man; the whole country doth what he doth. And although we made no particular choice of Adam to stand for us, yet the Lord made it for us; who, being goodness itself, bears more good will to man than he can or could bear to himself; and being wisdom itself, made the wisest choice, and took the wisest course for the good of man. (W 1:24)

*   *   *

A Short Story

GOVERNOR WINTHROP: She thinkes that the Soule is annihilated by the Judgement that was sentenced upon Adam. Her Error springs from her Mistaking of the Curse of God upon Adam, for that Curse doth not implye Annihilation of the soule and body, but only a dissolution of the Soul and Body.

MR. ELIOT: She thinks the Soule to be Nothinge but a Breath, and so vanisheth. I pray put that to her.

MRS. HUCHINSON: *I thinke the soule to be nothing but Light.* (AC 356)

* * *

The Erroneous Gentlewoman

GOVERNOR WINTHROP: We have thought good to send for you to understand how things are, that if you be in an erroneous way we may reduce you that so you may become a profitable member here among us. (AC 312)

THOMAS SHEPARD: I confes I am wholy unsatisfied in her Expressions to some of the Errors. Any Hereticke may bringe a slye Interpritation, upon any of thease Errors and yet hould them to thear Death: therefor I am unsatisfied. (AC 377)

ANNE HUTCHINSON: My Judgment is not altered though my Expression alters.

BROTHER WILSON: Your Expressions, whan your Expressions are soe contrary to the Truth. (AC 378)

NOAH WEBSTER: EX-PRES' SION, (eks-presh' un,) *n.* The act of expressing the act of forcing out by pressure, as juices and oils from plants.

2. The act of uttering, declaring, or representing; utterance; declaration; representation; as, an *expression* of the public will. (WD 426)

MRS. HUTCHINSON: I doe not acknowledge it to be an Error but a Mistake. *I doe acknowledge my Expression to be Ironious but my Judgment was not Ironious,* for I held befor as you did but could not express it soe. (AC 361)

NOAH WEBSTER: ER-RO' NE-OUS, *a.* [L. *erroneus,* from *erro,* to err.]

1. Wandering: roving; unsettled.

   They roam

   Erroneous and disconsolate. *Philips.*

2. Deviating; devious; irregular; wandering from the right course.

   Erroneous circulation of blood   *Arbuthnot.* (WD 408)

ANNE HUTCHINSON: *So thear was my Mistake. I tooke Soule for Life.* (AC 360)

NOAH WEBSTER: Noah is here called *Man.* (WD xxiii)

* * *

Key

AC   Hall, David D. *The Antinomian Controversy, 1636–1638: A Documentary History.* Edited by David D. Hall. Middletown, Conn.: Wesleyan University Press, 1968.

C   Shepard, Thomas. *Thomas Shepard's "Confessions."* Edited by George Selement and Bruce C. Woolley. In *Collections of the Colonial Society of Massachusetts,* vol. 58. Boston: The Society, 1981.

GM   Burke, Kenneth. *A Grammar of Motives.* New York: Georges Braziller, 1955.

L   Dickinson, Emily. *The Letters of Emily Dickinson.* 3 vols. Edited by Thomas H. Johnson and Theodora Ward. Cambridge, Mass.: The Belknap Press, Harvard University Press, 1958.

M Mather, Cotton. *Magnalia Christi Americana: or, the Ecclesiastical History of New-England.* 2 vols. Hartford, Conn.: Silus Andrus & Son, 1855.

MBED Dickinson, Emily. *The Manuscript Books of Emily Dickinson.* 2 vols. Edited by R. W. Franklin. Cambridge, Mass.: The Belknap Press, Harvard University Press, 1981.

ML Dickinson, Family. *The Master Letters of Emily Dickinson.* Edited by R. W. Franklin. Amherst, Mass.: Amherst College Press, 1986.

PT Melville, Herman. *The Piazza Tales, and Other Prose Pieces.* Edited by Harrison Hayford, Alma A. MacDougall, and G. Thomas Tanselle. Evanston and Chicago: Northwestern University Press and the Newberry Library, 1987.

S   Girard, Rene. *The Scapegoat.* Translated by Yvonne Freccero. Baltimore: Johns Hopkins University Press, 1986.

TP Macherey, Pierre. *A Theory of Literary Production.* Translated by Geoffrey Wall. London: Routledge & Kegan Paul, 1978.

V   Jakobson, Roman. *Verbal Art, Verbal Sign, Verbal Time.* Edited by Krystyna Pomorska and Stephen Rudy. Minneapolis: University of Minnesota Press, 1985.

W   Shepard, Thomas. *The Works of Thomas Shepard.* 3 vols. Edited by John A. Albro, 1853. Reprint, New York: AMS, 1967.

WD Webster, Noah *An American Dictionary of the English Language.* Revised and enlarged by Chauncey A. Goodrich. Springfield, Mass.: George and Charles Merriam, 1852.

YS Stein, Gertrude. *The Yale Gertrude Stein.* Edited by Richard Kostelanetz. New Haven, Conn.: Yale University Press, 1980.

FEDERAL INDIAN IDENTIFICATION POLICY: A USURPATION OF INDIGENOUS SOVEREIGNTY IN NORTH AMERICA

M. Annette Jaimes

I'm forever being asked not only my "tribe," but my "percentage of Indian blood." I've given the matter a lot of thought, and find I prefer to make the computation based on all of me rather than just the fluid coursing through my veins. Calculated in this way, I can report that I am precisely 52.5 pounds Indian— about 35 pounds Creek and the remainder Cherokee—88 pounds Teutonic, 43.5 pounds some sort of English, and the rest "undetermined." Maybe the last part should just be described as "human." It all seems rather silly as a means of assessing who I am, don't you think?

—Ward Churchill
Creek/Cherokee Métis, 1991

The question of my "identity" often comes up. I think I must be a mixed-blood. I claim to be male, although only one of my parents was male.

—Jimmie Durham
Cherokee, 1991

By all accepted standards of international jurisprudence and human decency, American Indian peoples whose territory lies within the borders of the United States hold compelling legal and moral rights to be treated as fully sovereign nations. It is axiomatic that any such national entity is inherently entitled to exercise the prerogative of determining for itself the criteria by which its citizenry, or "membership," is to be recognized by other sovereign nations. This is a principle that applies equally to superpowers such as the U.S. and to non-powers such as Grenada and Monaco. In fact, it is a tenet so widely understood and imbedded in international law, custom, and convention that it bears no particular elaboration here.

Contrary to virtually universal practice, the United States has opted to preempt unilaterally the rights of many North American indigenous nations to engage in this most fundamental level of internal decisionmaking. Instead, in pursuit of the interests of their own state rather than those of the nations that are thereby affected, federal policymakers have increasingly imposed "Indian identification standards" of their own design. Typically centering upon a notion of "blood quantum"—not especially different in its conception from the eugenics code once adopted by nazi Germany in its effort to achieve "racial purity," or currently utilized by South Africa to segregate Blacks and "coloreds"—this aspect of U.S. policy has increasingly wrought havoc with the American Indian sense of nationhood (and often the individual sense of self) over the past century. This chapter offers a brief analysis of the motivations underlying this federal usurpation of the American Indian expression of sovereignty and points out certain implications of it.

Federal Obligations

The more than 370 formally ratified treaties entered into by the United States with various Indian nations represent the basic real estate documents by which the federal government now claims legal title to most of its land base. In exchange for the lands ceded by Indians, the United States committed itself to the permanent provision of a range of services to Indian populations (i.e., the citizens of the Indian nations with which the treaty agreements were reached), which would assist them in adjusting their economies and ways of life to their newly constricted territories. For example, in the 1794 Treaty with the Oneida (also affecting the Tuscarora and Stockbridge Indians), the United States guaranteed provision of instruction "in the arts of the miller and sawyer," as well as regular annuities paid in goods and cash, in exchange for a portion of what is now the state of New York.[1] Similarly, the 1804 Treaty with the Delaware extended assurances of technical instruction in agriculture and the mechanical arts, as well as annuities.[2] As Evelyn C. Adams frames it:

> Treaties with the Indians varied widely, stipulating cash annuities to be paid over a specified period of time or perpetually; rations and clothing, farming implements and domestic animals, and instruction in agriculture along with other educational opportunities . . . [And eventually] the school supplemented the Federal program of practical teaching.[3]

The reciprocal nature of such agreements received considerable reinforcement when it was determined, early in the 19th century, that "the enlightenment and civilization of the Indian" might yield—quite aside from any need on the part of the United States to honor its international obligations—a certain utility in terms of subordinating North America's indigenous peoples to Euroamerican domination. Secretary of War John C. Calhoun articulated this quite clearly in 1818:

> By a proper combination of force and persuasion, of punishment and rewards, they [the Indians] ought to be brought within the pales of law and civilization. Left to themselves, they will never reach that desirable condition. Before the slow operation of reason and experience can convince them of its superior advantages, they must be overwhelmed by the mighty torrent of our population. Such small bodies, with savage customs and character, cannot, and ought not, to be allowed to exist in an independent society. Our laws and manners ought to supersede their present savage manners and customs . . . their [treaty] annuities would constitute an ample school fund; and education, comprehending as well as the common arts of life, reading, writing, and arithmetic, ought not to be left discretionary with the parents. . . . When sufficiently advanced in civilization, they would be permitted to participate in such civil and political rights as the respective States.[4]

The utter cynicism involved in Calhoun's position—that of intentionally using the treaty instruments by which the United States conveyed recognition of Indian sovereignty as the vehicle with which to destroy that same sovereignty—speaks for itself. The more important point for purposes of this study, however, is that by 1820 U.S. strategic interests had congealed around the notion of extending federal obligations to Indians. The tactic was therefore continued throughout the entirety of the period of U. S.

---

[1]Kappler, Charles J., ed., *Indian Treaties, 1778–1883,* Interland Publishing Co., New York, (Second Printing) 1973, pp. 3–5.

[2]Ibid., pp. 7–9.

[3]Adams, Evelyn G. *American Indian Education: Government Schools and Economic Progress,* King's Crown Press, New York, 1946, pp. 30–31.

[4]Calhoun is quoted in *American State Papers: Indian Affairs* (Volume II). Wilmington, Delaware, 1972, pp. 183–4.

internal territorial conquest and consolidation.[5] By 1900, the federal obligations to Indian nations were therefore quite extensive.

Financial Factors

As Vine Deloria., Jr., has observed:

> The original relationship between the United States government and American Indian (nations) was one of treaties. Beginning with the establishment of federal policy toward Indians in the Northwest Ordinance of 1787, which pledged that the utmost good faith would be exercised toward the Indian (nations), and continuing through many treaties and statutes, the relationship has gradually evolved into a strange and stifling union in which the United States has become responsible for all the programs and policies affecting Indian communities."[6]

What this meant in practice was that the government was being required to underwrite the cost of a proliferating bureaucratic apparatus overseeing "service delivery" to Indians, a process initiated on April 16, 1818, with the passage of an act (*U.S. Statutes at Large*, 13:461) requiring the placement of a federal agent with each Indian nation, to serve as liaison and to "administer the discharge of Governmental obligations thereto." As the number of Indian groups with which the United States held relations had increased, so too had the number of "civilizing" programs and services undertaken, ostensibly in their behalf. This was all well and good during the time-span when it was seen as a politico-military requirement, but by the turn of the century this need had passed. The situation was compounded by the fact that the era of Indian population decline engendered by war and disease had also come to an end; the population eligible for per capita benefits, which had been reduced to a quarter-million by the 1890s, could be expected to rebound steadily in the 20th century. With its land base secured, the United States was casting about for a satisfactory mechanism to avoid paying the ongoing costs associated with its acquisition.

The most obvious route to this end, of course, lay in simply and overtly refusing to comply with the terms of the treaties, thus abrogating them.[7] The problems in this regard were, however, both two-fold and extreme. First, the deliberate invalidation of the U.S. treaties with the Indians would (obviously) tend to simultaneously invalidate the legitimacy which the country attributed to its occupancy of much of North America. Second, such a move would immediately negate the useful and carefully nurtured image the U.S. had cultivated of itself as a country of progressive laws rather than raw force. The federal government had to appear to continue to meet its commitments, while at the same time avoiding them, or at least containing them at some acceptable level. A devious approach to the issue was needed.

This was found in the so-called "blood quantum" or "degree of Indian blood" standard of American Indian identification which had been adopted by Congress in 1887 as part of the General Allotment Act.

---

[5]The bulk of the obligations in question were established prior to Congress' 1871 suspension of treaty-making with "the tribes" (Title 25, Section 71, U.S. Code). Additional obligations were undertaken by the federal government thereafter by "agreement" and as part of its ongoing agenda of completing the socio-political subordination of Indians, with an eye toward their eventual "assimilation" into the dominant culture and polity.

[6]Deloria, Vine Jr., "The Place of Indians in Contemporary Education," *American Indian Journal,* Vol. 2, No. 21, February, 1976, p. 2.

[7]This strategy was actually tried in the wake of the passage of the House Concurrent Resolution 108 in June 1953. Predictably, the federal dissolution of American Indian nations such as the Klamath and Menominee so tarnished the U.S. image that implementation of the policy was shortly suspended (albeit the law remains an the books).

The function of this piece of legislation was to expedite the process of Indian "civilization" by unilaterally dissolving their collectively (i.e., nationally) held reservation land holdings. Reservation lands were reallocated in accordance with the "superior" (i.e., Euroamerican) concept of property: *individually* deeded land parcels, usually of 160 acres each. Each Indian, identified as being those documentably of *one-half or more Indian blood,* was entitled to receive title in fee of such a parcel; all others were simply disenfranchised altogether. Reserved Indian land that remained unallotted after all "blooded" Indians had received their individual parcels was to be declared "surplus" and opened up for non-Indian use and occupancy.

Needless to say, there were nowhere near enough Indians meeting the Act's genetic requirements to absorb by individual parcel the quantity of acreage involved in the formerly reserved land areas. Consequently, between 1887 and 1934, the aggregate Indian land base within the U.S. was "legally" reduced from about 138 million acres to about 48 million.[8] Moreover, the allotment process itself had been manipulated in such a way that the worst reservation acreage tended to be parceled out to Indians, while the best was opened to non-Indian homesteading and corporate use; nearly 20 million of the acres remaining in Indian hands by the latter year were arid or semi-arid, and thus marginal or useless for agricultural purposes.[9]

By the early 1900s, then, the eugenics mechanism of the blood quantum had already proven itself such a boon in the federal management of its Indian affairs that it was generally adapted as the "eligibility factor," triggering entitlement to any federal service from the issuance of commodity rations to health care, annuity payments, and educational benefits. If the government could not repeal its obligations to Indians, it could at least act to limit their number, thereby diminishing the cost associated with underwriting their entitlements on a per capita basis. Concomitantly, it must have seemed logical that if the overall number of Indians could be kept small, the administrative expenses involved in their service programs might also be held to a minimum. Much of the original impetus toward the federal preemption of the sovereign Indian prerogative of defining "who's Indian," and the standardization of the racist degree-of-blood method of Indian identification, derived from the budgetary considerations of a federal government anxious to avoid paying its bills.

Other Economic Factors

As the example of the General Allotment Act clearly demonstrates, economic determinants other than the mere outflow of cash from the federal treasury figure into the federal utilization of the blood quantum. The huge windfall of land expropriated by the United States as a result of the act was only the tip of the iceberg. For instance, in constricting the acknowledged size of Indian populations, the government could technically meet its obligations to reserve "first rights" to water usage for Indians while simultaneously siphoning off artificial "surpluses" to non-Indian agricultural, ranching, municipal, and industrial use in the arid west.[10] The same principle pertains to the assignment of fishing quotas in the Pacific Northwest, a matter directly related to the development of a lucrative non-Indian fishing industry there.[11]

---

[8]Collier, John, *Memorandum, Hearings and H.R. 7902 Before the House Committee on Indian Affairs,* (73rd Cong., 2d Sess.), U.S. Department of the Interior, Washington, D.C., 1934, pp. 16–18.

[9]Deloria, Vine, Jr., and Clifford M. Lytle, *American Indians, American Justice,* University of Texas Press, Austin, 1983, p. 10.

[10]See Hundley, Norris C. Jr., "The Dark and Bloody Ground of Indian Water Rights," in Roxanne Dunbar Ortiz and Larry Emerson, eds., *Economic Development in Indian Reservations,* University of New Mexico Press, Albuquerque, 1979.

[11]See American Friends Service Committee. *Uncommon Controversy: Fishing Rights of the Muckleshoot, Puyallup, and Nisqually Indians,* University of Washington Press, Seattle, 1970. Also see Cohen, Fay G., *Treaties on Trial: The Continuing Controversy over Northwest Indian Fishing Rights,* University of Washington Press, Seattle, 1986.

By the 1920s, it was also becoming increasingly apparent that much of the agriculturally worthless terrain left to Indians after allotment lay astride rich deposits of natural resources such as coal, copper, oil, and natural gas; later in the century, it was revealed that some 60 percent of all "domestic" uranium reserves also lay beneath reservation lands. It was therefore becoming imperative, from the viewpoint of federal and corporate economic planners, to gain unhindered access to these assets. Given that it would have been just as problematic to simply seize the resources as it would have been to abrogate the treaties, another expedient was required. This assumed the form of legislation unilaterally extending the responsibilities of citizenship (though not all the rights: Indians are still regulated by about 5,000 more laws than other citizens) over all American Indians within the United States.

> Approximately two-thirds of the Indian population had citizenship conferred upon them under the 1877 Allotment Act, as a condition of the allotment of their holdings . . . [In 1924] an act of Congress [8 U.S.C.A. 1402 (a) (2)] declared all Indians to be citizens of the United States and of the states in which they resided. . . .[12]

The Indian Citizenship Act greatly confused the circumstances even of many of the blooded and federally certified Indians insofar as it was held to bear legal force, and to carry legal obligations, whether or not any given Indian or group of Indians wished to be a U.S. citizen. As for the host of non-certified, mixed-blood people residing in the U.S., their status was finally "clarified"; they had been definitionally absorbed into the American mainstream at the stroke of the congressional pen. And, despite the fact that the act technically left certified Indians occupying the status of citizenship in their own indigenous nation as well as in the U.S. (a "dual form" of citizenship so awkward as to be sublime), the juridical door had been opened by which the weight of Indian obligations would begin to accrue more to the U.S. than to themselves. Resource negotiations would henceforth be conducted between "American citizens" rather than between representatives of separate nations, a context in which federal and corporate arguments "for the greater good" could be predicted to prevail.

In 1934, the effects of the citizenship act were augmented by the passage of the Indian Reorganization Act. The expressed purpose of this law was finally and completely to usurp the traditional mechanisms of American Indian governance (e.g., the traditional chiefs, council of elders, etc.), replacing them with a system of federally approved and regulated "tribal councils." These councils, in turn, were consciously structured more along the lines of corporate boards than of governmental entities. As Section 17 of the IRA, which spells out the council functions, puts the matter:

> [An IRA charter] may convey to the incorporated tribe the power to purchase, take by gift, or bequest, or otherwise, own, hold, manage, operate, and dispose of property of every description, real and personal, including the power to purchase restricted Indian lands and to issue in exchange for corporate property, and such further powers as may be incidental to the conduct of corporate business, not inconsistent with the law.

Indeed, since the exercise of such typical governmental attributes as jurisdiction over criminal law had already been stripped away from the councils by legislation such as the 1885 Major Crimes Act, there has been very little for the IRA form of Indian government to do but sign off on leasing and other business arrangements with external interests. The situation was and is compounded by the fact that grassroots Indian resistance to the act's "acceptance" on many reservations was overcome by federal manipulation of

---

[12]League of Women Voters, Indian Country, Publication No. 605, Washington, D.C., 1977, p. 24.

local referenda.[13] This has left the IRA governments in the position of owing Washington rather than their supposed constituents for whatever legitimacy they may possess. All in all, it was and is a situation made to order for the rubber-stamping of plans integral to U.S. economic development at the direct expense of Indian nations and individual Indian people. This is readily borne out by the fact that, as of 1984, American Indians received, on the average, less than 20 percent of the market royalty rates (i.e., the rates paid to non-Indians) for the extraction of minerals from their land. As Winona LaDuke observes:

> By official census counts, there are only about 1 1/2 million Indians in the United States. By conservative estimates a quarter of all the low sulphur coal in the United States lies under our reservation land. About 15 percent of all the oil and natural gas lies there, as well as two-thirds of the uranium. 100 percent of all U.S. uranium production since 1955 has been on Indian land. And we have a lot of copper, timber, water rights and other resources too. By any reasonable estimation, with this small number of people and vast amount of resources, we should be the richest group in the United States. But we are the poorest. Indians have the lowest per capita income of any population group in the U.S. We have the highest rate of unemployment and the lowest level of educational attainment. We have the highest rates of malnutrition, plague disease, death by exposure and infant mortality. On the other hand, we have the shortest life-span. Now, I think this says it all. Indian wealth is going somewhere, and that somewhere is definitely not to Indians. I don't know your definition of colonialism, but this certainly fits into mine.[14]

In sum, the financial advantages incurred by the United States in its appropriation of the definition of Indian identity have been neatly joined to even more powerful economic motivators during this century. The previously noted reluctance of the federal government to pay its bills cannot be uncoupled from its desire to profit from the resources of others.

Contemporary Political Factors

The utilization of treaties as instruments by which to begin the subordination of American Indian nations to U.S. hegemony, as well as subsequent legislation, such as the Major Crime Act, the General Allotment Act, and the Termination Act, all carry remarkably clear political overtones. This, to be sure, is the language of the colonizer and the colonized, to borrow a phrase from Albert Memmi,[15] and in each case the federal manipulation of the question of American Indian identity has played its role. These examples, however, may rightly be perceived as being both historical and parts of the "grand scheme" of U.S. internal colonialism (or "Manifest Destiny," as it was once called).

Today, the function of the Indian identity question appears to reside at the less rarified level of maintaining the status quo. First, it goes to the matter of keeping the aggregate number of Indians at less than 1 percent of the overall U.S. population and thus devoid of any potential electoral power. Second, and perhaps of equal importance, it goes to the classic "divide and conquer" strategy of keeping Indians at odds with one another, even within their own communities. As Tim Giago, conservative editor of the *Lakota Times,* asks:

---

[13]Probably the best overview of the IRA process may be found in Deloria, Vine Jr., and Clifford M. Lytle, *The Nations Within: The Past and Future of American Indian Sovereignty,* Pantheon Press, New York, 1984; on referenda fraud, see Chapter 11.

[14]LaDuke, Winona, presentation at International Women's Week activities, University of Colorado at Boulder, March 13, 1984; tape on file.

[15]Memmi, Albert, *The Colonizer and the Colonized,* Beacon Press, Boston, 1967.

Don't we have enough problems trying to unite without . . . additional headaches? Why must people be categorized as full-bloods, mixed-bloods, etc? Many years ago, the Bureau of Indian Affairs decided to establish blood quanta for the purpose of [tribal] enrollment. At that time, blood quantum was set at one-fourth degree for enrollment. Unfortunately, through the years this caused many people on the reservation to be categorized and labeled. . . . [The] situation [is] created solely by the BIA, with the able assistance of the Department of Interior.[16]

What has occurred is that the limitation of federal resources allocated to meeting U.S. obligations to American Indians has become so severe that Indians themselves have increasingly begun to enforce the race codes excluding the genetically marginalized from both identification as Indian citizens and consequent entitlements. In theory, such a posture leaves greater per capita shares for all remaining "bona fide" Indians. But, as American Indian Movement activist Russell Means has pointed out:

The situation is absurd. Our treaties say nothing about your having to be such-and-such a degree of blood in order to be covered . . . when the federal government made its guarantees to our nations in exchange for our land, it committed to provide certain services to us as we defined ourselves. As nations, and as a *people*. This seems to have been forgotten. Now we have Indian people who spend most of their time trying to prevent other Indian people from being recognized as such, just so that a few more crumbs—crumbs from the federal table—may be available to them, personally. I don't have to tell you that this isn't the Indian way of doing things. The Indian way would be to get together and demand what is coming to each and every one of us, instead of trying to cancel each other out. We are acting like colonized peoples, like subject peoples. . . .[17]

The nature of the dispute has followed the classic formulation of Frantz Fanon, wherein the colonizer contrives issues which pit the colonized against one another, fighting viciously for some presumed status within the colonial structure, never having time or audacity enough to confront their oppressors.[18] In the words of Stella Pretty Sounding Flute, a member of the Crow Creek band of Lakota, "My grandmother used to say that Indian blood was getting all mixed up, and some day there would be a terrible mess. . . . [Now] no matter which way we turn, the white man has taken over."[19]

The problem, of course, has been conscientiously exacerbated by the government through its policies of leasing individual reservation land parcels to non-Indians, increasingly "checkerboarding" tribal holdings since 1900. Immediate economic consequences aside, this has virtually ensured that a sufficient number of non-Indians would be residents in reservations, and that intermarriage would steadily result. During the 1950s, the federal relocation program—in which reservation-based Indians were subsidized to move to cities, where they might be anticipated as being subsumed within vastly larger non-Indian populations—accelerated the process of "biological hybridization." Taken in combination with the ongoing federal insistence that "Indianness" could be measured only by degree of blood, these policies tend to speak for themselves. Even in 1972 when, through the Indian Education Act (86 *Stat.* 334), the government seemed

[16]Giago, Tim. "Blood Quantum is a Degree of Discrimination," *Notes From Indian Country,* Vol. 1, State Publishing Co., Pierre, SD, 1984, p. 337.

[17]Means. Russell, speech at the law school of the University of Colorado at Boulder, April 19, 1985; tape on file.

[18]See Fanon, Frantz, *The Wretched of the Earth,* Grove Press, New York. 1966.

[19]Quoted in Martz, Ron. "Indians decry verification plan for federally-funded heath are," *Cox News Service,* Pierre, SD, October 7, 1986.

finally to be abandoning the blood quantum, there was a hidden agenda. As Lorelei DeCora (Means), a former Indian education program coordinator, put it:

> The question was really one of control, whether Indians would ever be allowed to control the identification of their own group members or citizens. First there was this strict blood quantum thing, and it was enforced for a hundred years, over the strong objections of a lot of Indians. Then, when things were sufficiently screwed up because of that, the feds suddenly reverse themselves completely, saying it's all a matter of self-identification. Almost anybody who wants to can just walk in and announce that he or she is Indian—no familiarity with tribal history, or Indian affairs, community recognition, or anything else really required—and, under the law, there's not a lot that Indians can do about it. The whole thing is suddenly just . . . really out of control. At that point, you really did have a lot of people showing up claiming that one of their ancestors, seven steps removed, had been some sort of "Cherokee princess." And we were obliged to accept that, and provide services. Hell, if all of that was real, there are more Cherokees in the world than there are Chinese.[20]

Predictably, Indians of all perspectives on the identity question reacted strongly against such gratuitous dilution of themselves. The result was a broad rejection of what was perceived as "the federal attempt to convert us from being the citizens of our own sovereign nations into benign members of some sort of all-purpose U.S. 'minority group,' without sovereign rights."[21] For its part, the government, without so much as a pause to consider the connotations of the word "sovereign" in this connection, elected to view such statements as an *Indian* demand for resumption of the universal application of the blood-quantum standard. Consequently, the Reagan administration, during the 1980s, set out to gut the Indian Education Act[22] and to enforce degree-of-blood requirements for federal services, such as those of the Indian Health Service.[23]

An even clearer example of the contemporary reassertion of eugenics principles in federal Indian identification policies came under the Bush administration. On November 30, 1990, Public Law 101–644 (104 *Stat.* 4662) went into effect. Grotesquely described as "an Act to promote development of Indian arts and crafts," the statute legally restricts definition of American Indian artists to those possessing a federally issued "Certificate of Degree of Indian Blood"—derogatorily-referred to as "pedigree slips" by opponents—or those certified as such by "federally recognized tribes" or the "Alaska Native Corporation." Excluded are not only those who fall below blood-quantum requirements, but anyone who has, for politico-philosophical reasons, refused to cooperate with federal pretensions to define for itself who will and who will not be considered a member and citizen of a recognized indigenous nation. Further, the entire populations of federally unrecognized nations such as the populous Lumbees of North Carolina, Abenakis of Vermont, and more than 200 others, are simply written out of existence even in terms of their internal membership identification as Indians.

In order to put "teeth" into the legislation, Congress imposed penalties of up to $1 million in fines and as much as fifteen years in a federal prison for anyone not meeting its definition to "offer to display for sale or to sell any good, with or without a Government trademark, which . . . suggests it is Indian pro-

---

[20]DeCora (Means), Lorelei, statement on radio station KILI, Porcupine, SD, October 12, 1986.

[21]Means, Ted, statement before the South Dakota Indian Education Association. Pierre, SD, November 16, 1975.

[22]See Jones. Richard, *American Indian Policy: Selected Major Issues in the 98th Congress.* Issue Brief No. 1B83083, Library of Congress. Government Division, Washington, D.C. (updated version. February 6.1984), pp. 3–4.

[23]Martz, op. cit.

duced." For galleries, museums, and other private concerns to display as "Indian arts or crafts" the work of any person not meeting the federal definition of Indian-ness, a fine of up to $5 million is imposed. Under such conditions, the Cherokee National Museum in Muskogee, Oklahoma was forced to close its doors when it was discovered that even the late Willard Stone—a talented sculptor, creator of the Great Seal of the Cherokee Nation, and a probable "full blood"—had never registered himself as a bona fide Indian according to federal standards.[24] At this juncture, things have become such a welter of confusion that:

> The Federal government, State governments and the Census Bureau all have different criteria for defining "Indians" for statistical purposes, and even Federal criteria are not consistent among Federal agencies. For example, a State desiring financial aid to assist Indian education receives the aid only for the number of people with one-quarter or more Indian blood. For preference in hiring, enrollment records from a Federally recognized tribe are required. Under regulations for law and order, anyone of "Indian descent" is counted as an Indian. If the Federal criteria are inconsistent, State guidelines are [at this point] even more chaotic. In the course of preparing this report, the Commission contacted several States with large Indian populations to determine their criteria. Two States accept the individual's own determination. Four accept individuals as Indian if they were "recognized in the community" as Native Americans. Five use residence on a reservation as criteria. One requires one-quarter blood, and still another uses the Census Bureau definition that Indians are who they say they are.[25]

This, without doubt, is a situation made to order for conflict, among Indians more than anyone else. Somehow, it is exceedingly difficult to imagine that the government would wish to see things turn out any other way.

Implications

The eventual outcome of federal blood-quantum policies can be described as little other than genocidal in their final implications. As historian Patricia Nelson Limerick recently summarized the process:

> Set the blood quantum at one-quarter, hold to it as a rigid definition of Indians, let intermarriage proceed as it had for centuries, and eventually Indians will be defined out of existence. When that happens, the federal government will be freed of its persistent "Indian problem."[26]

Already, this conclusion receives considerable validation in the experience of the Indians of California, such as the Juaneño. Pursuant to the "Pit River Consolidated Land Settlement" of the 1970s, in which the government purported to "compensate" many of the small California bands for lands expropriated during the course of non-Indian "settlement" in that state (at less than 50 cents per acre), the Juaneño and a number of other "Mission Indians" were simply declared to be "extinct." This policy was pursued despite the fact that substantial numbers of such Indians were known to exist, and that the government was at the time issuing settlement checks to them. The tribal rolls were simply ordered closed to any new additions, despite the fact that many of the people involved were still bearing children, and their population might well have

---

[24]Nichols, Lyn, "New Indian Art Regulations Shut Down Muskogee Museum," *San Francisco Examiner,* December 3, 1990.

[25]American Indian Policy Review Commission, *Final Report,* Vol. 1, May 17, 1977, U.S. Government Printing Office, Washington. D.C., 1977, p. 89.

[26]Limerick, Patricia Nelson, *The Legacy of Conquest: The Unbroken Past of the American West,* W. W. Norton and Co., New York, 1987, p. 338.

been expanding. It was even suggested in some instances that children born after an arbitrary cut-off date should be identified as "Hispanic" or "Mexican" in order that they benefit from federal and state services to minority groups.[27]

When attempting to come to grips with the issues raised by such federal policies, the recently "dissolved" California groups, as well as a number of previously unrecognized ones such as the Gay Head Wampanoags (long described as extinct), confronted a Catch-22 situation worthy of Joseph Heller. This rested in the federal criteria for recognition of Indian existence to the present day:

1. An Indian is a member of any federally recognized Indian Tribe. To be federally recognized, an Indian Tribe must be comprised of Indians.
2. To gain federal recognition, an Indian Tribe must have a land base. To secure a land base, an Indian Tribe must be federally recognized.:[28]

As Shoshone activist Josephine C. Mills put it in 1964, "There is no longer any need to shoot down Indians in order to take away their rights and land [or to wipe them out] . . . legislation is sufficient to do the trick legally."[29]

The notion of genocidal implications in all this receives firm reinforcement from the increasing federal propensity to utilize residual Indian land bases as dumping grounds for many of the more virulently toxic by-products of its advanced technology and industry.[30] By the early '70s, this practice had become so pronounced that the Four Corners and Black Hills regions, two of the more heavily populated locales (by Indians) in the country, had been semi-officially designated as prospective "National Sacrifice Areas" in the interests of projected U.S. energy development.[31] This, in turn, provoked Russell Means to observe that such a move would turn the Lakota, Navajo, Laguna, and other native nations in to "national sacrifice peoples.[32]

American Indian Response

Of late, there have been encouraging signs that American Indians of many perspectives and political persuasions have begun to arrive at common conclusions regarding the use to which the federal government had been putting their identity and the compelling need for Indians to finally reassert complete control over this vital aspect of their lives. For instance, Dr. Frank Ryan, a liberal and rather establishmentarian

---

[27]The author is an enrolled Juaneño, as is her eldest son. Her younger son, born after the closing of the Juaneño rolls, is not "federally recognized" as an Indian, despite the fact that his genealogy, cultural background, etc., is identical to that of his brother. The "suggestions" mentioned in the text were made to the author by a federal employee in 1979. The Juanaño band in California, in the 1990s, is initiating federal recognition procedures.

[28]Native American Consultants, Inc., *Indian Definition Study,* contracted pursuant to P. L. 95–581, Title IV. Section 1147, submitted to the Office of the Assistant Secretary of Education, U. S. Department of Education, Washington, D.C., January 1980, p. 2.

[29]Quoted in Armstrong, Virginia I., *I Have Spoken: American History Through the Voices of Indians,* Pocket Books, New York, 1975, p. 175.

[30]See Churchill, Ward, "American Indian Lands: The Native Ethic amid Resource Development." *Environment,* Vol. 28, No. 6, July/August 1986, pp. 12–7, 28–33.

[31]Ibid.

[32]Means, Russell, "The Same Old Song." in Ward Churchill, ed., *Marxism and Native Americans,* South End Press. Boston, 1983, p. 25.

Indian who has served as the director of the federal Office of Indian Education, began during the early 1980s to reach some rather hard conclusions about the policies of his employers. Describing the federal blood-quantum criteria for benefits eligibility in the educational arena as "a racist policy," Ryan went on to term it nothing more than "a shorthand method for denying Indian children admission to federal schools [and other programs]."[33] He concluded that, "The power to determine tribal membership has always been an essential attribute of inherent tribal sovereignty," and called for abolition of federal guidelines on the question of Indian identity without *any* lessening of federal obligations to the individuals and groups affected.[34] The question of the (re)adoption of blood-quantum standards by the Indian Health Service, proposed during the '80s by the Reagan administration, has served as even more of a catalyst. The National Congress of American Indians, never a bastion of radicalism, took up the issue at its 43rd Annual Convention, in October 1986. The NCAI produced a sharply worded statement rejecting federal identification policy:

> [T]he federal government, in an effort to erode tribal sovereignty and reduce the number of Indians to the point where they are politically, economically and culturally insignificant, [is being censured by] many of the more than 500 Indian leaders [attending the convention].[35]

The statement went on to condemn:

> . . . a proposal by the Indian Health Service to establish blood quotas for Indians, thus allowing the federal government to determine who is Indian and who is not, for the purpose of health care. Tribal leaders argue that *only* the individual tribe, not the federal government, should have this right, and many are concerned that this debate will overlap [as it has, long since] into Indian education and its regulation as well [emphasis added].[36]

Charles E. Dawes, Second Chief of the Ottawa Indian Tribe of Oklahoma, took the convention position much further at about the same time:

> What could not be completed over a three hundred year span [by force of arms] may now be completed in our life-span by administrative law. . . . What I am referring to is the continued and expanded use of blood quantum to determine eligibility of Indian people for government entitlement programs . . . [in] such areas as education, health care, management and economic assistance . . . [obligations] that the United States government imposed upon itself in treaties with sovereign Indian nations. . . . We as tribal leaders made a serious mistake in accepting [genetic] limits in educational programs, and we must not make the same mistake again in health programs. On the contrary, we must fight any attempt to limit any program by blood quantum every time there is mention of such a possibility . . . we simply cannot give up on this issue—ever . . . Our commitment as tribal leaders must be to eliminate any possibility of *genocide* for our people by administrative law. We must dedicate our efforts to insuring that . . . Native American people[s]

---

[33]Ryan, Frank A., *A Working Paper Prepared for the National Advisory Committee on Indian Education,* Paper No. 071279, Harvard American Indian Education Program. Harvard University Graduate School of Education, Cambridge, MA, July 18, 1979, p. 3.

[34]Ibid., pp. 41–44.

[35]Quoted in Martz, Ron, "Indians maintain U.S. trying to erode tribal sovereignty: cultural insignificance said to be goal." *Cox News Service,* Pierre, SD, October 26, 1986.

[36]Quoted in Martz. Ron. "Indians decry verification plan for federally-funded health care," *Cox News Service,* Pierre, SD, October 26, 1986.

will be clearly identified without reference to blood quantum . . . and that our sovereign Indian Nations will be recognized as promised [emphasis added].[37]

On the Pine Ridge Reservation in South Dakota, the Oglala Lakota have become leaders in totally abandoning blood quantum as a criterion for tribal enrollment, opting instead to consider factors such as residency on the reservation, affinity to and knowledge of, as well as service to the Oglala people.[38] This follows the development of a recent "tradition" of Oglala militancy in which tribal members played a leading role in challenging federal conceptions of Indian identity during the 1972 Trail of Broken Treaties takeover of BIA headquarters in Washington, and seven non-Indian members of the Vietnam Veterans Against the War were naturalized as citizens of the "Independent Oglala Nation" during the 1973 siege of Wounded Knee.[39] In 1986, at a meeting of the United Sioux Tribes in Pierre, South Dakota, Oglala representatives lobbied the leaders of other Lakota reservations to broaden their own enrollment criteria beyond federal norms. This is so, despite recognition that "in the past fifty years, since the Indian Reorganization Act of 1934, tribal leaders have been reluctant to recognize blood from individuals from other tribes [or any one else]."[40]

In Alaska, the Haida have produced a new draft constitution which offers a full expression of indigenous sovereignty, at least insofar as the identity of citizenry is concerned. The Haida draft begins with those who are now acknowledged as members of the Haida nation and posits that all those who marry Haidas will also be considered eligible for naturalized citizenship (just as in any other nation). The children of such unions would also be Haida citizens from birth, regardless of their degree of Indian blood, and children adopted by Haidas would also be considered citizens." On Pine Ridge, a similar "naturalization" plank had surfaced in the 1983 TREATY platform upon which Russell Means attempted to run for the Oglala Lakota tribal presidency before being disqualified at the insistence of the BIA.[42]

An obvious problem that might be associated with this trend is that even though Indian nations have begun to recognize their citizens by their own standards rather than those of the federal government, the government may well refuse to recognize the entitlement of unblooded tribal members to the same services and benefits as any other. In fact, there is every indication that this is the federal intent, and such a disparity of "status" stands to heighten tensions among Indians, destroying their fragile rebirth of unity and solidarity before it gets off the ground. Federal policy in this regard is, however, also being challenged.

Most immediately, this concerns the case of Dianne Zarr, an enrolled member of the Sherwood Valley Pomo Band of Indians, who is of less than one-quarter degree of Indian blood. On September 11, 1980, Zarr filed an application for higher educational grant benefits, and was shortly rejected as not meeting quantum requirements. Zarr went through all appropriate appeal procedures before filing, on July 15, 1983, a suit in federal court, seeking to compel award of her benefits. This was denied by the district court

---

[37]Dawes, Charles E., "Tribal leaders see danger in use of blood quantum as eligibility standard." *The Uset Calumet*. Nashville, TN. February/March, 1986, pp. 7–8.

[38]"Indians decry verification plan for federally-funded health care," op. cit.

[39]On the Trail of Broken Treaties Challenge. see Editors. *BIA, I'm Not Your Indian Any More, Akwesasne Notes,* Mohawk Nation via Rooseveltown, NY, 1973, p. 78. On VVAW naturalization, see Burnette, Robert, and John Koster, *The Road to Wounded Knee,* Bantam Books, New York, 1974, p. 238.

[40]"Indians maintain U.S. trying to erode tribal sovereignty," op. cit.

[41]Draft, Haida Constitution, circa 1982, xerox copy provided to the author by Pam Colorado.

[42]*TREATY: The Campaign of Russell Means for the Presidency of the Oglala Sioux Tribe,* Porcupine, SD, 1982, p. 3.

on April 2,1985. Zarr appealed and, on September 26,1985, the lower court was reversed on the basis of the "Snyder Act" (25 U.S.C. §297), which precludes discrimination based solely on racial criteria.[43] Zarr received her grant, setting a very useful precedent for the future.

Still, realizing that the utility of the U.S. courts will necessarily be limited, a number of Indian organizations have recently begun to seek to bring international pressure to bear on the federal government. The Indian Law Resource Center, National Indian Youth Council, and, for a time, the International Indian Treaty Council, have repeatedly taken Native American issues before the United Nations Working Group on Indigenous Populations (a component of the U.N. Commission on Human Rights) in Geneva, Switzerland, since 1977. Another forum that has been utilized for this purpose has been the Fourth Russell International Tribunal on the Rights of the Indians of the Americas, held in Rotterdam, Netherlands, in 1980. Additionally, delegations from various Indian nations and organizations have visited, often under auspices of the host governments, more than thirty countries during the past decade.[44]

Conclusion

The history of the U.S. imposition of its standards of identification upon American Indians is particularly ugly. Its cost to Indians has involved millions of acres of land, the water by which to make much of this land agriculturally useful, control over vast mineral resources that might have afforded them a comfortable standard of living, and the ability to form themselves into viable and meaningful political blocks at any level. Worse, it has played a prominent role in bringing about their generalized psychic disempowerment; if one is not allowed even to determine for one's self, or within one's peer group, the answer to the all-important question "Who am I?," what possible personal power can one feel s/he possesses? The negative impact, both physically and psychologically, of this process upon succeeding generations of Native Americans in the United States is simply incalculable.

The blood-quantum mechanism most typically used by the federal government to assign identification to individuals over the years is as racist as any conceivable policy. It has brought about the systematic marginalization and eventual exclusion of many more Indians from their own cultural/national designation than it has retained. This is all the more apparent when one considers that, while one-quarter degree of blood has been the norm used in defining *Indian-ness,* the quantum has varied from time to time and place to place; one-half blood was the standard utilized in the case of the Mississippi Choctaws and adopted in the Wheeler-Howard Act; one sixty-fourth was utilized in establishing the Santee rolls in Nebraska. It is hardly unnatural, under the circumstances, that federal policy has set off a ridiculous game of one-upmanship in Indian Country: "I'm more Indian than you" and "You aren't Indian enough to say (or do, or think) that" have become common assertions during the second half of the 20th century.

The restriction of federal entitlement funds to cover only the relatively few Indians who meet quantum requirements, essentially a cost-cutting policy at its inception, has served to exacerbate tensions over the identity issue among Indians. It has established a scenario in which it has been perceived as profitable for one Indian to cancel the identity of her/his neighbor as means of receiving her/his entitlement. Thus,

[43]*Zarr v. Barlow, et al.,* No. 85–2170, U.S. Ninth Circuit Court of Appeals. District Court for the Northern District of California. Judge John P. Vukasin presiding.

[44]These have included Austria, Cuba, Nicaragua, Poland, East Germany, Hungary, Rumania, Switzerland, Algeria, Grenada, El Salvador, Colombia, Tunisia, Libya, Syria, Jordan, Iran, the Maori of New Zealand, New Aotara (Australia), Belize, Mexico, Costa Rica, Guinea, Kenya, Micronesia, the USSR, Finland, Norway, Sweden, Canada, Great Britain, Netherlands, France, Belgium, Japan, West Germany, Bulgaria, Yugoslavia, and Papua (New Guinea). The list here is undoubtedly incomplete.

a bitter divisiveness has been built into Indian communities and national policies, sufficient to preclude our achieving the internal unity necessary to offer any serious challenge to the status quo. At every turn, U.S. practice vis-à-vis American Indians is indicative of an advanced and extremely successful system of colonialism.

Fortunately, increasing numbers of Indians are waking up to the fact that this is the case. The recent analysis and positions assumed by such politically diverse Indian nations, organizations, and individuals as Frank Ryan and Russell Means, the National Congress of American Indians and the Indian Law Resource Center, the Haida and the Oglala, are a very favorable sign. The willingness of the latter two nations simply to defy federal standards and adopt identification and enrollment policies in line with their own interests and traditions is particularly important. Recent U.S. court decisions, such as that in the *Zarr* case, and growing international attention and concern over the circumstances of Native Americans are also hopeful indicators that things may be at long last changing for the better.

We are currently at a crossroads. If American Indians are able to continue the positive trend in which we reassert our sovereign prerogative to control the criteria of our own membership, we may reasonably assume that we will be able to move onward, into a true process of decolonization and reestablishment of ourselves as functioning national entities. The alternative, of course, is that we will fail, continue to be duped into bickering over the question of "who's Indian" in light of federal guidelines, and thus facilitate not only our own continued subordination, expropriation, and colonization, but ultimately our own statistical extermination.

NOBODY MEAN MORE TO ME
THAN YOU AND THE
FUTURE LIFE OF WILLIE JORDAN

June Jordan

Black English is not exactly a linguistic buffalo; as children, most of the thirty-five million Afro-Americans living here depend on this language for our discovery of the world. But then we approach our maturity inside a larger social body that will not support our efforts to become anything other than the clones of those who are neither our mothers nor our fathers. We begin to grow up in a house where every true mirror shows us the face of somebody who does not belong there, whose walk and whose talk will never look or sound "right," because that house was meant to shelter a family that is alien and hostile to us. As we learn our way around this environment, either we hide our original word habits, or we completely surrender our own voice, hoping to please those who will never respect anyone different from themselves: Black English is not exactly a linguistic buffalo, but we should understand its status as an endangered species, as a perishing, irreplaceable system of community intelligence, or we should expect its extinction, and, along with that, the extinguishing of much that constitutes our own proud, and singular identity.

What we casually call "English" less and less defers to England and its "gentlemen." "English" is no longer a specific matter of geography or an element of class privilege; more than thirty-three countries use this tool as a means of "intranational communication." Countries as disparate as Zimbabwe and Malaysia, or Israel and Uganda, use it as their non-native currency of convenience. Obviously, this tool, this "English," cannot function inside thirty-three discrete societies on the basis of rules and values absolutely determined somewhere else, in a thirty-fourth other country, for example.

In addition to that staggering congeries of non-native users of English, there are five countries, or 333,746,000 people, for whom this thing called "English" serves as a native tongue. Approximately 10% of these native speakers of "English" are Afro-American citizens of the U.S.A. I cite these numbers and varieties of human beings dependent on "English" in order, quickly, to suggest how strange and how tenuous is any concept of "Standard English." Obviously, numerous forms of English now operate inside a natural, an uncontrollable, continuum of development. I would suppose "the standard" for English in Malaysia is not the same as "the standard" in Zimbabwe. I know that standard forms of English for Black people in this country do not copy those of whites. And, in fact, the structural differences between these two kinds of English have intensified, becoming more Black, or less white, despite the expected homogenizing effects of television and other mass media.

Nonetheless, white standards of English persist, supreme and unquestioned, in these United States. Despite our multi-lingual population, and despite the deepening Black and white cleavage within that conglomerate, white standards control our official and popular judgements of verbal proficiency and correct, or incorrect, language skills, including speech. In contrast to India, where at least fourteen languages co-exist as legitimate Indian languages, in contrast to Nicaragua, where all citizens are legally entitled to formal school instruction in their regional or tribal languages, compulsory education in America compels accommodation to exclusively white forms of "English." White English, in America, is "Standard English."

This story begins two years ago. I was teaching a new course, "In Search of the Invisible Black Woman," and my rather large class seemed evenly divided between young Black women and men. Five or six white students also sat in attendance. With unexpected speed and enthusiasm we had moved through historical narratives of the 19th century to literature by and about Black women, in the 20th. I had assigned the first forty pages of Alice Walker's *The Color Purple,* and I came, eagerly, to class that morning:

"So!" I exclaimed, aloud. "What did you think? How did you like it?"

The students studied their hands, or the floor. There was no response. The tense, resistant feeling in the room fairly astounded me.

At last, one student, a young woman still not meeting my eyes, muttered something in my direction:

"What did you say?" I prompted her.

"Why she have them talk so funny. It don't sound right."

"You mean the language?"

Another student lifted his head: "It don't look right, neither. I couldn't hardly read it."

At this, several students dumped on the book. Just about unanimously, their criticisms targeted the language. I listened to what they wanted to say and silently marvelled at the similarities between their casual speech patterns and Alice Walker's written version of Black English.

But I decided against pointing to these identical traits of syntax; I wanted not to make them self-conscious about their own spoken language—not while they clearly felt it was "wrong." Instead I decided to swallow my astonishment. Here was a negative Black reaction to a prize-winning accomplishment of Black literature that white readers across the country had selected as a best seller. Black rejection was aimed at the one irreducibly Black element of Walker's work: the language—Celie's Black English. I wrote the opening lines of *The Color Purple* on the blackboard and asked the students to help me translate these sentences into Standard English:

You better not never tell nobody but God. It'd kill your mammy.
Dear God,

  I am fourteen years old. I have always been a good girl. Maybe you can give me a sign letting me know what is happening to me.

  Last spring after Little Lucious come I heard them fussing. He was pulling on her arm. She say it too soon, Fonso. I ain't well. Finally he leave her alone. A week go by, he pulling on her arm again. She say, Naw, I ain't gonna. Can't you see I'm already half dead, an all of the children.

Our process of translation exploded with hilarity and even hysterical, shocked laughter: The Black writer, Alice Walker, knew what she was doing! If rudimentary criteria for good fiction includes the manipulation of language so that the syntax and diction of sentences will tell you the identity of speakers, the probable age and sex and class of speakers, and even the locale—urban/rural/southern/western—then Walker had written, perfectly. This is the translation into Standard English that our class produced:

Absolutely, one should never confide in anybody besides God. Your secrets could prove devastating to your mother.

Dear God,

  I am fourteen years old. I have always been good. But now, could you help me to understand what is happening to me?

Last spring, after my little brother, Lucious, was born, I heard my parents fighting. My father kept pulling at my mother's arm. But she told him, "It's too soon for sex, Alfonso. I am still not feeling well." Finally, my father left her alone. A week went by, and then he began bothering my mother again: pulling her arm. She told him, "No, I won't! Can't you see I'm already exhausted from all of these children?"

(Our favorite line was "It's too soon for sex, Alphonso.")

Once we could stop laughing, once we could stop our exponentially wild improvisations on the theme of Translated Black English, the students pushed me to explain their own negative first reactions to their spoken language on the printed page. I thought it was probably akin to the shock of seeing yourself in a photograph for the first time. Most of the students had never before seen a written facsimile of the way they talk. None of the students had ever learned how to read and write their own verbal system of communication: Black English. Alternatively, this fact began to baffle or else bemuse and then infuriate my students. Why not? Was it too late? Could they learn how to do it, now? And, ultimately, the final test question, the one testing my sincerity: Could I teach them? Because I had never taught anyone Black English and, as far as I knew, no one, anywhere in the United States, had ever offered such a course, the best I could say was "I'll try."

He looked like a wrestler.

He sat dead center in the packed room and, every time our eyes met, he quickly nodded his head as though anxious to reassure and encourage me.

Short, with strikingly broad shoulders and long arms, he spoke with a surprisingly high, soft voice that matched the soft bright movement of his eyes. His name was Willie Jordan. He would have seemed even more unlikely in the context of Contemporary Women's Poetry, except that ten or twelve other Black men were taking the course, as well. Still, Willie was conspicuous. His extreme fitness, the muscular density of his presence underscored the riveted, gentle attention that he gave to anything anyone said. Generally, he did not join the loud and rowdy dialogue flying back and forth, but there could be no doubt about his interest in our discussions. And, when he stood to present an argument he'd prepared, overnight, that nervous smile of his vanished and an irregular stammering replaced it, as he spoke with visceral sincerity, word by word.

That was how I met Willie Jordan. It was in between "In Search of the Invisible Black Woman" and "The Art of Black English." I was waiting for Departmental approval and I supposed that Willie might be, so to speak, killing time until he, too, could study Black English. But Willie really did want to explore Contemporary Women's Poetry and, to that end, volunteered for extra research and never missed a class.

Towards the end of that semester, Willie approached me for an independent study project on South Africa. It would commence the next semester. I thought Willie's writing needed the kind of improvement only intense practice will yield. I knew his intelligence was outstanding. But he'd wholeheartedly opted for "Standard English" at a rather late age, and the results were stilted and frequently polysyllabic, simply for the sake of having more syllables. Willie's unnatural formality of language seemed to me consistent with the formality of his research into South African apartheid. As he projected his studies, he would have little time, indeed, for newspapers. Instead, more than 90% of his research would mean saturation in strictly historical, if not archival, material. I was certainly interested. It would be tricky to guide him into a more confident and spontaneous relationship with both language and

apartheid. It was going to be wonderful to see what happened when he could catch up with himself, entirely, and talk back to the world.

September, 1984: Breezy fall weather and much excitement! My class, "The Art of Black English," was full to the limit of the fire laws. And, in Independent Study, Willie Jordan showed up, weekly, fifteen minutes early for each of our sessions. I was pretty happy to be teaching, altogether!

I remember an early class when a young brother, replete with his ever-present pork-pie hat, raised his hand and then told us that most of what he'd heard was "all right" except it was "too clean." "The brothers on the street," he continued, "they mix it up more. Like 'fuck' and 'motherfuck.' Or like 'shit.'" He waited. I waited. Then all of us laughed a good while, and we got into a brawl about "correct" and "realistic" Black English that led to Rule 1.

Rule 1: *Black English is about a whole lot more than mothafuckin.*

As a criterion, we decided, "realistic" could take you anywhere you want to go. Artful places. Angry places. Eloquent and sweetalkin places. Polemical places. Church. And the local Bar & Grill. We were checking out a language, not a mood or a scene or one guy's forgettable mouthing off.

It was hard. For most of the students, learning Black English required a fallback to patterns and rhythms of speech that many of their parents had beaten out of them. I mean *beaten*. And, in a majority of cases, correct Black English could be achieved only by striving for *incorrect* Standard English, something they were still pushing at, quite uncertainly. This state of affairs led to Rule 2.

Rule 2: *If it's wrong in Standard English it's probably right in Black English, or, at least, you're hot.*

It was hard. Roommates and family members ridiculed their studies, or remained incredulous. "You *studying* that shit? At school?" But we were beginning to feel the companionship of pioneers. And we decided that we needed another rule that would establish each one of us as equally important to our success. This was Rule 3.

Rule 3: *If it don't sound like something that come out somebody mouth then it don't sound right. If it don't sound right then it ain't hardly right. Period.*

This rule produced two weeks of compositions in which the students agonizingly tried to spell the sound of the Black English sentence they wanted to convey. But Black English is, preeminently, an oral/spoken means of communication. *And spelling don't talk.* So we needed Rule 4.

Rule 4: *Forget about the spelling. Let the syntax carry you.*

Once we arrived at Rule 4 we started to fly because syntax, the structure of an idea, leads you to the world view of the speaker and reveals her values. The syntax of a sentence equals the structure of your consciousness. If we insisted that the language of Black English adheres to a distinctive Black syntax, then we were postulating a profound difference between white and Black people, *per se*. Was it a difference to prize or to obliterate?

There are three qualities of Black English—the presence of life, voice, and clarity—that testify to a distinctive Black value system that we became excited about and self-consciously tried to maintain.

1. Black English has been produced by a pre-technocratic, if not anti-technological, culture. More, our culture has been constantly threatened by annihilation or, at least, the swallowed blurring of assimilation. Therefore, our language is a system constructed by people constantly needing to insist that we exist, that we are present. Our language devolves from a culture that abhors all abstraction, or anything tending to obscure or delete the fact of the human being who is here and now/the truth of the person who is speaking or listening. Consequently, *there is no passive voice construction possible in Black English*. For example, you cannot say, "Black English is being eliminated." You must say, instead, "White people eliminating Black English." The assumption of the presence of life governs all of Black English. Therefore,

overwhelmingly, *all action takes place in the language of the present indicative.* And every sentence assumes the living and active participation of at least two human beings, the speaker and the listener.

2. A primary consequence of the person-centered values of Black English is the delivery of voice. If you speak or write Black English, your ideas will necessarily possess that otherwise elusive attribute, *voice.*

3. One main benefit following from the person-centered values of Black English is that of *clarity.* If your idea, your sentence, assumes the presence of at least two living and active people, you will make it understandable because the motivation behind every sentence is the wish to say something real to somebody real.

As the weeks piled up, translation from Standard English into Black English or vice versa occupied a hefty part of our course work.

> Standard English (hereafter S.E.): "In considering the idea of studying Black English those questioned suggested—"
> (What's the subject? Where's the person? Is anybody alive in there, in that idea?)
> Black English (hereafter B.E.): "I been asking people what you think about somebody studying Black English and they answer me like this:"

But there were interesting limits. You cannot "translate" instances of Standard English preoccupied with abstraction or with nothing/nobody evidently alive, into Black English. That would warp the language into uses antithetical to the guiding perspective of its community of users. Rather you must first change those Standard English sentences, themselves, into ideas consistent with the person-centered assumptions of Black English.

Guidelines for Black English

1. Minimal number of words for every idea: This is the source for the aphoristic and/or poetic force of the language; eliminate every possible word.
2. Clarity: If the sentence is not clear it's not Black English.
3. Eliminate use of the verb *to be* whenever possible. This leads to the deployment of more descriptive and therefore more precise verbs.
4. Use *be* or *been* only when you want to describe a chronic, ongoing state of things.
   He *be* at the office, by 9. (He is always at the office by 9.)
   He *been* with her since forever.
5. Zero copula: Always eliminate the verb *to be* whenever it would combine with another verb, in Standard English.
   S.E.: She is going out with him.
   B.E.: She going out with him.
6. Eliminate *do* as in:
   S.E.: What do you think? What do you want?
   B.E.: What you think? What you want?

Rules number 3, 4, 5, and 6 provide for the use of the minimal number of verbs per idea and, therefore, greater accuracy in the choice of verb.

7. In general, if you wish to say something really positive, try to formulate the idea using emphatic negative structure.
   S.E.: He's fabulous.
   B.E.: He bad.

8. Use double or triple negatives for dramatic emphasis.
   S.E.: Tina Turner sings out of this world.
   B.E.: Ain nobody sing like Tina.
9. Never use the *-ed* suffix to indicate the past tense of a verb.
   S.E.: She closed the door.
   B.E.: She close the door. Or, she have close the door.
10. Regardless of intentional verb time, only use the third person singular, present indicative, for use of the verb to *have,* as an auxiliary.
    S.E.: He had his wallet then he lost it.
    B.E.: He have him wallet then he lose it.
    S.E.: We had seen that movie.
    B.E.: We seen that movie. Or, we have see that movie.
11. Observe a minimal inflection of verbs. Particularly, never change from the first person singular forms to the third person singular.
    S.E.: Present Tense Forms: He goes to the store.
    B.E.: He go to the store.
    S.E.: Past Tense Forms: He went to the store.
    B.E.: He go to the store. Or, he gone to the store. Or, he been to the store.
12. The possessive case scarcely ever appears in Black English. Never use an apostrophe ('s) construction. If you wander into a possessive case component of an idea, then keep logically consistent: *ours, his, theirs, mines.* But, most likely, if you bump into such a component, you have wandered outside the underlying worldview of Black English.
    S.E.: He will take their car tomorrow.
    B.E.: He taking they car tomorrow.
13. Plurality: Logical consistency, continued: If the modifier indicates plurality, then the noun remains in the singular case.
    S.E.: He ate twelve doughnuts.
    B.E.: He eat twelve doughnut.
    S.E.: She has many books.
    B.E.: She have many book.
14. Listen for, or invent, special Black English forms of the past tense, such as: "He losted it. That what she felted." If they are clear and readily understood, then use them.

   Do not hesitate to play with words, sometimes inventing them; e.g., "astropotomous" means huge like a hippo plus astronomical and, therefore, signifies real big.

15. In Black English, unless you keenly want to underscore the past tense nature of an action, stay in the present tense and rely on the overall context of your ideas for the conveyance of time and sequence.
16. Never use the suffix *-ly* form of an adverb in Black English.
    S.E.: The rain came down rather quickly.
    B.E.: The rain come down pretty quick.
17. Never use the indefinite article *an* in Black English.
    S.E.: He wanted to ride an elephant.
    B.E.: He want to ride him a elephant.

18. In variant syntax: In correct Black English it is possible to formulate an imperative, an interrogative, and a simple declarative idea with the same syntax:

    B.E.: You going to the store?

    You going to the store.

    You going to the store!

Where was Willie Jordan? We'd reached the mid-term of the semester. Students had formulated Black English guidelines, by consensus, and they were now writing with remarkable beauty, purpose, and enjoyment:

I ain hardly speakin for everybody but myself so understan that.

—Kim Parks

Samples from student writings:

"Janie have a great big ole hole inside her. Tea Cake the only thing that fit that hole. . . .

"That pear tree beautiful to Janie, especial when bees fiddlin with the blossomin pear there growin large and lovely. But personal speakin, the love she get from starin at that tree ain the love what starin back at her in them relationship." (Monica Morris)

"Love is a big theme in *They Eye Was Watching God*. Love show people new corners inside theyself. It pull out good stuff and stuff back bad stuff. . . . Joe worship the doing uh his own hand and need other people to worship him too. But he ain't think about Janie that she a person and ought to live like anybody common do. Queen life not for Janie." (Monica Morris)

"In both life and writin, Black womens have varietous experience of love that be cold like a iceberg or fiery like a inferno. Passion got for the other partner involve, man or woman, seem as shallow, ankle-deep water or the most profoundest abyss." (Constance Evans)

"Family love another bond that ain't never break under no pressure." (Constance Evans)

"You know it really cold/When the friend you/Always get out the fire/Act like they don't know you/When you in the heat." (Constance Evans)

"Big classroom discussion bout love at this time. I never take no class where us have any long arguin for and against for two or three day. New to me and great. I find the class time talkin a million time more interestin than detail bout the book." (Kathy Esseks)

As these examples suggest, Black English no longer limited the students, in any way. In fact, one of them, Philip Garfield, would shortly "translate" a pivotal scene from lbsen's *Doll House,* as his final term paper:

Nora: I didn't gived no shit. I thinked you a asshole back then, too, you make it so hard for me save mines husband life.

Krogstad: Girl, it clear you ain't any idea what you done. You done exact what once done, and I losed my reputation over it.

Nora: You asks me believe you once act brave save you wife life?

Krogstad: Law care less why you done it.

Nora: Law must suck.

Krogstad: Suck or no, if I wants, judge screw you wid dis paper.

Nora: No way, man. (Philip Garfield)

But where was Willie? Compulsively punctual, and always thoroughly prepared with neatly typed compositions, he had disappeared. He failed to show up for our regularly scheduled conference, and I received neither a note nor a phone call of explanation. A whole week went by. I wondered if Willie had finally been captured by the extremely current happenings in South Africa: passage of a new constitution that did not enfranchise the Black majority, and militant Black South African reaction to that affront. I wondered if he'd been hurt, somewhere. I wondered if the serious workload of weekly readings and writings had overwhelmed him and changed his mind about independent study. Where was Willie Jordan?

One week after the first conference that Willie missed, he called: "Hello, Professor Jordan? This is Willie. I'm sorry I wasn't there last week. But something has come up and I'm pretty upset. I'm sorry but I really can't deal right now."

I asked Willie to drop by my office and just let me see that he was okay: He agreed to do that. When I saw him I knew something hideous had happened. Something had hurt him and scared him to the marrow. He was all agitated and stammering and terse and incoherent. At last, his sadly jumbled account let me surmise as follows: Brooklyn police had murdered his unarmed, twenty-five-year-old brother, Reggie Jordan. Neither Willie nor his elderly parents knew what to do about it. Nobody from the press was interested. His folks had no money. Police ran his family around and around, to no point. And Reggie was really dead. And Willie wanted to fight, but he felt helpless.

With Willie's permission I began to try to secure legal counsel for the Jordan family. Unfortunately Black victims of police violence are truly numerous while the resources available to prosecute their killers are truly scarce. A friend of mine at the Center for Constitutional Rights estimated that just the preparatory costs for bringing the cops into court normally approaches $180,000. Unless the execution of Reggie Jordan became a major community cause for organizing and protest, his murder would simply become a statistical item.

Again with Willie's permission, I contacted every newspaper and media person I could think of. But the William Bastone feature article in *The Village Voice* was the only result from that canvassing.

Again with Willie's permission, I presented the case to my class in Black English. We had talked about the politics of language. We had talked about love and sex and child abuse and men and women. But the murder of Reggie Jordan broke like a hurricane across the room.

There are few "issues" as endemic to Black life as police violence. Most of the students knew and respected and liked Jordan. Many of them came from the very neighborhood where the murder had occurred. All of the students had known somebody close to them who had been killed by police, or had known frightening moments of gratuitous confrontation with the cops. They wanted to do everything at once to avenge death. Number One: They decided to compose personal statements of condolence to Willie Jordan and his family, written in Black English. Number Two: They decided to compose individual messages to the police, in Black English. These should be prefaced by an explanatory paragraph composed by the entire group. Number Three: These individual messages, with their lead paragraph, should be sent to *Newsday.*

The morning after we agreed on these objectives, one of the young women students appeared with an unidentified visitor, who sat through the class, smiling in a peculiar, comfortable way.

Now we had to make more tactical decisions. Because we wanted the messages published, and because we thought it imperative that our outrage be known by the police, the tactical question was this: Should the opening, group paragraph be written in Black English or Standard English?

I have seldom been privy to a discussion with so much heart at the dead heat of it. I will never forget the eloquence, the sudden haltings of speech, the fierce struggle against tears, the furious throwaways and useless explosions that this question elicited.

That one question contained several others, each of them extraordinarily painful to even contemplate. How best to serve the memory of Reggie Jordan? Should we use the language of the killers—Standard English—in order to make our ideas acceptable to those controlling the killers? But wouldn't what we had to say be rejected, summarily, if we said it in our own language, the language of the victim, Reggie Jordan? But if we sought to express ourselves by abandoning our language, wouldn't that mean our suicide on top of Reggie's murder? But if we expressed ourselves in our own language, wouldn't that be suicidal to the wish to communicate with those who, evidently, did not give a damn about us/Reggie/police violence in the Black community?

At the end of one of the longest, most difficult hours of my own life, the students voted, unanimously, to preface their individual messages with a paragraph composed in the language of Reggie Jordan. *"At least we don't give up nothing else. At least we stick to the truth: Be who we been. And stay all the way with Reggie."*

It was heartbreaking to proceed, from that point. Everyone in the room realized that our decision in favor of Black English had doomed our writings, even as the distinctive reality of our Black lives always has doomed our efforts to "be who we been" in this country.

I went to the blackboard and took down this paragraph, dictated by the class:

. . . You Cops!
We the brother and sister of Willie Jordan, a fellow stony brook student who the brother of the dead Reggie Jordan. Reggie, like many brother and sister, he a victim of brutal racist police, October 25, 1984. Us ap pall, fed up, because that another senseless death what occur in our community. This what we feel, this, from our heart, for we ain't stayin' silent no more.

With the completion of this introduction, nobody said anything. I asked for comments. At this invitation, the unidentified visitor, a young Black man, ceaselessly smiling, raised his hand. He was, it so happens, a rookie cop. He had just joined the force in September and, he said, he thought he should clarify a few things. So he came forward and sprawled easily into a posture of barroom, or fireside, nostalgia:

"See," Officer Charles enlightened us, "most times when you out on the street and something come down you do one of two things. Over-react or under-react. Now, if you under-react then you can get yourself kilt. And if you over-react then maybe you kill somebody. Fortunately it's about nine times out of ten and you will over-react. So the brother got kilt. And I'm sorry about that, believe me. But what you have to understand is what kilt him: over-reaction. That's all. Now you talk about Black people and white police but see, now, I'm a cop myself. And [big smile] I'm Black. And just a couple months ago I was on the other side. But see it's the same for me. You a cop, you the ultimate authority: the Ultimate Authority. And you on the street, most of the time you can only do one of two things: over-react or under-react. That's all it is with the brother. Over-reaction. Didn't have nothing to do with race."

That morning Officer Charles had the good fortune to escape without being boiled alive. But barely. And I remember the pride of his smile when I read about the fate of Black policemen and other collaborators in South Africa. I remember him, and I remember the shock and palpable feeling of shame that filled the room. It was as though that foolish, and deadly, young man had just relieved himself of his foolish, and deadly, explanation, face to face with the grief of Reggie Jordan's father and Reggie Jordan's mother. Class ended quietly. I copied the paragraph from the blackboard, collected the individual messages, and left to type them up.

Newsday rejected the piece.

The Village Voice could not find room in their "Letters" section to print the individual messages from the students to the police.

None of the tv news reporters picked up the story.

Nobody raised $180,000 to prosecute the murder of Reggie Jordan.

Reggie Jordan is really dead.

I asked Willie Jordan to write an essay pulling together everything important to him from that semester. He was still deeply beside himself with frustration and amazement and loss. This is what he wrote, un-edited, and in its entirety:

Throughout the course of this semester I have been researching the effects of oppression and exploitation along racial lines in South Africa and its neighboring countries. I have become aware of South African police brutalization of native Africans beyond the extent of the law, even though the laws themselves are catalyst affliction upon Black men, women and children. Many Africans die each year as a result of the deliberate use of police force to protect the white power structure.

Social control agents in South Africa, such as policemen, are also used to force compliance among citizens through both overt and covert tactics. It is not uncommon to find bold-faced coercion and cold-blooded killings of Blacks by South African police for undetermined and/or inadequate reasons. Perhaps the truth is that the only reason for this heinous treatment of Blacks rests in racial differences. We should also understand that what is conveyed through the media is not always accurate and may sometimes be construed as the tip of the iceberg at best.

I recently received a painful reminder that racism, poverty, and the abuse of power are global problems which are by no means unique to South Africa. On October 25, 1984 at approximately 3:00 p.m. my brother, Mr. Reginald Jordan, was shot and killed by two New York City policemen from the 75th precinct in the East New York section of Brooklyn. His life ended at the age of twenty-five. Even up to this current point in time the Police Department has failed to provide my family, which consists of five brothers, eight sisters, and two parents, with a plausible reason for Reggie's death. Out of the many stories that were given to my family by the Police Department, not one of them seems to hold water. In fact, I honestly believe that the Police Department's assessment of my brother's murder is nothing short of absolute bullshit, and thus far no evidence had been produced to alter this perception of the situation.

Furthermore, I believe that one of three cases may have occurred in this incident. First, Reggie's death may have been the desired outcome of the police officer's action, in which case the killing was premeditated. Or, it was a case of mistaken identity, which clarifies the fact that the two officers who killed my brother and their commanding parties are all grossly incompetent. Or, both of the above cases are correct, i.e., Reggie's murderers intended to kill him and the Police Department behaved insubordinately.

Part of the argument of the officers who shot Reggie was that he had attacked one of them and took his gun. This was their major claim. They also said that only one of them had actually shot Reggie. The facts, however, speak for themselves. According to the Death Certificate and autopsy report, Reggie was shot eight times from point-blank range. The Doctor who performed the autopsy told me himself that two bullets entered the side of my brother's head, four bullets were sprayed into his back, and two bullets struck him in the back of his legs. It is obvious that unnecessary force was used by the police and that it is extremely difficult to shoot someone in his back when he is attacking or approaching you.

After experiencing a situation like this and researching South Africa I believe that to a large degree, justice may only exist as rhetoric. I find it difficult to talk of true justice when the oppression of my people both at home and abroad attests to the fact that inequality and injustice are serious problems whereby

Blacks and Third World people are perpetually short-changed by society. Something has to be done about the way in which this world is set up. Although it is a difficult task, we do have the power to make a change.

—WILLIE J. JORDAN JR.
EGL 487, SECTION 58, NOVEMBER 14, 1984

It is my privilege to dedicate this book to the future life of Willie J. Jordan Jr.

August 8, 1985

IF YOU ARE WHAT YOU EAT, THEN WHAT AM I?

Geeta Kothari

To belong is to understand the tacit codes of the people you live with.

—Michael Ignatieff, *Blood and Belonging*

I

The first time my mother and I open a can of tuna, I am nine years old. We stand in the doorway of the kitchen, in semidarkness, the can tilted toward daylight. I want to eat what the kids at school eat: bologna, hot dogs, salami—foods my parents find repugnant because they contain pork and meat byproducts, crushed bone and hair glued together by chemicals and fat. Although she has never been able to tolerate the smell of fish, my mother buys the tuna, hoping to satisfy my longing for American food.

Indians, of course, do not eat such things.

The tuna smells fishy, which surprises me because I can't remember anyone's tuna sandwich actually smelling like fish. And the tuna in those sandwiches doesn't look like this, pink and shiny, like an internal organ. In fact, this looks similar to the bad foods my mother doesn't want me to eat. She is silent, holding her face away from the can while peering into it like a half-blind bird.

"What's wrong with it?" I ask.

She has no idea. My mother does not know that the tuna everyone else's mothers made for them was tuna *salad*.

"Do you think it's botulism?"

I have never seen botulism, but I have read about it, just as I have read about but never eaten steak and kidney pie.

There is so much my parents don't know. They are not like other parents, and they disappoint me and my sister. They are supposed to help us negotiate the world outside, teach us the signs, the clues to proper behavior: what to eat and how to eat it.

We have expectations, and my parents fail to meet them, especially my mother, who works full-time. I don't understand what it means, to have a mother who works outside and inside the home; I notice only the ways in which she disappoints me. She doesn't show up for school plays. She doesn't make chocolate-frosted cupcakes for my class. At night, if I want her attention, I have to sit in the kitchen and talk to her while she cooks the evening meal, attentive to every third or fourth word I say.

We throw the tuna away. This time my mother is disappointed. I go to school with tuna eaters. I see their sandwiches, yet cannot explain the discrepancy between them and the stinking, oily fish in my mother's hand. We do not understand so many things, my mother and I.

II

On weekends, we eat fried chicken from Woolworth's on the back steps of my father's first-floor office in Murray Hill. The back steps face a small patch of garden—hedges, a couple of skinny trees, and gravel instead of grass. We can see the back window of the apartment my parents and I lived in until my sister was born. There, the doorman watched my mother, several months pregnant and wearing a sari, slip on the ice in front of the building.

My sister and I pretend we are in the country, where our American friends all have houses. We eat glazed doughnuts, also from Woolworth's, and french fries with ketchup.

III

My mother takes a catering class and learns that Miracle Whip and mustard are healthier than mayonnaise. She learns to make egg salad with chopped celery, deviled eggs dusted with paprika, a cream cheese spread with bits of fresh ginger and watercress, chicken liver pate, and little brown-and-white checkerboard sandwiches that we have only once. She makes chicken a la king in puff pastry shells and eggplant Parmesan. She acquires smooth wooden paddles, whose purpose is never clear, two different egg dicers, several wooden spoons, icing tubes, cookie cutters, and an electric mixer.

IV

I learn to make tuna salad by watching a friend. My sister never acquires a taste for it. Instead, she craves

bologna
hot dogs
bacon
sausages

and a range of unidentifiable meat products forbidden by my parents. Their restrictions are not about sacred cows, as everyone around us assumes; in a pinch, we are allowed hamburgers, though lamb burgers are preferable. A "pinch" means choosing not to draw attention to ourselves as outsiders, impolite visitors who won't eat what their host serves. But bologna is still taboo.

V

Things my sister refuses to eat: butter, veal, anything with jeera. The baby-sitter tries to feed her butter sandwiches, threatens her with them, makes her cry in fear and disgust. My mother does not disappoint her; she does not believe in forcing us to eat, in using food as a weapon. In addition to pbj, my sister likes pasta and marinara sauce, bologna and Wonder Bread (when she can get it), and fried egg sandwiches with turkey, cheese, and horseradish. Her tastes, once established, are predictable.

VI

When we visit our relatives in India, food prepared outside the house is carefully monitored. In the hot, sticky monsoon months in New Delhi and Bombay, we cannot eat ice cream, salad, cold food, or any fruit that can't be peeled. Definitely no meat. People die from amoebic dysentery, unexplained fevers, strange boils on their bodies. We drink boiled water only, no ice. No sweets except for jalebi, thin fried twists of dough in dripping hot sugar syrup. If we're caught outside with nothing to drink, Fanta, Limca, Thums Up (after Coca-Cola is thrown out by Mrs. Gandhi) will do. Hot tea sweetened with sugar, served with thick creamy buffalo milk, is preferable. It should be boiled, to kill the germs on the cup.

My mother talks about "back home" as a safe place, a silk cocoon frozen in time where we are sheltered by family and friends. Back home, my sister and I do not argue about food with my parents. Home is where they know all the rules. We trust them to guide us safely through the maze of city streets for which they have no map, and we trust them to feed and take care of us, the way parents should.

Finally, though, one of us will get sick, hungry for the food we see our cousins and friends eating, too thirsty to ask for a straw, too polite to insist on properly boiled water.

At my uncle's diner in New Delhi, someone hands me a plate of aloo tikki, fried potato patties filled with mashed channa dal and served with a sweet and a sour chutney. The channa, mixed with hot chilies and spices, burns my tongue and throat. I reach for my Fanta, discard the paper straw, and gulp the sweet orange soda down, huge drafts that sting rather than soothe.

When I throw up later that day (or is it the next morning, when a stomachache wakes me from deep sleep?), I cry over the frustration of being singled out, not from the pain my mother assumes I'm feeling as she holds my hair back from my face. The taste of orange lingers in my mouth, and I remember my lips touching the cold glass of the Fanta bottle.

At that moment, more than anything, I want to be like my cousins.

VII

In New York, at the first Indian restaurant in our neighborhood, my father orders with confidence, and my sister and I play with the silverware until the steaming plates of lamb biryani arrive.

What is Indian food? my friends ask, their noses crinkling up.

Later, this restaurant is run out of business by the new Indo-Pak-Bangladeshi combinations up and down the street, which serve similar food. They use plastic cutlery and Styrofoam cups. They do not distinguish between North and South Indian cooking, or between Indian, Pakistani, and Bangladeshi cooking, and their customers do not care. The food is fast, cheap, and tasty. Dosa, a rice flour crepe stuffed with masala potato, appears on the same trays as chicken makhani.

Now my friends want to know, Do you eat curry at home?

One time my mother makes lamb vindaloo for guests. Like dosa, this is a South Indian dish, one that my Punjabi mother has to learn from a cookbook. For us, she cooks everyday food—yellow dal, rice, chapati, bhaji. Lentils, rice, bread, and vegetables. She has never referred to anything on our table as "curry" or "curried," but I know she has made chicken curry for guests. Vindaloo, she explains, is a curry too. I understand then that curry is a dish created for guests, outsiders, a food for people who eat in restaurants.

VIII

I have inherited brown eyes, black hair, a long nose with a crooked bridge, and soft teeth with thin enamel. I am in my twenties, moving to a city far from my parents, before it occurs to me that jeera, the spice my sister avoids, must have an English name. I have to learn that haldi = turmeric, methi = fenugreek. What to make with fenugreek, I do not know. My grandmother used to make methi roti for our breakfast, cornbread with fresh fenugreek leaves served with a lump of homemade butter. No one makes it now that she's gone, though once in a while my mother will get a craving for it and produce a facsimile ("The cornmeal here is wrong") that only highlights what she's really missing: the smells and tastes of her mother's house.

I will never make my grandmother's methi roti or even my mother's unsatisfactory imitation of it. I attempt chapati; it takes six hours, three phone calls home, and leaves me with an aching back. I have to write translations down: jeera = cumin. My memory is unreliable. But I have always known garam = hot.

IX

My mother learns how to make brownies and apple pie. My father makes only Indian food, except for loaves of heavy, sweet brown bread that I eat with thin slices of American cheese and lettuce. The recipe is a secret, passed on to him by a woman at work. Years later, when he finally gives it to me, when I finally ask for it, I end up with three bricks of gluten that even the birds and my husband won't eat.

X

My parents send me to boarding school, outside of London. They imagine that I will overcome my shyness and find a place for myself in this all-girls' school. They have never lived in England, but as former subjects of the British Empire, they find London familiar, comfortable in a way New York—my mother's home for over twenty years by now—is not. Americans still don't know what to call us; their Indians live on reservations, not in Manhattan. Because they understand the English, my parents believe the English understand us.

I poke at my first school lunch—thin, overworked pastry in a puddle of lumpy gravy. The lumps are chewy mushrooms, maybe, or overcooked shrimp.

"What is this?" I don't want to ask, but I can't go on eating without knowing.

"Steak and kidney pie."

The girl next to me, red-haired, freckled, watches me take a bite from my plate. She has been put in charge of me, the new girl, and I follow her around all day, a foreigner at the mercy of a reluctant and angry tour guide. She is not used to explaining what is perfectly and utterly natural.

"What, you've never had steak and kidney pie? Bloody hell."

My classmates scoff, then marvel, then laugh at my ignorance. After a year, I understand what is on my plate: sausage rolls, blood pudding, Spam, roast beef in a thin, greasy gravy, all the bacon and sausage I could possibly want. My parents do not expect me to starve.

The girls at school expect conformity; it has been bred into them, through years of uniforms and strict rules about proper behavior. I am thirteen and contrary, even as I yearn for acceptance. I declare myself a vegetarian and doom myself to a diet of cauliflower cheese and baked beans on toast. The administration does not question my decision; they assume it's for vague, undefined religious reasons, although my father, the doctor, tells them it's for my health. My reasons, from this distance of many years, remain murky to me.

Perhaps I am my parents' daughter after all.

XI

When she is three, sitting on my cousin's lap in Bombay, my sister reaches for his plate and puts a chili in her mouth. She wants to be like the grownups, who dip green chilies in coarse salt and eat them like any other vegetable. She howls inconsolable animal pain for what must be hours. She doesn't have the vocabulary for the oily heat that stings her mouth and tongue, burns a trail through her small tender body. Only hot, sticky tears on my father's shoulder.

As an adult, she eats red chili paste, mango pickle, kimchee, foods that make my eyes water and my stomach gurgle. My tastes are milder. I order raita at Indian restaurants and ask for food that won't sear the roof of my mouth and scar the insides of my cheeks. The waiters nod, and their eyes shift—a slight once-over that indicates they don't believe me. I am Indian, aren't I? My father seems to agree with them. He tells me I'm asking for the impossible, as if he believes the recipes are immutable, written in stone during the passage from India to America.

XII

I look around my boyfriend's freezer one day and find meat: pork chops, ground beef, chicken pieces, Italian sausage. Ham in the refrigerator, next to the homemade bolognese sauce. Tupperware filled with chili made from ground beef and pork.

He smells different from me. Foreign. Strange.

I marry him anyway.

He has inherited blue eyes that turn gray in bad weather, light brown hair, a sharp pointy nose, and excellent teeth. He learns to make chili with ground turkey and tofu, tomato sauce with red wine and portobello mushrooms, roast chicken with rosemary and slivers of garlic under the skin.

He eats steak when we are in separate cities, roast beef at his mother's house, hamburgers at work. Sometimes I smell them on his skin. I hope he doesn't notice me turning my face, a cheek instead of my lips, my nose wrinkled at the unfamiliar, musky smell.

XIII

And then I realize I don't want to be a person who can find Indian food only in restaurants. One day my parents will be gone and I will long for the foods of my childhood, the way they long for theirs. I prepare for this day the way people on TV prepare for the end of the world. They gather canned goods they will never eat while I stockpile recipes I cannot replicate. I am frantic, disorganized, grabbing what I can, filing scribbled notes haphazardly. I regret the tastes I've forgotten, the meals I have inhaled without a thought. I worry that I've come to this realization too late.

XIV

Who told my mother about Brie? One day we were eating Velveeta, the next day Brie, Gouda, Camembert, Port Salut, Havarti with caraway, Danish fontina, string cheese made with sheep's milk. Who opened the door to these foreigners that sit on the refrigerator shelf next to last night's dal?

Back home, there is one cheese only, which comes in a tin, looks like Bakelite, and tastes best when melted.

And how do we go from Chef Boyardee to fresh pasta and homemade sauce, made with Redpack tomatoes, crushed garlic, and dried oregano? Macaroni and cheese, made with fresh cheddar and whole milk, sprinkled with bread crumbs and paprika. Fresh eggplant and ricotta ravioli, baked with marinara sauce and fresh mozzarella.

My mother will never cook beef or pork in her kitchen, and the foods she knew in her childhood are unavailable. Because the only alternative to the supermarket, with its TV dinners and canned foods, is the gourmet Italian deli across the street, by default our meals become socially acceptable.

XV

If I really want to make myself sick, I worry that my husband will one day leave me for a meat-eater, for someone familiar who doesn't sniff him suspiciously for signs of alimentary infidelity.

XVI

Indians eat lentils. I understand this as absolute, a decree from an unidentifiable authority that watches and judges me.

So what does it mean that I cannot replicate my mother's dal? She and my father show me repeatedly, in their kitchen, in my kitchen. They coach me over the phone, buy me the best cookbooks, and finally write down their secrets. Things I'm supposed to know but don't. Recipes that should be, by now, engraved on my heart.

Living far from the comfort of people who require no explanation for what I do and who I am, I crave the foods we have shared. My mother convinces me that moong is the easiest dal to prepare, and yet it fails me every time: bland, watery, a sickly greenish yellow mush. These imperfect imitations remind me only of what I'm missing.

But I have never been fond of moong dal. At my mother's table it is the last thing I reach for. Now I worry that this antipathy toward dal signals something deeper, that somehow I am not my parents' daughter, not Indian, and because I cannot bear the touch and smell of raw meat, though I can eat it cooked (charred, dry, and overdone), I am not American either.

I worry about a lifetime purgatory in Indian restaurants where I will complain that all the food looks and tastes the same because they've used the same masala.

XVII

About the tuna and her attempts to feed us, my mother laughs. She says, "You were never fussy. You ate everything I made and never complained."

My mother is at the stove, wearing only her blouse and petticoat, her sari carefully folded and hung in the closet. She does not believe a girl's place is in the kitchen, but she expects me to know that too much hing can ruin a meal, to know without being told, without having to ask or write it down. Hing = asafetida.

She remembers the catering class. "Oh, that class. You know, I had to give it up when we got to lobster. I just couldn't stand the way it looked."

She says this apologetically, as if she has deprived us, as if she suspects that having a mother who could feed us lobster would have changed the course of our lives.

Intellectually, she understands that only certain people regularly eat lobster, people with money or those who live in Maine, or both. In her catering class there were people without jobs for whom preparing lobster was a part of their professional training as caterers. Like us, they wouldn't be eating lobster at home. For my mother, however, lobster was just another American food, like tuna—different, strange, not natural yet somehow essential to belonging.

I learned how to prepare and eat lobster from the same girl who taught me tuna salad. I ate bacon at her house too. And one day this girl, with her houses in the country and Martha's Vineyard, asked me how my uncle was going to pick me up from the airport in Bombay. In 1973, she was surprised to hear that he used a car, not an elephant. At home, my parents and I laughed, and though I never knew for sure if she was making fun of me, I still wanted her friendship.

My parents were afraid my sister and I would learn to despise the foods they loved, replace them with bologna and bacon and lose our taste for masala. For my mother, giving up her disgust of lobster, with its hard exterior and foreign smell, would mean renouncing some essential difference. It would mean becoming, decidedly, definitely, American—unafraid of meat in all its forms, able to consume large quantities of protein at any given meal. My willingness to toss a living being into boiling water and then get past its ugly appearance to the rich meat inside must mean to my mother that I am somehow someone she is not.

But I haven't eaten lobster in years. In my kitchen cupboards, there is a thirteen-pound bag of basmati rice, jars of lime pickle, mango pickle, and ghee, cans of tuna and anchovies, canned soups, coconut milk, and tomatoes, rice noodles, several kinds of pasta, dried mushrooms, and unlabeled bottles of spices: haldi, jeera, hing. When my husband tries to help me cook, he cannot identify all the spices. He gets confused when I forget their English names and remarks that my expectations of him are unreasonable.

I am my parents' daughter. Like them, I expect knowledge to pass from me to my husband without one word of explanation or translation. I want him to know what I know, see what I see, without having to tell him exactly what it is. I want to believe that recipes never change.

☙ STABAT MATER ☙

Julia Kristeva

Opening up a fascinating field of investigation, this essay is of particular interest to feminists. So far, Kristeva herself has not really followed up her own "program" for research into maternity, although Histoires d'amour *as a whole does contain many valuable observations on the topic.*

The Paradox: Mother or Primary Narcissism

If it is not possible to say of a *woman* she *is* (without running the risk of abolishing her difference), would it perhaps be different concerning the *mother,* since that is the only function of the "other sex" to which we can definitely attribute existence? And yet, there too, we are caught in a paradox. First, we live in a civilization where the *consecrated* (religious or secular) representation of femininity is absorbed by motherhood. If, however, one looks at it more closely, this motherhood is the *fantasy* that is nurtured by the adult, man or woman, of a lost territory; what is more, it involves less an idealized archaic mother than the idealization of the *relationship* that binds us to her, one that cannot be localized—an idealization of primary narcissism. Now, when feminism demands a new representation of femininity, it seems to identify motherhood with that idealized misconception and, because it rejects the image and its misuse, feminism circumvents the real experience that fantasy overshadows. The result?—A negation or rejection of motherhood by some avant-garde feminist groups. Or else an acceptance—conscious or not—of its traditional representations by the great mass of people, women and men.

FLASH—instant of time or of dream without time; inordinately swollen atoms of a bond, a vision, a shiver, a yet formless, unnameable embryo. Epiphanies. Photos of what is not yet visible and that language necessarily skims over from afar, allusively. Words that are always too distant, too abstract for this underground swarming of seconds, folding in unimaginable spaces. Writing them down is an ordeal of discourse, like love. What is loving, for a woman, the same thing as writing. Laugh. Impossible. Flash on the unnameable, weavings of abstractions to be torn. Let a body venture at last out of its shelter, take a chance with meaning under a veil of words. WORD FLESH. From one to the other, eternally, broken up visions, metaphors of the invisible.

Christianity is doubtless the most refined symbolic construct in which femininity, to the extent that it transpires through it—and it does so incessantly—is focused on *Maternality.*[1] Let us call "maternal" the ambivalent principle that is bound to the species, on the one hand, and on the other stems from an identity catastrophe that causes the Name to topple over into the unnameable that one imagines as femininity, nonlanguage, or body. Thus Christ, the Son of man, when all is said and done is "human" only through his mother—as if Christly or Christian humanism could only be a materialism (this is, besides, what some secularizing trends within its orbit do not cease claiming in their esotericism). And yet, the humanity of the Virgin mother is not always obvious, and we shall see how, in her being cleared of sin, for instance, Mary distinguishes herself from mankind. But at the same time the most intense revelation of God, which occurs in mysticism, is given only to a person who assumes himself as "maternal." Augustine,

---

[1]Between the lines of this section one should be able to detect the presence of Marina Warner, *Alone of All Her Sex: The Myth and Cult of the Virgin Mary* (New York: Knopf, 1976), and Ilse Barande, *Le Maternel sigulier* (Paris: Aubier-Montaigne, 1977), which underlay my reflections.

Bernard of Clairvaux, Meister Eckhart, to mention but a few, played the part of the Father's virgin spouses, or even, like Bernard, received drops of virginal milk directly on their lips. Freedom with respect to the maternal territory then becomes the pedestal upon which love of God is erected. As a consequence, mystics, those "happy Schrebers" (Sollers) throw a bizarre light on the psychotic sore of modernity: it appears as the incapability of contemporary codes to tame the maternal, that is, primary narcissism. Uncommon and "literary," their present-day counterparts are always somewhat oriental, if not tragical—Henry Miller who says he is pregnant, Artaud who sees himself as "his daughters" or "his mother." . . . It is the orthodox constituent of Christianity, through John Chrysostom's golden mouth, among others, that sanctioned the transitional function of the Maternal by calling the Virgin a "bond," a "middle," or an "interval," thus opening the door to more or less heretical identifications with the Holy Ghost.

This resorption of femininity within the Maternal is specific to many civilizations, but Christianity, in its own fashion, brings it to its peak. Could it be that such a reduction represents no more than a masculine appropriation of the Maternal, which, in line with our hypothesis, is only a fantasy masking primary narcissism? Or else, might one detect in it, in other respects, the workings of enigmatic sublimation? These are perhaps the workings of masculine sublimation, a sublimation just the same, if it be true that for Freud picturing Da Vinci, and even for Da Vinci himself, the taming of that economy (of the Maternal or of primary narcissism) is a requirement for artistic, literacy, or painterly accomplishment?

Within that perspective, however, there are two questions, among others, that remain unanswered. What is there, in the portrayal of the Maternal in general and particularly in its Christian, virginal, one, that reduces social anguish and gratifies a male being; what is there that also satisfies a woman so that a commonality of the sexes is set up, beyond and in spite of their glaring incompatibility and permanent warfare? Beyond social and political demands, this takes the well-known "discontents" of our civilization to a level where Freud would not follow—the discontents of the species.

A Triumph of the Unconscious in Monotheism

It would seem that the "virgin" attribute for Mary is a translation error, the translator having substituted for the Semitic term that indicates the sociolegal status of a young unmarried woman the Greek word *parthenos,* which on the other hand specifies a physiological and psychological condition: virginity. One might read into this the Indo-European fascination (which Dumezil analyzed).[2] with the virgin daughter as guardian of paternal power; one might also detect an ambivalent conspiracy, through excessive spiritualization, of the mother-goddess and the underlying matriarchy with which Greek culture and Jewish monotheism kept struggling. The fact remains that Western Christianity has organized that "translation error," projected its own fantasies into it, and produced one of the most powerful imaginary constructs known in the history of civilizations.

The story of the virginal cult in Christianity amounts in fact to the imposition of pagan-rooted beliefs on, and often against, dogmas of the official Church. It is true that the Gospels already posit Mary's existence. But they suggest only very discreetly the immaculate conception of Christ's mother, they say nothing concerning Mary's own background and speak of her only seldom at the side of her son or during crucifixion. Thus Matthew 1:20 (" . . . the angel of the Lord appeared to him in a dream and said 'Joseph, son of David, do not be afraid to take Mary home as your wife, because she has conceived what is in her by the Holy Spirit'"), and Luke 1:34 ("Mary said to the angel, 'But how can this come about since I do not know man?'"), open a door, a narrow opening for all that, but one that would soon widen

---

[2]Georges Dumezil, *La Religion romaine archaïque* (Paris: Payot, 1974).

thanks to apocryphal additions, on impregnation without sexuality; according to this notion a woman, preserved from masculine intervention, conceives alone with a "third party," a nonperson, the Spirit. In the rare instances when the Mother of Jesus appears in the Gospels, she is informed that filial relationship rests not with the flesh but with the name or, in other words, that any possible matrilinearism is to be repudiated and the symbolic link alone is to last. We thus have Luke 2:48–49 (". . . his mother said to him, 'My child, why have you done this to us? See how worried your father and I have been, looking for you.' 'Why were you looking for me?' he replied. 'Did you not know that I must be busy with my father's affairs?'"), and also John 2:3–5 (". . . the mother of Jesus said to him, 'They have no wine.' Jesus said, 'Woman, why turn to me?[3] My hour has not come yet.'"), and 19:26–27 ("Seeing his mother and the disciple he loved standing near her, Jesus said to his mother, 'Woman, this is your son.' Then to the disciple he said, 'This is your mother.' And from that moment the disciple made a place for her in his home.").

Starting from this programmatic material, rather skimpy nevertheless, a compelling imaginary construct proliferated in essentially three directions. In the first place, there was the matter of drawing a parallel between Mother and Son by expanding the theme of the immaculate conception, inventing a biography of Mary similar to that of Jesus said, by depriving her of sin, to deprive her of death: Mary leaves by way of Dormition or Assumption. Next, she needed letters patent of nobility, a power that, even though exercised in the beyond, is none the less political, since Mary was to be proclaimed queen, given the attributes and paraphernalia of royalty, and, in parallel fashion, declared Mother of the divine institution on earth, the Church. Finally, the relationship with Mary and from Mary was to be revealed as the prototype of love relationships and followed two fundamental aspects of Western love: courtly love and child love, thus fitting the entire range that goes from sublimation to asceticism and masochism.

Neither Sex nor Death

Mary's life, devised on the model of the life of Jesus, seems to be the fruit of apocryphal literature. The story of her own miraculous conception, called "immaculate conception," by Anne and Joachim, after a long, barren marriage, together with her biography as a pious maiden, show up in apocryphal sources as early as the end of the first century. Their entirety may be found in the *Secret Book of James* and also in one of pseudoepigrapha, the Gospel according to the Hebrews (which inspired Giotto's frescos, for instance). Those "facts" were quoted by Clement of Alexandria and Origen but not officially accepted; even though the Eastern Church tolerated them readily, they were translated into Latin only in the sixteenth century. Yet the West was not long before glorifying the life of Mary on its own but always under orthodox guidance. The first Latin poem, "Maria," on the birth of Mary was written by the nun Hrotswith von Gandersheim (who died before 1002), a playwright and poet.

Fourth-century asceticism, developed by the Fathers of the Church, was grafted on that apocryphal shoot in order to bring out and rationalize the immaculate conception postulate. The demonstration was abased on a simple logical relation: the intertwining of sexuality and death. Since they are mutually implicated with each other, one cannot avoid the one without fleeing the other. This asceticism, applicable to both sexes, was vigorously expressed by John Chrysostom (*On Virginity*: "For where there is death there is also sexual copulation, and where there is no death there is no sexual copulation either"); even though he was attacked by Augustine and Aquinas, he none the less fueled Christian doctrine. Thus, Augustine

---

[3][The French version quoted by Kristeva ("Woman, what is there in common between you and me?") is even stronger than the King James's translation, "Woman, what have I to do with thee?"—Trans.]

condemned "concupiscence" (*epithumia*) and posited that Mary's virginity is in fact only a logical precondition of Christ's chastity. The Orthodox Church, heir no doubt to a matriarchy that was more intense in Eastern European societies, emphasized Mary's virginity more boldly. Mary was contrasted with Eve, life with death (Jerome, *Letter 22*, "Death came through Eve but life came through Mary"; Irenaeus, "through Mary the snake becomes a dove and we are freed from the chains of death"). People even got involved in tortuous arguments in order to demonstrate that Mary remained a virgin after childbirth (thus the second Constantinople council, in 381, under Arianistic influence, emphasized the Virgin's role in comparison to official dogma and asserted Mary's perpetual virginity; the 451 council called her *Aeiparthenos*—ever virgin). Once this was established, Mary, instead of being referred to as Mother of man or Mother of Christ, would be proclaimed Mother of God: *Theotokos.* Nestorius, patriarch of Constantinople, refused to go along; Nestorianism, however, for all practical purposes died with the patriarch's own death in 451, and the path that would lead to Mary's deification was then clear.

Very soon, within the complex relationship between Christ and his Mother where relations of God to mankind, man to woman, son to mother, etc. are hatched, the problematics of *time* similar to that of cause loomed up. If Mary preceded Christ and he originated in her if only from the standpoint of his humanity, should not the conception of Mary herself have been immaculate? For, if that were not the case, how could a being conceived in sin and harboring it in herself produce a God? Some apocryphal writers had not hesitated, without too much caution, to suggest such an absence of sin in Mary's conception, but the Fathers of the Church were more careful. Bernard of Clairvaux is reluctant to extol the conception of Mary by Anne, and thus he tries to check the homologation of Mary with Christ. But it fell upon Duns Scotus to change the hesitation over the promotion of a mother goddess within Christianity into a logical problem, thus saving them both, the Great Mother as well as logic. He viewed Mary's birth as a *praeredemptio,* as a matter of congruency: if it be true that Christ alone saves us through his redemption on the cross, the Virgin who bore him can but be preserved from sin in "recursive" fashion, from the time of her own conception up to that redemption.

For or against, with dogma or logical shrewdness, the battle around the Virgin intensified between Jesuits and Dominicans, but the Counter-Reformation, as is well known, finally ended the resistance: henceforth, Catholics venerated Mary in herself. The Society of Jesus succeeded in completing a process of popular pressure distilled by patristic asceticism, and in reducing, with neither explicit hostility nor brutal rejection, the share of the Maternal (in the sense given above) useful to a certain balance between the two sexes. Curiously and necessarily, when that balance began to be seriously

---

Head reclining, nape finally relaxed, skin, blood, nerves warmed up, luminous flow: stream of hair made of ebony, of nectar, smooth darkness through her fingers, gleaming honey under the wings of bees, sparkling strands burning bright . . . silk, mercury, ductile copper: frozen light warmed under fingers. Mane of breast—squirrel, horse, and the happiness of a faceless head, Narcissuslike touching without eyes, slight dissolving in muscles, hair, deep, smooth, peaceful colors. Mamma: anamnesis.

Taut eardrum, tearing sound out of muted silence. Wind among grasses, a seagull's faraway call, echoes of waves, auto horns, voices, or nothing? Or his own tears, my newborn, spasm of syncopated void. I no longer hear anything, but the eardrum keeps transmitting this resonant vertigo to my skull, the hair. My body is no longer mine, it doubles up, suffers, bleeds, catches cold, puts its teeth in, slobbers, coughs, is covered with pimples, and it laughs. And yet, when its own joy, my child's, returns, its smile washes only my eyes. But the pain, its pain—it comes from inside, never remains apart, other, it inflames me at once, without a second's respite. As if that was what I had given birth to and, not willing to part from me, insisted on coming back, dwelled in me permanently. One does not give birth in pain, one gives birth to pain: the child represents it and henceforth it settles in, it is continuous. Obviously you may close your eyes, cover up your ears, teach courses, run errands, tidy up the house, think about objects, subjects. But a mother is always branded by pain, she

yields to it. "And a sword will pierce your own soul too. . . ."

Dream without glow, without sound, dream of brawn. Dark twisting, pain in the back, the arms, the thighs—pincers turned into fibers, infernos bursting veins, stones breaking bones: grinders of volumes, expanses, spaces, lines, points. All those words, now, ever visible things to register the roar of a silence that hurts all over. As if a geometry ghost could suffer when collapsing in a noiseless tumult. . . . Yet the eye picked up nothing, the ear remained deaf. But everything swarmed, and crumbled, and twisted, and broke—the grinding continued. . . . Then, slowly, a shadowy shape gathered, became detached, darkened, stood out: seen from what must be the true place of my head, it was the right side of my pelvis. Just bony, sleek, yellow, misshapen, a piece of my body jutting out unnaturally, unsymmetrically, but slit: severed scaly surface, revealing under this disproportionate pointed limb the fibers of a marrow. . . . Frozen placenta, live limb of a skeleton, monstrous graft of life on myself, a living dead. Life . . . death . . . undecidable. During delivery it went to the left with the afterbirth. . . . My removed marrow, which nevertheless acts as a graft, which wounds but increases me. Paradox: deprivation and benefit of childbirth. But calm finally hovers over pain, over the terror of this dried branch that comes back to life, cut off, wounded, deprived of its sparkling bark. The calm of another life, the life of that other who wends his way while I remain henceforth like a framework. Still life. There is him, however, his own flesh, which was mine yesterday. Death, then, how could I yield to it?

threatened in the nineteenth century, the Catholic Church—more dialectical and subtle here than the Protestants who were already spawning the first suffragettes—raised the Immaculate Conception to dogma status in 1854. It is often suggested that the blossoming of feminism in Protestant countries is due, among other things, to the greater initiative allowed women on the social and ritual plane. One might wonder if, in addition, such a flowering is not the result of a *lack* in the Protestant religious structure with respect to the Maternal, which, on the contrary, was elaborated within Catholicism with a refinement to which the Jesuits gave the final touch, and which still makes Catholicism very difficult to analyze.

The fulfillment, under the name of Mary, of a totality made of woman and God is finally accomplished through the avoidance of death. The Virgin Mary experiences a fate more radiant than her son's: she undergoes no Calvary, she has no tomb, she doesn't die and hence has no need to rise from the dead. Mary doesn't die but, as if to echo oriental beliefs, Taoist among others, according to which human bodies pass from one place to another in an eternal flow that constitutes a carbon copy of the maternal receptacle—she is transported.

Her transition is more passive in the Eastern Church: it is a Dormition (*Koimesis*) during which, according to a number of iconographic representations, Mary can be seen changed into a little girl in the arms of her son who henceforth becomes her father; she thus reverses her role as Mother into a Daughter's role for the greater pleasure of those who enjoy Freud's "Theme of the Three Caskets."

Indeed, *mother* of her son and his *daughter* as well, Mary is also, and besides, his *wife*: she therefore actualizes the threefold metamorphosis of a woman in the tightest parenthood structure. From 1135 on, transposing the Song of Songs, Bernard of Clairvaux glorifies Mary in her role of beloved and wife. But Catherine of Alexandria (said to have been martyred in 307) already pictured herself as receiving the wedding ring from Christ, with the Virgin's help, while Catherine of Siena (1347–1380) goes through a mystical wedding with him. Is it the impact of Mary's function as Christ's beloved and wife that is responsible for the blossoming out of the Marian cult of the West after Bernard and thanks to the Cistercians? *"Vergine Madre, figlia del tuo Figlio,"* Dante exclaims, thus probably best condensing the gathering of the three feminine functions (daughter-wife-mother) within a totality where they vanish as specific corporealities while retaining their psychological functions. Their bond makes up the basis of unchanging and timeless spirituality; "the set time limit of an eternal design" [*Termine fisso d'eterno consiglio*], as Dante masterfully points out in his *Divine Comedy.*

The transition is more active in the West, with Mary rising body and soul towards the other world in an *Assumption*. That feast, honored in Byzantium as early as the fourth century, reaches Gaul in the seventh under the influence of the Eastern Church; but the earliest Western visions of the Virgin's assumption, women's visions (particularly that of Elizabeth von Schonau who died in 1164), date only from the twelfth century. For the Vatican, the Assumption became dogma only in 1950. What death anguish was it intended to soothe after the conclusion of the deadliest of wars?

Image of Power

On the side of "power," *Maria Regina* appears in imagery as early as the sixth century in the church of Santa Maria Antiqua in Rome. Interestingly enough, it is she, woman and mother, who is called upon to represent supreme earthly power. Christ is king but neither he nor his father are pictured wearing crowns, diadems, costly paraphernalia and other external signs of abundant material goods. That opulent infringement to Christian idealism is centered on the Virgin Mother. Later, when she assumed the title of *Our Lady,* this will also be in analogy to the earthly power of the noble feudal lady of medieval courts. Mary's function as guardian of power, later checked when the Church became wary of it, nevertheless persisted in popular and pictural representation, witness Piero della Francesca's impressive painting, *Madonna della Misericordia,* which was disavowed by Catholic authorities at the time. And yet, not only did the papcy revere more and more the Christly mother as the Vatican's power over cities and municipalities was strengthened, it also openly identified its own institution with the Virgin: Mary was officially proclaimed Queen by Pius XII in 1954 and *Mater Ecclesiae* in 1964.

Eia Mater, Fons Amoris!

Fundamental aspects of Western love finally converged on Mary. In a first step, it indeed appears that the Marian cult homologizing Mary with Jesus and carrying asceticism to the extreme was opposed to courtly love for the noble lady, which, while representing social transgression, was not at all a physical or moral sin. And yet, at the very dawn of a "courtliness" that was still very carnal, Mary and the Lady shared one common trait: they are the focal point of men's desires and aspirations. Moreover, because they were unique and thus excluded all other women, both the Lady and the Virgin embodied an absolute authority the more attractive as it appeared removed from paternal sternness. This feminine power must have been experienced as denied power, more pleasant to seize because it was both archaic and secondary, a kind of substitute for effective power in the family and the city but no less authoritarian, the underhand double of explicit phallic power. As early as the thirteenth century, thanks to the implantation of ascetic Christianity and especially, as early as 1328, to the promulgation of Salic laws, which excluded daughters from the inheritance and thus made the loved one very vulnerable and colored one's love for her with all the hues of the impossible, the Marian and courtly streams came together. Around Blanche of Castile (who died in 1252) the Virgin explicitly became the focus of courtly love, thus gathering the attributes of the desired woman and of the holy mother in a totality as accomplished as it was inaccessible. Enough to make any woman suffer, any man dream. One finds indeed in a *Miracle de Notre Dame* the story of a young man who abandons his fiancée for the Virgin: the latter came to him in a dream and reproached him for having left her for an "earthly woman."

Scent of milk, dewed greenery, acid and clear, recall of wind, air, seaweed (as if a body lived without waste): it slides under the skin, does not remain in the mouth or nose but fondles the veins, detaches skin from bones, inflates me like an ozone balloon, and I hover with feet firmly planted on the ground in order to carry him, sure, stable, ineradicable, while he dances in my neck, flutters with my hair, seeks a smooth shoulder on the right, on the left, slips on the breast, swingles, silver vivid blossom of my belly, and finally flies away on my navel in his dream carried by my hands. My Nights of wakefulness, scattered sleep, sweetness of the child, warm mercury in my arms, cajolery, affection, defenseless body, his or mine, sheltered, protected. A wave swells again, when he goes to sleep, under my skin—tummy, thighs, legs: sleep of the muscles, not of the brain, sleep of the flesh. The wakeful tongue quietly remembers another withdrawal, mine: a blossoming heaviness in the middle of the bed, of a hollow, of the sea. . . . Recovered childhood, dreamed peace restored, in sparks, flash of cells, instants of laughter, smiles in the blackness of dreams, at night, opaque joy that roots me in her bed, my mother's, and projects him, a son, a butterfly soaking up dew from her hand, there, nearby, in the night. Alone: she, I, and he.

He returns from the depths of the nose, the vocal cords, the lungs, the ears, pierces their smothering stopping sickness swab, and awakens in his eyes. Gentleness of the sleeping face, contours of pinkish jade—forehead, eyebrows, nostrils, cheeks, parted features of the mouth, delicate, hard, pointed chin. Without fold or shadow, neither being nor unborn, neither present nor absent, but real, real inaccessible innocence, engaging weight and seraphic lightness. A child?—An angel, a glow on an Italian painting, impassive, peaceful dream—dragnet of Mediterranean fishermen. And then, the mother-of-pearl bead awakens: quicksilver. Shiver of the eyelashes, imperceptible twitch of the eyebrows, quivering skin, anxious reflections, seeking, knowing, casting their knowledge aside in the face of my non-knowledge: fleeting irony of childhood gentleness that awakens to meaning, surpasses it, goes past it, causes me to soar in music, in dance. Impossible

Nevertheless, besides that ideal totality that no individual woman could possibly embody, the Virgin also became the fulcrum of the humanization of the West in general and of love in particular. It is again about the thirteenth century, with Francis of Assisi, that this tendency takes shape with the representation of Mary as poor, modest, and humble—madonna of humility at the same time as a devoted, fond mother. The famous nativity of Piero della Francesca in London, in which Simone de Beauvoir too hastily saw a feminine defeat because the mother kneeled before her barely born son, in fact consolidates the new cult of humanistic sensitivity. It replaces the high spirituality that assimilated the Virgin to Christ with an earthly conception of a wholly human mother. As a source for the most popularized pious images, such material humility comes closer to "lived" feminine experience than the earlier representations did. Beyond this, however, it is true that it integrates a certain feminine masochism but also displays its counterpart in gratification and *jouissance*. The truth of it is that the lowered head of the mother before her son is accompanied by the immeasurable pride of the one who knows she is also his wife and daughter. She knows she is destined to that eternity (of the spirit or of the species), of which every mother is unconsciously aware, and with regard to which maternal devotion or even sacrifice is but an insignificant price to pay. A price that is borne all the more easily since, contrasted with the love that binds a mother to her son, all other "human relationships" burst like blatant shams. The Franciscan representation of the Mother conveys many essential aspects of maternal psychology, thus leading up to an influx of common people to the churches and also a tremendous increase in the Marian cult—witness the building of many churches dedicated to her ("Notre Dame"). Such a humanization of Christianity through the cult of the mother also led to an interest in the humanity of the fatherman: the celebration of "family life" showed Joseph to advantage as early as the fifteenth century.

What Body?

We are entitled only to the ear of the virginal body, the tears and the breast. With the female sexual organ changed into an innocent shell, holder of sound, there arises a possible tendency to eroticize hearing, voice, or even understanding. By the same token, however, sexuality is brought down to the level of innuendo. Feminine sexual experience is thus rooted in the universality of sound, since it is distributed *equally* among all men, all women. A woman will only have the choice to live her life either *hyperabstractly* ("immediately universal," Hegel said) in order thus to earn divine grace and homologation with symbolic order; or merely *different*, other, fallen refinement, subtle rape of inherited genes: before what has been learned comes to pelt him, harden him, ripen him. Hard, mischievous gentleness of the first ailment overcome, innocent wisdom of the first ordeal undergone, yet hopeful blame on account of the suffering I put you through, by calling for you, desiring, creating. . . . Gentleness, wisdom, blame: your face is already human, sickness has caused you to join our species, you speak without words but your throat no longer gurgles—it harkens with me to the silence of your born meaning that draws my tears toward a smile.

The lover gone, forgetfulness comes, but the pleasure of the sexes remains, and there is nothing lacking. No representation, sensation, or recall. Inferno of vice. Later, forgetfulness returns but this time as a fall—leaden—gray, dull, opaque. Forgetfulness: blinding, smothering foam, but on the quiet. Like the fog that devours the park, wolfs down the branches, erases the green, rusty ground, and mists up my eyes.

Absence, inferno, forgetfulness. Rhythm of our loves.

A hunger remains, in place of the heart. A spasm that spreads, runs through the blood vessels to the tips of the breasts, to the tips of the fingers. It throbs, pierces the void, erases it, and gradually settles in. My heart: a tremendous pounding wound. A thirst.

Anguished, guilty. Freud's *Vaterkomplex* on the Acropolis? The impossibility of being without repeated legitimation (without books, man, family). Impossibility—depressing possibility—of "transgression."

Either repression in which I hand the other what I want from others.

Or this squalling of the void, open wound in my heart, which allows me to be only in purgatory.

I yearn for the Law. And since it is not made for me alone, I venture to desire outside the law. Then, narcissism

("immediately particular," Hegel said). But she will not be able to accede to the complexity of being divided, of heterogeneity, of the catastrophic-fold-of-"being" ("never singular," Hegel said).

Under a full blue dress, the maternal, virginal body allowed only the breast to show, while the face, with the stiffness of Byzantine icons gradually softened, was covered with tears. Milk and tears became the privileged signs of the *Mater Dolorosa* who invaded the west beginning with the eleventh century, reaching the peak of its influx in the fourteenth. But it never ceased to fill the Marian visions of those, men or women (often children), who were racked by the anguish of a maternal frustration. Even though orality—threshold of infantile regression—is displayed in the area of the breast, while the spasm at the slipping away of eroticism is translated into tears, this should not conceal what milk and tears have in common: they are the metaphors of nonspeech, of a "semiotics" that linguistic communication does not account for. The Mother and her attributes, evoking sorrowful humanity, thus become representatives of a "return of the repressed" in monotheism. They reestablish what is nonverbal and show up as the receptacle of a signifying disposition that is closer to so-called primary processes. Without them the complexity of the Holy Ghost would have been mutilated. On the other hand, as they return by way of the Virgin Mother, they find their outlet in the arts—painting and music—of which the Virgin necessarily becomes both patron saint and privileged object.

The function of the "Virginal Maternal" may thus be seen taking shape in the Western symbolic economy. Starting with the high Christly sublimation for which it yearns and occasionally exceeds, and extending to the extralinguistic regions of the unnameable, the Virgin Mother occupied the tremendous territory hither and yon of the parenthesis of language. She adds to the Christian trinity and to the World that delineates their coherence the heterogeneity they salvage.

The ordering of the maternal libido reached its apotheosis when centered in the theme of death. The *Mater Dolorosa* knows no masculine body save that of her dead son, and her only pathos (which contrasts with the somewhat vacant, gentle serenity of the nursing Madonnas) is her shedding tears over a corpse. Since resurrection there is, and, as Mother of God, she must know this, nothing justifies Mary's outburst of pain at the foot of the cross, unless it be the desire to experience within her own body the death of a human being, which her feminine fate of being the source of life spares her. Could it be that the love, as puzzling as it is ancient, of mourners for corpses relates to the same longing of a woman whom nothing fulfills—the longing to experience the wholly mas-

thus awakened—the narcissism that wants to be sex—roams, astonished. In sensual rapture I am distraught. Nothing reassures, for only the law sets anything down. Who calls such a suffering *jouissance*? It is the pleasure of the damned.

Belief in the mother is rooted in fear, fascinated with a weakness—the weakness of language. If language is powerless to locate myself for and state myself to the other, I assume—I want to believe—that there is someone who makes up for that weakness. Someone, of either sex, *before* the id speaks, before language, who might make me be by means of borders, separations, vertigos. In asserting that "in the beginning was the Word," Christians must have found such a postulate sufficiently hard to believe and, for whatever it was worth, they added its compensation, its permanent lining: the material receptacle, purified as it might be by the virginal fantasy. Archaic maternal love would be an incorporation of my suffering that is unfailing, unlike what often happens with the lacunary network of signs. In that sense, any belief, anguished by definition, is upheld by the fascinated fear of language's impotence. Every God, even including the God of the Word, relies on a mother Goddess. Christianity is perhaps also the last of the religions to have displayed in broad daylight the bipolar structure of belief: on the one hand, the difficult experience of the Word—a passion; on the other, the reassuring wrapping in the proverbial mirage of the mother—a love. For that reason, it seems to me that there is only one way to go through the religion of the Word, or its counterpart, the more or less discreet cult of the Mother; it is the "artists" way, those who make up for the vertigo of language weakness with the oversaturation of sign-systems. By this token, all art is a kind of counterreformation, an accepted baroqueness. For is it not true that if the Jesuits

culine pain of a man who expires at every moment on account of *jouissance* due to obsession with his own death? And yet, Marian pain is in no way connected with tragic outburst: joy and even a kind of triumph follow upon tears, as if the conviction that death does not exist were an irrational but unshakable maternal certainty, on which the principle of resurrection had to rest. The brilliant illustration of the wrenching between desire for the masculine corpse and negation of death, a wrenching whose paranoid logic cannot be overlooked, is masterfully presented by the famous *Stabat Mater*. It is likely that all beliefs in resurrections are rooted in mythologies marked by the strong dominance of a mother goddess. Christianity, it is true, finds its calling in the displacement of that biomaternal determinism through the postulate that immorality is mainly that of the name of the Father. But it does not succeed in imposing *its* symbolic revolution without relying on the feminine representation of an immortal biology. Mary defying death is the theme that has been conveyed to us by the numerous variations of the *Stabat Mater,* which, in the text attributed to Jacopone da Tody, enthralls us today through the music of Palestrina, Pergolesi, Haydn, and Rossini.

Let us listen to the baroque style of the young Pergolesi (1710–1736) who was dying of tuberculosis when he wrote his immortal *Stabat Mater*. His musical inventiveness, which, through Haydn, later reverberated in the work of Mozart, probably constitutes his one and only claim to immortality. But when this cry burst forth, referring to Mary facing her son's death, *"Eia Mater, fons amoris!"* ("Hail mother, source of love!")—was it merely a remnant of the period? Man overcomes the unthinkable of death by postulating maternal love in its place—in the place and stead of death and thought. This love, of which divine love is merely a not always convincing derivation, psychologically is perhaps a recall, on the near side of early identifications, of the primal shelter that ensured the survival of the newborn. Such a love is in fact, logically speaking, a surge of anguish at the very moment when the identity of thought and living body collapses. The possibilities of communication having been swept away, only the subtle gamut of sound, touch, and visual traces, older than language and newly worked out, are preserved as an ultimate shield against death. It is only "normal" for a maternal representation to set itself up at the place of this subdued anguish called love. No one escapes it. Except perhaps the saint, the mystic, or the writer who, through the power of language, nevertheless succeeds in doing no better than to take apart the fiction of the mother as mainstay of love, and to identify with love itself and what he is in fact—*a fire of tongues,* an exit from representation. Might not modern art then be, for the

finally did persuade the official Church to accept the cult of the Virgin, following the puritanical wave of the Reformation, that dogma was in fact no more than a pretext, and its efficacy lay elsewhere? It did not become the opposite of the cult of the mother but its inversion through expenditure in the wealth of signs that constitutes the baroque. The latter renders belief in the Mother useless by overwhelming the symbolic weakness where she takes refuge, withdrawn from history, with an overabundance of discourse.

The immeasureable, unconfinable maternal body.

First there is the separation, previous to pregnancy, but which pregnancy brings to light and imposes without remedy.

On the one hand—the pelvis: center of gravity, unchanging ground, solid pedestal, heaviness and weight to which the thighs adhere, with no promise of agility on that score. On the other—the torso, arms, neck, head, face, calves, feet: unbounded liveliness, rhythm, and mask, which furiously attempt to compensate for the immutability of the central tree. We live on that border, crossroads beings, crucified beings. A woman is neither nomadic nor a male body that considers itself earthly only in erotic passion. A mother is a continuous separation, a division of the very flesh. And consequently a division of language—and it has always been so.

Then there is this other abyss that opens up between the body and what had been its inside: there is the abyss between the mother and the child. What connection is there between myself, or even more unassumingly between my body and this internal graft and fold, which, once the umbilical cord has been

few who are attached to it, the implementation of that maternal love—a veil of death, in death's very site and with full knowledge of the facts? A sublimated celebration of incest. . . .

Alone of Her Sex

Freud collected, among other objects of art and archeology, countless statuettes representing mother goddesses. And yet his interest in them comes to light only in discreet fashion in his work. It shows up when Freud examines artistic creation and homosexuality in connection with Leonardo da Vinci and deciphers there the ascendancy of an archaic mother, seen therefore from the standpoint of her effects on man and particularly on this strange function of his sometimes to change languages. Moreover, when Freud analyzes the advent and transformations of monotheism, he emphasizes that Christianity comes closer to pagan myths by integrating, through and against Judaic rigour, a preconscious acknowledgment of a maternal feminine. And yet, among the patients analyzed by Freud, one seeks in vain for mothers and their problems. One might be led to think that motherhood was a solution to neurosis and, by its very nature, ruled out psychoanalysis as a possible other solution. Or might psychoanalysis, at this point, make way for religion? In simplified fashion, the only thing Freud tells us concerning motherhood is that the desire for a child is a transformation of either penis envy or anal drive, and this allows her to discover the neurotic equation child-penis-feces. We are thus enlightened concerning an essential aspect of male phantasmatics with respect to childbirth, and female phantasmatics as well to the extent that it embraces, in large part and in its hysterical labyrinths, the male one. The fact remains, as far as the complexities and pitfalls of maternal experience are involved, that Freud offers only a massive *nothing*, which, for those who might care to analyze it, is punctuated with this or that remark on the part of Freud's mother, proving to him in the kitchen that his own body is anything but immortal and will crumble away like dough; or the sour photograph of Marthe Freud, the wife, a whole mute story. . . . There thus remained for his followers an entire continent to explore, a black one indeed, where Jung was the first to rush in, getting all his esoteric fingers burnt, but not without calling attention to some sore points of the imagination with regard to motherhood, points that are still resisting analytical rationality.[4]

---

[4]Jung thus noted the "hierogamous" relationship between Mary and Christ as well as the overprotection given the Virgin with respect to original sin, which places her on the margin of mankind; finally, he insisted very much on the Vatican's adoption of the Assumption as dogma, seeing it as one of the considerable merits of Catholicism as opposed to Protestantism (C. J. Jung, *Answer to Job,* Princeton: Princeton University Press, 1969).

severed, is an inaccessible other? My body and . . . him. No connection. Nothing to do with it. And this, as early as the first gestures, cries, steps, long before *its* personality has become my opponent. The child, whether *he* or *she* is irremediably an other. To say that there are no sexual relationships constitutes a skimpy assertion when confronting the flash that bedazzles me when I confront the abyss between what was mine and is henceforth but irreparably alien. Trying to think through that abyss: staggering vertigo. No identity holds up. A mother's identity is maintained only through the well-known closure of consciousness within the indolence of habit, when a woman protects herself from the borderline that severs her body and expatriates it from her child. Lucidity, on the contrary, would restore her as cut in half, alien to its other—and a ground favorable to delirium. But also and for that very reason, motherhood destines us to a demented jouissance that is answered, by chance, by the nursling's laughter in the sunny waters of the ocean. What connection is there between it and myself? No connection, except for that overflowing laughter where one senses the collapse of some ringing, subtle, fluid identity or other, softly buoyed by the waves.

Concerning that stage of my childhood, scented, warm, and soft to the touch, I have only a spatial memory. No time at all. Fragrance of honey, roundness of forms, silk and velvet under my fingers, on my cheeks.

Mummy. Almost no sight—a shadow that darkens, soaks me up, or vanishes amid flashes. Almost no voice in her placid presence. Except, perhaps, and more belatedly, the echo of quarrels: her exasperation, her being fed up, her

There might doubtless be a way to approach the dark area that motherhood constitutes for a woman; one needs to listen, more carefully than ever, to what mothers are saying today, through their economic difficulties and, beyond the guilt that a too existentialist feminism handed down, through their discomforts, insomnias, joys, angers, desires, pains, and pleasures. . . . One might, in similar fashion, try better to understand the incredible construct of the Maternal that the West elaborated by means of the Virgin, and of which I have just mentioned a few episodes in a never-ending history.

What is it then in this maternal representation that, alone of her sex, goes against both of the two sexes,[5] and was able to attract women's wishes for identification as well as the very precise interposition of those who assumed to keep watch over the symbolic and social order?

Let me suggest, by way of hypothesis, that the virginal maternal is a way (not among the less effective ones) of dealing with feminine paranoia.

- The Virgin assumes her feminine denial of the other sex (of man) but overcomes him by setting up a third person: *I* do not conceive with *you* but with *Him*. The result is an immaculate conception (therefore with neither man nor sex), conception of a God with whose existence a woman has indeed something to do, on condition that she acknowledge being subjected to it.
- The Virgin assumes the paranoid lust for power by changing a woman into a Queen in heaven and a Mother of the earthly institutions (of the Church). But she succeeds in stifling that megalomania by putting it on its knees before the child-god.
- The Virgin obstructs the desire for murder or devoration by means of a strong oral cathexis (the breast), valorization of pain (the sob), and incitement to replace the sexed body with the ear of understanding.
- The Virgin assumes the paranoid fantasy of being excluded from time and death through the very flattering representation of Dormition or Assumption.
- The Virgin especially agrees with the repudiation of the other woman (which doubtless amounts basically to a repudiation of the woman's mother) by suggesting the image of A Unique Woman: alone among women, alone among mothers, alone among humans since she is without sin. But the acknowledgment of a longing for uniqueness is immediately checked by the postulate according to which uniqueness is attained only through an exacerbated masochism: a concrete woman, worthy of the feminine ideal embodied by the Virgin as an inaccessible goal, could only be a nun, a martyr or, if she is married,

---

[5]As Caelius Sedulius wrote, "She . . . had no peer / Either in our first mother or in all women / Who were to come. But alone of all her sex / She pleased the Lord" ("Paschalis Carminis," Book II, II. 68ff. Of *Opera Omnia,* Vienna, 1885). Epigraph to Marina Warner, *Alone of all Her Sex.*

hatred. Never straightforward, always held back, as if, although the unmanageable child deserved it, the daughter could not accept the mother's hatred—it was not meant for her. A hatred without recipient or rather whose recipient was not "I" and which, perturbed by such a lack of recipience, was toned down into irony or collapsed into remorse before reaching its destination. With others, this maternal aversion may be worked up to a spasm that is held like a delayed orgasm. Women doubtless reproduce among themselves the strange gamut of forgotten body relationships with their mothers. Complicity in the unspoken, connivance of the inexpressible, of a wink, a tone of voice, a gesture, a tinge, a scent. We are in it, set free of our identification papers and names, on an ocean of preciseness, a computerization of the unnameable. No communication between individuals but connections between atoms, molecules, wisps of words, droplets of sentences. The community of women is a community of dolphins. Conversely, when the other woman posits herself as such, that is, as singular and inevitably in opposition, "I" am startled, so much that "I" no longer know what is going on. There are then two paths left open to the rejection that bespeaks the recognition of the other woman as such. Either, not wanting to experience her, I ignore her and, "alone of my sex," I turn my back on her in friendly fashion. It is a hatred that, lacking a recipient worthy enough of its power, changes to unconcerned complacency. Or else, outraged by her own stubbornness, by that other's belief that she is singular, I unrelentingly let go at her claim to address me and find respite only in the eternal return of power strokes, bursts of hatred—blind and dull but obstinate. I do not see her as herself but beyond her I aim at the claim to singularity, the unacceptable ambition to be something other than a child or a fold in the plasma that consti-

one

tutes who

leads a life that would remove her from the "earthly" condition and dedicate her to the highest sublimation alien to her body. A bonus, however: the promised *jouissance*.

A skillful balance of concessions and constraints involving feminine paranoia, the representation of virgin motherhood appears to crown the efforts of a society to reconcile the social remnants of matrilinearism and the unconscious needs of primary narcissism on the one hand, and on the other the requirements of a new society based on exchange and before long on increased production, which require the contribution of the superego and rely on the symbolic paternal agency.

While that clever balanced architecture today appears to be crumbling, one is led to ask the following: what are the aspects of the feminine psyche for which that representation of motherhood does not provide a solution or else provides one that is felt as too coercive by twentieth-century women?

The unspoken doubtless weighs first on the maternal body: as no signifier can uplift it without leaving a remainder, for the signifier is always meaning, communication, or structure, whereas a woman as mother would be, instead, a strange fold that changes culture into nature, the speaking into biology. Although it concerns every woman's body, the heterogeneity that cannot be subsumed in the signifier nevertheless explodes violently with pregnancy (the threshold of culture and nature) and the child's arrival (which extracts woman out of her oneness and gives her the possibility—but not the certainty—of reaching out to the other, the ethical). Those particularities of the maternal body compose woman into a being of folds, a catastrophe of being that the dialectics of the trinity and its supplements would be unable to subsume.

Silence weighs heavily none the less on the corporeal and psychological suffering of childbirth and especially the self-sacrifice involved in becoming anonymous in order to pass on the social norm, which one might repudiate for one's own sake but within which *one must* include the child in order to educate it along the chain of generations. A suffering lined with jubilation—ambivalence of masochism—on account of which a woman, rather refractory to perversion, in fact allows herself a coded, fundamental, perverse behavior, ultimate guarantee of society, without which society will not reproduce and will not maintain a constancy of standardized household. Feminine perversion does not reside in the parceling or the Don Juan-like multiplying of objects of desire; it is at once legalized, if not rendered paranoid, through the agency

tutes us, an echo of the cosmos that unifies us. What an inconceivable ambition it is to aspire to singularity, it is not natural, hence it is inhuman; the mania smitten with Oneness ("There is only One woman") can only impugn it by condemning it as "masculine." . . . Within this strange feminine seesaw that makes "me" swing from the unnameable community of women over to the war of individual singularities, it is unsettling to say "I." The languages of the great formerly matriarchal civilizations must avoid, do avoid, personal pronouns: they leave to the context the burden of distinguishing protagonists and take refuge in tones to recover an underwater, transverbal communication between bodies. It is a music from which so-called oriental civility tears away suddenly through violence, murder, blood baths. A woman's discourse, would that be it? Did not Christianity attempt, among other things, to freeze that seesaw? To stop it, tear women away from its rhythm, settle them permanently in the spirit? Too permanently . . .

The love of God and for God resides in a gap: the broken space made explicit by sin on the one side, the beyond on the other. Discontinuity, lack, and arbitrariness: topography of the sign, of the symbolic relation that posits my otherness as impossible. Love, here, is only for the impossible.

For a mother, on the other hand, strangely so, the other as arbitrary (the child) is taken for granted. As far as she is concerned—impossible, that is just the way it is: it is reduced to the implacable. The other is inevitable, she seems to say, turn it into a God if you wish, it is nevertheless natural, for such an other has come out of myself, which is yet not myself but a flow of unending germinations, an eternal cosmos. The other goes much without saying and without my saying that, at the limit, it

of masochism: all sexual "dissoluteness" will be accepted and hence become insignificant, provided a child seals up such outpours. Feminine perversion [*père-version*] is coiled up in the desire for law as desire for reproduction and continuity, it promotes feminine masochism to the rank of structure stabilizer (against its deviations); by assuring the mother that she may thus enter into an order that is above that of human will it gives her her reward of pleasure. Such coded perversion, such close combat between maternal masochism and the law have been utilized by totalitarian powers of all times to bring women to their side, and, of course, they succeed easily. And yet, it is not enough to "declaim against" the reactionary role of mothers in the service of "male dominating power." One would need to examine to what extent that role corresponds to the biosymbolic latencies of motherhood and, on that basis, to try to understand, since the myth of the Virgin does not subsume them, or no longer does, how their surge lays women open to the most fearsome manipulations, not to mention blinding, or pure and simple rejection by progressive activists who refuse to take a close look.

Among things left out of the virginal myth there is the war between mother and daughter, a war masterfully but too quickly settled by promoting Mary as universal and particular, but never singular—as "alone of her sex." The relation to the other woman has presented our culture, in massive fashion during the past century, with the necessity to reformulate its representations of love and hatred—inherited from Plato's *Symposium,* the troubadours, or Our Lady. On that level, too, motherhood opens out a vista: a woman seldom (although not necessarily) experiences her passion (love and hatred) for another woman without having taken her own mother's place—without having herself become a mother, and especially without slowly learning to differentiate between same beings—as being face to face with her daughter forces her to do.

Finally, repudiation of the other sex (the masculine) no longer seems possible under the aegis of the third person, hypostatized in the child as go-between: "neither me, nor you, but him, the child, the third person, the nonperson, God, which I still am in the final analysis. . . ." Since there is repudiation, and if the feminine being that struggles within it is to remain there, it henceforth calls for, not the deification of the third party, but countercathexes in strong values, in strong *equivalents of power.* Feminine psychosis today is sustained and absorbed through passion for politics, science, art. . . . The variant that accompanies motherhood might be analyzed perhaps more readily than the others from the standpoint of the

does not exist for itself. The "just the same" of motherly peace of mind, more persistent than philosophical doubt, gnaws, on account of its basic disbelief, at the symbolic's allmightiness. It bypasses perverse negation ("I know, but just the same") and constitutes the basis of the social bond in its generality, in the sense of "resembling others and eventually the species." Such an attitude is frightening when one imagines that it can crush everything the other (the child) has that is specifically irreducible: rooted in that disposition of motherly love, besides, we find the leaden strap it can become, smothering any different individuality. But it is there, too, that the speaking being finds a refuge when his/her symbolic shell cracks and a crest emerges where speech causes biology to show through: I am thinking of the time of illness, of sexual-intellectual-physical passion, of death . . .

rejection of the other sex that it compromises. To allow what? Surely not some understanding or other on the part of "sexual partners" within the preestablished harmony of primal androgyny. Rather, to lead to an acknowledgment of what is irreducible, of the irreconciliable interest of both sexes in asserting their differences, in the quest of each one—and of women, after all—for an appropriate fulfillment.

These, then, are a few questions among others concerning a motherhood that today remains, after the Virgin, without a discourse. They suggest, all in all, the need of an ethics for this "second" sex, which, as one asserts it, is reawakening.

Nothing, however, suggests that a feminine ethics is possible, and Spinoza excluded women from his (along with children and the insane). Now, if a contemporary ethics is no longer seen as being the same as morality; if ethics amounts to not avoiding the embarrassing and inevitable problematics of the law but giving it flesh, language, and *jouissance*—in that case its reformulation demands the contribution of women. Of women who harbor the desire to reproduce (to have stability). Of women who are available so that our speaking species, which knows it is moral, might withstand death. Of mothers. For an heretical ethics separated from morality, an *herethics,* is perhaps no more than that which in life makes bonds, thoughts, and therefore the thought of death, bearable: herethics is undeath [*a-mort*], love . . . *Eia Mater, fons amoris* . . . So let us again listen to the *Stabat Mater,* and the music, all the music . . . it swallows up the goddesses and removes their necessity.

❧ SHE UNNAMES THEM ❧

Ursula K. LeGuin

Most of them accepted namelessness with the perfect indifference with which they had so long accepted and ignored their names. Whales and dolphins, seals and sea otters consented with particular grace and alacrity, sliding into anonymity as into their element. A faction of yaks, however, protested. They said that "yak" sounded right, and that almost everyone who knew they existed called them that. Unlike the ubiquitous creatures such as rats and fleas, who had been called by hundreds or thousands of different names since Babel, the yaks could truly say, they said, that they had a name. They discussed the matter all summer. The councils of the elderly females finally agreed that though the name might be useful to others it was so redundant from the yak point of view that they never spoke it themselves and hence might as well dispense with it. After they presented the argument in this light to their bulls, a full consensus was delayed only by the onset of severe early blizzards. Soon after the beginning of the thaw, their agreement was reached and the designation "yak" was returned to the donor.

Among the domestic animals, few horses had cared what anybody called them since the failure of Dean Swift's attempt to name them from their own vocabulary. Cattle, sheep, swine, asses, mules, and goats, along with chickens, geese, and turkeys, all agreed enthusiastically to give their names back to the people to whom—as they put it—they belonged.

A couple of problems did come up with pets. The cats, of course, steadfastly denied ever having had any name other than those self-given, unspoken, ineffably personal names which, as the poet named Eliot said, they spend long hours daily contemplating—though none of the contemplators has ever admitted that what they contemplate is their names and some onlookers have wondered if the object of that meditative gaze might not in fact be the Perfect, or Platonic, Mouse. In any case, it is a moot point now. It was with the dogs, and with some parrots, lovebirds, ravens, and mynahs, that the trouble arose. These verbally talented individuals insisted that their names were important to them, and flatly refused to part with them. But as soon as they understood that the issue was precisely one of individual choice, and that anybody who wanted to be called Rover, or Froufrou, or Polly, or even Birdie in the personal sense, was perfectly free to do so, not one of them had the least objection to parting with the lowercase (or, as regards German creatures, uppercase) generic appellations "poodle," "parrot," "dog," or "bird," and all the Linnaean qualifiers that had tailed along behind them for two hundred years like tin cans tied to a tail.

The insects parted with their names in vast clouds and swarms of ephemeral syllables buzzing and stinging and humming and flitting and crawling and tunnelling away.

As for the fish of the sea, their names dispersed from them in silence throughout the oceans like faint, dark blurs of cuttlefish ink, and drifted off on the currents without a trace.

None were left now to unname, and yet how close I felt to them when I saw one of them swim or fly or trot or crawl across my way or over my skin, or stalk me in the night, or go along beside me for a while in the day. They seemed far closer than when their names had stood between myself and them like a clear barrier: so close that my fear of them and their fear of me became one same fear. And the attraction that many of us felt, the desire to smell one another's smells, feel or rub or caress one another's scales or skin or feathers or fur, taste one another's blood or flesh, keep one another warm—that attraction was now all one with the fear, and the hunter could not be told from the hunted, nor the eater from the food.

This was more or less the effect I had been after. It was somewhat more powerful than I had anticipated, but could not now, in all conscience, make an exception for myself. I resolutely put anxiety away, went to Adam, and said, "You and your father lent me this—gave it to me, actually. It's been really useful, but it doesn't exactly seem to fit very well lately. But thanks very much! It's really been very useful."

It is hard to give back a gift without sounding peevish or ungrateful, and I did not want to leave him with that impression of me. He was not paying much attention, as it happened, and said only. "Put it down over there, O.K." and went on with what he was doing.

One of my reasons for doing what I did was that talk was getting us nowhere, but all the same I felt a little let down. I had been prepared to defend my decision. And I thought that perhaps when he did notice he might be upset and want to talk. I put some things away and fiddled around a little, but he continued to do what he was doing and to take no notice of anything else. At last I said, "Well, goodbye, dear. I hope the garden key turns up."

He was fitting parts together, and said, without looking around, "O.K., fine, dear. When's dinner?"

"I'm not sure," I said. "I'm going now. With the—" I hesitated, and finally said, "With them, you know," and went on out. In fact, I had only just then realized how hard it would have been to explain myself. I could not chatter away as I used to do, taking it all for granted. My words now must be as slow, as new, as single, as tentative as the steps I took going down the path away from the house, between the dark-branched, tall dancers motionless against the winter shining.

HISTORY OF AN ENCOUNTER

Eunice Lipton

I don't remember when I first saw Victorine Meurent, but I wouldn't have recognized her or known her name at the time. No one would have. She was just another naked woman in a painting. Maybe I remarked that the man who made the picture was called Manet or that the work itself was named *Olympia*, but that would have been it. When I was at college in the late 1950s, works of art were considered things of beauty. Period. One would never pay attention to a painting's literal content. One wouldn't even risk noticing that De Kooning's *Woman II* had a woman in it.

Even as I became a professional art historian in the 1960s, the look of *Olympia* did not change. The naked white woman on the bed seemed like any odalisque, Venus, or Danaë—idealized flesh made into art. I was taught to appreciate Manet's particularly modern vocabulary, his tonal contrasts, flattened spaces, outlined forms, that is, his fundamentally abstract intentions. It was Manet who was placed first in the pantheon of modernist painting; we were told that before anyone else, he had seen people and events for what they really were, abstract forms.

But one day in 1970, try as I may, I could not shake the feeling that there was an event unfolding in *Olympia* and that the naked woman was staring quite alarmingly out of the picture. I could not make her recede behind the abstract forms I knew—I had been taught so fervently to believe—were the true content of the work. Her face kept swimming forward, her eyes demanded attention. I saw that unlike other naked woman in paintings, Olympia did not drape herself suggestively upon her bed, or supplicate prospective lovers, or droop resignedly. Nor did she smile flirtatiously. Rather she reigned imperiously, reclining upon silken pillows, her steady gaze a dare, her tight little body and proprietary hand an omen. Now I could see that even the stilted pose of the black maid and overarching cat gave the lie to scenarios of seduction. Olympia, alert and dignified, resembled a noble consort on an Etruscan funerary monument far more than an inviting Greek or Oriental courtesan. This was a woman who could say "yes," *or* she could say "no."

Her contemporaries knew this in the nineteenth century though they didn't say it in so many words. In fact, Manet was greatly distressed over how his painting was received; he even considered destroying it. What happened was this. In May of 1865 *Olympia* was exhibited in the Salon, the official exhibition forum of the time. The press took an instant and bellicose dislike to the work, using words like: "The vicious strangeness of [this] . . . woman of the night"; "a sort of female gorilla, a grotesque . . ." "Such indecency! . . ." Before anyone knew what was happening, respectable Parisians were sweeping through the Salon's drafty halls brandishing walking sticks and umbrellas; they were heading toward *Olympia* with murder on their minds. The authorities were taken aback, and took the unprecedented step of cordoning off the painting. But the damage was done. Manet fled to Spain thinking: Titian had done it, so had Giorgione and Velazquez—he meant painted naked women—why is everyone so angry at me? This may have been the first time in modern history that a painting incited people to such public agitation. . . .

I can't say when it was exactly that my wonder about Olympia and the treatment she received turned to impatience, but I began to hear the rampaging walking sticks and umbrellas, and to feel the heat and

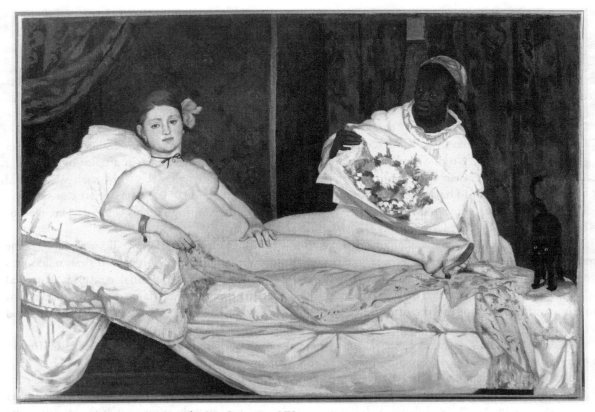

Edouard Manet. *Olympia,* 1863. Giraudan/Art Resources, NY

rage the painting produced in commentators, the barely contained anger squeezed into stylish commentary about artist-geniuses and their pathetic models. I know it was about the same time that I met Linda, and also read an article in the *Village Voice* entitled "The Next Great Moment in History Is Theirs." In it, Vivian Gornick wrote that "women in this country are gathering themselves into a sweat of civil revolt. . . . [Their] energy . . . lies trapped and dormant like a growing tumor, and at its center there is despair, hot, deep, wordless. . . . [They have been] deprived . . . of the right to say 'I' and have it mean something. This understanding . . . underlies the current wave of feminism. It is felt by thousands of women today, it will be felt by millions tomorrow."

The next thing I knew I was throwing Kate Millet's *Sexual Politics* across the room, demanding, "How can this be true, this silencing of women, this enforced invisibility? And what the hell did that professor mean when he said I had too many ideas?"

Then it was August 26, 1970, and a march was called to commemorate the Nineteenth Amendment to the Constitution, the establishing of women's right to vote. I went with my friend Marcia. We made our way to Fifth Avenue and Fifty-ninth Street. As we approached, what we saw took our breath away. Women were everywhere—thousands and thousands and thousands of women. Marcia grabbed my arm and said the oddest thing: "What *would* my mother have made of this?" I wouldn't have thought of my mother at such a moment. I never thought of my mother as a woman.

But what a sight the avenue was, women filling all the spaces, banishing the cars, the honking, the men. How we gazed upon each other. With what amazement and pleasure we talked and laughed and wept as we flooded that capacious boulevard. And with what confidence we lured the hesitant from the sidelines. How they fell into the arms of the river that we became that day, we women of all shapes, sizes, and ages marveling at each other.

We also handed each other leaflets and flyers that said: "Join the National Organization of Women!" "Come to meetings of Redstockings" ". . . The New York Radical Feminists" ". . . The Feminists!" And we did. We met in churches, in school rooms, in libraries. Then in each other's homes. We organized by neighborhood, ten to twelve in a cadre. We met weekly, and we talked our hearts out. We divulged secrets we didn't know we had. Nothing was off limits. We talked about sex and orgasm, ambition, marriage, homosexuality, our fathers, our siblings, our mothers. The rage at our families, our lovers, our teachers was staggering. And maybe for the first time in our lives, we turned that fury on to the world, away from ourselves.

The listening, the uninterrupted speaking, made us realize how smart we were, and how inhibited. For most of us, this talking—this consciousness-raising—was the first time we heard each other speaking discursively and analytically about our lives. Bit by little bit, our talking, our weeping, and our anger added up to an emotional and political history. And a strategy.

What better emblem for the time—those opening salvos of the Women's Movement—than *Olympia,* a woman whose naked body said: "See this? It's mine. I will not be the object of your gaze, invisible to my own. This is my body, my life."

Yes, I marveled at the intricate psychological drama surrounding *Olympia,* which on the one hand elicited men's attraction—so many had written *some*thing about her at a time when models were usually nameless and invisible—but on the other provoked ridicule and contempt. *All that writing about her.* In our own time, in 1977, an entire book on *Olympia* written by Theodore Reff, and again in 1985, T. J. Clark, the most dazzling bad boy in the Art History community, published a notably long, obfuscating, and tortured essay on *Olympia* in his book on Manet. Every prominent scholar of nineteenth-century art planted himself in front of her, writing paraphernalia at hand. All thought their engagement disinterested, but it wasn't. They circled her from above, close up, on top. What did they mean to do with all those words? Describe her? Analyze her? Situate her? *Or:* Possess her? Control her? Silence her? No one admitted his emotions, neither the irritation nor the fascination. None could acknowledge what amounted to a professional obsession that spanned a century and a half. And continues.

More and more I brought Meurent up in my classes as if I could somehow redress the balance by at least speaking her name, acknowledging her corporeality as Victorine Meurent, a real woman of the nineteenth century. Musingly, I'd say, "Some day I'm going to find this woman," and the more I said it, the more I meant it. It became a promise. I took her to myself, unconsciously, unwittingly. That face, those eyes. I wanted what she had: her confidence, her dignity, her "no."

Many things came between us though. My career for one, books and articles about geniuses—Picasso, Degas, Manet. And my own ambivalent self stuck in a conservative profession. And a culture that enjoined girls to behave themselves. Plus—I rationalized—all I know is Meurent's name, that she worked for Manet, traveled to the United States, exhibited a few times at the Paris Salon. She was only a model. What is there really to say?

I had no idea what the ramifications of the search would be. I didn't even realize that our names were the same: "Eunice" is a translation from the Greek of "Evnike;" it means "Happy Victory." And I certainly didn't *intend* to end up a redhead. All I knew was that I envied Meurent her autonomy even as I acknowledged the paradox that I was a well-paid American professor in the late twentieth century, and she was a working-class model in nineteenth-century Paris. I was convinced that she had had more choices than I, and that she had acted on them. The dare of her gaze was the proof.

As I set out in earnest to find Meurent, I kept losing my way. A two-step of desire and longing crossed by withdrawal and passivity. I had learned this dance as a child, but coming of age in the era of McCarthyism, Eisenhower, and Doris Day refined it immeasurably. Across this faraway history I started looking for Meurent.

This is the record of my search.

SHOW AND TELL

Scott McCloud

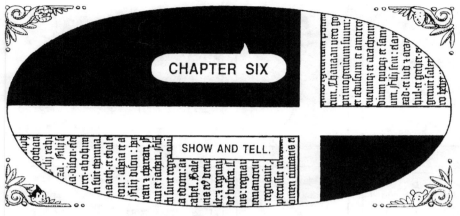

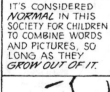

TRADITIONAL THINKING HAS LONG HELD THAT TRULY *GREAT* WORKS OF ART AND LITERATURE ARE ONLY POSSIBLE WHEN THE TWO ARE KEPT AT ARM'S LENGTH.

WORDS AND PICTURES *TOGETHER* ARE CONSIDERED, AT BEST, A *DIVERSION* FOR THE *MASSES*, AT WORST A PRODUCT OF *CRASS COMMERCIALISM.*

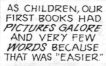

AS CHILDREN, OUR FIRST BOOKS HAD *PICTURES GALORE* AND VERY FEW *WORDS* BECAUSE THAT WAS "EASIER."

THEN, AS WE GREW, WE WERE EXPECTED TO GRADUATE TO BOOKS WITH MUCH *MORE* TEXT AND ONLY *OCCASIONAL* PICTURES--

--AND FINALLY TO ARRIVE AT *"REAL"* BOOKS-- THOSE WITH NO PICTURES *AT ALL.*

OR PERHAPS, AS IS SADLY THE CASE THESE DAYS, TO NO *BOOKS* AT ALL.

MEANWHILE, WORDS AND *MOVING* PICTURES HAVE HALF THE WORLD IN THRALL TO THEIR CHARMS, BUT MUST STRUGGLE TO MAKE *THEIR* POTENTIAL UNDERSTOOD.

WORDS AND PICTURES ARE AS POPULAR AS EVER, BUT THIS WIDESPREAD FEELING THAT THE COMBINATION IS SOMEHOW *BASE* OR *SIMPLISTIC* HAS BECOME A *SELF-FULFILLING PROPHECY.*

THE ROOTS OF THIS ATTITUDE RUN PRETTY *DEEP.*

AS NEAR AS WE CAN TELL, PICTURES *PREDATE* THE WRITTEN WORD BY A *LARGE MARGIN.* HERE ARE SOME BIG HITS FROM THE GOLDEN AGE OF CAVE PAINTING, ABOUT 15,000 YEARS AGO.

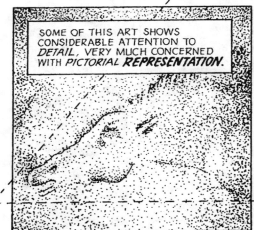

SOME OF THIS ART SHOWS CONSIDERABLE ATTENTION TO *DETAIL,* VERY MUCH CONCERNED WITH *PICTORIAL* **REPRESENTATION.**

BUT OTHERS WERE VERY *ICONIC,* ACTING AS *SYMBOLS* RATHER THAN *PICTURES* -- MORE LIKE A *PRIMITIVE LANGUAGE!*

AS MENTIONED IN OUR *LAST CHAPTER*,* THE EARLIEST *WORDS* WERE, IN FACT, *STYLIZED PICTURES.*

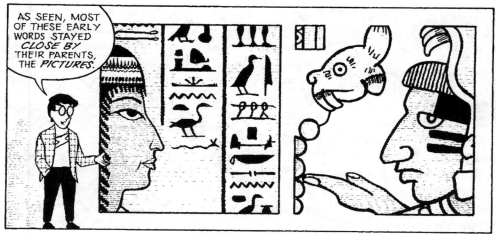

AS SEEN, MOST OF THESE EARLY WORDS STAYED *CLOSE BY* THEIR PARENTS, THE *PICTURES.*

IT DIDN'T TAKE *LONG*, THOUGH-- RELATIVELY SPEAKING-- BEFORE ANCIENT WRITING STARTED TO BECOME MORE *ABSTRACT.*

SOME WRITTEN LANGUAGES SURVIVE TO THIS DAY, BEARING TRACES OF THEIR ANCIENT PICTORIAL HERITAGE.

* SEE PAGE 129.

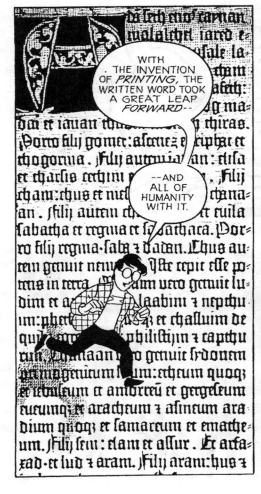

*IN ILLUMINATED MANUSCRIPTS, FOR EXAMPLE.

FACSIMILE DETAILS OF PORTRAITS BY DURER
(1519) REMBRANDT (1660) DAVID (1788) AND INGRES
(1810-15).

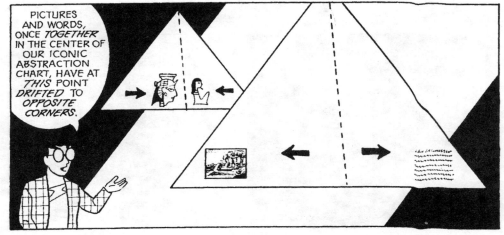

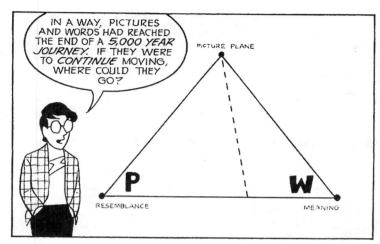

IN A WAY, PICTURES AND WORDS HAD REACHED THE END OF A *5,000 YEAR JOURNEY*. IF THEY WERE TO *CONTINUE* MOVING, WHERE COULD THEY GO?

PICTURE PLANE

P

W

RESEMBLANCE

MEANING

FOR *PICTURES*, THERE WAS ONLY *UP!*

IMPRESSIONISM SENT WESTERN ART TOWARD THE *ABSTRACT VERTEX*, BUT IN A WAY THAT *CLUNG* TO WHAT THE *EYE* SAW.

P

IMPRESSIONISM, WHILE IT COULD BE THOUGHT OF AS THE FIRST *MODERN* MOVEMENT, WAS MORE A *CULMINATION* OF THE *OLD*, THE *ULTIMATE STUDY* OF *LIGHT* AND *COLOR*.

FACSIMILE DETAIL OF "A SUNDAY AFTERNOON ON THE ISLAND OF LA GRANDE JATTE" BY GEORGES SEURAT.

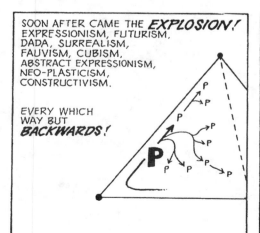

SOON AFTER CAME THE *EXPLOSION!* EXPRESSIONISM, FUTURISM, DADA, SURREALISM, FAUVISM, CUBISM, ABSTRACT EXPRESSIONISM, NEO-PLASTICISM, CONSTRUCTIVISM.

EVERY WHICH WAY BUT *BACKWARDS!*

P P P P P P P P P P

STRICT REPRESENTATIONAL STYLES WERE OF LITTLE IMPORTANCE TO THE NEW SCHOOLS. *ABSTRACTION*, BOTH ICONIC AND *NON*-ICONIC MADE A SPECTACULAR *COMEBACK!*

FACSIMILE DETAILS OF PORTRAITS BY PICASSO, LEGER AND KLEE.

SOME ARTISTS HEADED *UPWARD* TO THE *SUMMIT* OF THE PICTURE PLANE, WANTING NEITHER *RESEMBLANCE* NOR EXTERNAL "*MEANING*."

MONDRIAN A LA McCLOUD.

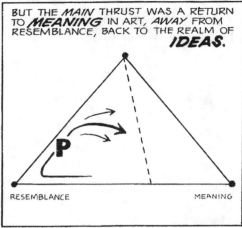

BUT THE *MAIN* THRUST WAS A RETURN TO *MEANING* IN ART, *AWAY* FROM RESEMBLANCE, BACK TO THE REALM OF *IDEAS.*

RESEMBLANCE

MEANING

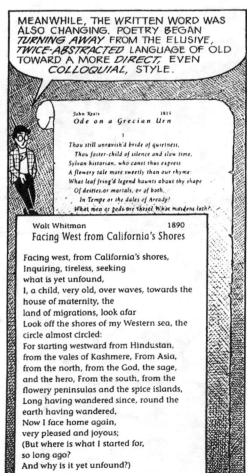

MEANWHILE, THE WRITTEN WORD WAS ALSO CHANGING. POETRY BEGAN *TURNING AWAY* FROM THE ELUSIVE, *TWICE-ABSTRACTED* LANGUAGE OF OLD TOWARD A MORE *DIRECT,* EVEN *COLLOQUIAL,* STYLE.

John Keats   1819
Ode on a Grecian Urn

1

Thou still unravish'd bride of quietness,
Thou foster-child of silence and slow time,
Sylvan historian, who canst thus express
A flowery tale more sweetly than our rhyme:
What leaf-fring'd legend haunts about thy shape
Of deities or mortals, or of both,
In Tempe or the dales of Arcady?
What men or gods are these? What maidens loth?

Walt Whitman   1890
Facing West from California's Shores

Facing west, from California's shores,
Inquiring, tireless, seeking
what is yet unfound,
I, a child, very old, over waves, towards the
house of maternity, the
land of migrations, look afar
Look off the shores of my Western sea, the
circle almost circled:
For starting westward from Hindustan,
from the vales of Kashmere, From Asia,
from the north, from the God, the sage,
and the hero, From the south, from the
flowery peninsulas and the spice islands,
Long having wandered since, round the
earth having wandered,
Now I face home again,
very pleased and joyous;
(But where is what I started for,
so long ago?
And why is it yet unfound?)

IN PROSE, LANGUAGE WAS BECOMING EVEN MORE DIRECT, CONVEYING MEANING *SIMPLY* AND *QUICKLY,* MORE LIKE *PICTURES.*

"MEANING" WAS NOT *ABANDONED* BY *ANY MEANS,* BUT AUTHORS WERE DEFINITELY MOVING *LEFT*--

W

-- AND HEADED FOR A *COLLISION!*

RESEMBLANCE

MEANING

DADA POSTER FOR THE PLAY
"THE BEARDED HEART"

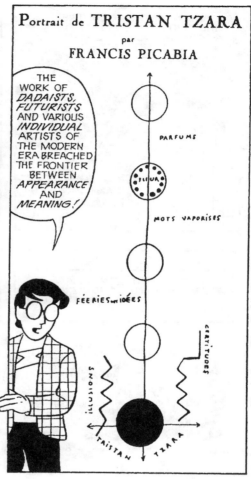

Portrait de TRISTAN TZARA
par
FRANCIS PICABIA

THE WORK OF *DADAISTS, FUTURISTS* AND VARIOUS *INDIVIDUAL* ARTISTS OF THE MODERN ERA BREACHED THE FRONTIER BETWEEN *APPEARANCE* AND *MEANING!*

FACSIMILE OF "ORIENTAL SWEETNESS" (1938) BY PAUL KLEE.

PAINTINGS INCREASINGLY TOOK ON *SYMBOLIC,* EVEN *CALLIGRAPHIC,* MEANINGS...

WHILE SOME ARTISTS ADDRESSED THE IRONIES OF WORDS AND PICTURES *HEAD-ON!*

AND IN *POPULAR* CULTURE THE TWO FORMS COLLIDED *AGAIN AND AGAIN* WITHOUT ANY PRETENSES OF *"HIGH"* ART.

NOWHERE IS THIS COLLISION MORE THOROUGHLY EXPLORED THAN THE MODERN COMIC. AND IT'S NOT A RECENT OBSESSION.

LET'S GO BACK TO THE EARLY 1800's BEFORE ANY OF THIS HAPPENED, WHEN WORDS AND PICTURES HAD DRIFTED AS FAR APART AS *POSSIBLE.*

UP TO THAT POINT, *EUROPEAN BROADSHEETS* HAD OFFERED *REMINDERS* OF WHAT WORDS AND PICTURES COULD DO WHEN COMBINED.

BUT AGAIN IT WAS *RODOLPHE TÖPFFER* WHO FORESAW THEIR *INTERDEPENDENCY* AND BROUGHT THE FAMILY *BACK TOGETHER* AT LAST.

M. CRÉPIN ADVERTISES FOR A TUTOR, AND MANY APPLY FOR THE JOB.

TRANSLATION BY E. WIESE.

I'M SURE THAT THESE IDEAS WERE THE *FURTHEST THING* FROM TÖPFFER'S MIND WHEN HE PUT *PEN TO PAPER*--

--BUT THE FACT THAT THE MODERN COMIC WAS BORN JUST AS ART AND WRITING WERE PREPARING TO CHANGE DIRECTION IS AT LEAST *INTRIGUING.*

AND PERHAPS THIS COMMON THREAD OF *UNIFICATION* DID GROW OUT OF A *SHARED INSTINCT* OF THE DAY...

...AN INSTINCT WHICH SAID THAT WE HAD REACHED THE END OF A *LONG JOURNEY* AND THAT IT WAS TIME AT LAST TO *HEAD FOR HOME.*

* NOT AS MUCH AS WE LIKE TO *THINK* IT HAS, ANYWAY.

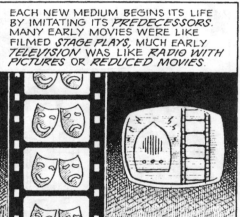

WORDS AND PICTURES IN COMBINATION MAY NOT BE MY *DEFINITION* OF COMICS, BUT THE COMBINATION HAS HAD *TREMENDOUS INFLUENCE* ON ITS *GROWTH.*

com·ics (kom'iks)**n.** p... ... form, used with a singula... ... Juxtaposed pictorial ... ...er images in deliberate ... ...ence, intended to convo... ... and/or to prod... ... response in th... ... **2.** Superheroes... costumes, fighti... villains who want ... ...he world in violent se... ...use...

A HUGE RANGE OF HUMAN EXPERIENCES CAN BE *PORTRAYED* IN COMICS THROUGH EITHER WORDS OR PICTURES.

AS A RESULT--AND DESPITE ITS MANY *OTHER* POTENTIAL USES -- COMICS HAVE BECOME *FIRMLY IDENTIFIED* WITH THE ART OF *STORYTELLING.*

AND *INDEED,* WORDS AND PICTURES HAVE *GREAT* POWERS TO TELL STORIES WHEN CREATORS FULLY EXPLOIT THEM *BOTH.*

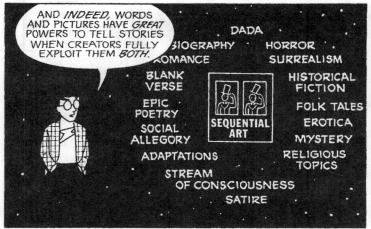

DADA

BIOGRAPHY

HORROR

ROMANCE

SURREALISM

BLANK VERSE

HISTORICAL FICTION

EPIC POETRY

FOLK TALES

SOCIAL ALLEGORY

SEQUENTIAL ART

EROTICA

MYSTERY

ADAPTATIONS

RELIGIOUS TOPICS

STREAM OF CONSCIOUSNESS

SATIRE

AND SO FAR, WE'VE ONLY SEEN THE *TIP OF THE ICEBERG!*

AS CHILDREN, WE "SHOW AND TELL" *INTERCHANGEABLY,* WORDS AND IMAGES COMBINING TO TRANSMIT A *CONNECTED SERIES OF IDEAS.*

IT'S GOT ONE OF *THESE* THINGS

THE *DIFFERENT WAYS* IN WHICH WORDS AND PICTURES CAN *COMBINE* IN COMICS IS VIRTUALLY *UNLIMITED.*

BUT LET'S TRY TO BREAK IT DOWN INTO SOME *DISTINCT CATEGORIES.*

PERHAPS THE MOST *COMMON* TYPE OF WORD/PICTURE COMBINATION IS THE *INTER-DEPENDENT*, WHERE WORDS AND PICTURES GO *HAND IN HAND* TO CONVEY AN IDEA THAT NEITHER COULD CONVEY *ALONE*.

MEANWHILE...

DID ANYONE *SEE* YOU?

THIS IS ALL I NEED TO *STOP* HIM!

I ASK YOU, DOES THIS GUY LOOK LIKE A *C.E.O.* TO *YOU?*?

"AND JUST *GUESS* WHO DROVE UP IN BOB'S TRUCK AN HOUR LATER!"

HEY, MARGE!

OH, MY *GOD!*

HE'S LYING.

UH-HUH.

"AFTER COLLEGE, I PURSUED A CAREER IN *HIGH FINANCE*."

HURRY UP, WILLYA?!

INTERDEPENDENT COMBINATIONS AREN'T ALWAYS AN *EQUAL BALANCE* THOUGH AND MAY FALL *ANYWHERE* ON A SCALE BETWEEN TYPES ONE AND TWO.

GENERALLY SPEAKING, THE MORE IS SAID WITH *WORDS*, THE MORE THE PICTURES CAN BE FREED TO GO EXPLORING AND *VICE VERSA*.

$$\frac{P}{W}$$

$$\frac{W}{P}$$

IN COMICS AT ITS *BEST,* WORDS AND PICTURES ARE LIKE *PARTNERS* IN A *DANCE* AND EACH ONE TAKES TURNS *LEADING.*

WHEN *BOTH* PARTNERS TRY TO LEAD, THE COMPETITION CAN *SUBVERT* THE OVERALL GOALS...

YOW!

...THOUGH A LITTLE *PLAYFUL* *COMPETITION* CAN SOMETIMES PRODUCE *ENJOYABLE RESULTS.*

BUT WHEN THESE PARTNERS EACH *KNOW* THEIR ROLES --

--AND *SUPPORT* EACH OTHER'S *STRENGTHS*--

--COMICS CAN MATCH *ANY* OF THE ART FORMS IT DRAWS SO MUCH OF ITS STRENGTH FROM.

WHEN *PICTURES* CARRY THE WEIGHT OF CLARITY IN A SCENE, THEY FREE WORDS TO EXPLORE A WIDER AREA.

LET'S SAY I SHOW YOU A WOMAN WALKING ACROSS THE STREET IN THE RAIN, BUYING A PINT OF ICE CREAM AND EATING IT IN HER APARTMENT--

--ALL IN *PICTURES.*

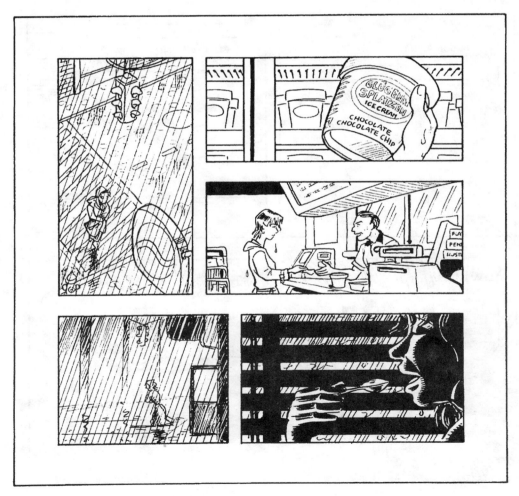

When a scene shows you all you *"NEED"* to know, like *THIS* one, the latitude for *SCRIPTING* grows *ENORMOUSLY.*

I MAY BE ALONE LIKE THIS FOR A VERY LONG TIME.

IT COULD BECOME AN *INTERNAL MONOLOGUE.*

(INTERDEPENDENT)

PERHAPS SOMETHING WILDLY *INCONGRUOUS*

"MISSION CONTROL, MISSION CONTROL, DO YOU READ ME?"

(PARALLEL)

MAYBE IT'S ALL JUST A BIG *ADVERTISEMENT!*

YOU'LL *Love* THE TASTE!

(INTERDEPENDENT)

OR A CHANCE TO RUMINATE ON *BROADER TOPICS.*

THIS IS THE WAY THE WORLD ENDS...

THIS IS THE WAY THE WORLD ENDS...

(INTERDEPENDENT)

ON THE *OTHER* HAND, IF THE **WORDS** LOCK IN THE *"MEANING"* OF A SEQUENCE, THEN THE *PICTURES* CAN REALLY TAKE OFF.

P W

SAME SCENE NOW, BUT THIS TIME ALL IN *WORDS!*

I CROSSED THE STREET TO THE CONVENIENCE STORE. *THE RAIN SOAKED INTO MY BOOTS.*

I FOUND THE LAST PINT OF CHOCOLATE CHOCOLATE CHIP IN THE FREEZER.

THE CLERK TRIED TO PICK ME UP. I SAID *NO THANKS.* HE GAVE ME THIS CREEPY LOOK...

I WENT BACK TO THE APARTMENT--

--AND FINISHED IT ALL IN AN HOUR.

ALONE AT LAST.

NOW, ONE COULD JUST *COMBINE* THE *PICTURES* FROM PAGE 157 WITH THE WORDS FROM PAGE 159 --

--BUT WHAT ARE SOME *OTHER* OPTIONS?

IF THE ARTIST WANTS TO, HE/SHE CAN NOW SHOW ONLY *FRAGMENTS* OF A SCENE.

(WORD SPECIFIC)

OR MOVE TOWARD GREATER LEVELS OF *ABSTRACTION* OR *EXPRESSION*.

THE CLERK TRIED TO PICK ME UP. I SAID *NO THANKS.* HE GAVE ME THIS CREEPY LOOK...

(AMPLIFICATION)

PERHAPS THE ARTIST CAN GIVE US SOME IMPORTANT *EMOTIONAL* INFORMATION.

I WENT BACK TO THE APARTMENT--

(INTERDEPENDENT)

OR SHIFT AHEAD OR BACKWARDS IN TIME.

--AND FINISHED IT ALL IN AN HOUR.

ALONE AT LAST.

(WORD SPECIFIC)

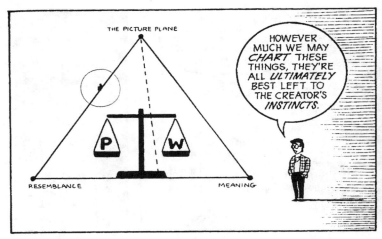

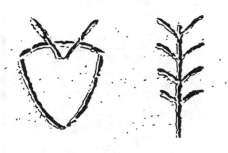

FROM SILENCE TO WORDS: WRITING AS STRUGGLE

Min-zhan Lu

> Imagine that you enter a parlor. You come late. When you arrive, others have long preceded you, and they are engaged in a heated discussion. . . .You listen for a while, until you decide that you have caught the tenor of the argument; then you put in your oar. Someone answers; you answer him; another comes to your defense; another aligns himself against you, to either the embarrassment or gratification of your opponent, depending upon the quality of your ally's assistance. However, the discussion is interminable. The hour grows late, you must depart. And you do depart, with the discussion still vigorously in progress.
>
> —Kenneth Burke, *The Philosophy of Literary Form*

> Men are not built in silence, but in word, in work, in action-reflection.
>
> —Paulo Freire, *Pedagogy of the Oppressed*

My mother withdrew into silence two months before she died. A few nights before she fell silent, she told me she regretted the way she had raised me and my sisters. I knew she was referring to the way we had been brought up in the midst of two conflicting worlds—the world of home, dominated by the ideology of the Western humanistic tradition, and the world of a society dominated by Mao Tse-tung's Marxism. My mother had devoted her life to our education, an education she knew had made us suffer political persecution during the Cultural Revolution. I wanted to find a way to convince her that, in spite of the persecution, I had benefited from the education she had worked so hard to give me. But I was silent. My understanding of my education was so dominated by memories of confusion and frustration that I was unable to reflect on what I could have gained from it.

This paper is my attempt to fill up that silence with words, words I didn't have then, words that I have since come to by reflecting on my earlier experience as a student in China and on my recent experience as a composition teacher in the United States. For in spite of the frustration and confusion I experienced growing up caught between two conflicting worlds, the conflict ultimately helped me to grow as a reader and writer. Constantly having to switch back and forth between the discourse of home and that of school made me sensitive and self-conscious about the struggle I experienced every time I tried to read, write, or think in either discourse. Eventually, it led me to search for constructive uses for such struggle.

From early childhood, I had identified the differences between home and the outside world by the different languages I used in each. My parents had wanted my sisters and me to get the best education they could conceive of—Cambridge. They had hired a live-in tutor, a Scot, to make us bilingual. I learned to speak English with my parents, my tutor, and my sisters. I was allowed to speak Shanghai dialect only with the servants. When I was four (the year after the Communist Revolution of 1949), my parents sent me to a local private school where I learned to speak, read, and write in a new language—Standard Chinese, the official written language of New China.

In those days I moved from home to school, from English to Standard Chinese to Shanghai dialect, with no apparent friction. I spoke each language with those who spoke the language. All seemed quite "natural"—servants spoke only Shanghai dialect because they were servants; teachers spoke Standard Chinese because they were teachers; languages had different words because they were different languages. I thought of English as my family language, comparable to the many strange dialects I didn't speak but had often heard some of my classmates speak with their families. While I was happy to have a special family language, until second grade I didn't feel that my family language was any different than some of my classmates' family dialects.

My second grade homeroom teacher was a young graduate from a missionary school. When she found out I spoke English, she began to practice her English on me. One day she used English when asking me to run an errand for her. As I turned to close the door behind me, I noticed the puzzled faces of my classmates. I had the same sensation I had often experienced when some stranger in a crowd would turn on hearing me speak English. I was more intensely pleased on this occasion, however, because suddenly I felt that my family language had been singled out from the family languages of my classmates. Since we were not allowed to speak any dialect other than Standard Chinese in the classroom, having my teacher speak English to me in class made English an official language of the classroom. I began to take pride in my ability to speak it.

This incident confirmed in my mind what my parents had always told me about the importance of English to one's life. Time and again they had told me of how my paternal grandfather, who was well versed in classic Chinese, kept losing good-paying jobs because he couldn't speak English. My grandmother reminisced constantly about how she had slaved and saved to send my father to a first-rate missionary school. And we were made to understand that it was my father's fluent English that had opened the door to his success. Even though my family had always stressed the importance of English for my future, I used to complain bitterly about the extra English lessons we had to take after school. It was only after my homeroom teacher had "sanctified" English that I began to connect English with my education. I became a much more eager student in my tutorials.

What I learned from my tutorials seemed to enhance and reinforce what I was learning in my classroom. In those days each word had one meaning. One day I would be making a sentence at school: "The national flag of China is red." The next day I would recite at home, "My love is like a red, red rose." There seemed to be an agreement between the Chinese "red" and the English "red," and both corresponded to the patch of color printed next to the word. "Love" was my love for my mother at home and my love for my "motherland" at school; both "loves" meant how I felt about my mother. Having two loads of homework forced me to develop a quick memory for words and a sensitivity to form and style. What I learned in one language carried over to the other. I made sentences such as, "I saw a red, red rose among the green leaves," with both the English lyric and the classic Chinese lyric—red flower among green leaves—running through my mind, and I was praised by both teacher and tutor for being a good student.

Although my elementary schooling took place during the fifties, I was almost oblivious to the great political and social changes happening around me. Years later, I read in my history and political philosophy textbooks that the fifties were a time when "China was making a transition from a semi-feudal, semi-capitalist, and semi-colonial country into a socialist country," a period in which "the Proletarians were breaking into the educational territory dominated by Bourgeois Intellectuals." While people all over the country were being officially classified into Proletarians, Petty-bourgeois, National-bourgeois, Poor-peasants, and Intellectuals, and were trying to adjust to their new social identities, my parents were allowed to continue the upper middle-class life they had established before the 1949 Revolution because of my father's affiliation with British firms. I had always felt that my family was different from the families of my classmates, but I didn't perceive society's view of my family until the summer vacation before I entered high school.

First, my aunt was caught by her colleagues talking to her husband over the phone in English. Because of it, she was criticized and almost labeled a Rightist. (This was the year of the Anti-Rightist movement, a movement in which the Intellectuals became the target of the "socialist class-struggle.") I had heard others telling my mother that she was foolish to teach us English when Russian had replaced English as the "official" foreign language. I had also learned at school that the American and British Imperialists were the arch-enemies of New China. Yet I had made no connection between the arch-enemies and the English our family spoke. What happened to my aunt forced the connection on me. I began to see my parents' choice of a family language as an anti-Revolutionary act and was alarmed that I had participated in such an act. From then on, I took care not to use English outside home and to conceal my knowledge of English from my new classmates.

Certain words began to play important roles in my new life at the junior high. On the first day of school, we were handed forms to fill out with our parents' class, job, and income. Being one of the few people not employed by the government, my father had never been officially classified. Since he was a medical doctor, he told me to put him down as an Intellectual. My homeroom teacher called me into the office a couple of days afterwards and told me that my father couldn't be an Intellectual if his income far exceeded that of a Capitalist. He also told me that since my father worked for Foreign Imperialists, my father should be classified as an Imperialist Lackey. The teacher looked nonplussed when I told him that my father couldn't be an Imperialist Lackey because he was a medical doctor. But I could tell from the way he took notes on my form that my father's job had put me in an unfavorable position in his eyes.

The Standard Chinese term "class" was not a new word for me. Since first grade, I had been taught sentences such as, "The Working class are the masters of New China." I had always known that it was good to be a worker, but until then, I had never felt threatened for not being one. That fall, "class" began to take on a new meaning for me. I noticed a group of Working-class students and teachers at school. I was made to understand that because of my class background, I was excluded from that group.

Another word that became important was "consciousness." One of the slogans posted in the school building read, "Turn our students into future Proletarians with socialist consciousness and education!" For several weeks we studied this slogan in our political philosophy course, a subject I had never had in elementary school. I still remember the definition of "socialist consciousness" that we were repeatedly tested on through the years: "Socialist consciousness is a person's political soul. It is the consciousness of the Proletarians represented by Marxist Mao Tse-tung thought. It takes expression in one's action, language, and lifestyle. It is the task of every Chinese student to grow up into a Proletarian with a socialist consciousness so that he can serve the people and the motherland." To make the abstract concept accessible to us, our teacher pointed out that the immediate task for students from Working-class families was to strengthen their socialist consciousnesses. For those of us who were from other class backgrounds, the task was to turn ourselves into Workers with socialist consciousnesses. The teacher never explained exactly how we were supposed to "turn" into Workers. Instead, we were given samples of the ritualistic annual plans we had to write at the beginning of each term. In these plans, we performed "self-criticism" on our consciousnesses and made vows to turn ourselves into Workers with socialist consciousnesses. The teacher's division between those who did and those who didn't have a socialist consciousness led me to reify the notion of "consciousness" into a thing one possesses. I equated this intangible "thing" with a concrete way of dressing, speaking, and writing. For instance, I never doubted that my political philosophy teacher had a socialist consciousness because she was from a steelworker's family (she announced this the first day of class) and was a party member who wore grey cadre suits and talked like a philosophy textbook. I noticed other things about her. She had beautiful eyes and spoke Standard Chinese with such a pure accent that I thought she should be a film star. But I was embarrassed that I had noticed things that ought not to have been associated with her. I blamed my observation on my Bourgeois consciousness.

At the same time, the way reading and writing were taught through memorization and imitation also encouraged me to reduce concepts and ideas to simple definitions. In literature and political philosophy classes, we were taught a large number of quotations from Marx, Lenin, and Mao Tse-tung. Each concept that appeared in these quotations came with a definition. We were required to memorize the definitions of the words along with the quotations. Every time I memorized a definition, I felt I had learned a word: "The national red flag symbolizes the blood shed by Revolutionary ancestors for our socialist cause"; "New China rises like a red sun over the eastern horizon." As I memorized these sentences, I reduced their metaphors to dictionary meanings: "red" meant "Revolution" and "red sun" meant "New China" in the "language" of the Working class. I learned mechanically but eagerly. I soon became quite fluent in this new language.

As school began to define me as a political subject, my parents tried to build up my resistance to the "communist poisoning" by exposing me to the "great books"—novels by Charles Dickens, Nathaniel Hawthorne, Emily Brontë, Jane Austen, and writers from around the turn of the century. My parents implied that these writers represented how I, their child, should read and write. My parents replaced the word "Bourgeois" with the word "cultured." They reminded me that I was in school only to learn math and science. I needed to pass the other courses to stay in school, but I was not to let the "Red doctrines" corrupt my mind. Gone were the days when I could innocently write, "I saw the red, red rose among the green leaves," collapsing, as I did, English and Chinese cultural traditions. "Red" came to mean Revolution at school, "the Commies" at home, and adultery in *The Scarlet Letter.* Since I took these symbols and metaphors as meanings natural to people of the same class, I abandoned my earlier definitions of English and Standard Chinese as the language of home and the language of school. I now defined English as the language of the Bourgeois and Standard Chinese as the language of the Working class. I thought of the language of the Working class as someone else's language and the language of the Bourgeois as my language. But I also believed that, although the language of the Bourgeois was my real language, I could and would adopt the language of the Working class when I was at school. I began to put on and take off my Working class language in the same way I put on and took off my school clothes to avoid being criticized for wearing Bourgeois clothes.

In my literature classes, I learned the Working-class formula for reading. Each work in the textbook had a short "Author's Biography": "X X X, born in 19—in the province of X X, is from a Worker's family. He joined the Revolution in 19—. He is a Revolutionary realist with a passionate love for the Party and Chinese Revolution. His work expresses the thoughts and emotions of the masses and sings praise to the prosperous socialist construction on all fronts of China." The teacher used the "Author's Biography" as a yardstick to measure the texts. We were taught to locate details in the texts that illustrated these summaries, such as words that expressed Workers' thoughts and emotions or events that illustrated the Workers' lives.

I learned a formula for Working-class writing in the composition classes. We were given sample essays and told to imitate them. The theme was always about how the collective taught the individual a lesson. I would write papers about labor-learning experiences or school-cleaning days, depending on the occasion of the collective activity closest to the assignment. To make each paper look different, I dressed it up with details about the date, the weather, the environment, or the appearance of the Master-worker who had taught me "the lesson." But as I became more and more fluent in the generic voice of the Working-class Student, I also became more and more self-conscious about the language we used at home.

For instance, in senior high we began to have English classes ("to study English for the Revolution," as the slogan on the cover of the textbook said), and I was given my first Chinese-English dictionary. There I discovered the English version of the term "class-struggle." (The Chinese characters for a school "class" and for a social "class" are different.) I had often used the English word "class" at home in sentences such as, "So and so has class," but I had not connected this sense of "class" with "class-struggle." Once the connection was made, I heard a second layer of meaning every time someone at home said a person had "class." The expression began to mean the person had the style and sophistication characteristic of the bourgeoisie. The word lost its innocence. I was uneasy about hearing that second layer of meaning because I was sure my parents did not hear the word that way. I felt that therefore I should not be hearing it that way either. Hearing the second layer of meaning made me wonder if I was losing my English.

My suspicion deepened when I noticed myself unconsciously merging and switching between the "reading" of home and the "reading" of school. Once I had to write a report on *The Revolutionary Family*, a book about an illiterate woman's awakening and growth as a Revolutionary through the deaths of her husband and all her children for the cause of the Revolution. In one scene the woman deliberated over whether or not she should encourage her youngest son to join the Revolution. Her memory of her husband's death made her afraid to encourage her son. Yet she also remembered her earlier married life and the first time her husband tried to explain the meaning of the Revolution to her. These memories made her feel she should encourage her son to continue the cause his father had begun.

I was moved by this scene. "Moved" was a word my mother and big sisters used a lot when we discussed books. Our favorite moments in novels were moments of what I would now call internal conflict, moments which we said "moved" us. I remember that we were "moved" by Jane Eyre when she was torn between her sense of ethics, which compelled her to leave the man she loved, and her impulse to stay with the only man who had ever loved her. We were also moved by Agnes in *David Copperfield* because of the way she restrained her love for David so that he could live happily with the woman he loved. My standard method of doing a book report was to model it on the review by the Publishing Bureau and to dress it up with detailed quotations from the book. The review of *The Revolutionary Family* emphasized the woman's Revolutionary spirit. I decided to use the scene that had moved me to illustrate this point. I wrote the report the night before it was due. When I had finished, I realized I couldn't possibly hand it in. Instead of illustrating her Revolutionary spirit, I had dwelled on her internal conflict, which could be seen as a moment of weak sentimentality that I should never have emphasized in a Revolutionary heroine. I wrote another report, taking care to illustrate the grandeur of her Revolutionary spirit by expanding on a quotation in which she decided that if the life of her son could change the lives of millions of sons, she should not begrudge his life for the cause of Revolution. I handed in my second version but kept the first in my desk.

I never showed it to anyone. I could never show it to people outside my family, because it had deviated so much from the reading enacted by the jacket review. Neither could I show it to my mother or sisters, because I was ashamed to have been so moved by such a "Revolutionary" book. My parents would have been shocked to learn that I could like such a book in the same way they liked Dickens. Writing this book report increased my fear that I was losing the command over both the "language of home" and the "language of school" that I had worked so hard to gain. I tried to remind myself that, if I could still tell when my reading or writing sounded incorrect, then I had retained my command over both languages. Yet I could no longer be confident of my command over either language because I had discovered that when I was not careful—or even when I was—my reading and writing often surprised me with its impurity. To prevent such impurity, I became very suspicious of my thoughts when I read or wrote. I was always asking myself why I was using this word, how I was using it, always afraid that I wasn't reading or writing correctly. What confused and frustrated me most was that I could not figure out why I was no longer able to read or write correctly without such painful deliberation.

I continued to read only because reading allowed me to keep my thoughts and confusion private. I hoped that somehow, if I watched myself carefully, I would figure out from the way I read whether I had really mastered the "languages." But writing became a dreadful chore. When I tried to keep a diary, I was so afraid that the voice of school might slip in that I could only list my daily activities. When I wrote for school, I worried that my Bourgeois sensibilities would betray me.

The more suspicious I became about the way I read and wrote, the more guilty I felt for losing the spontaneity with which I had learned to "use" these "languages." Writing the book report made me feel that my reading and writing in the "language" of either home or school could not be free of the interference of the other. But I was unable to acknowledge, grasp, or grapple with what I was experiencing, for both my parents and my teachers had suggested that, if I were a good student, such interference would and should not take place. I assumed that once I had "acquired" a discourse, I could simply switch it on and off every time I read and wrote as I would some electronic tool. Furthermore, I expected my readings and writings to come out in their correct forms whenever I switched the proper discourse on. I still regarded the discourse of home as natural and the discourse of school as alien, but I never had doubted before that I could acquire both and switch them on and off according to the occasion.

When my experience in writing conflicted with what I thought should happen when I used each discourse, I rejected my experience because it contradicted what my parents and teachers had taught me. I shied away from writing to avoid what I assumed I should not experience. But trying to avoid what should not happen did not keep it from recurring whenever I had to write. Eventually my confusion and frustration over these recurring experiences compelled me to search for an explanation: how and why had I failed to learn what my parents and teachers had worked so hard to teach me?

I now think of the internal scene for my reading and writing about *The Revolutionary Family* as a heated discussion between myself, the voices of home, and those of school. The review on the back of the book, the sample student papers I came across in my composition classes, my philosophy teacher—these I heard as voices of one group. My parents and my home readings were the voices of an opposing group. But the conversation between these opposing voices in the internal scene of my writing was not as polite and respectful as the parlor scene Kenneth Burke has portrayed (see epigraph). Rather, these voices struggled to dominate the discussion, constantly incorporating, dismissing, or suppressing the arguments of each other, like the battles between the hegemonic and counter-hegemonic forces described in Raymond Williams' *Marxism and Literature* (108–14).

When I read *The Revolutionary Family* and wrote the first version of my report, I began with a quotation from the review. The voices of both home and school answered, clamoring to be heard. I tried to listen to one group and turn a deaf ear to the other. Both persisted. I negotiated my way through these conflicting voices, now agreeing with one, now agreeing with the other. I formed a reading out of my interaction with both. Yet I was afraid to have done so because both home and school had implied that I should speak in unison with only one of these groups and stand away from the discussion rather than participate in it.

My teachers and parents had persistently called my attention to the intensity of the discussion taking place on the external social scene. The story of my grandfather's failure and my father's success had from my early childhood made me aware of the conflict between Western and traditional Chinese cultures. My political education at school added another dimension to the conflict; the war of Marxist-Maoism against them both. Yet when my parents and teachers called my attention to the conflict, they stressed the anxiety of having to live through China's transformation from a semi-feudal, semi-capitalist, and semi-colonial society to a socialist one. Acquiring the discourse of the dominant group was, to them, a means of seeking alliance with that group and thus of surviving the whirlpool of cultural currents around them. As a result, they modeled their pedagogical practices on this utilitarian view of language. Being the eager student, I adopted this view of language as a tool for survival. It came to dominate my understanding of the discussion on the social and historical scene and to restrict my ability to participate in that discussion.

To begin with, the metaphor of language as a tool for survival led me to be passive in my use of discourse, to be a bystander in the discussion. In Burke's "parlor," everyone is involved in the discussion. As it goes on through history, what we call "communal discourses"—arguments specific to particular political, social, economic, ethnic, sexual, and family groups—form, re-form and transform. To use a discourse in such a scene is to participate in the argument and to contribute to the formation of the discourse. But when I was growing up, I could not take on the burden of such an active role in the discussion. For both home and school presented the existent conventions of the discourse each taught me as absolute laws for my action. They turned verbal action into a tool, a set of conventions produced and shaped prior to and outside of my own verbal acts. Because I saw language as a tool, I separated the process of producing the tool from the process of using it. The tool was made by someone else and was then acquired and used by me. How the others made it before I acquired it determined and guaranteed what it produced when I used it. I imagined that the more experienced and powerful members of the community were the ones responsible for making the tool. They were the ones who participated in the discussion and fought with opponents. When I used what they made, their labor and accomplishments would ensure the quality of my reading and writing. By using it, I could survive the heated discussion. When my immediate experience in writing the book report suggested that knowing the conventions of school did not guarantee the form and content of my report, when it suggested that I had to write the report with the work and responsibility I had assigned to those who wrote book reviews in the Publishing bureau, I thought I had lost the tool I had earlier acquired.

Another reason I could not take up an active role in the argument was that my parents and teachers contrived to provide a scene free of conflict for practicing my various languages. It was as if their experience had made them aware of the conflict between their discourse and other discourses and of the struggle involved in reproducing the conventions of any discourse on a scene where more than one discourse exists. They seemed convinced that such conflict and struggle would overwhelm someone still learning the discourse. Home and school each contrived a purified space where only one discourse was spoken and heard. In their choice of textbooks, in the way they spoke, and in the way they required me to speak, each jealously silenced any voice that threatened to break the unison of the scene. The homogeneity of home and of school implied that only one discourse could and should be relevant in each place. It led me to believe I should leave behind, turn a deaf ear to, or forget the discourse of the other when I crossed the boundary dividing them. I expected myself to set down one discourse whenever I took up another just as I would take off or put on a particular set of clothes for school or home.

Despite my parents' and teachers' attempts to keep home and school discrete, the internal conflict between the two discourses continued whenever I read or wrote. Although I tried to suppress the voice of one discourse in the name of the other, having to speak aloud in the voice I had just silenced each time I crossed the boundary kept both voices active in my mind. Every "I think . . ." from the voice of home or school brought forth a "However . . ." or a "But. . ." from the voice of the opponents. To identify with the voice of home or school, I had to negotiate through the conflicting voices of both by restating, taking back, qualifying my thoughts. I was unconsciously doing so when I did my book report. But I could not use the interaction comfortably and constructively. Both my parents and my teachers had implied that my job was to prevent that interaction from happening. My sense of having failed to accomplish what they had taught silenced me.

To use the interaction between the discourses of home and school constructively, I would have to have seen reading or writing as a process in which I worked my way towards a stance through a dialectical process of identification and division. To identify with an ally, I would have to have grasped the distance between where he or she stood and where I was positioning myself. In taking a stance against an opponent, I would have to have grasped where my stance identified with the stance of my allies. Teetering along the "wavering line of pressure and counter-pressure" from both allies and opponents, I might have worked my way towards a stance of my own (Burke, *A Rhetoric of Motives*, 23). Moreover, I would have to have understood that the voices in my mind, like the participants in the parlor scene, were in constant flux. As I came into contact with new and different groups of people or read different books, voices entered and left. Each time I read or wrote, the stance I negotiated out of these voices would always be at some distance from the stances I worked out in my previous and my later readings or writings.

I could not conceive such a form of action for myself because I saw reading and writing as an expression of an established stance. In delineating the conventions of a discourse, my parents and teachers had synthesized the stance they saw as typical for a representative member of the community. Burke calls this the stance of a "god" or the "prototype"; Williams calls it the "official" or "possible" stance of the community. Through the metaphor of the survival tool, my parents and teachers had led me to assume I could automatically reproduce the official stance of the discourse I used. Therefore, when I did my book report on *The Revolutionary Family*, I expected my knowledge of the official stance set by the book review to ensure the actual stance of my report. As it happened, I began by trying to take the official stance of the review. Other voices interrupted. I answered back. In the process, I worked out a stance approximate but not identical to the official stance I began with. Yet the experience of having to labor to realize my knowledge of the official stance or to prevent myself from wandering away from it frustrated and confused me. For even though I had been actually reading and writing in a Burkean scene, I was afraid to participate actively in the discussion. I assumed it was my role to survive by staying out of it.

Not long ago, my daughter told me that it bothered her to hear her friend "talk wrong." Having come to the United States from China with little English, my daughter has become sensitive to the way English, as spoken by her teachers, operates. As a result, she has amazed her teachers with her success in picking up the language and in adapting to life at school. Her concern to speak the English taught in the classroom "correctly" makes her uncomfortable when she hears people using "ain't" or double negatives, which her teacher considers "improper." I see in her the me that had eagerly learned and used the discourse of the Working class at school. Yet while I was torn between the two conflicting worlds of school and home, she moves with seeming ease from the conversations she hears over the dinner table to her teacher's words in the classroom. My husband and I are proud of the good work she does at school. We are glad she is spared the kinds of conflict between home and school I experienced at her age. Yet as we watch her becoming more and more fluent in the language of the classroom, we wonder if, by enabling her to "survive" school, her very fluency will silence her when the scene of her reading and writing expands beyond that of the composition classroom.

For when I listen to my daughter, to students, and to some composition teachers talking about the teaching and learning of writing, I am often alarmed by the degree to which the metaphor of a survival tool dominates their understanding of language as it once dominated my own. I am especially concerned with the way some composition classes focus on turning the classroom into a monological scene for the students' reading and writing. Most of our students live in a world similar to my daughter's, somewhere between the purified world of the classroom and the complex world of my adolescence. When composition classes encourage these students to ignore those voices that seem irrelevant to the purified world of the classroom, most students are often able to do so without much struggle. Some of them are so adept at doing it that the whole process has for them become automatic.

However, beyond the classroom and beyond the limited range of these students' immediate lives lies a much more complex and dynamic social and historical scene. To help these students become actors in such a scene, perhaps we need to call their attention to voices that may seem irrelevant to the discourse we teach rather than encourage them to shut them out. For example, we might intentionally complicate the classroom scene by bringing into it discourses that stand at varying distances from the one we teach. We might encourage students to explore ways of practicing the conventions of the discourse they are learning by negotiating through these conflicting voices. We could also encourage them to see themselves as responsible for forming or transforming as well as preserving the discourse they are learning.

As I think about what we might do to complicate the external and internal scenes of our students' writing, I hear my parents and teachers saying: "Not now. Keep them from the wrangle of the marketplace until they have acquired the discourse and are skilled at using it." And I answer: "Don't teach them to 'survive' the whirlpool of crosscurrents by avoiding it. Use the classroom to moderate the currents. Moderate the currents, but teach them from the beginning to struggle." When I think of the ways in which the teaching of reading and writing as classroom activities can frustrate the development of students, I am almost grateful for the overwhelming complexity of the circumstances in which I grew up. For it was this complexity that kept me from losing sight of the effort and choice involved in reading or writing with and through a discourse.

References

Burke, Kenneth. *The Philosophy of Literary Form: Studies in Symbolic Action.* 2nd ed. Baton Rouge: Louisiana State UP, 1967.

_____. *A Rhetoric of Motives.* Berkeley: U of California P, 1969.

Freire, Paulo. *Pedagogy of the Oppressed.* Trans. M. B. Ramos. New York: Continuum, 1970.

Williams, Raymond. *Marxism and Literature.* New York: Oxford UP, 1977.

from THE WAY TO RAINY MOUNTAIN

N. Scott Momaday

I

You know, everything had to begin, and this is how it was: the Kiowas came one by one into the world through a hollow log. They were many more than now, but not all of them got out. There was a woman whose body was swollen up with child, and she got stuck in the log. After that, no one could get through, and that is why the Kiowas are a small tribe in number. They looked all around and saw the world. It made them glad to see so many things. They called themselves *Kwuda,* "coming out."

They called themselves Kwuda *and later* Tepda, *both of which mean "coming out." And later still they took the name Gaigwu, a name which can be taken to indicate something of which the two halves differ from each other in appearance. It was once a custom among Kiowa warriors that they cut their hair on the right side of the head only and on a line level with the lobe of the ear, while on the left they let the hair grow long and wore it in a thick braid wrapped in otter skin. "Kiowa" is indicated in sign language by holding the hand palm up and slightly cupped to the right side of the head and rotating it back and forth from the wrist. "Kiowa" is thought to derive from the softened Comanche form of* Gaigwu.

I remember coming out upon the northern Great Plains in the late spring. There were meadows of blue and yellow wildflowers on the slopes, and I could see the still, sunlit plain below, reaching away out of sight. At first there is no discrimination in the eye, nothing but the land itself, whole and impenetrable. But then smallest things begin to stand out of the depths—herds and rivers and groves—and each of these has perfect being in terms of distance and of silence and of age. Yes, I thought, now I see the earth as it really is; never again will I see things as I saw them yesterday or the day before.

III

Before there were horses the Kiowas had need of dogs. That was a long time ago, when dogs could talk. There was a man who lived alone; he had been thrown away, and he made his camp here and there on the high ground. Now it was dangerous to be alone, for there were enemies all around. The man spent his arrows hunting food. He had one arrow left, and he shot a bear; but the bear was only wounded and it ran away. The man wondered what to do. Then a dog came up to him and said that many enemies were coming; they were close by and all around. The man could think of no way to save himself. But the dog said: "You know, I have puppies. They are young and weak and they have nothing to eat. If you will take care of my puppies, I will show you how to get away." The dog led the man here and there, around and around, and they came to safety.

A hundred years ago the Comanche Ten Bears remarked upon the great number of horses which the Kiowas owned. "When we first knew you," he said, "you had nothing but dogs and sleds." It was so; the dog is primordial. Perhaps it was dreamed into being.

The principal warrior society of the Kiowas was the Ka-itsenko, *"Real Dogs," and it was made up of ten men only, the ten most brave. Each of these men wore a long ceremonial sash and carried a sacred arrow. In time of battle he must by means of this arrow impale the end of his sash to the earth and stand his ground to the death. Tradition has it that the founder of the* Ka-itsenko *had a dream in which he saw a band of warriors, outfitted after the fashion of the society, being led by a dog. The dog sang the song of the* Ka-itsenko, *then said to the dreamer: "You are a dog; make a noise like a dog and sing a dog song."*

There were always dogs about my grandmother's house. Some of them were nameless and lived a life of their own. They belonged there in a sense that the word "ownership" does not include. The old people paid them scarcely any attention, but they should have been sad, I think, to see them go.

XXI

Mammedaty was the grandson of Guipahgo, and he was well-known on that account. Now and then Mammedaty drove a team and wagon out over the plain. Once, in the early morning, he was on the way to Rainy Mountain. It was summer and the grass was high and meadowlarks were calling all around. You know, the top of the plain is smooth and you can see a long way. There was nothing but the early morning and the land around. Then Mammedaty heard something. Someone whistled to him. He looked up and saw the head of a little boy nearby above the grass. He stopped the horses and got down from the wagon and went to see who was there. There was no one; there was nothing there. He looked for a long time, but there was nothing there.

There is a single photograph of Mammedaty. He is looking past the camera and a little to one side. In his face there is calm and good will, strength and intelligence. His hair is drawn close to the scalp, and his braids are long and wrapped with fur. He wears a kilt, fringed leggings, and beaded moccasins. In his right hand there is a peyote fan. A family characteristic: the veins stand out in his hands, and his hands are small and rather long.

Mammedaty saw four things that were truly remarkable. This head of the child was one, and the tracks of the water beast another. Once, when he walked near the pecan grove, he saw three small alligators on a log. No one had ever seen them before and no one ever saw them again. Finally, there was this: something had always bothered Mammedaty, a small aggravation that was never quite out of mind, like a name on the tip of the tongue. He had always wondered how it is that the mound of earth which a mole makes around the opening of its burrow is so fine. It is nearly as fine as powder, and it seems almost to have been sifted. One day Mammedaty was sitting quietly when a mole came out of the earth. Its cheeks were puffed out as if it had been a squirrel packing nuts. It looked all around for a moment, then blew the fine dark earth out of its mouth. And this it did again and again, until there was a ring of black, powdery earth on the ground. That was a strange and meaningful thing to see. It meant that Mammedaty had got possession of a powerful medicine.

XXIV

East of my grandmother's house, south of the pecan grove, there is buried a woman in a beautiful dress. Mammedaty used to know where she is buried, but now no one knows. If you stand on the front porch of the house and look eastward towards Carnegie, you know that the woman is buried somewhere within the range of your vision. But her grave is unmarked. She was buried in a cabinet, and she wore a beautiful dress. How beautiful it was! It was one of those fine buckskin dresses, and it was decorated with elk's teeth and beadwork. That dress is still there, under the ground.

Aho's high moccasins are made of softest, cream-colored skins. On each instep there is a bright disc of beadwork—an eight-pointed star, red and pale blue on a white field—and there are bands of beadwork at the soles and ankles The flaps of the leggings are wide and richly ornamented with blue and red and green and white and lavender beads.

East of my grandmother's house the sun rises out of the plain. Once in his life a man ought to concentrate his mind upon the remembered earth, I believe. He ought to give himself up to a particular landscape in his experience, to look at it from as many angles as he can, to wonder about it, to dwell upon it. He ought to imagine that he touches it with his hands at every season and listens to the sounds that are made upon it. He ought to imagine the creatures there and all the faintest motions of the wind. He ought to recollect the glare of noon and all the colors of the dawn and dusk.

❧ "MOMMY, WHAT DOES 'NIGGER' MEAN?" ❧

Gloria Naylor

Language is the subject. It is the written form with which I've managed to keep the wolf away from the door and, in diaries, to keep my sanity. In spite of this, I consider the written word inferior to the spoken, and much of the frustration experienced by novelists is the awareness that whatever we manage to capture in even the most transcendent passages falls far short of the richness of life. Dialogue achieves its power in the dynamics of a fleeting moment of sight, sound, smell and touch.

I'm not going to enter the debate here about whether it is language that shapes reality or vice versa. That battle is doomed to be waged whenever we seek intermittent reprieve from the chicken and egg dispute. I will simply take the position that the spoken word, like the written word, amounts to a nonsensical arrangement of sounds letters without a consensus that assigns "meaning." And building from the meanings of what we hear, we order reality. Words themselves are innocuous; it is the consensus that gives them true power.

I remember the first time I heard the word nigger. In my third grade class, our math tests were being passed down the rows, and as I handed the papers to a little boy in back of me, I remarked that once again he had received a much lower mark than I did. He snatched his test from me and spit out that word. Had he called me a nymphomaniac or a necrophiliac, I couldn't have been more puzzled. I didn't know what a nigger was, but I knew that whatever it meant, it was something he shouldn't have called me. This was verified when I raised my hand, and in a loud voice repeated what he had said and watched the teacher scold him for using a "bad" word. I was later to go home and ask the inevitable question that every black parent must face: "Mommy, what does 'nigger' mean?"

And what exactly did it mean? Thinking back, I realize that this could not have been the first time the word was used in my presence. I was part of a large extended family that had migrated from the rural South after World War II and formed a close-knit network that gravitated around my maternal grandparents. Their ground-floor apartment in one of the buildings they owned in Harlem was a weekend mecca for my immediate family, along with countless aunts, uncles and cousins who brought along assorted friends. It was a bustling and open house with assorted neighbors and tenants popping in and out to exchange bits of gossip, pick up an old quarrel or referee the ongoing checkers game in which my grandmother cheated shamelessly. They were all there to let down their hair and put up their feet after a week of labor in the factories, laundries and shipyards of New York.

Amid the clamor, which could reach deafening proportions—two or three conversations going on simultaneously, punctuated by the sound of a baby's crying somewhere in the back rooms or out on the street—there was still a rigid set of rules about what was said and how. Older children were sent out of the living room when it was time to get into the juicy details about "you-know-who" up on the third floor who had gone and gotten herself "p-r-e-g-n-a-n-t!" But my parents, knowing that I could spell well beyond my years, always demanded that I follow the others out to play. Beyond sexual misconduct and death, everything else was considered harmless for our young ears. And so among the anecdotes of the triumphs and disappointments in the various workings of their lives, the word nigger was used in my presence, but it was set within contexts and inflections that caused it to register in my mind as something else.

In the singular, the word was always applied to a man who had distinguished himself in some situation that brought their approval for his strength, intelligence or drive:

"Did Johnny really do that?"

"I'm telling you, that nigger pulled in $6,000 of overtime last year. Said he got enough for a down payment on a house."

When used with a possessive adjective by a woman—"my nigger"—it became a term of endearment for husband or boyfriend. But it could be more than just a term applied to a man. In their mouths it became the pure essence of manhood—a disembodied force that channeled their past history of struggle and present survival against the odds into a victorious statement of being: "Yeah, that old foreman found out quick enough—you don't mess with a nigger."

In the plural, it became a description of some group within the community that had overstepped the bounds of decency as my family defined it: Parents who neglected their children, a drunken couple who fought in public, people who simply refused to look for work, those with excessively dirty mouths or unkempt households were all "trifling niggers." This particular circle could forgive hard times, unemployment, the occasional bout of depression—they had gone through all of that themselves—but the unforgivable sin was lack of self-respect.

A woman could never be a "nigger" in the singular, with its connotation of confirming worth. The noun girl was its closest equivalent in that sense, but only when used in direct address and regardless of the gender doing the addressing. "Girl" was a token of respect for a woman. The one-syllable word was drawn out to sound like three in recognition of the extra ounce of wit, nerve or daring that the woman had shown in the situation under discussion.

"G-i-r-l, stop. You mean you said that to his face?"

But if the word was used in a third-person reference or shortened so that it almost snapped out of the mouth, it always involved some element of communal disapproval. And age became an important factor in these exchanges. It was only between individuals of the same generation, or from an older person to a younger (but never the other way around), that "girl" would be considered a compliment.

I don't agree with the argument that use of the word nigger at this social stratum of the black community was an internalization of racism. The dynamics were the exact opposite: the people in my grandmother's living room took a word that whites used to signify worthlessness or degradation and rendered it impotent. Gathering there together, they transformed "nigger" to signify the varied and complex human beings they knew themselves to be. If the word was to disappear totally from the mouths of even the most racist of white society, no one in that room was naive enough to believe it would disappear from white minds. Meeting the word head-on, they proved it had absolutely nothing to do with the way they were determined to live their lives.

So there must have been dozens of times that the word "nigger" was spoken in front of me before I reached the third grade. But I didn't "hear" it until it was said by a small pair of lips that had already learned it could be a way to humiliate me. That was the word I went home and asked my mother about. And since she knew that I had to grow up in America, she took me in her lap and explained.

WHAT QUICKENS ME: SOME THOUGHTS ON IMAGE AND IDEA IN JAMES WRIGHT'S POEMS

Shane Seely

I am going to try to say something about movement in James Wright's poems. The term itself is a tricky one for me, even as I pronounce it the subject of my inquiry: movement happens in many ways in Wright's work, as it does in everybody's, as it does in every sentence, every word. We start somewhere, and we end up somewhere else. We move through language, through idea and emotion, as it moves through us. (I originally conceived 'movement' as a denotative term, but as I write, it accrues meaning: the moves a writer makes to move us; the way we move through the words of a poem, or any piece of language, and back and forth between language and emotion; the way the ideas illuminated or enshadowed by that language move through us, in an almost biological way, as, we like to say, we digest them. And: the a piece of music, divided into movements, and the movement of breath or bow, generating sound.)

The starting focus of my investigation, however, is the way Wright's poems are pieced together, specifically the ways he connects narrative or lyric elements with abstract or argumentative modes. I want to say that these moves startle us into questioning the division between the two sides: narrative serves argument, argument informs lyric. I want to say—and this may be going too far—that the two work together, become one.

Wright is often remembered for his "deep image" poems, semi-surrealist lyrics full of incandescent images of rural life—machines, animals, weather—that are striking in their refusal to explain themselves. A short example might be a few lines from "Spring Images": "Small antelopes / Fall asleep in the ashes / Of the moon." Also memorable are the early formal poems, many of which display a skill with prosody that must have set his later free verse more wholly free. A great example of this is "Saint Judas," notable here particularly not only as an example of his deft measure and rhyme, but as a sonnet—that most storied argumentative form—that is not an argument but a dramatic narrative in Judas' voice. The story itself argues for the ideas/themes—fate, redemption—which underlie the poem. In the poems that I will explore here, Wright's images retain their "deep" resonance and gravity. 357 are nouns that argue all by themselves, lending potency to his ideas.

One of the most striking examples of Wright's marriage of narrative and argument comes in one of his most famous poems, "Autumn Begins in Martin's Ferry, Ohio." This poem is widely anthologized and heartbreakingly beautiful, and it will serve as a reference point for much of the analysis in this essay. It's short, and I will quote it now in full:

Essay Seminar, May 14, 2001.

In the Shreve High football stadium,
I think of Polacks nursing long beers in Tiltonsville,
And gray faces of Negroes in the blast furnace at Benwood,
And the ruptured night watchman of Wheeling Steel,
Dreaming of heroes.

All the proud fathers are ashamed to go home.
Their women cluck like starved pullets,
Dying for love.

Therefore,
Their sons grow suicidally beautiful
At the beginning of October,
And gallop terribly against each other's bodies.

The first two stanzas construct a world that animates the poem via the speaker's thoughts. The first line establishes a place for the action (a high school football stadium) and immediately in the second shows us a person ('I') doing something (thinking). As soon as these elements are established, the poem leaves them behind and develops—in the way that film is developed—the speaker's thoughts into a vivid picture of the world that surrounds that football stadium. The women in the second stanza are connected to and separated from the men in the first. One can almost imagine a split screen the men on one side, "nursing long beers" and keeping the night watch, while on the other side, the women "cluck like starved pullets." Wright deftly underscores this parallel by echoing the last line of the first stanza in the last line of the second; "Dreaming of heroes" and "Dying for love" are nearly identical in sound and rhythm. Each is essentially a trochee followed by an iamb, though "of heroes" carries an extra syllable at the end. The clean iamb "for love" accentuates, I think, the first two stanzas' completeness as a portrait of a town's working-class population. The two beats between stressed syllables slow the lines, increasing their gravity. Repetition of the solemn D-sound adds to that effect, while it strengthens the connection. Dreaming and dying enact the outlooks of the men and women in this poem's world. After the first two stanzas, we have in our heads a full, wrenching picture of working-class people in Martin's Ferry, Ohio. We are shown not only their heartbreak, but that which would sustain them as well.

With the first word—which is the first line in its entirety—of the final stanza, the poem explodes into its true form: an argument. We have nearly forgotten after the first two stanzas that a speaker is thinking these townspeople and their emptiness, that this picture in our minds has been given to us within a narrative frame. (I use "narrative" loosely here, of course, and mean only to distinguish a dramatic specificity of person and place.) But "therefore" is an abstraction, the first of its kind in the poem (aside from love I suppose), and it throws us back immediately to the poem's beginning and reminds us that the world created for us is the product of the speaker's thought. Suddenly, the first two stanzas aren't merely portraits of Americans, like those of Sherwood Anderson or Edgar Lee Masters; they make up one side of a logical proof. On the other side of that proof, the picture of the "suicidally beautiful" boys "gallop[ing] terribly against each other's bodies" is, like the portraits in the prior stanzas, a picture of a segment of life in Martin's Ferry. It becomes significant that the speaker *thinks* of the people, intellectualizes them, rather than imagining or remembering them. It is only the unifying presence of the speaker, along with the conjunction "therefore," that organizes the portrait into an argument.

It is important to note also that the speaker's thoughts in the beginning of the poem are not on his setting, but on the men and women that populate the bars and blast furnaces of the area. It is not until the last stanza that his thoughts circle back to his setting, the football stadium from which he narrates. This 'full circle' gives the poem a satisfying feeling of completeness, I think, reminiscent of Chekhov's dictum that a gun on a table in the first act of a play had better be fired by the third. The tension created by the gun's presence until the third act helps keep the audience's focus. The structure of the poem's thought—the sequencing of the images and ideas—is integral to its effect; if the speaker first described the football players, then explained their violence and beauty by saying that their parents are dreaming of heroes and dying for love, the power of the poem's revelation—"therefore"—would disappear.

In another poem from the same collection, we can see Wright make similar moves. In "Lying in a Hammock at William Duffy's Farm in Pine Island, Minnesota," the attention to setting is heightened, and the traditional logical rhetorical moves are virtually gone. The physical description begins, obviously, with the title, which places the speaker. Here is the poem:

> Over my head, I see the bronze butterfly,
> Asleep on the black trunk,
> Blowing like a leaf in green shadow.
> Down the ravine behind the empty house,
> The cowbells follow one another
> Into the distances of the afternoon.
> To my right,
> In a field of sunlight between two pines,
> The droppings of last year's horses
> Blaze up into golden stones.
> I lean back, as the evening darkens and comes on.
> A chicken hawk floats over, looking for home.
> I have wasted my life.

The entire poem, save the last line, is devoted to a thorough description of the bucolic setting. The first three sentences begin with phrases indicating direction, and are lush with colorful images. Many of Wright's favorite words and images are here: the colors green, black, and gold, shadows, leaves, horses, incipient dark—all are absorbed with a careful eye and reported with little emotion, except perhaps for a reverence evidenced by the care with which the observation is reported. And then the last line shifts the poem's tone and discourse dramatically, defying our expectations with its sudden baldfaced despair. It is an argument, even more tersely stated and less explicit than the one in "Autumn Begins," but it is an argument nonetheless. When questioned about this poem, Wright said, "Isn't it enough just to say what's going on?" That comment, I think, hints that the poem may have been written fairly spontaneously, or at least that it aims to capture a spontaneity, which contributes to the visceral nature of the poem's ultimate argument.

And that argument is structured quite similarly to the one in "Autumn Begins." In this poem, the title does the work of the previous poem's first line; the speaker's attitude toward his subject is even more embedded, because the scene lacks an action (like "thinking"). Once again, the speaker's focus leaps from its initial subject immediately; instead of learning more about the person lying in the hammock, our attention goes to the bronze butterfly over his head. It is not until the end of the poem that the speaker's focus circles back around to himself in the hammock: and he is devastated by his sudden revelation. The speaker's realization in "Lying in a Hammock" is more visceral, less intellectual, than that of the speaker in "Autumn Begins." We see this in the absence of any word indicating the relationship of image to idea. Appropriately, the revelation at the end of "Lying in a Hammock" is a personal one, rather than an explanation of a frightening and beautiful social phenomenon.

Still, the speaker never tells us just how he managed to waste his life, nor does he provide for us any real evidence that he actually has done so. However, if he did indeed provide such evidence, we certainly wouldn't be moved by the poem's revelation, or the sudden welling of emotion it embodies. Any such report would have created an ironic situation in the poem, in which we knew the speaker had wasted his life before he himself came to the realization, and we would have felt no real catharsis when he caught up to us. The speaker's fixation on his physical surroundings creates a space in the poem for the emotion to burgeon, leaving the speaker to his despair while we listen to the cowbells. The mystery of this poem is in what happens emotionally, without speech, as the images are recounted; that mystery bursts into the poem in the final, lamenting line.

Retrospectively, we can pinpoint the symbolic power of the images: the butterfly (perhaps the most tired of symbols?), the droppings transforming into "golden stones," the encroaching evening, and so on. From such analysis we can create for ourselves a logical sequence of thought: the man lounging in the hammock sees the symbol of transformation and renewal resting beneath (and on, with the black trunk) the pall of death; symbolic sounds of death lead away to the symbol for eternity; the symbol for waste makes something of itself by coming back in beauty; he leans back and feels that death is on its way; the barnyard predator (ignoble bird) looks for somewhere to go die. It all adds up to this: death is imminent, and you're missing life lying there in your hammock. Thus, the speaker concludes that he has wasted his life.

But reading the poem only in that way robs it of much of its effect, I think. The directness of the description argues for its integrity as image—the poem, for the first twelve of its thirteen lines, is solely observation. That integrity of observation carries into the final line, where the observation is an intellectual one; the speaker's sense of his wasted life is as palpable to him as the bronze butterfly, and as unburdened by explanation. At the same time, the final line's presence as a piece of argument colors the preceding observation with an intellectual shade. The description becomes the argument, as the argument becomes the description.

I'd like to look at another poem that achieves its effects in slightly different ways. In "In Response to a Rumor That the Oldest Whorehouse in Wheeling, West Virginia, Has Been Condemned," Wright makes many of the same moves we have seen in the previous examples; however, the interplay of narrative and argument is less drastic and abrupt in this poem, and we are not startled the way we have been in the previous examples by the sudden walloping shift. The ideas of this poem blossom naturally and traceably from the poem's narrative.

The title begins to lay out the poem's logical apparatus; instead of placing the speaker in a physical situation, as it did in "Lying in a Hammock," this title establishes the poem's exigency, its reason for being written. Here are the first two stanzas:

I will grieve alone,
As I strolled alone,
years ago, down along
The Ohio shore.
I hid in the hobo jungle weeds
Upstream from the sewer main,
Pondering, gazing.

I saw, down river,
At Twenty-third and Water Streets
By the vinegar works,
The doors open in early evening.

Swinging their purses, the women
Poured down the long street to the river
And into the river.

We have seen already how Wright's poems often start with one focus, and move quickly to another; in this poem, we begin in the future and move immediately into the speaker's memory. The diction and prosody of the poem's first two phrases accentuate this shift. In addition to the repeated words and clause structure, the second phrase makes a slight but significant variation on the first. While "grieve alone" and "strolled alone" are identical rhythmic figures (stressed-unstressed-stressed), "I will" (stressed-unstressed) is the opposite of "As I" (unstressed-stressed). The result is a subtle feeling of change, mirroring the shift of tense, which itself mirrors the speaker's movement into memory. Also notable is the difference in sound between "grieve" and "strolled": the first consonants in "grieve" are voiced, while the first in "strolled" are unvoiced. Unvoiced sounds are softer to the ear and gentler to the spirit—as the move to memory is made with fondness and good humor. The stressed-unstressed-stressed pattern continues in the two remaining phrases of the second line, building the momentum of the budding memories. The third line echoes the rhythmic structure, though with a slight variation (two unstressed syllables at the beginning of the line); together with the lineation, this rhythmic pattern reinforces the poem's movement from the present to the past. We may imagine, by the third line, that the 'fade to memory' is complete, and that we are in the world of the speaker's past.

Wright lingers with this memory, paying it out a bit at a time. The focus at first is on the boy he was, hiding in the "hobo jungle weeds" (a phrase steeped in a boy's imaginations of adventure and danger). We learn what he is doing and, while we can certainly surmise the object of his attention, we don't see it in the first stanza. Nor do we see the whorehouse in the early lines of the second stanza, as the speaker builds up phrase after phrase in his enthusiasm and delicious anticipation, locating his interest with greater and greater precision. And finally, in the fifth line of the second stanza, we see the object of his attention, his affection, his awe, even after all these years: the women. His astonishment at the scene before him is echoed with the repetitive diction once again, as "to the river" is repeated in the stanza's last two lines.

At this point, Wright has once again enthralled us with his story telling. We know the scene, the pertinent details, and we know the speaker and the boy the speaker was—all of that is portrayed for us in his diction, his detail, and his prosody. After the first two stanzas, the poem takes a contemplative turn:

I do not know how it was
They could drown every evening.
What time near dawn did they climb up the other shore,
Drying their wings?

Here we see the point of view of the speaker merge with the point of view of the boy he was in his memory, as the speaker's action changes to present tense: he still (or perhaps only now, in memory) "do[es] not know" what happened to the women. (One of the beauties of this poem is the speaker's willingness not to be sensible in the situation—to act as though the logical explanation were a fantastic one. I make this caveat only because it feels strange to say that the speaker really thinks the women might drown every evening.) Now the speaker/boy wonders at the mystery in this memory, the women's seeming unearthliness. The shift from the narrative to the argumentative is less abrupt here, more firmly embedded in the narrative. The ideas that end the poem are those of speaker/boy, the character that the speaker has become in the third stanza. By way of comparison, the speaker in "Autumn Begins" stands outside the world created in the poem's first two stanzas.

The speaker/boy goes on to explain his consternation, and the ideas that inform the poem's narrative, in the final two stanzas.

> For the river at Wheeling, West Virginia,
> Has only two shores:
> The one in hell, the other
> In Bridgeport, Ohio.
>
> And nobody would commit suicide, only
> To find beyond death
> Bridgeport, Ohio.

And so we learn that the boy's fascination (and that of the speaker, who will grieve) with the women is neither their status as "bad women," nor their sensuality (undoubtedly alluded to in hissed whispers by the "good" locals). It is rather that they seem to the young voyeur to be supernatural creatures, and the strange logic whereby he reaches that conclusion is laid out at the poem's end. The third stanza's questions are cryptic and strange; why would he not jump to the outrageous conclusion that the women were simply bathing in the river? But Wright's watcher cannot do what Whitman's does; he cannot join the bathers, and know intimately their sport. Instead, his distance from them is such that he sees them differently than perhaps they were, or at least than we expect to see them: they transform, and shun death. And why they choose transformation is as humorous as the speaker's memory is tender: because, if the Ohio is the Styx, why die and go to Bridgeport, Ohio? (If you have been to Bridgeport, the logic makes sense.)

The final stanzas argue for the speaker's child-like interpretation of the scene; the poem's structure allows us to sit with the unusual ruminations of the speaker before we hear his equally unusual and lovely ideas about the river and its banks. Had the speaker explained to us about the river's shores before he pondered the nature of the women, his wonderment would have struck us less. The poem is really about two things, the women and the river; because the women are the speaker's focus in his narrative, the river carries its weight by occupying the end of the poem, acting as the logical imperative for the speaker's reality.

In the short poem, "A Prayer to Escape the Marketplace," the narrative-to-argument pattern is reversed, as a series of ideas are interrupted by a miniscule but compelling event. Here is the poem, in full:

> I renounce the blindness of the magazines.
> I want to lie down under a tree.
> This is the only duty that is not death.
> This is the everlasting happiness
> Of small winds.
> Suddenly,
> A pheasant flutters, and I turn
> Only to see him vanishing at the damp edge
> Of the road.

The first thing we might notice is the sixth line, "Suddenly," because it resonates strongly with the line "Therefore," from "Autumn Begins." Both single-word lines act as pivot points in their respective poems, and will provide a fine joint on which to hinge an analysis.

In "Autumn Begins," the speaker opens the poem by establishing a scene; the poem moves from there toward its argument. In "A Prayer," though, the speaker begins in abstraction. The first four lines of the poem are statements, generalizations. The lines repeat structurally ("I renounce" and "I want," then the phrase "This is the . . ." twice), reinforcing their prayer-like quality. The poem's first lines are a litany, but they lack the metrical quality of many poetic 'prayers.' Scansion of this poem reveals only its inconsistency of rhythm. The generalizations (and the fact that the poem opens with them) reflect the mood embodied by the "prayer to escape": the speaker wants things, has opinions, fears dying. Of course, he is talking about his disconnection from experience, from "the everlasting happiness/Of small winds"; this disconnection is mirrored in the poem's uneven metrics. Then, "Suddenly," the pounding of a pheasant's wings startles him from his abstraction and into experience, into narrative. Just as suddenly as the speaker hears the pheasant, the poem is transformed from one of idea, detached from time and place, to one of narrative. No matter how fleeting the interlude with the pheasant, it is more real than anything in "the market place," more potent than any of his protestations. In some sense, we could say that his prayer works, and he is released from "the blindness of the magazines" as he catches a glimpse of the bird at the road's edge. We might also say that the entire poem becomes, by its end, a narrative of its speaker's thought. Similar to the way "Autumn Begins" explodes into its argumentative structure, "A Prayer" locates the reader in a narrative in the final sentence, altering the way we read the initial lines. In this way, the sighting of the pheasant is at once the answer to the prayer and the prayer itself, and praying becomes a form of escape.

At the risk of going on too long, I'd like to bring in another poem that makes similar movements, one of which I am quite fond because of the relationship of its narrative to its ideas. (I love it also for its subject matter. In fact, I love all of these poems for their subject matter. I am dazzled and floored by the way these subjects are taken up in these forms.) This poem is not broken into stanzas, so I will quote the entire thing here, all at once. It is called "Northern Pike":

All right. Try this,
Then. Every body
I know and care for,
And every body
Else is going
To die in a loneliness
I can't imagine and a pain
I don't know. We had
Togo on living. We
Untangled the net, we slit
The body of this fish
Open from the hinge of the tail
To a place beneath the chin
I wish I could sing of.
I would just as soon we let
The living go on living.
An old poet whom we believe in
Said the same thing, and so
We paused among the dark cattails and prayed
For the muskrats,
For the ripples below their tails,
For the little movements that we knew the crawdads were making under water,
For the right-hand wrist of my cousin who is a policeman.
We prayed for the game warden's blindness.
We prayed for the road home.

We ate the fish.
There must be something very beautiful in my body,
I am so happy.

This poem is a justification. It is not merely a justification of an act, the act of killing and eating a fish; it is a justification of the emotions to which the speaker finally admits in the poem's last line. His happiness at having eaten this fish is something he himself has trouble justifying, and he takes a good while to do it. It is how he justifies his emotions to us and to himself that is of interest to us here.

The poem starts us off, say, four-fifths of the way through the argument; the emotional pitch is high in the first two lines. We have missed much: we have missed the uninflected telling of the catching and eating of the fish; we have missed the speaker's first moments of self-accusation. We aren't sure, at first read, what's going on. The speaker is almost at a point of exasperation: "All right. Try this, / Then." The clipped diction and syntax in the early lines reinforce the stridency in the speaker's voice, especially in the separating of the compound "everybody" into two words. Each word gets an added emphasis. The poem's opening disorients the reader, because the poem is at its beginning at once startlingly intimate and without clear reference— the title, for a change, provides no real anchor for the opening lines. The poet goes on to justify (what, we're not sure) with a despairing logic; the tension in the opening four lines overflows into vast emotional anguish in the next four. Finally, eight lines into the poem, the speaker gets around to just what in hell he is talking about. At first, he is still unclear: "We had / to go on living." The poem is an intimate utterance that stops just shy of saying 'you,' and the effect is to give the reader the notion that he is not the intended audience, or that he has just awakened into a conversation he has been already having. Or, the savvy reader may speculate, this argument is too intimate to be directed toward an outsider, and is directed instead toward the speaker himself, toward his own conscience.

Such a reading, which I think is sound, shades the speaker's description of the events in an interesting way: he is recounting them, perhaps for the thousandth time, trying, trying to make sense of them. His protestation, "We had / To go on living," transitions him from the argument that begins the poem to the description to which it moves; this protestation represents a focusing of the speaker's attention from the general to the specific. The first lines of description ("We / untangled the net . . ." and so forth) are without ornament, as the speaker's roiling emotions cool. He invokes a precision in his description of the opening of the fish's body that stands in contrast to his earlier statements about everyone dying in unknowable loneliness and pain.

This precision allows him to return to his ideas, which he does in the poem's fourteenth and fifteenth lines: "I would just as soon we let / The living go on living." The tone here his much more subdued than it was early in the poem, and the longer lines reflect the easier emotional ground. Thus far, experience has acted at once as the impetus for the speaker's anguish, and, in its recounting, as a stabilizer for it. But, as impetus, the experience lies outside of the poem; what we have before us is the stabilizer, the anchor by which the speaker holds himself upright. The act that he set out to defend becomes, in this way, what rescues him from his distress.

In the next lines, the speaker returns to the story and delivers the poem's emotional climax. Once again, it is a prayer. As in "A Prayer to Escape the Market Place," we see the repeated language and syntax; also similar to that poem is the power of the specific, of the image, the experience, to liberate from anguish. And the specificity of the images is really quite dazzling: the speaker attends not just to the muskrats, but to the ripples below their tails. We must imagine that this prayer blessed the eating of the fish which the speaker recounts, just as blesses him as he remembers it. In fact, the momentum of the repeated syntax ("we prayed," "we prayed," "we ate") blends the eating of the fish with the prayer, until it becomes a part of the prayer. And thus, the speaker makes his peace with the eating of the fish: as "We ate the fish" becomes a part of the poem's litany, the act of eating the fish becomes a prayerful one, as full of transcendent attention and pious awareness as the knowledge of the "little movements" of the crawdads underwater.

This transformation is achieved through the power of the narrative and the power of the image, and it allows the speaker to make his final confession. His attention to his world manifests itself in his retelling of the catching, killing, and eating of a northern pike, and it is this attention that ultimately fulfills his argument and unites him with that world. In some sense, the prayer in this poem begins with the first image of the fish. The seventeenth-century philosopher Nicholas Malebranche first posited that the paying of attention is the soul's natural prayer. It is truly that attention to the world, the poem tells us, that is the ultimate persuasion. The killing and eating of the northern pike is justified by the prayerful attitude in which it is done.

There are many wonderful poets who write many wonderful poems in which ideas dominate physical things. Carl Phillips, from whom I stole the information about Malebranche, is one. He can say smart things like this, from "Clay":

> If there can be one, the shape
> of any line
> is its direction.

Those are smart words, and well said. I could not say them. I could not say them without a line in my hand, or in my mind's hand, to measure and weigh. I would me much more likely to say:

> If it has one, the shape
> of this line
> is its direction.

And I would probably rather say something about what the line is for, where it exists in the world, what it thinks about itself. James Wright, somehow, does both. His arguments are of the world, and his world is verdant with ideas. The relationship between what he shows you and what he tells you is often abrupt, always tight. The reasons for things are best explained by the things themselves.

In an early draft of this essay, I included a story of conversation I once had about God. I grew up in a part of the country where God is on everyone's mind, sometimes in a peculiar way. One of my friends, at the end of her wits with me, asked, "Do you *believe* in God?"

We were sitting in my car, in a driveway. It was dark outside. The sky was clear and the moon was a sliver, so the stars blazed unabashedly. I got out of the car. "Look," I said, feeling profound, pointing up. "Look." I had meant to say with that grand gesture that I believed in God, because I couldn't look at something so astonishing and not believe in something, but that I didn't believe God kept a tally on how often I crossed the threshold of the local Presbyterian church. She didn't understand, of course, and later gave up on me altogether. But I still believe in the persuasive power of a constellation, in the intellectual heft of the waxing moon. If attentiveness is the natural attitude of prayer, then whatever God there is must have smiled on James Wright.

LANGUAGE AND LITERATURE FROM A PUEBLO INDIAN PERSPECTIVE

Leslie Marmon Silko

Where I come from, the words most highly valued are those spoken from the heart, unpremeditated and unrehearsed. Among the Pueblo people, a written speech or statement is highly suspect because the true feelings of the speaker remain hidden as she reads words that are detached from the occasion and the audience. I have intentionally not written a formal paper because I want you to *hear* and to experience English in a structure that follows patterns from the oral tradition. For those of you accustomed to being taken from point A to point B to point C, this presentation may be somewhat difficult to follow. Pueblo expression resembles something like a spider's web—with many little threads radiating from the center, crisscrossing each other. As with the web, the structure emerges as it is made and you must simply listen and trust, as the Pueblo people do, that meaning will be made.

My task is a formidable one: I ask you to set aside a number of basic approaches that you have been using, and probably will continue to use, and instead, to approach language from the Pueblo perspective, one that embraces the whole of creation and the whole of history and time.

What changes would Pueblo writers make to English as a language for literature? I have some examples of stories in English that I will use to address this question. At the same time, I would like to explain the importance of storytelling and how it relates to a Pueblo theory of language.

So, I will begin, appropriately enough, with the Pueblo Creation story, an all-inclusive story of how life began. In this story, Tséitsínako, Thought Woman, by thinking of her sisters, and together with her sisters, thought of everything that is. In this way, the world was created. Everything in this world was a part of the original creation; the people at home understood that far away there were other human beings, also a part of this world. The Creation story even includes a prophecy, which describes the origin of European and African peoples and also refers to Asians.

This story, I think, suggests something about why the Pueblo people are more concerned with story and communication and less concerned with a particular language. There are at least six, possibly seven, distinct languages among the twenty pueblos of the southwestern United States, for example, Zuñi and Hopi. And from mesa to mesa there are subtle differences in language. But the particular language being spoken isn't as important as what a speaker is trying to say, and this emphasis on the story itself stems, I believe, from a view of narrative particular to the Pueblo and other Native American peoples—that is, that language *is* story.

I will try to clarify this statement. At Laguna Pueblo, for example, many individual words have their own stories. So when one is telling a story, and one is using words to tell the story, each word that one is speaking has a story of its own, too. Often the speakers or tellers will go into these word-stories, creating an elaborate structure of stories-within-stories. This structure, which becomes very apparent in the actual telling of a story, informs contemporary Pueblo writing and storytelling as well as the traditional narratives. This perspective on narrative—of story within story, the idea that one story is only the beginning of many stories, and the sense that stories never truly end—represents an important contribution of Native American cultures to the English language.

Many people think of storytelling as something that is done at bedtime, that it is something done for small children. But when I use the term *storytelling*, I'm talking about something much bigger than that. I'm talking about something that comes out of an experience and an understanding of that original view of creation—that we are all part of a whole; we do not differentiate or fragment stories and experiences. In the beginning, Tséitsínako, Thought Woman, thought of all things, and all of these things are held together as one holds many things together in a single thought.

So in the telling (and you will hear a few of the dimensions of this telling) first of all, as mentioned earlier, the storytelling always includes the audience, the listeners. In fact, a great deal of the story is believed to be inside the listener; the storyteller's role is to draw the story out of the listeners. The storytelling continues from generation to generation.

Basically, the origin story constructs our identity—within this story, we know who we are. We are the Lagunas. This is where we come from. We came this way. We came by this place. And so from the time we are very young, we hear these stories, so that when we go out into the world, when one asks who we are, or where we are from, we immediately know: we are the people who came from the north. We are the people of these stories.

In the Creation story, Antelope says that he will help knock a hole in the earth so that the people can come up, out into the next world. Antelope tries and tries; he uses his hooves, but is unable to break through. It is then that Badger says, "Let me help you." And Badger very patiently uses his claws and digs a way through, bringing the people into the world. When the Badger clan people think of themselves, or when the Antelope people think of themselves, it is as people who are of *this* story, and this is *our* place, and we fit into the very beginning when the people first came, before we began our journey south.

Within the clans there are stories that identify the clan. One moves, then, from the idea of one's identity as a tribal person into clan identity, then to one's identity as a member of an extended family. And it is the notion of "extended family" that has produced a kind of story that some distinguish from other Pueblo stories, though Pueblo people do not. Anthropologists and ethnologists have, for a long time, differentiated the types of stories the Pueblos tell. They tended to elevate the old, sacred, and traditional stories and to brush aside family stories, the family's account of itself. But in Pueblo culture, these family stories are given equal recognition. There is no definite, present pattern for the way one will hear the stories of one's own family, but it is a very critical part of one's childhood, and the storytelling continues throughout one's life. One will hear stories of importance to the family—sometimes wonderful stories—stories about the time a maternal uncle got the biggest deer that was ever seen and brought it back from the mountains. And so an individual's identity will extend from the identity constructed around the family—"I am from the family of my uncle who brought in this wonderful deer and it was a wonderful hunt."

Family accounts include negative stories, too; perhaps an uncle did something unacceptable. It is very important that one keep track of all these stories—both positive and not so positive—about one's own family and other families. Because even when there is no way around it—old Uncle Pete *did* do a terrible thing—by knowing the stories that originate in other families, one is able to deal with terrible sorts of things that might happen within one's own family. If a member of the family does something that cannot be excused, one always knows stories about similar inexcusable things done by a member of another family. But this knowledge is not communicated for malicious reasons. It is very important to understand this. Keeping track of all the stories within the community gives us all a certain distance, a useful perspective, that brings incidents down to a level we can deal with. If others have done it before, it cannot be so terrible. If others have endured, so can we.

The stories are always bringing us together, keeping this whole together, keeping this family together, keeping this clan together. "Don't go away, don't isolate yourself, but come here, because we have all had these kinds of experiences." And so there is this constant pulling together to resist the tendency to run or hide or separate oneself during a traumatic emotional experience. This separation not only endangers the group but the individual as well—one does not recover by oneself.

Because storytelling lies at the heart of Pueblo culture, it is absurd to attempt to fix the stories in time. "When did they tell the stories?" or "What time of day does the storytelling take place?"—these questions are nonsensical from a Pueblo perspective, because our storytelling goes on constantly: as some old grandmother puts on the shoes of a child and tells her the story of a little girl who didn't wear her shoes, for instance, or someone comes into the house for coffee to talk with a teenage boy who has just been in a lot of trouble, to reassure him that someone else's son has been in that kind of trouble, too. Storytelling is an ongoing process, working on many different levels.

Here's one story that is often told at a time of individual crisis (and I want to remind you that we make no distinctions between types of story—historical, sacred, plain gossip—because these distinctions are not useful when discussing the Pueblo *experience* of language). There was a young man who, when he came back from the war in Vietnam, had saved up his army pay and bought a beautiful red Volkswagen. He was very proud of it. One night he drove up to a place called the King's Bar right across the reservation line. The bar is notorious for many reasons, particularly for the deep *arroyo* located behind it. The young man ran in to pick up a cold six-pack, but he forgot to put on his emergency brake. And his little red Volkswagen rolled back into the *arroyo* and was all smashed up. He felt very bad about it, but within a few days everybody had come to him with stories about other people who had lost cars and family members to that *arroyo,* for instance, George Day's station wagon, with his mother-in-law and kids inside. So everybody was saying, "Well, at least your mother-in-law and kids weren't in the car when it rolled in," and one can't argue with that kind of story. The story of the young man and his smashed-up Volkswagen was now joined with all the other stories of cars that fell into that *arroyo.*

Now I want to tell you a very beautiful little story. It is a very old story that is sometimes told to people who suffer great family or personal loss. This story was told by my Aunt Susie. She is one of the first generation of people at Laguna who began experimenting with English—who began working to make English speak for us—that is, to speak from the heart. (I come from a family intent on getting the stories told.) As you read the story, I think you will hear that. And here and there, I think, you will also hear the influence of the Indian school at Carlisle, Pennsylvania, where my Aunt Susie was sent (like being sent to prison) for six years.

This scene is set partly in Acoma, partly in Laguna. Waithea was a little girl living in Acoma and one day she said, "Mother, I would like to have some *yashtoah* to eat." *Yashtoah* is the hardened crust of corn mush that curls up. *Yashtoah* literally means "curled up." She said, "I would like to have some *yashtoah,*" and her mother said, "My dear little girl, I can't make you any *yashtoah* because we haven't any wood, but if you will go down off the mesa, down below, and pick up some pieces of wood and bring them home, I will make you some *yashtoah.*" So Waithea was glad and ran down the precipitous cliff of Acoma mesa. Down below, just as her mother had told her, there were pieces of wood, some curled, some crooked in shape, that she was to pick up and take home. She found just such wood as these.

She brought them home in a little wicker basket. First she called to her mother as she got home, "*Nayah, deeni!* Mother, upstairs!" The Pueblo people always called "upstairs" because long ago their homes were two, three stories, and they entered from the top. She said, "*Deeni!* UPSTAIRS!" and her mother came. The little girl said, "I have brought the wood you wanted me to bring." And she opened her little wicker basket to lay out the pieces of wood but here they were snakes. They were snakes instead of crooked sticks of wood. And her mother said, "Oh my dear child, you have brought snakes instead!" She said, "Go take them back and put them back just where you got them." And the little girl ran down the mesa again, down below to the flats. And she put those snakes back just where she got them. They were snakes instead and she was very hurt about this and so she said, "I'm not going home. I'm going to *Kawaik,* the beautiful lake place, *Kawaik,* and drown myself in the lake, *byn'yah'nah* [the "west lake"]. I will go there and drown myself."

So she started off, and as she passed the Enchanted Mesa near Acoma she met an old man, very aged, and he saw her running, and he said , My dear child, where are you going?" "I'm going to *Kawaik* and jump into the lake there." "Why?" "Well, because," she said, "my mother didn't want to make any *yashtoah* for me." The old man said, "Oh, no! You must not go my child. Come with me and I will take you home." He tried to catch her, but she was very light and skipped along. And every time he would try to grab her she would skip faster away from him.

The old man was coming home with some wood strapped to his back and tied with yucca. He just let the strap go and let the wood drop. He went as fast as he could up the cliff to the little girl's home. When he got to the place where she lived, he called to her mother. "*Deeni!*" "Come on up!" And he said, "I can't. I just came to bring you a message. Your little daughter is running away. She is going to *Kawaik* to drown herself in the lake there." "Oh my dear little girl!" the mother said. So she busied herself with making the *yashtoah* her little girl liked so much. Corn mush curled at the top. (She must have found enough wood to boil the corn meal and make the *yashtoah.*)

While the mush was cooking off, she got the little girl's clothing, her *manta* dress and buckskin moccasins and all her other garments, and put them in a bundle—probably a yucca bag. And she started down as fast as she could on the east side of Acoma. (There used to be a trail there, you know. It's gone now, but it was accessible in those days.) She saw her daughter way at a distance and she kept calling: "Stsamaku! My daughter! Come back! I've got your *yashtoah* for you." But the little girl would not turn. She kept on ahead and she cried: "My mother, my mother, she didn't want me to have any *yashtoah.* So now I'm going to *Kawaik* and drown myself." Her mother heard her cry and said, My little daughter, come back here!" "No," and she kept a distance away from her. And they came nearer and nearer to the lake. And she could see her daughter now, very plain. "Come back, my daughter! I have your *yashtoah.*" But no, she kept on, and finally she reached the lake and she stood on the edge.

She had tied a little feather in her hair, which is traditional (in death they tie this feather on the head). She carried a feather, the little girl did, and she tied it in her hair with a piece of string, right on top of her head she put the feather. Just as her mother was about to reach her, she jumped into the lake. The little feather was whirling around and around in the depths below. Of course the mother was very sad. She went, grieved, back to Acoma and climbed her mesa home. She stood on the edge of the mesa and scattered her daughter's clothing, the little moccasins, the *yashtoah.* She scattered them to the east, to the west, to the north, to the south. And the pieces of clothing and the moccasins and yashtoah, all turned into butterflies. And today they say that Acoma has more beautiful butterflies: red ones, white ones, blue ones, yellow ones. They came from this little girl's clothing.

Now this is a story anthropologists would consider very old. The version I have given you is just as Aunt Susie tells it. You can occasionally hear some English she picked up at Carlisle—words like "precipitous." You will also notice that there is a great deal of repetition, and a little reminder about *yashtoah,* and how it is made. There is a remark about the cliff trail at Acoma—that it was once there, but is there no longer. This story may be told at a time of sadness or loss, but within this story many other elements are brought together. Things are not separated out and categorized; all things are brought together. So that the reminder about the *yashtoah* is valuable information that is repeated—a recipe, if you will. The information about the old trail at Acoma reveals that stories are, in a sense, maps, since even to this day there is little information or material about trails that is passed around with writing. In the structure of this story the repetitions are, of course, designed to help you remember. It is repeated again and again, and then it moves on.

The next story I would like to tell is by Simon Ortiz, from Acoma Pueblo. He is a wonderful poet who also works in narrative. One of the things I find very interesting in this short story is that if you listen very closely, you begin to hear what I was talking about in terms of a story never beginning at the beginning, and certainly never ending. As the Hopis sometimes say, "Well, it has gone this far for a while." There is always that implication of a continuing. The other thing I want you to listen for is the many stories within one story. Listen to the kinds of stories contained within the main story—stories that give one a family identity and an individual identity, for example. This story is called "Home Country":

"Well, it's been a while. I think in 1947 was when I left. My husband had been killed in Okinawa some years before. And so I had no more husband. And I had to make a living. O I guess I could have looked for another man but I didn't want to. It looked like the war had made some of them into a bad way anyway. I saw some of them come home like that. They either got drunk or just stayed around a while or couldn't seem to be satisfied anymore with what was there. I guess now that I think about it, that happened to me although I wasn't in the war not in the Army or even much off the reservation just that several years at the Indian School. Well there was that feeling things were changing not only the men the boys, but things were changing.

"One day the home nurse the nurse that came from the Indian health service was at my mother's home my mother was getting near the end real sick and she said that she had been meaning to ask me a question. I said what is the question. And the home nurse said well your mother is getting real sick and after she is no longer around for you to take care of, what will you be doing you and her are the only ones here. And I said I don't know. But I was thinking about it what she said made me think about it. And then the next time she came she said to me Eloise the government is hiring Indians now in the Indian schools to take care of the boys and girls I heard one of the supervisors saying that Indians are hard workers but you have to supervise them a lot and I thought of you well because you've been taking care of your mother real good and you follow all my instructions. She said I thought of you because you're a good Indian girl and you would be the kind of person for that job. I didn't say anything I had not ever really thought about a job but I kept thinking about it.

"Well my mother she died and we buried her up at the old place the cemetery there it's real nice on the east side of the hill where the sun shines warm and the wind doesn't blow too much sand around right there. Well I was sad we were all sad for a while but you know how things are. One of my aunties came over and she advised me and warned me about being too sorry about it and all that she wished me that I would not worry too much about it because old folks they go along pretty soon life is that way and then she said that maybe I ought to take in one of my aunties kids or two because there was a lot of them kids and I was all by myself now. But I was so young and I thought that I might do that you know take care of someone but I had been thinking too of what the home nurse said to me about working. Hardly anybody at our home was working at something like that no woman anyway. And I would have to move away.

"Well I did just that. I remember that day very well. I told my aunties and they were all crying and we all went up to the old highway where the bus to town passed by everyday. I was wearing an old kind of bluish sweater that was kind of big that one of my cousins who was older had got from a white person a tourist one summer in trade for something she had made a real pretty basket. She gave me that and I used to have a picture of me with it on it's kind of real ugly. Yeah that was the day I left wearing a baggy sweater and carrying a suitcase that someone gave me too I think or maybe it was the home nurse there wasn't much in it anyway either. I was scared and everybody seemed to be sad I was so young and skinny then. My aunties said one of them who was real fat you make sure you eat now make your own tortillas drink the milk and stuff like candies is no good she learned that from the nurse. Make sure you got your letter my auntie said. I had it folded into my purse. Yes I have one too a brown one that my husband when he was still alive one time on furlough he brought it on my birthday it was a nice purse and still looked new because I never used it.

"The letter said that I had a job at Kearns Canyon the boarding school there but I would have to go to the Agency first for some papers to be filled and that's where I was going first. The Agency. And then they would send me out to Kearns Canyon. I didn't even know where it was except that someone of our relatives said that it was near Hopi. My uncles teased me about watching out for the Hopi men and boys don't let them get too close they said well you know how they are and they were pretty strict too about those things and then they were joking and then they were not too and so I said aw they won't get near to me I'm too ugly and I promised I would be careful anyway.

"So we all gathered for a while at my last auntie's house and then the old man my grandfather brought his wagon and horses to the door and we all got in and sat there for a while until my auntie told her father okay father let's go and shook his elbow because the poor old man was old by then and kind of going to sleep all the time you had to talk to him real loud. I had about ten dollars I think that was a lot of money more than it is now you know and when we got to the highway where the Indian road which is just a dirt road goes off the pave road my grandfather reached into his blue jeans and pulled out a silver dollar and put it into my hand. I was so shocked. We were all so shocked. We all looked around at each other we didn't know where the old man had gotten it because we were real poor two of my uncles had to borrow on their accounts at the trading store for the money I had in my purse but there it was a silver dollar so big and shrinking in my grandfather's hand and then in my hand.

"Well I was so shocked and everybody was so shocked that we all started crying right there at the junction of that Indian road and the pave highway I wanted to be a little girl again running after the old man when he hurried with his long legs to the cornfields or went for water down to the river. He was old then and his eye was turned gray and he didn't do much anymore except drive the wagon and chop a little bit of wood but I just held him and I just held him so tightly.

"Later on I don't know what happened to the silver dollar it had a date of 1907 on it but I kept it for a long time because I guess I wanted to have it to remember when I left my home country. What I did in between then and now is another story but that's the time I moved away,"

is what she said.

There are a great many parallels between Pueblo experiences and those of African and Caribbean peoples—one is that we have all had the conqueror's language imposed on us. But our experience with English has been somewhat different in that the Bureau of Indian Affairs schools were not interested in teaching us the canon of Western classics. For instance, we never heard of Shakespeare. We were given Dick and Jane, and I can remember reading that the robins were heading south for the winter. It took me a long time to figure out what was going on. I worried for quite a while about our robins in Laguna because they didn't leave in the winter, until I finally realized that all the big textbook companies are up in Boston and *their* robins do go south in the winter. But in a way, this dreadful formal education freed us by encouraging us to maintain our narratives. Whatever literature we were exposed to at school (which was damn little), at home the storytelling, the special regard for telling and bringing together through the telling, was going on constantly.

And as the old people say, "If you can remember the stories, you will be all right. Just remember the stories." When I returned to Laguna Pueblo after attending college, I wondered how the storytelling was continuing (anthropologists say that Laguna Pueblo is one of the more acculturated pueblos), so I visited an English class at Laguna Acoma High School. I knew the students had cassette tape recorders in their lockers and stereos at home, and that they listened to Kiss and Led Zeppelin and were all informed about popular culture in general. I had with me an anthology of short stories by Native American writers, *The Man to Send Rain Clouds.* One story in the book is about the killing of a state policeman in New Mexico by three Acoma Pueblo men in the early 1950s. I asked the students how many had heard this story and steeled myself for the possibility that the anthropologists were right, that the old traditions were indeed dying out and the students would be ignorant of the story. But instead, all but one or two raised their hands—they had heard the story, just as I had heard it when I was young, some in English, some in Laguna.

One of the other advantages that we Pueblos have enjoyed is that we have always been able to stay with the land. Our stories cannot be separated from their geographical locations, from actual physical places on the land. We were not relocated like so many Native American groups who were torn away from their ancestral land. And our stories are so much a part of these places that it is almost impossible for future generations to lose them—there is a story connected with every place, every object in the landscape.

Dennis Brutus has talked about the "yet unborn" as well as "those from the past," and how we are still *all* in *this* place, and language—the storytelling—is our way of passing through or being with them, or being together again. When Aunt Susie told her stories, she would tell a younger child to go open the door so that our esteemed predecessors might bring in their gifts to us. "They are out there," Aunt Susie would say. "Let them come in. They're here, they're here with us within the stories."

A few years ago, when Aunt Susie was 106, 1 paid her a visit, and while I was there she said, "Well, I'll be leaving here soon. I think I'll be leaving here next week, and I will be going over to the Cliff House." She said, "It's going to be real good to get back over there." I was listening, and I was thinking that she must be talking about her house at Paguate Village, just north of Laguna. And she went on, "Well, my mother's sister (and she gave her Indian name) will be there. She has been living there. She will be there and we will be over there, and I will get a chance to write down these stories I've been telling you." Now you must understand, of course, that Aunt Susie's mother's sister, a great storyteller herself, has long since passed over into the land of the dead. But then I realized, too, that Aunt Susie wasn't talking about death the way most of us do. She was talking about "going over" as a journey, a journey that perhaps we can only begin to understand through an appreciation for the boundless capacity of language that, through storytelling, brings us together, despite great distances between cultures, despite great distances in time.

LULLABY

Leslie Marmon Silko

The sun had gone down but the snow in the wind gave off its own light. It came in thick tufts like new wool—washed before the weaver spins it. Ayah reached out for it like her own babies had, and she smiled when she remembered how she had laughed at them. She was an old woman now, and her life had become memories. She sat down with her back against the wide cottonwood tree, feeling the rough bark on her back bones; she faced east and listened to the wind and snow sing a high-pitched Yelbechei song. Out of the wind she felt warmer, and she could watch the wide, fluffy snow fill in her tracks, steadily, until the direction she had come from was gone. By the light of the snow she could see the dark outline of the big arroyo a few feet away. She was sitting on the edge of Cebolleta Creek, where in the springtime the thin cows would graze on grass already chewed flat to the ground. In the wide, deep creek bed where only a trickle of water flowed in the summer, the skinny cows would wander, looking for new grass along winding paths splashed with manure.

Ayah pulled the old Army blanket over her head like a shawl. Jimmie's blanket—the one he had sent to her. That was a long time ago and the green wool was faded, and it was unraveling on the edges. She did not want to think about Jimmie. So she thought about the weaving and the way her mother had done it. Oil the tall wooden loom set into the sand under a tamarack tree for shade. She could see it clearly. She had been only a little girl when her grandma gave her the wooden combs to pull the twigs and burrs from the raw, freshly washed wool. And while she combed the wool, her grandma sat beside her spinning a silvery strand of yarn around the smooth cedar spindle. Her mother worked at the loom with yarns dyed bright yellow and red and gold. She watched them dye the yarn in boiling black pots full of bee-weed petals, juniper berries, and sage. The blankets her mother made were soft and woven so tight that rain rolled off them like birds' feathers. Ayah remembered sleeping warmly on cold windy nights, wrapped in her mother's blankets on the hogan's sandy floor.

The snow drifted now, with the northwest wind hurling it in gusts. It drifted up around her black overshoes—old ones with little metal buckles. She smiled at the snow which was trying to cover her little by little. She could remember when they had no black rubber overshoes; only the high buckskin leggings that they wrapped over their elkhide moccasins. If the snow was dry or frozen, a person could walk all day and not get wet; and in the evenings the beams of the ceiling would hang with lengths of pale buckskin leggings drying out slowly.

She felt peaceful remembering. She didn't feel cold any more. Jimmie's blanket seemed warmer than it had ever been. And she could remember the morning he was born. She could remember whispering to her mother, who was sleeping on the other side of the hogan, to tell her it was time now. She did not want to wake the others. The second time she called to her, her mother stood up and pulled on her shoes; she knew. They walked to the old stone hogan together, Ayah walking a step behind her mother. She waited alone learning the rhythms of the pains while her mother went to call the old woman to help them. The morning was already warm even before dawn and Ayah smelled the bee flowers blooming and the young willow growing at the springs. She could remember that so clearly, but his birth merged into

391

the births of the other children and to her it became all the same birth. They named him for the summer morning and in English they called him Jimmie.

It wasn't like Jimmie died. He just never came back, and one day a dark blue sedan with white writing on its doors pulled up in front of the boxcar shack where the rancher let the Indians live. A man in a khaki uniform trimmed in gold gave them a yellow piece of paper and told them that Jimmie was dead. He said the Army would try to get the body back and then it would be shipped to them; but it wasn't likely because the helicopter had burned after it crashed. All of this was told to Chato because he could understand English. She stood inside the doorway holding the baby while Chato listened. Chato spoke English like a white man and he spoke Spanish too. He was taller than the white man and he stood straighter too. Chato didn't explain why; he just told the military man they could keep the body if they found it. The white man looked bewildered; he nodded his head and left. Then Chato looked at her and shook his head, and then he told her, "Jimmie isn't coming home anymore, and when he spoke, he used the words to speak of the dead. She didn't cry then, but she hurt inside with anger. And she mourned him as the years passed, when a horse fell with Chato and broke his leg, and the white rancher told them he wouldn't pay Chato until he could work again. She mourned Jimmie because he would have worked for his father then; he would have saddled the big bay horse and ridden the fence lines each day, with wire cutters and heavy gloves, fixing the breaks in the barbed wire and putting the stray cattle back inside again.

She mourned him after the white doctors came to take Danny and Ella away. She was at the shack alone that day they came. It was back in the days before they hired Navajo women to go with them as interpreters. She recognized one of the doctors. She had seen him at the children's clinic at Cañoncito about a month ago. They were wearing khaki uniforms and they waved papers at her and a black ballpoint pen, trying to make her understand their English words. She was frightened by the way they looked at the children, like the lizard watches the fly. Danny was swinging on the tire swing on the elm tree behind the rancher's house, and Ella was toddling around the front door, dragging the broomstick horse Chato made for her. Ayah could see they wanted her to sign the papers, and Chato had taught her to sign her name. It was something she was proud of. She only wanted them to go, and to take their eyes away from her children.

She took the pen from the man without looking at his face and she signed the papers in three different places he pointed to. She stared at the ground by their feet and waited for them to leave. But they stood there and began to point and gesture at the children. Danny stopped swinging. Ayah could see his fear. She moved suddenly and grabbed Ella into her arms; the child squirmed, trying to get back to her toys. Ayah ran with the baby toward Danny; she screamed for him to run and then she grabbed him around his chest and carried him too. She ran south into the foothills of juniper trees and black lava rock. Behind her she heard the doctors running, but they had been taken by surprise, and as the hills became steeper and the cholla cactus were thicker, they stopped. When she reached the top of the hill, she stopped to listen in case they were circling around her. But in a few minutes she heard a car engine start and they drove away. The children had been too surprised to cry while she ran with them. Danny was shaking and Ella's little fingers were gripping Ayah's blouse.

She stayed up in the hills for the rest of the day, sitting on a black lava boulder in the sunshine where she could see for miles all around her. The sky was light blue and cloudless, and it was warm for late April. The sun warmth relaxed her and took the fear and anger away. She lay back on the rock and watched the sky. It seemed to her that she could walk into the sky, stepping through clouds endlessly. Danny played with little pebbles and stones, pretending they were birds' eggs and then little rabbits. Ella sat at her feet and dropped fistfuls of dirt into the breeze, watching the dust and particles of sand intently. Ayah watched a hawk soar high above them, dark wings gliding; hunting or only watching, she did not know. The hawk was patient and he circled all afternoon before he disappeared around the high volcanic peak the Mexicans called Guadalupe.

Late in the afternoon, Ayah looked down at the gray boxcar shack with the paint all peeled from the wood: the stove pipe on the roof was rusted and crooked. The fire she had built that morning in the oil drum stove had burned out. Ella was asleep in her lap now and Danny sat close to her, complaining that he was hungry; he asked when they would go to the house. "We will stay up here until your father comes," she told him, "because those white men were chasing us." The boy remembered then and he nodded at her silently.

If Jimmie had been there he could have read those papers and explained lo to her what they said. Ayah would have known then, never to sign them. The doctors came back the next day and they brought a BIA policeman with them. They told Chato they had her signature and that was all they needed. Except for the kids. She listened to Chato sullenly; she hated him when he told her it was the old woman who died in the winter, spitting blood; it was her old grandma who have given the children this disease. "They don't spit blood," she said coldly. "The whites lie." She held Ella and Danny, close to her, ready to run to the hills again. "I want a medicine man first," she said to Chato, not looking at him. He shook his head. "It's too late now. The policeman is with them. You signed the paper." His voice was gentle.

It was worse than if they had died: to lose the children and to know that somewhere, in a place called Colorado, in a place full of sick and dying strangers, her children were without her. There had been babies that died soon after they were born, and one that died before he could walk. She had carried them herself, up to the boulders and great pieces of the cliff that long ago crashed down from Long Mesa; she laid them in the crevices of sandstone and buried them in fine brown sand with round quartz pebbles that washed down the hills in the rain. She had endured it because they had been with her. But she could not bear this pain. She did not sleep for a long time after they took her children. She stayed on the hill where they had fled the first time, and she slept rolled up in the blanket Jimmie had sent her. She carried the pain in her belly and it was fed by everything she saw: the blue sky of their last day together and the dust and pebbles they played with; the swing in the elm tree and broomstick horse choked life from her. The pain filled her stomach and there was no room for food or for her lungs to fill with air. The air and the food would have been theirs.

She hated Chato, not because he let the policeman and doctors put the screaming children in the government car, but because he had taught her to sign her name. Because it was like the old ones always told her about learning their language or any of their ways: It endangers you. She slept alone on the hill until the middle of November when the first snows came. Then she made a bed for herself where the children had slept. She did not lie down beside Chato again until many years later, when he was sick and shivering and only her body could keep him warm. The illness came after the white rancher told Chato he was too old to work for him anymore, and Chato and his old woman should be out of the shack by the next afternoon because the rancher had hired new people to work there. That had satisfied her. To see how the white man repaid Chato's years of loyalty and work. All of Chato's fine-sounding English talk didn't change things.

It snowed steadily and the luminous light from the snow gradually diminished into the darkness. Somewhere in Ceboletta a dog barked and other village dogs joined with it. Ayah looked in the direction she had come, from the bar where Chato was buying the wine. Sometimes he told her to go on ahead and wait; and then he never came. And when she finally went back looking for him, she would find him passed out at the bottom of the wooden steps to Azzle's Bar. All the wine would be gone and most of the money too, from the pale blue check that came to them once a month in a government envelope. It was then that she would look at his face and his hands, scarred by ropes and the barbed wire of all those years, and she would think, this man is a stranger; for forty years she had smiled at him and cooked his food, but he remained a stranger. She stood up again, with the snow almost to her knees, and she walked back to find Chato.

It was hard to walk in the deep snow and she felt the air burn in her lungs. She stopped a short distance from the bar to rest and readjust the blanket. But this time he wasn't waiting for her at the bottom step with his old Stetson hat pulled down and his shoulders hunched up in his long wool overcoat.

She was careful not to slip on the wooden steps. When she pushed the door open, warm air and cigarette smoke hit her face. She looked around slowly and deliberately, in every corner, in every dark place that the old man might find to sleep. The bar owner didn't like Indians in there, especially Navajos, but he let Chato come in because he could talk Spanish like he was one of them. The men at the bar stared at her, and the bartender saw that she left the door open wide. Snowflakes were flying inside like moths and melting into a puddle on the oiled wood floor. He motioned to her to close the door, but she did not see him. She held herself straight and walked across the room slowly, searching the room with every step. The snow in her hair melted and she could feel it on her forehead. At the far corner of the room, she saw red flames at the mica window of the old stove door; she looked behind the stove just to make sure. The bar got quiet except for the Spanish polka music playing on the jukebox. She stood by the stove and shook the snow from her blanket and held it near the stove to dry. The wet wool smell reminded her of newborn goats in early March, brought inside to warm near the fire. She felt calm.

In past years they would have told her to get out. But her hair was white now and her face was wrinkled. They looked at her like she was a spider crawling slowly across the room. They were afraid; she could feel the fear. She looked at their faces steadily. They reminded her of the first time the white people brought her children back to her that winter. Danny had been shy and hid behind the thin white woman who brought them. And the baby had not known her until Ayah took her into her arms, and then Ella had nuzzled close to her as she had when she was nursing. The blonde woman was nervous and kept looking at a dainty gold watch on her wrist. She sat on the bench near the small window and watched the dark snow clouds gather around the mountains; she was worrying about the unpaved road. She was frightened by what she saw inside too: the strips of venison drying on a rope across the ceiling and the children jabbering excitedly in a language she did not know. So they stayed for only a few hours. Ayah watched the government car disappear down the road and she knew they were already being weaned from these lava hills and from this sky. The last time they came was in early June, and Ella stared at her the way the men in the bar were now staring. Ayah did not try to pick her up; she smiled at her instead and spoke cheerfully to Danny. When he tried to answer her, he could not seem to remember and he spoke English words with the Navajo. But he gave her a scrap of paper that he had found somewhere and carried in his pocket; it was folded in half, and he shyly looked up at her and said it was a bird. She asked Chato if they were home for good this time. He spoke to the white woman and she shook her head. "How much longer?" he asked, and she said she didn't know; but Chato saw how she stared at the box-car shack. Ayah turned away then. She did not say good-bye.

She felt satisfied that the men in the bar feared her. Maybe it was her face and the way she held her mouth with teeth clenched tight, like there was nothing anyone could do to her now. She walked north down the road, searching for the old man. She did this because she had the blanket, and there would be no place for him except with her and the blanket in the old adobe barn near the arroyo. They always slept there when they came to Cebolleta. If the money and the wine were gone, she would be relieved because then they could go home again; back to the old hogan with a dirt roof and rock walls where she herself had been born. And the next day the old man could go back to the few sheep they still had, to follow along behind them, guiding them, into dry sandy arroyos where sparse grass grew. She knew he did not like walking behind old ewes when for so many years he rode big quarter horses and worked with cattle. But she wasn't sorry for him; he should have known all along what would happen.

There had not been enough rain for their garden in five years; and that was when Chato finally hitched a ride into the town and brought back brown boxes of rice and sugar and big tin cans of welfare peaches. After that, at the first of the month they went to Ceboletta to ask the postmaster for the check; and then Chato would go to the bar and cash it. They did this as they planted the garden every May, not because anything would survive the summer dust, but because it was time to do this. The journey passed the days that smelled silent and dry like the caves above the canyon with yellow painted buffaloes on their walls.

He was walking along the pavement when she found him. He did not stop or turn around when he heard her behind him. She walked beside him and she noticed how slowly he moved now. He smelled strong of woodsmoke and urine. Lately he had been forgetting. Sometimes he called her by his sister's name and she had been gone for a long time. Once she had found him wandering on the road to the white man's ranch, and she asked him why he was going that way; he laughed at her and said, "You know they can't run that ranch without me," and he walked on determined, limping on the leg that had been crushed many years before. Now he looked at her curiously, as if for the first time, but he kept shuffling along, moving slowly along the side of the highway. His gray hair had grown long and spread out on the shoulders of the long overcoat. He wore the old felt hat pulled down over his ears. His boots were worn out at the toes and he had stuffed pieces of an old red shirt in the holes. The rags made his feet look like little animals up to their ears in snow. She laughed at his feet; the snow muffled the sound of her laugh. He stopped and looked at her again. The wind had quit blowing and the snow was falling straight down; the southeast sky was beginning to clear and Ayah could see a star.

"Let's rest awhile," she said to him. They walked away from the road and up the slope to the giant boulders that had tumbled down from the red sandrock mesa throughout the centuries of rainstorms and earth tremors. In a place where the boulders shut out the wind, they sat down with their backs against the rock. She offered half of the blanket to him and they sat wrapped together.

The storm passed swiftly. The clouds moved east. They were massive and full, crowding together across the sky. She watched them with the feeling of horses—steely blue-gray horses startled across the sky. The powerful haunches pushed into the distances and the tall hairs streamed white mist behind them. The sky cleared. Ayah saw that there was nothing between her and the stars. The light was crystalline. There was no shimmer, no distortion through earth haze. She breathed the clarity of the night sky; she smelled the purity of the half moon and the stars. He was lying on his side with his knees pulled up near his belly for warmth. His eyes were closed now, and in the light from the stars and the moon, he looked young again.

She could see it descend out of the night sky: an icy stillness from the edge of the thin moon. She recognized the freezing. It came gradually, sinking snowflake by snowflake until the crust was heavy and deep. It had the strength of the stars in Orion, and its journey was endless. Ayah knew that with the wine he would sleep. He would not feel it. She tucked the blanket around him, remembering how it was when Ella had been with her; and she felt the rush so big inside her heart for the babies. And she sang the only song she knew to sing for babies. She could not remember if she had ever sung it to her children, but she knew that her grandmother had sung it and her mother had sung it:

The earth is your mother,
   she holds you.

The sky, is your father,
    he protects you.
Sleep,
sleep.
Rainbow, is your sister,
    she loves you.
The winds are your brothers,
    they sing to you.
Sleep,
sleep.
We are together always
We are together always
There never was a time
when this
was not so.

from ON PHOTOGRAPHY

Susan Sontag

Recently, photography has become almost as widely practiced an amusement as sex and dancing—which means that, like every mass art form, photography is not practiced by most people as an art. It is mainly a social rite, a defense against anxiety, and a tool of power.

Memorializing the achievements of individuals considered as members of families (as well as of other groups) is the earliest popular use of photography. For at least a century, the wedding photograph has been as much a part of the ceremony as the prescribed verbal formulas. Cameras go with family life. According to a sociological study done in France, most households have a camera, but a household with children is twice as likely to have at least one camera as a household in which there are no children. Not to take pictures of one's children, particularly when they are small, is a sign of parental indifference, just as not turning up for one's graduation picture is a gesture of adolescent rebellion.

Through photographs, each family constructs a portrait-chronicle of itself—a portable kit of images that bears witness to its connectedness. It hardly matters what activities are photographed so long as photographs get taken and are cherished. Photography becomes a rite of family life just when, in the industrializing countries of Europe and America, the very institution of the family starts undergoing radical surgery. As that claustrophobic unit, the nuclear family, was being carved out of a much larger family aggregate, photography came along to memorialize, to restate symbolically, the imperiled continuity and vanishing extendedness of family life. Those ghostly traces, photographs, supply the token presence of the dispersed relatives. A family's photograph album is generally about the extended family—and, often, is all that remains of it.

As photographs give people an imaginary possession of a past that is unreal, they also help people to take possession of space in which they are insecure. Thus, photography develops in tandem with one of the most characteristic of modern activities: tourism. For the first time in history, large numbers of people regularly travel out of their habitual environments for short periods of time. It seems positively unnatural to travel for pleasure without taking a camera along. Photographs will offer indisputable evidence that the trip was made, that the program was carried out, that fun was had. Photographs document sequences of consumption carried on outside the view of family, friends, neighbors. But dependence on the camera, as the device that makes real what one is experiencing, doesn't fade when people travel more. Taking photographs fills the same need for the cosmopolitans accumulating photograph-trophies of their boat trip up the Albert Nile or their fourteen days in China as it does for lower-middle-class vacationers taking snapshots of the Eiffel Tower or Niagara Falls.

A way of certifying experience, taking photographs is also a way of refusing it—by limiting experience to a search for the photogenic, by converting experience into an image, a souvenir. Travel becomes a strategy for accumulating photographs. The very activity of taking pictures is soothing, and assuages general feelings of disorientation that are likely to be exacerbated by travel. Most tourists feel compelled to put the camera between themselves and whatever is remarkable that they encounter. Unsure of other responses, they take a picture. This gives shape to experience: stop, take a photograph, and move on. The method especially appeals to people handicapped by a ruthless work ethic—Germans, Japanese, and Americans. Using a camera appeases the anxiety which the work-driven feel about not working when they are on vacation and supposed to be having fun. They have something to do that is like a friendly imitation of work: they can take pictures.

People robbed of their past seem to make the most fervent picture takers, at home and abroad. Everyone who lives in an industrialized society is obliged gradually to give up the past, but in certain countries, such as the United States and Japan, the break with the past has been particularly traumatic. In the early 1970s, the fable of the brash American tourist of the 1950s and 1960s, rich with dollars and Babbittry,[1] was replaced by the mystery of the group-minded Japanese tourist, newly released from his island prison by the miracle of overvalued yen, who is generally armed with two cameras, one on each hip.

Photography has become one of the principal devices for experiencing something, for giving an appearance of participation. One full-page ad shows a small group of people standing pressed together, peering out of the photograph, all but one looking stunned, excited, upset. The one who wears a different expression holds a camera to his eye; he seems self-possessed, is almost smiling. While the others are passive, clearly alarmed spectators, having a camera has transformed one person into something active, a voyeur: only he has mastered the situation. What do these people see? We don't know. And it doesn't matter. It is an Event: something worth seeing—and therefore worth photographing. The ad copy, white letters across the dark lower third of the photograph like news coming over a teletype machine, consists of just six words: ". . . Prague . . . Woodstock . . . Vietnam . . . Sapporo . . . Londonderry . . . LEICA." Crushed hopes, youth antics, colonial wars, and winter sports are alike—are equalized by the camera. Taking photographs has set up a chronic voyeuristic relation to the world which levels the meaning of all events.

A photograph is not just the result of an encounter between an event and a photographer; picture-taking is an event in itself, and one with ever more peremptory rights—to interfere with, to invade, or to ignore whatever is going on. Our very sense of situation is now articulated by the camera's interventions. The omnipresence of cameras persuasively suggests that time consists of interesting events, events worth photographing. This, in turn, makes it easy to feel that any event, once underway, and whatever its moral character, should be allowed to complete itself—so that something else can be brought into the world, the photograph. After the event has ended, the picture will still exist, conferring on the event a kind of immortality (and importance) it would never otherwise have enjoyed. While real people are out there killing themselves or other real people, the photographer stays behind his or her camera, creating a tiny element of another world: the image-world that bids to outlast us all.

Photographing is essentially an act of non-intervention. Part of the horror of such memorable coups of contemporary photojournalism as the pictures of a Vietnamese bonze[2] reaching for the gasoline can, of a Bengali guerrilla in the act of bayoneting a trussed-up collaborator, comes from the awareness of how plausible it has become, in situations where the photographer has the choice between a photograph and a life, to choose the photograph. The person who intervenes cannot record; the person who is recording cannot intervene. Dziga Vertov's great film, *Man with a Movie Camera* (1929), gives the ideal image of the photographer as someone in perpetual movement, someone moving through a panorama of disparate events with such agility and speed that any intervention is out of the question. Hitchcock's *Rear Window* (1954) gives the complementary image: the photographer played by James Stewart has an intensi-

---

[1] *Babbittry* is a term, based on Sinclair Lewis's novel *Babbit* (1975), for Americans who define themselves by ready-made products and opinions. [ed.]

[2] A *bonze* is a Buddhist monk. [ed.]

fied relation to one event, through his camera, precisely because he has a broken leg and is confined to a wheelchair; being temporarily immobilized prevents him from acting on what he sees, and makes it even more important to take pictures. Even if incompatible with intervention in a physical sense, using a camera is still a form of participation. Although the camera is an observation station, the act of photographing is more than passive observing. Like sexual voyeurism, it is a way of at least tacitly, often explicitly, encouraging whatever is going on to keep on happening. To take a picture is to have an interest in things as they are, in the status quo remaining unchanged (at least for as long as it takes to get a "good" picture), to be in complicity with whatever makes a subject interesting, worth photographing—including, when that is the interest, another person's pain or misfortune.

❧ BLACK MEN AND PUBLIC SPACE ❧

Brent Staples

My first victim was a woman—white, well dressed, probably in her late twenties. I came upon her late one evening on a deserted street in Hyde Park, a relatively affluent neighborhood in an otherwise mean, impoverished section of Chicago. As I swung onto the avenue behind her, there seemed to be a discreet, uninflammatory distance between us. Not so. She cast back a worried glance. To her, the youngish black man—a broad six feet two inches with a beard and billowing hair, both hands shoved into the pockets of a bulky military jacket—seemed menacingly close. After a few more quick glimpses, she picked up her pace and was soon running in earnest. Within seconds she disappeared into a cross street.

That was more than a decade ago. I was twenty-two years old, a graduate student newly arrived at the University of Chicago. It was in the echo of that terrified woman's footfalls that I first began to know the unwieldy inheritance I'd come into—the ability to alter public space in ugly ways. It was clear that she thought herself the quarry of a mugger, a rapist, or worse. Suffering a bout of insomnia, however, I was stalking sleep, not defenseless wayfarers. As a softy who is scarcely able to take a knife to a raw chicken— let alone hold one to a person's throat—I was surprised, embarrassed, and dismayed all at once. Her flight made me feel like an accomplice in tyranny. It also made it clear that I was indistinguishable from the muggers who occasionally seeped into the area from the surrounding ghetto. That first encounter, and those that followed, signified that a vast, unnerving gulf lay between nighttime pedestrians—particularly women—and me. And I soon gathered that being perceived as dangerous is a hazard in itself. I only needed to turn a corner into a dicey situation, or crowd some frightened, armed person in a foyer somewhere, or make an errant move after being pulled over by a policeman. Where fear and weapons meet—and they often do in urban America—there is always the possibility of death.

In that first year, my first away from my hometown, I was to become thoroughly familiar with the language of fear. At dark, shadowy intersections, I could cross in front of a car stopped at a traffic light and elicit the *thunk, thunk, thunk, thunk* of the driver—black, white, male, or female—hammering down the door locks. On less traveled streets after dark, I grew accustomed to but never comfortable with people crossing to the other side of the street rather than pass me. Then there were the standard unpleasantries with policemen, doormen, bouncers, cabdrivers, and others whose business it is to screen out troublesome individuals *before* there is any nastiness.

I moved to New York nearly two years ago and I have remained an avid night walker. In central Manhattan, the near constant crowd cover minimizes tense one-on-one street encounters. Elsewhere—in SoHo, for example, where sidewalks are narrow and tightly spaced buildings shut out the sky—things can get very taut indeed.

After dark, on the warrenlike streets of Brooklyn where I live, I often see women who fear the worst from me. They seem to have set their faces on neutral, and with their purse straps strung across their chests bandolier-style, they forge ahead as though bracing themselves against being tackled. I understand, of course, that the danger they perceive is not a hallucination. Women are particularly vulnerable to street violence, and young black males are drastically overrepresented among the perpetrators of that violence.

401

Yet these truths are no solace against the kind of alienation that comes of being ever the suspect, a fearsome entity with whom pedestrians avoid making eye contact.

It is not altogether clear to me how I reached the ripe old age of twenty-two without being conscious of the lethality nighttime pedestrians attributed to me. Perhaps it was because in Chester, Pennsylvania, the small, angry industrial town where I came of age in the 1960s, I was scarcely noticeable against a backdrop of gang warfare, street knifings, and murders. I grew up one of the good boys, had perhaps a half-dozen fistfights. In retrospect, my shyness of combat has clear sources.

As a boy, I saw countless tough guys locked away; I have since buried several, too. They were babies, really—a teenage cousin, a brother of twenty-two, a childhood friend in his mid-twenties—all gone down in episodes of bravado played out in the streets. I came to doubt the virtues of intimidation early on. I chose, perhaps unconsciously, to remain a shadow—timid, but a survivor.

The fearsomeness mistakenly attributed to me in public places often has a perilous flavor. The most frightening of these confusions occurred in the late 1970s and early 1980s, when I worked as a journalist in Chicago. One day, rushing into the office of a magazine I was writing for with a deadline story in hand, I was mistaken for a burglar. The office manager called security and, with an ad hoc posse, pursued me through the labyrinthine halls, nearly to my editor's door. I had no way of proving who I was. I could only move briskly toward the company of someone who knew me.

Another time I was on assignment for a local paper and killing time before an interview. I entered a jewelry store on the city's affluent Near North Side. The proprietor excused herself and returned with an enormous red Doberman pinscher straining at the end of a leash. She stood, the dog extended toward me, silent to my questions, her eyes bulging nearly out of her head. I took a cursory look around, nodded, and bade her good night.

Relatively speaking, however, I never fared as badly as another black male journalist. He went to nearby Waukegan, Illinois, a couple of summers ago to work on a story about a murderer who was born there. Mistaking the reporter for the killer, police officers hauled him from his car at gunpoint and but for his press credentials would probably have tried to book him. Such episodes are not uncommon. Black men trade tales like this all the time.

Over the years, I learned to smother the rage I felt at so often being taken for a criminal. Not to do so would surely have led to madness. I now take precautions to make myself less threatening. I move about with care, particularly late in the evening. I give a wide berth to nervous people on subway platforms during the wee hours, particularly when I have exchanged business clothes for jeans. If I happen to be entering a building behind some people who appear skittish, I may walk by, letting them clear the lobby before I return, so as not to seem to be following them. I have been calm and extremely congenial on those rare occasions when I've been pulled over by the police.

And on late-evening constitutionals I employ what has proved to be an excellent tension-reducing measure: I whistle melodies from Beethoven and Vivaldi and the more popular classical composers. Even steely New Yorkers hunching toward nighttime destinations seem to relax, and occasionally they even join in the tune. Virtually everybody seems to sense that a mugger wouldn't be warbling bright, sunny selections from Vivaldi's *Four Seasons*. It is my equivalent of the cowbell that hikers wear when they know they are in bear country.

HEROIN/E

Cheryl Strayed

When my mother died, I stripped her naked. Plush round belly and her pale breasts rising above. Her arms were black-and-blue from all the needles going in. Needles with clear liquid and needles that only the nurses had a hold of and other needles gripping constantly into her, held tight with tape to the translucent skin of her hand or the silk skin of her wrist. And not one of those needles trying to save her. I picked her dead hand up, the arm slack and draping below. It did not want to be held. Her skin was dry and cracked and stabbed. When she died the nurse took the needle out forever. But I wanted it back, and eventually I would get it.

The day they told us my mother had cancer I was wearing green. Green pants, green shirt, green bow in my hair. My mother had sewn this outfit for me. I did not like such a themed look, but I wore it anyway, to the Mayo Clinic, as a penance, an offering, a talisman. We found a vacant wheelchair, and I got into it and raced and spun down the hallway. Cancer, at this point, was something we did not have to take seriously. My mother was forty-five. She looked fine, beautiful, I would later think, *alive*. It was just the two of us, me and my mother. There were others too, my stepfather working his job, wondering, my grandparents waiting by the phone, wanting to know if it was true, if perhaps the oncologist in Duluth had been mistaken after all. But now, as before, as it would always be, it was only me and my mother. In the elevator she sat in the wheelchair and reached out to tug at my pants. She rubbed the fabric between her fingers proprietarily. "Perfect," she said.

I was twenty-two. I believed that if a doctor told you that you were going to die soon, you'd be taken to a room with a gleaming wooden desk. This was not so. My mother sat with her shirt off on top of the table with paper stretched over it. When she moved, the room was on fire with the paper ripping and crinkling beneath her. She wore a pale yellow smock with strings meant to be tied. I could see her soft back, the small shelf of flesh that curved down at her waist. The doctor said she'd be lucky if she lived a year. My mother blinked her wet eyes but did not cry. She sat with her hands folded tightly together and her ankles hooked one to the other. Shackled to herself. She'd asked the doctor if she could continue riding her horse. He then took a pencil in his hand and stood it upright on the edge of the sink and tapped it down on the surface hard. "This is your spine after radiation," he said. "One jolt and your bones will crumble like a dry cracker."

First we went to the women's restroom. Each of us locked in a separate stall, weeping. We didn't say a word. Not because we felt alone in our grief, but because we were so together in it, as if we were one body instead of two. I could feel her weight leaning against the door, her hands slapping slowly against it, causing the entire frame of the bathroom stalls to shake. Later we came out to wash our hands and faces, standing side by side in the ladies' room mirror.

We were sent to the pharmacy to wait. I sat next to my mother in my green pantsuit. There was a big bald boy in an old man's lap. There was a woman who had an arm that swung wildly from the elbow. She held it stiffly with the other hand, trying to calm it. She waited. We waited. There was a beautiful dark-haired woman who sat in a wheelchair. She wore a purple hat and a handful of diamond rings. We could not take our eyes off her. She spoke in Spanish to the people gathered around her, her family and perhaps her husband. "Do you think she has cancer?" my mother whispered loudly to me. There was a song coming quietly over the speakers. A song without words, but my mother knew the words anyway and sang them softly to herself. "Paper roses, paper roses, oh they're only paper roses to me," she sang. She put her hand on mine and said, "I used to listen to that song when I was young. It's funny to think of that. To think about listening to the same song now. I would've never known." My mother's name was called then: her prescriptions were ready. "Go get them for me," she said. "Tell them who you are. Tell them you're my daughter."

My mother said I could have her jewelry box. She said, "When I am done with it." She was lying in the bed my stepfather had made for her, for them, with branches twisting and arching up behind her, leaves and jumping bugs carved discreetly into them. There was a dancing pink girl who lived in the jewelry box. She stood and twirled around to the song that played when you wound it up and opened the box. The song changed as it slowed, became sorrowful and destitute. The girl tottered and then stopped as if it hurt her. She had lips the size of a pinhead painted red and a scratchy pink tutu. When we shut the box she went down into it, stiff as a board, bending at the feet.

"I always wonder what the ballerina is thinking," my mother said dreamily.

When my mother got cancer I'd folded my life down. I was a senior in college in Minneapolis, and I'd convinced my professors to allow me to be in class only two days each week. As soon as those days were over, I drove north to the house in rural Minnesota where I had grown up, racing home, to my mother. I could not bear to be away from her. Plus I was needed. My stepfather was with my mother when he could be, when he wasn't working as a carpenter in an attempt to pay the bills. I cooked food that my mother tried to eat. She'd say: pork chops and stuffed green peppers, cherry cheesecake and chicken with rice, and then holler the recipes out to me from her bed. When I'd finished she'd sit like a prisoner staring down at her steaming plate. "It smells good," she'd say. "I think I'll be able to eat it later." I scrubbed the floors. I took everything from the cupboards and put new paper down. My mother slept and moaned and counted and swallowed her pills, or on good days she sat in a chair and talked to me, she paged through books.

"Put these on for me." My mother sat up and reached for a pair of socks. It had been a few weeks since we'd learned of her cancer, and already she could not reach her own feet without great pain. I bent at my mother's feet. She held the ball of socks in her hand. "Here," she said. I had never put socks onto another person, and it was harder than you might think. They don't slide over the skin. They go on crooked and you have to work to get them right. I became frustrated with my mother, as if she were holding her foot in a manner that made it impossible for me. She sat back with her body leaning on her hands on the bed, her eyes closed. I could hear her breathing deeply, slowly. "Goddammit," I said, "help me." My mother looked down at me, silently.

We didn't know it then, but this would be the last time she was home. Her movements were slow and thick as she put her coat on, and she held on to the walls and edges of doors as she made her way out of the house. On the drive to the hospital in Duluth she looked out the window. She said, "Look at the snow there on those pines." She told me to toot my horn when we went past Cindy's house in Moose Lake. She said, "Be careful of the ice. It's black ice." She held an old plastic milk jug with the top cut off so she could vomit into it during the drive. My mother put one hand up to her ribs, where the cancer lived, and pressed gently. "Wouldn't that be something, to get into an accident now?"

Three years after my mother died I fell in love with a man who had electric blue hair. I'd gone to Portland, Oregon, to visit a friend, seeking respite from the shambles my life had become. I had thought that by then

I'd have recovered from the loss of my mother and also that the single act of her death would constitute the only loss. It is perhaps the greatest misperception of the death of a loved one: that it will end there, that death itself will be the largest blow. No one told me that in the wake of that grief other griefs would ensue. I had recently separated from the husband I loved. My stepfather was no longer a father to me. I was alone in the world and acutely aware of that. I went to Portland for a break.

We'll call the man with electric blue hair Joe. I met him on his twenty-fourth birthday and drank sangria with him. In the morning he wanted to know if I'd like some heroin. He lived on a street called Mississippi, in North Portland. There was a whole gathering of people who'd rigged up apartments above what thirty years before had been a thriving Rexall drugstore. Within days I lived there with him. In the beginning, for about a week, we smoked it. We made smooth pipes out of aluminum foil and sucked the smoke of burning black tar heroin up into them. "This is called chasing the dragon!" Joe said, and clapped his hands. The first time I smoked heroin it was a hot, sunny day in July. I got down on my knees in front of Joe where he sat on the couch. "More," I said, and laughed like a child. "More, more, more," I chanted. I had never cared much for drugs. I'd experimented with each kind once or twice, and drank alcohol with moderation and reserve. Heroin was different. I loved it. It was the first thing that worked. 1t took away every scrap of hurt that I had inside of me. When I think of heroin now, it is like remembering a person I met and loved intensely. A person I know I must live without.

The first time they offered my mother morphine, she said no. "Morphine is what they give to dying people," she said. "Morphine means there is no hope."

We were at the hospital in Duluth. We could not get the pillows right. My mother cried in pain and frustration when the nurses came into the room. The doctor told her that she shouldn't hold out any longer, that he had to give her morphine. He told her she was *actively dying*. He was young, perhaps thirty. He stood next to my mother, a gentle hairy hand slung into his pocket, looking down at her in the bed.

The nurses came one by one and gave her the morphine with a needle. Within a couple weeks my mother was dead. In those weeks she couldn't get enough of the drug. She wanted more morphine, more often. The nurses liked to give her as little as they could. One of the nurses was a man, and I could see the shape of his penis through his tight white nurse's trousers. I wanted desperately to pull him into the small bathroom beyond the foot of my mother's bed and offer myself up to him, to do anything at all if he would help us. And also I wanted to take pleasure from him, to feel the weight of his body against me, to feel his mouth in my hair and hear him say my name to me over and over again, to force him to acknowledge me, to make this matter to him, to crush his heart with mercy for us. I held my closed book on my lap and watched him walk softly into the room in his padded white shoes. My mother asked him for more morphine. She asked for it in a way that I have never seen anyone ask for anything. A mad dog. He did not look at my mother when she asked him this, but at his wrist watch. He held the same expression on his face regardless of the answer. Sometimes he gave it to her without a word, and sometimes he told her no in a voice as soft as his shoes and his penis curled up in his pants. My mother begged and whimpered then. She cried and her tears fell in the wrong direction, not down over the lush light of her cheeks to the corners of her mouth but away from the edges of her eyes to her ears and into the nest of her hair on the bed.

I wanted it and I got it, and the more heroin we got, the stingier we became with it. Perhaps if we snorted it, we thought, we'd get higher on less. And then, of course, the needle. The hypodermic needle, I'd read, was the barrier that kept the masses from heroin. The opposite was true with me. I loved the clean smell of it, the tight clench around my arm, the stab of hurt, the dull badge of ache. It made me think of my mother. It made me think of her, and then that thought would go away into the loveliest bliss. A bliss I had not imagined.

There was a man named Santos whom we called when we wanted heroin. He would make us wait by the telephone for hours, and then he'd call and instruct us to meet him in the parking lot of a Safeway. I sat in the car while Joe took a short drive with Santos in his yellow Pinto, and then Joe would calmly get back in the car with me and we'd go home. On some occasions we went to Santos's house. Once he sat in his front window with a shotgun across his lap. Once he clutched my thigh when Joe left the room and told me that if I came to see him alone he'd give me heroin free. Another time he held his baby daughter, just a month old. I looked at her and smiled and told Santos how beautiful she was, and inside of me I felt the presence of my real life. The woman who I actually was. The kind of woman who knows the beauty of a baby, who will have a baby, who once was a baby.

The days of my mother's death, the morphine days, and those that followed, the heroin days, lasted only weeks, months—but each day was an eternity, one stacked up on the other, a cold clarity inside of a deep haze. And unoccupied as well. Just me and my mother, or the ghost of her, though others surely came and went.

Some days flowers came to my mother's hospital room, and I set them on the edges of tables and windowsills. Women came too. Women who volunteered for the hospital. Old Catholic women, with hair cut close to the scalp or woven into long braids and pinned to their heads. My mother greeted them as she did the flowers: impervious, unmoved, resolute.

The women thought it would be for the best when my mother died. They sat next to me on the vinyl furniture and told me in low tones about the deaths of their own mothers. Mothers who had died standing at kitchen sinks, in the back seats of cars, in beds lit with candles. And also about the ones who made it. The ones with the *will to live*. Of tumors vanishing and clean blood and opaque bones. People who fought it, who refused to die. The ones who went and then came back. The survivors. The heroes. It would be for the best, they whispered, when it was over. Her life, that is. My mother's.

People whom I knew came, and I did not recognize them at first. It seemed they all wore strange hats or other disguises during this time, though I am certain that is not true. They were friends of my mother's. They couldn't bear to stay in the room, so instead they left chicken pot pies and bread. Scalloped potatoes and blocks of cheddar cheese. By then my mother could not eat half a banana. Couldn't lick a lick of a popsicle without retching it back up. They said her name to her, and she said their names back to them, hoarse and confused. She said, "How nice you came." And she put a wan smile on her face. Her hair was flattened against her head, and I reached to smooth it into place.

I asked my mother if she would like for me to read to her. I had two books: *The Awakening,* by Kate Chopin, and *The Optimist's Daughter,* by Eudora Welty. These were books we'd read before, books we'd loved. So I started in, but I could not go on. Each word I said erased itself in the air. It was the same when I tried to pray. I prayed fervently, rabidly, to God, any god, to a god I could not identify or find. I prayed to the whole wide universe and thought perhaps God would be in it. I prayed and I faltered. God, I realized, had no intention of making things happen or not, of saving my mother's life. God would come later, perhaps, to help me bear it.

She taught me to knit, my mother, and I did this in the room while she slept and lived the last while. It occurred to me that she had taught me to knit for this particular occasion. So that I would have a place to put my hands and my eyes. "What are you making?" she asked.

"A scarf."

"For who?" Her hand pinched the sheet that covered her.

"I don't know," I said. "I am simply knitting a scarf."

The best part about knitting is the tapping, tapping, tapping of the needles. A sound so silent that it is like the language of snakes or rabbits or deer.

Eventually the nurses and doctors stopped paying any mind to what my mother said or wanted. They looked to me to decide how much morphine to give her. They said I had a choice: she could be in great pain but fairly conscious, or she could be comfortable but higher than a kite, and usually passed out. Ultimately, it was not up to me.

"Promise me one thing," she said. My mother was not dramatic or concise in her dying. She hadn't offered a single directive in the past days, and I was desperate for guidance. "That you won't allow me to be in pain anymore. I've had too much pain."

"Yes," I said, "yes."

There was using heroin and also not using it. In the mornings when I woke, groggy and drained, I'd stand in front of the mirror and talk to myself. I was shocked by my own life. *This was not meant to be,* I'd think in the mornings. *Stop it,* I said. *No more.* And then I would shower and dress in my black pants and white shirt and black bow tie and take a bus downtown to serve people coffee and pancakes. At two in the afternoon I'd take the bus home again with hopefully sixty bucks in my pocket for another score of heroin. This is how it went.

Joe waited for me to get home. He cooked me macaroni and cheese and called Santos. He pulled me into his bed and jumped up when the phone rang. I made him stick the needle into me the first time, and then he taught me how to do it myself. What I loved about Joe is that he didn't love me, or himself. I loved that he would not only let me but help me destroy myself. I'd never shared that with another person. The dark glory of our united self-destruction had the force of something like love. *I get to do this,* I thought. *I get to waste my life.* I felt a terrible power within me. The power of controlling the uncontrollable. *I get to be junk,* I thought.

But this was not to be. My husband, Mark, called me. He was in town and wanted to see me. The friend I'd come to visit in Portland had told him about Joe and about my using heroin, and in response he drove from Minneapolis to talk to me. I met him within the hour at our friend's house. He sat at a table in the kitchen with the branches of a fig tree tapping on the window nearby. He said, "You look, you look . . . different. You seem so, how can I say this—you seem like you aren't here." First he put his hands on mine, and we held on to one another, locked hand to hand. I couldn't explain it to him, the why. And then we fought. He stood up and screamed at me so loudly that I put my hands over my head for cover. His arms gestured madly into the air, at nothing. He clawed at himself and ripped the shirt from his own back and threw it at me. He wanted me to go home with him in an hour. Not for a reunion but to get away, not from Joe but from heroin.

I told Mark I needed to think. I drove back to Joe's apartment and sat in the lawn chair on the sidewalk. Heroin made me dumb, or distant, rather. A thought would form and then evaporate. I couldn't get a hold of my mind. I sat in the lawn chair on the sidewalk, and a man walked up to me and said his name was Tim. He took my hand and shook it and told me I could trust him. He asked if I could give him three dollars for diapers, then if he could use my phone, and then if I had change for a five-dollar bill, and on and on in a series of twisting requests and sorry stories that confused and compelled me to stand and pull the last ten dollars I had out of my jeans pocket. He saw the money and pulled a knife out of his shirt. He held it gently up to my chest and said, "Give me that money, sweetheart."

I packed a few things and called Mark. When he pulled up to the corner where I was waiting, I got into his car. By sunset Portland was long gone. In Montana we checked into a motel to sleep. I held myself in bed, rocking with a headache, a sickness in my gut. Mark brought me water and chocolate and watched television. I sat in the car as we drove across the country, and I felt my real life present but unattainable, as if heroin had taken me entirely from myself. Mark and I fought and cried and shook the car with our fighting. We were monstrous in our cruelty. We talked kindly afterward, shocked at ourselves and each other. We decided that we would get divorced. I hated him and I loved him. He had known my mother. I felt trapped, branded, held, and beloved. Like a daughter. "I didn't ask you to come to Portland," I screamed. "You came for your own reasons," I said.

"Maybe," he said.

"You love me that much?" I asked. "You came all this way to get me? Why?"

"Because," he said, 'just because."

I wanted my mother to love me, but more. I wanted her to prove it, to live. To go to battle and win. And if she was going to die, I wanted her to tell me, in the end, how I should live, without her. Until that point I had wanted just the opposite. I could not bear for her to tell me what to do or how to live. I had wanted to be unknown by her, opaque to her wondering eyes.

The last days, my mother was not so much high as down under. When she woke, she'd say, "Oh, oh." Or she'd let out a sad gulp of air. She'd look at me, and there would be a flash of love. Other times she'd roll back into sleep as if I were not there. Sometimes when my mother woke she did not know where she was. She demanded an enchilada and then some applesauce. She'd say, "That horse darn near stepped on me," and look around the room for it accusingly. During this time I wanted my mother to say to me that I had been the best daughter in the world. I did not want to want this, but I did, inexplicably, as if I had a great fever that could only be cooled by those words. I went so far as to ask her directly. "Have I been the best daughter in the world?" She said yes, I had, of course. But this was not enough. I wanted those words to knit together in my mother's mind and for them to be delivered, fresh, to me. I was ravenous for love.

One day a woman with a clipboard asked if I'd go with her to the cafeteria. She said that she wanted to talk to me about a donation my mother had made. Her name was Janet and she was dressed in a navy-colored shirt with little white fringes on each shoulder, as if she were the captain of something. Her fingernails were long and red and they clicked together when she moved her hands in certain ways.

When we sat down with two cups of coffee between us, she told me that my mother was an organ donor but that because she had cancer throughout her body they would only take her eyes.

"Her eyes?"

"Well, not the whole eye, of course, but parts of the organ." Janet took her cup up into her hands; one fingernail tapped against it. "We make it a policy to inform people close to the donor. In your mother's case, upon death, we will need to place ice on her eyes in order to preserve them." She thought about this a moment. This way you will understand what is happening when you see that we must put the bags of ice on her face. The removal is performed within a few hours after death." Her fingernails went up to the sides of her face, hovering in midair. "Small incisions will be made at the side of each eye." Janet showed me this, pointing with her own sharp nails. "The skin will be sutured carefully to disguise signs of this procedure." She swallowed a sip of coffee and looked at me. "It does not preclude an open-casket viewing."

I dreamed of heroin. I woke in the middle of the night with a wanting so deep I was breathless. I had started seeing a therapist to talk about heroin. She told me that this wanting was normal, that indeed when you use heroin the brain responds by activating pleasure neurons that would normally remain dormant. She said it would take months for them to calm. Until then, they go on aching to be fed. Trying to trick your body into it. I could see them, spindly arms with mouths like flowers, blooming or wilting and then blooming again. "What about pain?" I asked her. "Are there neurons in the brain that come alive only with agony? And if so, how long does it take for them to die, to fold back into themselves and float away?"

I saw Joe two more times. I'd kept in touch with him; calling him late at night from Minneapolis, I could hear the heroin in his voice, making it soft and open. Within a month he was at my door. He looked weak and pale. He sat on my couch and shot up and then lurched into my kitchen and bent to vomit into my sink. He wiped his face and smiled. "It's worth it," he said, "getting sick. Because you feel so good through it all." We spent a week in my apartment using the supply of heroin he'd brought with him. I knew I had to end this, and finally I did. He left when I asked him to. The second time I saw him, a year had passed and I was moving to Portland for reasons unrelated to him. We went to the beach for the day. He was no longer the smart, sexy, simpering man I'd fallen for, but a junkie. Joe had scabs on his skin from constant scratching; his bony arms were bruised and punctured. He didn't care anymore what color his hair was. I sat on the cool sand watching the Pacific Ocean roar in while Joe locked himself in the public restroom to shoot up. I held myself stiff against the desire to join him. The ocean inched nearer and nearer to me with each passing minute. I was both sickened by Joe and compelled. I felt in the presence of a dying man, a young, dying man, and I knew that I could never see him again if I wanted to live. And I did.

My mother didn't have time to get skinny. Her death was a relentless onward march. The hero's journey is one of return, but my mother's was all forward motion. She was altered but still fleshy when she died, the body of a woman among the living. She had her hair too, brown and brittle and frayed from being in bed for weeks.

From the room where she died I could see the great Lake Superior out her window. The biggest lake in the world, and the coldest. To see it, I had to work. I pressed my face sideways, hard, against the glass, and I'd catch a slice of it going on forever into the horizon. "A room with a view!" my mother exclaimed. "All of my life I've waited for a room with a view."

I arranged the flowers closer into my mother, to the edges of the tables, so that she could see them without having to turn her head. Bouquets of pink carnations, yellow roses, daisies, and tiger lilies. Flowers that originated on other continents and were brought here to witness my mother's dying.

My mother wanted to die sitting up, so I took all the pillows I could get my hands on and made a backrest for her. I wanted to take my mother and prop her in a field of yarrow to die. I covered her with a quilt that I had brought from home, one she had sewn herself out of pieces of our old clothing. "Get that out of here," she said savagely, and then kicked her legs like a swimmer to make it go away.

I watched my mother. It was March, and outside, the sun glinted off the sidewalks and the icy edges of the snow. It was Saint Patrick's Day, and the nurses brought my mother a square block of green Jell-O that sat quivering on the table beside her. It was the last day of her life, and my mother did not sleep, she did not wake. She held her eyes still and open. They were the bluest thing in the room, perhaps in all of Duluth. Bluer than the lake. They were the color of the sky on the best day of your life.

My mother died fast but not all of a sudden. A slow-burning fire when flames disappear to smoke and then smoke to air. She never once closed her eyes. First they were bitter and then they were bewildered and they changed again to something else, to a state that I have had, finally, to see as heroic. Blue, blue eyes. Daggers of blue wanting and wanting. To stay, to stay.

CODE OF STUDENT CONDUCT

Syracuse University Student Handbook

Students at Syracuse University are expected to conduct themselves in a manner supportive of the educational mission of the institution. Integrity, respect for the person and property of others, and a commitment to intellectual and personal growth in a diverse population are values deemed fundamental to membership in this University community.

Syracuse University considers the following behavior, or attempts thereof, by any student or student organization, whether acting alone or with any other persons, to violate the Code of Student Conduct:

1. Physical harm or threat of physical harm to any person or persons, including but not limited to: assault, sexual abuse, or other forms of physical abuse.
2. Harassment, whether physical or verbal, oral or written, which is beyond the bounds of protected free speech, directed at a specific individual(s), easily construed as "fighting words," and likely to cause an immediate breach of the peace.
3. Conduct which threatens the mental health, physical health or safety of any person or persons including but not limited to: hazing, drug or alcohol abuse, and other forms of destructive behavior.
4. Academic dishonesty,* including but not limited to: plagiarism and cheating, and other forms of academic misconduct, for example; misuse of academic resources or facilities; misuse of computer software, data, equipment, or networks.
5. Intentional disruption or obstruction of lawful activities of the University or its members including their exercise of the right to assemble and to peaceful protest.
6. Theft of or damage to personal or University property or services or illegal possession or use of the same.
7. Forgery, alteration, fabrication or misuse of identification cards, records, grades, diplomas, University documents, or misrepresentation of any kind to a University office or official.
8. Unauthorized entry, use, or occupation of University facilities that are locked, closed, or otherwise restricted as to use.
9. Disorderly conduct including, but not limited to: public intoxication, lewd, indecent or obscene behavior, libel, slander, and illegal gambling.
10. Illegal purchase, use, possession, or distribution of alcohol, drugs, or controlled substances.
11. Failure to comply with the lawful directives of University officials who are performing the duties of their office, especially as they are related to the maintenance of safety or security.
12. Unauthorized possession or use of firearms, explosive devices, fireworks, dangerous or illegal weapons, or hazardous materials.
13. Interference with or misuse of fire alarms, blue lights, elevators, or other safety and security equipment or programs.

From *Syracuse University Rights and Responsibilities Handbook.*

*Cases involving academic dishonesty are handled within the student's school or college.

14. Violation of any federal, state, or local law which has a negative impact on the well-being of Syracuse University or its individual members.

15. Violation of University policies, rules, or regulations that are published in the *Student Handbook,* or any other official University publications or agreements.

Culpability is not diminished for acts in violation of this Code that are committed in ignorance of the Code or under the influence of alcohol, illegal drugs, or improper use of controlled substances.

WHAT'S SO BAD ABOUT HATE?

Andrew Sullivan

I

I wonder what was going on in John William King's head two years ago when he tied James Byrd, Jr.'s feet to the back of a pickup truck and dragged him three miles down a road in rural Texas. King and two friends had picked up Byrd, who was black, when he was walking home, half drunk, from a party. As part of a bonding ritual in their fledgling white supremacist group, the three men took Byrd to a remote part of town, beat him, and chained his legs together before attaching them to the truck. Pathologists at King's trial testified that Byrd was probably alive and conscious until his body finally hit a culvert and split in two. When King was offered a chance to say something to Byrd's family at the trial, he smirked and uttered an obscenity.

We know all these details now, many months later. We know quite a large amount about what happened before and after. But I am still drawn, again and again, to the flash of ignition, the moment when fear and loathing became hate, the instant of transformation when King became hunter and Byrd became prey.

What was that? And what was it when Buford Furrow, Jr., longtime member of the Aryan Nations, calmly walked up to a Filipino-American mailman he happened to spot, asked him to mail a letter, and then shot him at point-blank range? Or when Russell Henderson beat Matthew Shepard, a young gay man, to a pulp, removed his shoes, and then, with the help of a friend, tied him to a post, like a dead coyote, to warn off others?

For all our documentation of these crimes and others, our political and moral disgust at them, our morbid fascination with them, our sensitivity to their social meaning, we seem at times to have no better idea now than we ever had of what exactly they were about. About what that moment means when, for some reason or other, one human being asserts absolute, immutable superiority over another. About not the violence, but what the violence expresses. About what—exactly—hate is. And what our own part in it may be.

I find myself wondering what hate actually is in part because we have created an entirely new offense in American criminal law—a "hate crime"—to combat it. And barely a day goes by without someone somewhere declaring war against it. Last month President Clinton called for an expansion of hate-crime laws as "what America needs in our battle against hate." A couple of weeks later, Senator John McCain used a campaign speech to denounce the "hate" he said poisoned the land. New York's mayor, Rudolph Giuliani, recently tried to stop the Million Youth March in Harlem on the grounds that the event was organized by people "involved in hate marches and hate rhetoric."

The media concur in their emphasis. In 1985, there were eleven mentions of "hate crimes" in the national media database Nexis. By 1990, there were more than a thousand. In the first six months of 1999, there were seven thousand. "Sexy fun is one thing," wrote a *New York Times* reporter about sexual assaults in Woodstock '99's mosh pit. "But this was an orgy of lewdness tinged with hate." And when Benjamin Smith marked the Fourth of July this year by targeting blacks, Asians, and Jews for murder in Indiana and Illinois, the story wasn't merely about a twisted young man who had emerged on the scene. As the

413

Times put it, "Hate arrived in the neighborhoods of Indiana University, in Bloomington, in the early-morning darkness."

But what exactly was this thing that arrived in the early-morning darkness? For all our zeal to attack hate, we still have a remarkably vague idea of what it actually is. A single word, after all, tells us less, not more. For all its emotional punch, "hate" is far less nuanced an idea than prejudice, or bigotry, or bias, or anger, or even mere aversion to others. Is it to stand in for all these varieties of human experience—and everything in between? If so, then the war against it will be so vast as to be quixotic. Or is "hate" to stand for a very specific idea or belief, or set of beliefs, with a very specific object or group of objects? Then waging war against it is almost certainly unconstitutional. Perhaps these kinds of questions are of no concern to those waging war on late. Perhaps it is enough for them that they share a sentiment that there is too much hate and never enough vigilance in combating it. But sentiment is a poor basis for law and a dangerous tool in politics. It is better to leave some unwinnable wars unfought.

II

Hate is everywhere. Human beings generalize all the time, ahead of time, about everyone and everything. A large part of it may even be hard-wired. At some point in our evolution, being able to know beforehand who was friend or foe was not merely a matter of philosophical reflection. It was a matter of survival. And even today it seems impossible to feel a loyalty without also feeling a disloyalty, a sense of belonging without an equal sense of unbelonging. We're social beings. We associate. Therefore we disassociate. And although it would be comforting to think that the one could happen without the other, we know in reality that it doesn't. How many patriots are there who have never felt a twinge of xenophobia?

Of course, by hate we mean something graver and darker than this kind of lazy prejudice. But the closer you look at this distinction, the fuzzier it gets. Much of the time, we harbor little or no malice toward people of other backgrounds or places or ethnicities or ways of life. But then a car cuts you off at an intersection and you find yourself noticing immediately that the driver is a woman, or black, or old, or fat, or white, or male. Or you are walking down a city street at night and hear footsteps quickening behind you. You look around and see that it is a white woman and not a black man, and you are instantly relieved. These impulses are so spontaneous they are almost involuntary. But where did they come from? The mindless need to be mad at someone—anyone—or the unconscious eruption of a darker prejudice festering within?

In 1993, in San Jose, California, two neighbors, one heterosexual, one homosexual, were engaged in a protracted squabble over grass clippings. (The full case is recounted in *Hate Crimes,* by James B. Jacobs and Kimberly Potter.) The gay man regularly mowed his lawn without a grass catcher, which prompted his neighbor to complain on many occasions that grass clippings spilled over onto his driveway. Tensions grew until one day the gay man mowed his front yard, spilling clippings onto his neighbor's driveway, prompting the straight man to yell an obscene and common antigay insult. The wrangling escalated. At one point the gay man agreed to collect the clippings from his neighbor's driveway but then later found them dumped on his own porch. A fracas ensued, with the gay man spraying the straight man's son with a garden hose and the son hitting and kicking the gay man several times, yelling antigay slurs. The police were called, and the son was eventually convicted of a hate-motivated assault, a felony. But what was the nature of the hate, antigay bias or suburban property-owner madness?

Or take the Labor Day parade last year in Broad Channel, a small island in Jamaica Bay, Queens. Almost everyone there is white, and in recent years a group of local volunteer firefighters has taken to decorating a pickup truck for the parade in order to win the prize for "funniest float." Their themes have tended toward the outrageously provocative. Beginning in 1995, they won prizes for floats depicting "Hasidic Park," "Gooks of Hazzard," and "Happy Gays." Last year they called their float "Black to the Future, Broad Channel 2098." They imagined their community a century hence as a largely black enclave, with every stereotype imaginable: watermelons, basketballs, and so on. At one point during the parade, one of them mimicked the dragging death of James Byrd. It was caught on videotape, and before long the entire community was depicted as a caldron of hate.

It's an interesting case, because the float was indisputably in bad taste and the improvisation on the Byrd killing was grotesque. But was it hate? The men on the float were local heroes for their volunteer work; they had no record of bigoted activity and were not members of any racist organizations. In previous years they had made fun of many other groups, and they saw themselves more as provocateurs than bigots. When they were described as racists, it came as a shock to them. They apologized for poor taste but refused to confess to bigotry. "The people involved aren't horrible people," protested a local woman. "Was it a racist act? I don't know. Are they racists? I don't think so."

If hate is a self-conscious activity, she has a point. The men were primarily motivated by the desire to shock and to reflect what they thought was their community's culture. Their display was not aimed at any particular black people or at any blacks who lived in Broad Channel—almost none do. But if hate is primarily an unconscious activity, then the matter is obviously murkier. And by taking the horrific lynching of a black man as a spontaneous object of humor, the men were clearly advocating indifference to it. Was this an aberrant excess? Or the real truth about the men's feelings toward African-Americans? Hate or tastelessness? And how on earth is anyone, even perhaps the firefighters themselves, going to know for sure?

Or recall H. L. Mencken. He shared in the anti-Semitism of his time with more alacrity than most and was an indefatigable racist. "It is impossible," he wrote in his diary, "to talk anything resembling discretion or judgment into a colored woman. They are all essentially childlike, and even hard experience does not teach them anything." He wrote at another time of the "psychological stigmata" of the "Afro-American race." But it is also true that during much of his life, day to day, Mencken conducted himself with no regard to race and supported a politics that was clearly integrationist. As the editor of his diary has pointed out, Mencken published many black authors in his magazine, *The Mercury,* and lobbied on their behalf with his publisher, Alfred A. Knopf. The last thing Mencken ever wrote was a diatribe against racial segregation in Baltimore's public parks. He was good friends with leading black writers and journalists, including James Weldon Johnson, Walter White, and George S. Schuyler, and played an underappreciated role in promoting the Harlem Renaissance.

What would our modern view of hate do with Mencken? Probably ignore him, or change the subject. But with regard to hate, I know lots of people like Mencken. He reminds me of conservative friends who oppose almost every measure for homosexual equality yet genuinely delight in the company of their gay friends. It would be easier for me to think of them as haters, and on paper, perhaps, there is a good case that they are. But in real life, I know they are not. Some of them clearly harbor no real malice toward me or other homosexuals whatsoever.

They are as hard to figure out as those liberal friends who support every gay rights measure they have ever heard of but do anything to avoid going into a gay bar with me. I have to ask thyself in the same frustrating kind of way, are they liberal bigots or bigoted liberals? Or are they neither bigots nor liberals, but merely people?

III

Hate used to be easier to understand. When Sartre described anti-Semitism in his 1946 essay "Anti-Semite and Jew," he meant a very specific array of firmly held prejudices, with a history, an ideology, and even a pseudoscience to back them up. He meant a systematic attempt to demonize and eradicate an entire race. If you go to the Web site of the World Church of the Creator, the organization that inspired young Benjamin Smith to murder in Illinois earlier this year, you will find a similarly bizarre, pseudo-rational ideology. The kind of literature read by Buford Furrow before he rained terror on a Jewish kindergarten last month and then killed a mailman because of his color is full of the same paranoid loopiness. And when we talk about hate, we often mean this kind of phenomenon.

But this brand of hatred is mercifully rare in the United States. These professional maniacs are to hate what serial killers are to murder. They should certainly not be ignored, but they represent what Harold Meyerson, writing in *Salon,* called "niche haters": cold-blooded, somewhat deranged, often poorly socialized psychopaths. In a free society with relatively easy access to guns, they will always pose a menace.

But their menace is a limited one, and their hatred is hardly typical of anything very widespread. Take Buford Furrow. He famously issued a "wake-up call" to "kill Jews" in Los Angeles before he peppered a Jewish community center with gunfire. He did this in a state with two Jewish female senators, in a city with a large, prosperous Jewish population, in a country where out of several million Jewish Americans, a total of sixty-six were reported by the FBI as the targets of hate-crime assaults in 1997. However despicable Furrow's actions were, it would require a very large stretch to describe them as representative of anything but the deranged fringe of an American subculture.

Most hate is more common and more complicated, with as many varieties as there are varieties of love. Just as there are possessive love and needy love, family love and friendship, romantic love and unrequited love, passion and respect, affection and obsession, so hatred has its shadings. There is hate that fears, and hate that merely feels contempt; there is hate that expresses power, and hate that comes from powerlessness; there is revenge, and there is hate that comes from envy. There is hate that was love, and hate that is a curious expression of love. There is hate of the other, and hate of something that reminds us too much of ourselves. There is the oppressor's hate and the victim's hate. There is hate that burns slowly and hate that fades. And there is hate that explodes and hate that never catches fire.

The modern words that we have created to describe the varieties of hate—"sexism," "racism," "anti-Semitism," "homophobia"—tell us very little about any of this. They tell us merely the identities of the victims; they don't reveal the identities of the perpetrators, or what they think, or how they feel. They don't even tell us how the victims feel. And this simplicity is no accident. Coming from the theories of Marxist and post-Marxist academics, these isms are far better at alleging structures of power than at delineating the workings of the individual heart or mind. In fact, these isms can exist without mentioning individuals at all.

We speak of institutional racism, for example, as if an institution can feel anything. We talk of "hate" as an impersonal noun, with no hater specified. But when these abstractions are actually incarnated, when someone feels something as a result of them, when a hater actually interacts with a victim, the picture changes. We find that hates are often very different phenomena one from another, that they have very different psychological dynamics, that they might even be better understood by not seeing them as varieties of the same thing at all.

There is, for example, the now unfashionable distinction between reasonable hate and unreasonable hate. In recent years we have become accustomed to talking about hates as if they were all equally indefensible, as if it could never be the case that some hates might be legitimate, even necessary. But when some 800,000 Tutsis are murdered under the auspices of a Hutu regime in Rwanda, and when a few thousand Hutus are killed in revenge, the hates are not commensurate. Genocide is not an event like a hurricane, in which damage is random and universal; it is a planned and often merciless attack of one group upon another. The hate of the perpetrators is a monstrosity. The hate of the victims, and their survivors, is justified. What else, one wonders, were surviving Jews supposed to feel toward Germans after the Holocaust? Or, to a different degree, South African blacks after apartheid? If the victims overcome this hate, it is a supreme moral achievement. But if they don't, the victims are not as culpable as the perpetrators. So the hatred of Serbs for Kosovars today can never be equated with the hatred of Kosovars for Serbs.

Hate, like much of human feeling, is not rational, but it usually has its reasons. And it cannot be understood, let alone condemned, without knowing them. Similarly, the hate that comes from knowledge is always different from the hate that comes from ignorance. It is one of the most foolish clichés of our time that prejudice is always rooted in ignorance and can usually be overcome by familiarity with the objects of our loathing. The racism of many Southern whites under segregation was not appeased by familiarity with Southern blacks; the virulent loathing of Tutsis by many Hutus was not undermined by living next door to them for centuries. Theirs was a hatred that sprang, for whatever reasons, from experience. It cannot easily be compared with, for example, the resilience of anti-Semitism in Japan, or hostility to immigration in areas where immigrants are unknown, or fear of homosexuals by people who have never knowingly met one.

The same familiarity is an integral part of what has become known as "sexism." Sexism isn't, properly speaking, a prejudice at all. Few men live without knowledge or constant awareness of women. Every single sexist man was born of a woman and is likely to be sexually attracted to women. His hostility is going to be very different from that of, say, a reclusive member of the Aryan Nations toward Jews he has never met.

In her book *The Anatomy of Prejudices,* the psychotherapist Elisabeth Young-Bruehl proposes a typology of three distinct kinds of hate: obsessive, hysterical, and narcissistic. It's not an exhaustive analysis, but it's a beginning in any serious attempt to understand hate rather than merely declaring war on it. The obsessives, for Young-Bruehl, are those, like the Nazis or Hutus, who fantasize a threat from a minority and obsessively try to rid themselves of it. For them, the very existence of the hated group is threatening. They often describe their loathing in almost physical terms: they experience what Patrick Buchanan, in reference to homosexuals, once described as a "visceral recoil" from the objects of their detestation. They often describe those they hate as diseased or sick, in need of a cure. Or they talk of "cleansing" them, as the Hutus talked of the Tutsis, or call them "cockroaches," as Yitzhak Shamir called the Palestinians. If you read material from the Family Research Council, it is clear that the group regards homosexuals as similar contaminants. A recent posting on its Web site about syphilis among gay men was headlined "Unclean."

Hysterical haters have a more complicated relationship with the objects of their aversion. In Young-Bruehl's words, hysterical prejudice is a prejudice that "a person uses unconsciously to appoint a group to act out in the world forbidden sexual and sexually aggressive desires that the person has repressed." Certain kinds of racists fit this pattern. White loathing of blacks is for some people at least partly about sexual and physical envy. A certain kind of white racist sees in black America all those impulses he wishes most to express himself but cannot. He idealizes in "blackness" a sexual freedom, a physical power, a Dionysian release that he detests but also longs for. His fantasy may not have any basis in reality, but it is powerful nonetheless. It is a form of love-hate, and it is impossible to understand the nuances of racism in, say, the American South, or in British imperial India, without it.

Unlike the obsessives, the hysterical haters do not want to eradicate the objects of their loathing; rather, they want to keep them in some kind of permanent and safe subjugation in order to indulge the attraction of their repulsion. A recent study, for example, found that the men most likely to be opposed to equal rights for homosexuals were those most likely to be aroused by homoerotic imagery. This makes little rational sense, but it has a certain psychological plausibility. If homosexuals were granted equality, then the hysterical gay-hater might panic that his repressed passions would run out of control, overwhelming him and the world he inhabits.

A narcissistic hate, according to Young-Bruehl's definition, is sexism. In its most common form, it is rooted in many men's inability even to imagine what it is to be a woman, a failing rarely challenged by men's control of our most powerful public social institutions. Women are not so much hated by most men as simply ignored in nonsexual contexts, or never conceived of as true equals. The implicit condescension is mixed, in many cases, with repressed and sublimated erotic desire. So the unawareness of women is sometimes commingled with a deep longing or contempt for them.

Each hate, of course, is more complicated than this, and in any one person hate can assume a uniquely configured combination of these types. So there are hysterical sexists who hate women because they need them so much, and narcissistic sexists who hardly notice that women exist, and sexists who oscillate between one of these positions and another. And there are gay-bashers who are threatened by masculine gay men and gay-haters who feel repulsed by effeminate ones. The soldier who beat his fellow soldier Barry Winchell to death with a baseball bat in July had earlier lost a fight to him. It was the image of' a macho gay man—and the shame of being bested by him—that the vengeful soldier had to obliterate, even if he needed a gang of accomplices and a weapon to do so. But the murderers of Matthew Shepard seem to have had a different impulse: a visceral disgust at the thought of any sexual contact with an effeminate homosexual. Their anger was mixed with mockery, as the cruel spectacle at the side of the road suggested.

In the same way, the pathological anti-Semitism of Nazi Germany was obsessive, inasmuch as it tried to cleanse the world of Jews, but also, as Daniel Jonah Goldhagen shows in his book, *Hitler's Willing Executioners,* hysterical. The Germans were mysteriously compelled as well as repelled by Jews, devising elaborate ways, like death camps and death marches, to keep them alive even as they killed them. And the early Nazi phobia of interracial sex suggests as well a lingering erotic quality to the relationship, partaking of exactly the kind of sexual panic that persists among some homosexual-haters and antimiscegenation racists. So the concept of "homophobia," like that of "sexism" and "racism," is often a crude one. All three are essentially cookie-cutter formulas that try to understand human impulses merely through the one-dimensional identity of the victims, rather than through the thoughts and feelings of the haters and hated.

This is deliberate. The theorists behind these isms want to ascribe all blame to one group in society—the "oppressors"—and render specific others—the "victims"—completely blameless. And they want to do this in order in part to side unequivocally with the underdog. But it doesn't take a genius to see how this approach too can generate its own form of bias. It can justify blanket condemnations of whole groups of people—white straight males, for example—purely because of the color of their skin or the nature of their sexual orientation. And it can condescendingly ascribe innocence to whole groups of others. It does exactly what hate does: it hammers the uniqueness of each individual into the anvil of group identity. And it postures morally over the result.

In reality, human beings and human acts are far more complex, which is why these isms and the laws they have fomented are continually coming under strain and challenge. Once again, hate wriggles free of its definers. It knows no monolithic groups of haters and hated. Like a river, it has many eddies, backwaters, and rapids. So there are anti-Semites who actually admire what they think of as Jewish power, and there are gay-haters who look up to homosexuals and some who want to sleep with them. And there are black racists, racist Jews, sexist women, and anti-Semitic homosexuals. Of course there are.

IV

Once you start thinking of these phenomena less as the isms of sexism, racism, and homophobia, once you think of them as independent psychological responses, it's also possible to see how they can work in a bewildering variety of ways in a bewildering number of people. To take one obvious and sad oddity: people who are demeaned and objectified in society may develop an aversion to their tormentors that is more hateful in its expression than the prejudice they have been subjected to. The FBI statistics on hate crimes throw up an interesting point. In America in the 1990s, blacks were up to three times as likely as whites to commit a hate crime, to express their hate by physically attacking their targets or their property. Just as sexual abusers have often been victims of sexual abuse and wife-beaters often grew up in violent households, so hate criminals may often be members of hated groups.

Even the Columbine murderers were in some sense victims of hate before they were purveyors of it. Their classmates later admitted that Dylan Klebold and Eric Harris were regularly called "faggots" in the corridors and classrooms of Columbine High and that nothing was done to prevent or stop the harassment. This climate of hostility doesn't excuse the actions of Klebold and Harris, but it does provide a more plausible context. If they had been black, had routinely been called "nigger" in the school, and had then exploded into a shooting spree against white students, the response to the matter might well have been different. But the hate would have been the same. In other words, hate victims are often hate victimizers as well. This doesn't mean that all hates are equivalent, or that some are not more justified than others. It means merely that hate goes both ways; and if you try to regulate it among some, you will find yourself forced to regulate it among others.

It is no secret, for example, that some of the most vicious anti-Semites in America are black, and that some of the most virulent anti-Catholic bigots in America are gay. At what point, we are increasingly forced to ask, do these phenomena become as indefensible as white racism or religious toleration of antigay bigotry? That question becomes all the more difficult when we notice that it is often minorities who commit some of the most hate-filled offenses against what they see as their oppressors. It was the mainly gay AIDS activist group Act Up that perpetrated the hateful act of desecrating communion hosts at a mass at St. Patrick's Cathedral in New York. And here is the playwright Tony Kushner, who is gay, responding to the Matthew Shepard beating in *The Nation* magazine: "Pope John Paul II endorses murder. He, too, knows the price of discrimination, having declared anti-Semitism a sin. . . . He knows that discrimination kills. But when the Pope heard the news about Matthew Shepard, he, too, worried about spin. And so, on the subject of gay-bashing, the Pope and his cardinals and his bishops and priests maintain their cynical political silence. . . . To remain silent is to endorse murder." Kushner went on to describe the pope as a "homicidal liar."

Maybe the passion behind these words is justified. But it seems clear enough to me that Kushner is expressing hate toward the institution of the Catholic Church and all those who perpetuate its doctrines. How else to interpret the way in which he accuses the pope of cynicism, lying, and murder? And how else either to understand the brutal parody of religious vocations expressed by the Sisters of Perpetual Indulgence, a group of gay men who dress in drag as nuns and engage in sexually explicit performances in public? Or T-shirts with the words "Recovering Catholic" on them, hot items among some gay and lesbian activists? The implication that someone's religious faith is a mental illness is clearly an expression of contempt. If that isn't covered under the definition of hate speech, what is?

Or take the following sentences: "The act male homosexuals commit is ugly and repugnant and afterwards they are disgusted with themselves. They drink and take drugs to palliate this, but they are disgusted with the act and they are always changing partners and cannot be really happy." The thoughts of Pat Robertson or Patrick Buchanan? Actually, that sentence was written by Gertrude Stein, one of the century's most notable lesbians. Or take the following, about how beating up "black boys like that made us feel *good* inside. . . . Every time I drove my foot into his [expletive], I felt better." It was written to describe the brutal assault on an innocent bystander for the sole reason of his race. By the end of the attack, the victim had blood gushing from his mouth as his attackers stomped on his genitals. Are we less appalled when we learn that the actual sentence was how beating up "white boys like that made us feel *good* inside. . . . Every time I drove my foot into his [expletive], I felt better"? It was written by Nathan McCall, an African-American who later in life became a successful journalist at the *Washington Post* and published his memoir of this "hate crime" to much acclaim.

In fact, one of the stranger aspects of hate is that the prejudice expressed by a group in power may often be milder in expression than the prejudice felt by the marginalized. After all, if you already enjoy privilege, you may not feel the anger that turns bias into hate. You may not need to. For this reason, most white racism may be more influential in society than most black racism—but also more calmly expressed.

So may other forms of minority loathing—especially hatred within minorities. I'm sure that black conservatives like Clarence Thomas and Thomas Sowell have experienced their fair share of white racism. But I wonder whether it has ever reached the level of intensity of the hatred directed toward them by other blacks? In several years of being an openly gay writer and editor, I have experienced the gamut of responses to my sexual orientation. But I have only directly experienced articulated, passionate hate from other homosexuals. I have been accused over the years by other homosexuals of being a sellout, a hypocrite, a traitor, a sexist, a racist, a narcissist, a snob. I've been called selfish, callous, hateful, self-hating, and malevolent. At a reading, a group of lesbian activists portrayed my face on a poster within the crosshairs of a gun. Nothing from the religious right has come close to such vehemence.

I am not complaining. No harm has ever come to me or my property, and much of the criticism is rooted in the legitimate expression of political differences. But the visceral tone and style of the gay criticism can only be described as hateful. It is designed to wound personally, and it often does. But its intensity comes in part, one senses, from the pain of being excluded for so long, of anger long restrained bubbling up and directing itself more aggressively toward an alleged traitor than an alleged enemy. It is the hate of the hated. And it can be the most hateful hate of all. For this reason, hate-crime laws may themselves be an oddly biased category—biased against the victims of hate. Racism is everywhere, but the already victimized might be more desperate, more willing to express it violently. And so more prone to come under the suspicious eye of the law.

V

And why is hate for a group worse than hate for a person? In Laramie, Wyoming, the now-famous "epicenter of homophobia," where Matthew Shepard was brutally beaten to death, vicious murders are not unknown. In the previous twelve months, a fifteen-year-old pregnant girl was found east of the town with seventeen stab wounds. Her thirty-eight-year-old boyfriend was apparently angry that she had refused an abortion and left her in the Wyoming foothills to bleed to death. In the summer of 1998, an eight-year-old Laramie girl was abducted, raped, and murdered by a pedophile, who disposed of her young body in a garbage dump. Neither of these killings was deemed a hate crime, and neither would be designated as such under any existing hate-crime law. Perhaps because of this, one crime is an international legend; the other two are virtually unheard of.

But which crime was more filled with hate? Once you ask the question, you realize how difficult it is to answer. Is it more hateful to kill a stranger or a lover? Is it more hateful to kill a child than an adult? Is it more hateful to kill your own child than another's? Under the law before the invention of hate crimes, these decisions didn't have to be taken. But under the law after hate crimes, a decision is essential. A decade ago, a murder was a murder. Now, in the era when group hate has emerged as our cardinal social sin, it all depends.

The supporters of laws against hate crimes argue that such crimes should be disproportionately punished because they victimize more than the victim. Such crimes, these advocates argue, spread fear, hatred, and panic among whole populations and therefore merit more concern. But of course all crimes victimize more than the victim and spread alarm in the society at large. Just think of the terrifying church shooting in Texas only two weeks ago. In fact, a purely random murder may be even more terrifying than a targeted one, since the entire community and not just a part of it feels threatened. High rates of murder, robbery, assault, and burglary victimize everyone, by spreading fear, suspicion, and distress everywhere. Which crime was more frightening to more people this summer: the mentally ill Buford Furrow's crazed attacks in Los Angeles, killing one, or Mark Barton's murder of his own family and several random day-traders in Atlanta, killing twelve? Almost certainly the latter. But only Furrow was guilty of "hate."

One response to this objection is that certain groups feel fear more intensely than others because of a history of persecution or intimidation. But doesn't this smack of a certain condescension toward minorities? Why, after all, should it be assumed that gay men or black women or Jews, for example, are as a group more easily intimidated than others? Surely in any of these communities there will be a vast range of responses, from panic to concern to complete indifference. The assumption otherwise is the kind of crude generalization the law is supposed to uproot in the first place. And among these groups, there are also likely to be vast differences. To equate a population once subjected to slavery with a population of Mexican immigrants or third-generation Holocaust survivors is to equate the unequatable. In fact, it is to set up a contest of vulnerability in which one group vies with another to establish its particular variety of suffering, a contest that can have no dignified solution.

Rape, for example, is not classified as a hate crime under most existing laws, pitting feminists against ethnic groups in a battle for recognition. If, as a solution to this problem, everyone except the white straight able-bodied male is regarded as a possible victim of a hate crime, then we have simply created a two-tier system of justice in which racial profiling is reversed, and white straight men are presumed guilty before being proved innocent, and members of minorities are free to hate them as gleefully as they like. But if we include the white straight male in the litany of potential victims, then we have effectively abolished the notion of a hate crime altogether, for if every crime is possibly a hate crime, then it is simply another name for crime. All we will have done is widened the search for possible bigotry, ratcheted up the sentences for everyone, and filled the jails up even further.

Hate-crime law advocates counter that extra penalties should be imposed on hate crimes because our society is experiencing an "epidemic" of such crimes. Mercifully, there is no hard evidence to support this notion. The federal government has only been recording the incidence of hate crimes in this decade, and the statistics tell a simple story. In 1992, there were 6,623 hate-crime incidents reported to the FBI by a total of 6,181 agencies, covering 51 percent of the population. In 1996, there were 8,734 incidents reported by 11,355 agencies, covering 84 percent of the population. That number dropped to 8,049 in 1997. These numbers are of course hazardous. They probably underreport the incidence of such crimes, but they are the only reliable figures we have. Yet even if they are faulty as an absolute number, they do not show an epidemic of hate crimes in the 1990s.

Is there evidence that the crimes themselves are becoming more vicious? None. More than 60 percent of recorded hate crimes in America involve no violent physical assault against another human being at all, and again, according to the FBI, that proportion has not budged much in the 1990s. These impersonal attacks are crimes against property or crimes of intimidation. Murder, which dominates media coverage of hate crimes, is a tiny proportion of the total. Of the 8,049 hate crimes reported to the FBI in 1997, a total of 8 were murders. Eight. The number of hate crimes that were aggravated assaults (generally involving a weapon) in 1997 is less than 15 percent of the total. That's 1,237 assaults too many, of course, but to put it in perspective, compare it with a reported 1,022,492 "equal opportunity" aggravated assaults in America in the same year. The number of hate crimes that were physical assaults is half the total. That's 4,000 assaults too many, of course, but to put it in perspective, it compares with around 3.8 million "equal opportunity" assaults in America annually.

The truth is, the distinction between a crime filled with personal hate and a crime filled with group hate is an essentially arbitrary one. It tells us nothing interesting about the psychological contours of the specific actor or his specific victim. It is a function primarily of politics, of special-interest groups carving out particular protections for themselves, rather than a serious response to a serious criminal concern. In such an endeavor, hate-crime law advocates cram an entire world of human motivations into an immutable, tiny box called hate and hope to have solved a problem. But nothing has been solved, and some harm may even have been done.

In an attempt to repudiate a past that treated people differently because of the color of their skin or their sex or religion or sexual orientation, we may merely create a future that permanently treats people differently because of the color of their skin or their sex, religion, or sexual orientation. This notion of a hate crime, and the concept of hate that lies behind it, takes a psychological mystery and turns it into a facile political artifact. Rather than compounding this error and extending it even further, we should seriously consider repealing the concept altogether.

To put it another way: violence can and should be stopped by the government. In a free society, hate can't and shouldn't be. The boundaries between hate and prejudice and between prejudice and opinion and between opinion and truth are so complicated and blurred that any attempt to construct legal and political fire walls is a doomed and illiberal venture. We know by now that hate will never disappear from human consciousness; in fact, it is probably, at some level, definitive of it. We know after decades of education measures that hate is not caused merely by ignorance and, after decades of legislation, that it isn't cured entirely by law.

To be sure, we have made much progress. Anyone who argues that America is as inhospitable to minorities and to women today as it has been in the past has not read much history. And we should of course be vigilant that our most powerful institutions, most notably the government, do not actively or formally propagate hatred, and insure that the violent expression of hate is curtailed by the same rules that punish all violent expression.

But after that, in an increasingly diverse culture, it is crazy to expect that hate, in all its variety, can be eradicated. A free country will always mean a hateful country. This may not be fair, or perfect, or admirable, but it is reality, and while we need not endorse it, we should not delude ourselves into thinking we can prevent it. That is surely the distinction between toleration and tolerance. Tolerance is the eradication of hate; toleration is coexistence despite it. We might do better as a culture and as a polity if we concentrated more on achieving the latter than the former. We would certainly be less frustrated.

And by aiming lower, we might actually reach higher. In some ways, some expression of prejudice serves a useful social purpose. It lets off steam; it allows natural tensions to express themselves incrementally; it can siphon off conflict through words rather than actions. Anyone who has lived in the ethnic shouting match that is New York City knows exactly what I mean. If New Yorkers disliked each other less, they wouldn't be able to get on so well. We may not all be able to pull off a Mencken—bigoted in words, egalitarian in action—but we might achieve a lesser form of virtue: a human acceptance of our need for differentiation without a total capitulation to it.

Do we not owe something more to the victims of hate? Perhaps we do. But it is also true that there is nothing that government can do for the hated that the hated cannot better do for themselves. After all, most bigots are not foiled when they are punished specifically for their beliefs. In fact, many of the worst haters crave such attention and find vindication in such rebukes. Indeed, our media's obsession with "hate," our elevation of it above other social misdemeanors and crimes, may even play into the hands of the pathetic and the evil, may breathe air into the smoldering embers of their paranoid loathing. Sure, we can help create a climate in which such hate is disapproved of—and we should. But there is a danger that if we go too far, if we punish it too much, if we try to abolish it altogether, we may merely increase its mystique, and entrench the very categories of human difference that we are trying to erase.

For hate is only foiled not when the haters are punished but when the hated are immune to the bigot's power. A hater cannot psychologically wound if a victim cannot psychologically be wounded. And that immunity to hurt can never be given; it can merely be achieved. The racial epithet only strikes at someone's core if he lets it, if he allows the bigot's definition of him to be the final description of his life and his person—if somewhere in his heart of hearts, he believes the hateful slur to be true. The only final answer to this form of racism, then, is not majority persecution of it but minority indifference to it. The only permanent rebuke to homophobia is not the enforcement of tolerance but gay equanimity in the face of prejudice. The only effective answer to sexism is not a morass of legal proscriptions but the simple fact of female success. In this, as in so many other things, there is no solution to the problem. There is only a transcendence of it. For all our rhetoric, hate will never be destroyed. Hate, as our predecessors knew better, can merely be overcome.

MEN AND WOMEN
TALKING ON THE JOB

Deborah Tannen

Amy was a manager with a problem: She had just read a final report written by Donald, and she felt it was woefully inadequate. She faced the unsavory task of telling him to do it over. When she met with Donald, she made sure to soften the blow by beginning with praise, telling him everything about his report that was good. Then she went on to explain what was lacking and what needed to be done to make it acceptable. She was pleased with the diplomatic way she had managed to deliver the bad news. Thanks to her thoughtfulness in starting with praise, Donald was able to listen to the criticism and seemed to understand what was needed. But when the revised report appeared on her desk, Amy was shocked. Donald had made only minor, superficial changes, and none of the necessary ones. The next meeting with him did not go well. He was incensed that she was now telling him his report was not acceptable and accused her of having misled him. "You told me before it was fine," he protested.

Amy thought she had been diplomatic; Donald thought she had been dishonest. The praise she intended to soften the message "This is unacceptable" sounded to him like the message itself: "This is fine." So what she regarded as the main point—the needed changes—came across to him as optional suggestions, because he had already registered her praise as the main point. She felt he hadn't listened to her. He thought she had changed her mind and was making him pay the price.

Work days are filled with conversations about getting the job done. Most of these conversations succeed, but too many end in impasses like this. It could be that Amy is a capricious boss whose wishes are whims, and it could be that Donald is a temperamental employee who can't hear criticism no matter how it is phrased. But I don't think either was the case in this instance. I believe this was one of innumerable misunderstandings caused by differences in conversational style. Amy delivered the criticism in a way that seemed to her self-evidently considerate, a way she would have preferred to receive criticism herself: taking into account the other person's feelings, making sure he knew that her ultimate negative assessment of his report didn't mean she had no appreciation of his abilities. She offered the praise as a sweetener to help the nasty-tasting news go down. But Donald didn't expect criticism to be delivered in that way, so he mistook the praise as her overall assessment rather than a preamble to it.

This conversation could have taken place between two women or two men. But I do not think it is a coincidence that it occurred between a man and a woman. This book will explain why. First, it gives a view of the role played by talk in our work lives. To do this, I show the workings of conversational style, explaining the ritual nature of conversation[1] and the confusion that arises when rituals are not shared

---

[1] "*. . . the ritual nature of conversation . . .*" As my colleague Rom Harré pointed out to me, it would be useful to note, for readers interested in finer distinctions, that I am using the term "ritual" rather loosely to capture the automatic, nonliteral, conventionalized nature of conversational language. There are, of course, a number of different levels on which this operates. Technically, a "ritual" per se is a symbolic means of accomplishing a social act. Other ways in which talk is not meant literally include what scholars refer to as "phatic speech," which refers to relatively "empty" verbiage whose main purpose is the maintenance of social relations, or recognizing the other as a person.

and therefore not recognized as such, I take into account the many influences on conversational style, but I focus in particular on the differing rituals that typify women and men (although, of course, not all individual men and women behave in ways that are typical). Conversational rituals common among men often involve using opposition such as banter, joking, teasing, and playful put-downs, and expending effort to avoid the one-down position in the interaction. Conversational rituals common among women are often ways of maintaining an appearance of equality, taking into account the effect of the exchange on the other person, and expending effort to downplay the speaker's authority so they can get the job done without flexing their muscles in an obvious way.

When everyone present is familiar with these conventions, they work well. But when ways of speaking are not recognized as conventions, they are taken literally, with negative results on both sides. Men whose oppositional strategies are interpreted literally may be seen as hostile when they are not, and their efforts to ensure that they avoid appearing one-down may be taken as arrogance. When women use conversational strategies designed to avoid appearing boastful and to take the other person's feelings into account, they may be seen as less confident and competent than they really are. As a result, both women and men often feel they are not getting sufficient credit for what they have done, are not being listened to, are not getting ahead as fast as they should.

When I talk about women's and men's characteristic ways of speaking, I always emphasize that both styles make sense and are equally valid in themselves, though the difference in styles may cause trouble in interaction. In a sense, when two people form a private relationship of love or friendship, the bubble of their interaction is a world unto itself, even though they both come with the prior experience of their families, their community, and a lifetime of conversations. But someone who takes a job is entering a world that is already functioning, with its own characteristic style already in place. Although there are many influences such as regional background, the type of industry involved, whether it is a family business or a large corporation, in general, workplaces that have previously had men in positions of power have already established male-style interaction as the norm. In that sense, women, and others whose styles are different, are not starting out equal, but are at a disadvantage. Though talking at work is quite similar to talking in private, it is a very different enterprise in many ways.

Negotiating from the Inside Out or the Outside In

Two co-workers who were on very friendly terms with each other were assigned to do a marketing survey together. When they got the assignment, the man began by saying, "I'll do the airline and automobile industry, and you can do the housewares and direct-mail market." The woman was taken aback. "Hey," she said. "It sounds like you've got it all figured out. As a matter of fact, *I'd* like to do airlines and autos. I've already got a lot of contacts in those areas." "Oh," he said, a little chagrined and a lot surprised. She continued, "I wish you wouldn't come on so strong." "Well, how would you have started?" he asked. She said, "I wouldn't have just said what I wanted to do. I would have asked, 'What parts do you want to do?' " This made no sense to him. "Then what are you complaining about? If you had asked me what parts I wanted to do, I would have said, 'I'll do the airlines and autos.' We would have ended up in the same place anyway."

The woman saw his point. But if the conversation had gone that way, she still would have been frustrated. To her, the question "What parts of the survey would you like to do?" is not an invitation to grab the parts he wants and run away with them. It's an invitation to talk about the various parts—which ones interest him, which he has experience in, which he would like to learn more about. Then he would ask, "What do you want to do?" and she would say what interests her, where her experience lies, and where she'd like to get more experience. Finally, they would divvy up the parts in a way that gave them both some of what they wanted, while taking advantage of both their expertise.

Making decisions is a crucial part of any workday. Daily, weekly, monthly, decisions must be made with never enough information and never enough time. People have very different ways of reaching decisions, and none is clearly better than others. But when two people with different styles have to make decisions together, both styles may have worse results than either would have if their styles were shared, unless the differences are understood and accommodated.

Beginning by stating what you will do is a style of negotiating that starts inside and works its way out. If others have different ideas, you expect them to say so, and you'll negotiate. Opening with a question like "What would you like to do?" or "What do you think?" is a style that begins by being vague and works its way in. It specifically invites others to express their perspective. Either style can work well. What makes the machine go TILT! is the difference in styles. Someone who expects negotiation to proceed from the inside and work its way out hears a vague question as an invitation to decide; someone who tends to negotiate from the outside in hears a specific claim as a nonnegotiable demand. In this sense, both styles are indirect—they depend on an unspoken understanding of how the subsequent conversation is expected to go. This is a sense in which conversation is ritualized: It follows a preset sequencing scheme that seems self-evidently appropriate.

More on Negotiating Styles

The managers of a medium-size company got the go-ahead to hire a human-resources coordinator, and two managers who worked well together were assigned to make the choice. As it turned out, Maureen and Harold favored different applicants, and both felt strongly about their preferences. Maureen argued with assurance and vigor that the person she wanted to hire was the most creative and innovative, and that he had the most appropriate experience. Harold argued with equal conviction that the applicant he favored had a vision of management that fit with the company's, whereas her candidate might be a thorn in their side. They traded arguments for some time, neither convincing the other. Then Harold said that hiring the applicant Maureen wanted would make him so uncomfortable that he would have to consider resigning. Maureen respected Harold. What's more, she liked him and considered him a friend. So she felt that his admission of such strong feelings had to be taken into account. She said what seemed to her the only thing she could say under the circumstances: "Well, I certainly don't want you to feel uncomfortable here; you're one of the pillars of the place. If you feel that strongly about it, I can't argue with that." Harold's choice was hired.

In this case, the decision-making power went not to the manager who had the highest rank in the firm (their positions were parallel) and not necessarily to the one whose judgment was best, but to the one whose arguing strategies were most effective in the negotiation. Maureen was an ardent and persuasive advocate for her view, but she assumed that she and Harold would have to come to an agreement in order to make a decision, and that she had to take his feelings into account. Since Harold would not back down, she did. Most important, when he argued that he would have to quit if she got her way, she felt she had no option but to yield.

What was crucial was not Maureen's and Harold's individual styles in isolation but how their styles interacted—how they played in concert with the other's style. Harold's threat to quit ensured his triumph—when used with someone who would not call his bluff. If he had been arguing with someone who regarded this threat as simply another move in the negotiation rather than as a nonnegotiable expression of deep feelings that had to be respected, the result might have been different. For example, had she said, "That's ridiculous; of course you're not going to quit!" or "If that's how shallow your commitment to this firm is, then we'd be better off without you," the decision might well have gone the other way.

When you talk to someone whose style is similar to yours, you can fairly well predict the response you are going to get. But when you talk to someone whose style is different, you can't predict, and often can't make sense of, the response. Hearing the reaction you get, if it's not the one you expected, often makes you regret what you said. Harold later told Maureen that he was sorry he had used the argument he did. In retrospect he was embarrassed, even a bit ashamed of himself. His retrospective chagrin was like what you feel if you slam down something in anger and are surprised and regretful to see that it breaks. You wanted to make a gesture, but you didn't expect it to come out with such force. Harold regretted what he said precisely because it caused Maureen to back down so completely. He'd known he was upping the ante—he felt he had to do something to get them out of the loop of recycling arguments they were in—but he had not expected it to end the negotiation summarily; he expected Maureen to meet his move with a balancing move of her own. He did not predict the impact that personalizing his argument would have on her. For her part, Maureen did not think of Harold's threat as just another move in a negotiable argument; she heard it as a personal plea that she could not reject. Their different approaches to negotiation put her at a disadvantage in negotiating with him.

"How Certain Are You of That?"

Negotiating is only one kind of activity that is accomplished through talk at work. Other kinds of decision-making are also based as much on ways of talking as on the content of the arguments. The CEO of a corporation explained to me that he regularly has to make decisions based on insufficient information—and making decisions is a large part of his work life. Much of his day is spent hearing brief presentations following which he must either approve or reject a course of action. He has to make a judgment in five minutes about issues the presenters have worked on for months. "I decide," he explained, "based on how confident they seem. If they seem very confident, I call it a go. If they seem unsure, I figure it's too risky and nix it."

Here is where the rule of competence and the role of communication go hand in hand. Confidence, after all, is an internal feeling. How can you judge others' confidence? The only evidence you have to go on is circumstantial—how they talk about what they know. You judge by a range of signs, including facial expression and body posture, but most of all, speech. Do they hesitate? Do they speak up or swallow half their words? Is their tone of voice declamatory or halting? Do they make bald statements ("This is a winner! We've got to go for it!") or hedge ("Um . . . from what I can tell, I think it'll work, but we'll never know for sure until we try")? This seems simple enough. Surely, you can tell how confident people are by paying attention to how they speak, just as you can tell when someone is lying.

Well, maybe not. Psychologist Paul Ekman has spent years studying lying, and he has found that most people are very sure they can tell when others are lying. The only trouble is, most can't. With a few thus-far inexplicable exceptions, people who tell him they are absolutely sure they can tell if someone is lying are as likely to be wrong as to be right—and he has found this to be as true for judges as for the rest of us.

In the same way, our ability to determine how confident others are is probably quite limited. The CEO who does not take into account the individual styles of the people who make presentations to him will find it difficult, if not impossible, to make the best judgment. Different people will talk very differently, not because of the absolute level of their confidence or lack of it, but because of their habitual ways of speaking. There are those who sound sure of themselves even when inside they're not sure at all, and others who sound tentative even when they're very sure indeed. So being aware of differences in ways of speaking is a prerequisite for making good decisions as well as good presentations.

Feasting on Humble Pie

Although these factors affecting decision-making are the same for men and women, and every individual has his or her own style, it seems that women are more likely to downplay their certainty, men more likely to downplay their doubts. From childhood, girls learn to temper what they say so as not to sound too aggressive—which means too certain. From the time they are little, most girls learn that sounding too sure of themselves will make them unpopular with their peers. Groups of girls, as researchers who have studied girls at play have found, will penalize and even ostracize a girl who seems too sure she's right. Anthropologist Marjorie Harness Goodwin found that girls criticize other girls who stand out by saying, "She thinks she's cute," or "She thinks she's something." Talking in ways that display self-confidence is not approved for girls.[2]

It is not only peers who disapprove of girls talking in ways that call attention to their accomplishments. Adults too can be critical of such behavior in girls, as was a woman who wrote a letter that was published in a magazine. The letter-writer was responding to an article about a ten-year-old girl named Heather DeLoach who became a child celebrity by tap-dancing in a bee costume on a rock video.[3] Heather was portrayed in the magazine as still being awed by others' fame ("I got to meet Pauly Shore and Janet Jackson, and I got Madonna's autograph, but I wasn't allowed to take pictures") and unawed by her own ("I see myself so much on TV that when the Bee Girl comes on, I just click right through the channel"). Sounding very much like other girls, she hedged when mentioning her good grades ("sort of like straight-A"). But she was also quoted as saying, "I'm extremely talented. I guess when the director first set eyes on me, he liked me. I try my best to be an actress, and I'm just great. I'm the one and only Bee Girl."

Although the article did not explain what question the interviewer asked to elicit Heather's truthful description of herself, the disapproving reader zeroed in on those words and admonished, "Heather DeLoach, the Bee Girl, describes herself as 'extremely talented' and 'just great.' Perhaps 10-year-old Heather should stop being a *bumble*bee and start being a *humble* bee." Not only did this reader tell the child star to start being more humble, but she also told her to stop being a bumblebee—that is, doing what she's so good at that it's bringing her attention, reward, and too much—or too obvious—self-confidence.

Reactions like these teach girls how they are expected to talk in order to be liked. It is not surprising that when she spoke in this guileless way, Heather DeLoach was ten. By the time she gets through junior high school and puberty, chances are she will have learned to talk differently, a transformation—and loss of confidence—that white middle-class American girls experience at that stage of their lives, according to

---

[2] "... *girls criticize other girls who stand out* ..." Marjorie Harness Goodwin spent a year and a half observing the girls and boys in her inner-city black Philadelphia neighborhood and found the girls sanctioning other girls who seemed to stand out by saying, in the dialect of their community, "She thinks she cute." Goodwin found, for example, that girls criticized a girl who dressed too well and did too well in school.

[3] The article about ten-year-old Heather DeLoach appeared in *People* magazine, November 29, 1993, p. 102. The letter criticizing her for not being humble was published in the same magazine, December 20, 1993, p. 8.

a great deal of current research.[4] But it is crucial to bear in mind that ways of talking are not literal representations of mental states, and refraining from boasting may not reveal a true lack of confidence. A pair of studies by a team of psychologists makes this clear.

Laurie Heatherington and her colleagues had student experimenters ask hundreds of incoming college students to predict how they thought their first year at college would go by forecasting the grades they expected to get. In some cases, the predictions were made anonymously: They were put in writing and placed in an envelope. In others, they were made publicly, either orally to the experimenter or by writing on a paper that the experimenter promptly read. The researchers found that women predicted lower grades for themselves than men did—but only when they made their predictions publicly. The predictions the women students made in private did not differ from the men's, just as the grades they actually earned as the year progressed did not differ from the men's. In other words, their lower predictions evidenced not lack of confidence but reluctance to reveal the level of confidence they felt.

The same researchers conducted a second study that captured women's characteristic balancing act between their own interests and those of the person they are talking to. In half the cases, the experimenters told their own grade-point averages to the students they interviewed, and the grades they claimed to have gotten were comparatively low. Lo and behold, when women students thought they were talking to someone who had gotten low grades, they lowered their predictions of what they expected their own grades to be. Whether or not the experimenter claimed to have gotten low grades did not affect the predictions made by men students.

The first of these ingenious experiments dramatizes that the social inhibition against seeming to boast can make women appear less confident than they really are. And the second study shows that part of the reason many women censor themselves from proclaiming their confidence is that they are balancing their own interests with those of the person they are talking to. In other words, they modify their speech to take into account the impact of what they say on the other person's feelings.

There may be something peculiarly white, middle-class, and American about the cultural constraint against women boasting. Those who have studied the remarkable change in how girls talk about their own talents and prospects during the crucial junior high school years have noted that the pattern is not necessarily found, or is not as strong, among black American teenage girls.[5] And anthropologist Thomas Kochman notes that talking about one's own accomplishments can be a highly valued source of humor for members of the cultural group he calls "community blacks," as illustrated by the widely publicized self-congratulatory verbal performances of the African-American prize-fighter Muhammad Ali. But every culture makes distinctions that outsiders may miss. Kochman contrasts acceptable African-American "boasting" to the kind of self-aggrandizement that is negatively sanctioned by the same community as "bragging."

To emphasize the cultural relativity of attitudes toward boasting, I should mention, too, the reaction of a British man who was certain that in his country, a boy who spoke like Heather DeLoach would be as likely as a girl to be chastised. Indeed, this Briton remarked, the British often find Americans annoyingly boastful.

---

[4]The crisis of confidence that girls undergo during adolescence was first brought to public attention by psychologist Carol Gilligan and her colleagues (see the essays in *Making Connections,* edited by Gilligan, Lyons, and Haruner). Journalist Judy Mann discusses the evidence for and causes of this troubling phenomenon in *The Difference,* and provides an eloquent personal expansion on it with reference to her own daughter. Psychotherapist Mary Pipher tells the stories of adolescent girls she has seen in psychotherapy in *Reviving Ophelia.*

[5]" . . . *have noted that the pattern is not necessarily found, or is not as strong, among black American teenage girls.*" See, for example, The AAUW Report, *How Schools Shortchange Girls,* p. 13.

For middle-class American women, though, the constraint is clear: Talking about your own accomplishments in a way that calls attention to yourself is not acceptable. This social constraint became both a source of criticism and a dodge for figure-skater Nancy Kerrigan when an inordinate amount of media attention was focused on her during the 1994 winter Olympics. *Newsweek* magazine called her "ungracious" for saying of her own performance, "I was flawless," and of her competitor's, "Oksana wasn't clean." But when a microphone picked up what Kerrigan thought was private grumbling about how "corny" and "dumb" it was to parade through Disney World with life-size cartoon characters, her "handlers" issued a statement that "she was referring merely to her mom's insistence that she wear her silver medal. She feared it would 'look like bragging.' "[6]

The expectation that women should not display their own accomplishments brings us back to the matter of negotiating that is so important in the workplace. A man who owned a medium-sized company remarked that women who came to ask him for raises often supported their requests by pointing to a fellow worker on the same level who earned more. He considered this a weak bargaining strategy because he could always identify a different coworker at that level who earned less. They would do better, he felt, to argue for a raise on the basis of how valuable their own work is to the company. Yet it is likely that many women would be less comfortable "blowing their own horn" than making a claim based on fairness.

Follow the Leader

Similar expectations constrain how girls express leadership. Being a leader often involves giving directions to others, but girls who tell other girls what to do are called "bossy." It is not that girls do not exert influence on their group—of course they do—but, as anthropologists like Marjorie Harness Goodwin have found, many girls discover they get better results if they phrase their ideas as suggestions rather than orders, and if they give reasons for their suggestions in terms of the good of the group. But while these ways of talking make girls—and, later, women—more likable, they make women seem less competent and self-assured in the world of work. And women who do seem competent and self-assured are as much in danger of being negatively labeled as are girls. After her retirement, Margaret Thatcher was described in the press as "bossy." Whereas girls are ready to stick this label on each other because they don't think any girl should boss the others around, it seems odd to apply it to Thatcher, who, after all, was the boss. And this is the rub: Standards of behavior applied to women are based on roles that do not include being boss.

Boys are expected to play by different rules, since the social organization of boys is different. Boys' groups tend to be more obviously hierarchical: Someone is one-up, and someone is one-down. Boys don't typically accuse each other of being "bossy" because the high-status boys are expected to give orders and push the low-status boys around. Daniel Maltz and Ruth Borker summarize research by many scholars showing that boys tend to jockey for center stage, challenge those who get it, and deflect challenges. Giving orders and telling the others what to do are ways of getting and keeping the high-status role. Another way of getting high status is taking center stage by telling stories, jokes, and information. Along with this, many boys learn to state their opinions in the strongest possible terms and find out if they're wrong by seeing if others challenge them. These ways of talking translate into an impression of confidence.

---

[6]*"She feared it would 'look like bragging.' " Newsweek*, March 14, 1994, p. 79.

The styles typical of women and men both make sense given the context in which they were learned, but they have very different consequences in the workplace. In order to avoid being put in the one-down position, many men have developed strategies for making sure they get the one-up position instead, and this results in ways of talking that serve them well when it comes to hiring and promotion. In relation to the examples I have given, women are more likely to speak in the styles that are less effective in getting recognized and promoted. But if they speak in the styles that are effective when used by men—being assertive, sounding sure of themselves, talking up what they have done to make sure they get credit for it—they run the risk that everyone runs if they do not fit their culture's expectations for appropriate behavior: They will not be liked and may even be seen as having psychological problems.

Both women and men pay a price if they do not behave in ways expected of their gender: Men who are not very aggressive are called "wimps," whereas women who are not very aggressive are called "feminine." Men who are aggressive are called "go-getters," though if they go too far, from the point of view of the viewer, they may be called "arrogant." This can hurt them, but not nearly as much as the innumerable labels for women who are thought to be too aggressive—starting with the most hurtful one: bitch.

Even the compliments that we receive are revealing. One woman who had designed and implemented a number of innovative programs was praised by someone who said, "You have such a gentle way of bringing about radical change that people don't realize what's happening—or don't get threatened by it." This was a compliment, but it also hinted at the downside of the woman's gentle touch: Although it made it possible for her to be effective in instituting the changes she envisioned, her unobtrusive style ensured a lack of recognition. If people don't realize what's happening, they won't give her credit for what she has accomplished.

Not only advancement and recognition, but hiring is affected by ways of speaking. A woman who supervised three computer programmers mentioned that her best employee was another woman whom she had hired over the objections of her own boss. Her boss had preferred a male candidate, because he felt the man would be better able to step into her supervisory role if needed. But she had taken a dislike to the male candidate. For one thing, she had felt he was inappropriately flirtatious with her. But most important, she had found him arrogant, because he spoke as if he already had the job, using the pronoun "we" to refer to the group that had not yet hired him.

I have no way of knowing whether the woman hired was indeed the better of these two candidates, or whether either she or the man was well suited to assume the supervisory role, but I am intrigued that the male boss was impressed with the male candidate's take-charge self-presentation, while the woman supervisor was put off by it. And it seems quite likely that whatever it was about his way of talking that struck her as arrogant was exactly what led her boss to conclude that this man would be better able to take over her job if needed.

This example brings to mind a small item in an unusual memoir: the autobiography of an Australian woman with autism. In her remarkable memoir *Somebody Somewhere,* Donna Williams explains that although her autism made it difficult for her to process language, she managed to function in the world by mimicking the speech she heard around her. However, she regarded her successful performances not as her own doing but as the work of two imaginary personas, Carol and Willie. Although there is no evidence that Williams herself thought of these two "characters" (as she called them) as female and male, when reading her account of the kinds of things they could say and do, I repeatedly noticed that Carol performed stereotypically female behavior (she cocked her head, filled the air with social chatter, and, above all, smiled), while Willie played the stereotypically male part (he was strong, detached, and accumulated facts to impress people). So it struck me as amusing, but also troubling, when I read in Williams's memoir that it was Willie who went for interviews but Carol who held down jobs. This is not to imply that men do not deserve the jobs they get, but that ways of talking typically associated with men are more likely to impress many job interviewers as well as those making decisions about promotions to managerial levels.

I believe these patterns explain why it is common to hear that a particular woman lacks confidence or that a particular man is arrogant. Though we think of these as individual weaknesses, underconfidence and arrogance are disproportionately observed in women and men respectively, because they result from an overabundance of ways of speaking that are expected of females and males. Boys are expected to put themselves forward, emphasize the qualities that make them look good, and deemphasize those that would show them in a less favorable light. Too much of this is called arrogance. Girls are expected to be "humble"—not try to take the spotlight, emphasize the ways they are just like everyone else, and deemphasize ways they are special. A woman who does this really well comes off as lacking in confidence. Ironically, those who learn the lessons best are most in danger of falling into traps laid by conversational conventions.

DOONESBURY

Garry Trudeau

Doonesbury

G. B. TRUDEAU

TENSE PRESENT:
DEMOCRACY, ENGLISH, AND
THE WARS OVER USAGE

David Foster Wallace

"Save up to 50%—and More!" Between you and I. On accident. Somewhat of a Kustom Kar Kare Autowash. "The cause was due to numerous factors." "Orange Crush—A Taste That's All It's Own." "Vigorex: Helping men conquer sexual issues." "Equal numbers of both men and women oppose the amendment." Feedback. "As drinking water becomes more and more in short supply." "IMATION—Borne of 3M Innovation." Point in time. Time frame. "At this point in time, the individual in question was observed, and subsequently apprehended by authorities." Here for you, there for you. *Fail to comply with* for *violate*. Comprised of. From whence. *Quote* for *quotation*. *Nauseous* for *nauseated*. Besides the point. To mentor, to parent. To partner. To critique. *Indicated* for *said*. *Parameters* for *limits* and *options* for *choices* and *viable options* for *options* and *workable solution* for *solution*. In point of fact. Prior to this time. As of this point in the time frame. Serves to. Tends to be. *Convince* for *persuade*. *Append* for *attach*, *portion* for *part*. Commence, cease. Expedite. *Request* for *ask*. *Eventuate* for *happen*. Subsequent to this time. Productive. Facilitate. Aid in. Utilize. Detrimental. Equates with. In regards to. Tragic, tragedy. *Grow* as transitive. *Keep* for *stay*. "To demonstrate the power of Epson's new Stylus Color Inkjet Printer with 1440 d.p.i., just listen:" Could care less. Issues, core issues. Fellow colleagues. Goal-orientated. Resources. Unproductive. Feelings. *Share* for *speak*. Nurture, empower, recover. *Valid* for *true*. Authentic. Productive, unproductive. "I choose to view my opponent's negative attacks as unproductive to the real issues facing the citizens of this campaign." Incumbent upon. Mandate. Plurality. *Per anum*. Conjunctive adverbs in general. Instantaneous. *Quality* as adj. Proactive. Proactive Mission-Statement. Positive feedback. A positive role-model. Compensation. Validation. As for example. True facts are often impactful. "Call now for your free gift!" I only wish. Not too good of a. Pay the consequences of. At this juncture. "Third-leading cause of death of both American men and women." To reference. To process. Process. The process of. The healing process. The grieving process. "Processing of feelings is a major component of the grieving process." Commensurant. "Till the stars fall from the sky/For you and I" Working together. Efficacious, effectual. Lifestyle. This phenomena, these criterion. Irregardless. *If* for *whether*. "Both sides are working together to achieve a workable consensus." Functional, dysfunctional. Family of origin. S. O. To nest. Relationship. Merge together. KEEP IN LANE. Whomever wants it. "My wife and myself wish to express our gratitude and thanks to you for being here to support us at this difficult time in our life." Eventuate. Diversity. Quality time. Values, family values. To conference. "French provincial twin bed with canape and box spring, $150." Take a wait-and-see attitude. Cum-N-Go Quik Mart. Travelodge. Self-confessed. Precise estimate. "Travel-times on the expressways are reflective of its still being bad out there." Budgetel. EZPAY. RENT2OWN. MENS' ROOM. LADY'S ROOM. *Individual* for *person*. *Whom* for *who, that* for *who*. "The accident equated to a lot of damage." *Ipse dixie*. Falderol. "'Waiting on' is a dialectical locution on the rise and splitting its meaning." Staunch the flow.

A.M. in the morning. *Forte* as "forté." Advisement. Most especially. Sum total. Final totals. Complete dearth. "You can donate your used car or truck in any condition." "DiBlasi's work shows how sex can bring people together and pull them apart." "Come in and take advantage of our knowledgeable staff." "We get the job done, not make excuses." "Chances of rain are prevalent." National Highway Traffic Safety Administration Rule and Regulation Amendment Task Force. *Further* for *farther.* "The Fred Pryor Seminar has opened my eyes to better time management techniques. Also it has given real life situations and how to deal with them effectively." Hands-on, can-do. "Each of the variants indicated in boldface type count as an entry." Visualization. "Insert and tighten metric calibrated hexscrews (K) into arc (C) comprised of intersecting vertical pieces (A) along transverse section of Structure. (see Diagram for #(3–4 inv.)" Creative, creativity. To message, to send a message, to bring our message to. To reach out to. Context. Straightlaced. A factor, a decisive factor. Myriads of decisive factors. "It is a federal requirement to comply with all safety regulations on this flight." In this context, of this context. On a __ly basis. From the standpoint of. Contextualization. Within the parameters of this context. Decontextualization. Defamiliarize. Orientated. "The artist's employment of a radical visual idiom serves to decontextualize both conventional modes of representation and the patriarchal contexts on which such traditional hegemonic notions as representation, tradition, and even conventional contextualization have come to be seen as depending for their privileged status as aestheto-interpretive mechanisms." I don't feel well and hope I recoup. "As parents, the responsibility of talking to your kids about drugs is up to you." Who would of thought? Last and final call. As to. Achieve. Achievement. Competitive. Challenge, challenged, challenges. Excellence. Pursuit of a standard of total excellence. An astute observance. *Misrepresent* for *lie.* A longstanding tradition of achievement in the arena of excellence. "All copier stores are not the same." Visible to the eye. *Which* for *that, I* for *me.* That which. In regards to. Data as singular, *media* as singular, *graffiti* as singular. *Remain* for *stay.* On-task. Escalate as transitive. Closure. Community. "Iran must realize that it cannot flaunt with impunity the expressed will and law of the world community." Community support. Community-based. Broad appeal. Rally support. Outpourings of support. "Tried to lay the cause at the feet of Congress." Epidemic proportions. Proportionate response. Feasibility. "This anguishing national ordeal." Bipartisan, nonpartisan. Widespread outbreaks. To appeal to. To impact. Author's Foreward. Hew and cry. From this aspect. Hayday. Appropriate, inappropriate. Contingency. Contingent upon. Every possible contingency. Audible to the ear. *As* for *since.* Palpably. "The enormity of his accomplishment." Frigid temperatures. Loud volume. Surrounded on all sides, my workable options are at this time few in number. Chaise lounge, nucular, deep-seeded, bedroom suit, reek havoc. Her ten-year rein atop the competition. The reason is because she still continues to hue to the basic fundamentals. Ouster. Lucrative salaries, expensive prices. *Forbear* for *forebear; forgo* for *forego.* Breech of conduct. Award for meretricious service. Substantiate, unsubstantiated, substantial. Reelected to another term. Fulsome praise. Service. Public service. "A tradition of servicing your needs." A commitment to accountability in a lifetime of public service. As best as we can. WAVE ALL INTEREST FOR 90 DAYS "But I also want to have—be the president that protects the rights of, of people to, to have arms. And that—so you don't go so far that the legitimate rights on some legislation are, are, you know, impinged on." "Dr. Charles Frieses'." Conflict. Conflict-resolution. The mutual advantage of both sides in this widespread conflict. "We will make a determination in terms of an appropriate response." Future plans. Don't go there! PLEASE WAIT HERE UNTIL NEXT AVAILABLE CLERK. I thought to myself. Fellow countrymen. "Your efforts to recover from the experience of growing up in an alcoholic family may be very difficult and threatening for your family to hear about and accept, especially if they are still in the midst of their own survival." *Misappropriate* for *steal.* Nortorious. I'll be there momentarily. At some later point in time. I'm not adverse to that. "Hello-o?" Have a good one. Luv Ya. :)

Discussed in this essay:

A Dictionary of Modern American Usage, by Bryan A. Garner. Oxford University Press, 1998. 723 pages. $35.

A Dictionary of Modern English Usage, by H. W Fowler. Oxford University Press, 1926. Rev. by Sir Ernest Gowers, 1965. 725 pages.

The Language Instinct: How the Mind Creates Language, by Steven Pinker. William Morrow and Company, 1994. 494 pages.

Webster's Dictionary of English Usage, E. W Gilman, ed. Merriam-Webster Inc., 1989. 978 pages.

Usage and Abusage: A Guide to Good English, by Eric Partridge. Hamish Hamilton, 1957. 392 pages.

Webster's Third New International Dictionary of the English Language, Philip Gove, ed. G. & C. Merriam Company, 1961. 2,662 pages.

> Dilige et quod vis fac.
> —ST. AUGUSTINE

Did you know that probing the seamy underbelly of U.S. lexicography reveals ideological strife and controversy and intrigue and nastiness and fervor on a nearly hanging-chad scale? For instance, did you know that some modern dictionaries are notoriously liberal and others notoriously conservative, and that certain conservative dictionaries were actually conceived and designed as corrective responses to the "corruption" and "permissiveness" of certain liberal dictionaries? That the oligarchic device of having a special "Distinguished Usage Panel . . . of outstanding professional speakers and writers" is an attempted compromise between the forces of egalitarianism and traditionalism in English, but that most linguistic liberals dismiss the Usage Panel as mere sham-populism?

Did you know that U.S. lexicography even *had* a seamy underbelly?

The occasion for this article is Oxford University Press's semi-recent release of Bryan A. Garner's *A Dictionary of Modern American Usage.* The fact of the matter is that Garner's dictionary is extremely good, certainly the most comprehensive usage guide since E. W Gilman's *Webster's Dictionary of English Usage;* now a decade out of date.[1] Its format, like that of Gilman and the handful of other great American usage guides of the last century, includes entries on individual words and phrases and expostulative small-cap MINI-ESSAYS on any issue broad enough to warrant more general discussion. But the really distinctive and ingenious features of *A Dictionary of Modern American Usage* involve issues of rhetoric and ideology and style, and it is impossible to describe why these issues are important and why Garner's management of them borders on genius without talking about the historical context[2] in which *ADMAU* appears, and this context

---

[1] With the advent of online databases, Garner has access to far more examples of actual usage than did Gilman, and he deploys them to great effect. (FYI, Oxford's 1996 *New Fowler's Modern English Usage* is also extremely comprehensive and good, but its emphasis is on British usage.)

[2] Sorry about this phrase; I hate this phrase, too. This happens to be one of those very rare times when "historical context" is the phrase to use and there is no equivalent phrase that isn't even worse. (I actually tried "lexico-temporal backdrop" in one of the middle drafts, which I think you'll agree is not preferable.)

INTERPOLATION

The above ¶ is motivated by the fact that this reviewer almost always sneers and/or winces when he sees "historical context" deployed in a piece of writing and thus hopes to head off any potential sneers/winces from the reader here, especially in an article about felicitous usage.

turns out to be a veritable hurricane of controversies involving everything from technical linguistics to public education to political ideology, and these controversies take a certain amount of time to unpack before their relation to what makes Garner's usage guide so eminently worth your hard-earned reference-book dollar can even be established; and in fact there's no way even to begin the whole harrowing polymeric discussion without taking a moment to establish and define the highly colloquial term *SNOOT.*

From one perspective, a certain irony attends the publication of any good new book on American usage. It is that the people who are going to be interested in such a book are also the people who are least going to need it, i.e., that offering counsel on the finer points of U.S. English is Preaching to the Choir. The relevant Choir here comprises that small percentage of American citizens who actually care about the current status of double modals and ergative verbs. The same sorts of people who watched *Story of English* on PBS (twice) and read W Safire's column with their half-caff every Sunday. The sorts of people who feel that special blend of wincing despair and sneering superiority when they see EXPRESS LANE—10 ITEMS OR LESS or hear *dialogue* used as a verb or realize that the founders of the Super 8 motel chain must surely have been ignorant of the meaning of *suppurate.* There are lots of epithets for people like this—Grammar Nazis, Usage Nerds, Syntax Snobs, the Language Police. The term I was raised with is *SNOOT.*[3] The word might be slightly self-mocking, but those other terms are outright dysphemisms. A SNOOT can be defined as somebody who knows what *dysphemism* means and doesn't mind letting you know it.

I submit that we SNOOTs are just about the last remaining kind of truly elitist nerd. There are, granted, plenty of nerd-species in today's America, and some of these are elitist within their own nerdy purview (e.g., the skinny, carbuncular, semi-autistic Computer Nerd moves instantly up on the totem pole of status when your screen freezes and now you need his help, and the bland condescension with which he performs the two occult keystrokes that unfreeze your screen is both elitist and situationally valid). But the SNOOT's purview is interhuman social life itself. You don't, after all (despite withering cultural pressure), have to use a computer, but you can't escape language: Language is everything and everywhere; it's what lets us have anything to do with one another; it's what separates us from the animals; Genesis 11:7–10 and so on. And we SNOOTs know when and how to hyphenate phrasal adjectives and to keep participles from dangling, and we know that we know, and we know how very few other Americans know this stuff or even care, and we judge them accordingly.

In ways that certain of us are uncomfortable about, SNOOTs' attitudes about contemporary usage resemble religious/political conservatives' attitudes about contemporary culture:[4] We combine a missionary zeal and a near-neural faith in our beliefs' importance with a curmudgeonly hell-in-a-handbasket de-

---

[3]*SNOOT* (n) (*highly colloq*) is this reviewer's nuclear family's nickname *à clef* for a really extreme usage fanatic, the sort of person whose idea of Sunday fun is to look for mistakes in Safire's column's prose itself. This reviewer's family is roughly 70 percent SNOOT, which term itself derives from an acronym, with the big historical family joke being that whether S.N.O.O.T. stood for "*Sprachgefühl* Necessitates Our Ongoing Tendance" or "Syntax Nudniks of Our Time" depended on whether or not you were one.

[4]This is true in my own case at any rate—plus also the "uncomfortable" part. I teach college English part-time—mostly Lit, not Comp. But I am also so pathologically anal about* usage that every semester the same thing happens: The minute I have read my students' first set of papers, we immediately abandon the regular Lit syllabus and have a three-week Emergency Remedial Usage Unit, during which my demeanor is basically that of somebody teaching HIV prevention to intravenous-drug users. When it emerges (as it does, every time) that 95 percent of these intelligent upscale college students have never been taught, e.g., what a clause is or why a misplaced *only* can make a sentence confusing, I all but pound my head on the blackboard: I exhort them to sue their hometown school boards. The kids end up scared, both of me and for me.

Editor's Note: Author insisted this phrase replace "obsessed with" and took umbrage at the suggestion that this change clearly demonstrated the very quality he wished to denigrate.

spair at the way English is routinely manhandled and corrupted by supposedly educated people. The Evil is all around us: boners and clunkers and solecistic howlers and bursts of voguish linguistic methane that make any SNOOT's cheek twitch and forehead darken. A fellow SNOOT I know likes to say that listening to most people's English feels like watching somebody use a Stradivarius to pound nails. We[5] are the Few, the Proud, the Appalled at Everyone Else.

Thesis Statement for Whole Article

Issues of tradition vs. egalitarianism in U.S. English are at root political issues and can be effectively addressed only in what this article hereby terms a "Democratic Spirit." A Democratic Spirit is one that combines rigor and humility, i.e., passionate conviction plus sedulous respect for the convictions of others. As any American knows, this is a very difficult spirit to cultivate and maintain, particularly when it comes to issues you feel strongly about. Equally tough is a D.S.'s criterion of 100 percent intellectual integrity— you have to be willing to look honestly at yourself and your motives for believing what you believe, and to do it more or less continually.

   This kind of stuff is advanced U.S. citizenship. A true Democratic Spirit is up there with religious faith and emotional maturity and all those other top-of-the-Maslow-Pyramid-type qualities people spend their whole lives working on. A Democratic Spirit's constituent rigor and humility and honesty are in fact so hard to maintain on certain issues that it's almost irresistibly tempting to fall in with some established dogmatic camp and to follow that camp's line on the issue and to let your position harden within the camp

---

[5]Please note that the strategically repeated 1-P pronoun is meant to iterate and emphasize that this reviewer is very much one too, a SNOOT, plus to connote the nuclear family mentioned supra. SNOOTitude runs in families. In, *ADMAU*'s Preface, Bryan Garner mentions both his father and grandfather and actually uses the word *genetic,* and it's probably true: 95 percent of the SNOOTs I know have at least one parent who is, by profession or temperament or both, a SNOOT. In my own case, my mom is a Comp teacher and has written remedial usage books and is a SNOOT of the most rabid and intractable sort. At least part of the reason I am a SNOOT is that for years Mom brainwashed us in all sorts of subtle ways. Here's an example. Family suppers often involved a game: If one of us children made a usage error, Mom would pretend to have a coughing fit that would go on and on until the relevant child had identified the relevant error and corrected it. It was all very self-ironic and lighthearted; but still, looking back, it seems a bit excessive to pretend that your child is actually *denying you oxygen* by speaking incorrectly. But the really chilling thing is that I now sometimes find myself playing this same "game" with my own students, complete with pretend pertussion.

INTERPOLATION

As something I'm all but sure *Harper's* will excise, I'll also insert that we even had a lighthearted but retrospectively chilling little family *song* that Mom and we little SNOOTlets would sing in the car on long trips while Dad silently rolled his eyes and drove (you have to remember the title theme of *Underdog* in order to follow the song):

When idiots in this world appear
And fail to be concise or clear
And solecisms rend the ear
The cry goes up both far and near
For Blunder Dog
Blunder Dog
Blunder Dog
Blunder Dog
[etc.] *

*(Since this'll almost surely get cut, I'll admit that, yes, I, as a kid, was the actual author of this song. But by this time I'd been thoroughly brainwashed. And just about the whole car sang along. It was sort of our family's version of "100 Bottles . . . Wall.")

and become inflexible and to believe that any other camp is either evil or insane and to spend all your time and energy trying to shout over them.

I submit, then, that it is indisputably easier to be dogmatic than Democratic, especially about issues that are both vexed and highly charged. I submit further that the issues surrounding "correctness" in contemporary American usage are both vexed and highly charged, and that the fundamental questions they involve are ones whose answers have to be "worked out" instead of simply found.

A distinctive feature of *ADMAU* is that its author is willing to acknowledge that a usage dictionary is not a bible or even a textbook but rather just the record of one smart person's attempts to work out answers to certain very difficult questions. This willingness appears to me to be informed by a Democratic Spirit. The big question is whether such a spirit compromises Garner's ability to present himself as a genuine "authority" on issues of usage. Assessing Garner's book, then, involves trying to trace out the very weird and complicated relationship between Authority and Democracy in what we as a culture have decided is English. That relationship is, as many educated Americans would say, still in process at this time.

A *Dictionary of Modern American Usage* has no Editorial Staff or Distinguished Panel. It's conceived, researched, and written *ab ovo usque ad mala* by Bryan Garner. This is an interesting guy. He's both a lawyer and a lexicographer (which seems a bit like being both a narcotics dealer and a DEA agent). His 1987 *A Dictionary of Modern Legal Usage* is already a minor classic; now, instead of practicing law anymore, he goes around conducting writing seminars for J.D.'s and doing prose-consulting for various judicial bodies. Garner's also the founder of something called the H. W Fowler Society,[6] a worldwide group of usage-Trekkies who like to send one another linguistic boners clipped from different periodicals. You get the idea. This Garner is one serious and very hard-core SNOOT.

The lucid, engaging, and extremely sneaky Preface to *ADMAU* serves to confirm Garner's SNOOTitude in fact while undercutting it in tone. For one thing, whereas the traditional usage pundit cultivates a sort of remote and imperial persona—the kind who uses *one* or *we* to refer to himself—Garner gives us an almost Waltonishly endearing sketch of his own background:

> I realized early—at the age of 15[7]—that my primary intellectual interest was the use of the English language. . . . It became an all-consuming passion. . . . I read everything I could find on the subject. Then, on a wintry evening while visiting New Mexico at the age of 16, I discovered Eric Partridge's *Usage and Abusage*. I was enthralled. Never had I held a more exciting book. . . . Suffice it to say that by the time I was 18, I had committed to memory most of Fowler, Partridge, and their successors. . . .

Although this reviewer regrets the biosketch's failure to mention the rather significant social costs of being an adolescent whose overriding passion is English usage,[8] the critical hat is off to yet another person-

---

[6]If Samuel Johnson is the Shakespeare of English usage, think of Henry Watson Fowler as the Eliot or Joyce. His 1926 *A Dictionary of Modern English Usage* is the granddaddy of modern usage guides, and its dust-dry wit and blushless imperiousness have been models for every subsequent classic in the field, from Eric Partridge's *Usage and Abusage* to Theodore Bernstein's *The Careful Writer* to Wilson Follett's *Modern American Usage* to Gilman's '89 *Webster's*.

[7](Garner prescribes spelling out only numbers under ten. I was taught that this rule applies just to Business Writing and that in all other modes you spell out one through nineteen and start using cardinals at 20.* *De gustibus non est disputandum*.)

Editor's Note: The Harper's style manual prescribes spelling out all numbers up to 100.

[8]From personal experience, I can assure you that any kid like this is going to be at best marginalized and at worst savagely and repeatedly Wedgied.

able section of the Preface, one that Garner entitles "First Principles": "Before going any further, I should explain my approach. That's an unusual thing for the author of a usage dictionary to do—unprecedented, as far as I know. But a guide to good writing is only as good as the principles on which it's based. And users should be naturally interested in those principles. So, in the interests of full disclosure. . . ."[9]

The "unprecedented" and "full disclosure" here are actually good-natured digs at Garner's Fowlerite predecessors, and a subtle nod to one camp in the wars that have raged in both lexicography and education ever since the notoriously liberal *Webster's Third New International Dictionary* came out in 1961 and included such terms as *heighth* and *irregardless* without any monitory labels on them. You can think of *Webster's Third* as sort of the Fort Sumter of the contemporary Usage Wars. These Wars are both the context and the target of a very subtle rhetorical strategy in *A Dictionary of Modern American Usage,* and without talking about them it's impossible to explain why Garner's book is both so good and so sneaky.

We regular citizens tend to go to The Dictionary for authoritative guidance.[10] Rarely, however, do we ask ourselves who decides what gets in The Dictionary or what words or spellings or pronunciations get deemed "substandard" or "incorrect." Whence the authority of dictionary-makers to decide what's OK[11] and what isn't? Nobody elected them, after all. And simply appealing to precedent or tradition won't work, because what's considered correct changes over time. In the 1600s, for instance, the second-singular pronoun took a singular conjugation—"You is." Earlier still, the standard 2-S pronoun wasn't *you* but *thou*. Huge numbers of now acceptable words like *clever, fun, banter,* and *prestigious* entered English as what usage authorities considered errors or egregious slang. And not just usage conventions but English itself changes over time; if it didn't, we'd all still be talking like Chaucer. Who's to say which changes are natural and which are corruptions? And when Bryan Garner or E. Ward Gilman do in fact presume to say, why should we believe them?

These sorts of questions are not new, but they do now have a certain urgency. America is in the midst of a protracted Crisis of Authority in matters of language. In brief, the same sorts of political upheavals that produced everything from Kent State to Independent Counsels have produced an influential contra-SNOOT school for whom normative standards of English grammar and usage are functions of nothing but custom and superstition and the ovine docility of a populace that lets self-appointed language authorities boss them around. See for example MIT's Steven Pinker in a famous *New Republic* article—"Once introduced, a prescriptive rule is very hard to eradicate, no matter how ridiculous. Inside the writing establishment, the rules survive by the same dynamic that perpetuates ritual genital mutilations"—or, at a somewhat lower pitch, Bill Bryson in *Mother Tongue: English and How It Got That Way:*

> Who sets down all those rules that we all know about from childhood—the idea that we must never end a sentence with a preposition or begin one with a conjunction, that we must use *each other* for two things and *one another* for more than two. . . ? The answer, surprisingly often, is that no one does, that when you look into the background of these "rules" there is often little basis for them.

---

[9]What follow in the Preface are " . . . the ten critical points that, after years of working on usage problems, I've settled on." These points are too involved to treat separately, but a couple of them are slippery in the extreme—e.g., "10. **Actual Usage.** In the end, the actual usage of educated speakers and writers is the overarching criterion for correctness," of which both "educated" and "actual" would require several pages of abstract clarification and qualification to shore up against Usage Wars—related attacks, but which Garner rather ingeniously elects to define and defend via their application in his dictionary itself.

[10]There's no better indication of The Dictionary's authority than that we use it to settle wagers. My own father is still to this day living down the outcome of a high-stakes bet on the correct spelling of *meringue,* a wager made on 14 September 1978.

[11]*Editor's Note:* The Harper's *style manual* prescribes okay.

In *ADMAU*'s Preface, Garner himself addresses the Authority Question with a Trumanesque simplicity and candor that simultaneously disguise the author's cunning and exemplify it:

> As you might already suspect, I don't shy away from making judgments. I can't imagine that most readers would want me to. Linguists don't like it, of course, because judgment involves subjectivity.[12] It isn't scientific. But rhetoric and usage, in the view of most professional writers, aren't scientific endeavors. You don't want dispassionate descriptions; you want sound guidance. And that requires judgment.

Whole monographs could be written just on the masterful rhetoric of this passage. Note for example the ingenious equivocation of judgment in "I don't shy away from making judgments" vs. "And that requires judgment." Suffice it to say that Garner is at all times *keenly* aware of the Authority Crisis in modern usage; and his response to this crisis is—in the best Democratic Spirit—rhetorical.

So . . .

Corollary to Thesis Statement for Whole Article

The most salient and timely feature of Garner's book is that it's both lexicographical and rhetorical. Its main strategy involves what is known in classical rhetoric as the Ethical Appeal. Here the adjective, derived from the Greek *ethos,* doesn't mean quite what we usually mean by *ethical.* But there are affinities. What the Ethical Appeal amounts to is a complex and sophisticated "Trust me." It's the boldest, most ambitious, and also most distinctively American of rhetorical Appeals, because it requires the rhetor to convince us not just of his intellectual acuity or technical competence but of his basic decency and fairness and sensitivity to the audience's own hopes and fears.[13]

These are not qualities one associates with the traditional SNOOT usage-authority, a figure who pretty much instantiates snobbishness and bow-tied anality, and one whose modern image is not improved by stuff like *American Heritage Dictionary* Distinguished Usage Panelist Morris Bishop's "The arrant solecisms of the ignoramus are here often omitted entirely, 'irregardless' of how he may feel about this neglect" or critic John Simon's "The English language is being treated nowadays exactly as slave traders once handled their merchandise. . . ." Compare those lines' authorial personas with Garner's in, e.g., "English usage is so challenging that even experienced writers need guidance now and then."

The thrust here is going to be that *A Dictionary of Modern American Usage* earns Garner pretty much all the trust his Ethical Appeal asks us for. The book's "feel-good" spirit (in the very best sense of "feel-good") marries rigor and humility in such a way as to allow Garner to be extremely prescriptive without any appearance of evangelism or elitist put-down. This is an extraordinary accomplishment. Understanding why it's basically a *rhetorical* accomplishment, and why this is both historically significant and (in this reviewer's opinion) politically redemptive, requires a more detailed look at the Usage Wars.

You'd sure know lexicography had an underbelly if you read the little introductory essays in modem dictionaries—pieces like *Webster's DEU*'s "A Brief History of English Usage" or *Webster's Third*'s "Linguistic Advances and Lexicography" or *AHD-3*'s "Usage in the American Heritage Dictionary: The Place of Crit-

---

[12]This is a clever half-truth. Linguists compose only one part of the anti-judgment camp, and their objections to usage judgments involve way more than just "subjectivity."

[13]In this last respect, recall for example W. J. Clinton's famous "I feel your pain," which was a blatant if not particularly masterful Ethical Appeal.

icism." But almost nobody ever bothers with these little intros, and it's not just their six-point type or the fact that dictionaries tend to be hard on the lap. It's that these intros aren't actually written for you or me or the average citizen who goes to The Dictionary just to see how to spell (for instance) *meringue*. They're written for other lexicographers and critics, and in fact they're not really introductory at all but polemical. They're salvos in the Usage Wars that have been under way ever since editor Philip Gove first sought to apply the value-neutral principles of structural linguistics to lexicography in *Webster's Third*. Gove's famous response to conservatives who howled[14], when *Webster's Third* endorsed *OK* and described *ain't* as "used orally in most parts of the U.S. by many cultivated speakers [*sic*]" was this: "A dictionary should have no traffic with . . . artificial notions of correctness or superiority. It should be descriptive and not prescriptive." These terms stuck and turned epithetic, and linguistic conservatives are now formally known as Prescriptivists and linguistic liberals as Descriptivists.

The former are far better known. When you read the columns of William Safire or Morton Freeman or books like Edwin Newman's *Strictly Speaking* or John Simon's *Paradigms Lost,* you're actually reading Popular Prescriptivism, a genre sideline of certain journalists (mostly older ones, the vast majority of whom actually do wear bow ties) whose bemused irony often masks a Colonel Blimp's rage at the way the beloved English of their youth is being trashed in the decadent present. The plutocratic tone and styptic wit of Safire and Newman and the best of the Prescriptivists is often modeled after the mandarin-Brit personas of Eric Partridge and H. W. Fowler, the same Twin Towers of scholarly Prescriptivism whom Garner talks about revering as a kid.[15]

Descriptivists, on the other hand, don't have weekly columns in the *Times*. These guys tend to be hard-core academics, mostly linguists or Comp theorists. Loosely organized under the banner of structural (or "descriptive") linguistics, they are doctrinaire positivists who have their intellectual roots in the work of Auguste Comte and Ferdinand de Saussure and their ideological roots firmly in the U.S. sixties. The brief explicit mention Garner's Preface gives this crew—

> Somewhere along the line, though, usage dictionaries got hijacked by the descriptive linguists,[16] who observe language scientifically. For the pure descriptivist, it's impermissible to say that one form of language

---

[14]Really, *howled*: blistering reviews and outraged editorials from across the country—from the *Times* and *The New Yorker* and good old *Life,* or q.v. this from the January '62 *Atlantic:* "We have seen a novel dictionary formula improvised, in great part, out of snap judgments and the sort of theoretical improvement that in practice impairs; and we have seen the gates propped wide open in enthusiastic hospitality to miscellaneous confusions and corruptions. In fine, the anxiously awaited work that was to have crowned cisatlantic linguistic scholarship with a particular glory turns out to be a scandal and a disaster."

[15]Note for example the mordant pith (and royal *we*) of this random snippet from Partridge's *Usage and Abusage:* **anxious of.** 'I am not hopeless of our future. But I am profoundly anxious of it', Beverley Nichols, *News of England,* 1938, which made us profoundly anxious *for* (or *about*)—not *of*—Mr Nichols's literary future.

Or see the near-Himalayan condescension of Fowler, here on some other people's use of words to mean things the words don't really mean:

slipshod extension . . . is especially likely to occur when some accident gives currency among the uneducated to words of learned origin, & the more if they are isolated or have few relatives in the vernacular. . . . The original meaning of *feasible* is simply doable (L *facare* do); but to the unlearned it is a mere token, of which he has to infer the value from the contexts in which he hears it used, because such relatives as it has in English—*feat, feature, faction,* &c.—either fail to show the obvious family likeness to which he is accustomed among families of indigenous words, or are (like *malfeasance*) outside his range.

[16]Utter bushwa: As *ADMAU*'s body makes clear, Garner knows exactly when the Descriptivists started influencing language guides.

is any better than another: as long as a native speaker says it, it's OK—and anyone who takes a contrary stand is a dunderhead. . . . Essentially, descriptivists and prescriptivists are approaching different problems. Descriptivists want to record language as it's actually used, and they perform a useful function—though their audience is generally limited to those willing to pore through vast tomes of dry-as-dust research.

—is disingenuous in the extreme, especially the "approaching different problems" part, because it vastly underplays the Descriptivists' influence on U.S. culture. For one thing, Descriptivism so quickly and thoroughly took over English education in this country that just about everybody who started junior high after c. 1970 has been taught to write Descriptively—via "freewriting," "brainstorming," "journaling," a view of writing as self-exploratory and -expressive rather than as communicative, an abandonment of systematic grammar, usage, semantics, rhetoric, etymology. For another thing, the very language in which today's socialist, feminist, minority, gay, and environmentalist movements frame their sides of political debates is informed by the Descriptivist belief that traditional English is conceived and perpetuated by Privileged WASP Males[17] and is thus inherently capitalist, sexist, racist, xenophobic, homophobic, elitist: unfair. Think Ebonics. Think of the involved contortions people undergo to avoid *he* as a generic pronoun, or of the tense deliberate way white males now adjust their vocabularies around non-w.m.'s. Think of today's endless battles over just the *names* of things—"Affirmative Action" vs. "Reverse Discrimination," "Pro-Life" vs. "Pro-Choice," "Undercount" vs. "Vote Fraud," etc.

The Descriptivist revolution takes a little time to unpack, but it's worth it. The structural linguists' rejection of conventional usage rules depends on two main arguments. The first is academic and methodological. In this age of technology, Descriptivists contend, it's the Scientific Method—clinically objective, value-neutral, based on direct observation and demonstrable hypothesis—that should determine both the content of dictionaries and the standards of "correct" English. Because language is constantly evolving, such standards will always be fluid. Gove's now classic introduction to *Webster's Third* outlines this type of Descriptivism's five basic edicts: "1—Language changes constantly; 2—Change is normal; 3—Spoken language is the language; 4—Correctness rests upon usage; 5—All usage is relative."

These principles look *prima facie* OK—commonsensical and couched in the bland simple s.-v.-o. prose of dispassionate Science—but in fact they're vague and muddled and it takes about three seconds to think of reasonable replies to each one of them, viz.:

1—OK, but how much and how fast?

2—Same thing. Is Heraclitean flux as normal or desirable as gradual change? Do some changes actually serve the language's overall pizzazz better than others? And how many people have to deviate from how many conventions before we say the language has actually changed? Fifty percent? Ten percent?

3—This is an old claim, at least as old as Plato's *Phaedrus*. And it's specious. If Derrida and the infamous Deconstructionists have done nothing else, they've debunked the idea that speech is language's primary instantiation.[18] Plus consider the weird arrogance of Gove's (3) w/r/t correctness. Only the most mullahlike Prescriptivists care very much about spoken English; most Prescriptive usage guides concern Standard *Written* English.[19]

---

[17](which is fact is true)

[18](Q.v. "The Pharmakon" in Derrida's *La dissémination*—but you'd probably be better off just trusting me.)

[19]Standard Written English (SWE) is also sometimes called Standard English (SE) or Educated English, but the inditement-emphasis is the same.

4—Fine, but whose usage? Gove's (4) begs the whole question. What he wants to imply here, I think, is a reversal of the traditional entailment-relation between abstract rules and concrete usage: Instead of usage ideally corresponding to a rigid set of regulations, the regulations ought to correspond to the way real people are actually using the language. Again, fine, but which people? Urban Latinos? Boston Brahmins? Rural Midwesterners? Appalachian Neogaelics?

5—*Huh?* If this means what it seems to mean, then it ends up biting Gove's whole argument in the ass. (5) appears to imply that the correct answer to the above "which people?" is: "All of them!" And it's easy to show why this will not stand up as a lexicographical principle. The most obvious problem with it is that not everything can go in The Dictionary. Why not? Because you can't observe every last bit of every last native speaker's "language behavior," and even if you could, the resultant dictionary would weigh 4 million pounds and have to be updated hourly.[20] The fact is that any lexicographer is going to have to make choices about what gets in and what doesn't. And these choices are based on . . . what? And now we're right back where we started.

It is true that, as a SNOOT, I am probably neurologically predisposed to look for flaws in Gove et al.'s methodological argument. But these flaws seem awfully easy to find. Probably the biggest one is that the Descriptivists' "scientific lexicography"—under which, keep in mind, the ideal English dictionary is basically number-crunching; you somehow observe every linguistic act by every native/naturalized speaker of English and put the sum of all these acts between two covers and call it The Dictionary—involves an incredibly simplistic and outdated understanding of what *scientific* means. It requires a naive belief in scientific objectivity, for one thing. Even in the physical sciences, everything from quantum mechanics to Information Theory has shown that an act of observation is itself part of the phenomenon observed and is analytically inseparable from it.

If you remember your old college English classes, there's an analogy here that points up the trouble scholars get into when they confuse observation with interpretation. Recall the New Critics.[21] They believed that literary criticism was best conceived as a "scientific" endeavor: The critic was a neutral, careful, unbiased, highly trained observer whose job was to find and objectively describe meanings that were right there—literally inside—pieces of literature. Whether you know what happened to the New Criticism's reputation depends on whether you took college English after c. 1975; suffice it to say that its star has dimmed. The New Critics had the same basic problem as Gove's Methodological Descriptivists: They believed that *scientific* meant the same thing as *neutral* or *unbiased*. And that linguistic meanings could exist "objectively," separate from any interpretive act.

SEMI-INTERPOLATION

Plus note that Garner's Preface explicitly names *ADMAU*'s intended audience as "writers and editors." And even ads for the dictionary in such organs as *The New York Review of Books* are built around the slogan "If you like to WRITE . . . Refer to us."*

*(Yr. SNOOT rev. cannot help observing, w/r/t these ads, that the opening r in **Refer** here should not be capitalized after a dependent clause + ellipses—*Quandoque bonus dormitat Homerus.*)

[20]True, some sort of 100 percent compendious real-time Mega-dictionary might be possible online, though it'd take a small army of lexical webmasters and a much larger army of *in situ* actual-use reporters and surveillance techs; plus it'd be GNP-level expensive.

[21]*New Criticism* refers to T. S. Eliot and I. A. Richards and F. R. Leavis and Cleanth Brooks and Wimsatt & Beardsley and the whole "close reading" school that dominated literary criticism from WWI well into the seventies.

The point of the analogy is that claims to objectivity in language study are now the stuff of jokes and shudders. The epistemological assumptions that underlie Methodological Descriptivism have been thoroughly debunked and displaced—in Lit by the rise of post-structuralism, Reader-Response Criticism, and Jaussian Reception Theory; in linguistics by the rise of Pragmatics—and it's now pretty much universally accepted that (a) meaning is inseparable from some act of interpretation and (b) an act of interpretation is always somewhat biased, i.e., informed by the interpreter's particular ideology. And the consequence of (a) and (b) is that there's no way around it—decisions about what to put in The Dictionary and what to exclude are going to be based on a lexicographer's ideology. And every lexicographer's got one. To presume that dictionary-making can somehow avoid or transcend ideology is simply to subscribe to a particular ideology, one that might aptly be called Unbelievably Naive Positivism.

There's an even more important way Descriptivists are wrong in thinking that the Scientific Method is appropriate to the study of language:

Even if, as a thought experiment, we assume a kind of nineteenth-century scientific realism—in which, even though some scientists' interpretations of natural phenomena might be biased,[22] the natural phenomena themselves can be supposed to exist wholly independent of either observation or interpretation—no such realist supposition can be made about "language behavior," because this behavior is both *human* and fundamentally *normative*. To understand this, you have only to accept the proposition that language is by its very nature public—i.e., that there can be no such thing as a Private Language[23]—and then to observe the way Methodological Descriptivists seem either ignorant of this fact or oblivious to its consequences, as in for example one Charles Fries's introduction to an epigone of *Webster's Third* called *The American College Dictionary*:

> A dictionary can be an "authority" only in the sense in which a book of chemistry or of physics or of botany can be an "authority"—by the accuracy and the completeness of its record of the observed facts of the field examined, in accord with the latest principles and techniques of the particular science.

---

[22]("EVIDENCE OF CANCER LINK REFUTED BY TOBACCO INSTITUTE RESEARCHERS")

[23]This proposition is in fact true, as is interpolatively demonstrated below, and although the demonstration is extremely persuasive it is also, you can see from the size of this FN, lengthy and involved and rather, umm, dense, so that again you'd probably be better off simply granting the truth of the proposition and forging on with the main text.

INTERPOLATIVE DEMONSTRATION OF THE FACT THAT THERE IS NO SUCH THING AS A PRIVATE LANGUAGE

It's sometimes tempting to imagine that there can be such a thing as a Private Language. Many of us are prone to lay-philosophizing about the weird privacy of our own mental states, for example, and from the fact that when my knee hurts only I can feel it, it's tempting to conclude that for me the word *pain* has a very subjective internal meaning that only I can truly understand. This line of thinking is sort of like the adolescent pot-smoker's terror that his own inner experience is both private and unverifiable, a syndrome that is technically known as Cannabic Solipsism. Eating Chips Ahoy! and staring intently at the television's network PGA event, for instance, the adolescent pot-smoker is struck by the ghastly possibility that, e.g., what he sees as the color green and what other people call "the color green" may in fact not be the same color experiences at all: The fact that both he and someone else call Pebble Beach's fairways green and a stoplight's GO signal green appears to guarantee only that there is a similar consistency in their color experience of fairways and GO lights, not that the actual subjective quality of those color experiences is the same; it could be that what the ad. pot-smoker experiences as green everyone else actually experiences as blue, and what we "mean" by the word *blue* is what he "means" by *green,* etc., etc., until the whole line of thinking gets so vexed and exhausting that the a.p.-s. ends up slumped crumb-strewn and paralyzed in his chair.

The point here is that the idea of a Private Language, like Private Colors and most of the other solipsistic conceits with which this particular reviewer has at various times been afflicted, is both deluded and demonstrably false.

This is so stupid it practically drools. An "authoritative" physics text presents the results of *physicists'* observations and *physicists'* theories about those observations. If a physics textbook operated on Descriptivist principles, the fact that 'some Americans believe that electricity flows better downhill (based on the observed fact that power lines tend to run high above the homes they serve) would require the Electricity Flows Better Downhill Theory to be included as a "valid" theory in the textbook—just as, for Dr. Fries, if some Americans use *infer* for *imply,* the use becomes an ipso facto "valid" part of the language. Structural linguists like Gove and Fries are not, finally, scientists but census-takers who happen to misconstrue the importance of "observed facts." It isn't scientific phenomena they're tabulating but rather a set of human behaviors, and a lot of human behaviors are—to be blunt—moronic. Try, for instance, to imagine an "authoritative" ethics textbook whose principles were based on what most people actually do.

Norm-wise, let's keep in mind that language didn't come into being because our hairy ancestors were sitting around the veldt with nothing better to do. Language was invented to serve certain specific purposes:[24] "That mushroom is poisonous"; "Knock these two rocks together and you can start a fire"; "This shelter is mine!" And so on. Clearly, as linguistic communities evolve over time, they discover that some ways of using language are "better" than others—meaning better with respect to the community's purposes. If we assume that one such purpose might be communicating which kinds of food are safe to eat, then you can see how, for example, a misplaced modifier might violate an important norm:

"People who eat that kind of mushroom often get sick" confuses the recipient about whether he'll get sick only if he eats the mushroom frequently or whether he stands a good chance of getting sick the very first time he eats it. In other words, the community has a vested practical interest in excluding this kind of misplaced modifier from acceptable usage; and even if a certain percentage of tribesmen screw up and use them, this still doesn't make m.m.'s a good idea.

Maybe now the analogy between usage and ethics is clearer. Just because people sometimes lie, cheat on their taxes, or scream at their kids, this doesn't mean that they think those things are "good." The whole point of norms is to help us evaluate our actions (including utterances) according to what we as a community have decided our real interests and purposes are. Granted, this analysis is oversimplified; in practice it's incredibly hard to arrive at norms and to keep them at least minimally fair or sometimes even to agree on what they are (q.v. today's Culture Wars). But the Descriptivists' assumption that all usage norms are arbitrary and dispensable leads to—well, have a mushroom.

The connotations of *arbitrary* here are tricky, though, and this sort of segues into the second argument Descriptivists make. There is a sense in which specific linguistic conventions *are* arbitrary. For instance, there's no particular metaphysical reason why our word for a four-legged mammal that gives milk

---

In the case of Private Language, the delusion is usually based on the belief that a word such as *pain* has the meaning it does because it is somehow "connected" to a feeling in my knee. But as Mr. L. Wittgenstein's *Philosophical Investigations* proved in the 1950s, words actually have the meanings they do because of certain rules and verification tests that are imposed on us from outside our own subjectivities, viz., by the community in which we have to get along and communicate with other people. Wittgenstein's argument, which is admittedly very complex and gnomic and opaque, basically centers on the fact that a word like *pain* means what it does for me because of the way the community I'm part of has tacitly agreed to use *pain.*

If you're thinking that all this seems not only abstract but also pretty irrelevant to the Usage Wars or to anything you have any real interest in at all, you are very much mistaken. If words' meanings depend on transpersonal rules and these rules on community consensus, language is not only conceptually non-Private but also irreducibly *public, political,* and *ideological.* This means that questions about our national consensus on grammar and usage are actually bound up with every last social issue that millennial America's about—class, race, gender, morality, tolerance, pluralism, cohesion, equality, fairness, money: You name it.

[24]Norms, after all, are just practices people have agreed on as optimal ways of doing things for certain purposes. They're not laws but they're not laissez-faire, either.

and goes Moo is *cow* and not, say, *prtlmpf.* The uptown phrase for this is "the arbitrariness of the linguistic sign," and it's used, along with certain principles of cognitive science and generative grammar, in a more philosophically sophisticated version of Descriptivism that holds the conventions of SWE to be more like the niceties of fashion than like actual norms. This "Philosophical Descriptivism" doesn't care much about dictionaries or method; its target is the standard SNOOT claim *supra*—that prescriptive rules have their ultimate justification in the community's need to make its language meaningful.

The argument goes like this. An English sentence's being *meaningful* is not the same as its being *grammatical.* That is, such clearly ill-formed constructions as "Did you seen the car keys of me?" or "The show was looked by many people" are nevertheless comprehensible; the sentences do, more or less, communicate the information they're trying to get across. Add to this the fact that nobody who isn't damaged in some profound Oliver Sacksish way actually ever makes these sorts of very deep syntactic errors.[25] and you get the basic proposition of Noam Chomsky's generative linguistics, which is that there exists a Universal Grammar beneath and common to all languages, plus that there is probably an actual part of the human brain that's imprinted with this Universal Grammar the same way birds' brains are imprinted with Fly South and dogs' with Sniff Genitals. There's all kinds of compelling evidence and support for these ideas, not least of which are the advances that linguists and cognitive scientists and A.I. researchers have been able to make with them, and the theories have a lot of credibility, and they are adduced by the Philosophical Descriptivists to show that since the really *important* rules of language are at birth already hard-wired into people's neocortex, SWE prescriptions against dangling participles or mixed metaphors are basically the linguistic equivalent of whalebone corsets and short forks for salad. As Descriptivist Steven Pinker puts it, "When a scientist considers all the high-tech mental machinery needed to order words into everyday sentences, prescriptive rules are, at best, inconsequential decorations."

This argument is not the barrel of drugged trout that Methodological Descriptivism was, but it's still vulnerable to some objections. The first one is easy. Even if it's true that we're all wired with a Universal Grammar, it simply doesn't follow that *all* prescriptive rules are superfluous. Some of these rules really do seem to serve clarity and precision. The injunction against two-way adverbs ("People who eat this often get sick") is an obvious example, as are rules about other kinds of misplaced modifiers ("There are many reasons why lawyers lie, some better than others") and about relative pronouns' proximity to the nouns they modify ("She's the mother of an infant daughter who works twelve hours a day").

Granted, the Philosophical Descriptivist can question just how absolutely necessary these rules are— it's quite likely that a recipient of clauses like the above could figure out what the sentences mean from the sentences on either side or from the "overall context" or whatever. A listener can usually figure out what I really mean when I misuse *infer* for *imply* or say *indicate* for *say,* too. But many of these solecisms require at least a couple extra nanoseconds of cognitive effort, a kind of rapid sift-and-discard process, before the recipient gets it. Extra work. It's debatable just how much extra work, but it seems indisputable that we put *some* extra neural burden on the recipient when we fail to follow certain conventions. W/r/t confusing clauses like the above, it simply seems more "considerate" to follow the rules of correct SWE . . . just as it's more "considerate" to de-slob your home before entertaining guests or to brush your teeth before picking up a date. Not just more considerate but more *respectful* somehow—both of your listener and of what you're trying to get across. As we sometimes also say about elements of fashion and etiquette, the way you use

---

[25]In his *The Language Instinct: How the Mind Creates Language* (1994), Steven Pinker puts it this way: "No one, not even a valley girl, has to be told not to say *Apples the eat boy* or *The child seems sleeping* or *Who did you meet John and?* or the vast, vast majority of the millions of trillions of mathematically possible combinations of words."

English "Makes a Statement" or "Sends a Message"—even though these Statements/Messages often have nothing to do with the actual information you're trying to transmit.

We've now sort of bled into a more serious rejoinder to Philosophical Descriptivism: From the fact that linguistic communication is not strictly dependent on usage and grammar it does not necessarily follow that the traditional rules of usage and grammar are nothing but "inconsequential decorations." Another way to state the objection is that just because something is "decorative" does not necessarily make it "inconsequential." Rhetorically, Pinker's flip dismissal is bad tactics, for it invites the very question it begs: inconsequential to *whom*?

Take, for example, the Descriptivist claim that so-called correct English usages such as *brought* rather than *brung*, and *felt* rather than *feeled* are arbitrary and restrictive and unfair and are supported only by custom and are (like irregular verbs in general) archaic and incommodious and an all-around pain in the ass. Let us concede for the moment that these objections are 100 percent reasonable. Then let's talk about pants. Trousers, slacks. I suggest to you that having the "correct" subthoracic clothing for U.S. males be pants instead of skirts is arbitrary (lots of other cultures let men wear skirts), restrictive and unfair (U.S. females get to wear pants), based solely on archaic custom (I think it's got something to do with certain traditions about gender and leg position, the same reasons girls' bikes don't have a crossbar), and in certain ways not only incommodious but illogical (skirts are more comfortable than pants; pants ride up; pants are hot; pants can squish the genitals and reduce fertility; over time pants chafe and erode irregular sections of men's leg hair and give older men hideous half-denuded legs, etc. etc.). Let us grant—as a thought experiment if nothing else—that these are all reasonable and compelling objections to pants as an androsartorial norm. Let us in fact in our minds and hearts say yes—*shout* yes—to the skirt, the kilt, the toga, the sarong, the jupe. Let us dream of or even in our spare time work toward an America where nobody lays any arbitrary sumptuary prescriptions on anyone else and we can all go around as comfortable and aerated and unchafed and unsquished and motile as we want.

And yet the fact remains that, in the broad cultural mainstream of millennial America, men do not wear skirts. If you, the reader, are a U.S. male, and even if you share my personal objections to pants and dream as I do of a cool and genitally unsquishy American Tomorrow, the odds are still 99.9 percent that in 100 percent of public situations you wear pants/slacks/shorts/trunks. More to the point, if you are a U.S. male and also have a U.S. male child, and if that child were to come to you one evening and announce his desire/intention to wear a skirt rather than pants to school the next day, I am 100-percent confident that you are going to discourage him from doing so. *Strongly* discourage him. You could be a Molotov-tossing anti-pants radical or a kilt manufacturer or Steven Pinker himself—you're going to stand over your kid and be prescriptive about an arbitrary, archaic, uncomfortable, and inconsequentially decorative piece of clothing. Why? Well, because in modern America any little boy who comes to school in a skirt (even, say, a modest all-season midi) is going to get stared at and shunned and beaten up and called a Total Geekoid by a whole lot of people whose approval and acceptance are important to him.[26] In our culture, in other words, a boy who wears a skirt is Making a Statement that is going to have all kinds of gruesome social and emotional consequences.

You see where this is going. I'm going to describe the intended point of the pants analogy in terms I'm sure are simplistic—doubtless there are whole books in Pragmatics or psycholinguistics or something

---

[26]In the case of Steve Pinker Jr., those people are the boy's peers and teachers and crossing guards, etc. In the case of adult cross-dressers and drag queens who have jobs in the Straight World and wear pants to those jobs, it's coworkers and clients and people on the subway. For the die-hard slob who nevertheless wears a coat and a tie to work, it's mostly his boss, who himself doesn't want his employee's clothes to send clients "the wrong message." But of course it's all basically the same thing.

devoted to unpacking this point. The weird thing is that I've seen neither Descriptivists nor SNOOTs deploy it in the Wars.[27]

When I say or write something, there are actually a whole lot of different things I am communicating. The propositional content (the actual information I'm trying to convey) is only one part of it. Another part is stuff about me, the communicator. Everyone knows this. It's a function of the fact that there are uncountably many well-formed ways to say the same basic thing, from e.g. "I was attacked by a bear!" to "Goddamn bear tried to kill me!" to "That ursine juggernaut bethought to sup upon my person!" and so on. And different levels of diction and formality are only the simplest kinds of distinction; things get way more complicated in the sorts of interpersonal communication where social relations and feelings and moods come into play. Here's a familiar sort of example. Suppose that you and I are acquaintances and we're in my apartment having a conversation and that at some point I want to terminate the conversation and not have you be in my apartment anymore. Very delicate social moment. Think of all the different ways I can try to handle it: "Wow, look at the time"; "Could we finish this up later?"; "Could you please leave now?"; "Go"; "Get out"; "Get the hell out of here"; "Didn't you say you had to be someplace?"; "Time for you to hit the dusty trail, my friend"; "Off you go then, love"; or that sly old telephone-conversation ender: "Well, I'm going to let you go now"; etc. And then think of all the different factors and implications of each option.

The point here is obvious. It concerns a phenomenon that SNOOTs blindly reinforce and that Descriptivists badly underestimate and that scary vocab-tape ads try to exploit. People really do "judge" one another according to their use of language. Constantly. Of course, people judge one another on the basis of all kinds of things—weight, scent, physiognomy, occupation, make of vehicle[28]—and, again, doubtless it's all terribly complicated and occupies whole battalions of sociolinguists. But it's clear that at least one component of all this interpersonal semantic judging involves *acceptance,* meaning not some touchy-feely emotional affirmation but actual acceptance or rejection of somebody's bid to be regarded as a peer, a member of somebody else's collective or community or Group. Another way to come at this is to acknowledge something that in the Usage Wars gets mentioned only in very abstract terms: "Correct" English usage is, as a practical matter, a function of whom you're talking to and how you want that person to respond—not just to your utterance but also to *you.* In other words, a large part of the agenda of any communication is rhetorical and depends on what some rhet-scholars call "Audience" or "Discourse Community."[29] And the United States obviously has a huge number of such Discourse Communities, many of them regional and/or cultural dialects of English: Black English, Latino English, Rural Southern, Urban Southern, Standard Upper-Midwest, Maine Yankee, East-Texas Bayou, Boston Blue-Collar, on and on. Everybody knows this. What not everyone knows—especially not certain Prescriptivists—is that many of these non-SWE dialects have their own highly developed and internally consistent grammars, and that some of these dialects' usage norms actually make more linguistic/aesthetic sense than do their Standard counterparts (see INTERPOLATION). Plus, of course, there are innumerable sub- and subsubdialects based on all sorts of things that have nothing to do with locale or ethnicity—Medical-School English, Peorians-Who-Follow-Pro-Wrestling-Closely English, Twelve-Year-Old-Males-Whose-Worldview-Is-Deeply-Informed-By-*South-Park* English—and that are

---

[27]In fact, the only time one ever hears the issue made explicit is in radio ads for tapes that promise to improve people's vocabulary. These ads are extremely ominous and intimidating and always start out with "DID YOU KNOW PEOPLE JUDGE YOU BY THE WORDS YOU USE?"

[28](. . . not to mention color, gender, creed—you can see how fraught and charged all this is going to get)

[29]*Discourse Community* is an example of that rare kind of academic jargon that's actually a valuable addition to SWE because it captures something at once very complex and very specific that no other English term quite can.*

*(The above is an obvious attempt to preempt readerly sneers/winces at the term's continued deployment in this article.)

452

nearly incomprehensible to anyone who isn't inside their very tight and specific Discourse Community (which of course is part of their function[30]).

Interpolation: Example of Grammatical Advantages of a Non-Standard Dialect That This Reviewer Actually Knows About Firsthand

This rev. happens to have two native English dialects—the SWE of my hypereducated parents and the hard-earned Rural Midwestern of most of my peers. When I'm talking to R.M.'s, I usually use, for example, the construction "Where's it at?" instead of "Where is it?" Part of this is a naked desire to fit in and not get rejected as an egghead or fag (see *sub*). But another part is that I, SNOOT or no, believe that this and other R.M.isms are in certain ways superior to their Standard equivalents.

For a dogmatic Prescriptivist, "Where's it at?" is double-damned as a sentence that not only ends with a preposition but whose final preposition forms a redundancy with *where* that's similar to the redundancy in "the reason is because" (which latter usage I'll admit makes me dig my nails into my palms). Rejoinder: First off, the avoid-terminal-prepositions rule is the invention of one Fr. R. Lowth, an eighteenth-century British preacher and indurate pedant who did things like spend scores of pages arguing for *hath* over the trendy and degenerate *has*. The a.-t.-p. rule is antiquated and stupid and only the most ayatolloid SNOOT takes it seriously. Garner himself calls the rule "stuffy" and lists all kinds of useful constructions like, "the man you were listening to" that we'd have to discard or distort if we really enforced it.

Plus the apparent redundancy of "Where's it at?"[31] is offset by its metrical logic. What the *at* really does is license the contraction of *is* after the interrogative adverb. You can't say "Where's it?" So the choice is between "Where is it?" and "Where's it at?", and the latter, a strong anapest, is prettier and trips off the tongue better than "Where is it?", whose meter is either a clunky monosyllabic-foot + trochee or it's nothing at all.

This is probably the place for your SNOOT reviewer openly to concede that a certain number of traditional prescriptive rules really are stupid and that people who insist on them (like the legendary assistant to P.M. Margaret Thatcher who refused to read any memo with a split infinitive in it, or the jr.-high teacher I had who automatically graded you down if you started a sentence with *Hopefully*) are that very most pathetic and dangerous sort of SNOOT, the SNOOT Who Is Wrong. The injunction against split infinitives, for instance, is a consequence of the weird fact that English grammar is modeled on Latin even though Latin is a synthetic language and English is an analytic language.[32] Latin infinitives consist of one word and are impossible to as it were split, and the earliest English Prescriptivists—so enthralled with Latin that their English usage guides were actually written in Latin[33]—decided that English infinitives shouldn't be split either. Garner himself takes out after the s.i. rule in both SPLIT

---

[30](Plus it's true that whether something gets called a "subdialect" or "jargon" seems to depend on bow much it annoys people outside its Discourse Community. Garner himself has miniessays on AIRLINESE, COMPUTERESE, LEGALESE, and BUREAUCRATESE, and he more or less calls all of them jargon. There is no *ADMAU* miniessay on DIALECTS, but there is one on JARGON, in which such is Garner 's self-restraint that you can almost hear his tendons straining, as in "[Jargon] arises from the urge to save time and space—and occasionally to conceal meaning from the uninitiated.") [1](a redundancy that's a bit arbitrary, since "Where's it *from*?" isn't redundant [mainly because *whence* has vanished into semiarchaism]).

[31](a redundancy that's a bit arbitrary, since "Where's it *from*?" isn't redundant [mainly because *whence* has vanished into semiarchaism]).

[32]A synthetic language uses inflections to dictate syntax, whereas an analytic language uses word order. Latin, German, and Russian are synthetic; English and Chinese, analytic.

[33](Q.v. for example Sir Thomas Smith's cortext-withering *De Recta et Emendata Linguae Anglicae Scriptione Diologus* of 1568.)

INFINITIVES and SUPERSTITIONS.[34] And *Hopefully* at the beginning of a sentence, as a certain cheeky eighth-grader once pointed out to his everlasting social cost, actually functions not as a misplaced modal auxiliary or as a manner adverb like *quickly* or *angrily* but as a "sentence adverb" that indicates the speaker's attitude about the state of affairs described by the sentence (examples of perfectly OK sentence adverbs are *Clearly, Basically, Luckily*), and only SNOOTs educated in the high-pedantic years up to 1960 blindly proscribe it or grade it down.

The cases of split infinitives and *Hopefully* are in fact often trotted out by dogmatic Descriptivists as evidence that all SWE usage rules are arbitrary and stupid (which is a bit like pointing to Pat Buchanan as evidence that all Republicans are maniacs). Garner rejects *Hopefully*'s knee-jerk proscription, too, albeit grudgingly, including the adverb in his miniessay on SKUNKED TERMS, which is his phrase for a usage that is "hotly disputed . . . any use of it is likely to distract some readers." (Garner also points out something I'd never quite realized, which is that *hopefully*, if misplaced/mispunctuated in the body of a sentence, can create some of the same two-way ambiguities as other adverbs, as in the clause "I will borrow your book and hopefully read it soon.")

Whether we're conscious of it or not, most of us are fluent in more than one major English dialect and in a large number of subdialects and are probably at least passable in countless others. Which dialect you choose to use depends, of course, on whom you're addressing. More to the point, I submit that the dialect you use depends mostly on what sort of Group your listener is part of and whether you wish to present yourself as a fellow member of that Group. An obvious example is that traditional upper-class English has certain dialectal differences from lower-class English and that schools used to have courses in Elocution whose whole point was to teach people how to speak in an upper-class way. But usage-as-inclusion is about much more than class. Here's another thought experiment: A bunch of U.S. teenagers in clothes that look far too large for them are sitting together in the local mall's Food Court, and a 53-year-old man with a combover and clothes that fit comes over to them and says that he was scoping them and thinks they're totally rad and/or phat and is it cool if he just kicks it and does the hang here with them. The kids' reaction is going to be either scorn or embarrassment for the guy—most likely a mix of both. Q: Why? Or imagine that two hard-core urban black guys are standing there talking and I, who am resoundingly and in all ways white, come up and greet them with "Yo" and call them "Brothers" and ask "s'up, s'goin on," pronouncing on with that NYCish $\overline{oo}$-o diphthong that Young Urban Black English deploys for a standard o. Either these guys are going to be offended or they are going to be offended or they are going to think I am simply out of my mind. No other reaction is remotely foreseeable. Q: Why?

Why: A dialect of English is learned and used either because it's your native vernacular or because it's the dialect of a Group by which you wish (with some degree of plausibility) to be accepted. And although it is the major and arguably the most important one, SWE is only one dialect. And it is never, or at least hardly ever, anybody's only dialect. This is because there are—as you and I both know and yet no one in

---

[34]But note that he's sane about it. Some split infinitives really are clunky and hard to parse, especially when there are a whole bunch of words between *to* and the verb—"We will attempt to swiftly and to the best of our ability respond to these charges"—which Garner calls "wide splits" and sensibly discourages. His overall verdict on s.i.'s—which is that some are "perfectly proper" and some iffy and some just totally bad news, and that no one wide tidy dogmatic ukase can handle all s.i. cases, and thus that "knowing when to split an infinitive requires a good ear and a keen eye"—is a good example of the way Garner distinguishes sound and helpful Descriptivist objects from wacko or dogmatic objections and then incorporates the sound objections into a smarter and more flexible Prescriptivism.

the Usage Wars ever seems to mention—situations in which faultlessly correct SWE is clearly not the appropriate dialect.

Childhood is full of such situations. This is one reason why SNOOTlets tend to have a very hard social time of it in school. A SNOOTlet is a little kid who's wildly, precociously fluent in SWE (he is often, recall, the offspring of SNOOTs). Just about every class has a SNOOTlet, so I know you've seen them— these are the sorts of six- to twelve-year-olds who use *whom* correctly and whose response to striking out in T-ball is to cry out "How incalculably dreadful!" etc. The elementary-school SNOOTlet is one of the earliest identifiable species of academic Geekoid and is duly despised by his peers and praised by his teachers. These teachers usually don't see the incredible amounts of punishment the SNOOTlet is receiving from his classmates, or if they do see it they blame the classmates and shake their heads sadly at the vicious and arbitrary cruelty of which children are capable.

But the other children's punishment of the SNOOTlet is not arbitrary at all. There are important things at stake. Little kids in school are learning about Group-inclusion and -exclusion and about the respective rewards and penalties of same and about the use of dialect and syntax and slang as signals of affinity and inclusion.[35] They're learning about Discourse Communities. Kids learn this stuff not in English or Social Studies but on the playground and at lunch and on the bus. When his peers are giving the SNOOTlet monstrous quadruple Wedgies or holding him down and taking turns spitting on him, there's serious learning going on . . . for everyone except the little SNOOT, who in fact is being punished for precisely his *failure* to learn. What neither he nor his teacher realizes is that the SNOOTlet is *deficient* in Language Arts. He has only one dialect. He cannot alter his vocabulary, usage, or grammar, cannot use slang or vulgarity; and it's these abilities that are really required for "peer rapport," which is just a fancy Elementary-Ed term for being accepted by the most important Group in the little kid's life.

This reviewer acknowledges that there seems to be some, umm, personal stuff getting dredged up and worked out here;[36] but the stuff is relevant. The point is that the little A+ SNOOTlet is actually in the same dialectal position as the class's "slow" kid who can't learn to stop using *ain't* or *bringed*. One is punished in class, the other on the playground, but both are deficient in the same linguistic skill—viz., the ability to move between various dialects and levels of "correctness," the ability to communicate one way with peers and another way with teachers and another with family and another with Little League coaches and so on. Most of these dialectal adjustments are made below the level of conscious awareness, and our ability to make them seems part psychological and part something else—perhaps something hardwired into the same motherboard as Universal Grammar—and in truth this ability is a far better indicator of a kid's "Verbal I.Q." than test scores or grades, since U.S. English classes do far more to retard dialectal talent than to cultivate it.

Well-known fact: In neither K-12 nor college English are systematic SWE grammar and usage much taught anymore. It's been this way for more than 20 years. The phenomenon drives Prescriptivists nuts,

---

[35]The SNOOTlet is, as it happens, an indispensable part of other kids' playground education. The kids are learning that a Group's identity depends as much on exclusion as inclusion. They are, in other words, starting to learn about Us and Them, and about how an Us always needs a Them because being not-Them is essential to being Us. Because they're kids and it's school, the obvious Them is the teachers and all the values and appurtenances of the teacher world. This teacher-Them helps the kids see how to start to be an Us, but the SNOOTlet completes the puzzle by providing the as it were missing link: He is the Traitor, the Us who is in fact not Us but *Them*.

In sum, the SNOOTlet is teaching his peers that the criteria for membership in Us are not just age, station, inability to stay up past 9:00, etc.—that in fact Us is primarily a state of mind and a set of sensibilities. An ideology.

[36](The skirt-in-school scenario was not personal stuff, FYI.)

and it's one of the big things they cite as evidence of America's gradual murder of English. Descriptivists and English-Ed specialists counter that grammar and usage have been abandoned because scientific research proved that studying SWE grammar and usage simply doesn't help make kids better writers. Each side in the debate tends to regard the other as mentally ill or/and blinded by political ideology. Neither camp appears ever to have considered whether maybe the way prescriptive SWE was traditionally taught had something to do with its inutility.

By *way* here I'm referring not so much to actual method as to spirit or attitude. Most traditional teachers of English grammar have, of course, been dogmatic SNOOTs, and like most dogmatists they've been incredibly stupid about the rhetoric they used and the Audience they were addressing.[37] I refer specifically to their assumption that SWE is the sole appropriate English dialect and that the only reasons anyone could fail to see this are ignorance or amentia or grave deficiencies in character. As rhetoric, this sort of attitude works only in sermons to the Choir, and as pedagogy it's just disastrous. The reality is that an average U.S. student is going to go to the trouble of mastering the difficult conventions of SWE only if he sees SWE's relevant Group or Discourse Community as one he'd like to be part of. And in the absence of any sort of argument for why the correct-SWE Group is a good or desirable one (an argument that, recall, the traditional teacher hasn't given, because he's such a dogmatic SNOOT he sees no need to), the student is going to be reduced to evaluating the desirability of the SWE Group based on the one obvious member of the Group he's encountered, namely the SNOOTy teacher himself.

I'm not suggesting here that an effective SWE pedagogy would require teachers to wear sunglasses and call students "Dude." What I am suggesting is that the rhetorical situation of an English class—a class composed wholly of young people whose Group identity is rooted in defiance of Adult-Establishment values, plus also composed partly of minorities whose primary dialects are different from SWE—requires the teacher to come up with overt, honest, compelling arguments for why SWE is a dialect worth learning.

These arguments are hard to make—not intellectually but emotionally, politically. Because they are baldly elitist.[38] The real truth, of course, is that SWE is the dialect of the American elite. That it was invented, codified, and promulgated by Privileged WASP Males and is perpetuated as "Standard" by same. That it is the shibboleth of the Establishment and an instrument of political power and class division and racial discrimination and all manner of social inequity. These are shall we say rather *delicate* subjects to bring up in an English class, especially in the service of a pro-SWE argument, and *extra*-especially if you yourself are both a Privileged WASP Male and the Teacher and thus pretty much a walking symbol of the Adult Establishment. This reviewer's opinion, though, is that both students and SWE are better served if the teacher makes his premises explicit and his argument overt, presenting himself as an advocate of SWE's utility rather than as a prophet of its innate superiority.

Because this argument is both most delicate and (I believe) most important with respect to students of color, here is one version of a spiel I've given in private conference[39] with certain black students who were (a) bright and inquisitive and (b) deficient in what U.S. higher education considers written English facility:

---

[37]There are still some of these teachers around, at least here in the Midwest. You know the type: lipless, tweedy, cancrine—Old Maids of both genders. If you had one (as I did, 1976–77), you surely remember him.

[38](Or rather the arguments require us to acknowledge and talk about elitism, whereas a dogmatic SNOOT's pedagogy is merely elitism in action.)

[39](I'm not a total idiot.)

I don't know whether anybody's told you this or not, but when you're in a college English class you're basically studying a foreign dialect. This dialect is called Standard Written English. From talking with you and reading your essays, I've concluded that your own primary dialect is [one of three variants of SBE common to our region]. Now, let me spell something out in my official Teacher-voice: The SBE you're fluent in is different from SWE in all kinds of important ways. Some of these differences are grammatical—for example, double negatives are OK in Standard Black English but not in SWE, and SBE and SWE conjugate certain verbs in totally different ways. Other differences have more to do with style—for instance, Standard Written English tends to use a lot more subordinate clauses in the early parts of sentences, and it sets off most of these early subordinates with commas, and, under SWE rules, writing that doesn't do this is "choppy." There are tons of differences like that. How much of this stuff do you already know? [STANDARD RESPONSE: some variation on "I know from the grades and comments on my papers that English profs don't think I'm a good writer."] Well, I've got good news and bad news. There are some otherwise smart English profs who aren't very aware that there are real dialects of English other than SWE, so when they're reading your papers they'll put, like, "Incorrect conjugation" or "Comma needed" instead of "SWE conjugates this verb differently" or "SWE calls for a comma here." That's the good news—it's not that you're a bad writer, it's that you haven't learned the special rules of the dialect they want you to write in. Maybe that's not such good news, that they were grading you down for mistakes in a foreign language you didn't even know was a foreign language. That they won't let you write in SBE. Maybe it seems unfair. If it does, you're not going to like this news: I'm not going to let you write in SBE either. In my class, you have to learn and write in SWE. If you want to study your own dialect and its rules and history and how it's different from SWE, fine—there are some great books by scholars of Black English, and I'll help you find some and talk about them with you if you want. But that will be outside class. In class—in my English class—you will have to master and write in Standard Written English, which we might just as well call "Standard White English," because it was developed by white people and is used by white people, especially educated, powerful white people. [RESPONSES by this point vary too widely to standardize.] I'm respecting you enough here to give you what I believe is the straight truth. In this country, SWE is perceived as the dialect of education and intelligence and power and prestige, and anybody of any race, ethnicity, religion, or gender who wants to succeed in American culture has got to be able to use SWE. This is How It Is. You can be glad about it or sad about it or deeply pissed off. You can believe it's racist and unjust and decide right here and now to spend every waking minute of your adult life arguing against it, and maybe you should, but I'll tell you something: If you ever want those arguments to get listened to and taken seriously, you're going to have to communicate them in SWE, because SWE is the dialect our country uses to talk to itself. African Americans who've become successful and important in U.S. culture know this; that's why King's and X's and Jackson's speeches are in SWE, and why Morrison's and Angelou's and Baldwin's and Wideman's and West's books are full of totally ass-kicking SWE, and why black judges and politicians and journalists and doctors and teachers communicate professionally in SWE. Some of these people grew up in homes and communities where SWE was the native dialect, and these black people had it much easier in school, but the ones who didn't grow up with SWE realized at some point that they had to learn it and become able to write in it, and so they did. And [INSERT NAME HERE], you're going to learn to use it, too, because I am going to make you.

I should note here that a couple of the students I've said this stuff to were offended—one lodged an Official Complaint—and that I have had more than one colleague profess to find my spiel "racially insensitive." Perhaps you do, too. My own humble opinion is that some of the cultural and political realities of American life are themselves racially insensitive and elitist and offensive and unfair, and that pussyfooting around these realities with euphemistic doublespeak is not only hypocritical but toxic to the project of ever actually changing them. Such pussyfooting has of course now achieved the status of a dialect—one powerful enough to have turned the normal politics of the Usage Wars sort of inside out.

I refer here to Politically Correct English (PCE), under whose conventions failing students become "high-potential" students and poor people "economically disadvantaged" and people in wheelchairs "differently abled" and a sentence like "White English and Black English are different and you better learn White English if you don't want to flunk" is not blunt but "insensitive." Although it's common to make jokes about PCE (referring to ugly people as "aesthetically challenged" and so on), be advised that Politically Correct English's various pre- and proscriptions are taken very seriously *indeed* by colleges and corporations and government agencies, whose own institutional dialects now evolve under the beady scrutiny of a whole new kind of Language Police.

From one perspective, the history of PCE evinces a kind of Lenin-to-Stalinesque irony. That is, the same ideological principles that informed the original Descriptivist revolution—namely, the sixties-era rejections of traditional authority and traditional inequality—have now actually produced a far more inflexible Prescriptivism, one unencumbered by tradition or complexity and backed by the threat of real-world sanctions (termination, litigation) for those who fail to conform. This is sort of funny in a dark way, maybe, and most criticism of PCE seems to consist in making fun of its trendiness or vapidity. This reviewer's own opinion is that prescriptive PCE is not just silly but confused and dangerous.

Usage is always political, of course, but it's complexly political. With respect, for instance, to political change, usage conventions can function in two ways: On the one hand they can be a *reflection* of political change, and on the other they can be an *instrument* of political change. These two functions are different and have to be kept straight. Confusing them—in particular, mistaking for political efficacy what is really just a language's political symbolism—enables the bizarre conviction that America ceases to be elitist or unfair simply because Americans stop using certain vocabulary that is historically associated with elitism and unfairness. This is PCE's central fallacy—that a society's mode of expression is productive of its attitudes rather than a product of those attitudes—and of course it's nothing but the obverse of the politically conservative SNOOT's delusion that social change can be retarded by restricting change in standard usage.[40]

Forget Stalinization or Logic 101-level equivocations, though. There's a grosser irony about Politically Correct English. This is that PCE purports to be the dialect of progressive reform but is in fact—in its Orwellian substitution of the euphemisms of social equality for social equality itself—of vastly more help to conservatives and the U.S. status quo than traditional SNOOT prescriptions ever were. Were I, for instance, a political conservative who opposed taxation as a means of redistributing national wealth, I would be delighted to watch PCE progressives spend their time and energy arguing over whether a poor person should be described as "low-income" or "economically disadvantaged" or "pre-prosperous" rather than constructing effective public arguments for redistributive legislation or higher marginal tax rates on corporations. (Not to mention that strict codes of egalitarian euphemism serve to burke the sorts of painful, unpretty, and sometimes offensive discourse that in a pluralistic democracy leads to actual political change rather than symbolic political change. In other words, PCE functions as a form of censorship, and censorship always serves the status quo.)

As a practical matter, I strongly doubt whether a guy who has four small kids and makes $12,000 a year feels more empowered or less ill-used by a society that carefully refers to him as "economically disadvantaged" rather than "poor." Were I he, in fact, I'd probably find the PCE term insulting—not just because it's patronizing but because it's hypocritical and self-serving. Like many forms of Vogue

---

[40]E.G., this is the reasoning behind many Pop Prescriptivists' complaint that shoddy usage signifies the Decline of Western Civilization.

Usage,[41] PCE functions primarily to signal and congratulate certain virtues in the speaker—scrupulous egalitarianism, concern for the dignity of all people, sophistication about the political implications of language—and so serves the selfish interests of the PC far more than it serves any of the persons or groups renamed.

Interpolation on a Related Issue in the Face of Whose Ghastly Malignancy This Reviewer's Democratic Spirit Just Gives Out Altogether, Admittedly

This issue is Academic English, a cancer that has metastasized now to afflict both scholarly writing—

> If such a sublime cyborg would insinuate the future as post-Fordist subject, his palpably masochistic locations as ecstatic agent of the sublime superstate need to be decoded as the "now all-but-unreadable DNA" of the fast industrializing Detroit, just as his Robocop-like strategy of carceral negotiation and street control remains the tirelessly American one of inflicting regeneration through violence upon the racially heteroglassic wilds and others of the inner city.[42]

—and prose as mainstream as *The Village Voice's*:

> At first encounter, the poems' distanced cerebral surfaces can be daunting, evading physical location or straightforward emotional arc. But this seeming remoteness quickly reveals a very real passion, centered in the speaker's struggle to define his evolving self-construction.

Maybe it's a combination of my SNOOTitude and the fact that I end up having to read a lot of it for my job, but I'm afraid I regard Academic English not as a dialectal variation but as a grotesque debasement of SWE, and loathe it even more than the stilted incoherences of Presidential English ("This is the best and only way to uncover, destroy, and prevent Iraq from reengineering weapons of mass destruction") or the mangled pieties of BusinessSpeak ("Our Mission: to proactively search and provide the optimum networking skills and resources to meet the needs of your growing business"); and in support of this utter contempt and intolerance I cite no less an authority than Mr. G. Orwell, who 50 years ago had AE pegged as a "mixture of vagueness and sheer incompetence" in which "it is normal to come across long passages which are almost completely lacking in meaning."[43]

---

[41]*A Dictionary of Modern American Usage* includes a miniessay on VOGUE WORDS, but it's a disappointing one in that Garner does little more than list VW's that bug him and say that "vogue words have such a grip on the popular mind that they come to be used in contexts in which they serve little purpose." This is one of the rare places in *ADMAU* where Garner is simply wrong. The real problem is that every sentence blends and balances at least two different communicative functions—one the transmission of raw info, the other the transmission of certain stuff about the speaker—and Vogue Usage throws this balance off. Garner's "serve little purpose" is exactly incorrect; vogue words serve too much the purpose of presenting the speaker in a certain light (even if this is merely as with-it or hip), and people's subliminal B.S.-antennae pick this imbalance up, and that's why even nonSNOOTs often find Vogue Usage irritating and creepy.

[42]FYI, this passage, which appears in *ADMAU's* entry on OBSCURITY, is quoted from a 1997 *Sacramento Bee* article entitled "No Contest: English Professor Are Worst Writers on Campus."

[43]This was in his 1946 "Politics and the English Language," an essay that despite its date (and its title a basic redundancy) remains the definitive SNOOT statement on Academese. Orwell's famous AE translation of the gorgeous "I saw under the sun that the race is not to the swift" in Ecclesiastes as "Objective considerations of contemporary phenomena compel the conclusion that success or failure in competition activities exhibits no tendency to be commensurate with innate capacity, but that a considerable element of the unpredictable must invariably be taken into account" should be tattooed on the left wrist of every grad student in the anglophone world.

It probably isn't the whole explanation, but, as with the voguish hypocrisy of PCE, the obscurity and pretension of Academic English can be attributed in part to a disruption in the delicate rhetorical balance between language as a vector of meaning and language as a vector of the writer's own résumé. In other words, it is when a scholar's vanity/insecurity leads him to write *primarily* to communicate and reinforce his own status as an Intellectual that his English is deformed by pleonasm and pretentious diction (whose function is to signal the writer's erudition) and by opaque abstraction (whose function is to keep anybody from pinning the writer down to a definite assertion that can maybe be refuted or shown to be silly). The latter characteristic, a level of obscurity that often makes it just about impossible to figure out what an AE sentence is really saying, so closely resembles political and corporate doublespeak ("revenue enhancement," "downsizing," "pre-owned," "proactive resource-allocation restructuring") that it's tempting to think AE's real purpose is concealment and its real motivation fear.

The insecurity that drives AE, PCE, and vocab-tape ads is far from groundless, though. These are tense linguistic times. Blame it on Heisenbergian Uncertainty or postmodern relativism or Image Over Substance or the ubiquity of advertising and P .R. or the rise of Identity Politics or whatever you will—we live in an era of terrible preoccupation with presentation and interpretation. In rhetorical terms, certain long-held distinctions between the Ethical Appeal, Logical Appeal (= an argument's plausibility or soundness), and Pathetic Appeal (= an argument's emotional impact) have now pretty much collapsed—or rather the different sorts of Appeals now affect and are affected by one another in ways that make it almost impossible to advance an argument on "reason" alone.

A vividly concrete illustration here concerns the Official Complaint a black undergraduate filed against this rev. after one of my little *in camera* spiels. The complainant was (I opine) wrong, but she was not crazy or stupid; and I was able later to see that I did bear some responsibility for the whole nasty administrative swivet. My culpability lay in gross rhetorical naïveté. I'd seen my speech's primary Appeal as Logical: The aim was to make a conspicuously blunt, honest argument for SWE's utility. It wasn't pretty, maybe, but it was true, plus so manifestly bullshit-free that I think I anticipated not just acquiescence but gratitude for my candor.[44] The problem I failed to see, of course, lay not with the argument per se but with the person making it—namely me, a Privileged WASP Male in a position of power, thus someone whose statements about the primacy and utility of the Privileged WASP Male dialect appeared not candid/hortatory/authoritative/true but elitist/highhanded/authoritarian/racist. Rhetoric-wise, what happened was that I allowed the substance and style of my Logical Appeal to completely torpedo my Ethical Appeal: What the student heard was just another PWM rationalizing why his Group and his English were top dog and ought "logically" to stay that way (plus, worse, trying to use his academic power over her to coerce her assent[45]).

If for any reason you happen to find yourself sharing this particular student's perceptions and reaction,[46] I would ask that you bracket your feelings long enough to recognize that the PWM instructor's very modern rhetorical dilemma in that office was really no different from the dilemma faced by a male who makes a Pro-Life argument, or an atheist who argues against Creation Science, or a Caucasian who

---

[44]Please just don't even say it.

[45](She professed to have been especially traumatized by the climactic "I am going to make you," which in retrospect was indeed a mammoth rhetorical boner.)

[46](The Dept. head and Dean did not, as it happens, share her reaction . . . though it would be disingenuous not to tell you that they happened also to be PWM's, which fact did not go unremarked by the complainant, such that the whole proceeding got pretty darn tense, indeed, before it was all over.).

opposes Affirmative Action, or an African American who decries Racial Profiling, or anyone over eighteen who tries to make a case for raising the legal driving age to eighteen, etc. The dilemma has nothing to do with whether the arguments themselves are plausible or right or even sane, because the debate rarely gets that far—any opponent with sufficiently strong feelings or a dogmatic bent can discredit the arguments and pretty much foreclose all further discussion with a single, terribly familiar rejoinder: "Of course *you'd* say that"; "Easy for *you* to say"; "What right do *you* have. . . ?"

Now (still bracketing) consider the situation of any reasonably intelligent and well-meaning SNOOT who sits down to prepare a prescriptive usage guide. It's the millennium, post-Everything: Whence the authority to make any sort of credible Appeal for SWE at all?

Article's Crux: Why Bryan A. Garner Is a Genius, Though of a Rather Particular Kind

It isn't that *A Dictionary of Modern American Usage* is perfect. It doesn't seem to cover *conversant in* vs. *conversant with,* for example, or *abstruse* vs. *obtuse,* or to have anything on *hereby* and *herewith* (which I tend to use interchangeably but always have the uneasy feeling I'm screwing up). Garner's got a good discussion of *used to* but nothing on *supposed to.* Nor does he give any examples to help explain irregular participles and transitivity ("The light shone" vs. "I shined the light," etc.), and these would seem to be more important than, say, the correct spelling of *huzzah* or the plural of *animalculum,* both of which get discussed. Plus there's the VOGUE WORDS snafu and the absence of a pronunciation entry on *trough.*[47] In other words, a SNOOT is going to be able to find stuff to quibble about in any usage dictionary, and *ADMAU* is no exception.

But it's still really, really good—and not just lexicographically but rhetorically, politically (if it even makes sense to distinguish these any more). As a collection of judgments, *ADMAU* is in no way Descriptivist, but Garner structures his judgments very carefully to avoid the elitism and anality of traditional SNOOTitude. He does not deploy irony or scorn or caustic wit, nor tropes or colloquialisms or contractions . . . or really any sort of verbal style at all. In fact, even though Garner talks openly about himself and uses the 1-S pronoun throughout the whole dictionary, his personality is oddly effaced, neutralized. It's like he's so bland he's barely there. E.g., as this reviewer was finishing the book's final entry,[48] it struck me that I had no idea whether Bryan Garner was black or white, gay or straight, Democrat or Dittohead. What was even more striking was that I hadn't once wondered about any of this up to now; something about Garner's lexical persona kept me ever from asking where the guy was coming from or what particular agendas or ideologies were informing what he had admitted right up front were "value judgments."

Bryan Garner is a genius because *A Dictionary of Modern American Usage* pretty much resolves the Usage Wars' Crisis of Authority. Garner manages to control the compresence of rhetorical Appeals so

---

[47]To be honest, I noticed this omission only because midway through working on this article I happened to use the word *trough* in front of the same SNOOT friend who likes to compare public English to violin-hammering, and he fell sideways out of his chair, and it emerged that I have somehow all my life misheard *trough* as ending with a *th* instead of an *f* and thus have publicly mispronounced it God knows how many scores of times, and I all but burned rubber getting home to see whether perhaps the error was so common and human and understandable that Garner himself had a good-natured entry on it, but no such luck, which in fairness I don't suppose I can really blame Garner for.

[48](on *zwieback* vs. *zweiback*).

cleverly that he appears able to transcend both Usage Wars camps and simply tell the truth, and in a way that does not torpedo his own credibility but actually enhances it. His argumentative strategy is totally brilliant and totally sneaky, and part of both qualities is that it usually doesn't seem like there's even an argument going on at all.

Garner recognizes something that neither of the dogmatic camps appears to get: Given 40 years of the Usage Wars, "authority" is no longer something a lexicographer can just presume *ex officio.* In fact, a large part of the project of any contemporary usage dictionary will consist in establishing this authority. If that seems rather obvious, be apprised that nobody before Garner seems to have figured it out— that the lexicographer's challenge now is to be not just accurate and comprehensive but *credible.* That in the absence of unquestioned Authority in language, the reader must now be moved or persuaded to *grant* a dictionary its authority, freely and for what appear to be good reasons.

Garner's *A Dictionary of Modern American Usage* is thus both a collection of information and a piece of Democratic rhetoric.[49] Its goal is to recast the Prescriptivist's persona: The author presents himself as an authority not in an *autocratic* sense but in a *technocratic* sense. And the technocrat is not only a thoroughly modern and palatable image of Authority but also immune to the charges of elitism/classism that have hobbled traditional Prescriptivism.

Of course, Garner really *is* a technocrat. He's a lawyer, recall, and in *ADMAU* he consciously projects a sort of wise juridical persona: knowledgeable, dispassionate, fair, with an almost Enlightenment-grade passion for reason. His judgments about usage tend to be rendered like legal opinions—exhaustive citation of precedent (other dictionaries' judgments, published examples of actual usage) combined with clear, logical reasoning that's always informed by the larger consensual purposes SWE is meant to serve.

Also thoroughgoingly technocratic is Garner's approach to the issue of whether anybody's even going to be interested in his 700 pages of fine-pointed counsel. Like any specialist, he simply presumes that there are practical reasons why some people choose to concern themselves with SWE usage; and his attitude about the fact that most Americans "could care less" isn't scorn or disapproval but the phlegmatic resignation of a doctor or lawyer who realizes that he can give good advice but can't make you take it:

> The reality I care about most is that some people still want to use the language well.[50] They want to write effectively; they want to speak effectively. They want their language to be graceful at times and powerful at times. They want to understand how to use words well, how to manipulate sentences, and how to move about in the language without seeming to flail. They want good grammar, but they want more: they want rhetoric[51] in the traditional .sense. That is, they want to use the language deftly so that it's fit for their purposes.

It's now possible to see that all the autobiographical stuff in *ADMAU*'s Preface does more than just humanize Mr. Bryan A. Garner. It also serves to detail the early and enduring passion that helps make someone a credible technocrat—we tend to like and trust experts whose expertise is born of a real love for their specialty instead of just a desire to be expert at something. In fact, it turns out that *ADMAU*'s Preface quietly and steadily invests Garner with every single qualification of modern technocratic Authority: passion-

---

[49](meaning *literally* Democratic—It Wants Your Vote)

[50]The last two words of this sentence, of course, are what the Usage Wars are about—whose "language" and whose "well"? The most remarkable thing about this sentence is that coming from Garner it doesn't sound naïve or obnoxious but just . . . reasonable.

[51]Did you think I was kidding?

ate devotion, reason, and accountability (recall "in the interests of full disclosure, here are the ten critical points . . ."), experience ("that, after years of working on usage problems, I've settled on"), exhaustive and tech-savvy research ("For contemporary usage, the files of our greatest dictionary makers pale in comparison with the full-text search capabilities now provided by NEXIS and WESTLAW"), an even and judicious temperament (see e.g. this from HYPERCORRECTION: "Sometimes people strive to abide by the strictest etiquette, but in the process behave inappropriately"[52]), and the sort of humble integrity (for instance, including in one of the entries a past published usage-error of his own) that not only renders Garner likable but transmits the same kind of reverence for English that good jurists have for the law, both of which are bigger and more important than any one person.

Probably the most attractive thing about *ADMAU*'s Ethical Appeal, though, is Garner's scrupulous consideration of the reader's concern about his (or her) *own* linguistic authority and rhetorical persona and ability to convince an Audience that he cares. Again and again, Garner frames his prescriptions in rhetorical terms, e.g.: "To the writer or speaker for whom credibility is important, it's a good idea to avoid distracting *any* readers or listeners." *A Dictionary of Modern American Usage*'s real thesis, in other words, is that the purposes of the expert authority and the purposes of the lay reader are identical, and identically rhetorical—which I submit is about as Democratic these days as you're going to get.

---

[52](Here this reviewer's indwelling and ever-vigilant SNOOT can't help but question why Garner uses a comma before the conjunction in this sentence, since what follows the conjunction is neither an independent clause nor any kind of plausible complement for *strive to*. But respectful disagreement between people of goodwill is of course Democratically natural and healthy and, when you come right down to it, kind of fun.)

ODE TO AN ORANGE

Larry Woiwode

Oh, those oranges arriving in the midst of the North Dakota winters of the forties—the mere color of them, carried through the door in a net bag or a crate from out of the white winter landscape. Their appearance was enough to set my brother and me to thinking that it might be about time to develop an illness, which was the surest way of receiving a steady supply of them.

"Mom, we think we're getting a cold."

"*We?* You mean, you two want an orange?"

This was difficult for us to answer or dispute; the matter seemed moved beyond our mere wanting.

"If you want an orange," she would say, "why don't you ask for one?"

"We want an orange."

"'We' again. '*We want an orange.*'"

"May we have an orange, please."

"That's the way you know I like you to ask for one. Now, why don't each of you ask for one in that same way, but separately?"

"Mom . . ." And so on. There was no depth of degradation that we wouldn't descend to in order to get one. If the oranges hadn't wended their way northward by Thanksgiving, they were sure to arrive before the Christmas season, stacked first in crates at the depot, filling that musty place, where pews sat back to back, with a springtime acidity, as if the building had been rinsed with a renewing elixir that set it right for yet another year. Then the crates would appear at the local grocery store, often with the top slats pried back on a few of them, so that we were aware of a resinous smell of fresh wood in addition to the already orangy atmosphere that foretold the season more explicitly than any calendar.

And in the broken-open crates (as if burst by the power of the oranges themselves), one or two of the lovely spheres would lie free of the tissue they came wrapped in—always purple tissue, as if that were the only color that could contain the populations of them in their nestled positions. The crates bore paper labels at one end—of an orange against a blue background, or of a blue goose against an orange background—signifying the colorful otherworld (unlike our wintry one) that these phenomena had arisen from. Each orange, stripped of its protective wrapping, as vivid in your vision as a pebbled sun, encouraged you to picture a whole pyramid of them in a bowl on your dining room table, glowing in the light, as if giving off the warmth that came through the windows from the real winter sun. And all of them came stamped with a blue-purple name as foreign as the otherworld that you might imagine as their place of origin, so that on Christmas day you would find yourself digging past everything else in your Christmas stocking, as if tunneling down to the country of China, in order to reach the rounded bulge at the tip of the toe which meant that you had received a personal reminder of another state of existence, wholly separate from your own.

The packed heft and texture, finally, of an orange in your hand—this is it!—and the eruption of smell and the watery fireworks as a knife, in the hand of someone skilled, like our mother, goes slicing through the skin so perfect for slicing. This gaseous spray can form a mist like smoke, which can then be lit with a match to create actual fireworks if there is a chance to hide alone with a match (matches being forbidden) and the peel from one. Sputtery ignitions can also be produced by squeezing a peel near a candle (at least one candle is generally always going at Christmastime), and the leftover peels are set on the stove top to scent the house.

And the ingenious way in which oranges come packed into their globes! The green nib at the top, like a detonator, can be bitten off, as if disarming the orange, in order to clear a place for you to sink a tooth under the peel. This is the best way to start. If you bite at the peel too much, your front teeth will feel scraped, like dry bone, and your lips will begin to burn from the bitter oil. Better to sink a tooth into this greenish or creamy depression, and then pick at that point with the nail of your thumb, removing a little piece of the peel at a time. Later, you might want to practice to see how large a piece you can remove intact. The peel can also be undone in one continuous ribbon, a feat which maybe your father is able to perform, so that after the orange is freed, looking yellowish, the peel, rewound, will stand in its original shape, although empty.

The yellowish whole of the orange can now be divided into sections, usually about a dozen, by beginning with a division down the middle; after this, each section, enclosed in its papery skin, will be able to be lifted and torn loose more easily. There is a stem up the center of the sections like a mushroom stalk, but tougher; this can be eaten. A special variety of orange, without any pits, has an extra growth, or nubbin, like half of a tiny orange, tucked into its bottom. This nubbin is nearly as bitter as the peel, but it can be eaten, too; don't worry. Some of the sections will have miniature sections embedded in them and clinging as if for life, giving the impression that babies are being hatched, and should you happen to find some of these you've found the sweetest morsels of any.

If you prefer to have your orange sliced in half, as some people do, the edges of the peel will abrade the corners of your mouth, making them feel raw, as you eat down into the white of the rind (which is the only way to do it) until you can see daylight through the orangy bubbles composing its outside. Your eyes might burn; there is no proper way to eat an orange. If there are pits, they can get in the way, and the slower you eat an orange, the more you'll find your fingers sticking together. And no matter how carefully you eat one, or bite into a quarter, juice can always fly or slip from a corner of your mouth; this happens to everyone. Close your eyes to be on the safe side, and for the eruption in your mouth of the slivers of watery meat, which should be broken and rolled fine over your tongue for the essence of orange. And if indeed you have sensed yourself coming down with a cold, there is a chance that you will feel it driven from your head—your nose and sinuses suddenly opening—in the midst of the scent of a peel and eating an orange.

And oranges can also be eaten whole—rolled into a spongy mass and punctured with a pencil (if you don't find this offensive) or a knife, and then sucked upon. Then, once the juice is gone, you can disembowel the orange as you wish and eat away its pulpy remains, and eat once more into the whitish interior of the peel, which scours the coating from your teeth and makes your numbing lips and tip of your tongue start to tingle and swell up from behind, until, in the light from the windows (shining through an empty glass bowl), you see orange again from the inside. Oh, oranges, solid *o*'s, light from afar in the midst of the freeze, and not unlike that unspherical fruit which first went from Eve to Adam and from there (to abbreviate matters) to my brother and me.

"Mom, we think we're getting a cold."

"You mean, you want an orange?"

This is difficult to answer or dispute or even to acknowledge, finally, with the fullness that the subject deserves, and that each orange bears, within its own makeup, into this hard-edged yet insubstantial, incomplete, cold, wintry world.